SUPERBOY

SMALLVILLE ATTACKS

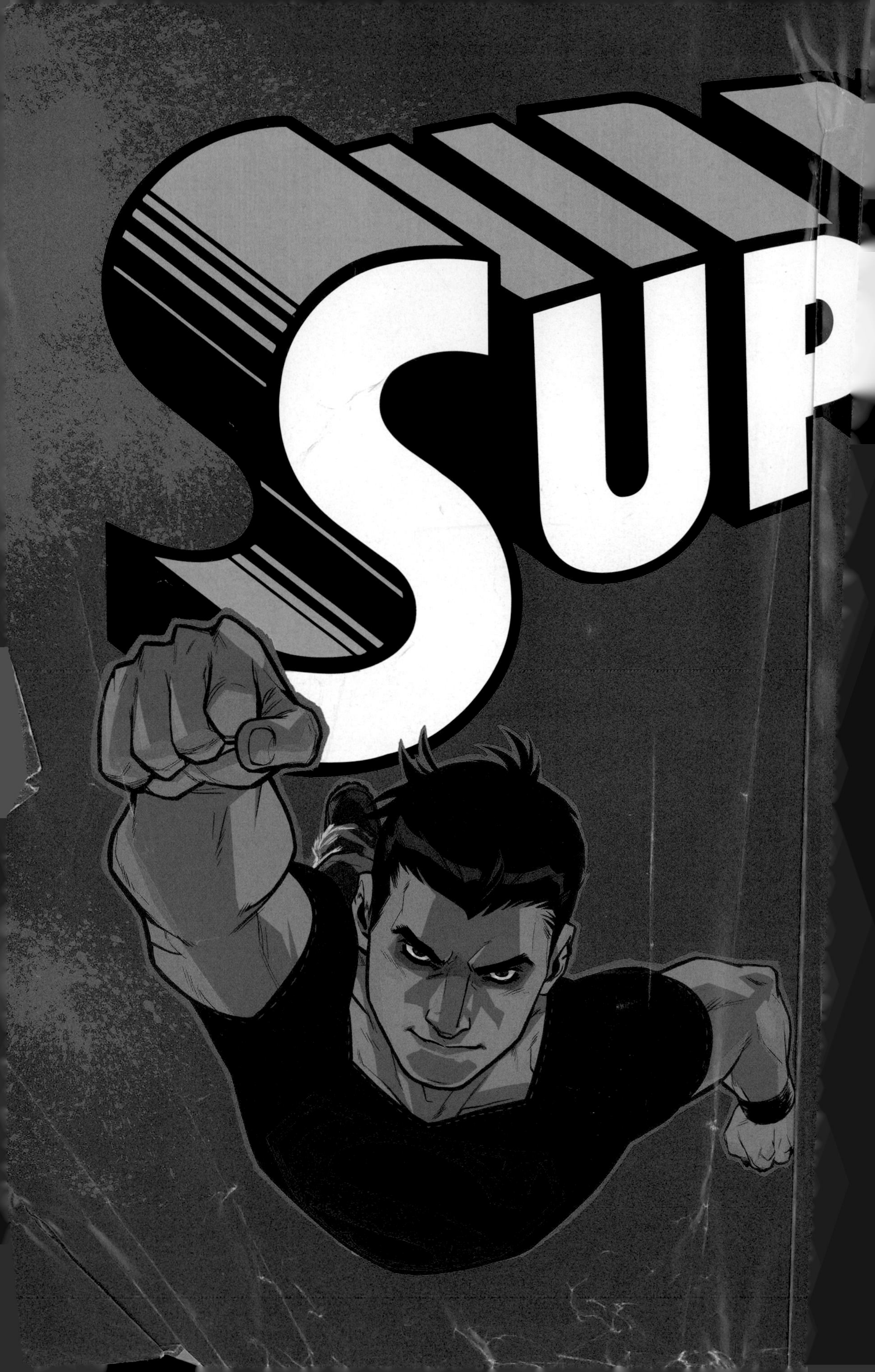
SUP

ERBOY

SMALLVILLE ATTACKS

WRITER   ARTISTS

JEFF LEMIRE   PIER GALLO

MARCO RUDY
DANIEL HDR
PETE WOODS
CAFU
BIT
PAULO SIQUEIRA
ANDREW MANGUM

COLORISTS

JAMIE GRANT
DOM REGAN
MARCO RUDY

LETTERERS

JOHN J. HILL
SAL CIPRIANO
SWANDS
CARLOS M. MANGUAL
TRAVIS LANHAM

COLLECTION COVER KARL KERSCHL AFTER RAFAEL ALBUQUERQUE

Matt Idelson	Editor – Original Series
Wil Moss	Associate Editor – Original Series
Ian Sattler	Director – Editorial, Special Projects and Archival Editions
Robin Wildman	Editor
Robbin Brosterman	Design Director – Books
Brainchild Studios/NYC	Publication Design
Eddie Berganza	Executive Editor
Bob Harras	VP – Editor in Chief
Diane Nelson	President
Dan DiDio and Jim Lee	Co-Publishers
Geoff Johns	Chief Creative Officer
John Rood	Executive VP – Sales, Marketing and Business Development
Amy Genkins	Senior VP – Business and Legal Affairs
Nairi Gardiner	Senior VP – Finance
Jeff Boison	VP – Publishing Operations
Mark Chiarello	VP – Art Direction and Design
John Cunningham	VP – Marketing
Terri Cunningham	VP – Talent Relations and Services
Alison Gill	Senior VP – Manufacturing and Operations
David Hyde	VP – Publicity
Hank Kanalz	Senior VP – Digital
Jay Kogan	VP – Business and Legal Affairs, Publishing
Jack Mahan	VP – Business Affairs, Talent
Nick Napolitano	VP – Manufacturing Administration
Sue Pohja	VP – Book Sales
Courtney Simmons	Senior VP – Publicity
Bob Wayne	Senior VP – Sales

SUPERBOY: SMALLVILLE ATTACKS

DC Comics, 1700 Broadway, New York, NY 10019
A Warner Bros. Entertainment Company.
Printed by RR Donnelley, Salem, VA, USA. 11/04/11. First Printing.
ISBN: 978-1-4012-3251-1

SUSTAINABLE
FORESTRY
INITIATIVE

Certified Chain of Custody
Promoting Sustainable
Forest Management
www.sfiprogram.org

Fiber used in this product line meets the
sourcing requirements of the SFI program.
www.sfiprogram.org SGS-SFI/COC-US10/81072

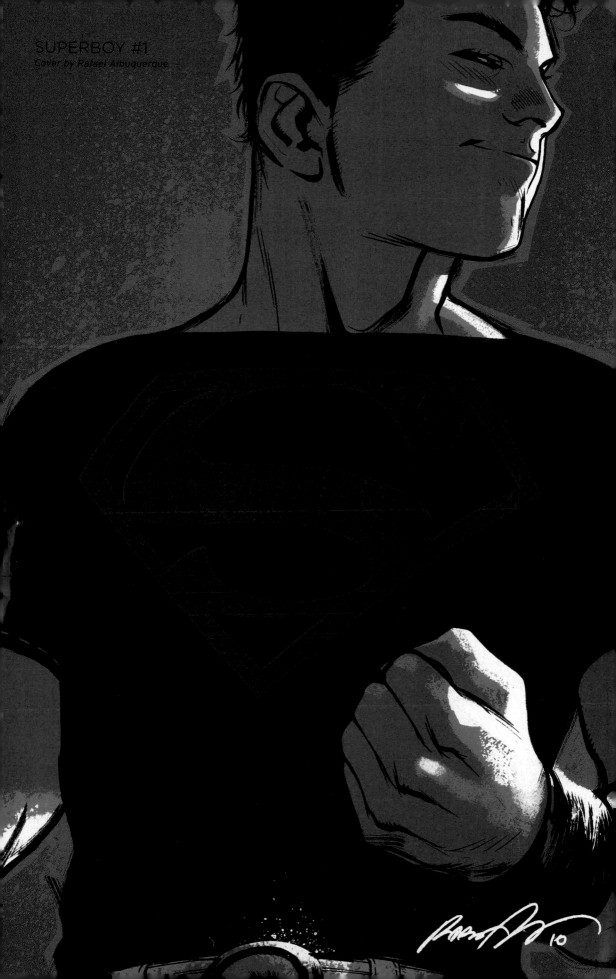

SUPERBOY #1
Cover by Rafael Albuquerque

SUPERBOY #1 | VARIANT

Cover by John Cassaday & Andre Szymanowicz

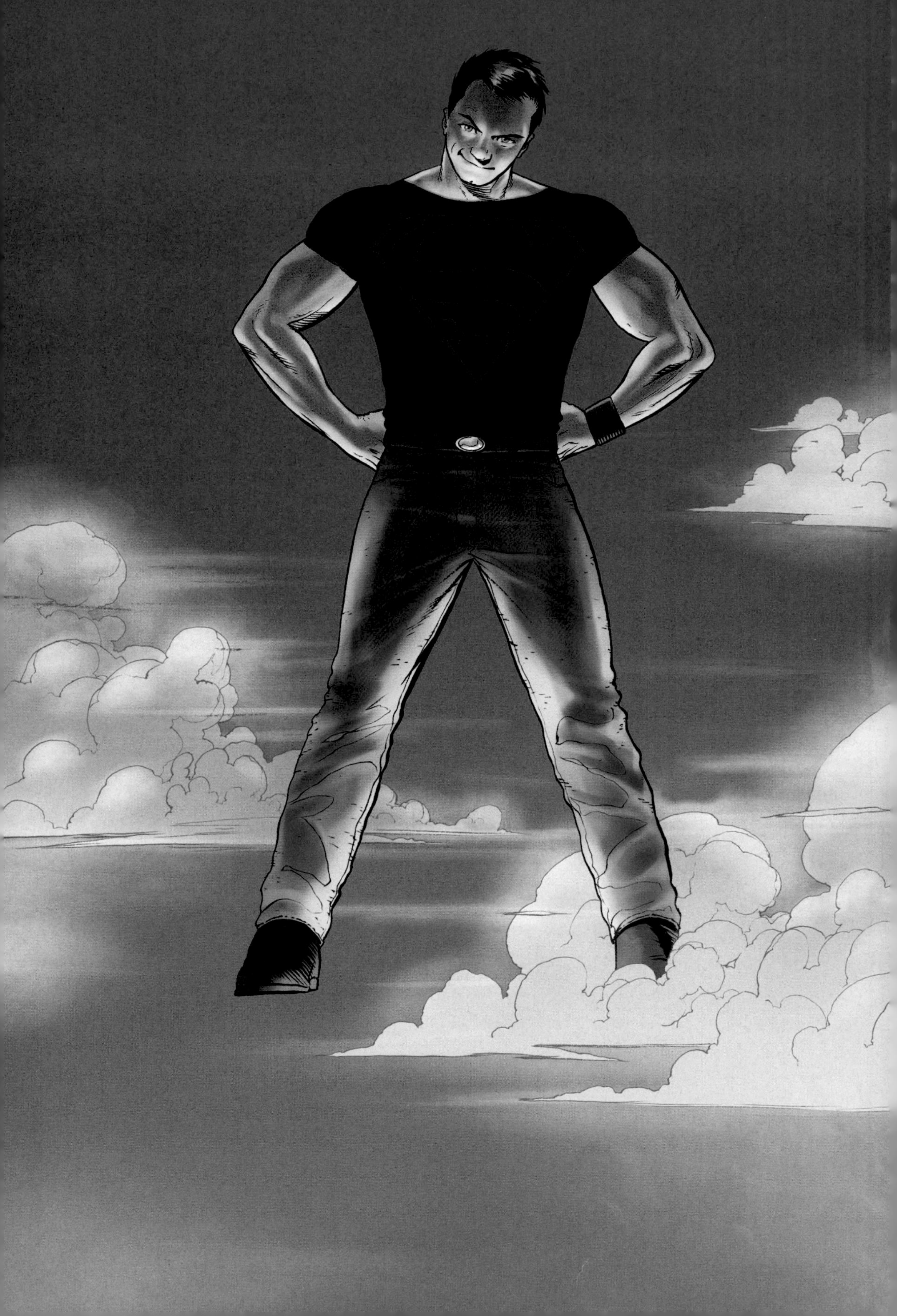

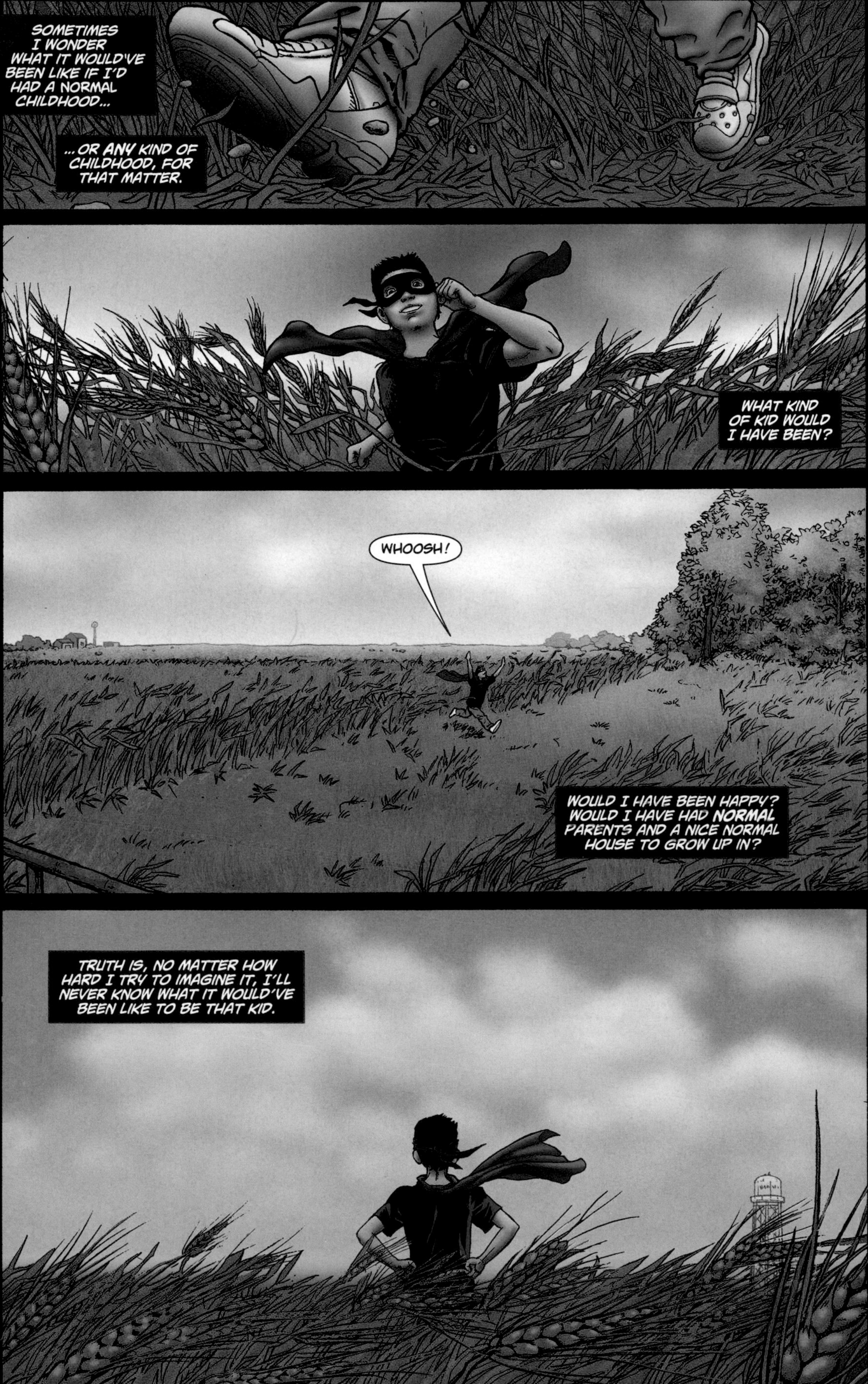
SOMETIMES I WONDER WHAT IT WOULD'VE BEEN LIKE IF I'D HAD A NORMAL CHILDHOOD...
...OR ANY KIND OF CHILDHOOD, FOR THAT MATTER.
WHAT KIND OF KID WOULD I HAVE BEEN?
WHOOSH!
WOULD I HAVE BEEN HAPPY? WOULD I HAVE HAD NORMAL PARENTS AND A NICE NORMAL HOUSE TO GROW UP IN?
TRUTH IS, NO MATTER HOW HARD I TRY TO IMAGINE IT, I'LL NEVER KNOW WHAT IT WOULD'VE BEEN LIKE TO BE THAT KID.

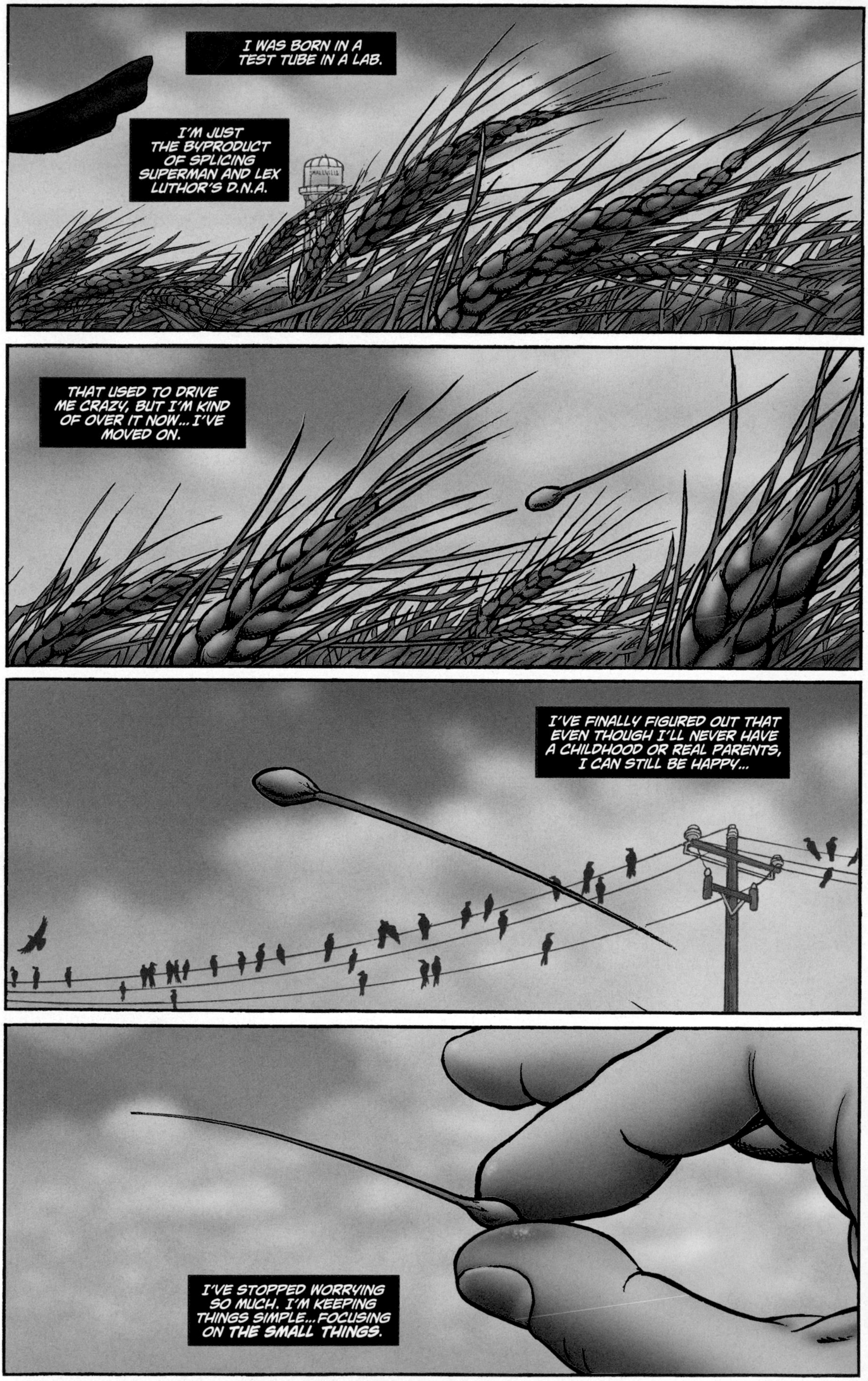
I WAS BORN IN A TEST TUBE IN A LAB.
I'M JUST THE BYPRODUCT OF SPLICING SUPERMAN AND LEX LUTHOR'S D.N.A.
SMALLVILLE
THAT USED TO DRIVE ME CRAZY, BUT I'M KIND OF OVER IT NOW... I'VE MOVED ON.
I'VE FINALLY FIGURED OUT THAT EVEN THOUGH I'LL NEVER HAVE A CHILDHOOD OR REAL PARENTS, I CAN STILL BE HAPPY...
I'VE STOPPED WORRYING SO MUCH. I'M KEEPING THINGS SIMPLE... FOCUSING ON THE SMALL THINGS.

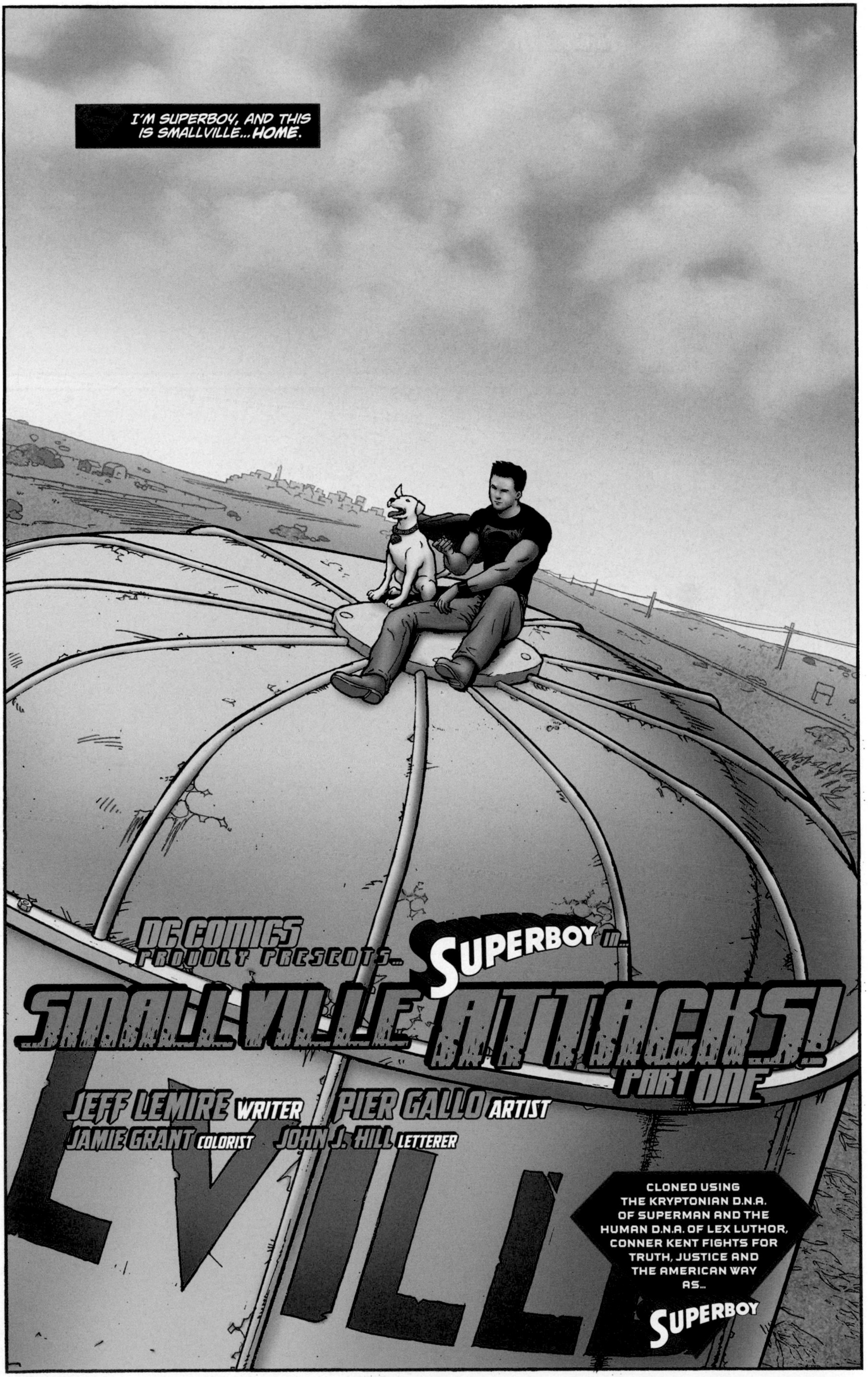
I'M SUPERBOY, AND THIS IS SMALLVILLE... HOME.
DC COMICS PROUDLY PRESENTS... SUPERBOY IN...
SMALLVILLE ATTACKS! PART ONE
JEFF LEMIRE WRITER PIER GALLO ARTIST
JAMIE GRANT COLORIST JOHN J. HILL LETTERER
CLONED USING THE KRYPTONIAN D.N.A. OF SUPERMAN AND THE HUMAN D.N.A. OF LEX LUTHOR, CONNER KENT FIGHTS FOR TRUTH, JUSTICE AND THE AMERICAN WAY AS... SUPERBOY

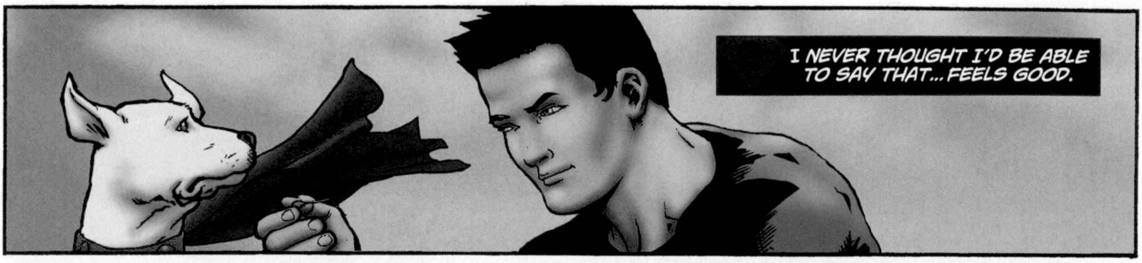
I NEVER THOUGHT I'D BE ABLE TO SAY THAT... FEELS GOOD.

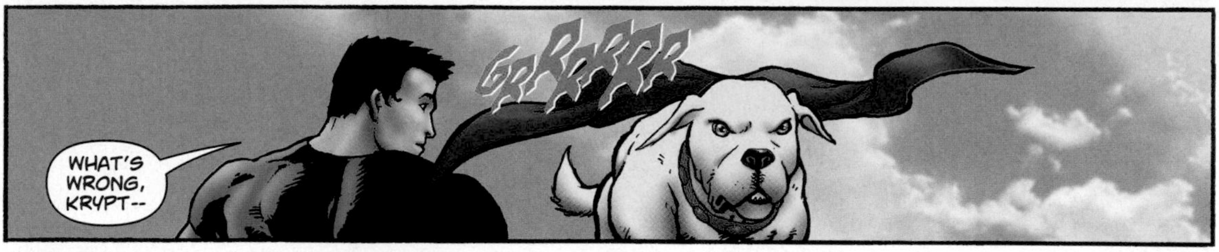
GRRRRRR
WHAT'S WRONG, KRYPT--

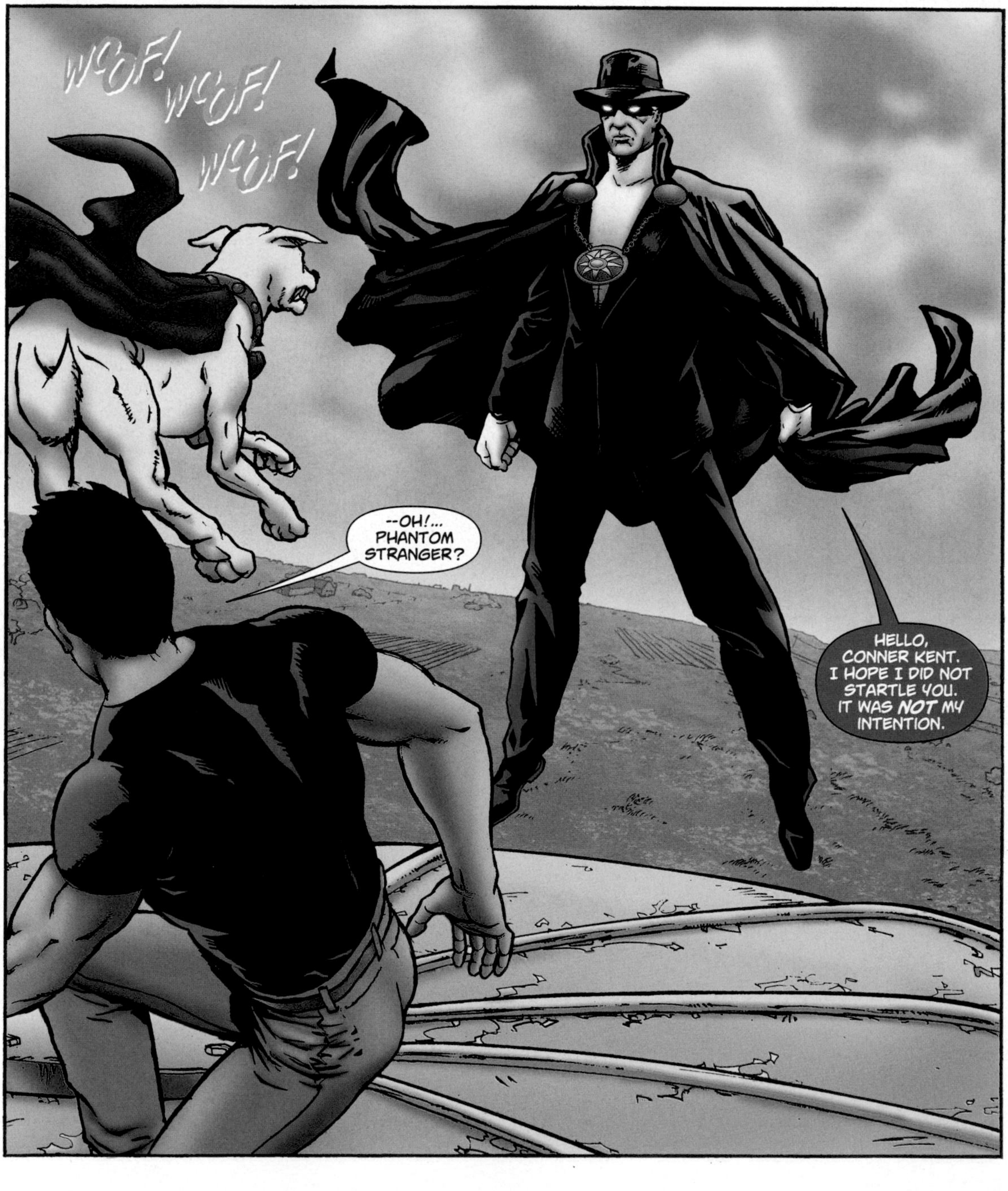
WOOF! WOOF! WOOF!
--OH!... PHANTOM STRANGER?
HELLO, CONNER KENT. I HOPE I DID NOT STARTLE YOU. IT WAS *NOT* MY INTENTION.

UH...NO. I'M COOL. SO WHAT'S UP?

GRRRR

WHAT IS "UP" IS THAT I HAVE TRAVELED VERY FAR TO SEE *YOU*... HERE...*TODAY.*

THERE IS A DARKNESS BLOWING IN ON THESE GENTLE KANSAS WINDS. SOMETHING SINISTER INCUBATES WITHIN THESE RICH OLD FIELDS...

...AND *YOUR ACTIONS* WILL SOON DRAW IT OUT INTO THE OPEN, CONNER KENT.

MINE? HOW ABOUT YOU JUST DROP THE OMINOUS, CRYPTIC SHTICK AND TELL ME WHAT *EXACTLY* YOU'RE TALKING ABOUT, MAN.

SNIFF SNIFF

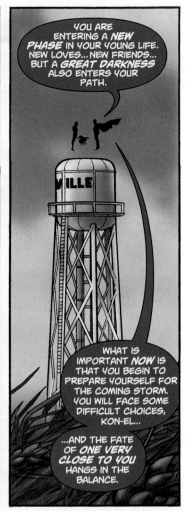

YOU ARE ENTERING A *NEW PHASE* IN YOUR YOUNG LIFE. NEW LOVES... NEW FRIENDS... BUT A *GREAT DARKNESS* ALSO ENTERS YOUR PATH.

'VILLE

WHAT IS IMPORTANT *NOW* IS THAT YOU BEGIN TO PREPARE YOURSELF FOR THE COMING STORM. YOU WILL FACE SOME DIFFICULT CHOICES, KON-EL...

...AND THE FATE OF *ONE VERY CLOSE TO YOU* HANGS IN THE BALANCE.

WHEN NEXT WE MEET, I WILL BE ABLE TO EXPLAIN MORE, BUT NOW YOU MUST GO.

GO? GO WHERE?

HOME. THE KENT FARM. YOU ARE URGENTLY NEEDED.

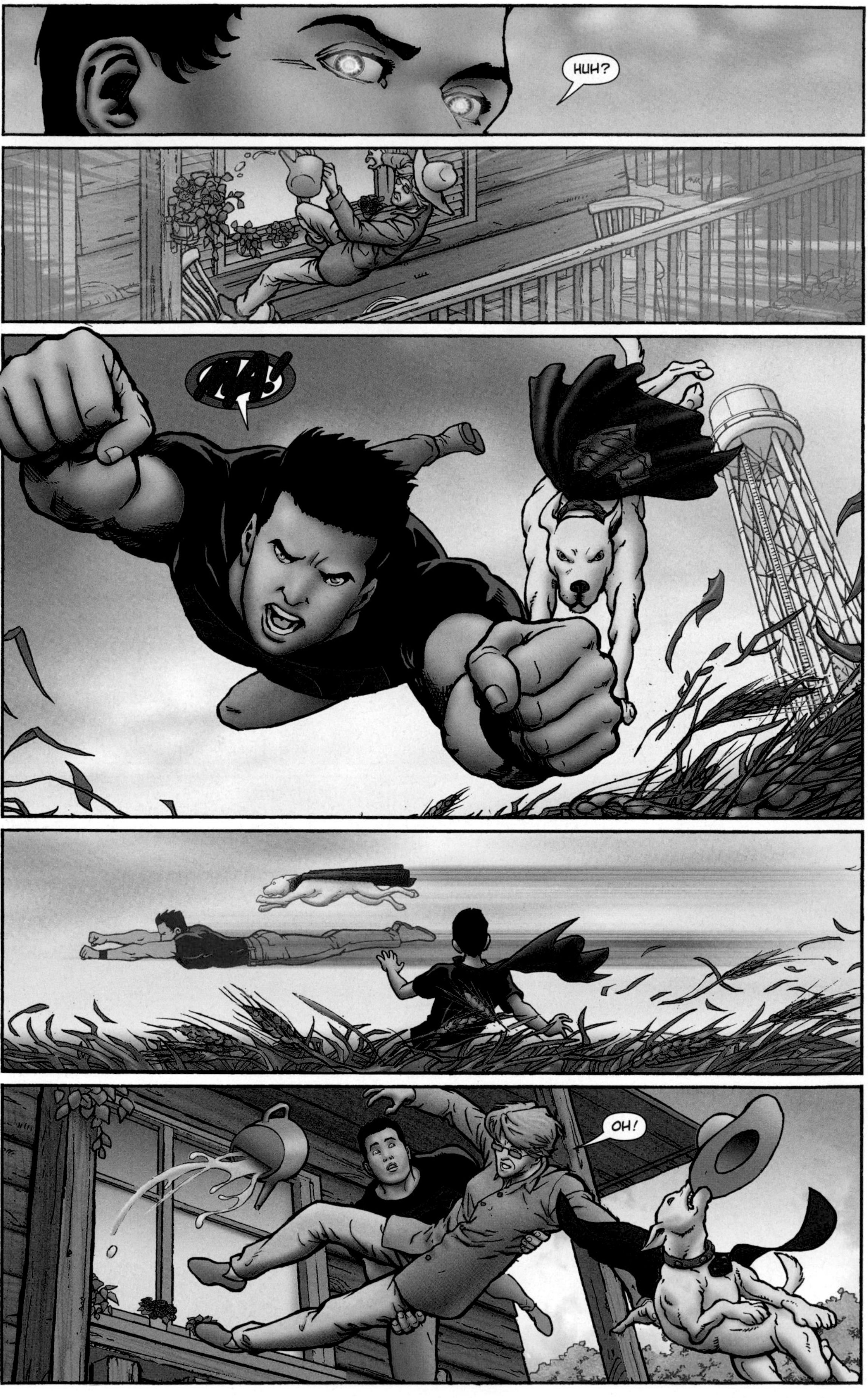
HUH?
OH!

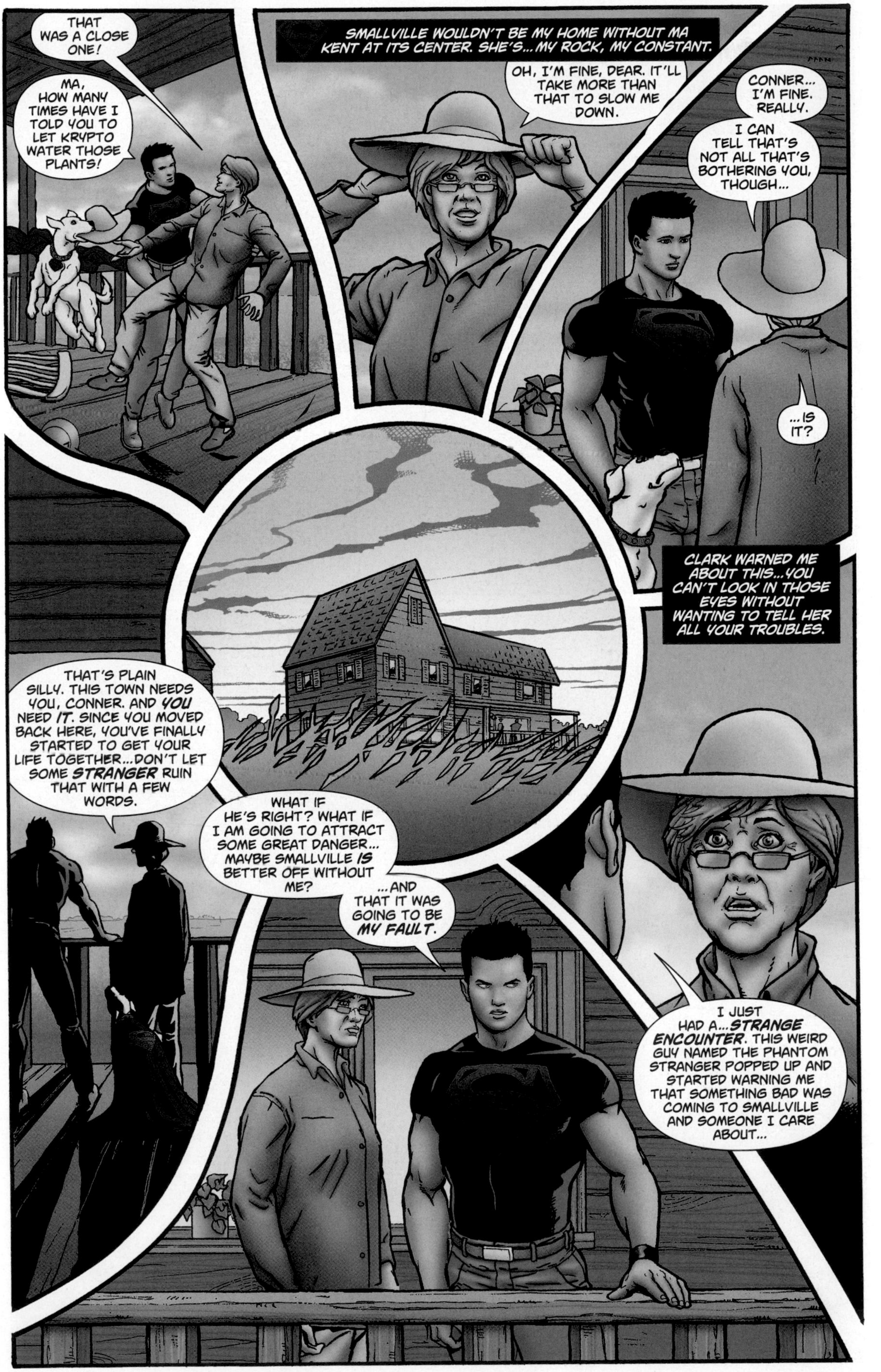
THAT WAS A CLOSE ONE!
MA, HOW MANY TIMES HAVE I TOLD YOU TO LET KRYPTO WATER THOSE PLANTS!
SMALLVILLE WOULDN'T BE MY HOME WITHOUT MA KENT AT ITS CENTER. SHE'S... MY ROCK, MY CONSTANT.
OH, I'M FINE, DEAR. IT'LL TAKE MORE THAN THAT TO SLOW ME DOWN.
CONNER... I'M FINE. REALLY.
I CAN TELL THAT'S NOT ALL THAT'S BOTHERING YOU, THOUGH...
...IS IT?
CLARK WARNED ME ABOUT THIS...YOU CAN'T LOOK IN THOSE EYES WITHOUT WANTING TO TELL HER ALL YOUR TROUBLES.
I JUST HAD A...STRANGE ENCOUNTER. THIS WEIRD GUY NAMED THE PHANTOM STRANGER POPPED UP AND STARTED WARNING ME THAT SOMETHING BAD WAS COMING TO SMALLVILLE AND SOMEONE I CARE ABOUT...
...AND THAT IT WAS GOING TO BE MY FAULT.
WHAT IF HE'S RIGHT? WHAT IF I AM GOING TO ATTRACT SOME GREAT DANGER... MAYBE SMALLVILLE IS BETTER OFF WITHOUT ME?
THAT'S PLAIN SILLY. THIS TOWN NEEDS YOU, CONNER. AND YOU NEED IT. SINCE YOU MOVED BACK HERE, YOU'VE FINALLY STARTED TO GET YOUR LIFE TOGETHER...DON'T LET SOME STRANGER RUIN THAT WITH A FEW WORDS.

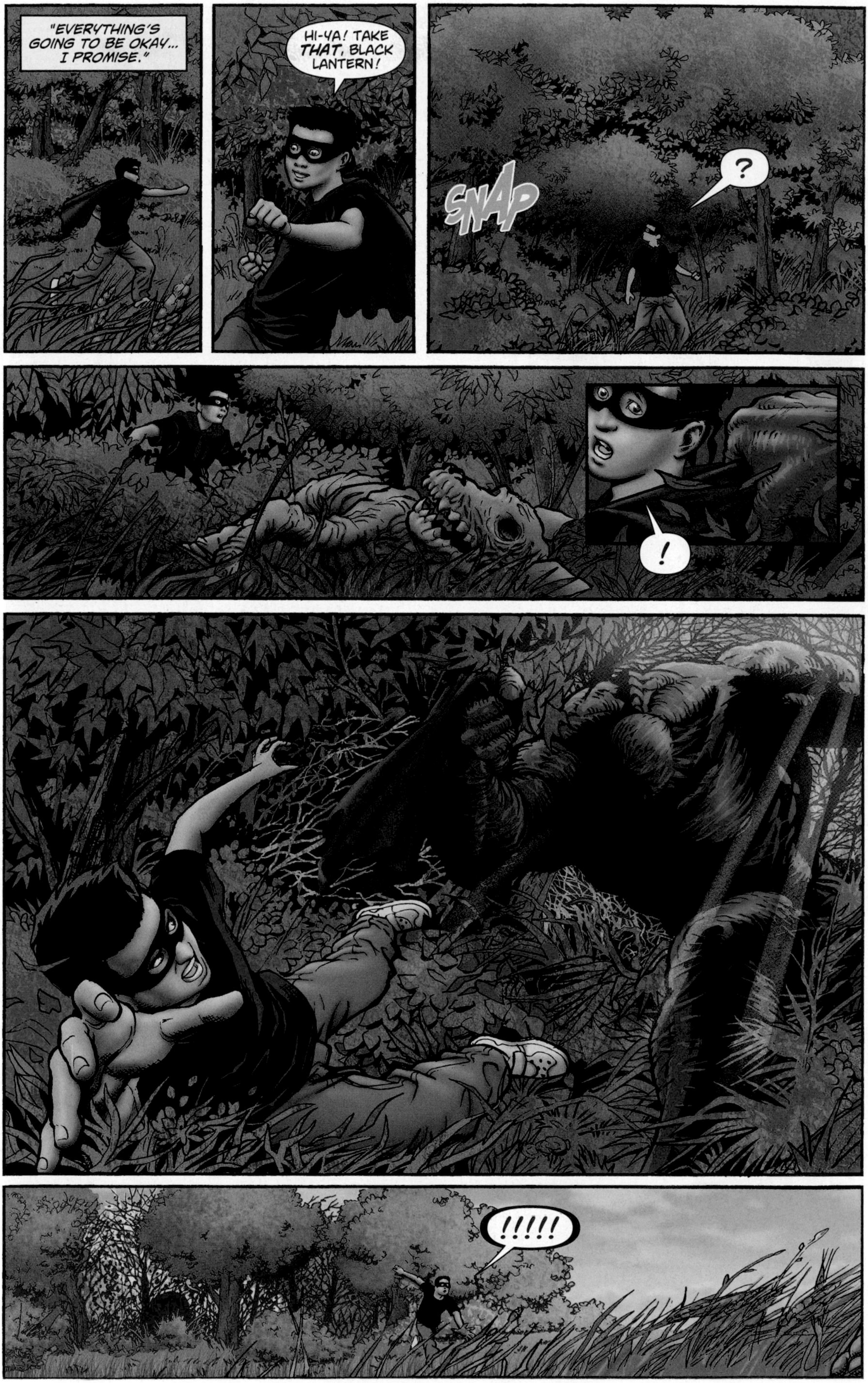
"EVERYTHING'S GOING TO BE OKAY... I PROMISE."
HI-YA! TAKE THAT, BLACK LANTERN!
SNAP
?
!
!!!!!

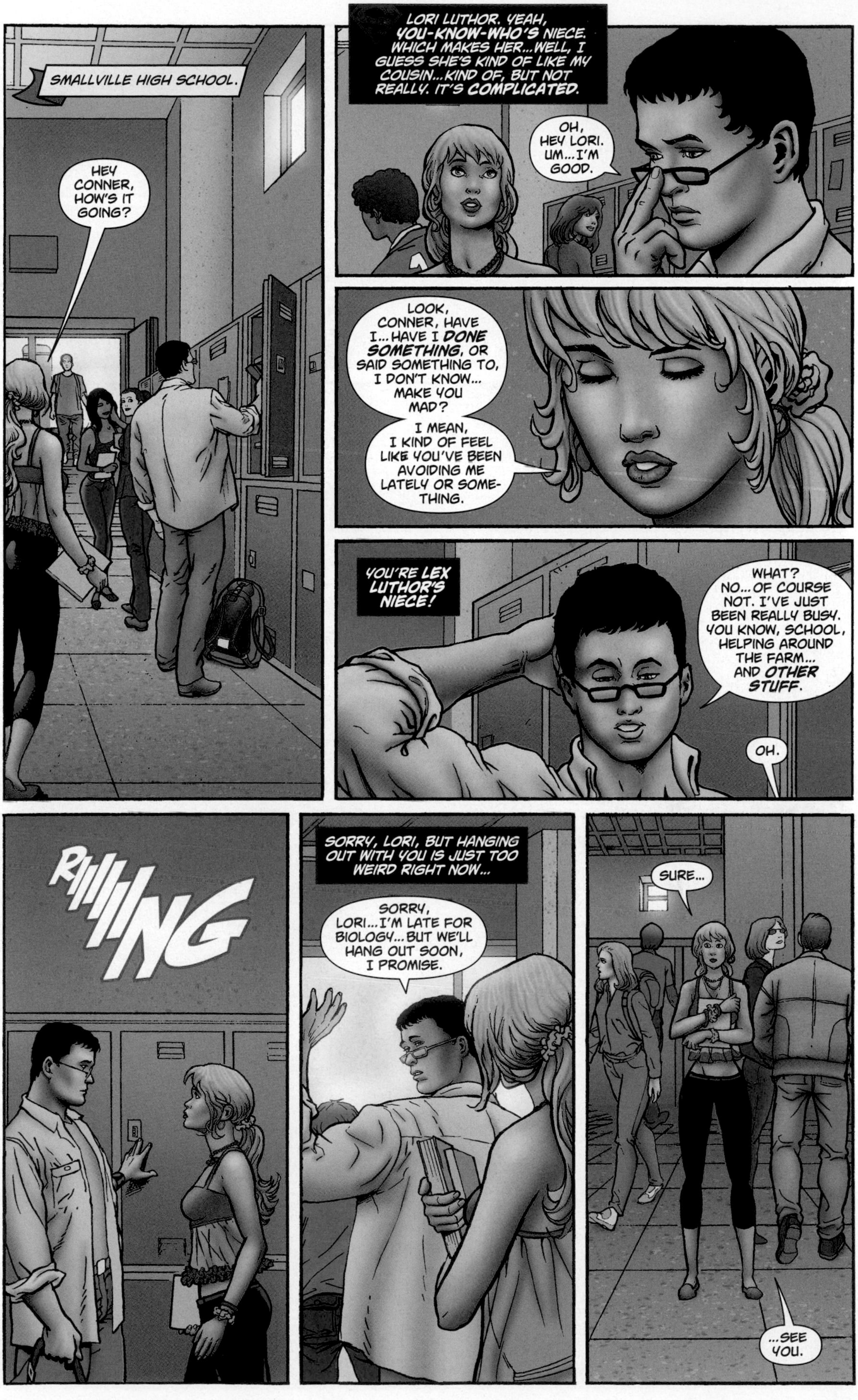
SMALLVILLE HIGH SCHOOL.
HEY CONNER, HOW'S IT GOING?
LORI LUTHOR. YEAH, YOU-KNOW-WHO'S NIECE. WHICH MAKES HER...WELL, I GUESS SHE'S KIND OF LIKE MY COUSIN...KIND OF, BUT NOT REALLY. IT'S COMPLICATED.
OH, HEY LORI. UM...I'M GOOD.
LOOK, CONNER, HAVE I...HAVE I DONE SOMETHING, OR SAID SOMETHING TO, I DON'T KNOW... MAKE YOU MAD?
I MEAN, I KIND OF FEEL LIKE YOU'VE BEEN AVOIDING ME LATELY OR SOME-THING.
YOU'RE LEX LUTHOR'S NIECE!
WHAT? NO...OF COURSE NOT. I'VE JUST BEEN REALLY BUSY. YOU KNOW, SCHOOL, HELPING AROUND THE FARM... AND OTHER STUFF.
OH.
RIIIING
SORRY, LORI, BUT HANGING OUT WITH YOU IS JUST TOO WEIRD RIGHT NOW...
SORRY, LORI...I'M LATE FOR BIOLOGY...BUT WE'LL HANG OUT SOON, I PROMISE.
SURE...
...SEE YOU.

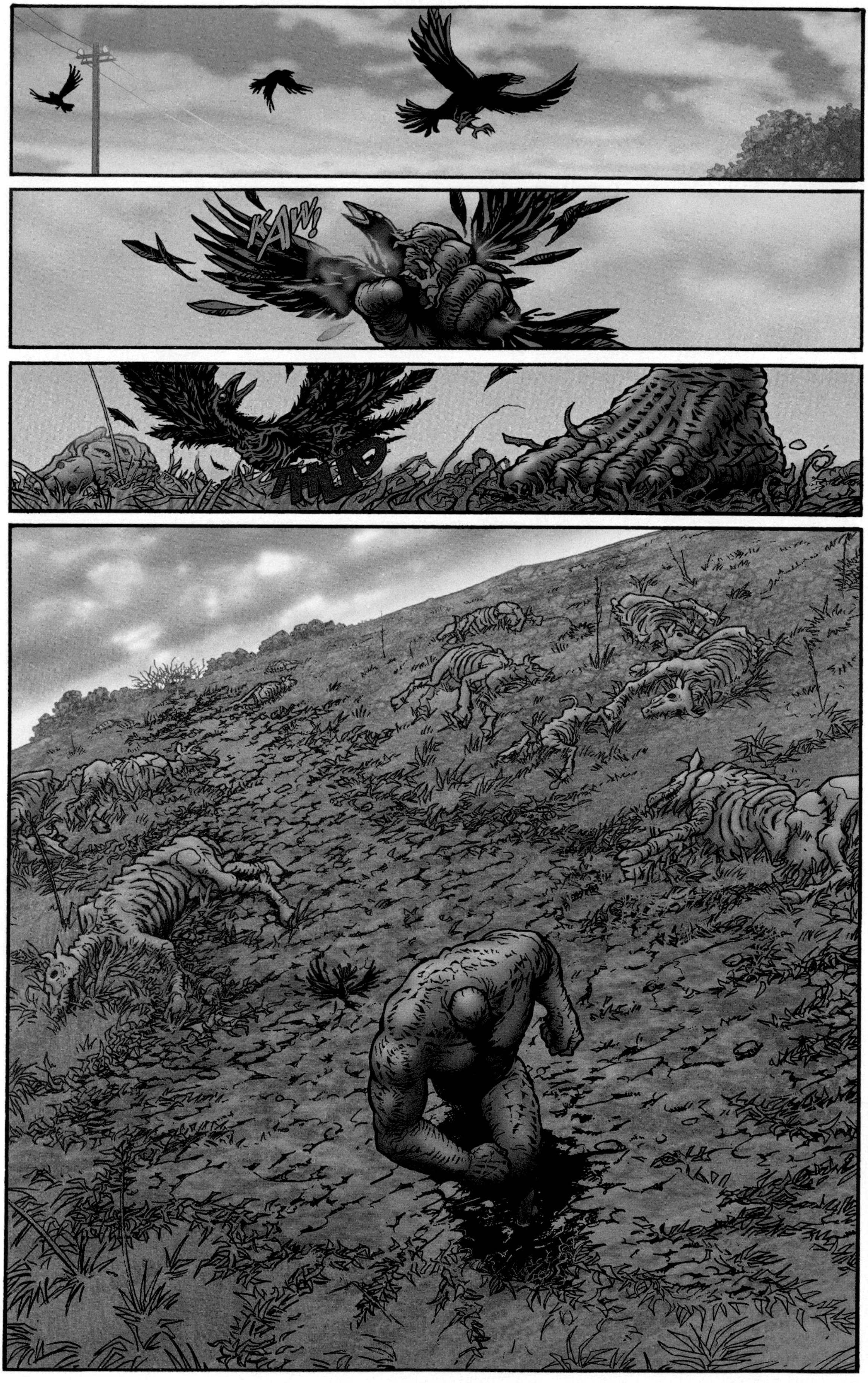
KAW!
THUD

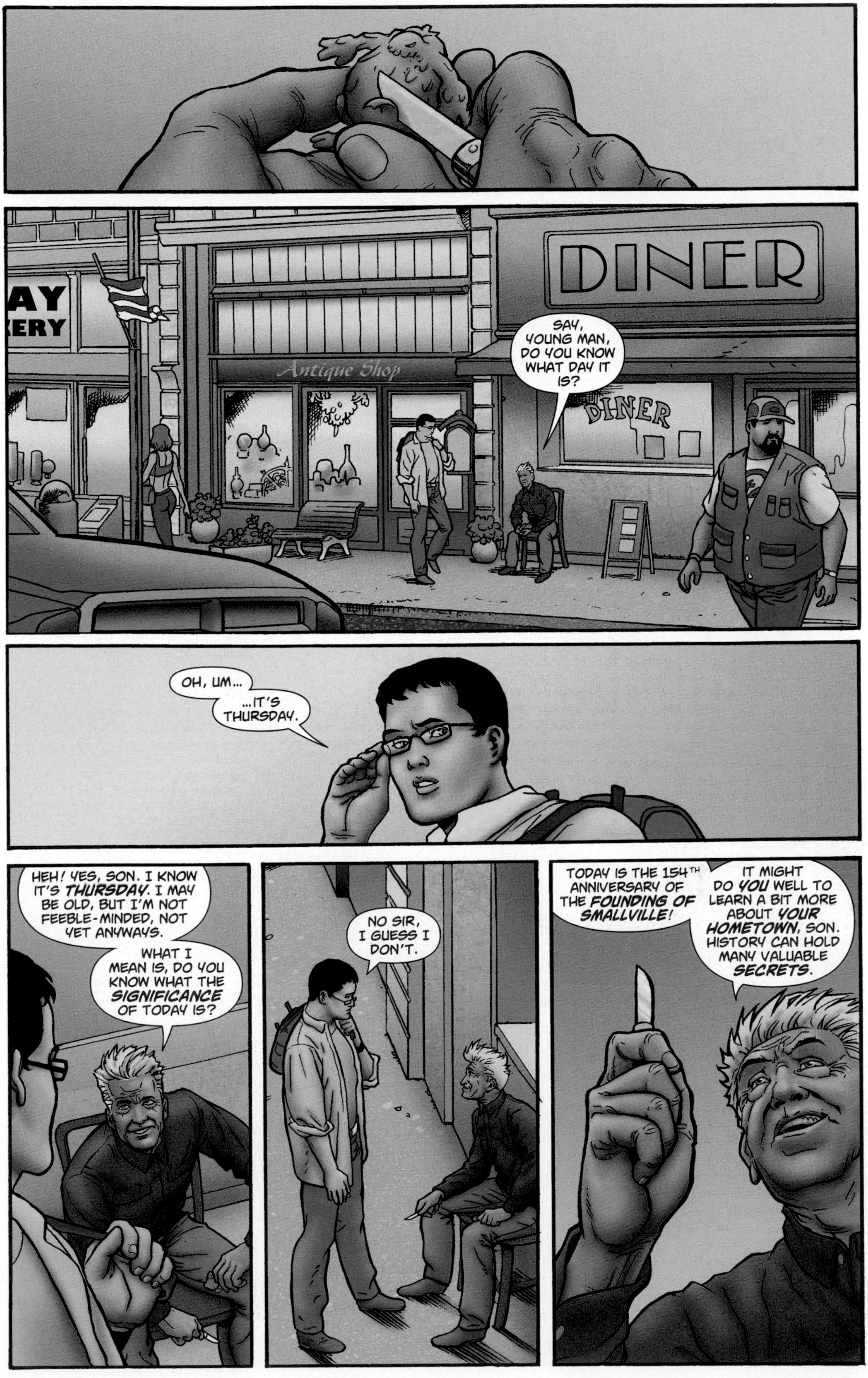
AY
KERY
Antique Shop
DINER
SAY, YOUNG MAN, DO YOU KNOW WHAT DAY IT IS?
DINER
OH, UM...
...IT'S THURSDAY.
HEH! YES, SON. I KNOW IT'S THURSDAY. I MAY BE OLD, BUT I'M NOT FEEBLE-MINDED, NOT YET ANYWAYS.
WHAT I MEAN IS, DO YOU KNOW WHAT THE SIGNIFICANCE OF TODAY IS?
NO SIR, I GUESS I DON'T.
TODAY IS THE 154TH ANNIVERSARY OF THE FOUNDING OF SMALLVILLE!
IT MIGHT DO YOU WELL TO LEARN A BIT MORE ABOUT YOUR HOMETOWN, SON. HISTORY CAN HOLD MANY VALUABLE SECRETS.

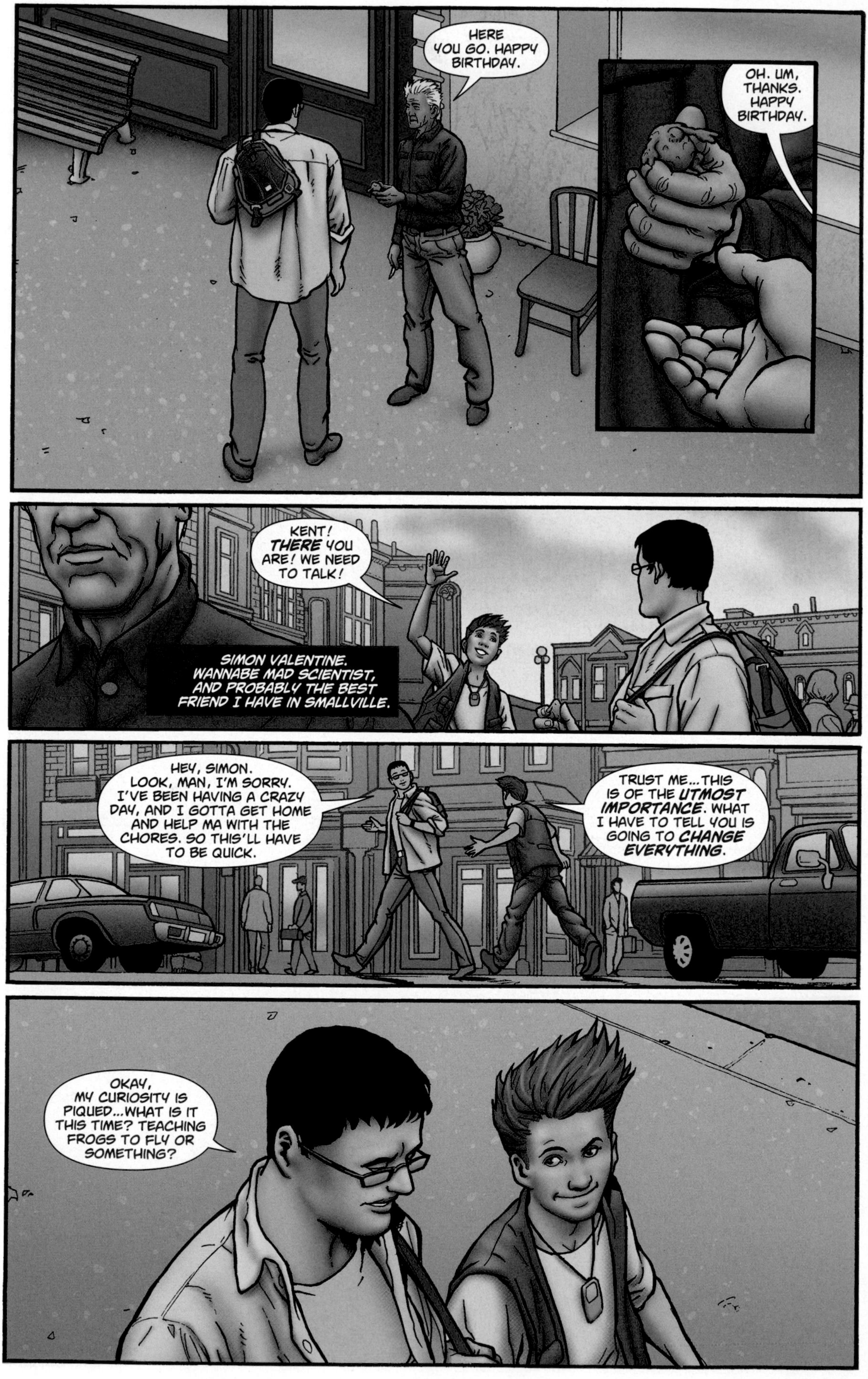
HERE YOU GO. HAPPY BIRTHDAY.
OH. UM, THANKS. HAPPY BIRTHDAY.
KENT! THERE YOU ARE! WE NEED TO TALK!
SIMON VALENTINE. WANNABE MAD SCIENTIST, AND PROBABLY THE BEST FRIEND I HAVE IN SMALLVILLE.
HEY, SIMON. LOOK, MAN, I'M SORRY. I'VE BEEN HAVING A CRAZY DAY, AND I GOTTA GET HOME AND HELP MA WITH THE CHORES. SO THIS'LL HAVE TO BE QUICK.
TRUST ME...THIS IS OF THE UTMOST IMPORTANCE. WHAT I HAVE TO TELL YOU IS GOING TO CHANGE EVERYTHING.
OKAY, MY CURIOSITY IS PIQUED...WHAT IS IT THIS TIME? TEACHING FROGS TO FLY OR SOMETHING?

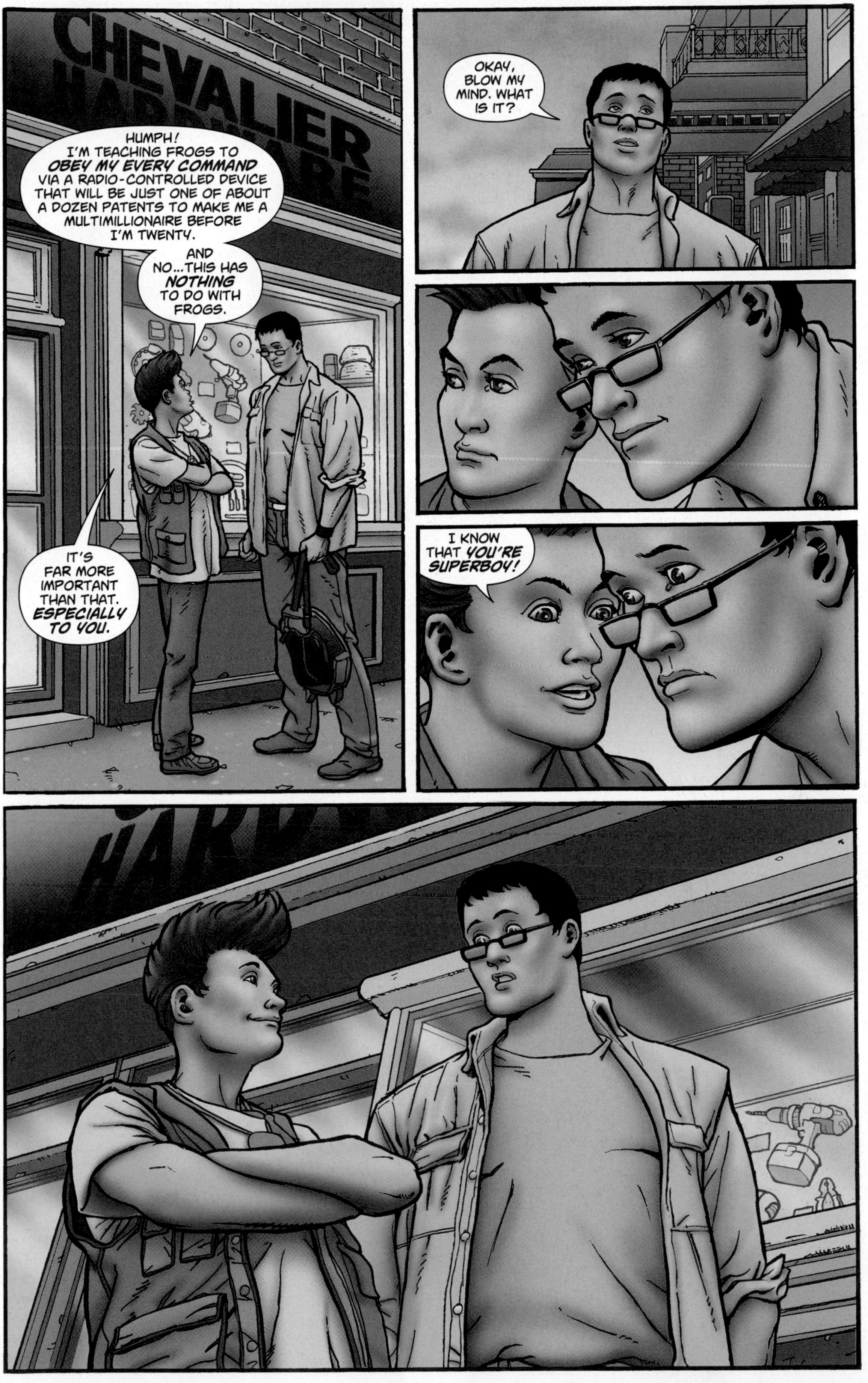
CHEVALIER HARDWARE
HUMPH! I'M TEACHING FROGS TO OBEY MY EVERY COMMAND VIA A RADIO-CONTROLLED DEVICE THAT WILL BE JUST ONE OF ABOUT A DOZEN PATENTS TO MAKE ME A MULTIMILLIONAIRE BEFORE I'M TWENTY.
AND NO...THIS HAS NOTHING TO DO WITH FROGS.
IT'S FAR MORE IMPORTANT THAN THAT. ESPECIALLY TO YOU.
OKAY, BLOW MY MIND. WHAT IS IT?
I KNOW THAT YOU'RE SUPERBOY!

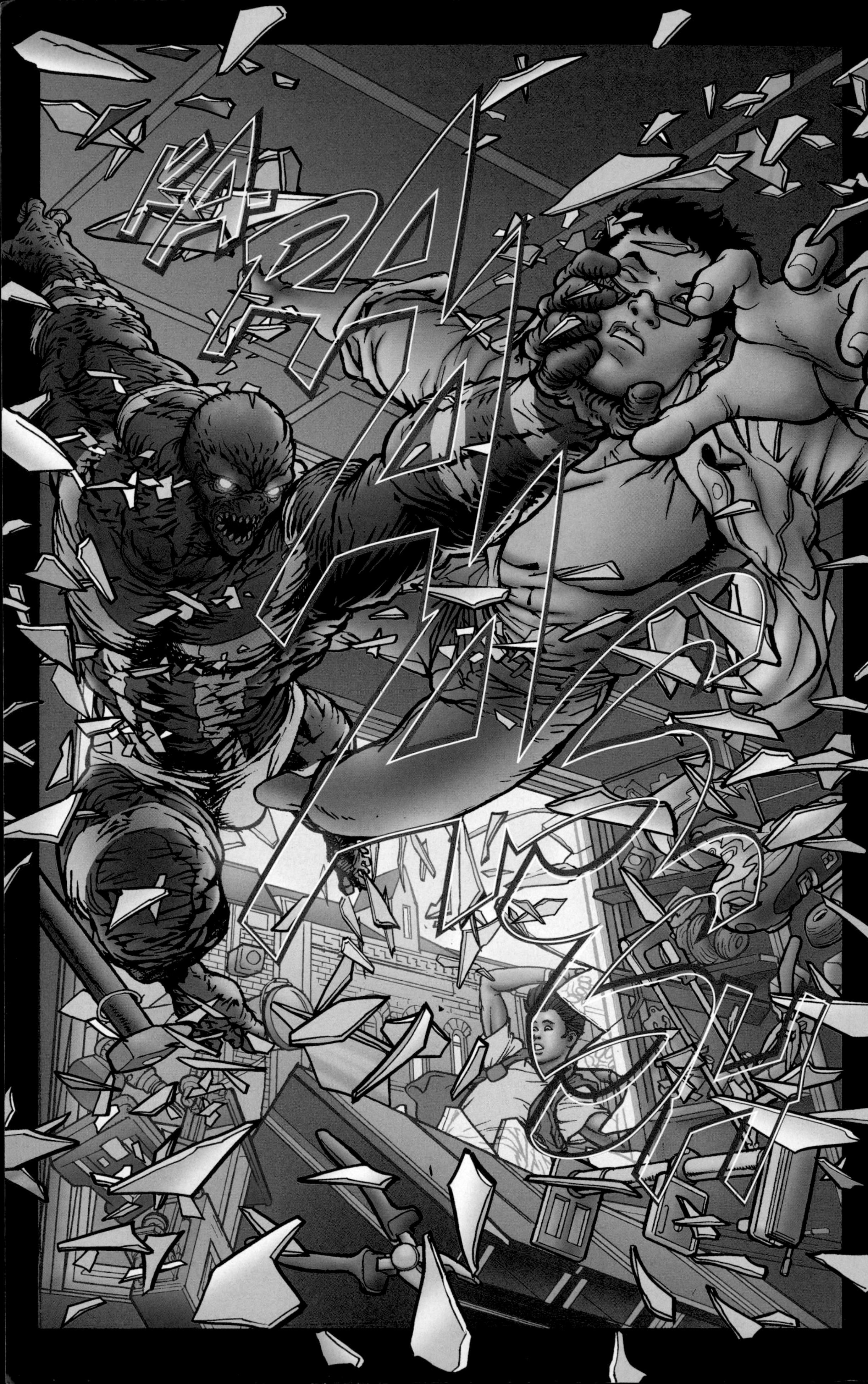

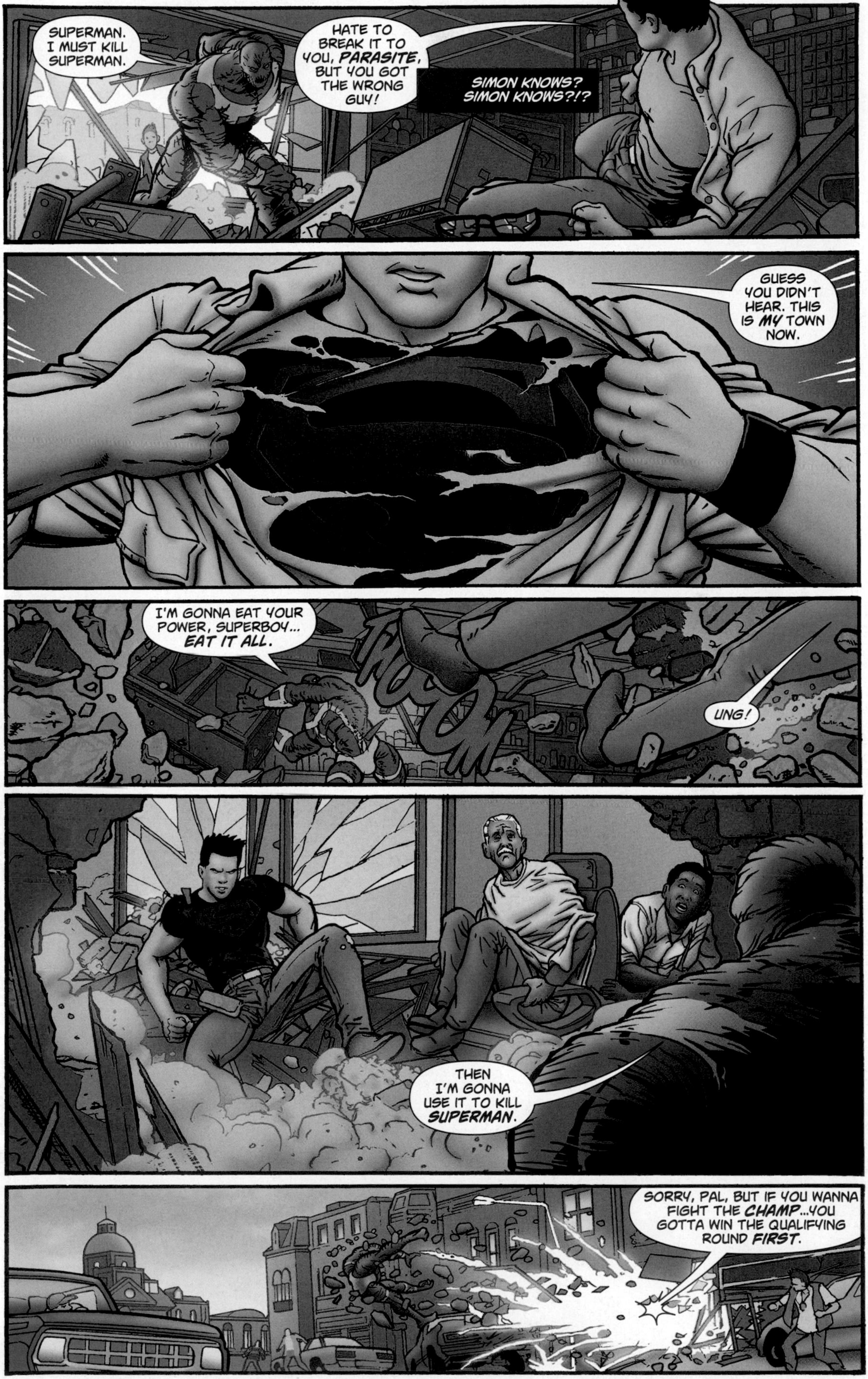
SUPERMAN. I MUST KILL SUPERMAN.
HATE TO BREAK IT TO YOU, PARASITE, BUT YOU GOT THE WRONG GUY!
SIMON KNOWS? SIMON KNOWS?!?
GUESS YOU DIDN'T HEAR. THIS IS MY TOWN NOW.
I'M GONNA EAT YOUR POWER, SUPERBOY... EAT IT ALL.
UNG!
THEN I'M GONNA USE IT TO KILL SUPERMAN.
SORRY, PAL, BUT IF YOU WANNA FIGHT THE CHAMP...YOU GOTTA WIN THE QUALIFYING ROUND FIRST.

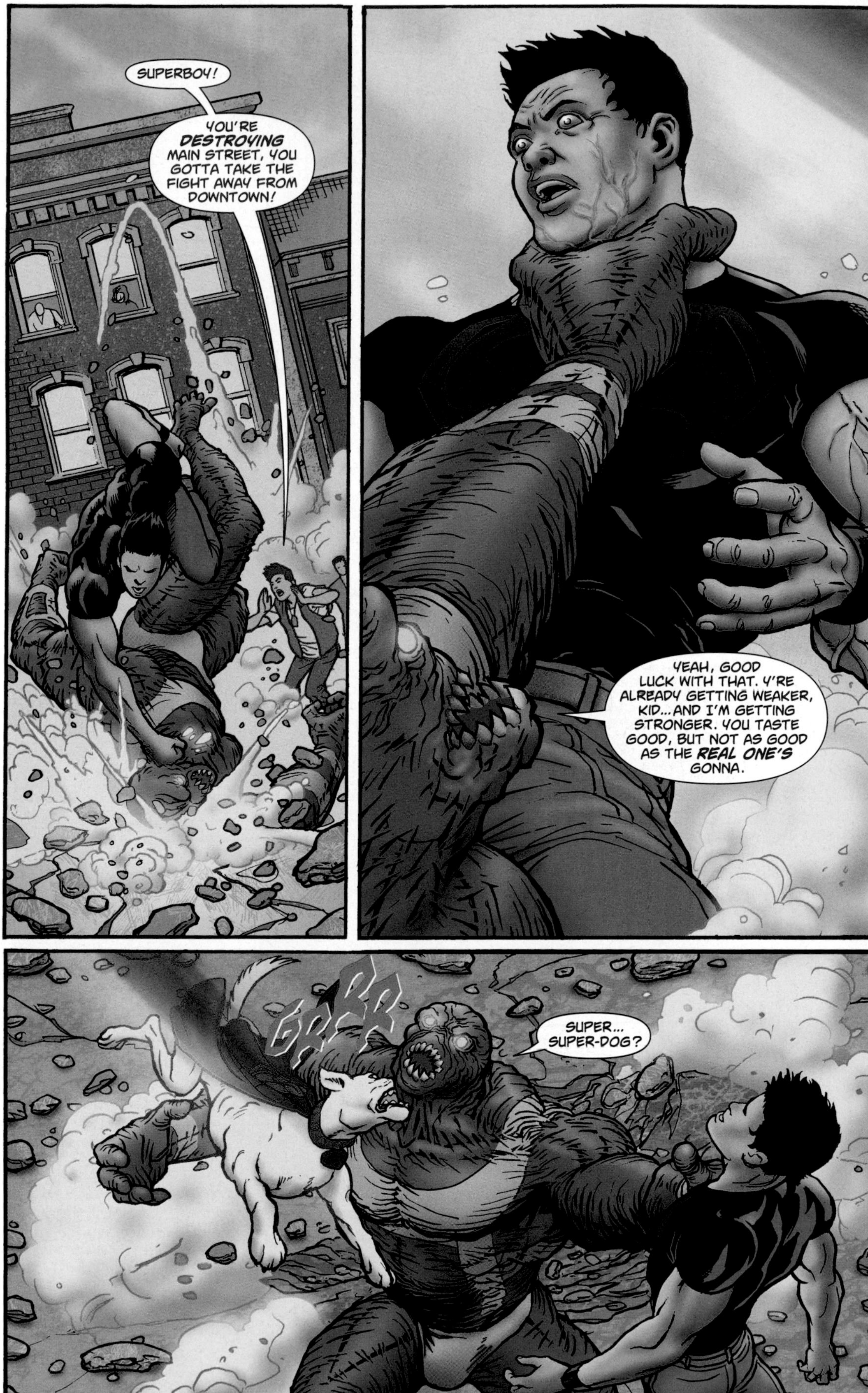
SUPERBOY!
YOU'RE DESTROYING MAIN STREET, YOU GOTTA TAKE THE FIGHT AWAY FROM DOWNTOWN!
YEAH, GOOD LUCK WITH THAT. Y'RE ALREADY GETTING WEAKER, KID...AND I'M GETTING STRONGER. YOU TASTE GOOD, BUT NOT AS GOOD AS THE REAL ONE'S GONNA.
GRRR
SUPER... SUPER-DOG?

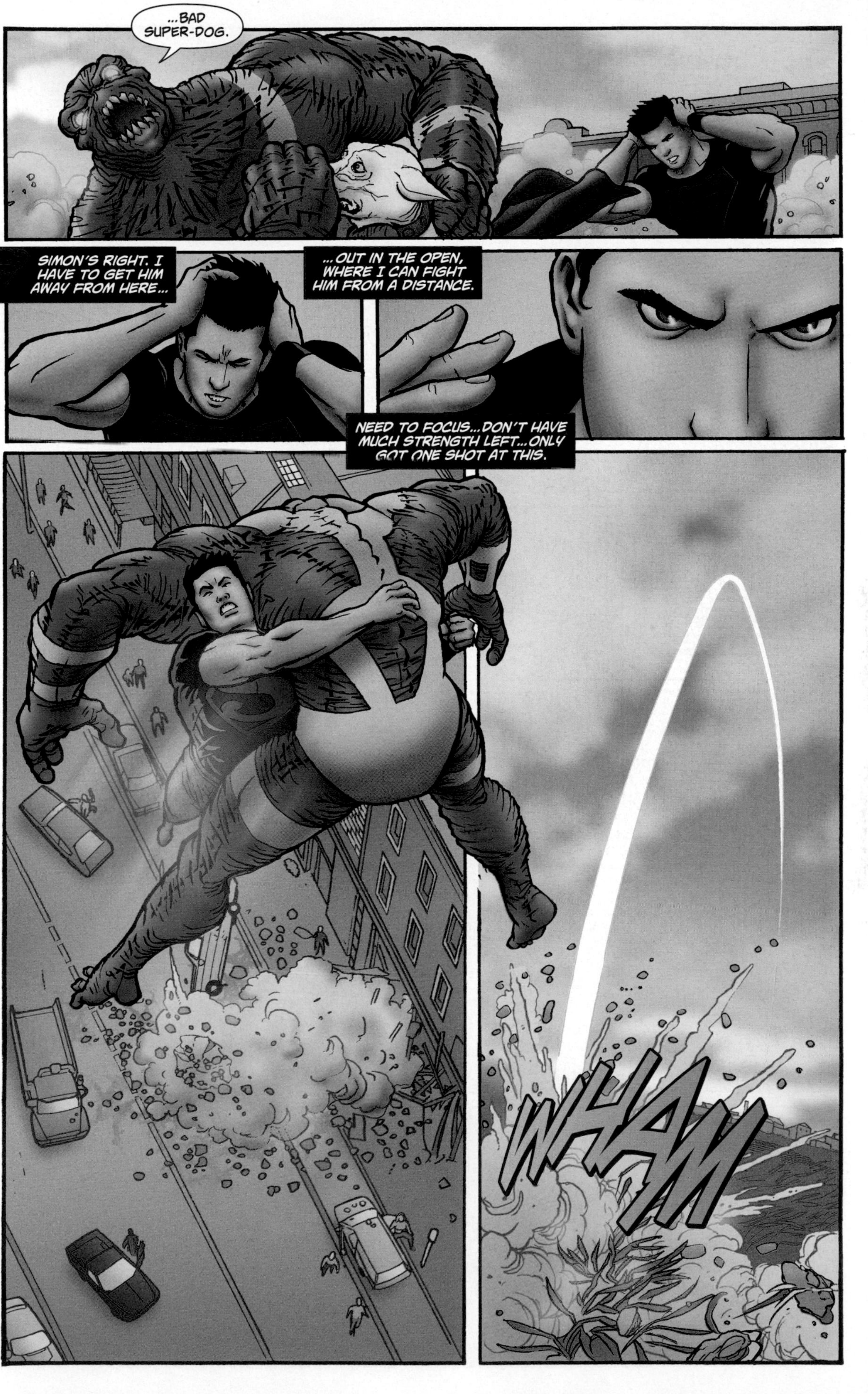
...BAD SUPER-DOG.
SIMON'S RIGHT. I HAVE TO GET HIM AWAY FROM HERE...
...OUT IN THE OPEN, WHERE I CAN FIGHT HIM FROM A DISTANCE.
NEED TO FOCUS...DON'T HAVE MUCH STRENGTH LEFT...ONLY GOT ONE SHOT AT THIS.
WHAM

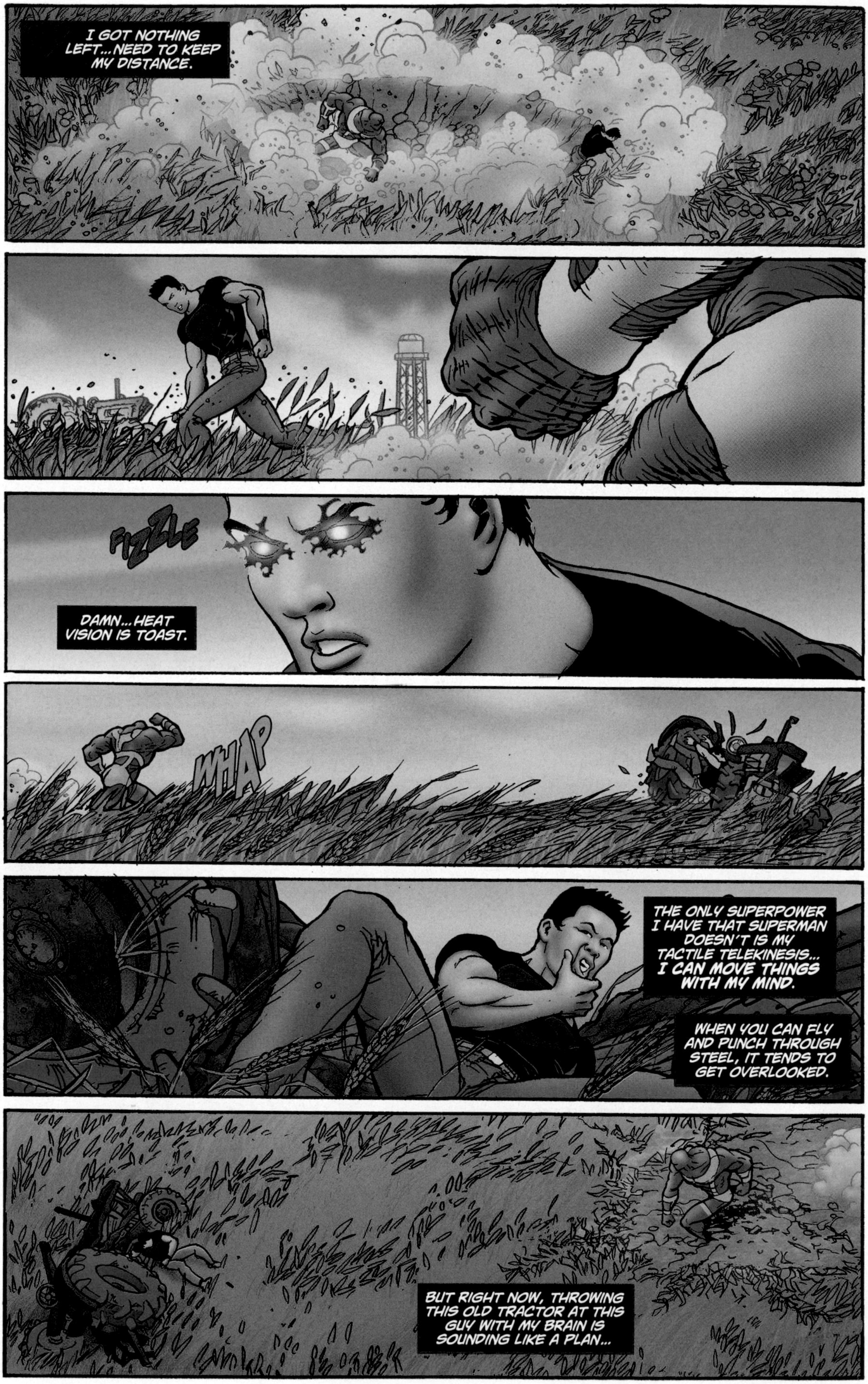
I GOT NOTHING LEFT...NEED TO KEEP MY DISTANCE.
FIZZLE
DAMN...HEAT VISION IS TOAST.
WHAP
THE ONLY SUPERPOWER I HAVE THAT SUPERMAN DOESN'T IS MY TACTILE TELEKINESIS... I CAN MOVE THINGS WITH MY MIND.
WHEN YOU CAN FLY AND PUNCH THROUGH STEEL, IT TENDS TO GET OVERLOOKED.
BUT RIGHT NOW, THROWING THIS OLD TRACTOR AT THIS GUY WITH MY BRAIN IS SOUNDING LIKE A PLAN...

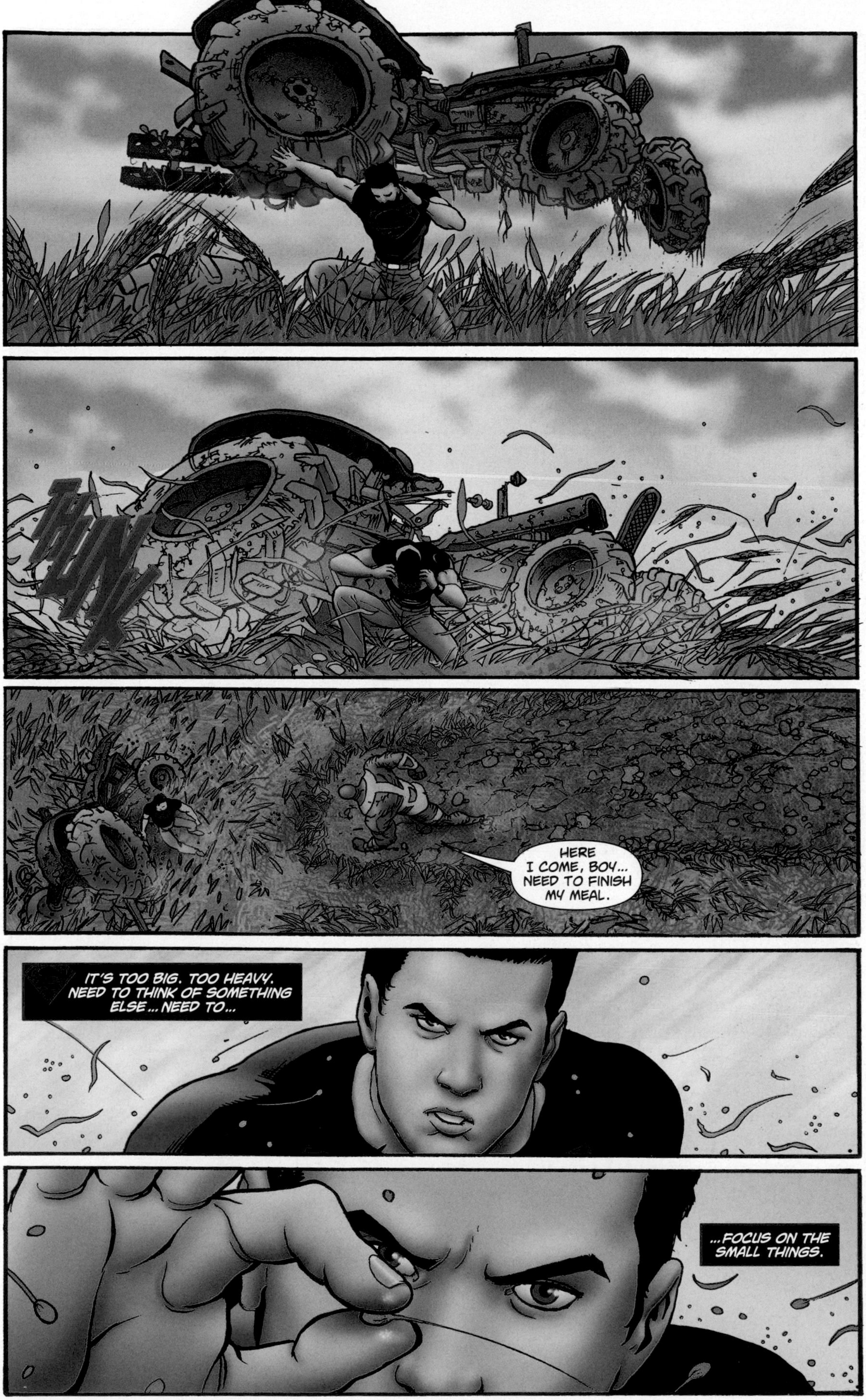
THUNK
HERE I COME, BOY... NEED TO FINISH MY MEAL.
IT'S TOO BIG. TOO HEAVY. NEED TO THINK OF SOMETHING ELSE... NEED TO...
...FOCUS ON THE SMALL THINGS.

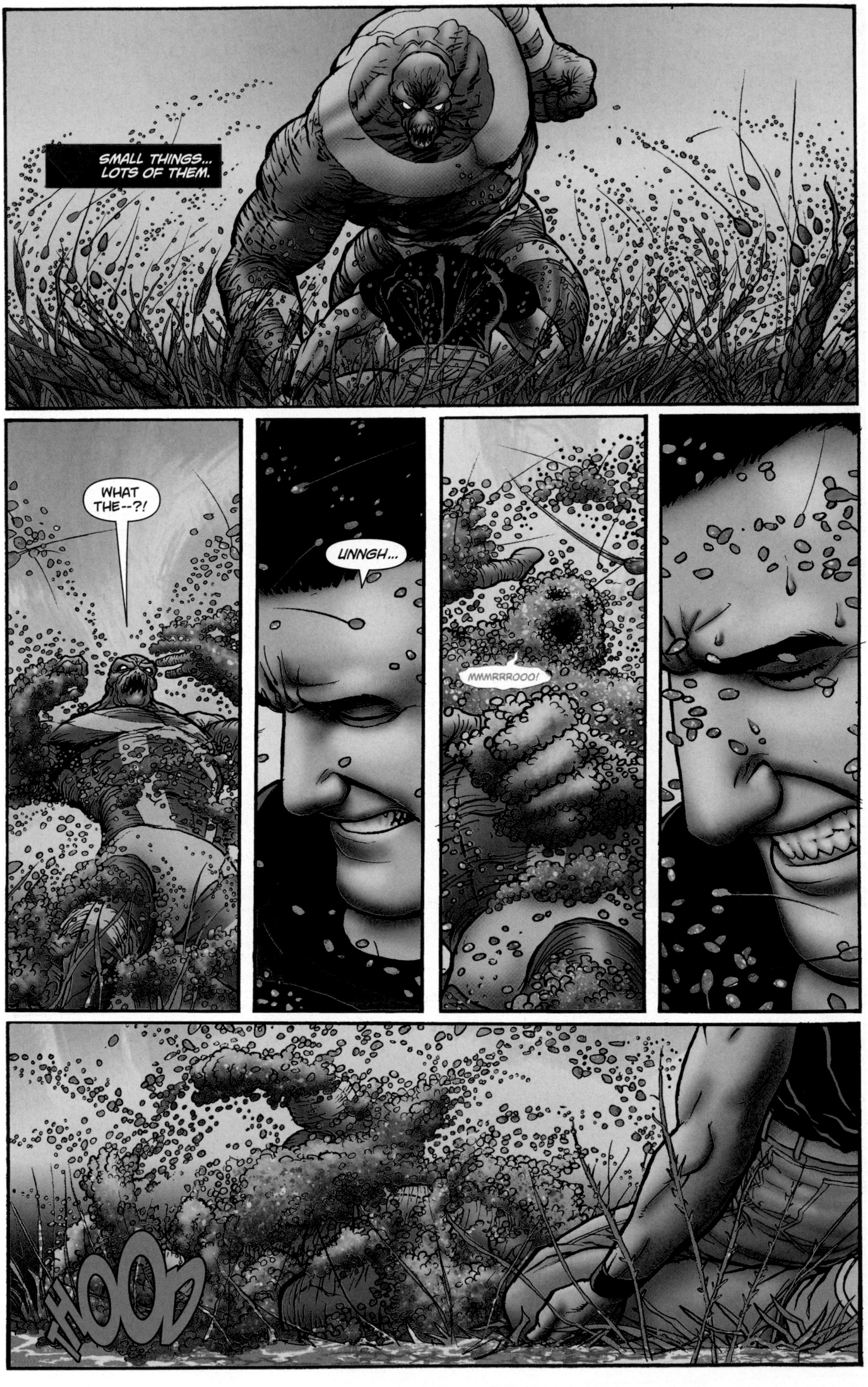
SMALL THINGS... LOTS OF THEM.
WHAT THE--?!
UNNGH...
MMMRRROOO!
HOOD

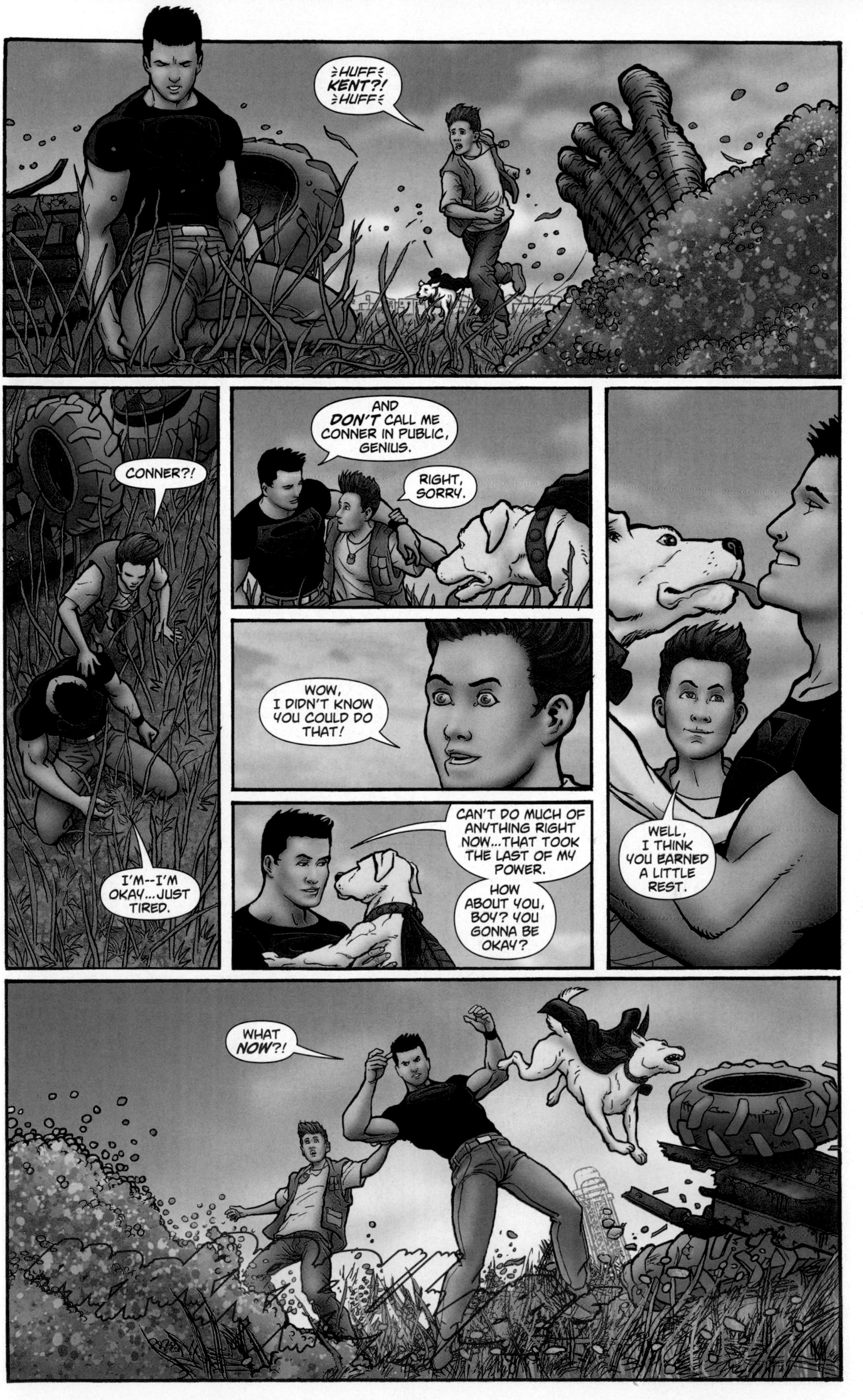
HUFF
KENT?!
HUFF
CONNER?!
I'M--I'M OKAY...JUST TIRED.
AND DON'T CALL ME CONNER IN PUBLIC, GENIUS.
RIGHT, SORRY.
WOW, I DIDN'T KNOW YOU COULD DO THAT!
CAN'T DO MUCH OF ANYTHING RIGHT NOW...THAT TOOK THE LAST OF MY POWER.
HOW ABOUT YOU, BOY? YOU GONNA BE OKAY?
WELL, I THINK YOU EARNED A LITTLE REST.
WHAT NOW?!

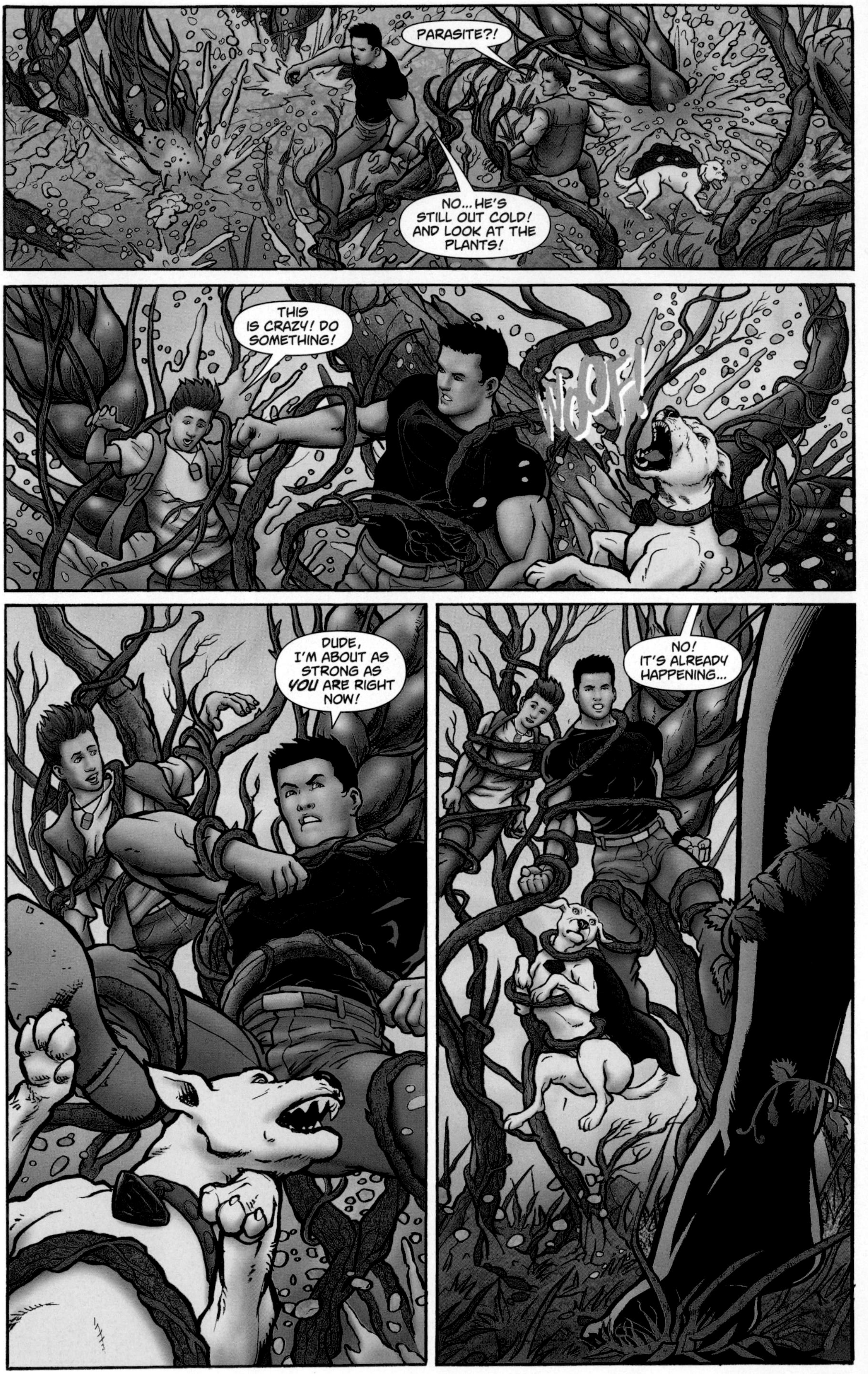
PARASITE?!
NO... HE'S STILL OUT COLD! AND LOOK AT THE PLANTS!
THIS IS CRAZY! DO SOMETHING!
WOOF!
DUDE, I'M ABOUT AS STRONG AS *YOU* ARE RIGHT NOW!
NO! IT'S ALREADY HAPPENING...

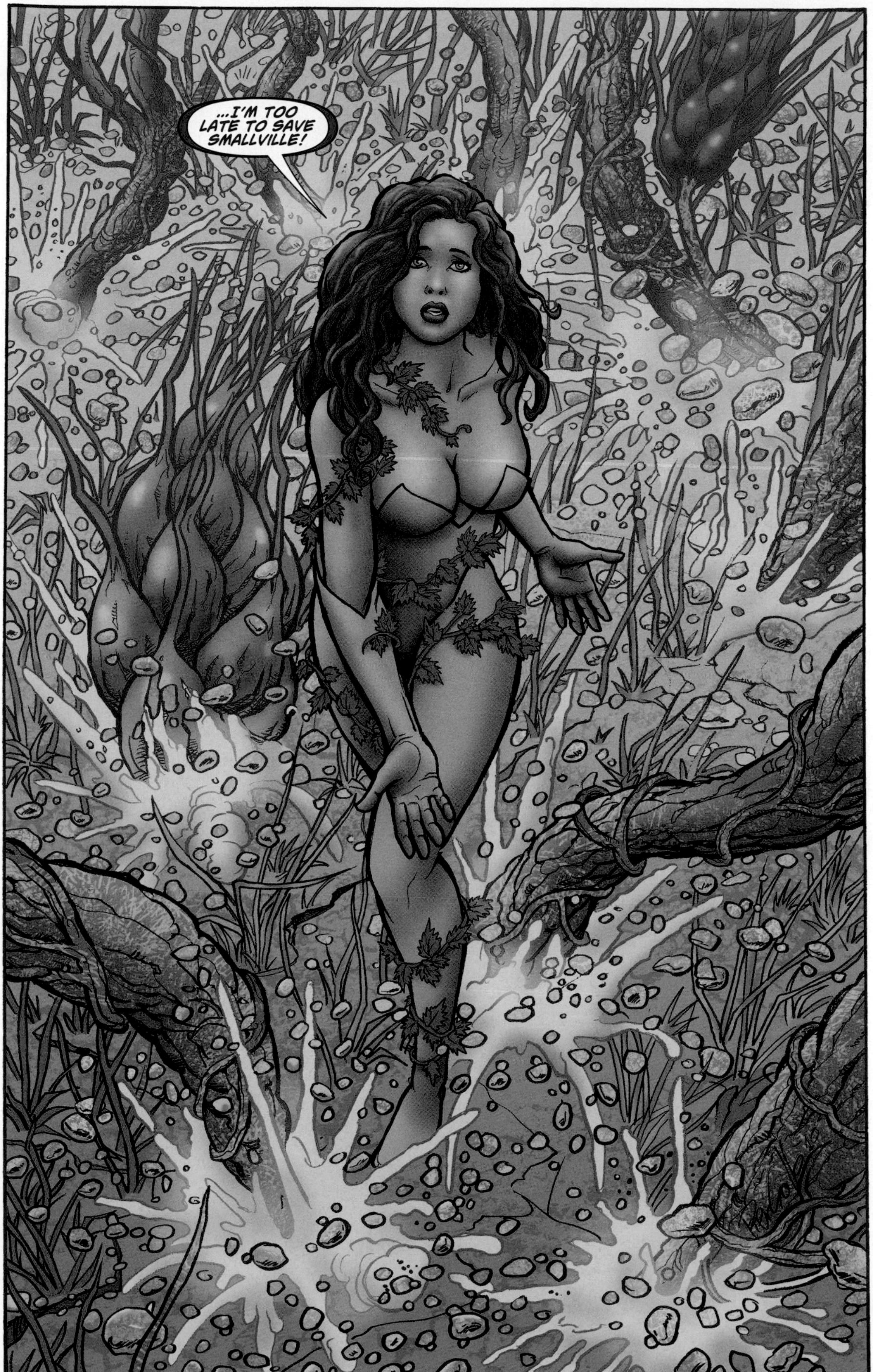
...I'M TOO LATE TO SAVE SMALLVILLE!

SUPERBOY #2
Cover by Phil Noto

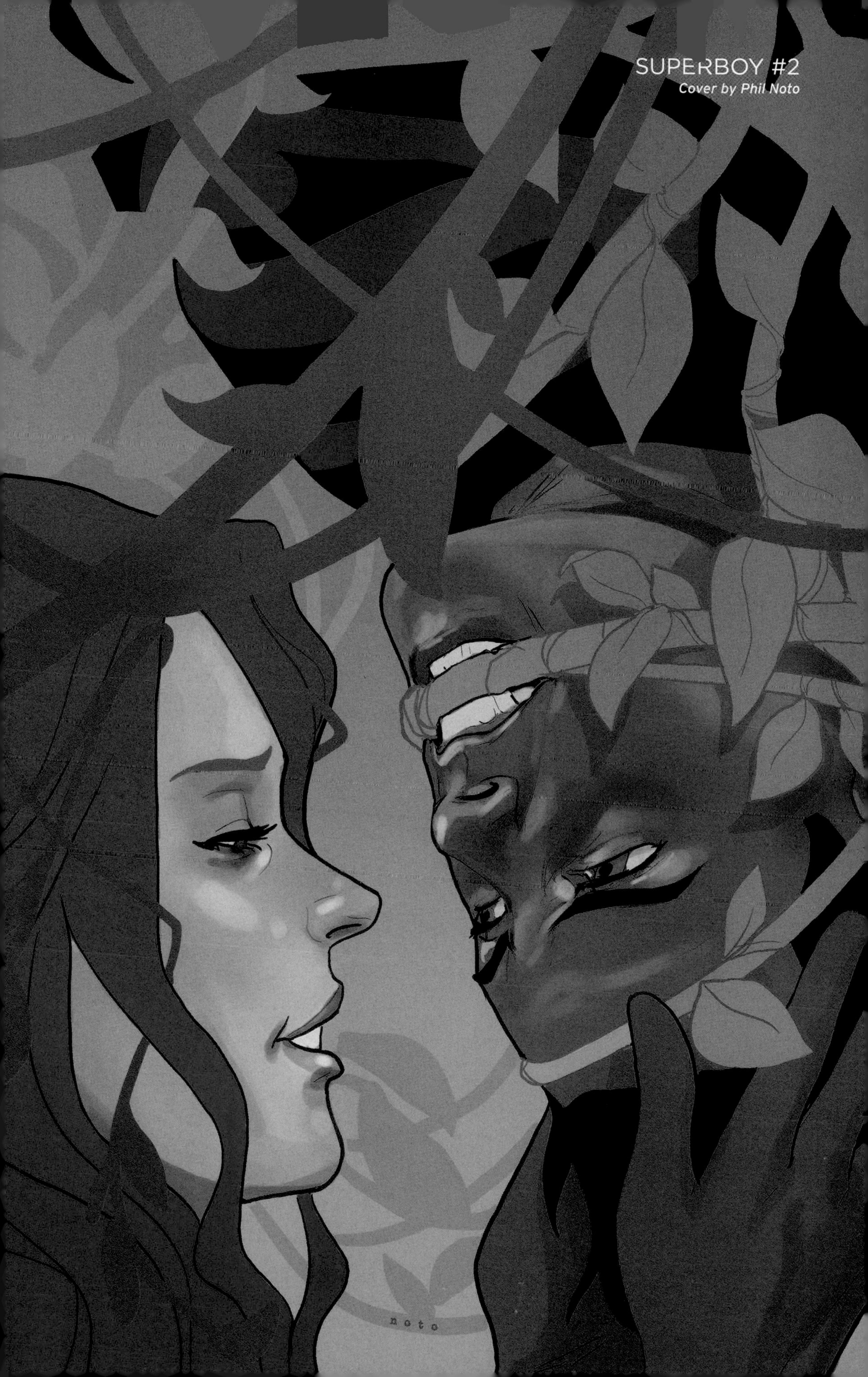
noto

SUPERBOY #2 | VARIANT

Cover by Guillem March

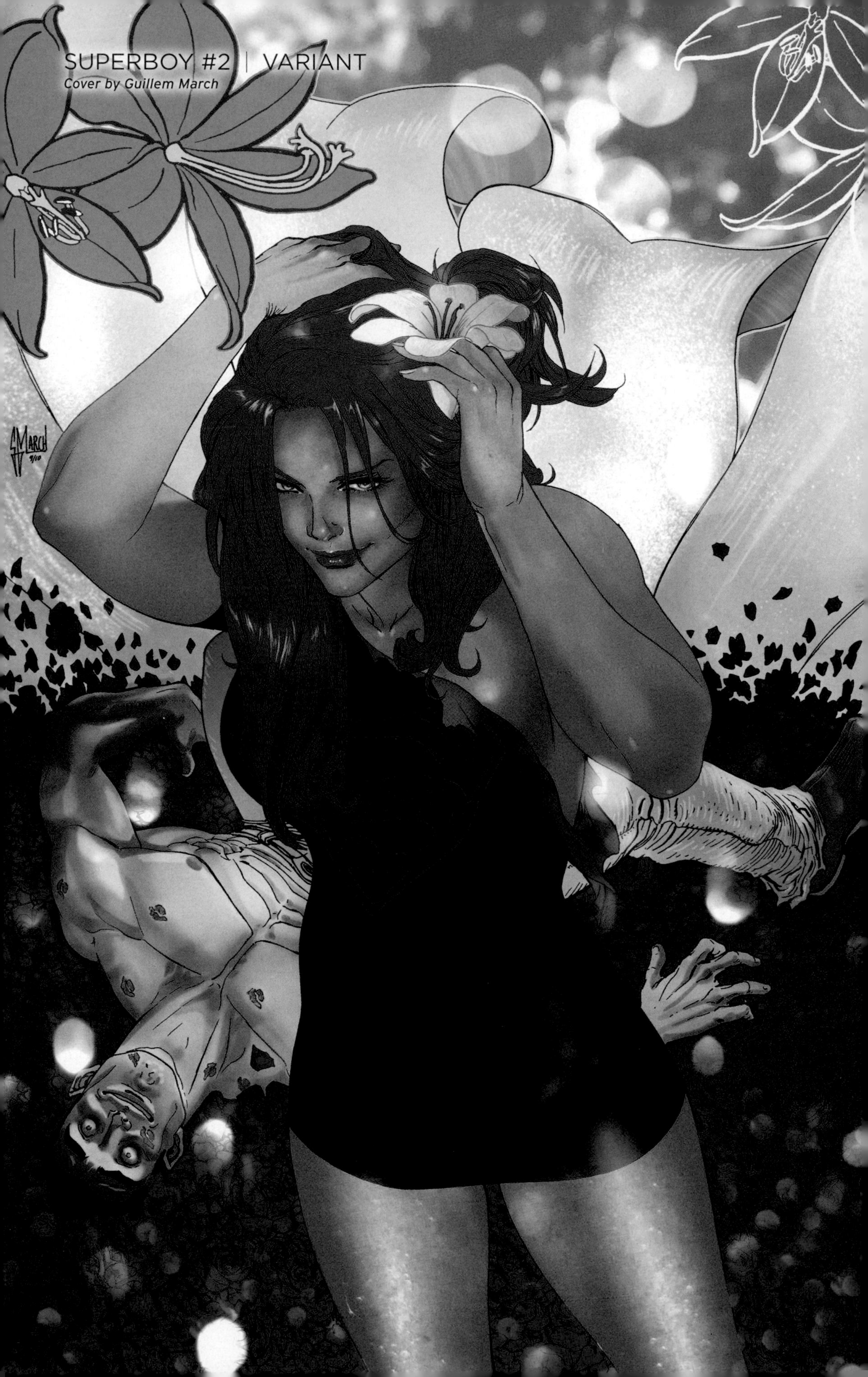

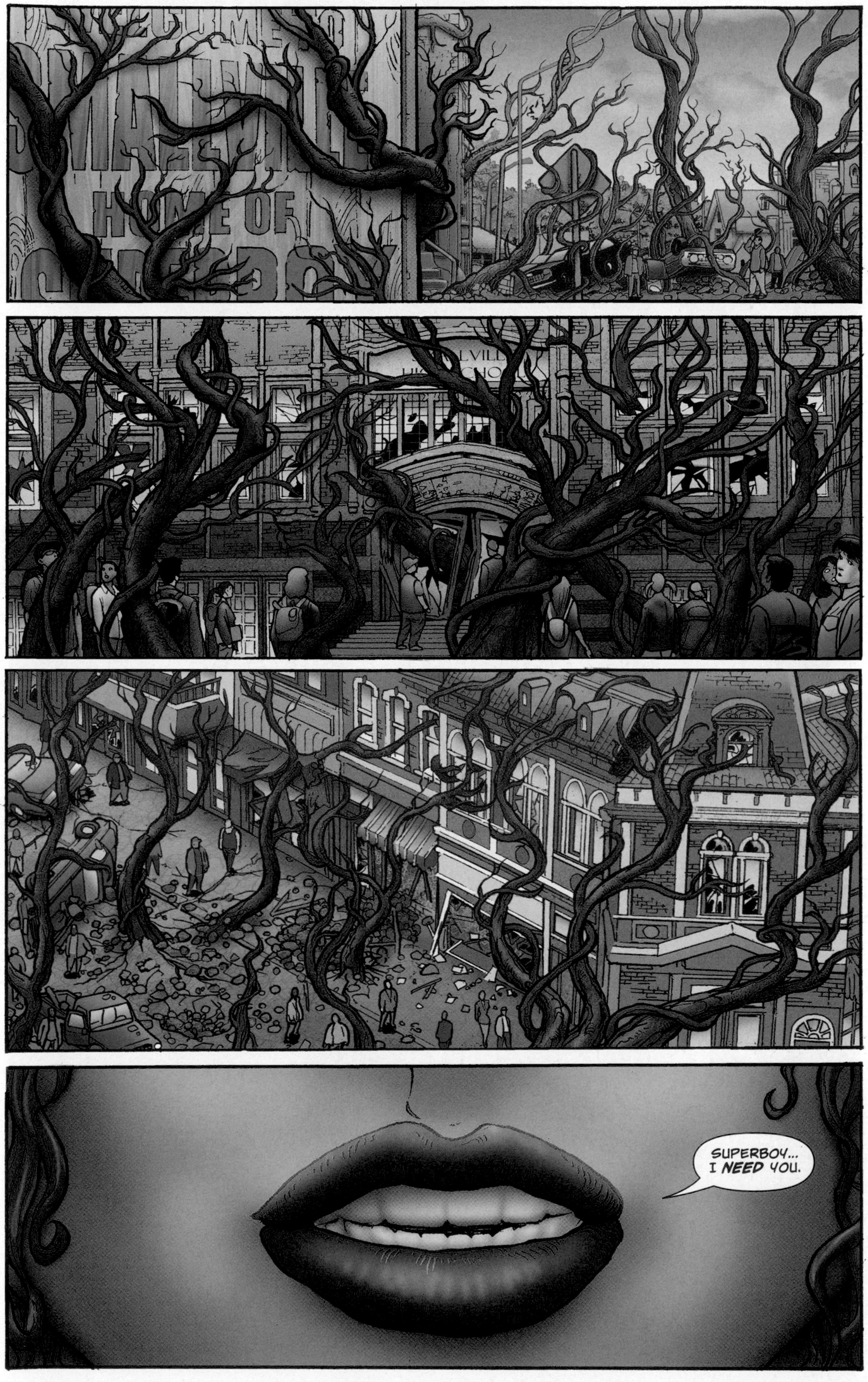
SUPERBOY... I NEED YOU.

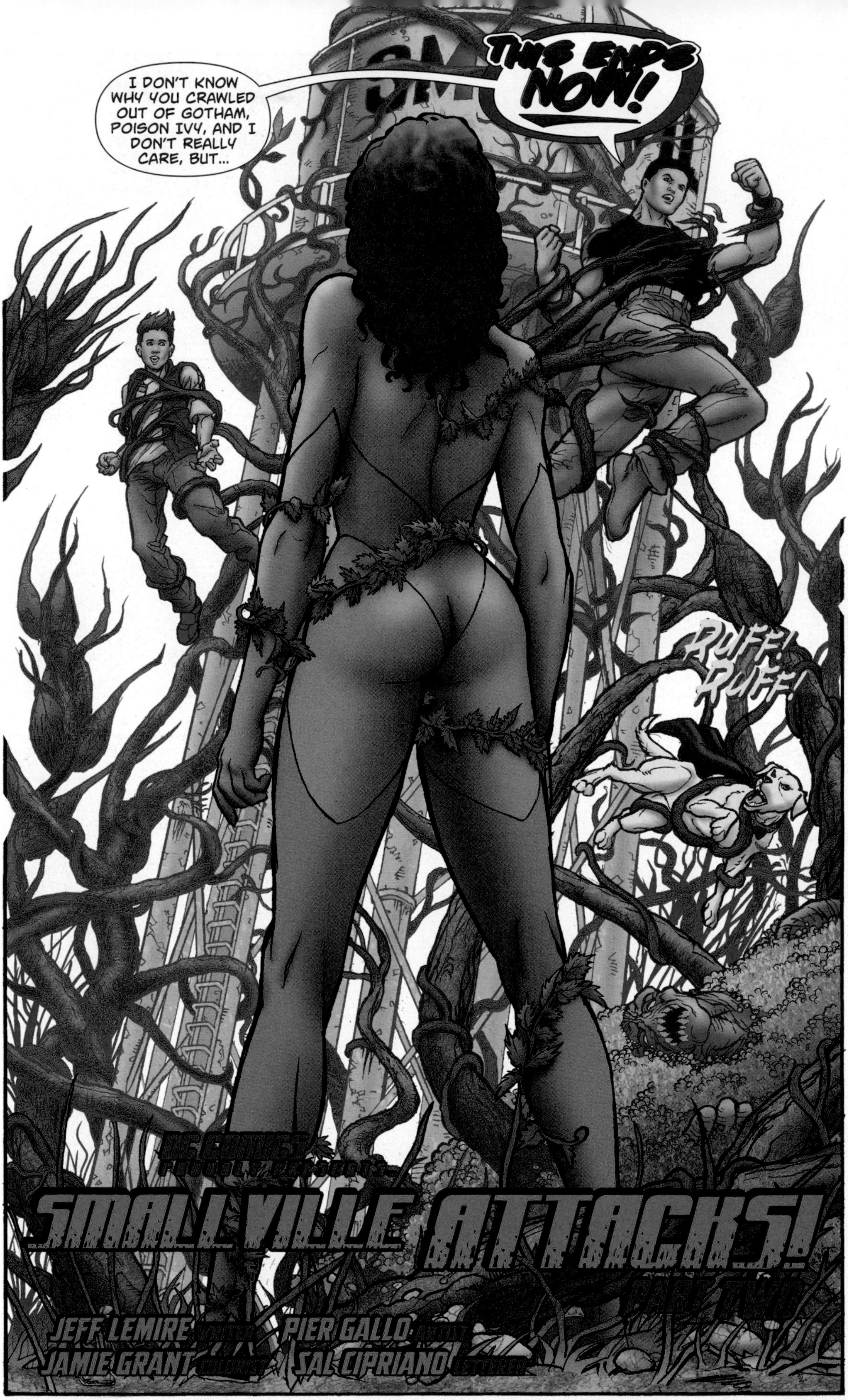
I DON'T KNOW WHY YOU CRAWLED OUT OF GOTHAM, POISON IVY, AND I DON'T REALLY CARE, BUT...
THIS ENDS NOW!
RUFF! RUFF!
SMALLVILLE ATTACKS!
JEFF LEMIRE
PIER GALLO
JAMIE GRANT
SAL CIPRIANO

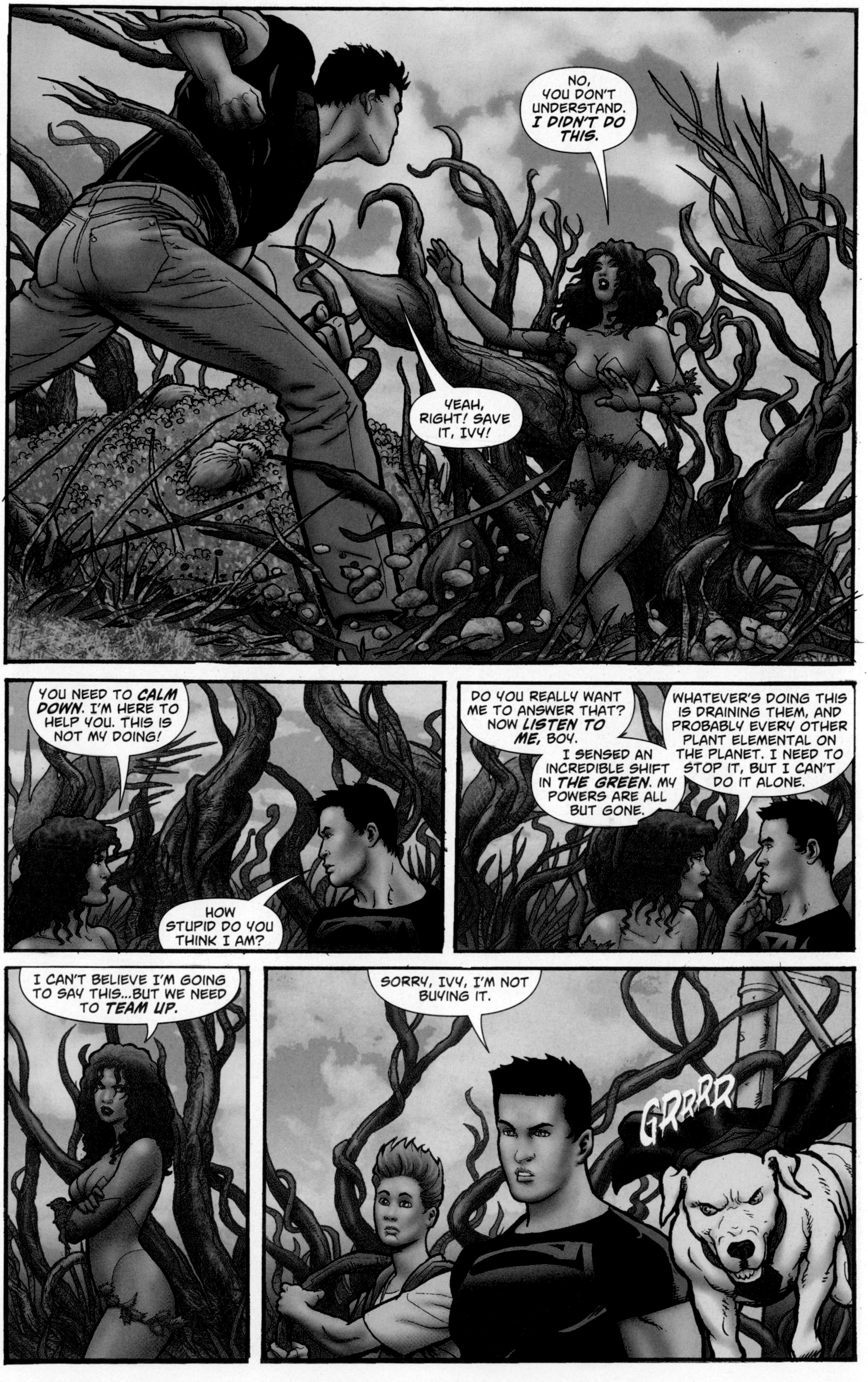
NO, YOU DON'T UNDERSTAND. I DIDN'T DO THIS.
YEAH, RIGHT! SAVE IT, IVY!
YOU NEED TO CALM DOWN. I'M HERE TO HELP YOU. THIS IS NOT MY DOING!
HOW STUPID DO YOU THINK I AM?
DO YOU REALLY WANT ME TO ANSWER THAT? NOW LISTEN TO ME, BOY.
I SENSED AN INCREDIBLE SHIFT IN THE GREEN. MY POWERS ARE ALL BUT GONE.
WHATEVER'S DOING THIS IS DRAINING THEM, AND PROBABLY EVERY OTHER PLANT ELEMENTAL ON THE PLANET. I NEED TO STOP IT, BUT I CAN'T DO IT ALONE.
I CAN'T BELIEVE I'M GOING TO SAY THIS...BUT WE NEED TO TEAM UP.
SORRY, IVY, I'M NOT BUYING IT.
GRRRR

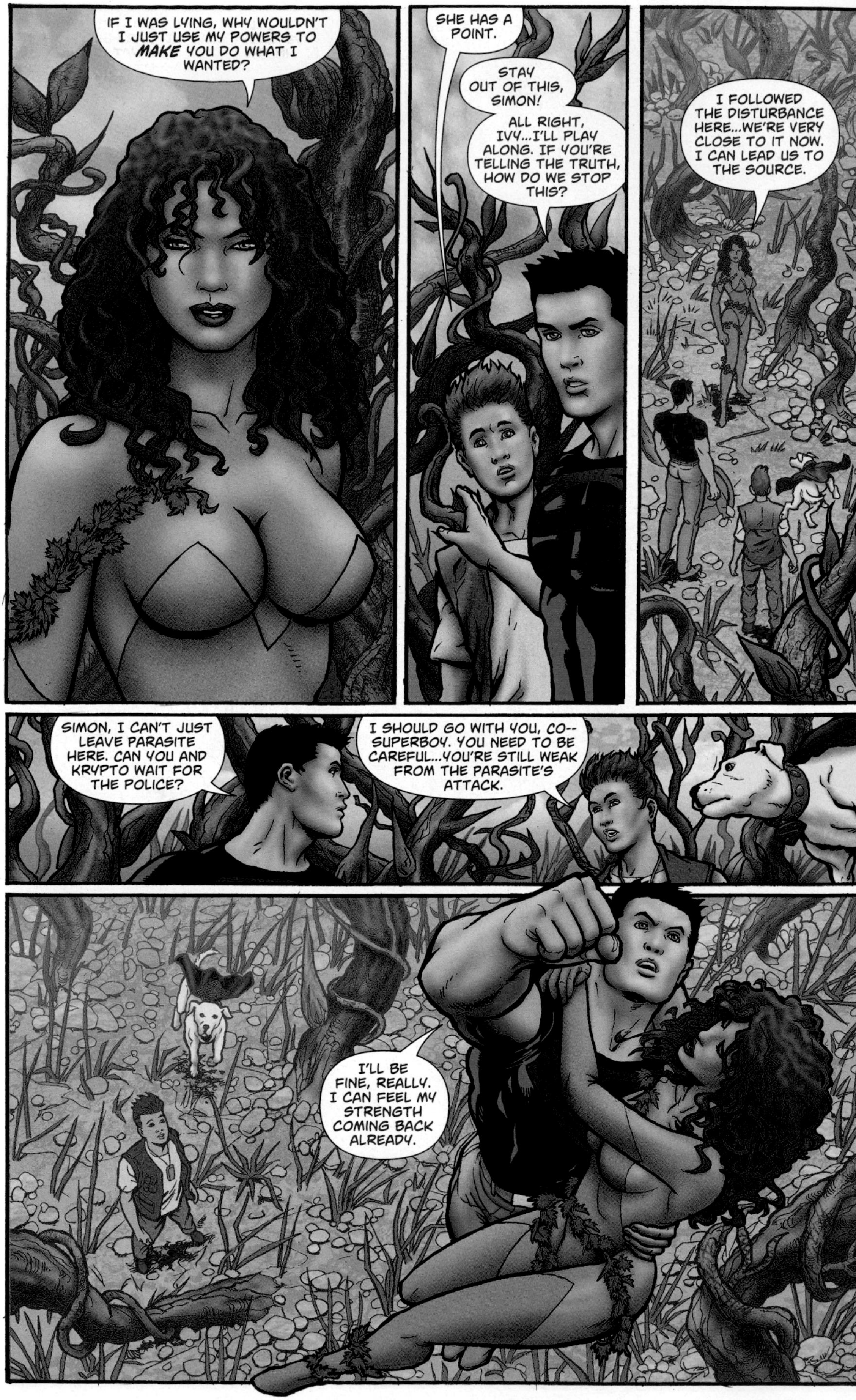
IF I WAS LYING, WHY WOULDN'T I JUST USE MY POWERS TO MAKE YOU DO WHAT I WANTED?
SHE HAS A POINT.
STAY OUT OF THIS, SIMON!
ALL RIGHT, IVY...I'LL PLAY ALONG. IF YOU'RE TELLING THE TRUTH, HOW DO WE STOP THIS?
I FOLLOWED THE DISTURBANCE HERE...WE'RE VERY CLOSE TO IT NOW. I CAN LEAD US TO THE SOURCE.
SIMON, I CAN'T JUST LEAVE PARASITE HERE. CAN YOU AND KRYPTO WAIT FOR THE POLICE?
I SHOULD GO WITH YOU, CO-- SUPERBOY. YOU NEED TO BE CAREFUL...YOU'RE STILL WEAK FROM THE PARASITE'S ATTACK.
I'LL BE FINE, REALLY. I CAN FEEL MY STRENGTH COMING BACK ALREADY.

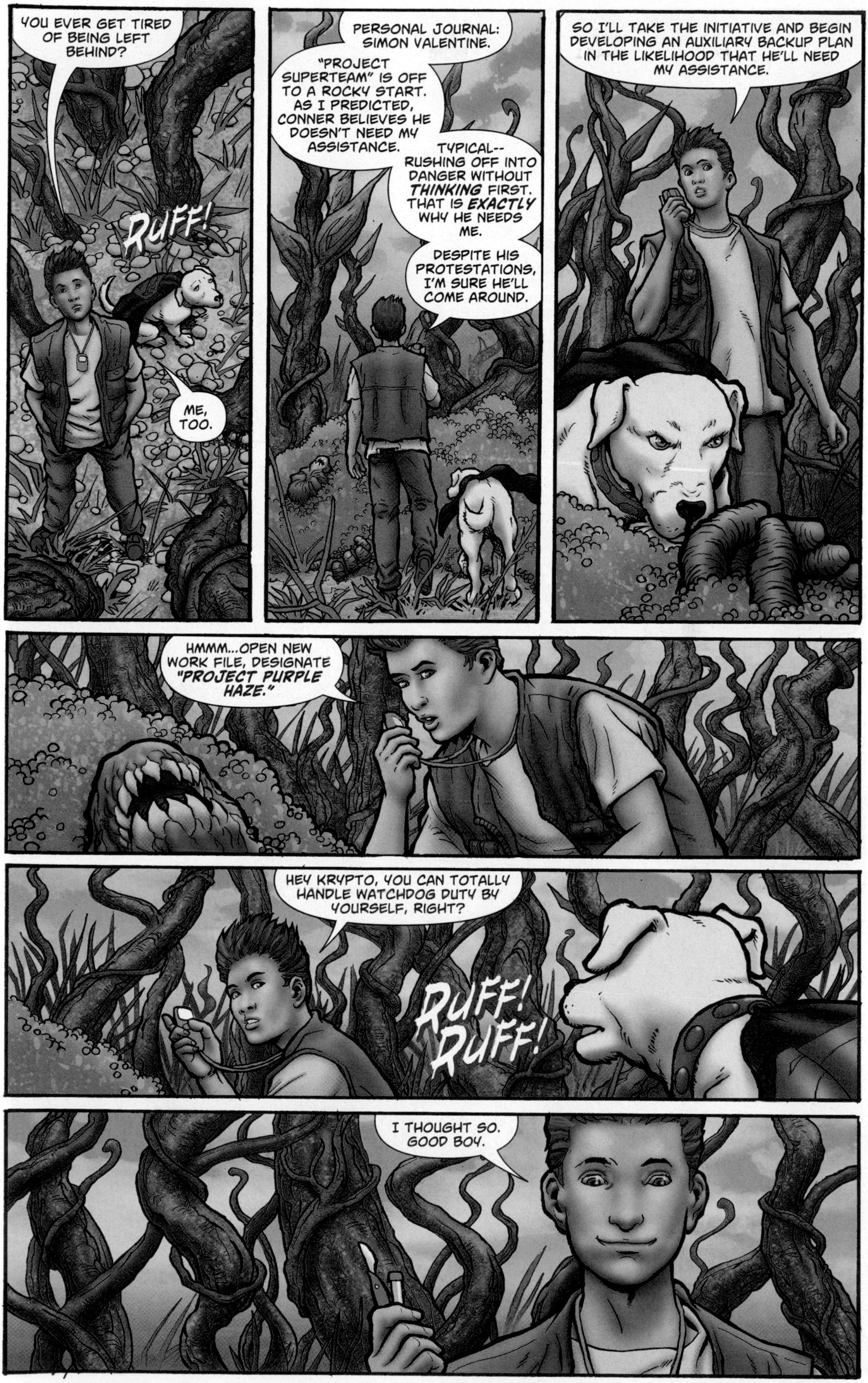
YOU EVER GET TIRED OF BEING LEFT BEHIND?
RUFF!
ME, TOO.
PERSONAL JOURNAL: SIMON VALENTINE.
"PROJECT SUPERTEAM" IS OFF TO A ROCKY START. AS I PREDICTED, CONNER BELIEVES HE DOESN'T NEED MY ASSISTANCE.
TYPICAL-- RUSHING OFF INTO DANGER WITHOUT THINKING FIRST. THAT IS EXACTLY WHY HE NEEDS ME.
DESPITE HIS PROTESTATIONS, I'M SURE HE'LL COME AROUND.
SO I'LL TAKE THE INITIATIVE AND BEGIN DEVELOPING AN AUXILIARY BACKUP PLAN IN THE LIKELIHOOD THAT HE'LL NEED MY ASSISTANCE.
HMMM...OPEN NEW WORK FILE, DESIGNATE "PROJECT PURPLE HAZE."
HEY KRYPTO, YOU CAN TOTALLY HANDLE WATCHDOG DUTY BY YOURSELF, RIGHT?
RUFF! RUFF!
I THOUGHT SO. GOOD BOY.

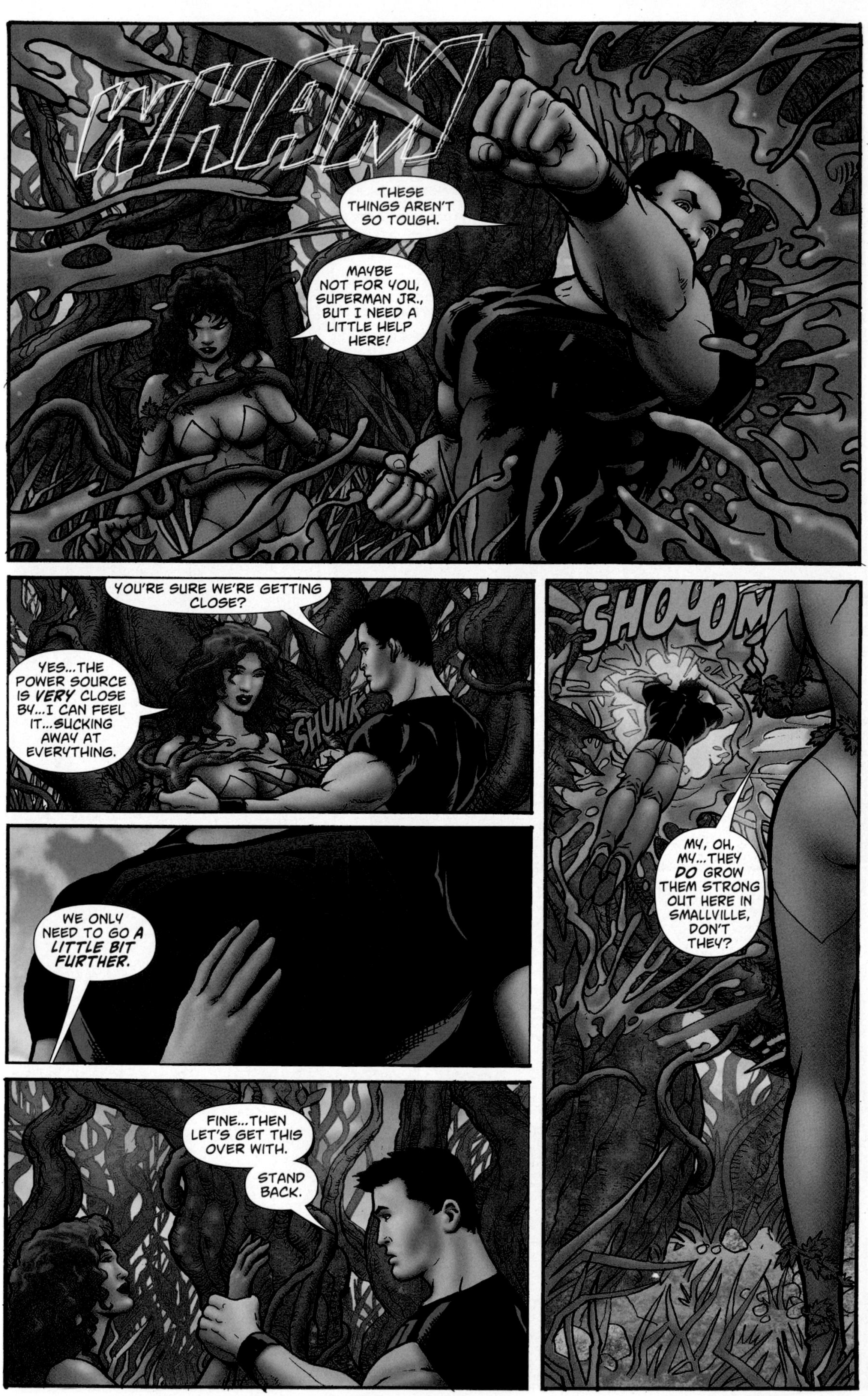
WHAM
THESE THINGS AREN'T SO TOUGH.
MAYBE NOT FOR YOU, SUPERMAN JR., BUT I NEED A LITTLE HELP HERE!
YOU'RE SURE WE'RE GETTING CLOSE?
YES...THE POWER SOURCE IS VERY CLOSE BY...I CAN FEEL IT...SUCKING AWAY AT EVERYTHING.
SHUNK
WE ONLY NEED TO GO A LITTLE BIT FURTHER.
FINE...THEN LET'S GET THIS OVER WITH.
STAND BACK.
SHOOOM
MY, OH, MY...THEY DO GROW THEM STRONG OUT HERE IN SMALLVILLE, DON'T THEY?

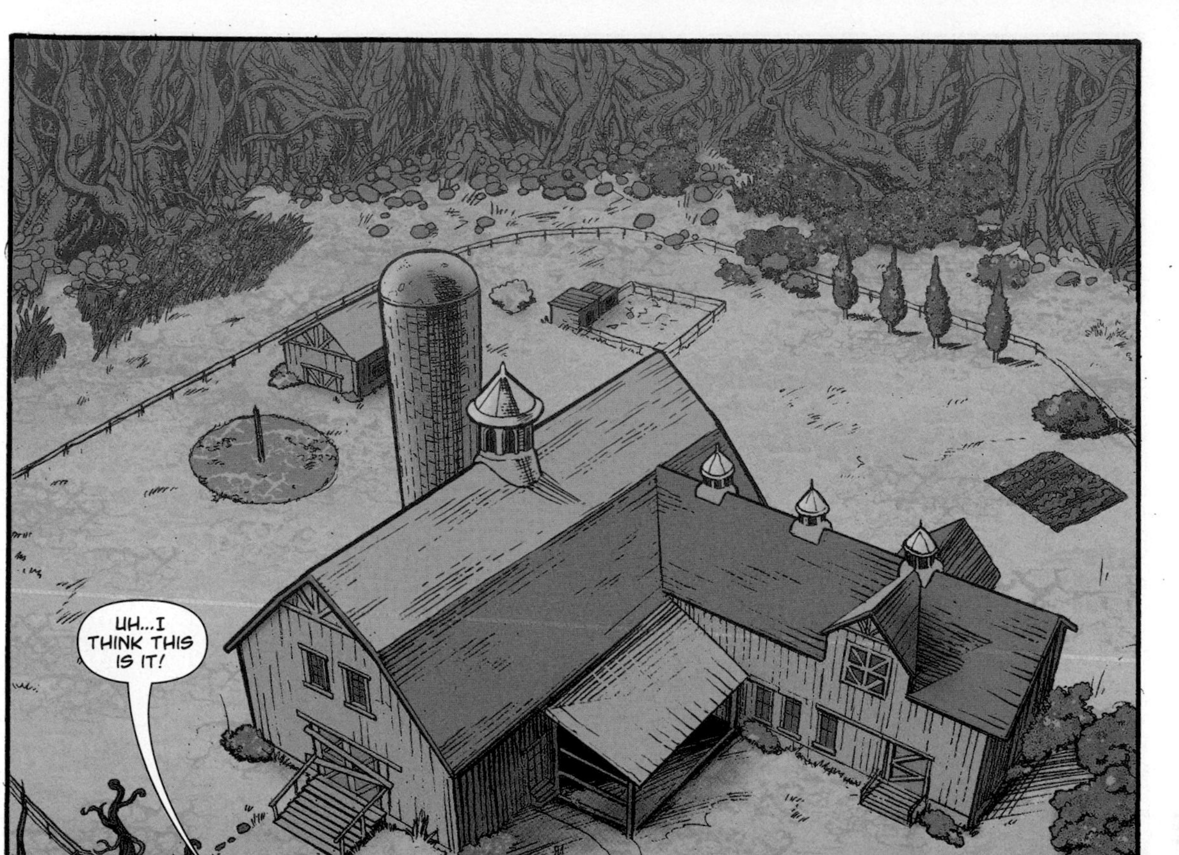
UH...I THINK THIS IS IT!

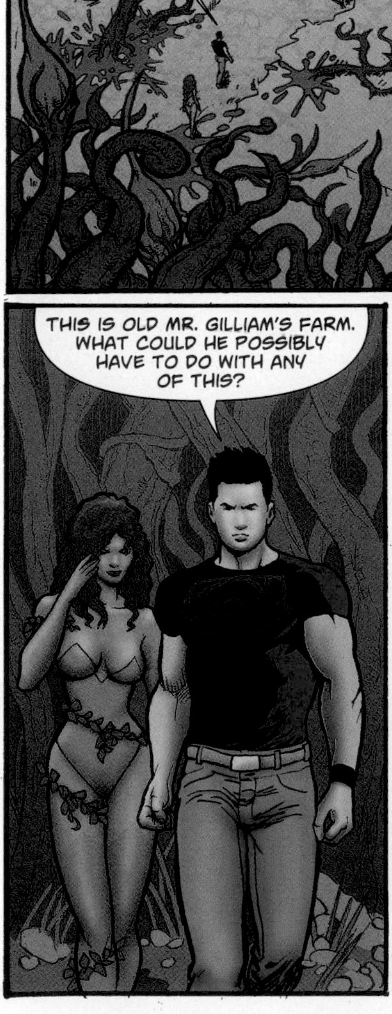
THIS IS OLD MR. GILLIAM'S FARM. WHAT COULD HE POSSIBLY HAVE TO DO WITH ANY OF THIS?

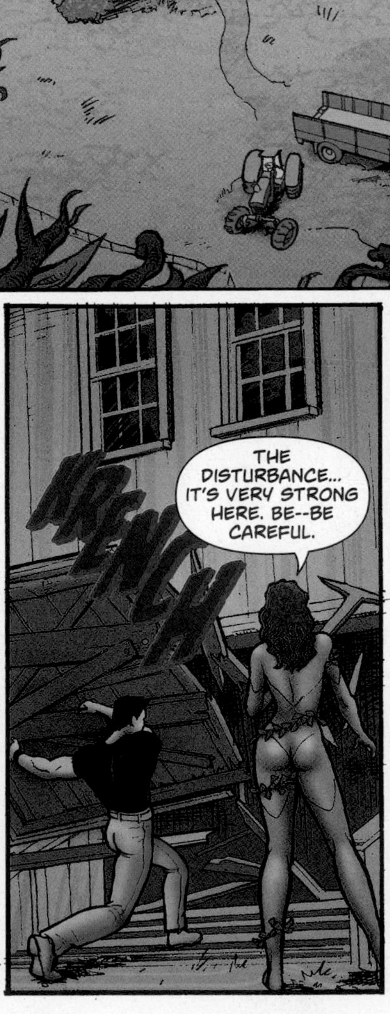
THE DISTURBANCE... IT'S VERY STRONG HERE. BE--BE CAREFUL.

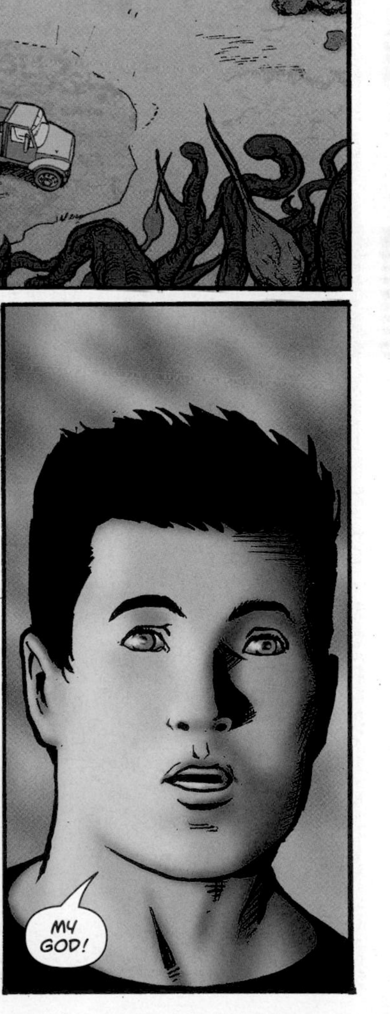
MY GOD!

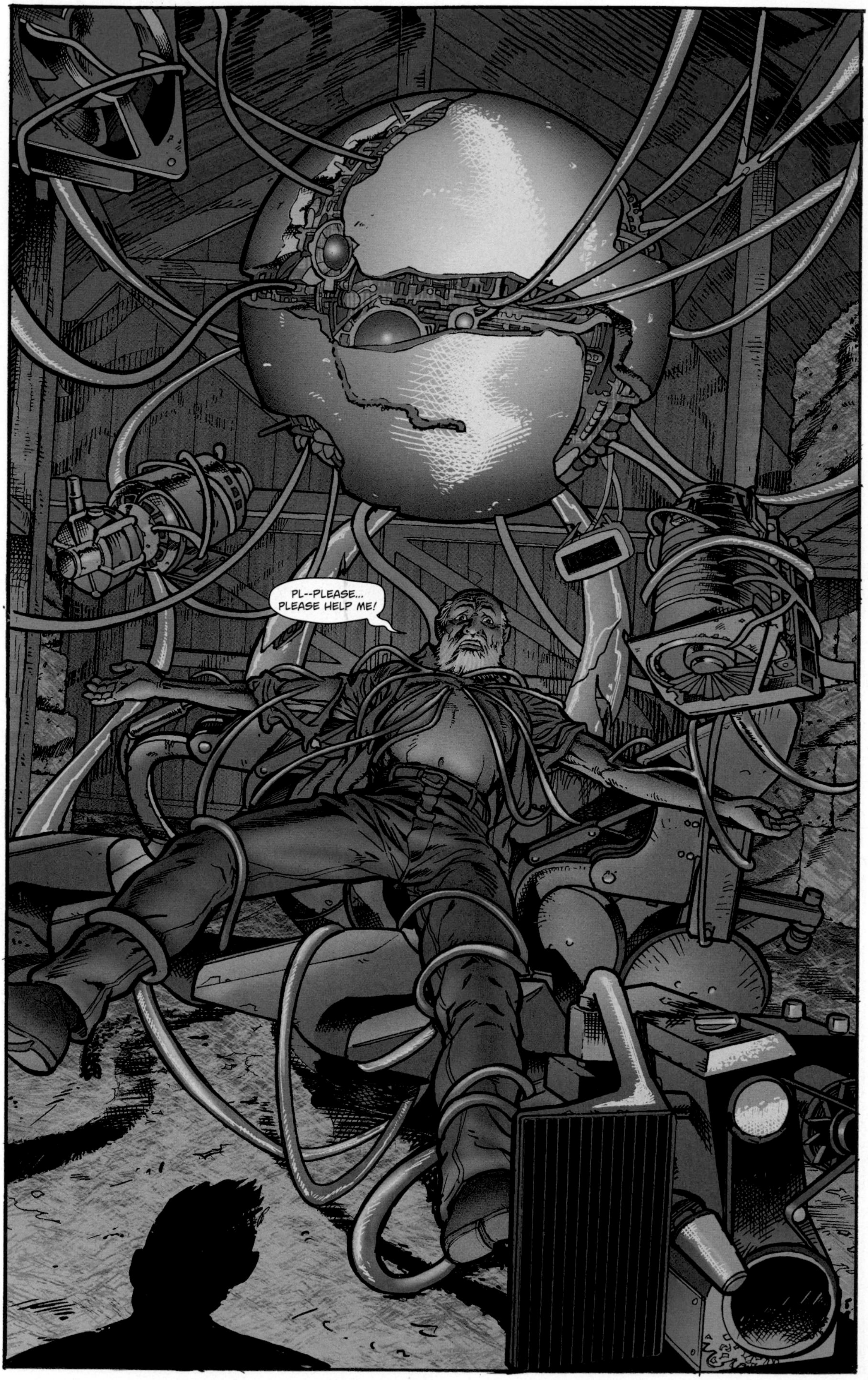
PL--PLEASE...
PLEASE HELP ME!

"THE JOURNAL OF SIMON VALENTINE: ENTRY #1254. THE CHAOS OUTSIDE HAS MADE IT DIFFICULT TO CONCENTRATE. BUT I SUPPOSE THAT IS ALL PART OF THE SUPERHERO LIFESTYLE...CALM UNDER PRESSURE."

"PROJECT PURPLE HAZE" IS PROCEEDING MUCH BETTER-- AND MUCH QUICKER--THAN I EVER COULD HAVE HOPED FOR.

ASIDE FROM THEIR OBVIOUS POWER-LEECHING ABILITIES, THE BLOOD AND TISSUE SAMPLES TAKEN FROM THE PARASITE ARE DEMONSTRATING SOME ABSOLUTELY AMAZING BEHAVIOR.

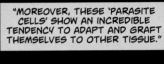

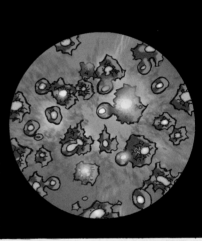

"MOREOVER, THESE 'PARASITE CELLS' SHOW AN INCREDIBLE TENDENCY TO ADAPT AND GRAFT THEMSELVES TO OTHER TISSUE."

THE POTENTIAL HERE IS INCREDIBLE!

HMMM...

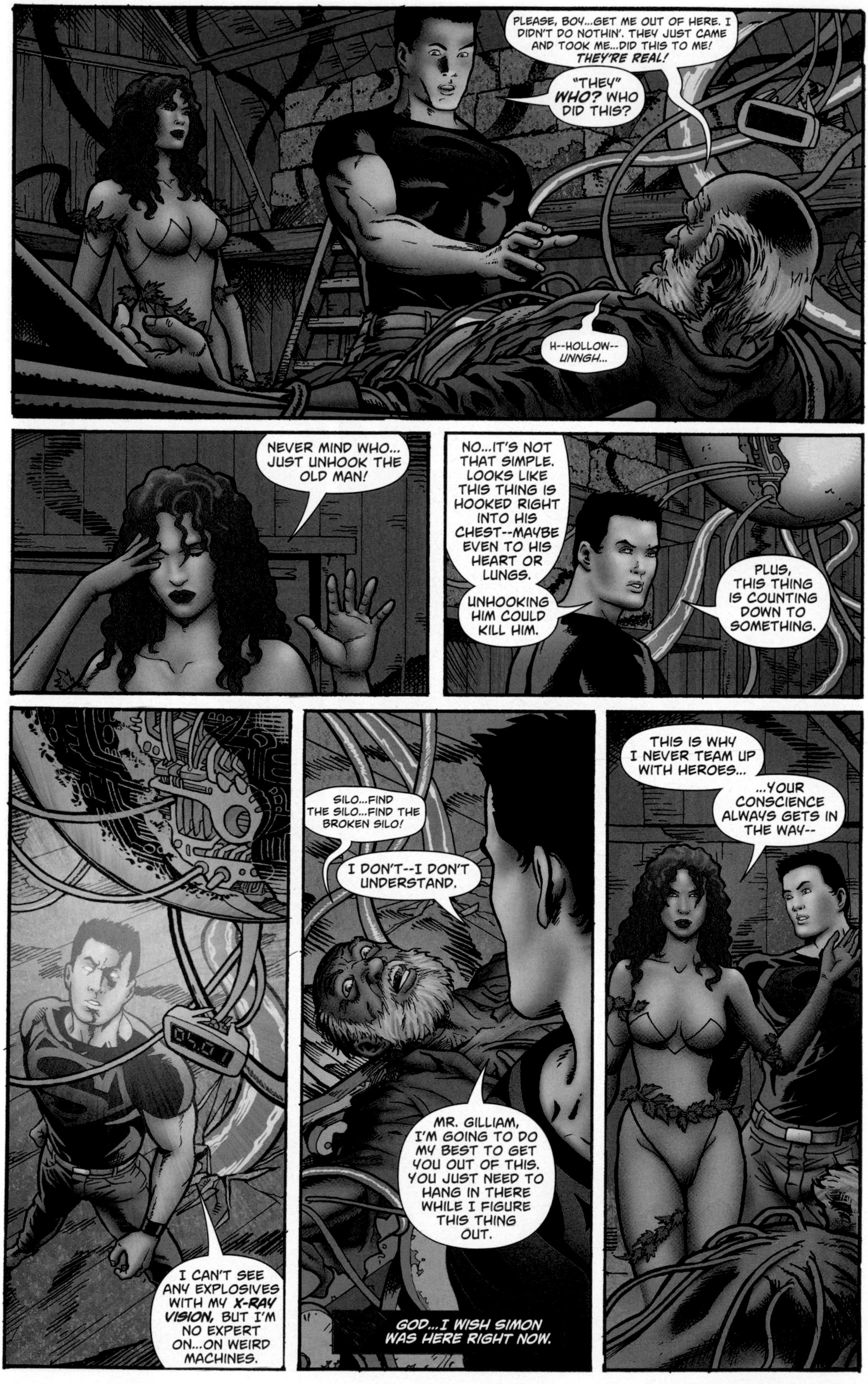
PLEASE, BOY...GET ME OUT OF HERE. I DIDN'T DO NOTHIN'. THEY JUST CAME AND TOOK ME...DID THIS TO ME! THEY'RE REAL!
"THEY" WHO? WHO DID THIS?
H--HOLLOW-- UNNGH...
NEVER MIND WHO... JUST UNHOOK THE OLD MAN!
NO...IT'S NOT THAT SIMPLE. LOOKS LIKE THIS THING IS HOOKED RIGHT INTO HIS CHEST--MAYBE EVEN TO HIS HEART OR LUNGS.
UNHOOKING HIM COULD KILL HIM.
PLUS, THIS THING IS COUNTING DOWN TO SOMETHING.
I CAN'T SEE ANY EXPLOSIVES WITH MY X-RAY VISION, BUT I'M NO EXPERT ON...ON WEIRD MACHINES.
SILO...FIND THE SILO...FIND THE BROKEN SILO!
I DON'T--I DON'T UNDERSTAND.
MR. GILLIAM, I'M GOING TO DO MY BEST TO GET YOU OUT OF THIS. YOU JUST NEED TO HANG IN THERE WHILE I FIGURE THIS THING OUT.
GOD...I WISH SIMON WAS HERE RIGHT NOW.
THIS IS WHY I NEVER TEAM UP WITH HEROES...
...YOUR CONSCIENCE ALWAYS GETS IN THE WAY--

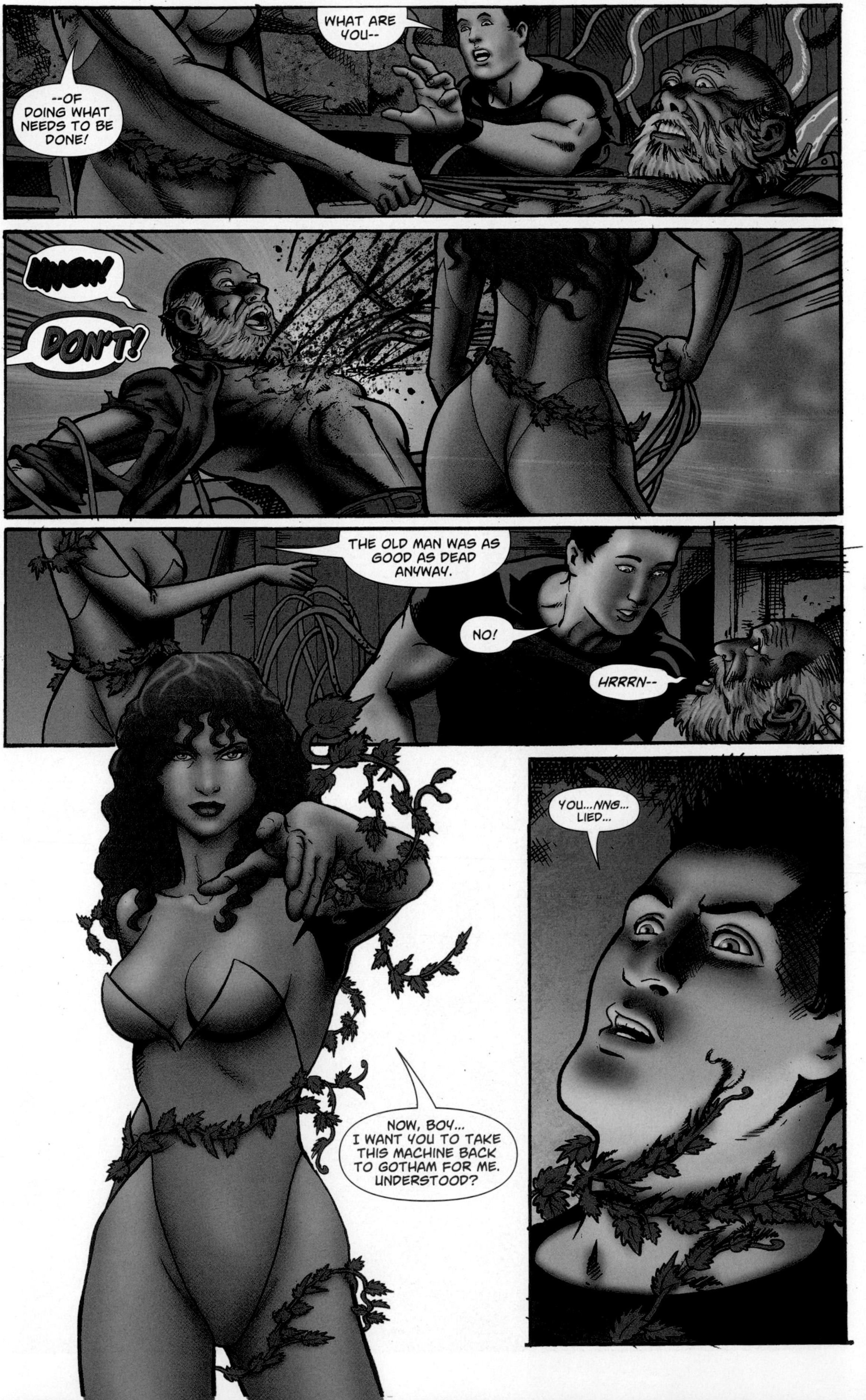
WHAT ARE YOU--
--OF DOING WHAT NEEDS TO BE DONE!
UNGH!
DON'T!
THE OLD MAN WAS AS GOOD AS DEAD ANYWAY.
NO!
HRRRN--
YOU...NNG... LIED...
NOW, BOY... I WANT YOU TO TAKE THIS MACHINE BACK TO GOTHAM FOR ME. UNDERSTOOD?

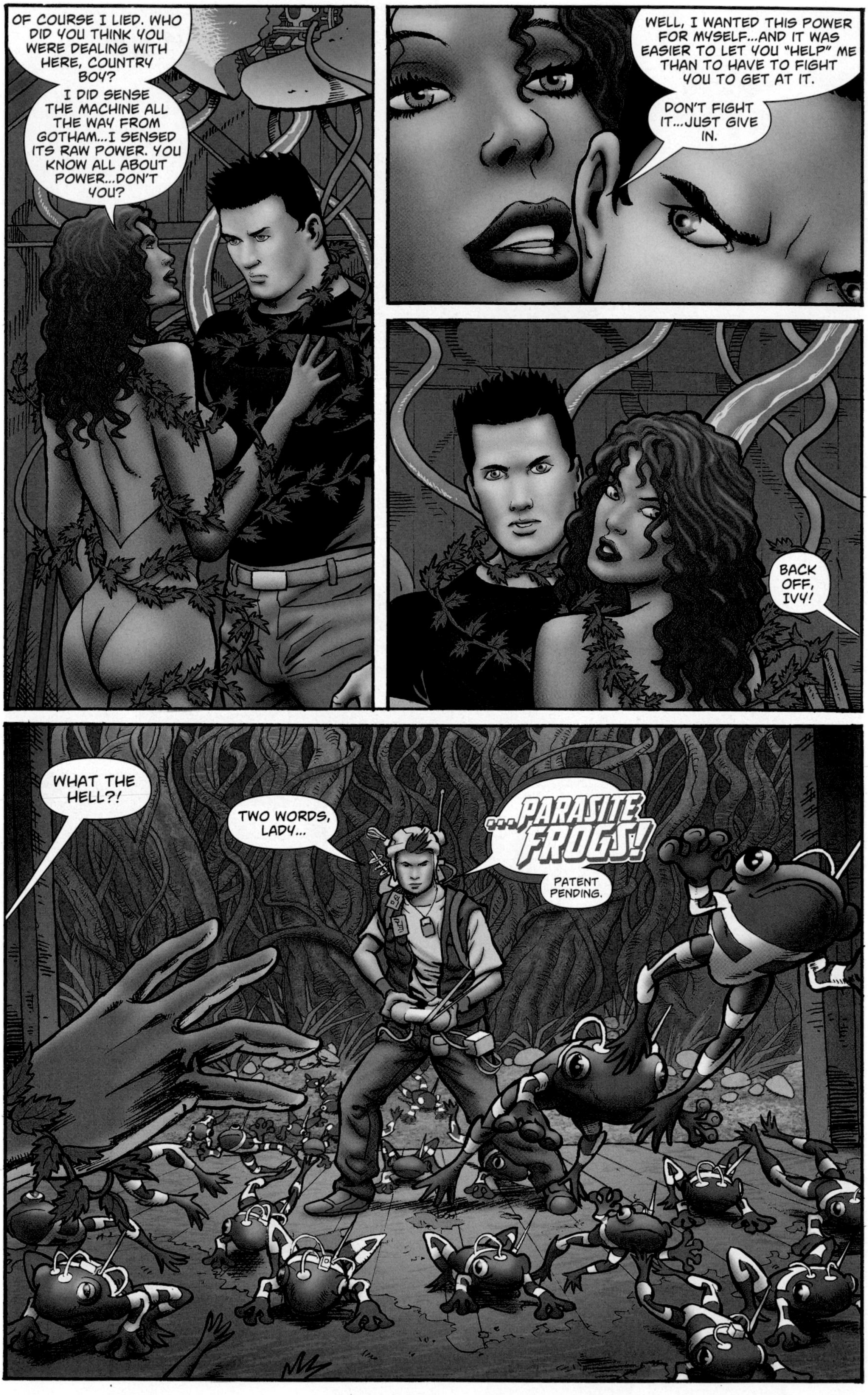
OF COURSE I LIED. WHO DID YOU THINK YOU WERE DEALING WITH HERE, COUNTRY BOY?
I DID SENSE THE MACHINE ALL THE WAY FROM GOTHAM...I SENSED ITS RAW POWER. YOU KNOW ALL ABOUT POWER...DON'T YOU?
WELL, I WANTED THIS POWER FOR MYSELF...AND IT WAS EASIER TO LET YOU "HELP" ME THAN TO HAVE TO FIGHT YOU TO GET AT IT.
DON'T FIGHT IT...JUST GIVE IN.
BACK OFF, IVY!
WHAT THE HELL?!
TWO WORDS, LADY...
...PARASITE FROGS!
PATENT PENDING.

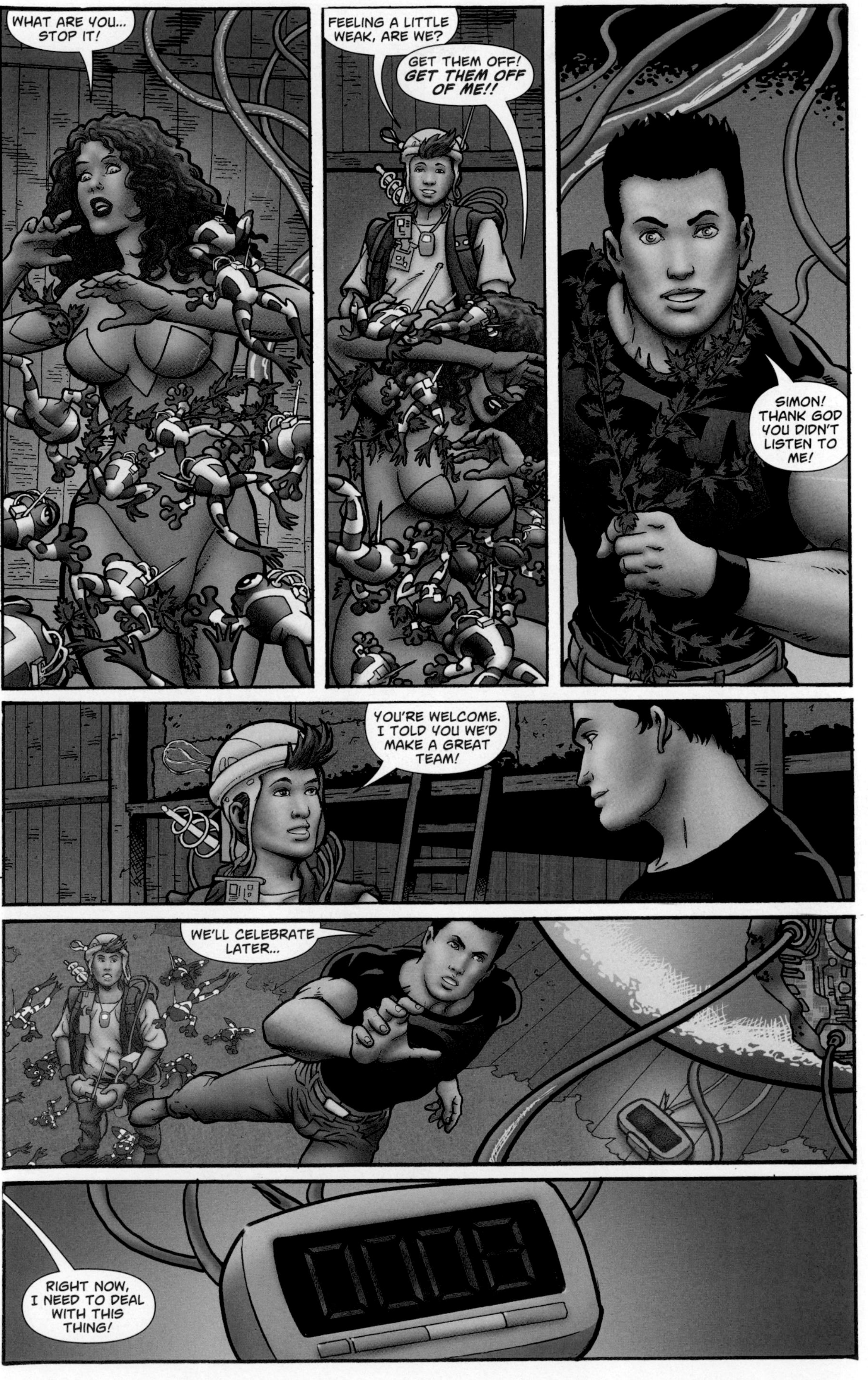
WHAT ARE YOU... STOP IT!
FEELING A LITTLE WEAK, ARE WE?
GET THEM OFF! GET THEM OFF OF ME!!
SIMON! THANK GOD YOU DIDN'T LISTEN TO ME!
YOU'RE WELCOME. I TOLD YOU WE'D MAKE A GREAT TEAM!
WE'LL CELEBRATE LATER...
RIGHT NOW, I NEED TO DEAL WITH THIS THING!

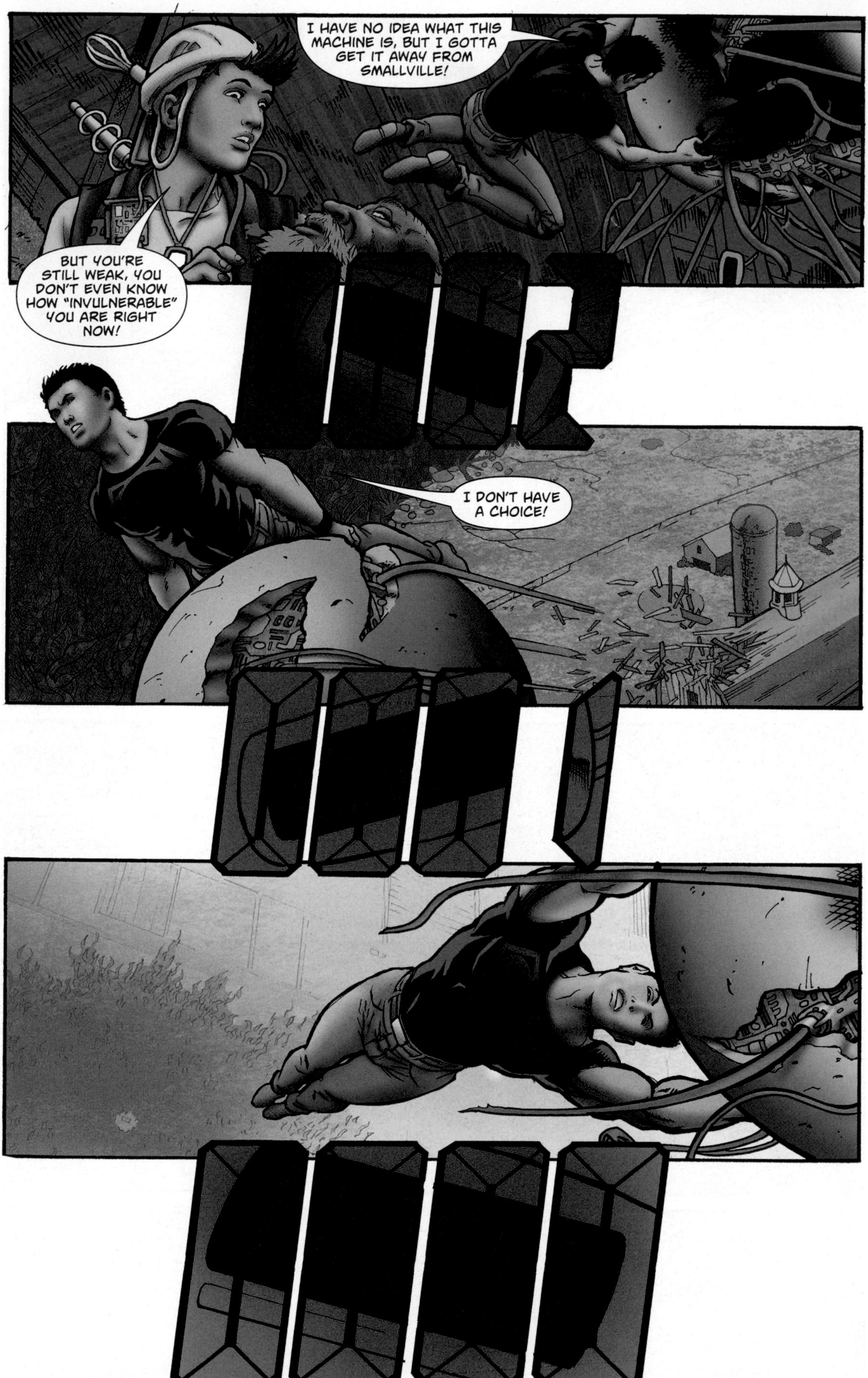
I HAVE NO IDEA WHAT THIS MACHINE IS, BUT I GOTTA GET IT AWAY FROM SMALLVILLE!
BUT YOU'RE STILL WEAK, YOU DON'T EVEN KNOW HOW "INVULNERABLE" YOU ARE RIGHT NOW!
I DON'T HAVE A CHOICE!

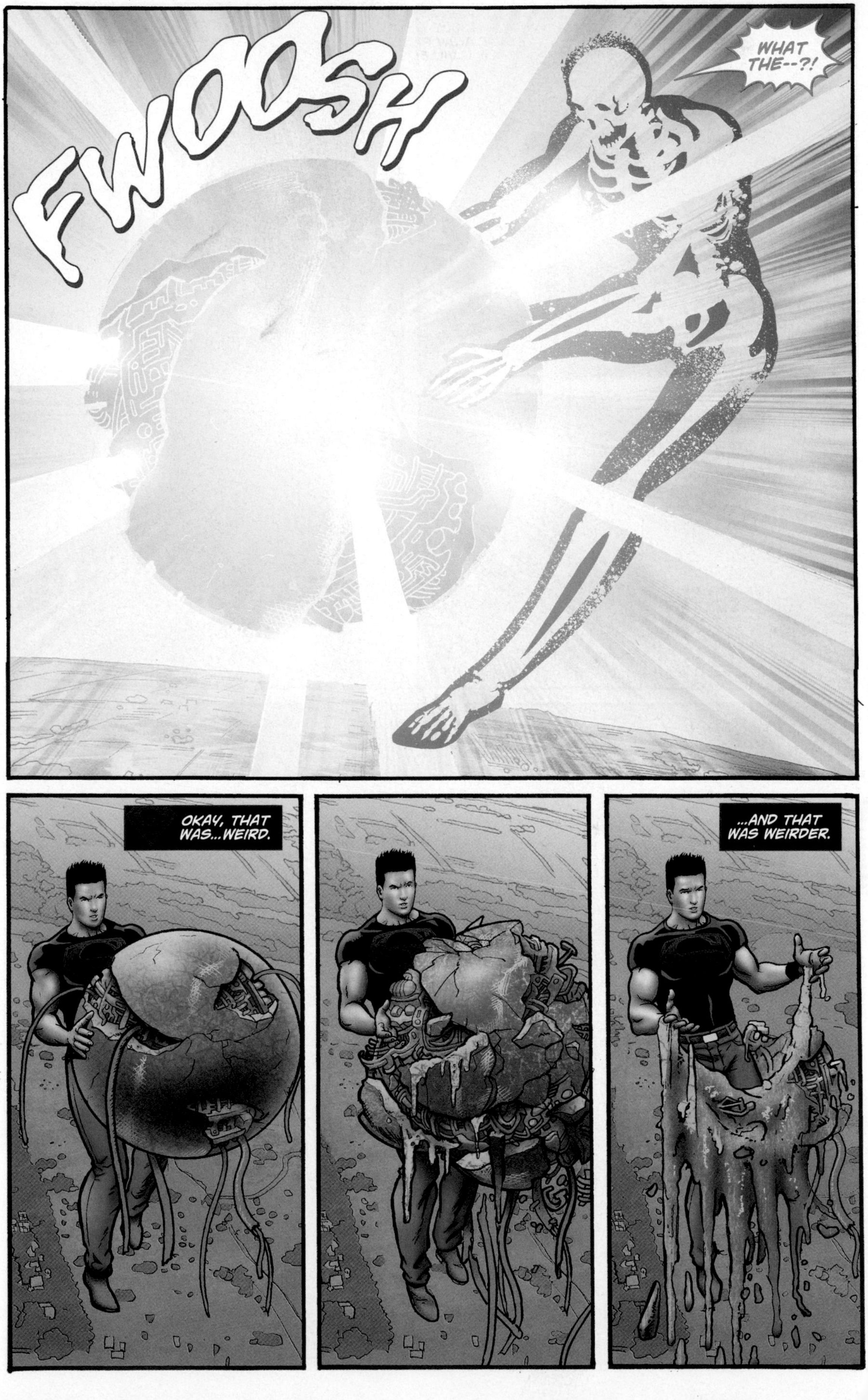
FWOOSH
WHAT THE--?!
OKAY, THAT WAS...WEIRD.
...AND THAT WAS WEIRDER.

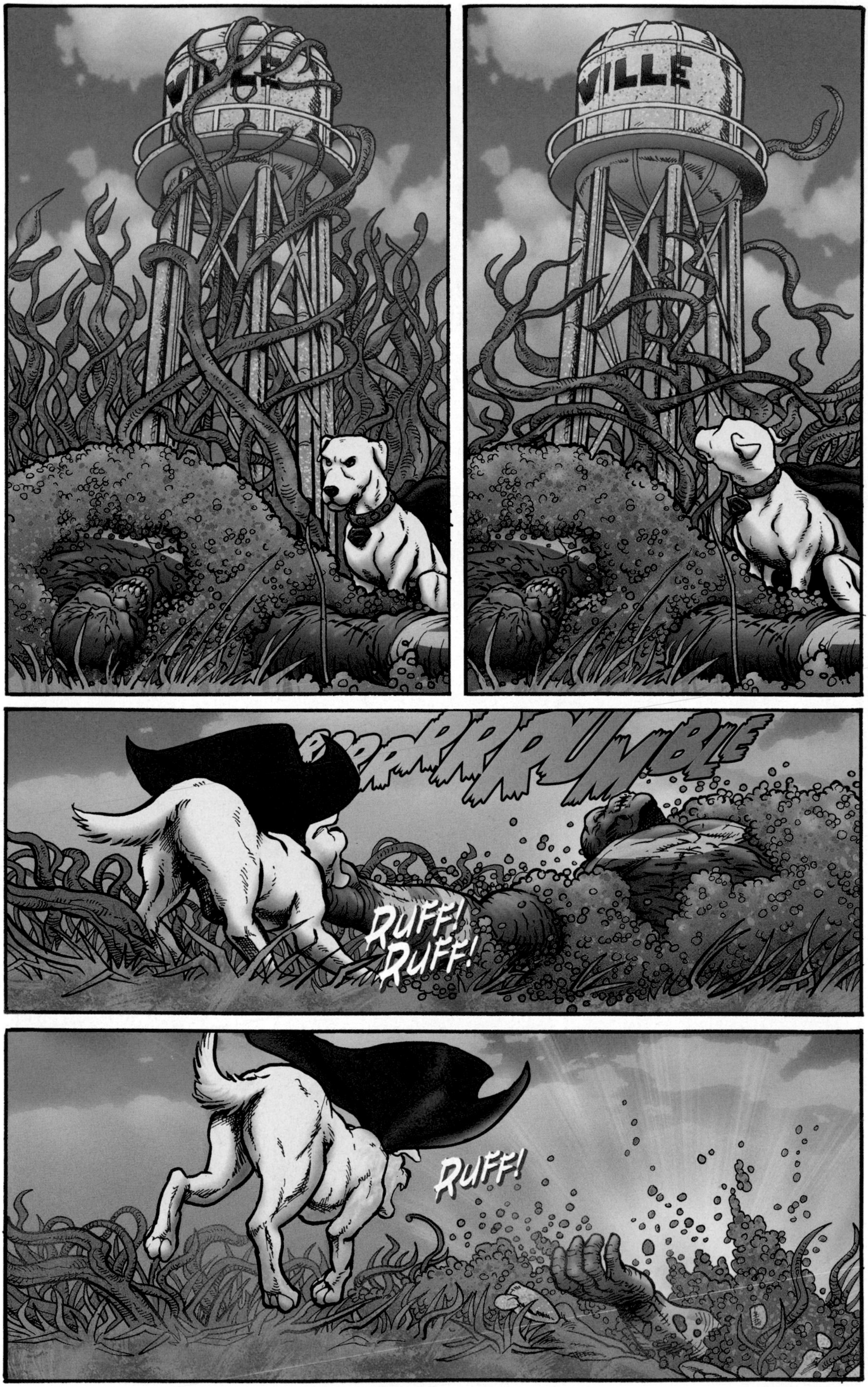

VILLE
VILLE
RRRRRUMBLE
RUFF! RUFF!
RUFF!

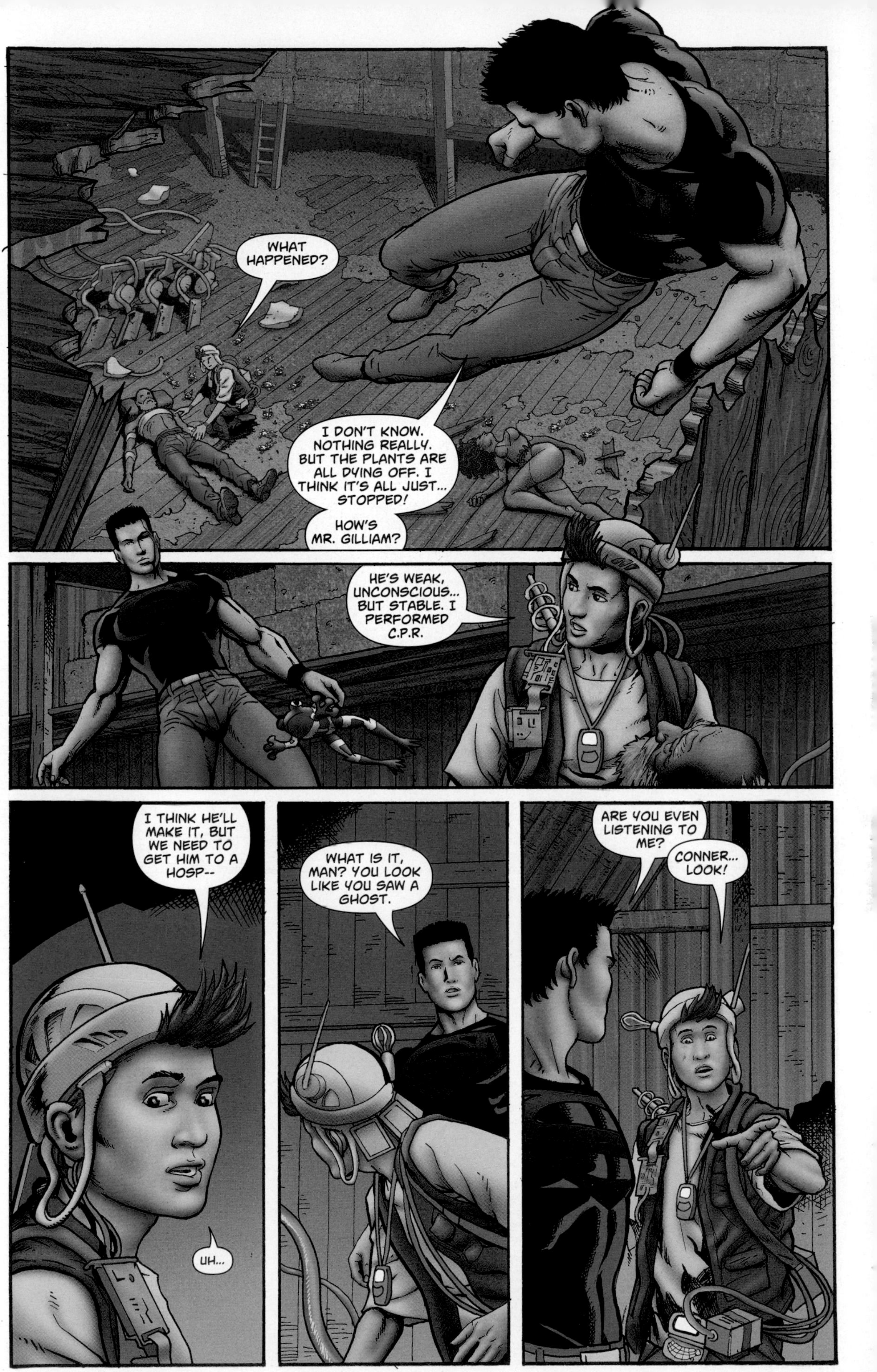
WHAT HAPPENED?
I DON'T KNOW. NOTHING REALLY. BUT THE PLANTS ARE ALL DYING OFF. I THINK IT'S ALL JUST... STOPPED!
HOW'S MR. GILLIAM?
HE'S WEAK, UNCONSCIOUS... BUT STABLE. I PERFORMED C.P.R.
I THINK HE'LL MAKE IT, BUT WE NEED TO GET HIM TO A HOSP--
UH...
WHAT IS IT, MAN? YOU LOOK LIKE YOU SAW A GHOST.
ARE YOU EVEN LISTENING TO ME?
CONNER... LOOK!

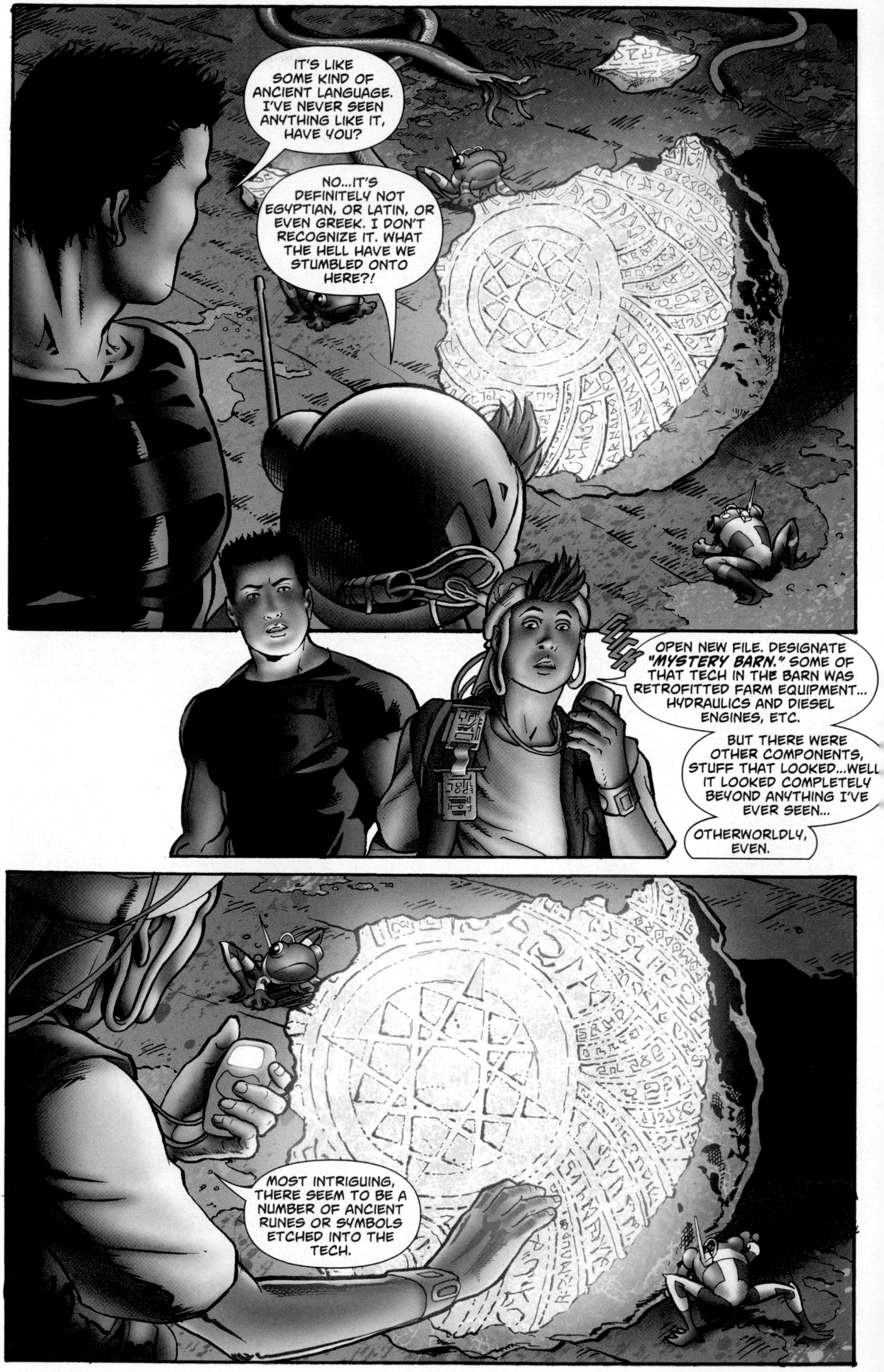
IT'S LIKE SOME KIND OF ANCIENT LANGUAGE. I'VE NEVER SEEN ANYTHING LIKE IT, HAVE YOU?
NO...IT'S DEFINITELY NOT EGYPTIAN, OR LATIN, OR EVEN GREEK. I DON'T RECOGNIZE IT. WHAT THE HELL HAVE WE STUMBLED ONTO HERE?!
CLICK
OPEN NEW FILE. DESIGNATE "MYSTERY BARN." SOME OF THAT TECH IN THE BARN WAS RETROFITTED FARM EQUIPMENT... HYDRAULICS AND DIESEL ENGINES, ETC.
BUT THERE WERE OTHER COMPONENTS, STUFF THAT LOOKED...WELL IT LOOKED COMPLETELY BEYOND ANYTHING I'VE EVER SEEN...
OTHERWORLDLY, EVEN.
MOST INTRIGUING, THERE SEEM TO BE A NUMBER OF ANCIENT RUNES OR SYMBOLS ETCHED INTO THE TECH.

WHAT ARE YOU DOING?

I'M TAKING NOTES.

WELL, STOP IT, IT'S ANNOYING. LISTEN, BEFORE GILLIAM BLACKED OUT...HE SAID SOME THINGS TO ME. I THOUGHT IT WAS GIBBERISH AT FIRST, BUT--

WE NEED TO FIND "THE BROKEN SILO."

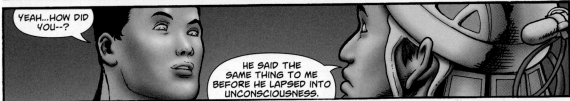

YEAH...HOW DID YOU--?

HE SAID THE SAME THING TO ME BEFORE HE LAPSED INTO UNCONSCIOUSNESS.

SO WHAT DO YOU THINK IT MEANS?

I--I DON'T KNOW, BUT BEFORE WE DO ANYTHING, I NEED TO GET HIM TO THE HOSPITAL. HE MAY HAVE MORE ANSWERS.

WE NEED TO FIND THIS "BROKEN SILO" BEFORE SOMETHING ELSE HAPPENS.

LOOK, MAN, WHATEVER'S GOING ON HERE IS WAY OVER MY HEAD. AND I THINK THIS IS ONLY THE BEGINNING...

WHICH IS ALL THE MORE REASON YOU'LL NEED ME. WHY IS IT SO HARD FOR YOU TO ACCEPT HELP?

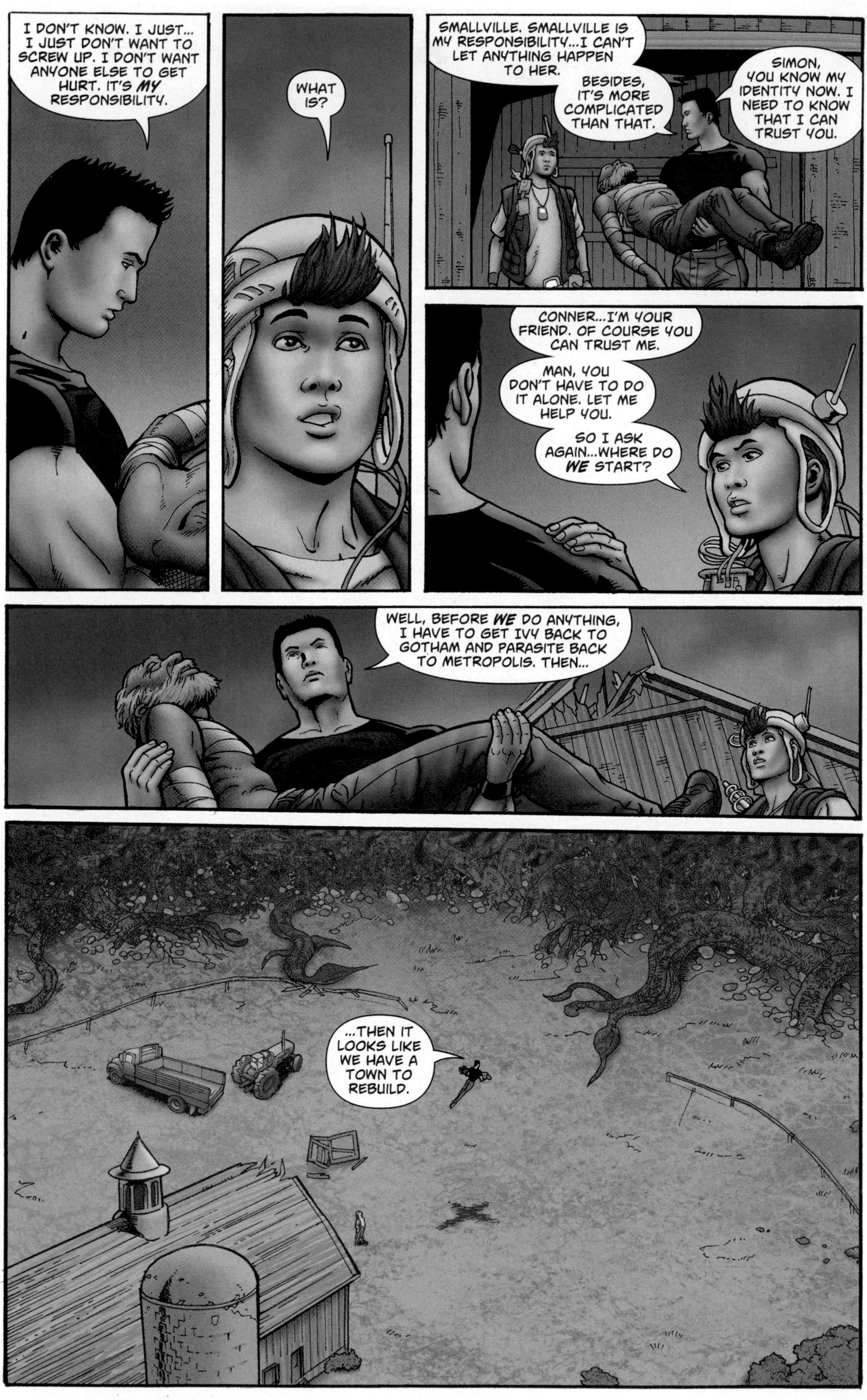
I DON'T KNOW. I JUST... I JUST DON'T WANT TO SCREW UP. I DON'T WANT ANYONE ELSE TO GET HURT. IT'S MY RESPONSIBILITY.
WHAT IS?
SMALLVILLE. SMALLVILLE IS MY RESPONSIBILITY...I CAN'T LET ANYTHING HAPPEN TO HER.
BESIDES, IT'S MORE COMPLICATED THAN THAT.
SIMON, YOU KNOW MY IDENTITY NOW. I NEED TO KNOW THAT I CAN TRUST YOU.
CONNER...I'M YOUR FRIEND. OF COURSE YOU CAN TRUST ME.
MAN, YOU DON'T HAVE TO DO IT ALONE. LET ME HELP YOU.
SO I ASK AGAIN...WHERE DO WE START?
WELL, BEFORE WE DO ANYTHING, I HAVE TO GET IVY BACK TO GOTHAM AND PARASITE BACK TO METROPOLIS. THEN...
...THEN IT LOOKS LIKE WE HAVE A TOWN TO REBUILD.

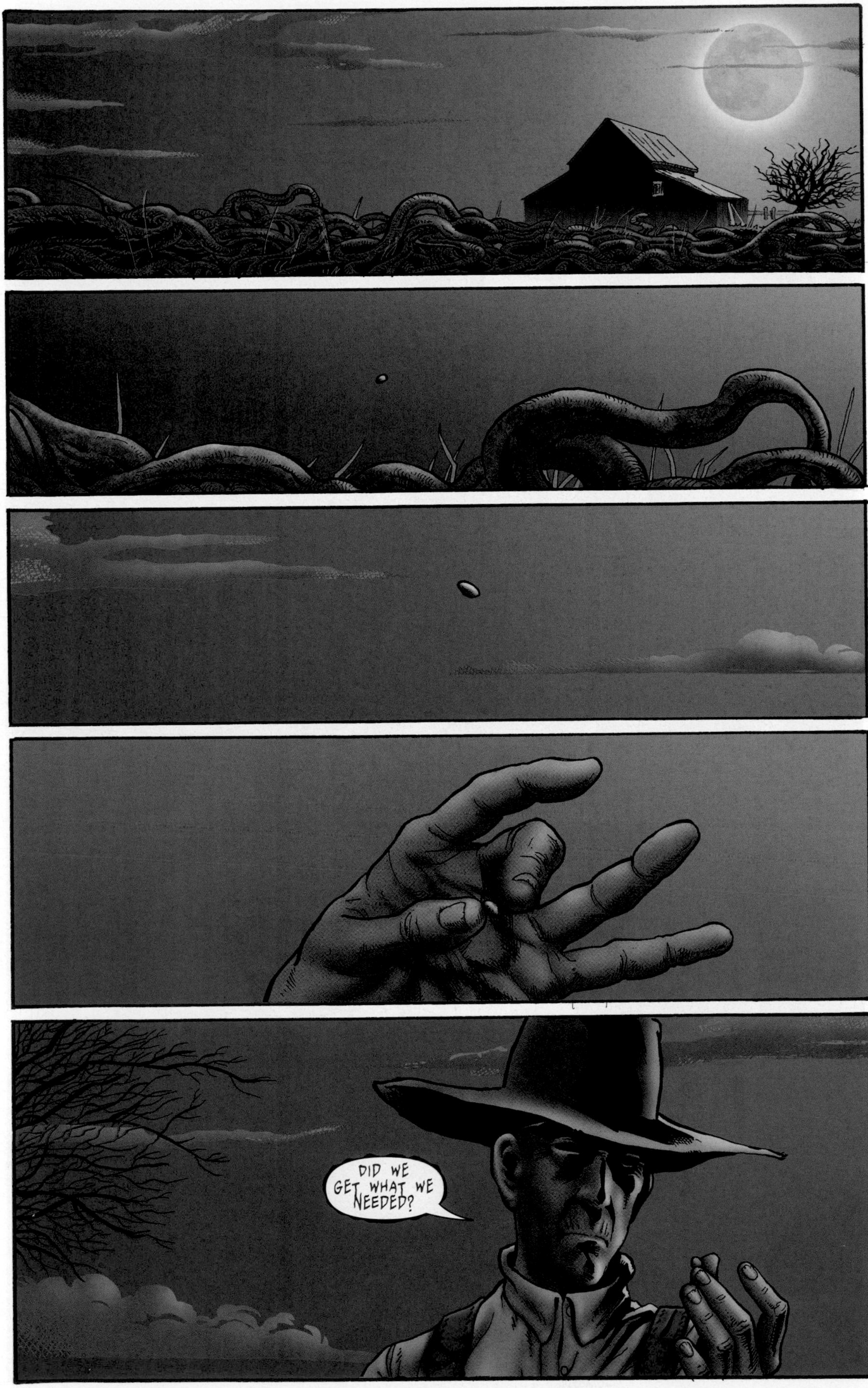
DID WE GET WHAT WE NEEDED?

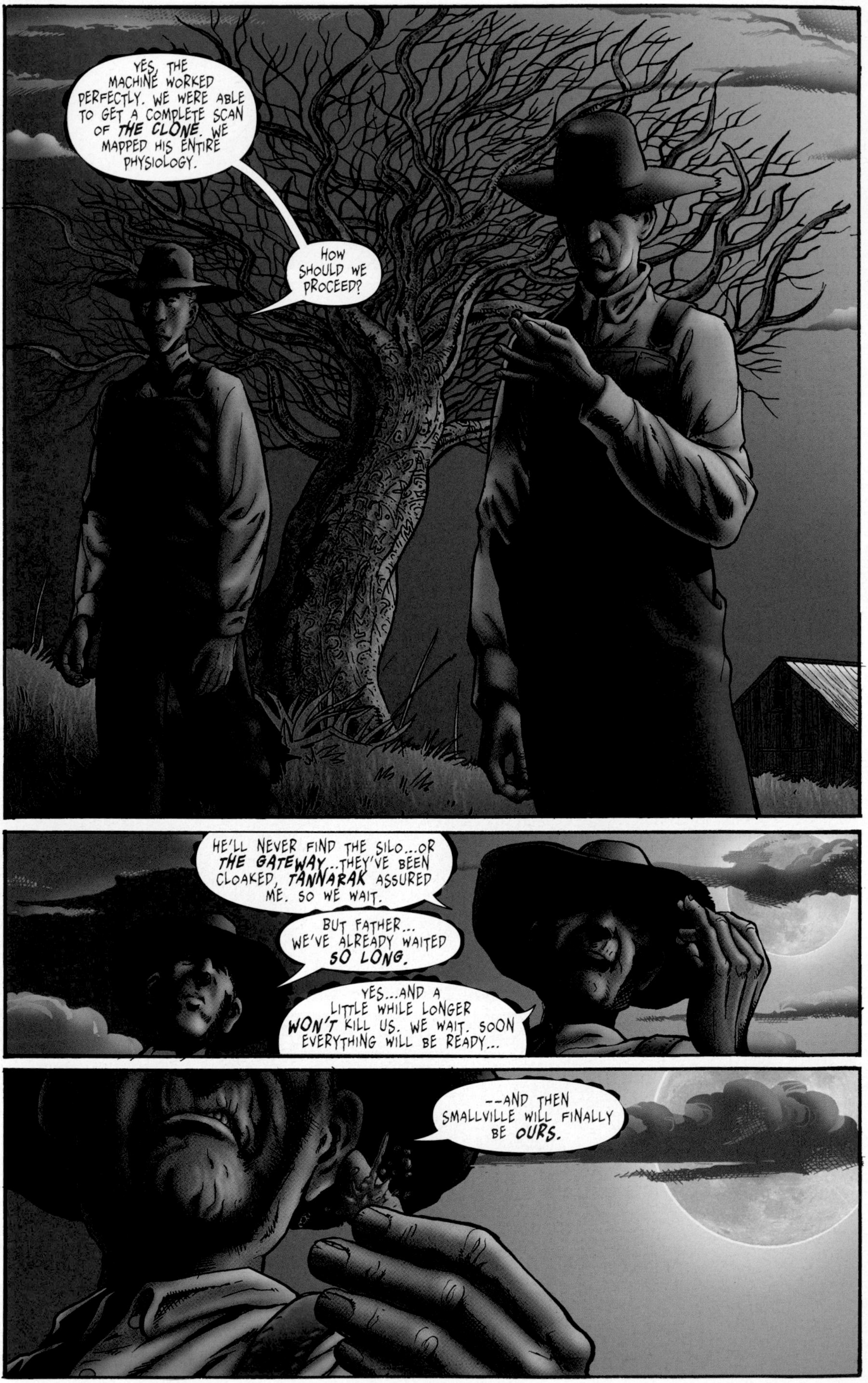
YES, THE MACHINE WORKED PERFECTLY. WE WERE ABLE TO GET A COMPLETE SCAN OF THE CLONE. WE MAPPED HIS ENTIRE PHYSIOLOGY.
HOW SHOULD WE PROCEED?
HE'LL NEVER FIND THE SILO...OR THE GATEWAY...THEY'VE BEEN CLOAKED, TANNARAK ASSURED ME. SO WE WAIT.
BUT FATHER... WE'VE ALREADY WAITED SO LONG.
YES...AND A LITTLE WHILE LONGER WON'T KILL US. WE WAIT. SOON EVERYTHING WILL BE READY...
--AND THEN SMALLVILLE WILL FINALLY BE OURS.

SUPERBOY #3

Cover by Phil Noto

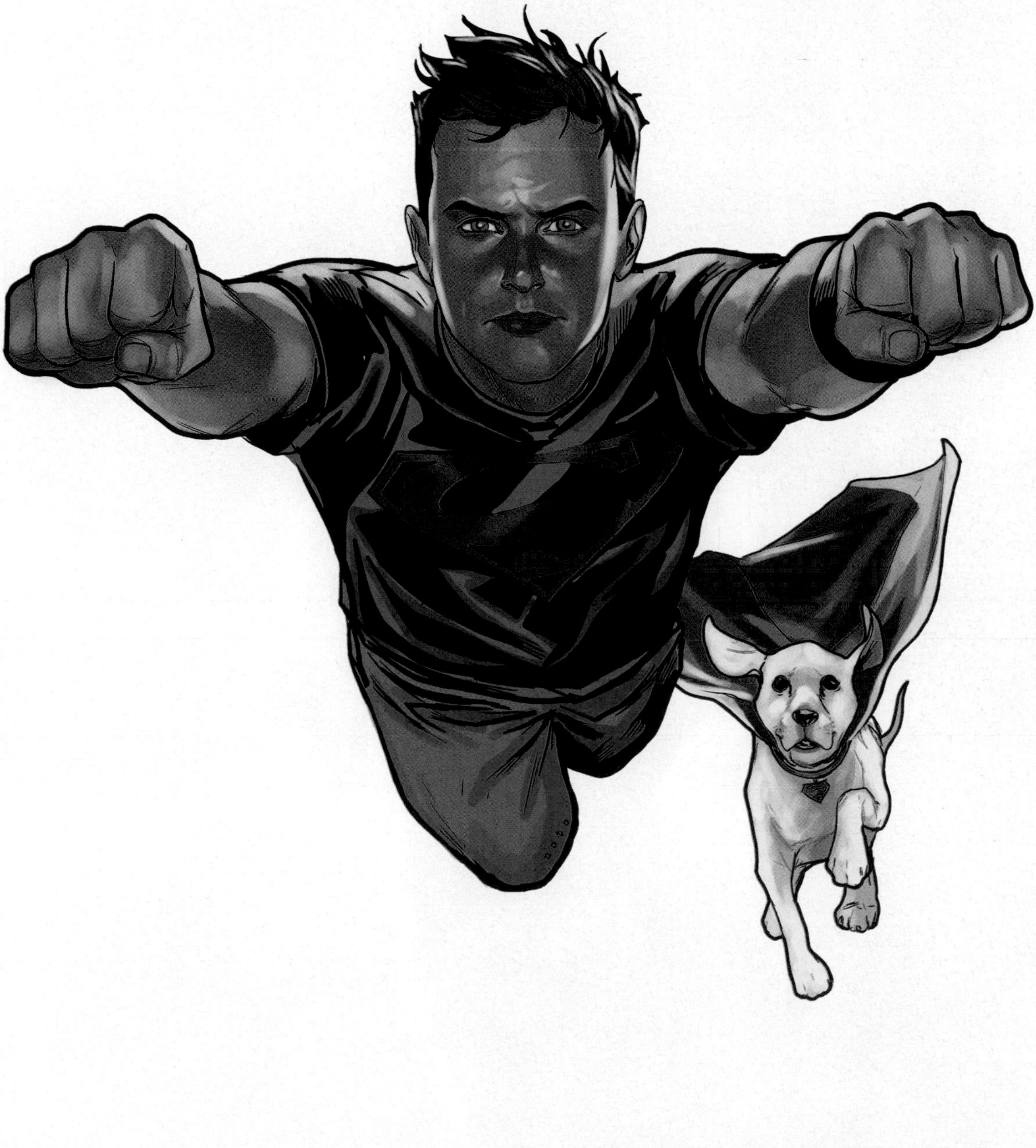

SUPERBOY #3 | VARIANT
Cover by Dustin Nguyen

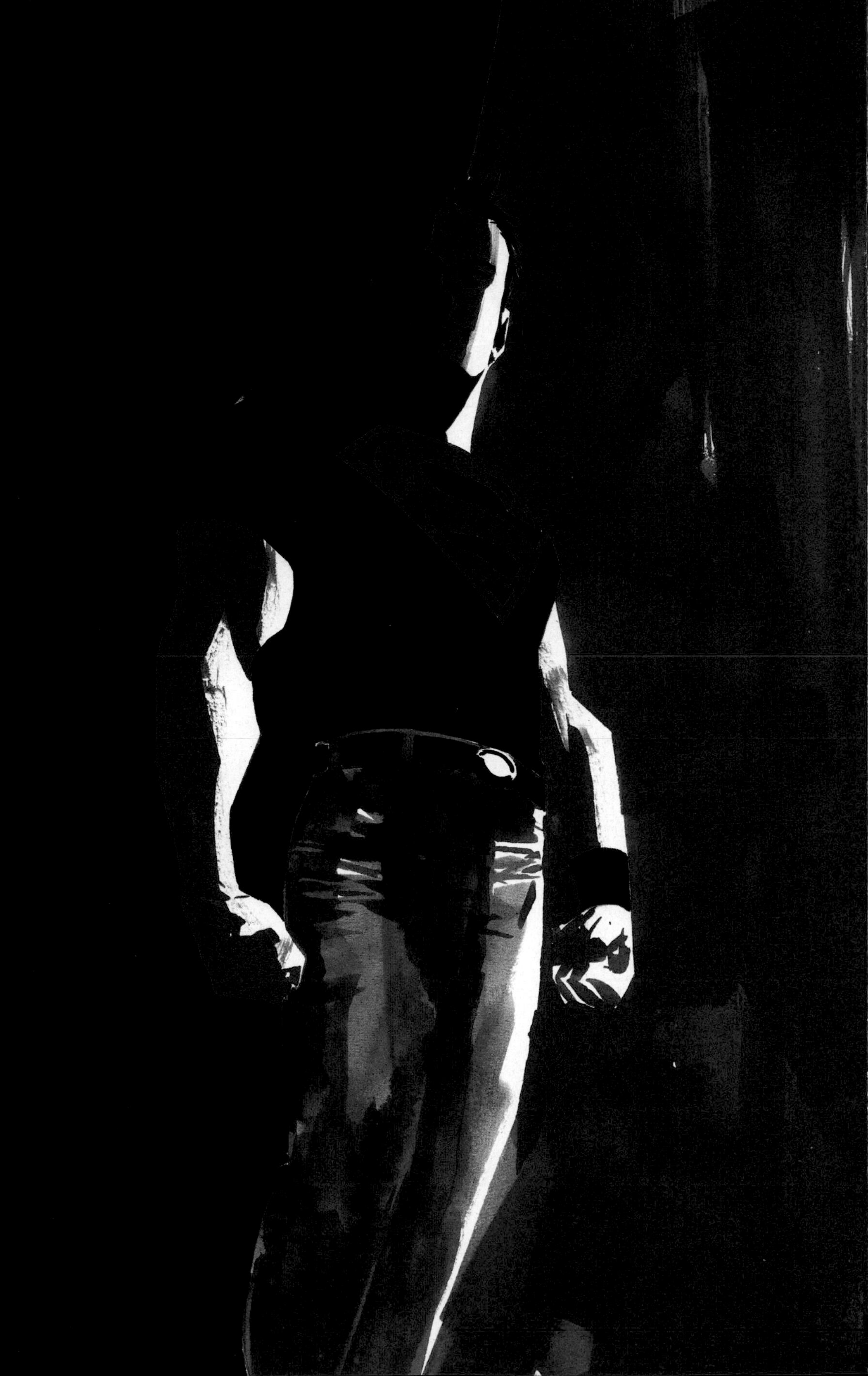

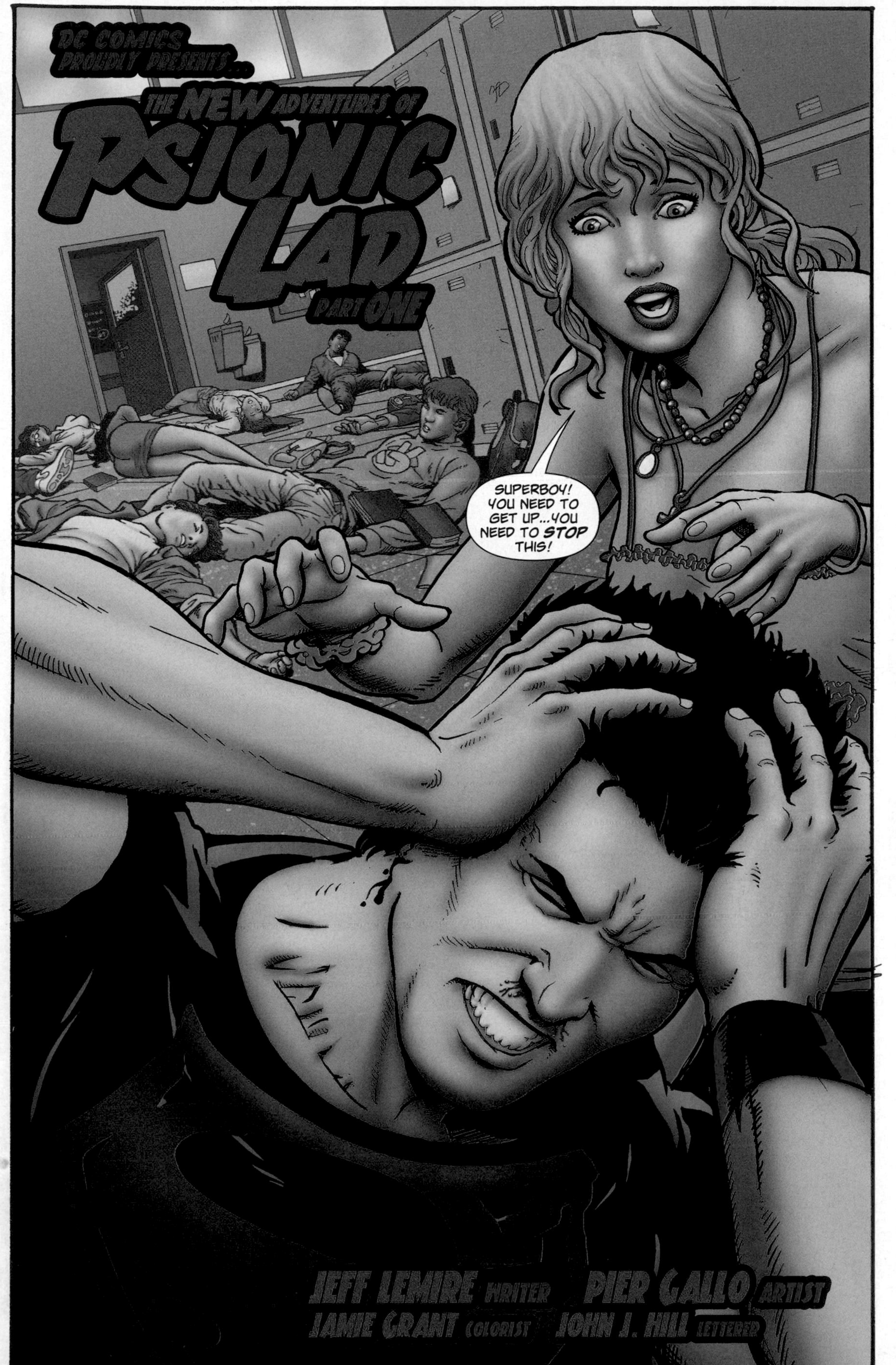
DC COMICS PROUDLY PRESENTS...
THE NEW ADVENTURES OF
PSIONIC LAD
PART ONE
SUPERBOY! YOU NEED TO GET UP...YOU NEED TO STOP THIS!
JEFF LEMIRE WRITER PIER GALLO ARTIST
JAMIE GRANT COLORIST JOHN J. HILL LETTERER

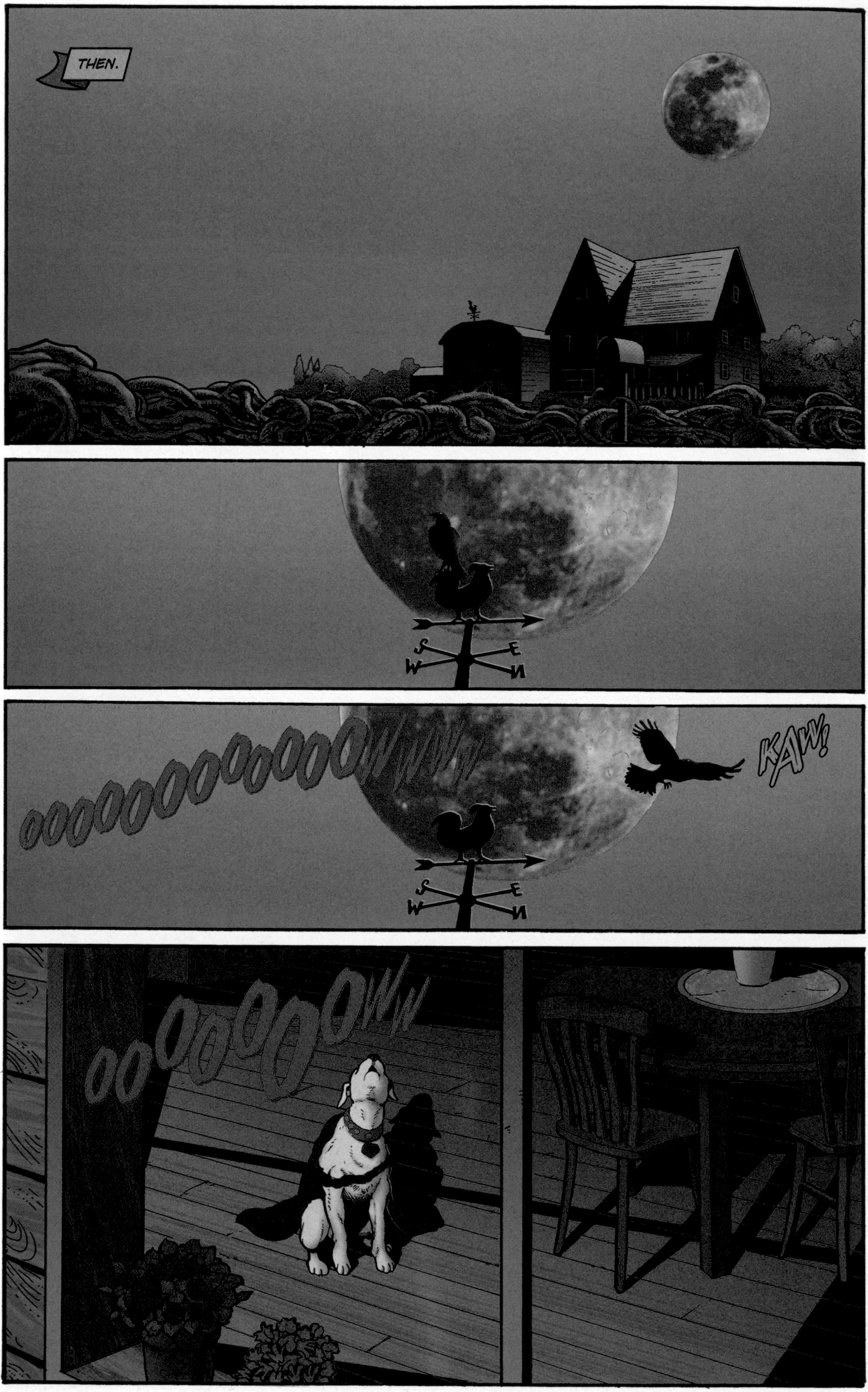
THEN.
KAW!

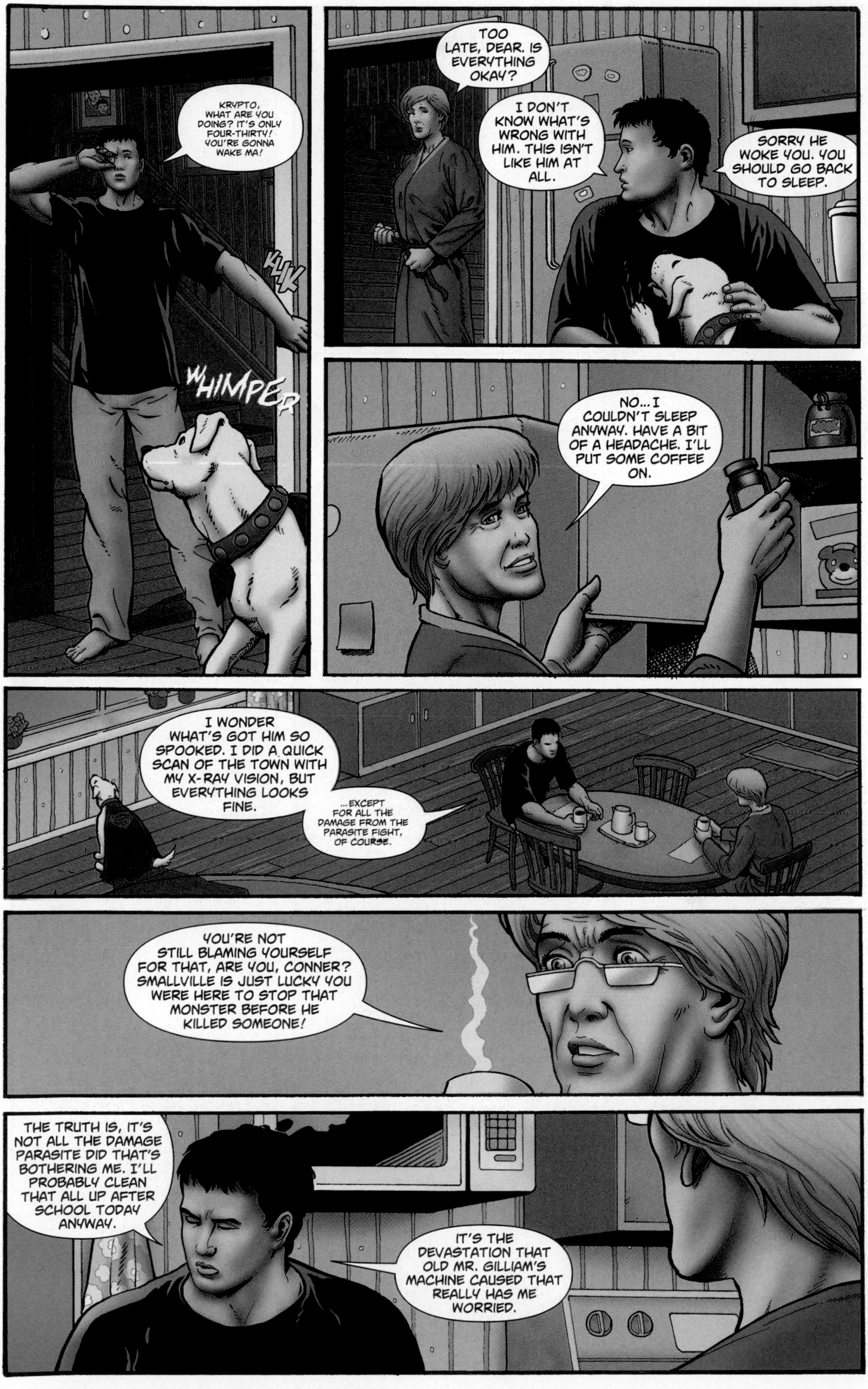
KRYPTO, WHAT ARE YOU DOING? IT'S ONLY FOUR-THIRTY! YOU'RE GONNA WAKE MA!
WHIMPER
TOO LATE, DEAR. IS EVERYTHING OKAY?
I DON'T KNOW WHAT'S WRONG WITH HIM. THIS ISN'T LIKE HIM AT ALL.
SORRY HE WOKE YOU. YOU SHOULD GO BACK TO SLEEP.
NO... I COULDN'T SLEEP ANYWAY. HAVE A BIT OF A HEADACHE. I'LL PUT SOME COFFEE ON.
I WONDER WHAT'S GOT HIM SO SPOOKED. I DID A QUICK SCAN OF THE TOWN WITH MY X-RAY VISION, BUT EVERYTHING LOOKS FINE.
...EXCEPT FOR ALL THE DAMAGE FROM THE PARASITE FIGHT, OF COURSE.
YOU'RE NOT STILL BLAMING YOURSELF FOR THAT, ARE YOU, CONNER? SMALLVILLE IS JUST LUCKY YOU WERE HERE TO STOP THAT MONSTER BEFORE HE KILLED SOMEONE!
THE TRUTH IS, IT'S NOT ALL THE DAMAGE PARASITE DID THAT'S BOTHERING ME. I'LL PROBABLY CLEAN THAT ALL UP AFTER SCHOOL TODAY ANYWAY.
IT'S THE DEVASTATION THAT OLD MR. GILLIAM'S MACHINE CAUSED THAT REALLY HAS ME WORRIED.

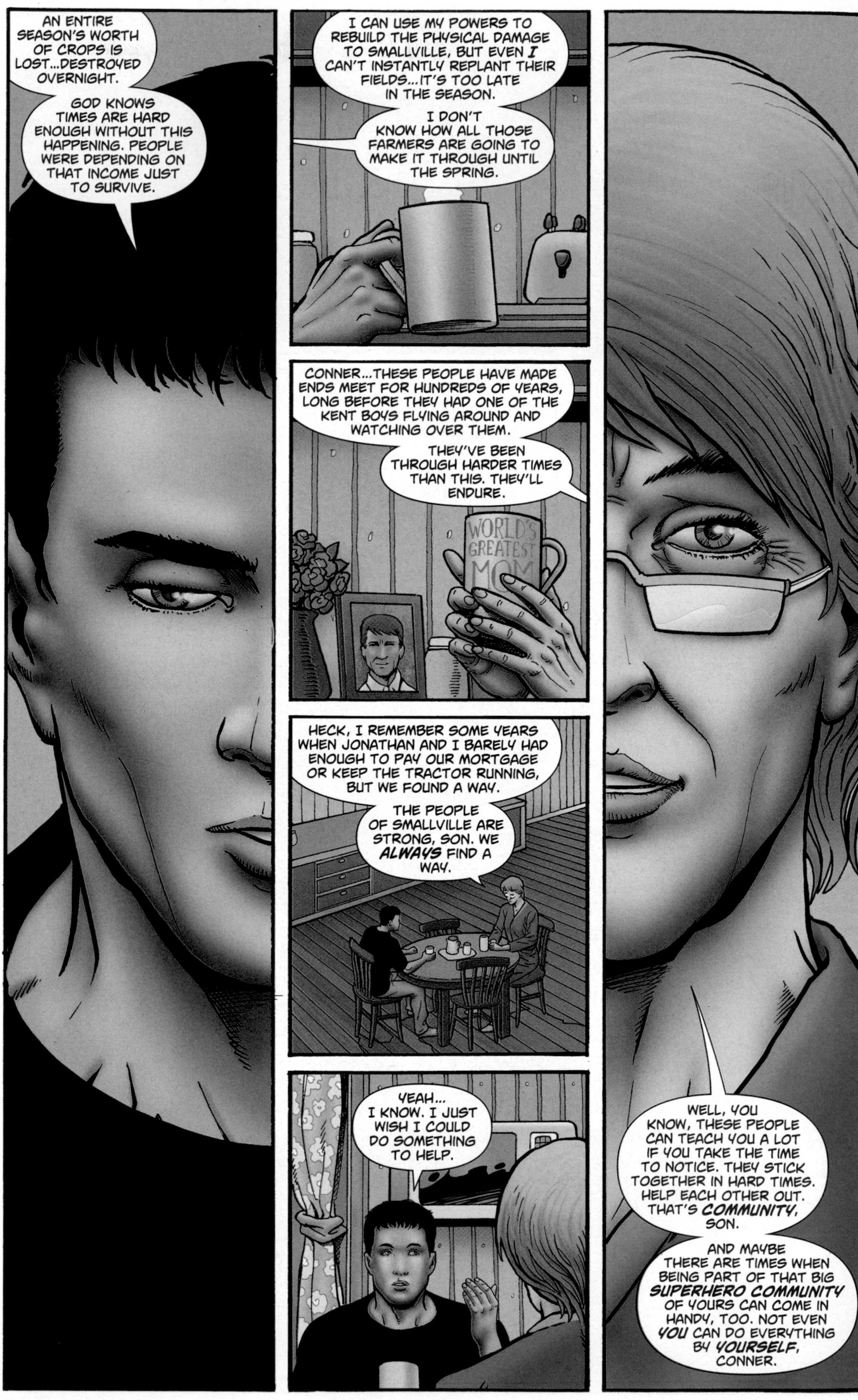
AN ENTIRE SEASON'S WORTH OF CROPS IS LOST...DESTROYED OVERNIGHT.
GOD KNOWS TIMES ARE HARD ENOUGH WITHOUT THIS HAPPENING. PEOPLE WERE DEPENDING ON THAT INCOME JUST TO SURVIVE.
I CAN USE MY POWERS TO REBUILD THE PHYSICAL DAMAGE TO SMALLVILLE, BUT EVEN *I* CAN'T INSTANTLY REPLANT THEIR FIELDS...IT'S TOO LATE IN THE SEASON.
I DON'T KNOW HOW ALL THOSE FARMERS ARE GOING TO MAKE IT THROUGH UNTIL THE SPRING.
CONNER...THESE PEOPLE HAVE MADE ENDS MEET FOR HUNDREDS OF YEARS, LONG BEFORE THEY HAD ONE OF THE KENT BOYS FLYING AROUND AND WATCHING OVER THEM.
THEY'VE BEEN THROUGH HARDER TIMES THAN THIS. THEY'LL ENDURE.
WORLD'S GREATEST MOM
HECK, I REMEMBER SOME YEARS WHEN JONATHAN AND I BARELY HAD ENOUGH TO PAY OUR MORTGAGE OR KEEP THE TRACTOR RUNNING, BUT WE FOUND A WAY.
THE PEOPLE OF SMALLVILLE ARE STRONG, SON. WE ***ALWAYS*** FIND A WAY.
YEAH... I KNOW. I JUST WISH I COULD DO SOMETHING TO HELP.
WELL, YOU KNOW, THESE PEOPLE CAN TEACH YOU A LOT IF YOU TAKE THE TIME TO NOTICE. THEY STICK TOGETHER IN HARD TIMES. HELP EACH OTHER OUT. THAT'S ***COMMUNITY***, SON.
AND MAYBE THERE ARE TIMES WHEN BEING PART OF THAT BIG ***SUPERHERO COMMUNITY*** OF YOURS CAN COME IN HANDY, TOO. NOT EVEN ***YOU*** CAN DO EVERYTHING BY ***YOURSELF***, CONNER.

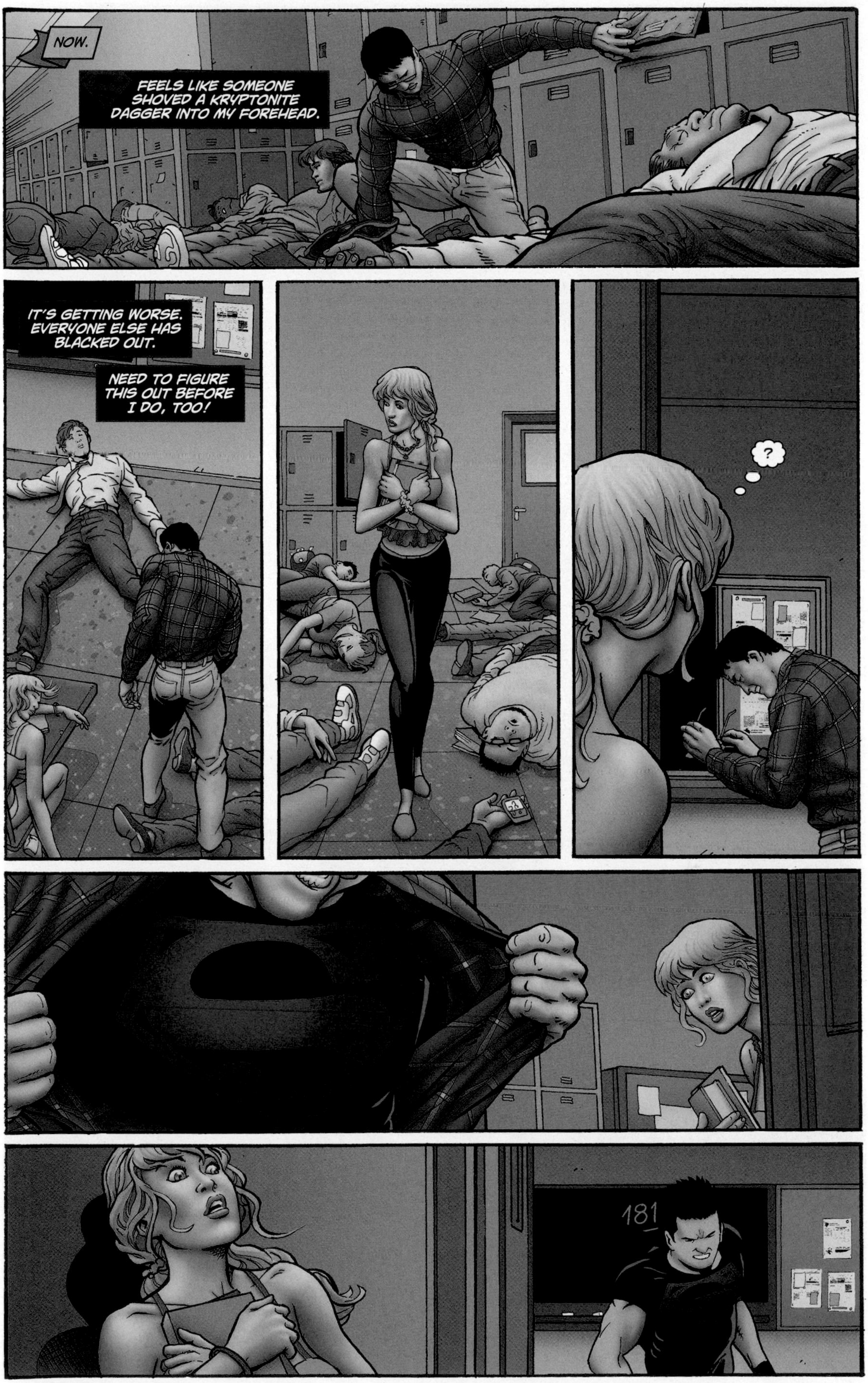
NOW.
FEELS LIKE SOMEONE SHOVED A KRYPTONITE DAGGER INTO MY FOREHEAD.
IT'S GETTING WORSE. EVERYONE ELSE HAS BLACKED OUT.
NEED TO FIGURE THIS OUT BEFORE I DO, TOO!
?
181

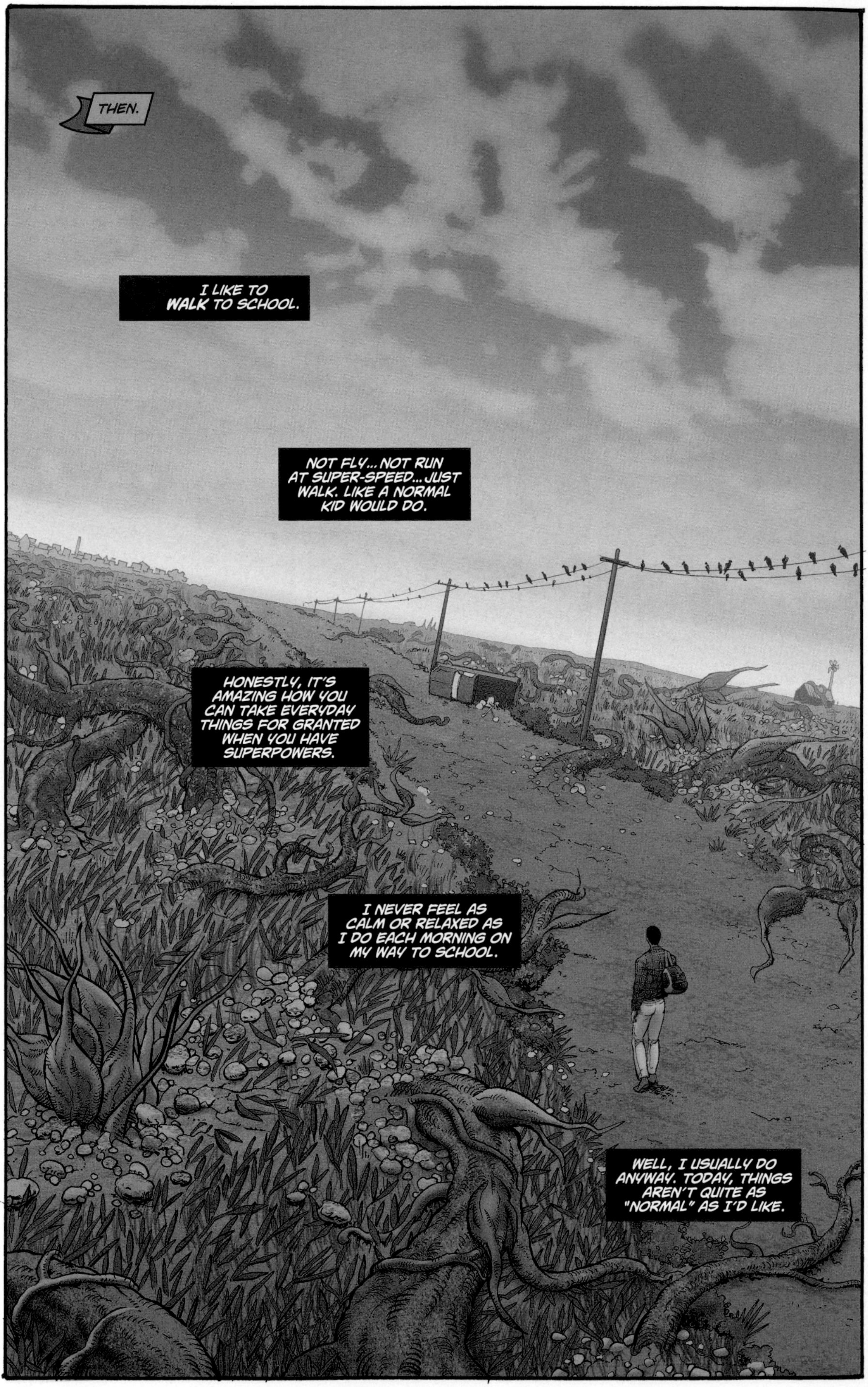
THEN.
I LIKE TO WALK TO SCHOOL.
NOT FLY... NOT RUN AT SUPER-SPEED... JUST WALK. LIKE A NORMAL KID WOULD DO.
HONESTLY, IT'S AMAZING HOW YOU CAN TAKE EVERYDAY THINGS FOR GRANTED WHEN YOU HAVE SUPERPOWERS.
I NEVER FEEL AS CALM OR RELAXED AS I DO EACH MORNING ON MY WAY TO SCHOOL.
WELL, I USUALLY DO ANYWAY. TODAY, THINGS AREN'T QUITE AS "NORMAL" AS I'D LIKE.

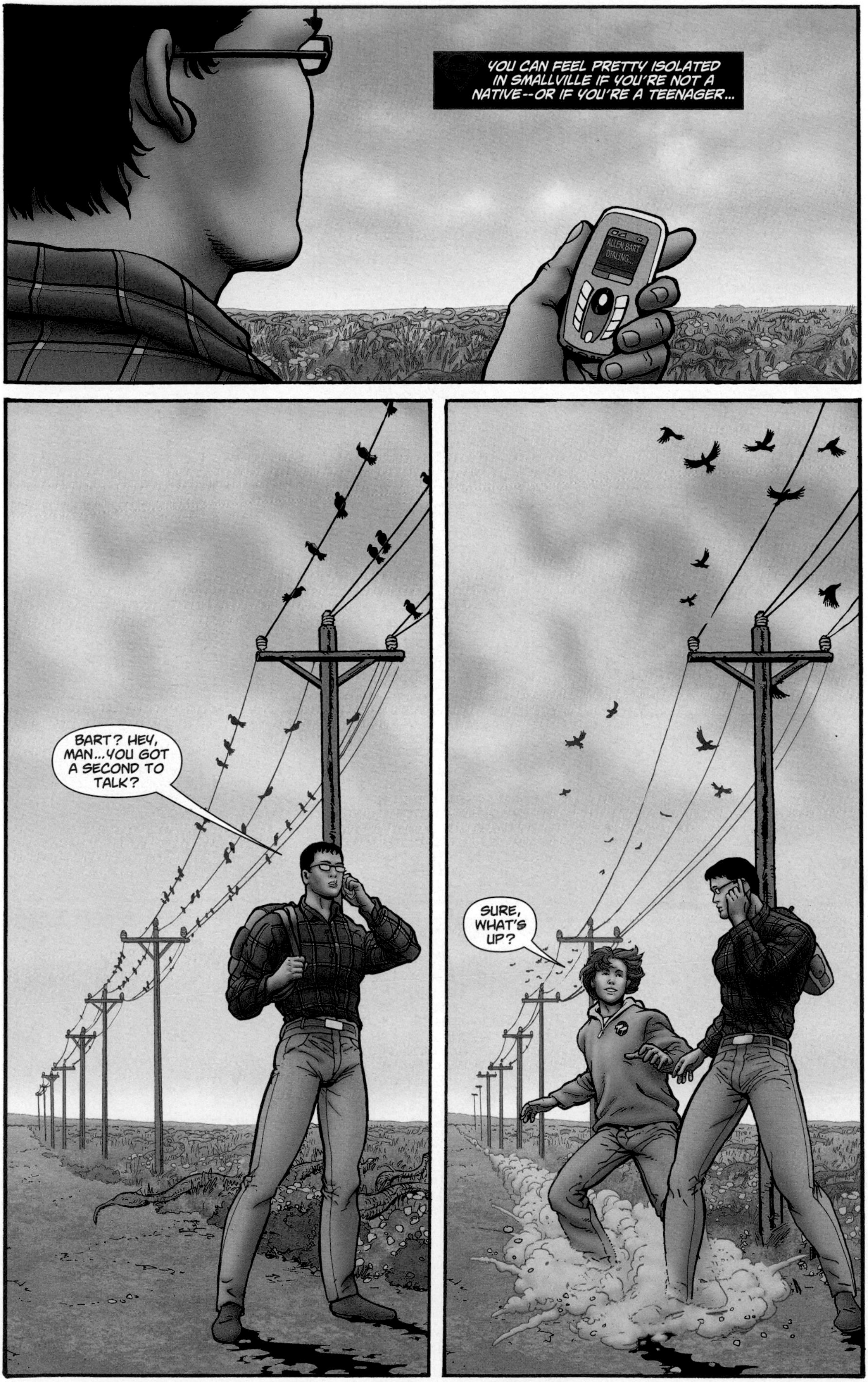
YOU CAN FEEL PRETTY ISOLATED IN SMALLVILLE IF YOU'RE NOT A NATIVE--OR IF YOU'RE A TEENAGER...
ALLEN,BART DIALING...
BART? HEY, MAN...YOU GOT A SECOND TO TALK?
SURE, WHAT'S UP?

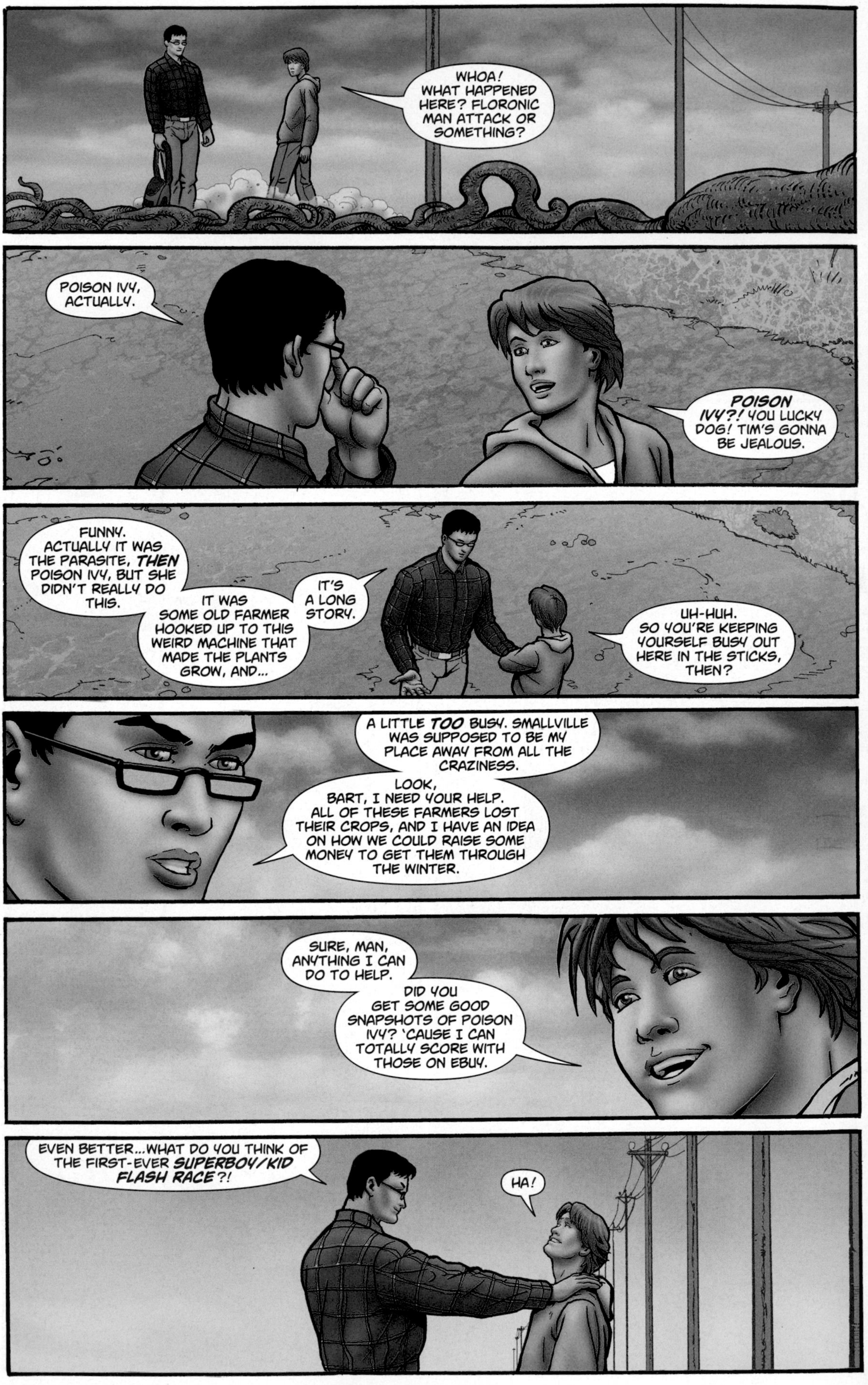
WHOA! WHAT HAPPENED HERE? FLORONIC MAN ATTACK OR SOMETHING?
POISON IVY, ACTUALLY.
POISON IVY?! YOU LUCKY DOG! TIM'S GONNA BE JEALOUS.
FUNNY. ACTUALLY IT WAS THE PARASITE, THEN POISON IVY, BUT SHE DIDN'T REALLY DO THIS.
IT WAS SOME OLD FARMER HOOKED UP TO THIS WEIRD MACHINE THAT MADE THE PLANTS GROW, AND...
IT'S A LONG STORY.
UH-HUH. SO YOU'RE KEEPING YOURSELF BUSY OUT HERE IN THE STICKS, THEN?
A LITTLE TOO BUSY. SMALLVILLE WAS SUPPOSED TO BE MY PLACE AWAY FROM ALL THE CRAZINESS.
LOOK, BART, I NEED YOUR HELP. ALL OF THESE FARMERS LOST THEIR CROPS, AND I HAVE AN IDEA ON HOW WE COULD RAISE SOME MONEY TO GET THEM THROUGH THE WINTER.
SURE, MAN, ANYTHING I CAN DO TO HELP.
DID YOU GET SOME GOOD SNAPSHOTS OF POISON IVY? 'CAUSE I CAN TOTALLY SCORE WITH THOSE ON EBUY.
EVEN BETTER...WHAT DO YOU THINK OF THE FIRST-EVER SUPERBOY/KID FLASH RACE?!
HA!

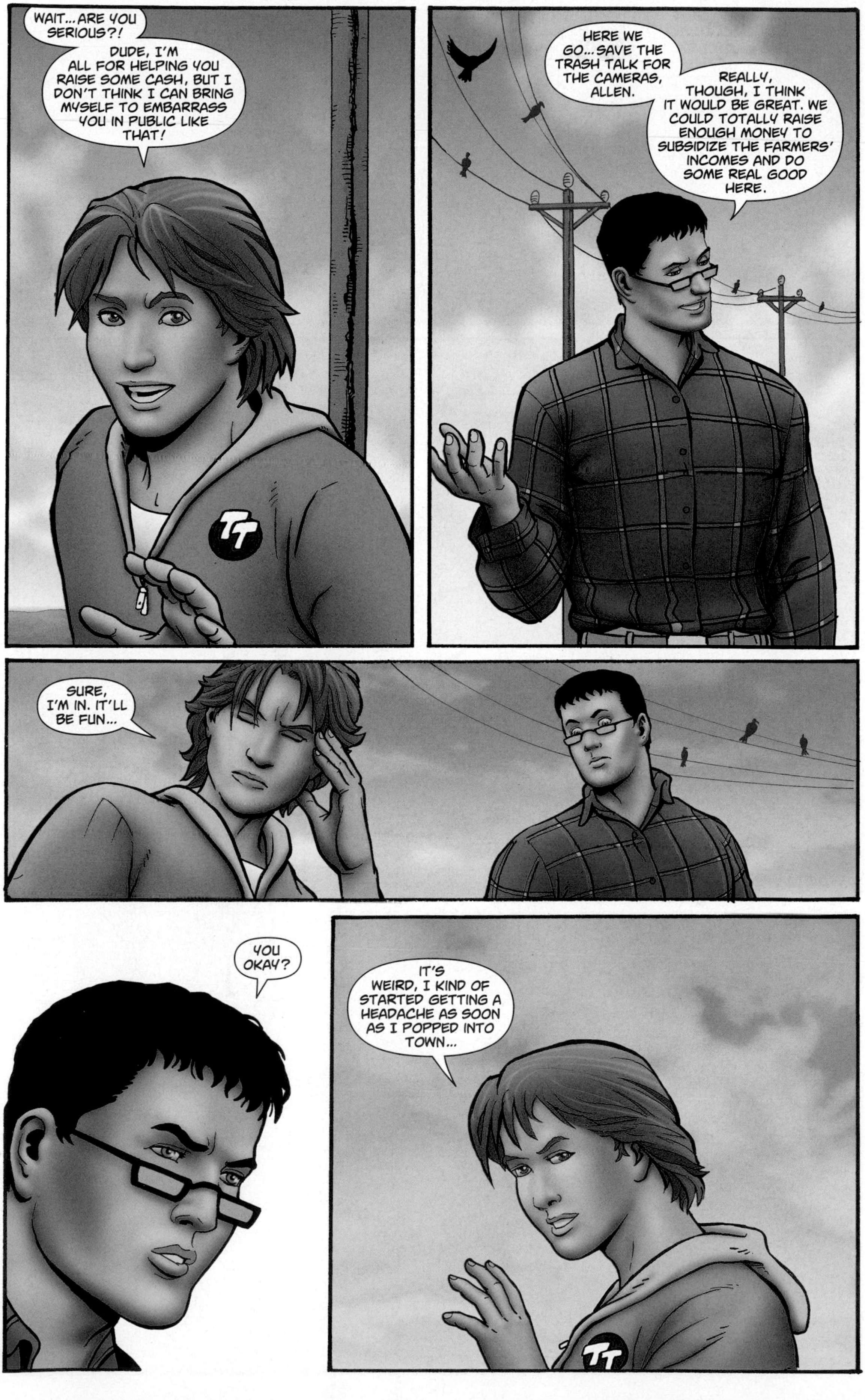
WAIT... ARE YOU SERIOUS?!
DUDE, I'M ALL FOR HELPING YOU RAISE SOME CASH, BUT I DON'T THINK I CAN BRING MYSELF TO EMBARRASS YOU IN PUBLIC LIKE THAT!
HERE WE GO... SAVE THE TRASH TALK FOR THE CAMERAS, ALLEN.
REALLY, THOUGH, I THINK IT WOULD BE GREAT. WE COULD TOTALLY RAISE ENOUGH MONEY TO SUBSIDIZE THE FARMERS' INCOMES AND DO SOME REAL GOOD HERE.
SURE, I'M IN. IT'LL BE FUN...
YOU OKAY?
IT'S WEIRD, I KIND OF STARTED GETTING A HEADACHE AS SOON AS I POPPED INTO TOWN...

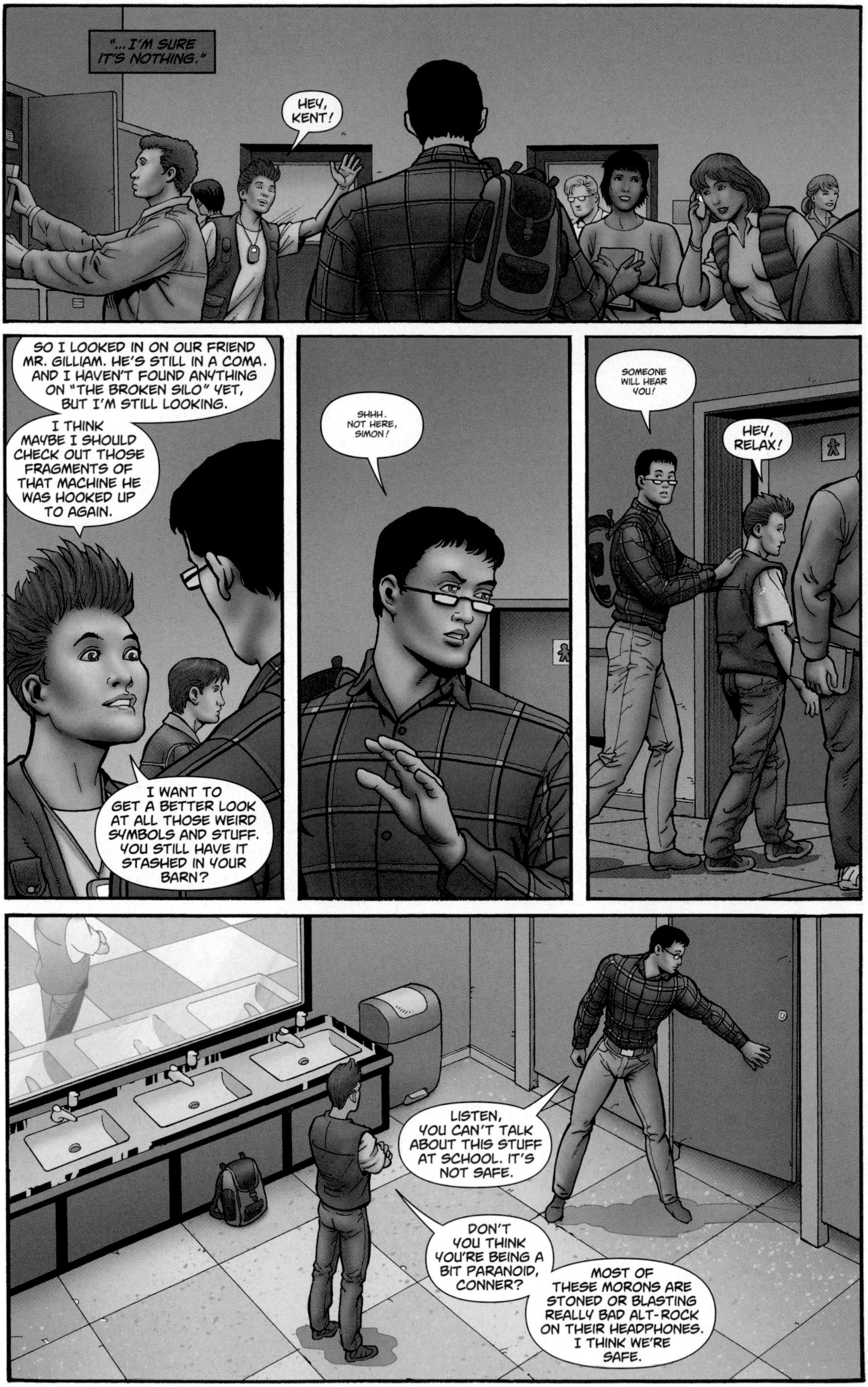
"...I'M SURE IT'S NOTHING."
HEY, KENT!
SO I LOOKED IN ON OUR FRIEND MR. GILLIAM. HE'S STILL IN A COMA. AND I HAVEN'T FOUND ANYTHING ON "THE BROKEN SILO" YET, BUT I'M STILL LOOKING.
I THINK MAYBE I SHOULD CHECK OUT THOSE FRAGMENTS OF THAT MACHINE HE WAS HOOKED UP TO AGAIN.
I WANT TO GET A BETTER LOOK AT ALL THOSE WEIRD SYMBOLS AND STUFF. YOU STILL HAVE IT STASHED IN YOUR BARN?
SHHH. NOT HERE, SIMON!
SOMEONE WILL HEAR YOU!
HEY, RELAX!
LISTEN, YOU CAN'T TALK ABOUT THIS STUFF AT SCHOOL. IT'S NOT SAFE.
DON'T YOU THINK YOU'RE BEING A BIT PARANOID, CONNER?
MOST OF THESE MORONS ARE STONED OR BLASTING REALLY BAD ALT-ROCK ON THEIR HEADPHONES. I THINK WE'RE SAFE.

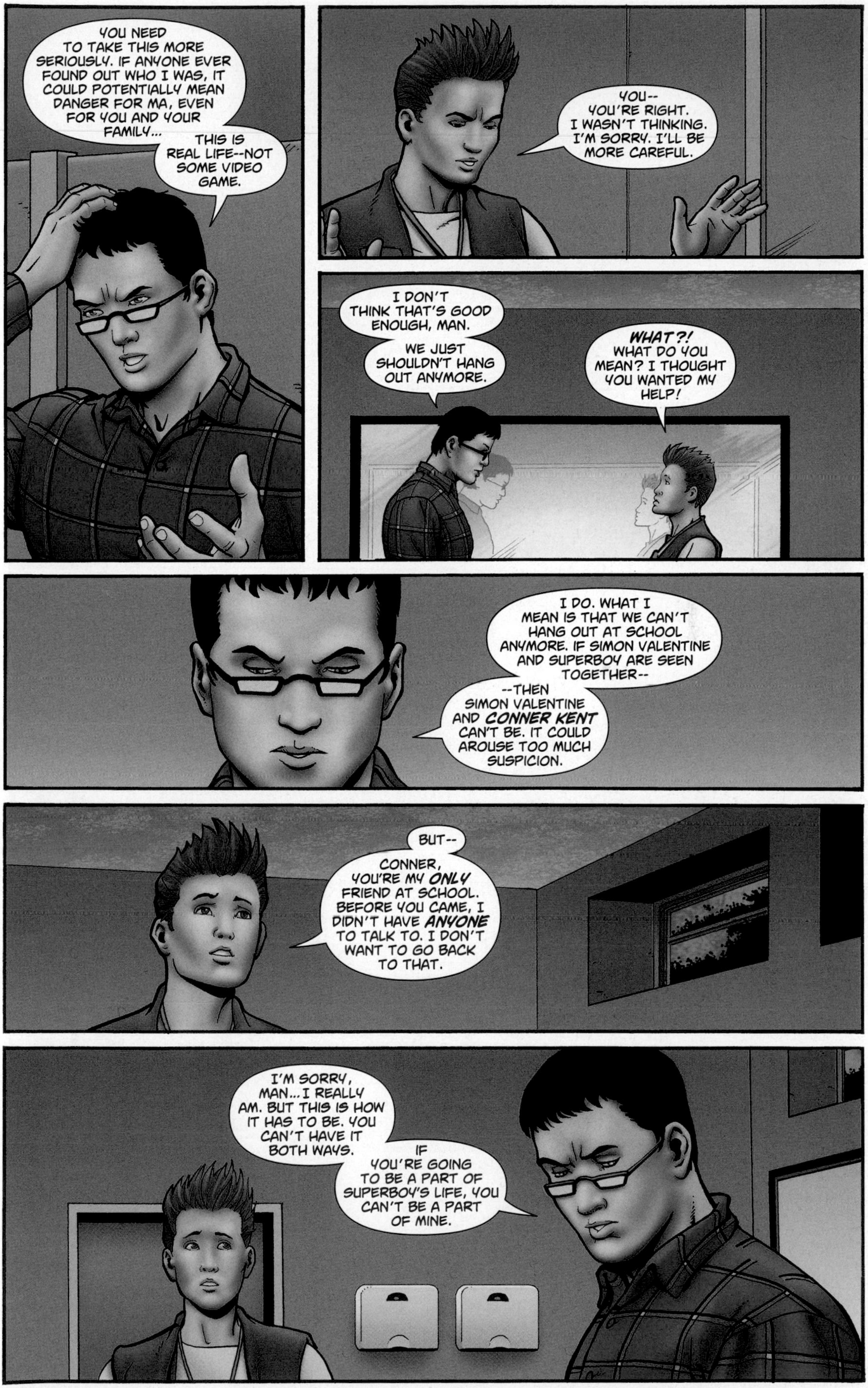
YOU NEED TO TAKE THIS MORE SERIOUSLY. IF ANYONE EVER FOUND OUT WHO I WAS, IT COULD POTENTIALLY MEAN DANGER FOR MA, EVEN FOR YOU AND YOUR FAMILY...
THIS IS REAL LIFE--NOT SOME VIDEO GAME.
YOU-- YOU'RE RIGHT. I WASN'T THINKING. I'M SORRY. I'LL BE MORE CAREFUL.
I DON'T THINK THAT'S GOOD ENOUGH, MAN.
WE JUST SHOULDN'T HANG OUT ANYMORE.
WHAT?! WHAT DO YOU MEAN? I THOUGHT YOU WANTED MY HELP!
I DO. WHAT I MEAN IS THAT WE CAN'T HANG OUT AT SCHOOL ANYMORE. IF SIMON VALENTINE AND SUPERBOY ARE SEEN TOGETHER--
--THEN SIMON VALENTINE AND CONNER KENT CAN'T BE. IT COULD AROUSE TOO MUCH SUSPICION.
BUT--
CONNER, YOU'RE MY ONLY FRIEND AT SCHOOL. BEFORE YOU CAME, I DIDN'T HAVE ANYONE TO TALK TO. I DON'T WANT TO GO BACK TO THAT.
I'M SORRY, MAN... I REALLY AM. BUT THIS IS HOW IT HAS TO BE. YOU CAN'T HAVE IT BOTH WAYS.
IF YOU'RE GOING TO BE A PART OF SUPERBOY'S LIFE, YOU CAN'T BE A PART OF MINE.

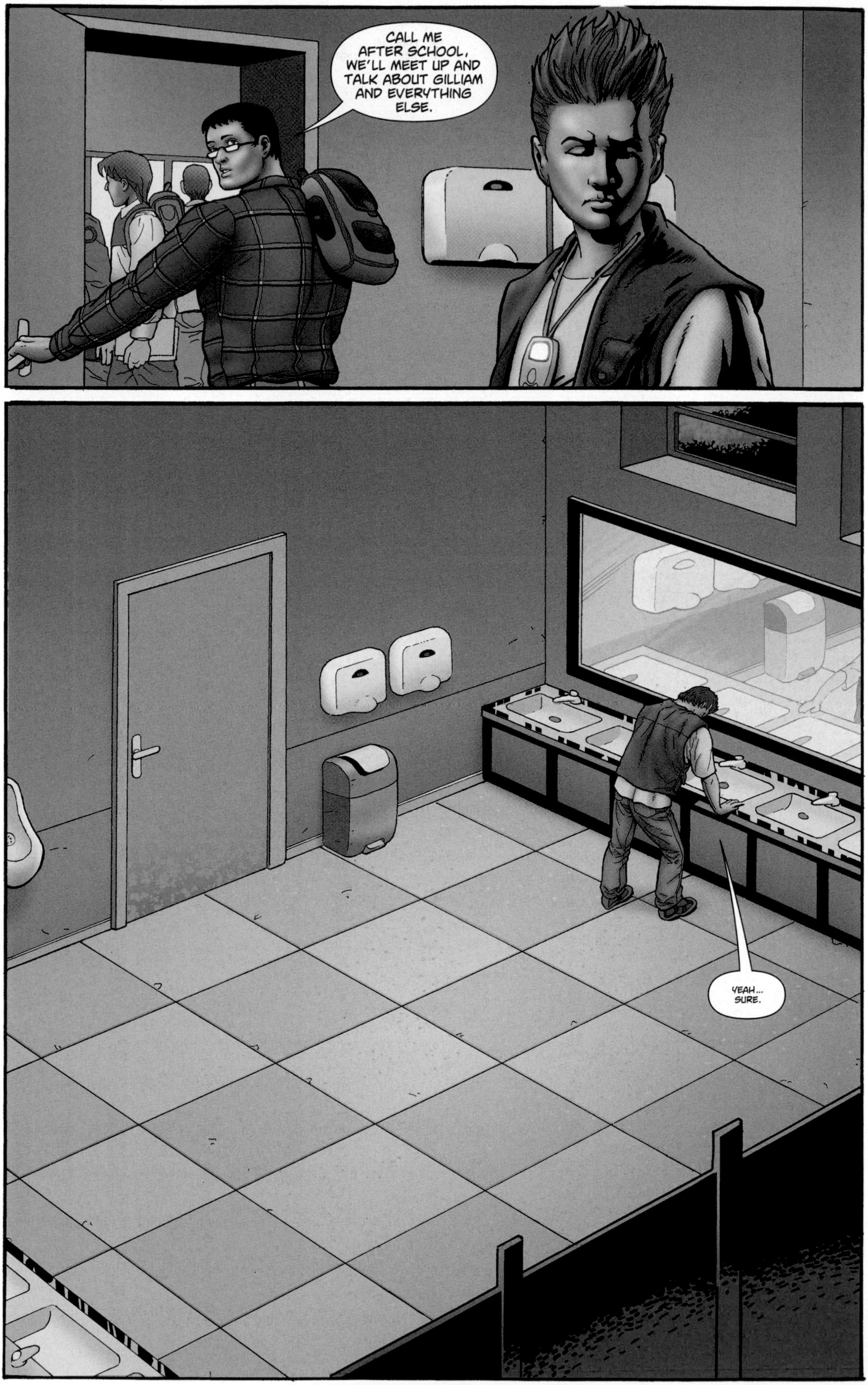
CALL ME AFTER SCHOOL, WE'LL MEET UP AND TALK ABOUT GILLIAM AND EVERYTHING ELSE.
YEAH... SURE.

NOW.

THIS...THIS IS CRAZY. I MEAN, I KIND OF SUSPECTED THAT CONNER MIGHT BE SUPERBOY AFTER EVERYTHING THAT HAPPENED WITH MY MOM AND UNCLE LEX*...BUT I NEVER *REALLY* THOUGHT IT WAS TRUE!

I CAN'T LET *HIM KNOW* THAT I *KNOW*...

*SEE *SUPERBOY: THE BOY OF STEEL*

...THINGS ARE WEIRD *ENOUGH* BETWEEN US!

LORI?!

SUPERBOY! THANK *GOD* YOU'RE HERE! I DON'T KNOW WHAT HAPPENED.

I WAS IN CLASS, THEN EVERYONE JUST STARTED SCREAMING AND PASSING OUT!

DON'T YOU--DON'T YOU FEEL IT... THE PAIN?

I FEEL FINE.

WELL... WHATEVER IT IS, IT'S GETTING WORSE. AND IF YOU'RE NOT AFFECTED, MAYBE YOU CAN HELP ME FIGURE IT OUT... ≥UNGH≤

SUPERBOY?

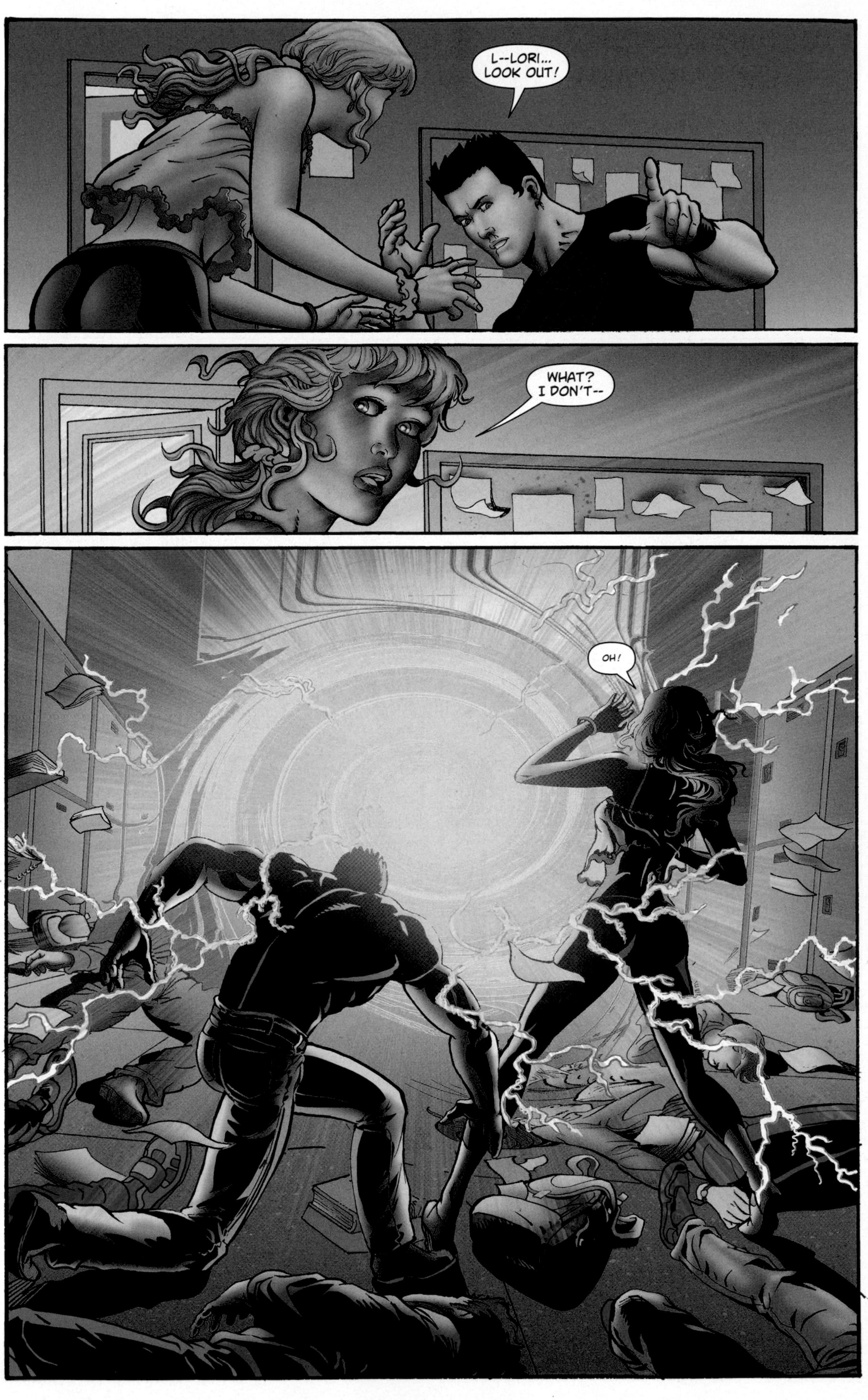
L--LORI...
LOOK OUT!
WHAT?
I DON'T--
OH!

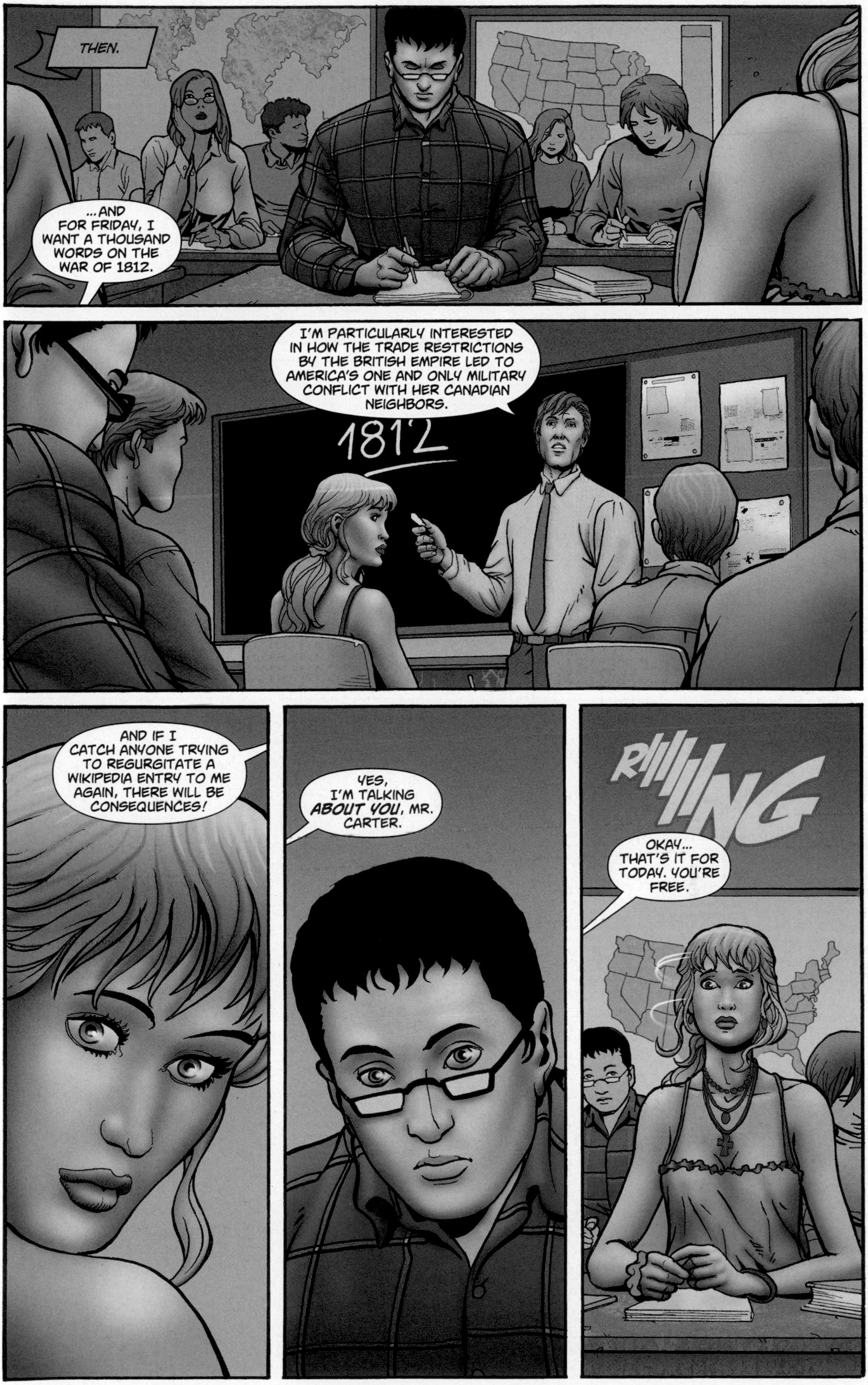
THEN.
...AND FOR FRIDAY, I WANT A THOUSAND WORDS ON THE WAR OF 1812.
I'M PARTICULARLY INTERESTED IN HOW THE TRADE RESTRICTIONS BY THE BRITISH EMPIRE LED TO AMERICA'S ONE AND ONLY MILITARY CONFLICT WITH HER CANADIAN NEIGHBORS.
1812
AND IF I CATCH ANYONE TRYING TO REGURGITATE A WIKIPEDIA ENTRY TO ME AGAIN, THERE WILL BE CONSEQUENCES!
YES, I'M TALKING *ABOUT YOU*, MR. CARTER.
RIIIING
OKAY... THAT'S IT FOR TODAY. YOU'RE FREE.

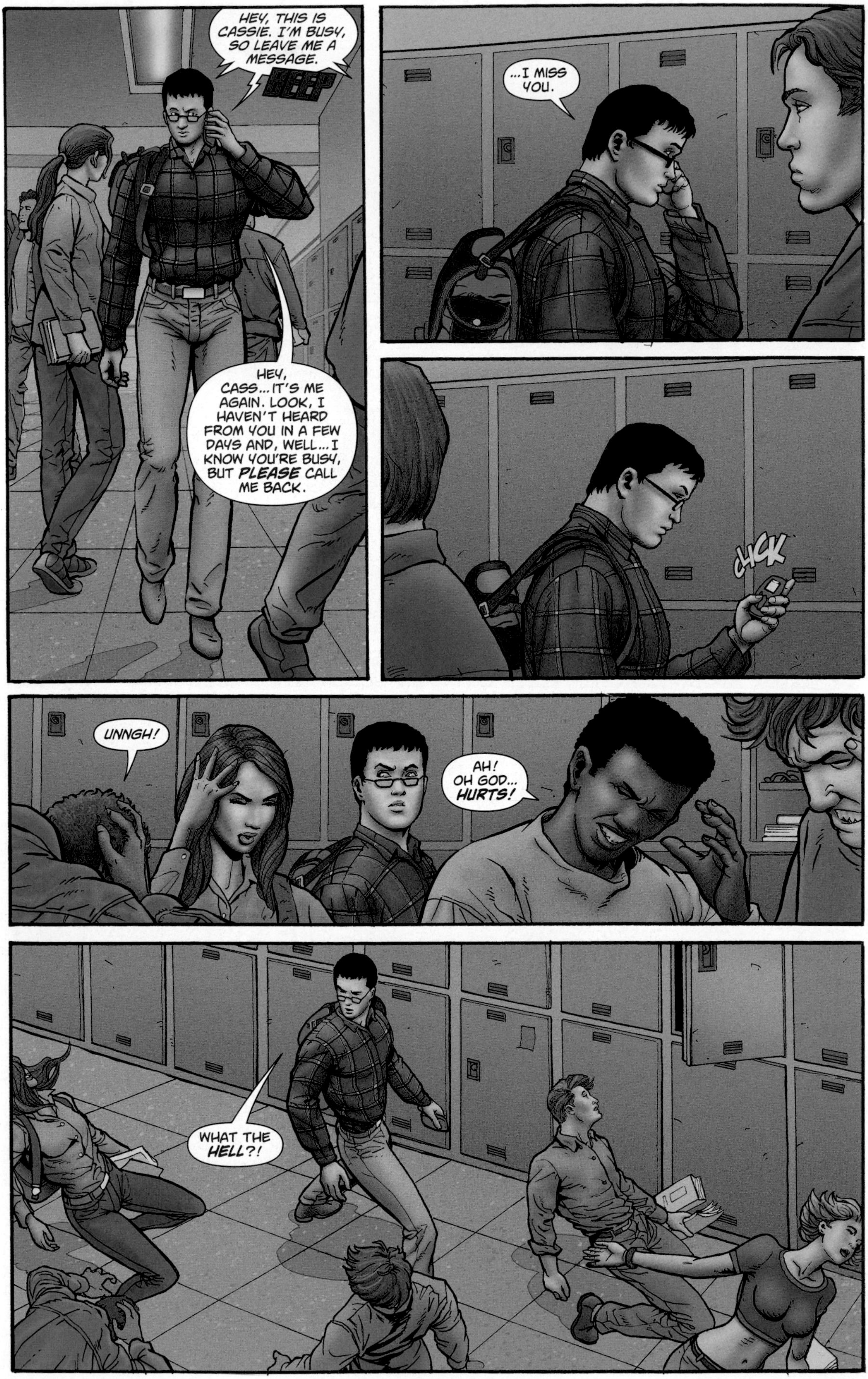
HEY, THIS IS CASSIE. I'M BUSY, SO LEAVE ME A MESSAGE.
BEEP
HEY, CASS... IT'S ME AGAIN. LOOK, I HAVEN'T HEARD FROM YOU IN A FEW DAYS AND, WELL... I KNOW YOU'RE BUSY, BUT PLEASE CALL ME BACK.
...I MISS YOU.
CLICK
UNNGH!
AH! OH GOD... HURTS!
WHAT THE HELL?!

NOW.

WHAT... IS IT?

I DON'T KNOW...SOME KIND OF PORTAL OR RIFT OR SOMETHING. I THINK YOU NEED TO GET AS FAR AWAY FROM HERE AS YOU CAN, LORI!

OH MY GOD--

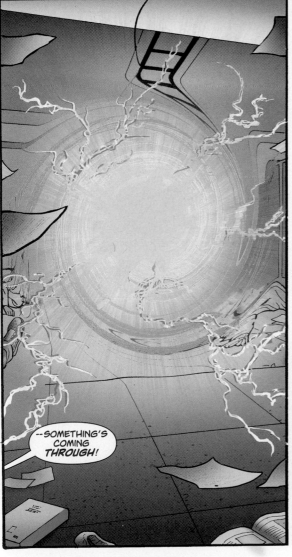

--SOMETHING'S COMING THROUGH!

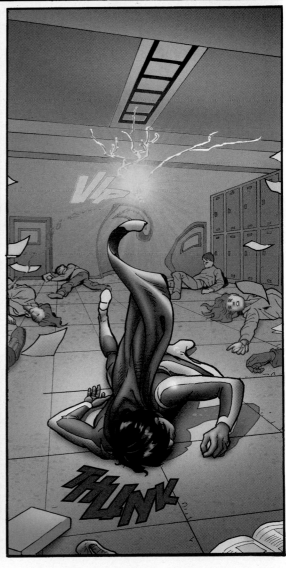

THLINK

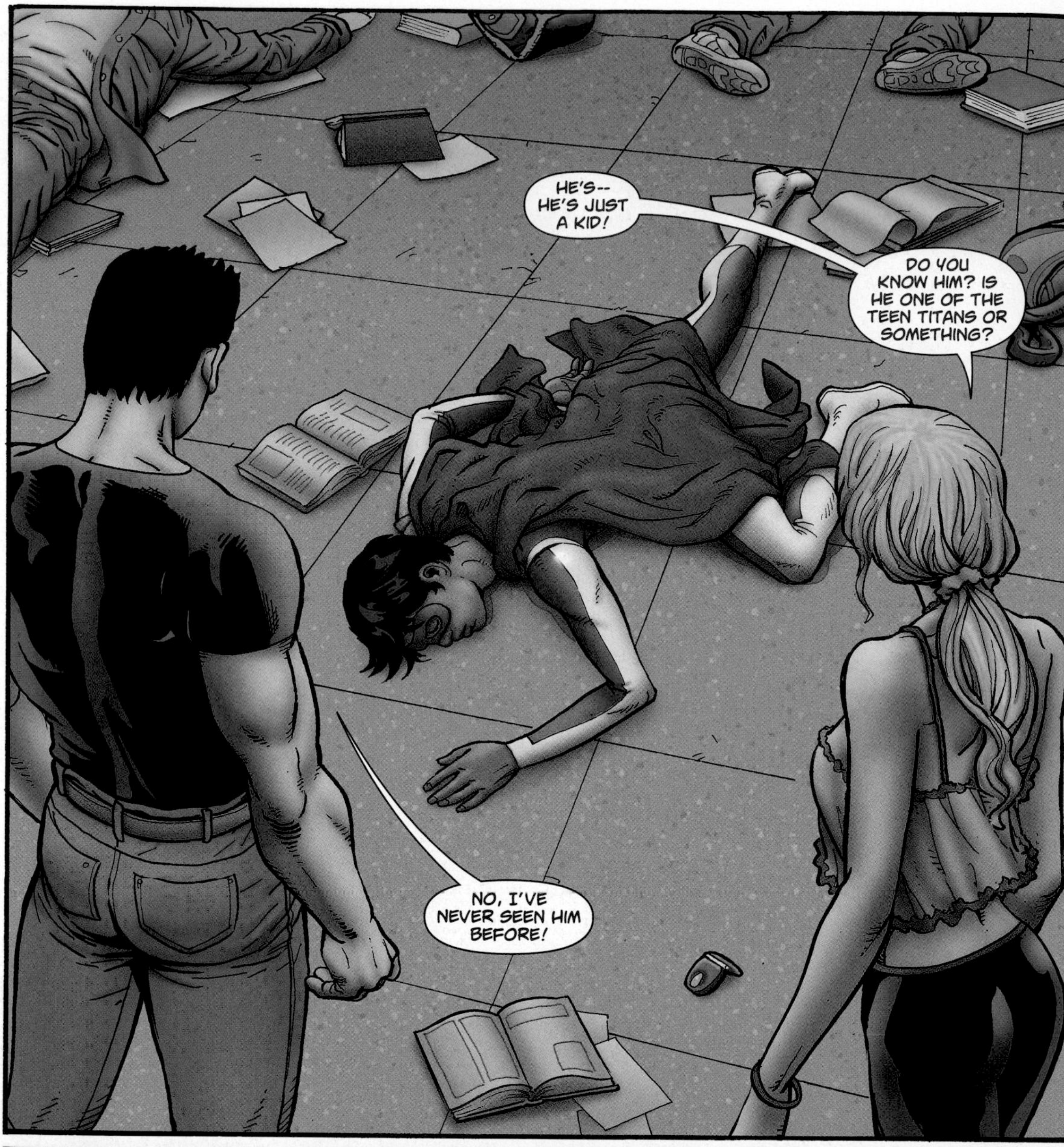
HE'S-- HE'S JUST A KID!
DO YOU KNOW HIM? IS HE ONE OF THE TEEN TITANS OR SOMETHING?
NO, I'VE NEVER SEEN HIM BEFORE!

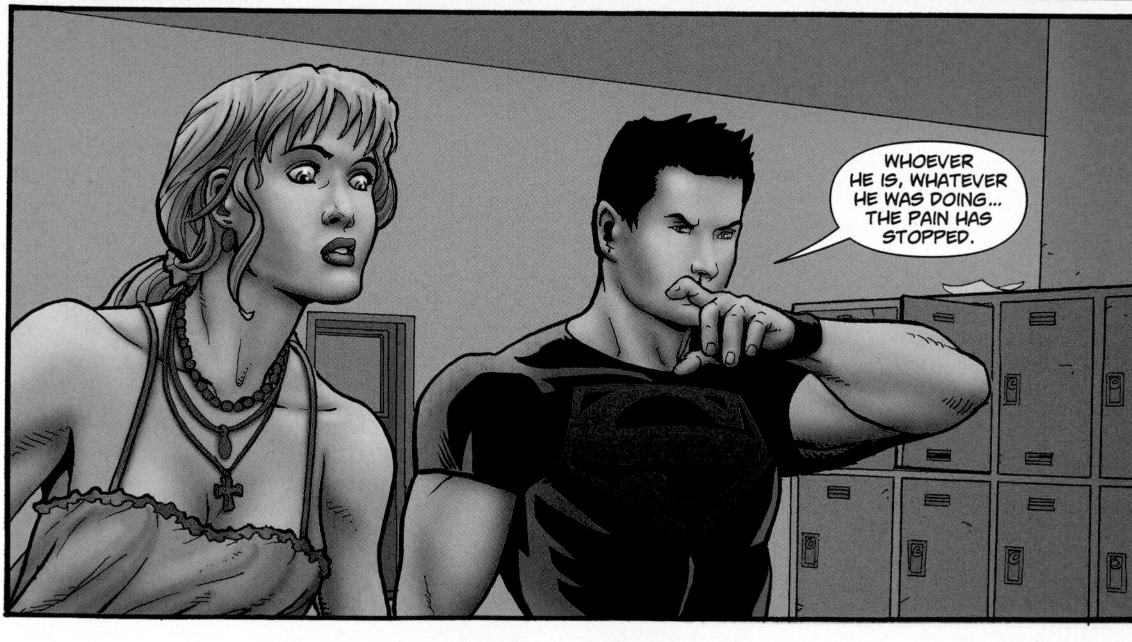
WHOEVER HE IS, WHATEVER HE WAS DOING... THE PAIN HAS STOPPED.

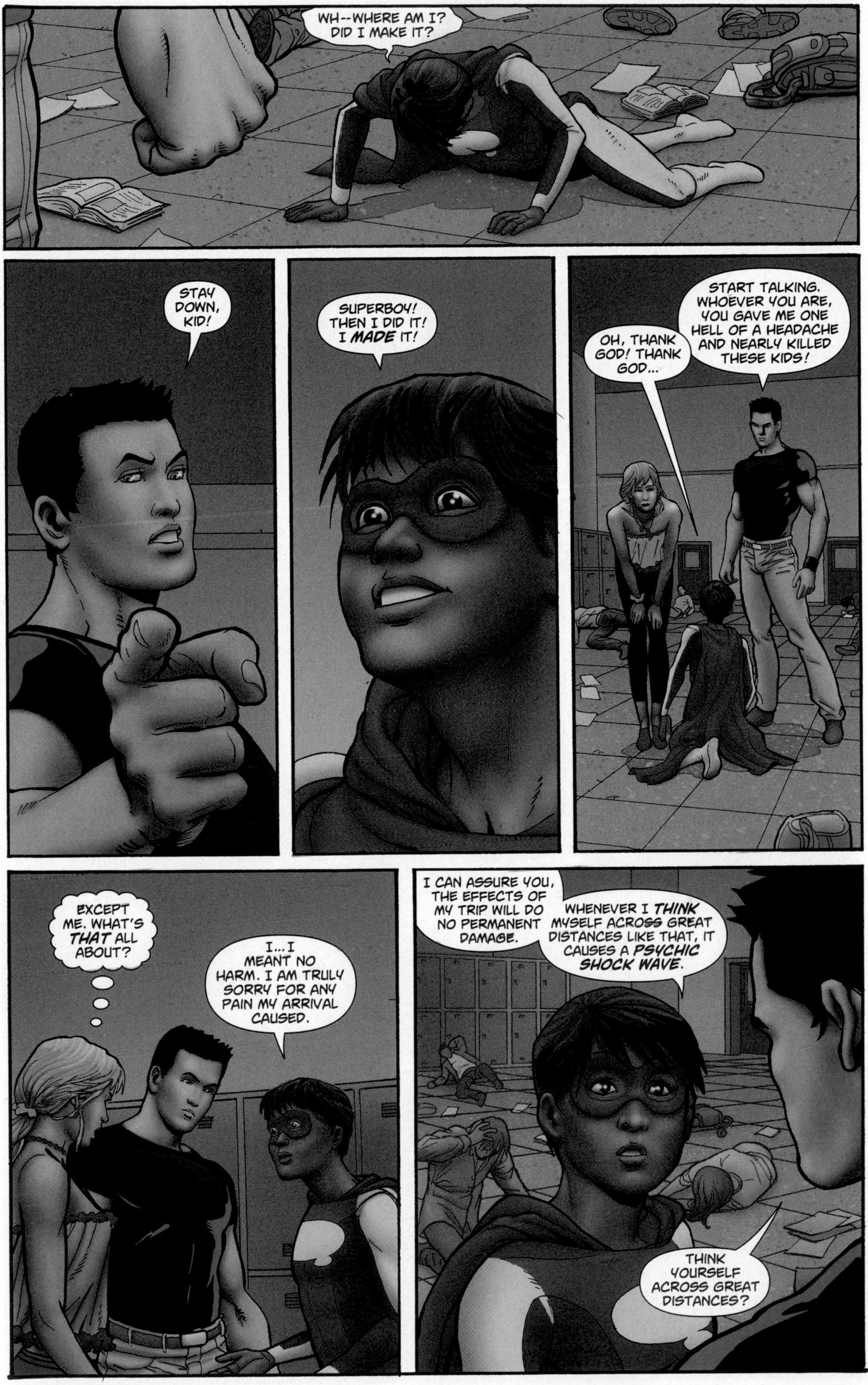
WH--WHERE AM I? DID I MAKE IT?
STAY DOWN, KID!
SUPERBOY! THEN I DID IT! I MADE IT!
START TALKING. WHOEVER YOU ARE, YOU GAVE ME ONE HELL OF A HEADACHE AND NEARLY KILLED THESE KIDS!
OH, THANK GOD! THANK GOD...
EXCEPT ME. WHAT'S THAT ALL ABOUT?
I...I MEANT NO HARM. I AM TRULY SORRY FOR ANY PAIN MY ARRIVAL CAUSED.
I CAN ASSURE YOU, THE EFFECTS OF MY TRIP WILL DO NO PERMANENT DAMAGE.
WHENEVER I THINK MYSELF ACROSS GREAT DISTANCES LIKE THAT, IT CAUSES A PSYCHIC SHOCK WAVE.
THINK YOURSELF ACROSS GREAT DISTANCES?

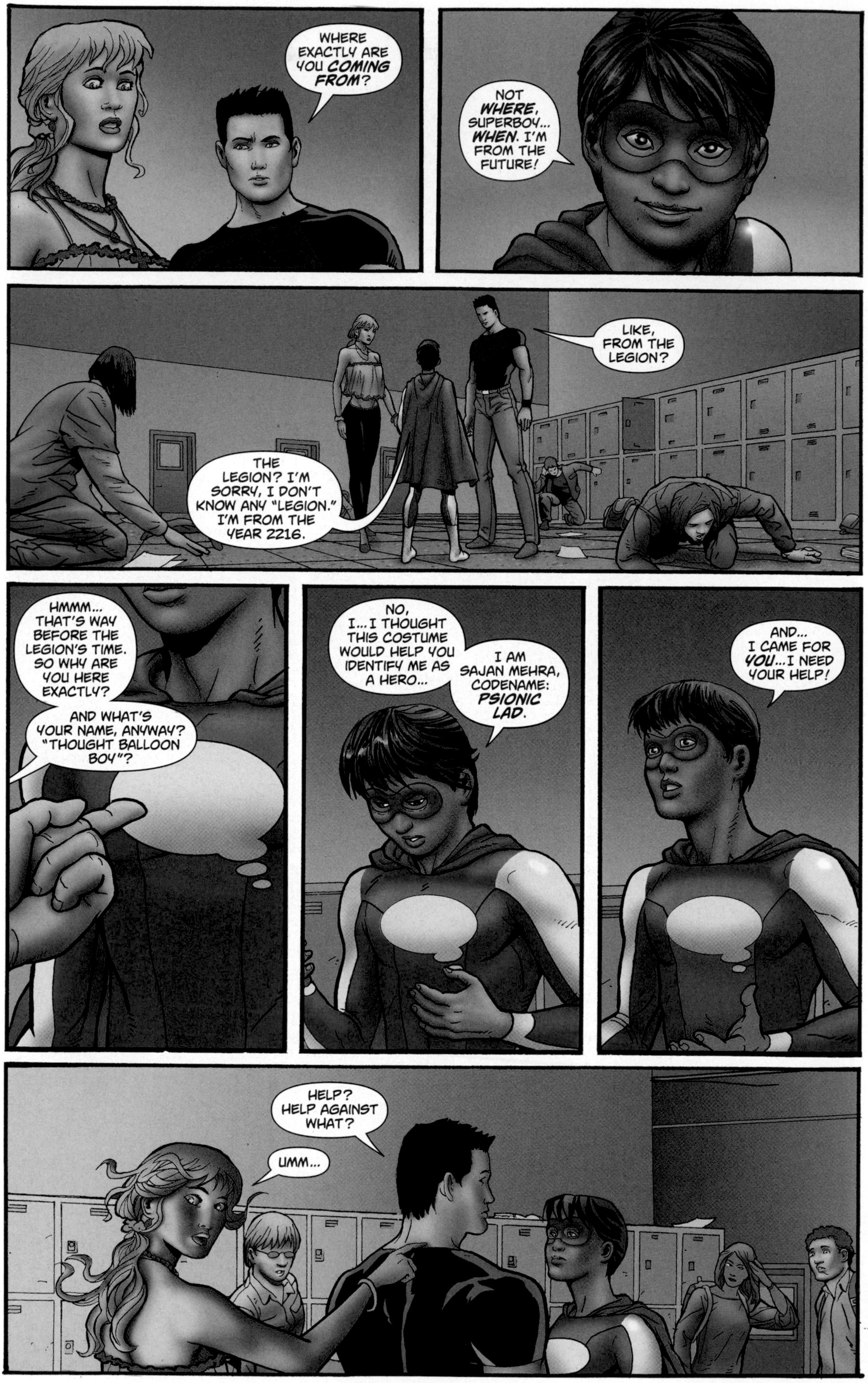
WHERE EXACTLY ARE YOU COMING FROM?
NOT WHERE, SUPERBOY... WHEN. I'M FROM THE FUTURE!
LIKE, FROM THE LEGION?
THE LEGION? I'M SORRY, I DON'T KNOW ANY "LEGION." I'M FROM THE YEAR 2216.
HMMM... THAT'S WAY BEFORE THE LEGION'S TIME. SO WHY ARE YOU HERE EXACTLY?
AND WHAT'S YOUR NAME, ANYWAY? "THOUGHT BALLOON BOY"?
NO, I... I THOUGHT THIS COSTUME WOULD HELP YOU IDENTIFY ME AS A HERO...
I AM SAJAN MEHRA, CODENAME: PSIONIC LAD.
AND... I CAME FOR YOU... I NEED YOUR HELP!
HELP? HELP AGAINST WHAT?
UMM...

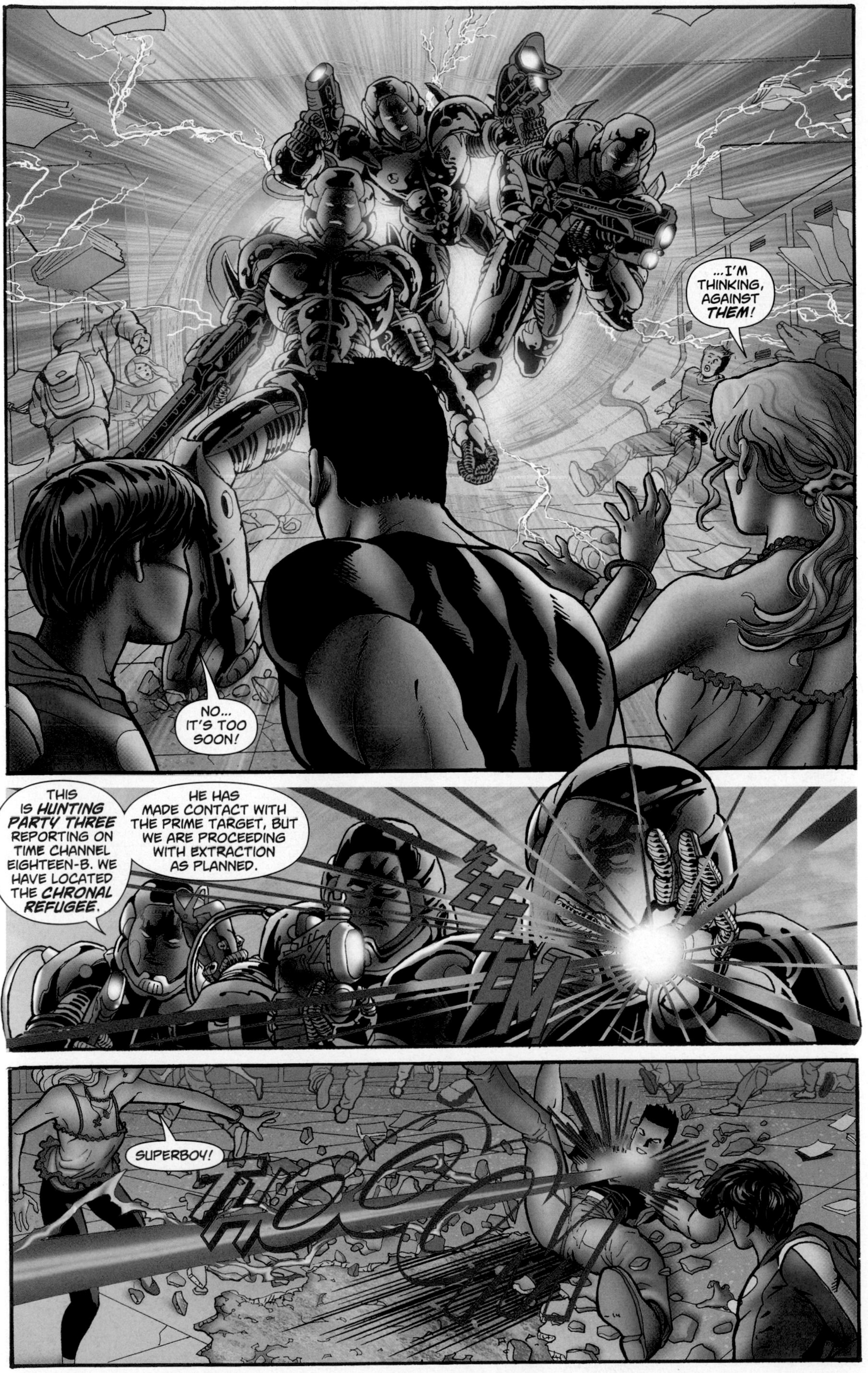
...I'M THINKING, AGAINST THEM!
NO... IT'S TOO SOON!
THIS IS HUNTING PARTY THREE REPORTING ON TIME CHANNEL EIGHTEEN-B. WE HAVE LOCATED THE CHRONAL REFUGEE.
HE HAS MADE CONTACT WITH THE PRIME TARGET, BUT WE ARE PROCEEDING WITH EXTRACTION AS PLANNED.
YEEEEEEEM
SUPERBOY!
THOOOOM

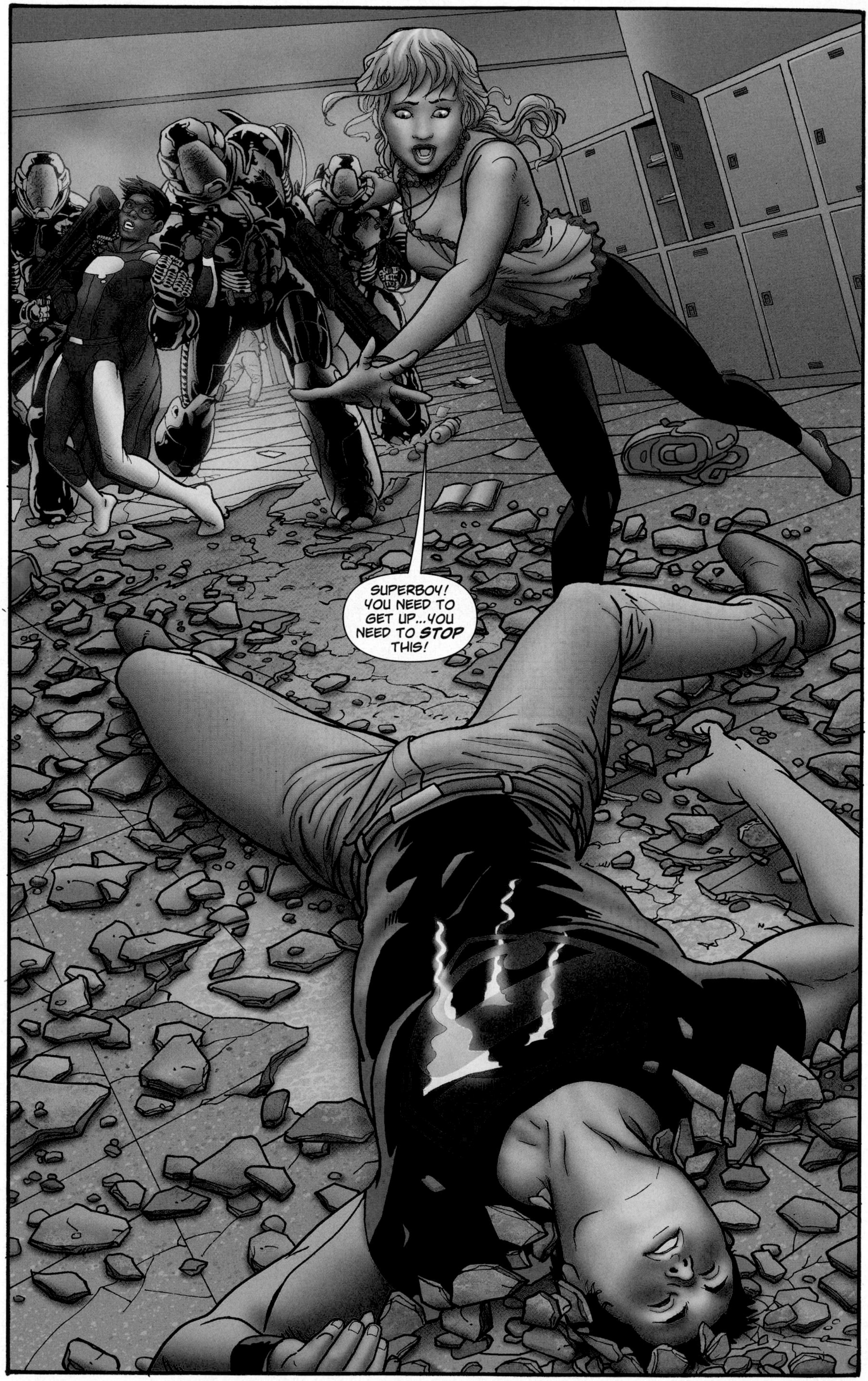
SUPERBOY! YOU NEED TO GET UP...YOU NEED TO STOP THIS!

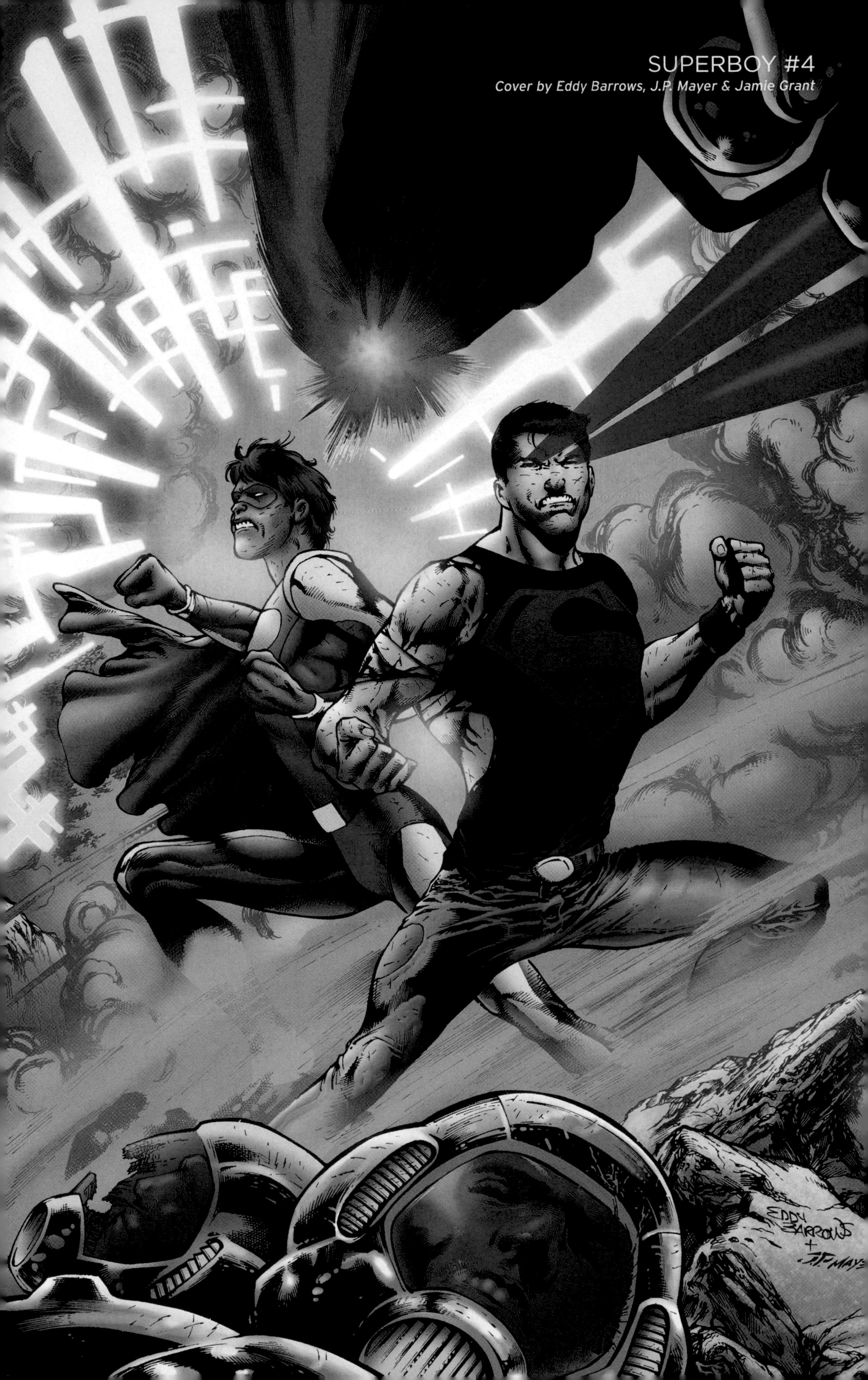

SUPERBOY #4

Cover by Eddy Barrows, J.P. Mayer & Jamie Grant

SUPERBOY #4 | VARIANT

Cover by Stanley "Artgerm" Lau

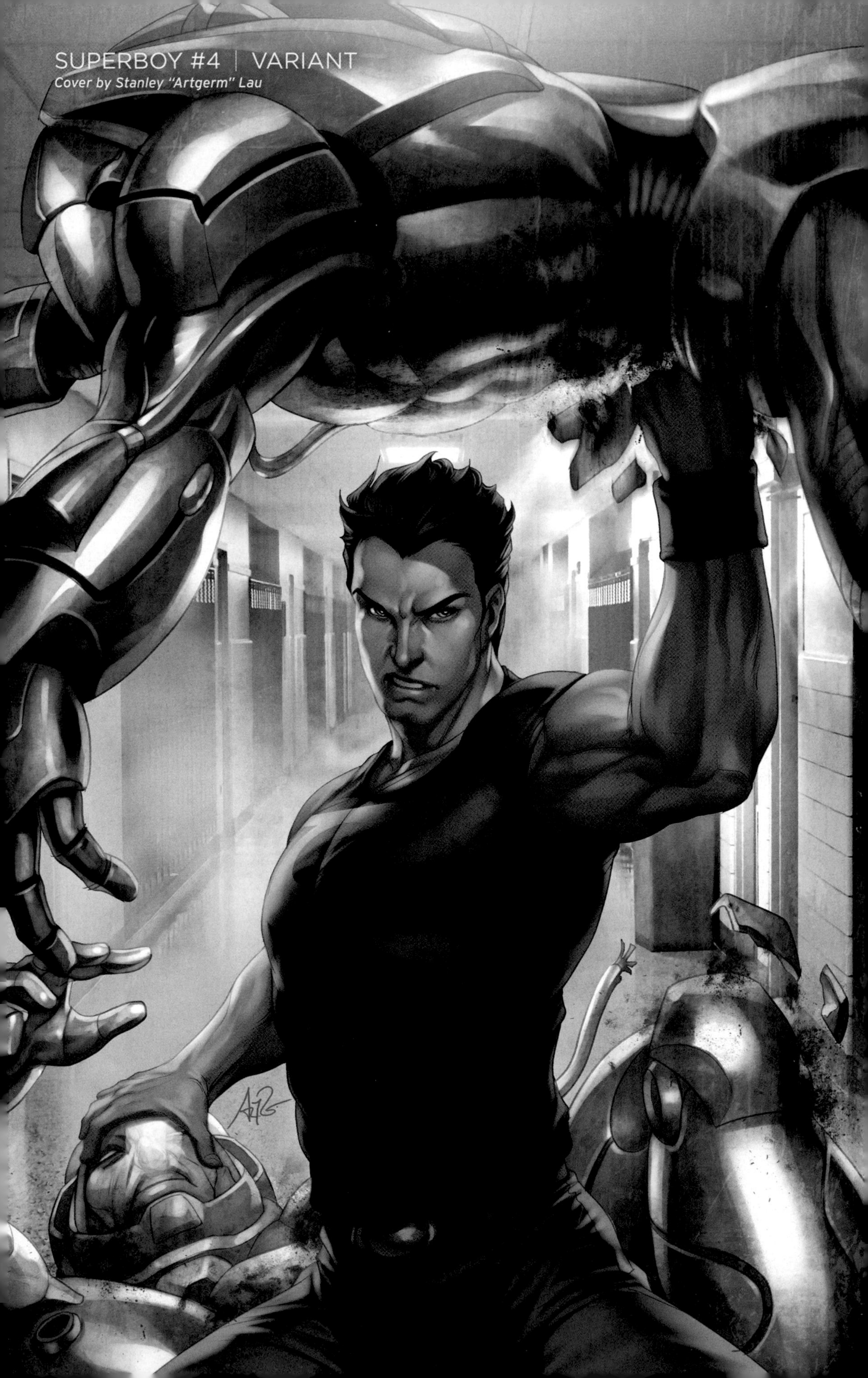

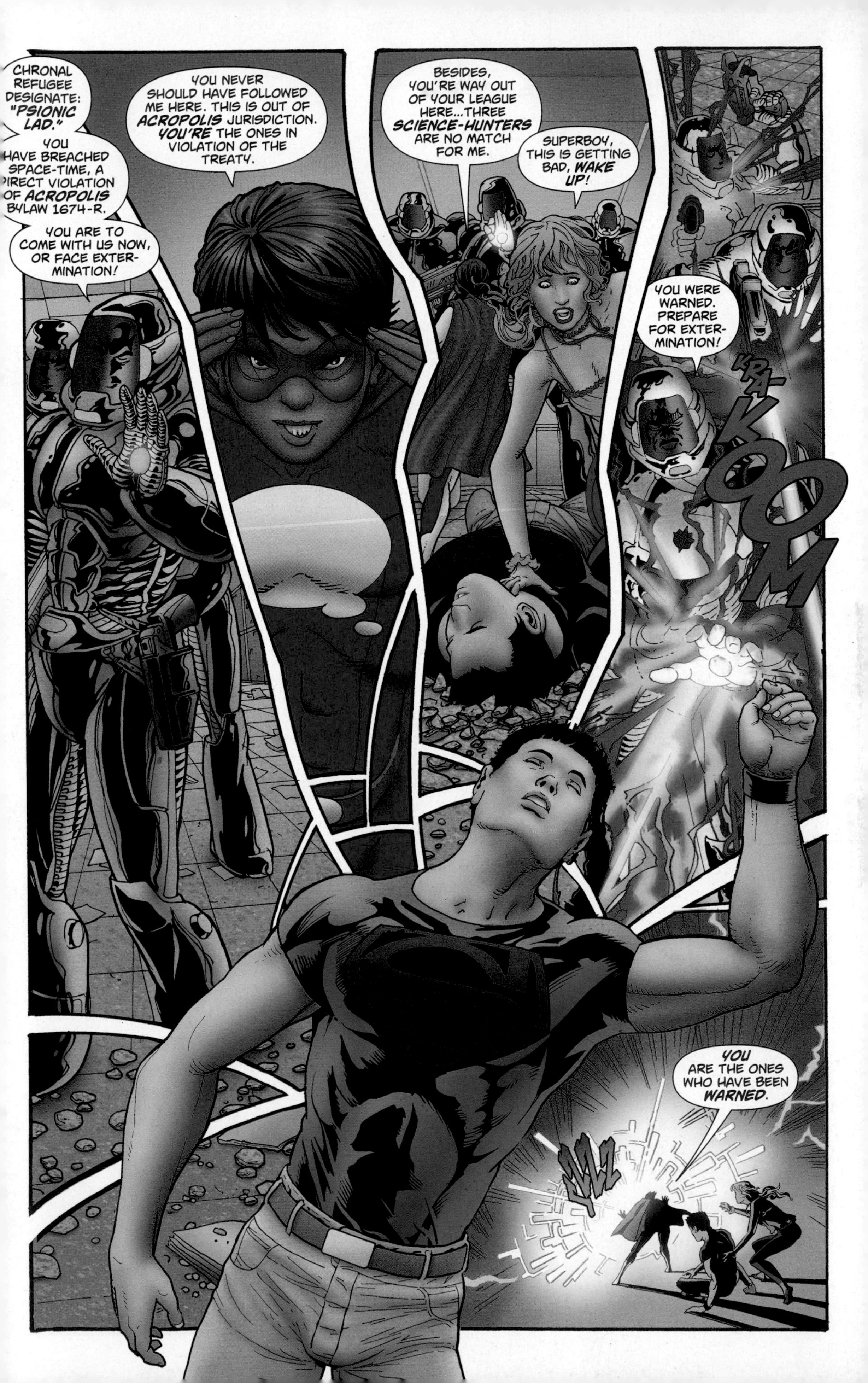
CHRONAL REFUGEE DESIGNATE: "PSIONIC LAD."
YOU HAVE BREACHED SPACE-TIME, A DIRECT VIOLATION OF ACROPOLIS BYLAW 1674-R.
YOU ARE TO COME WITH US NOW, OR FACE EXTERMINATION!
YOU NEVER SHOULD HAVE FOLLOWED ME HERE. THIS IS OUT OF ACROPOLIS JURISDICTION. YOU'RE THE ONES IN VIOLATION OF THE TREATY.
BESIDES, YOU'RE WAY OUT OF YOUR LEAGUE HERE...THREE SCIENCE-HUNTERS ARE NO MATCH FOR ME.
SUPERBOY, THIS IS GETTING BAD, WAKE UP!
YOU WERE WARNED. PREPARE FOR EXTERMINATION!
KRA-KOOM
YOU ARE THE ONES WHO HAVE BEEN WARNED.
ZZZ

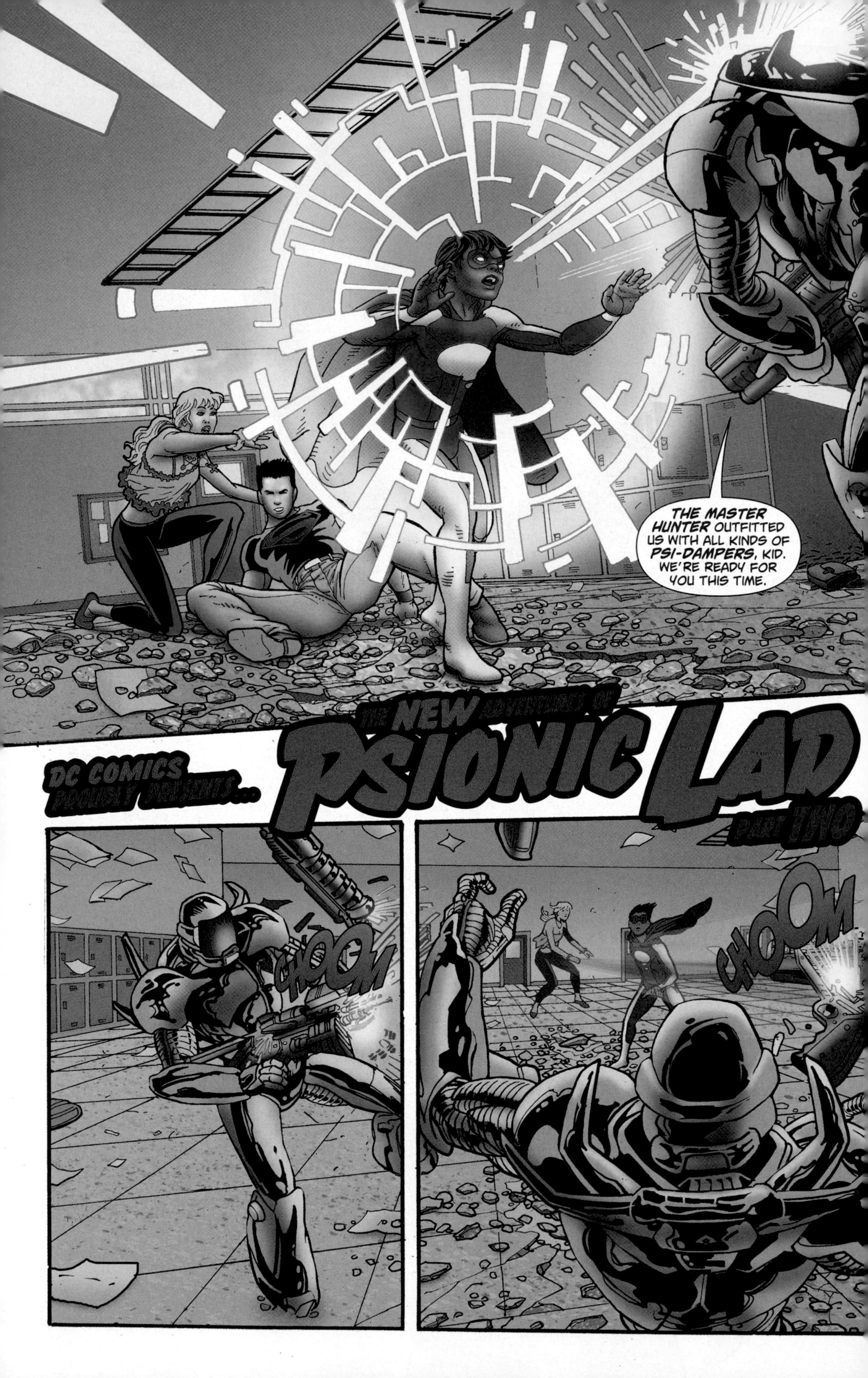
THE MASTER HUNTER OUTFITTED US WITH ALL KINDS OF PSI-DAMPERS, KID. WE'RE READY FOR YOU THIS TIME.
DC COMICS PROUDLY PRESENTS...
THE NEW ADVENTURES OF PSIONIC LAD
PART TWO
CHOOM
CHOOOM

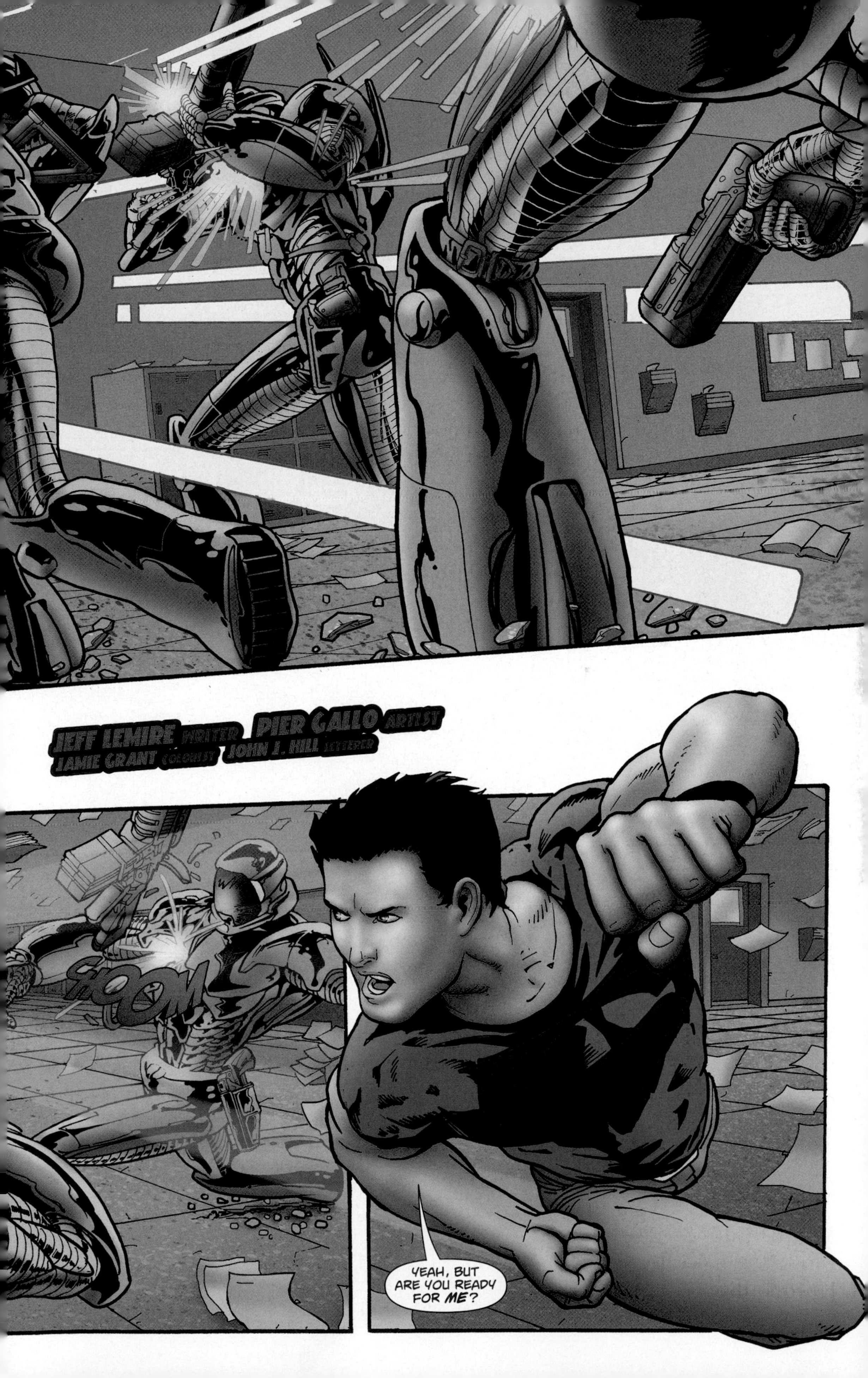

JEFF LEMIRE WRITER PIER GALLO ARTIST
JAMIE GRANT COLORIST JOHN J. HILL LETTERER
SHOOM
YEAH, BUT ARE YOU READY FOR ME?

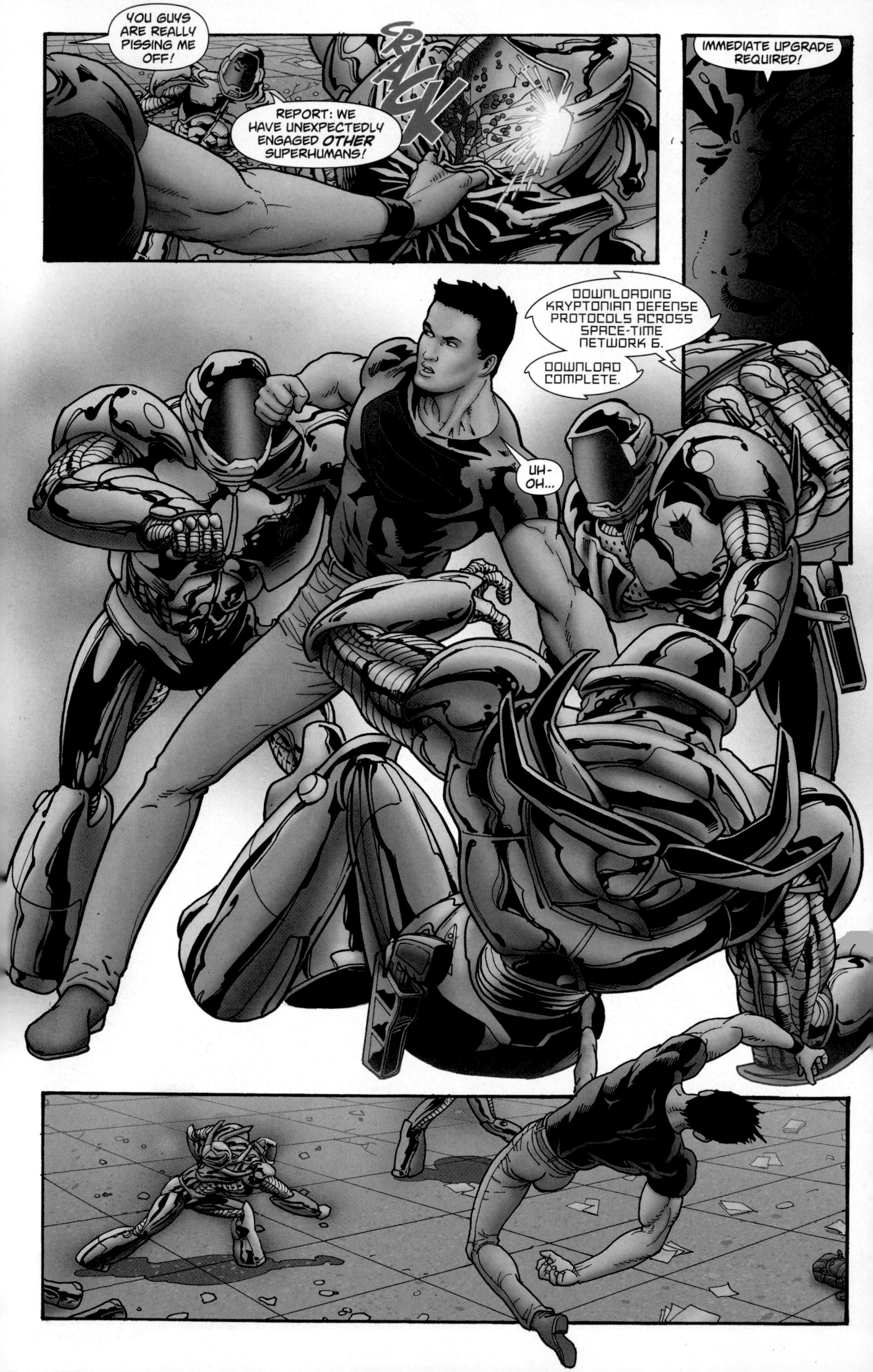
YOU GUYS ARE REALLY PISSING ME OFF!
CRACK
REPORT: WE HAVE UNEXPECTEDLY ENGAGED OTHER SUPERHUMANS!
IMMEDIATE UPGRADE REQUIRED!
DOWNLOADING KRYPTONIAN DEFENSE PROTOCOLS ACROSS SPACE-TIME NETWORK 6.
DOWNLOAD COMPLETE.
UH-OH...

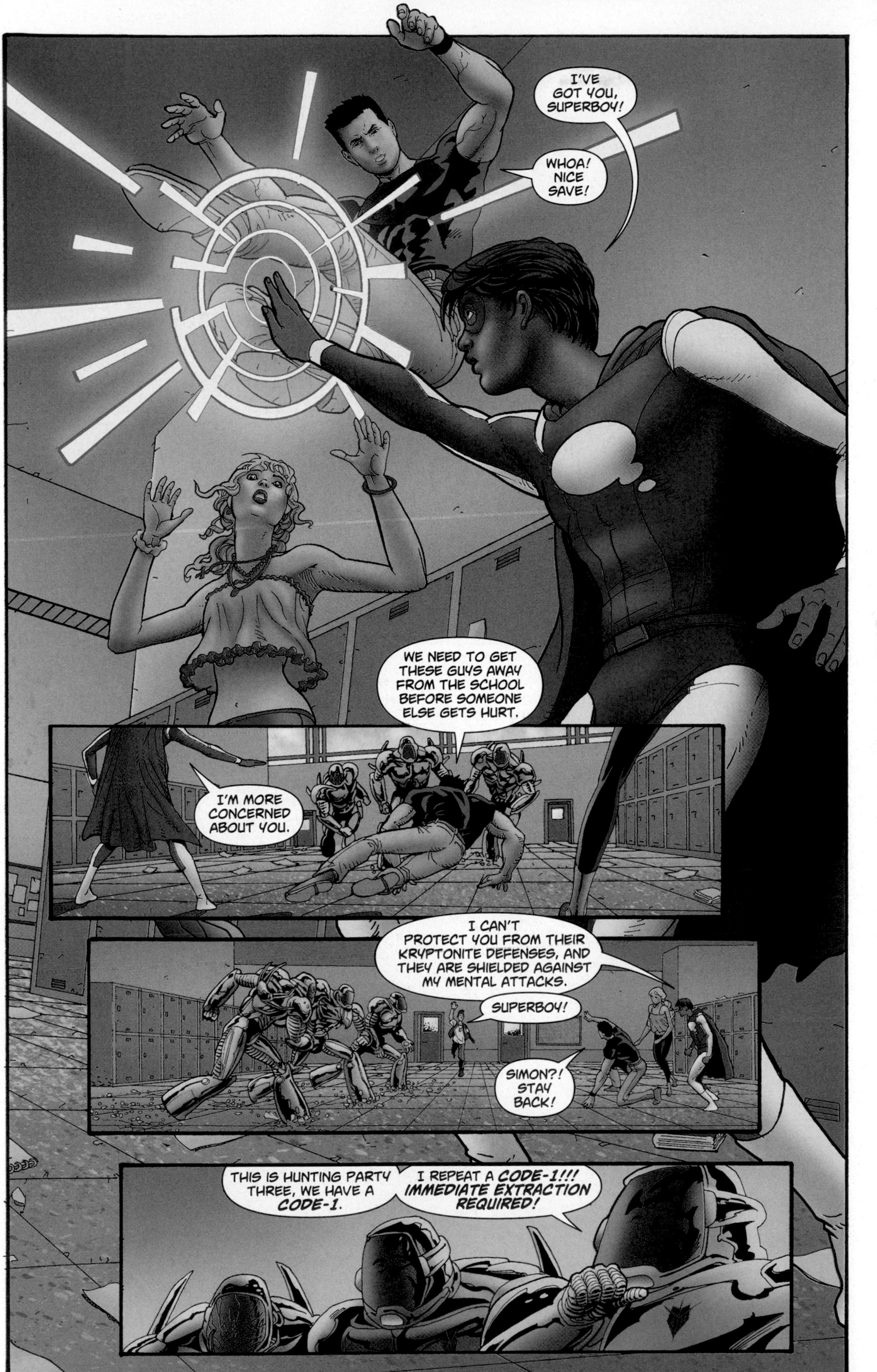
I'VE GOT YOU, SUPERBOY!
WHOA! NICE SAVE!
WE NEED TO GET THESE GUYS AWAY FROM THE SCHOOL BEFORE SOMEONE ELSE GETS HURT.
I'M MORE CONCERNED ABOUT YOU.
I CAN'T PROTECT YOU FROM THEIR KRYPTONITE DEFENSES, AND THEY ARE SHIELDED AGAINST MY MENTAL ATTACKS.
SUPERBOY!
SIMON?! STAY BACK!
THIS IS HUNTING PARTY THREE, WE HAVE A *CODE-1*.
I REPEAT A *CODE-1!!! IMMEDIATE EXTRACTION REQUIRED!*

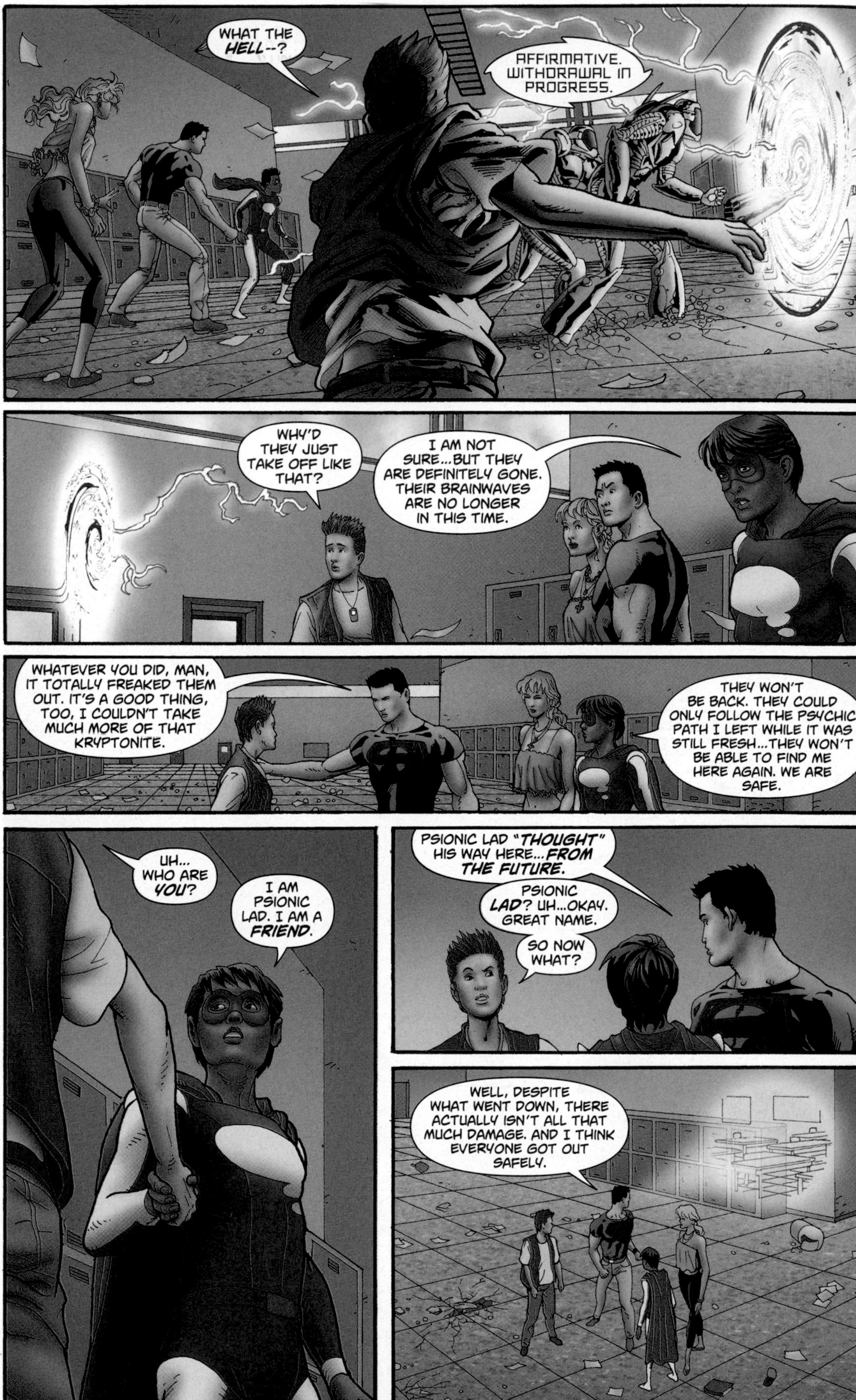
WHAT THE HELL--?
AFFIRMATIVE. WITHDRAWAL IN PROGRESS.
WHY'D THEY JUST TAKE OFF LIKE THAT?
I AM NOT SURE...BUT THEY ARE DEFINITELY GONE. THEIR BRAINWAVES ARE NO LONGER IN THIS TIME.
WHATEVER YOU DID, MAN, IT TOTALLY FREAKED THEM OUT. IT'S A GOOD THING, TOO, I COULDN'T TAKE MUCH MORE OF THAT KRYPTONITE.
THEY WON'T BE BACK. THEY COULD ONLY FOLLOW THE PSYCHIC PATH I LEFT WHILE IT WAS STILL FRESH...THEY WON'T BE ABLE TO FIND ME HERE AGAIN. WE ARE SAFE.
UH... WHO ARE YOU?
I AM PSIONIC LAD. I AM A FRIEND.
PSIONIC LAD "THOUGHT" HIS WAY HERE...FROM THE FUTURE.
PSIONIC LAD? UH...OKAY. GREAT NAME.
SO NOW WHAT?
WELL, DESPITE WHAT WENT DOWN, THERE ACTUALLY ISN'T ALL THAT MUCH DAMAGE. AND I THINK EVERYONE GOT OUT SAFELY.

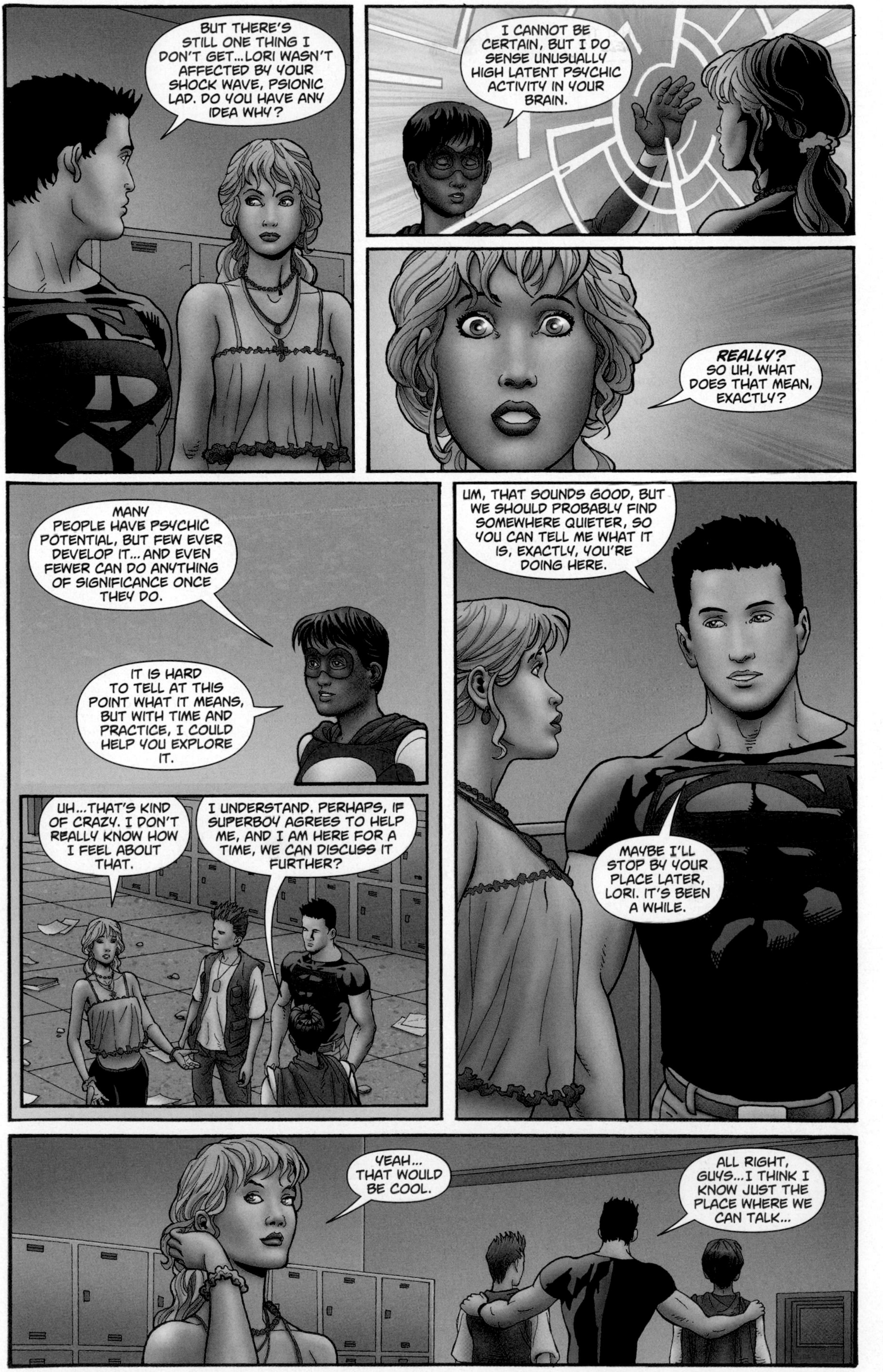
BUT THERE'S STILL ONE THING I DON'T GET...LORI WASN'T AFFECTED BY YOUR SHOCK WAVE, PSIONIC LAD. DO YOU HAVE ANY IDEA WHY?
I CANNOT BE CERTAIN, BUT I DO SENSE UNUSUALLY HIGH LATENT PSYCHIC ACTIVITY IN YOUR BRAIN.
REALLY? SO UH, WHAT DOES THAT MEAN, EXACTLY?
MANY PEOPLE HAVE PSYCHIC POTENTIAL, BUT FEW EVER DEVELOP IT... AND EVEN FEWER CAN DO ANYTHING OF SIGNIFICANCE ONCE THEY DO.
IT IS HARD TO TELL AT THIS POINT WHAT IT MEANS, BUT WITH TIME AND PRACTICE, I COULD HELP YOU EXPLORE IT.
UH...THAT'S KIND OF CRAZY. I DON'T REALLY KNOW HOW I FEEL ABOUT THAT.
I UNDERSTAND. PERHAPS, IF SUPERBOY AGREES TO HELP ME, AND I AM HERE FOR A TIME, WE CAN DISCUSS IT FURTHER?
UM, THAT SOUNDS GOOD, BUT WE SHOULD PROBABLY FIND SOMEWHERE QUIETER, SO YOU CAN TELL ME WHAT IT IS, EXACTLY, YOU'RE DOING HERE.
MAYBE I'LL STOP BY YOUR PLACE LATER, LORI. IT'S BEEN A WHILE.
YEAH... THAT WOULD BE COOL.
ALL RIGHT, GUYS...I THINK I KNOW JUST THE PLACE WHERE WE CAN TALK...

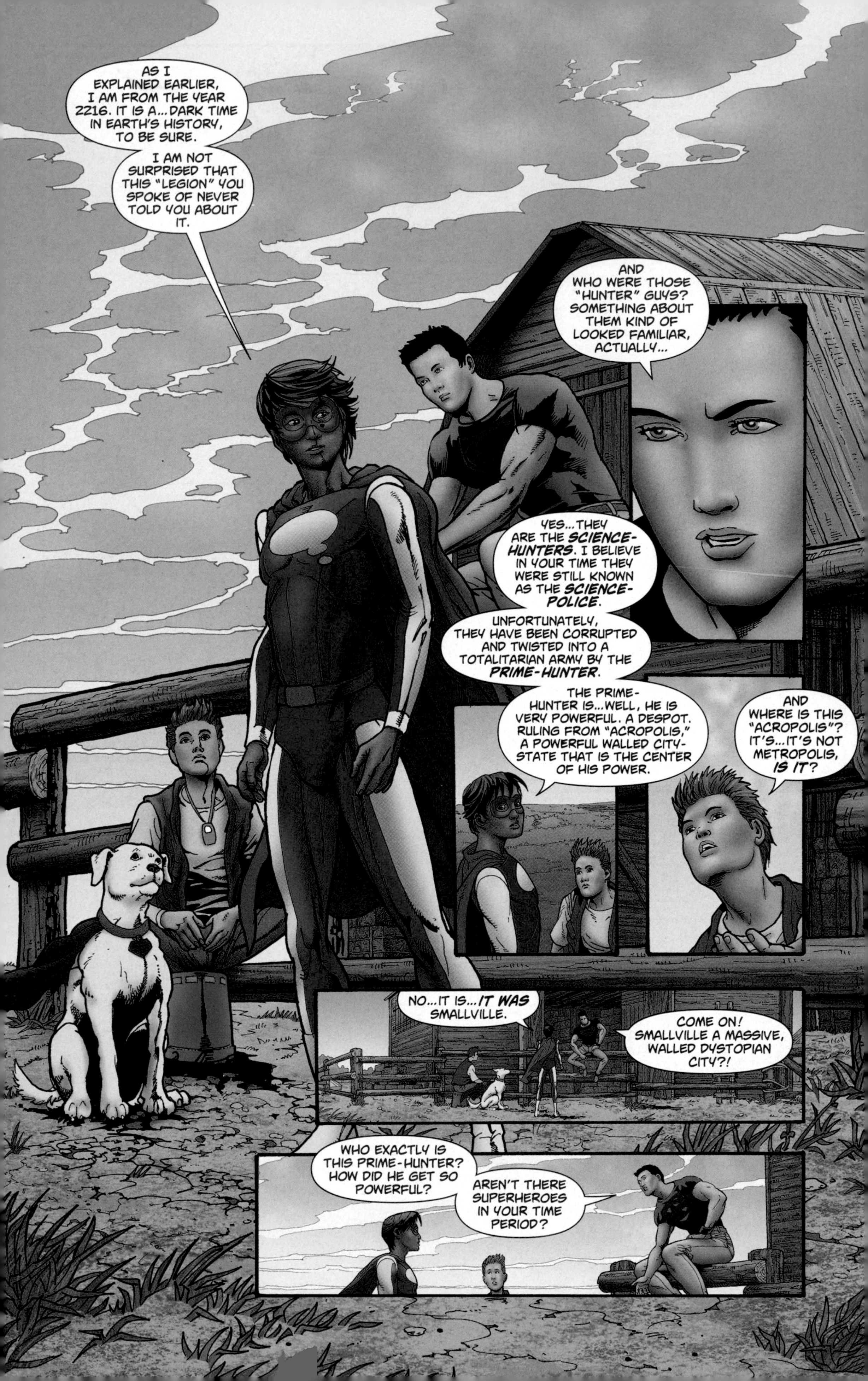
AS I EXPLAINED EARLIER, I AM FROM THE YEAR 2216. IT IS A...DARK TIME IN EARTH'S HISTORY, TO BE SURE.
I AM NOT SURPRISED THAT THIS "LEGION" YOU SPOKE OF NEVER TOLD YOU ABOUT IT.
AND WHO WERE THOSE "HUNTER" GUYS? SOMETHING ABOUT THEM KIND OF LOOKED FAMILIAR, ACTUALLY...
YES...THEY ARE THE SCIENCE-HUNTERS. I BELIEVE IN YOUR TIME THEY WERE STILL KNOWN AS THE SCIENCE-POLICE.
UNFORTUNATELY, THEY HAVE BEEN CORRUPTED AND TWISTED INTO A TOTALITARIAN ARMY BY THE PRIME-HUNTER.
THE PRIME-HUNTER IS...WELL, HE IS VERY POWERFUL. A DESPOT. RULING FROM "ACROPOLIS," A POWERFUL WALLED CITY-STATE THAT IS THE CENTER OF HIS POWER.
AND WHERE IS THIS "ACROPOLIS"? IT'S...IT'S NOT METROPOLIS, IS IT?
NO...IT IS...IT WAS SMALLVILLE.
COME ON! SMALLVILLE A MASSIVE, WALLED DYSTOPIAN CITY?!
WHO EXACTLY IS THIS PRIME-HUNTER? HOW DID HE GET SO POWERFUL?
AREN'T THERE SUPERHEROES IN YOUR TIME PERIOD?

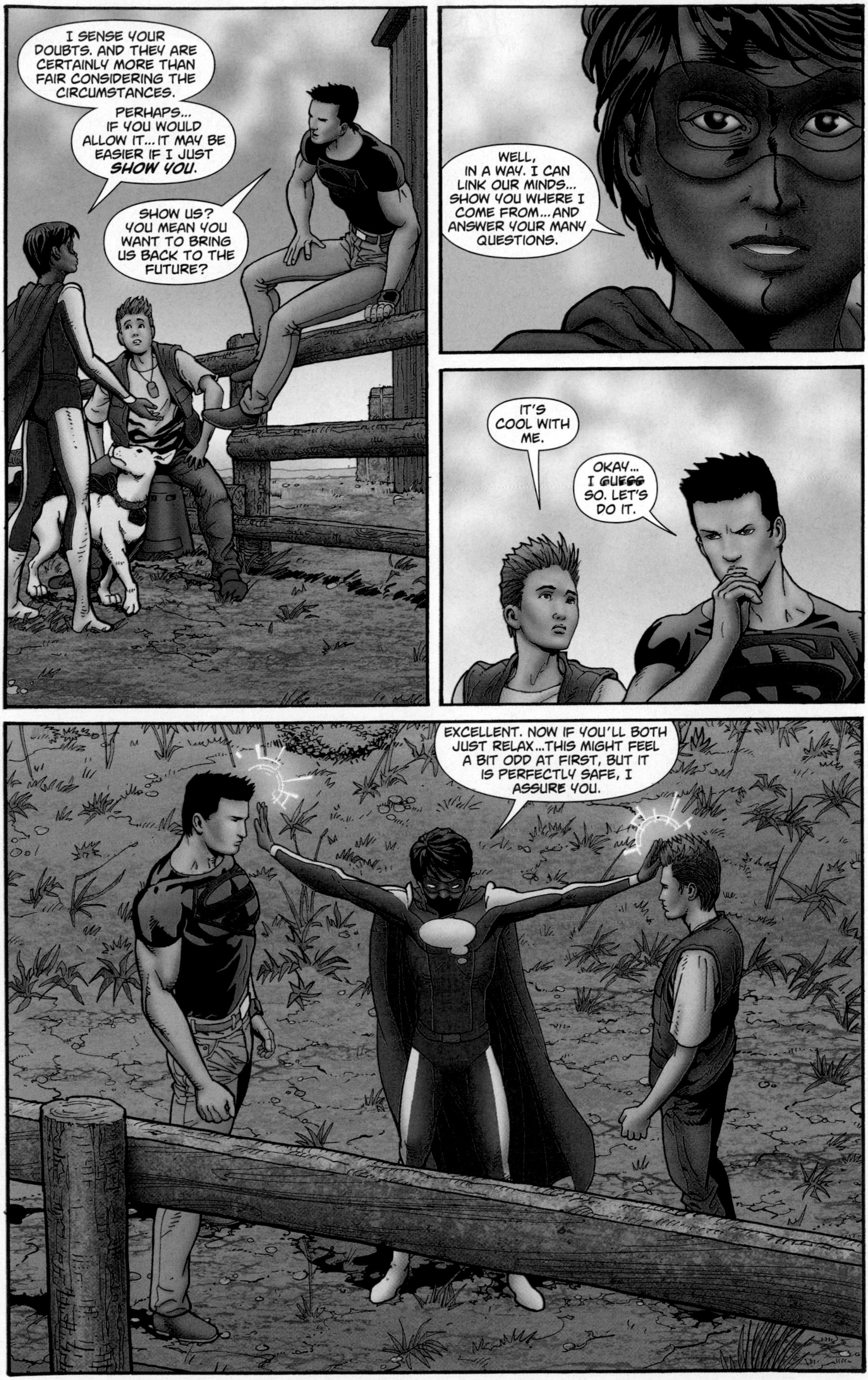
I SENSE YOUR DOUBTS. AND THEY ARE CERTAINLY MORE THAN FAIR CONSIDERING THE CIRCUMSTANCES.
PERHAPS... IF YOU WOULD ALLOW IT... IT MAY BE EASIER IF I JUST SHOW YOU.
SHOW US? YOU MEAN YOU WANT TO BRING US BACK TO THE FUTURE?
WELL, IN A WAY. I CAN LINK OUR MINDS... SHOW YOU WHERE I COME FROM... AND ANSWER YOUR MANY QUESTIONS.
IT'S COOL WITH ME.
OKAY... I GUESS SO. LET'S DO IT.
EXCELLENT. NOW IF YOU'LL BOTH JUST RELAX... THIS MIGHT FEEL A BIT ODD AT FIRST, BUT IT IS PERFECTLY SAFE, I ASSURE YOU.

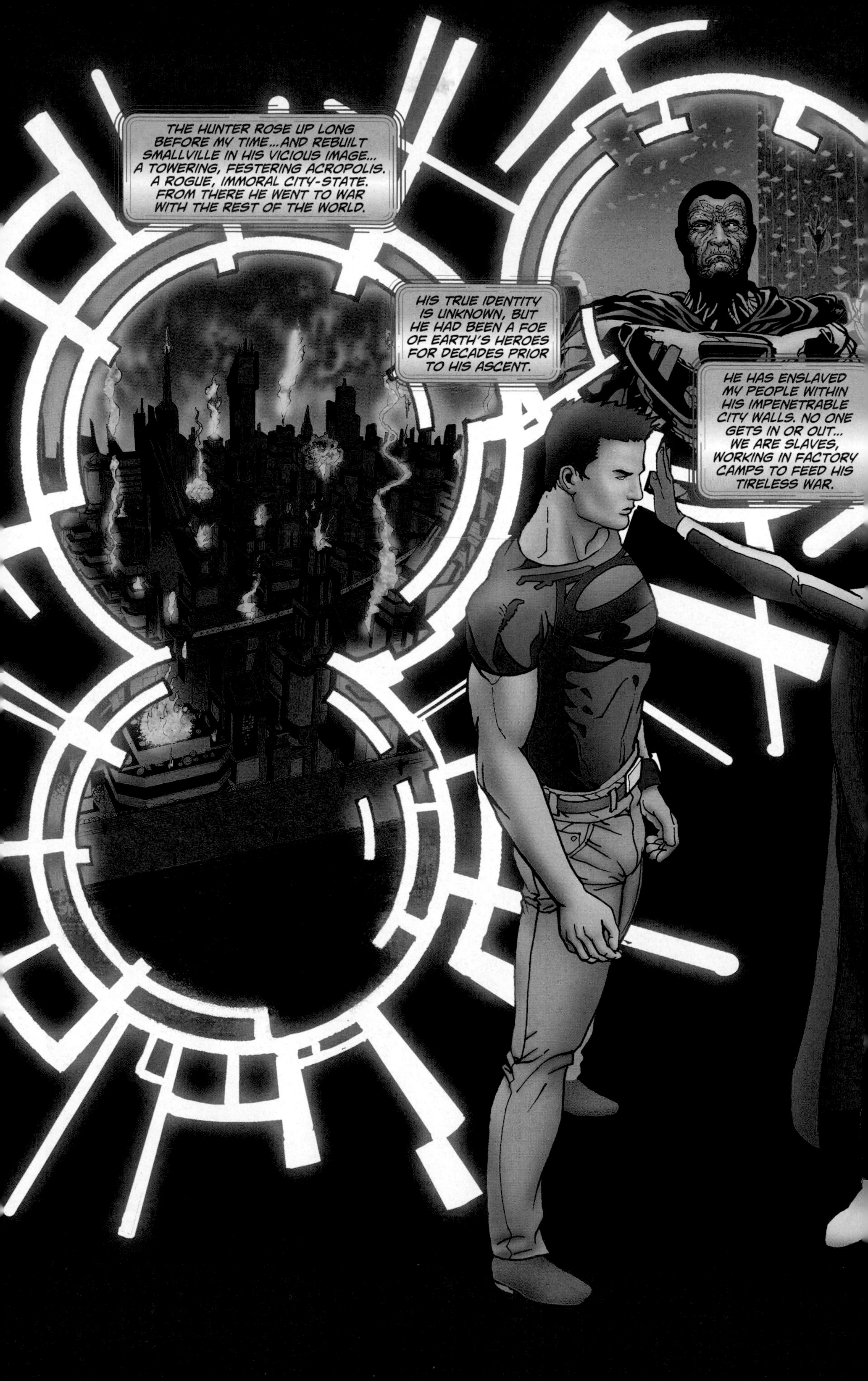
THE HUNTER ROSE UP LONG BEFORE MY TIME...AND REBUILT SMALLVILLE IN HIS VICIOUS IMAGE... A TOWERING, FESTERING ACROPOLIS. A ROGUE, IMMORAL CITY-STATE. FROM THERE HE WENT TO WAR WITH THE REST OF THE WORLD.
HIS TRUE IDENTITY IS UNKNOWN, BUT HE HAD BEEN A FOE OF EARTH'S HEROES FOR DECADES PRIOR TO HIS ASCENT.
HE HAS ENSLAVED MY PEOPLE WITHIN HIS IMPENETRABLE CITY WALLS. NO ONE GETS IN OR OUT... WE ARE SLAVES, WORKING IN FACTORY CAMPS TO FEED HIS TIRELESS WAR.

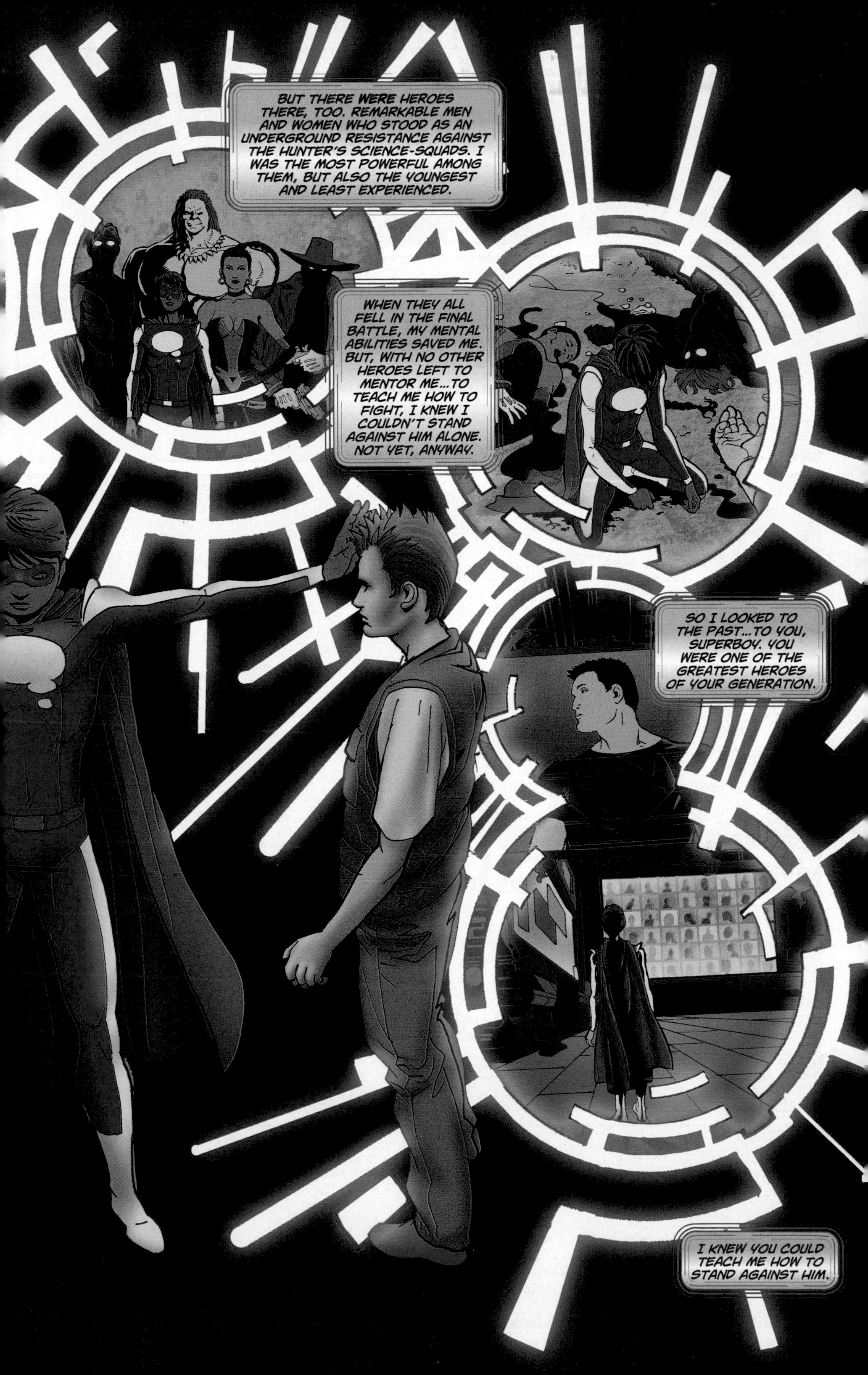
BUT THERE WERE HEROES THERE, TOO. REMARKABLE MEN AND WOMEN WHO STOOD AS AN UNDERGROUND RESISTANCE AGAINST THE HUNTER'S SCIENCE-SQUADS. I WAS THE MOST POWERFUL AMONG THEM, BUT ALSO THE YOUNGEST AND LEAST EXPERIENCED.
WHEN THEY ALL FELL IN THE FINAL BATTLE, MY MENTAL ABILITIES SAVED ME. BUT, WITH NO OTHER HEROES LEFT TO MENTOR ME...TO TEACH ME HOW TO FIGHT, I KNEW I COULDN'T STAND AGAINST HIM ALONE. NOT YET, ANYWAY.
SO I LOOKED TO THE PAST...TO YOU, SUPERBOY. YOU WERE ONE OF THE GREATEST HEROES OF YOUR GENERATION.
I KNEW YOU COULD TEACH ME HOW TO STAND AGAINST HIM.

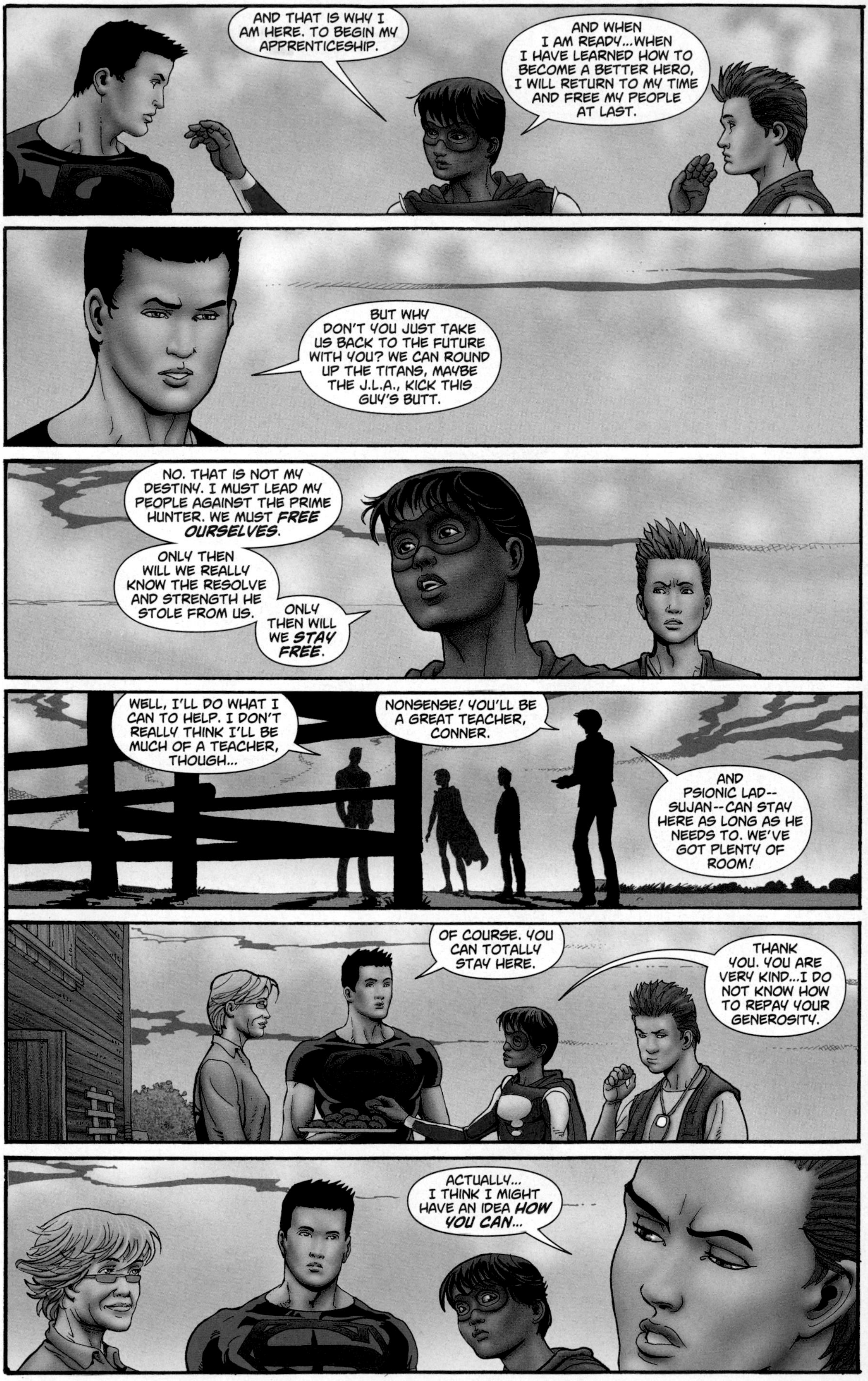
AND THAT IS WHY I AM HERE. TO BEGIN MY APPRENTICESHIP.
AND WHEN I AM READY...WHEN I HAVE LEARNED HOW TO BECOME A BETTER HERO, I WILL RETURN TO MY TIME AND FREE MY PEOPLE AT LAST.
BUT WHY DON'T YOU JUST TAKE US BACK TO THE FUTURE WITH YOU? WE CAN ROUND UP THE TITANS, MAYBE THE J.L.A., KICK THIS GUY'S BUTT.
NO. THAT IS NOT MY DESTINY. I MUST LEAD MY PEOPLE AGAINST THE PRIME HUNTER. WE MUST FREE OURSELVES.
ONLY THEN WILL WE REALLY KNOW THE RESOLVE AND STRENGTH HE STOLE FROM US.
ONLY THEN WILL WE STAY FREE.
WELL, I'LL DO WHAT I CAN TO HELP. I DON'T REALLY THINK I'LL BE MUCH OF A TEACHER, THOUGH...
NONSENSE! YOU'LL BE A GREAT TEACHER, CONNER.
AND PSIONIC LAD--SUJAN--CAN STAY HERE AS LONG AS HE NEEDS TO. WE'VE GOT PLENTY OF ROOM!
OF COURSE. YOU CAN TOTALLY STAY HERE.
THANK YOU. YOU ARE VERY KIND...I DO NOT KNOW HOW TO REPAY YOUR GENEROSITY.
ACTUALLY... I THINK I MIGHT HAVE AN IDEA HOW YOU CAN...

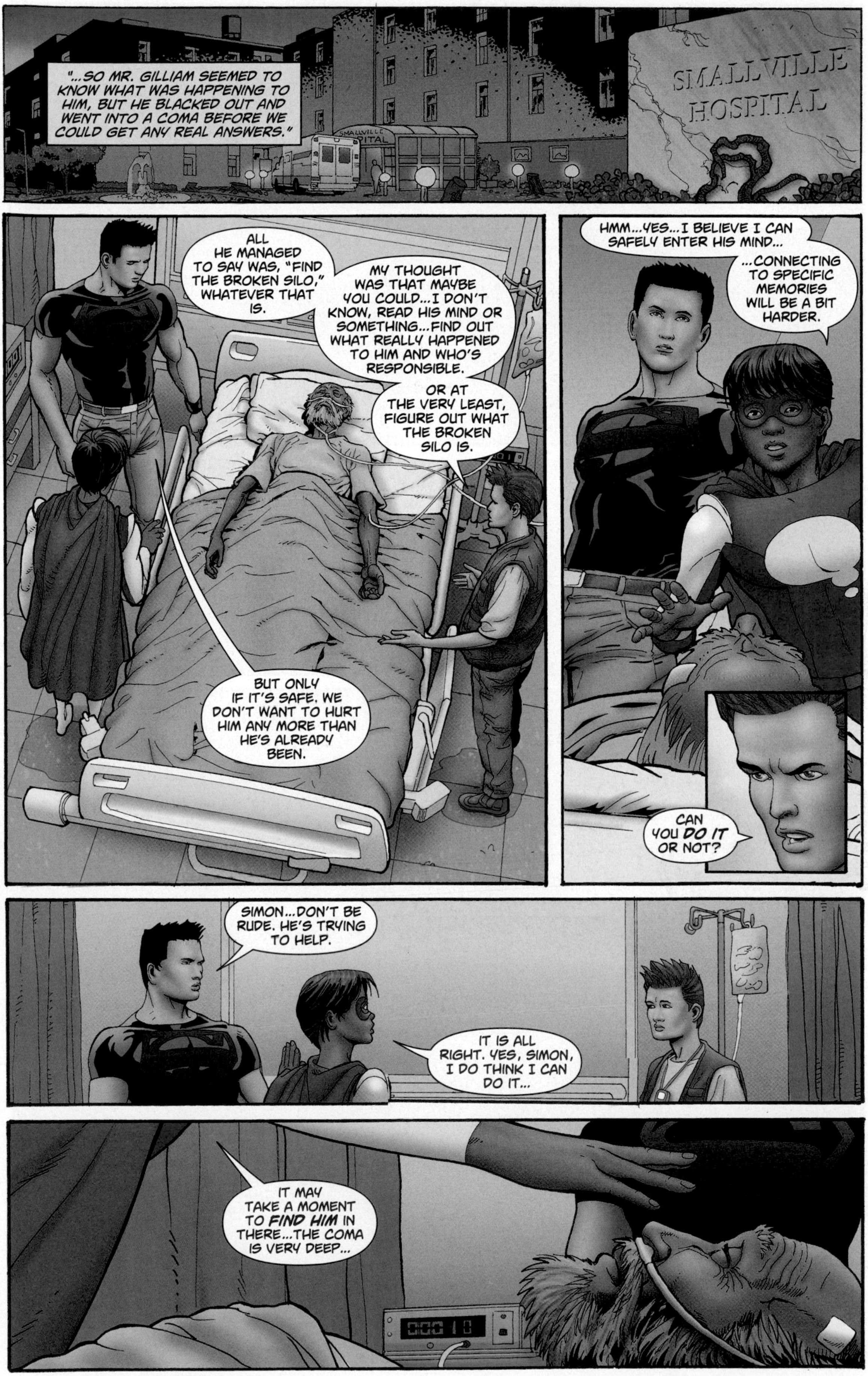
"...SO MR. GILLIAM SEEMED TO KNOW WHAT WAS HAPPENING TO HIM, BUT HE BLACKED OUT AND WENT INTO A COMA BEFORE WE COULD GET ANY REAL ANSWERS."
SMALLVILLE HOSPITAL
ALL HE MANAGED TO SAY WAS, "FIND THE BROKEN SILO," WHATEVER THAT IS.
MY THOUGHT WAS THAT MAYBE YOU COULD...I DON'T KNOW, READ HIS MIND OR SOMETHING...FIND OUT WHAT REALLY HAPPENED TO HIM AND WHO'S RESPONSIBLE.
OR AT THE VERY LEAST, FIGURE OUT WHAT THE BROKEN SILO IS.
BUT ONLY IF IT'S SAFE. WE DON'T WANT TO HURT HIM ANY MORE THAN HE'S ALREADY BEEN.
HMM...YES...I BELIEVE I CAN SAFELY ENTER HIS MIND...
...CONNECTING TO SPECIFIC MEMORIES WILL BE A BIT HARDER.
CAN YOU DO IT OR NOT?
SIMON...DON'T BE RUDE. HE'S TRYING TO HELP.
IT IS ALL RIGHT. YES, SIMON, I DO THINK I CAN DO IT...
IT MAY TAKE A MOMENT TO FIND HIM IN THERE...THE COMA IS VERY DEEP...

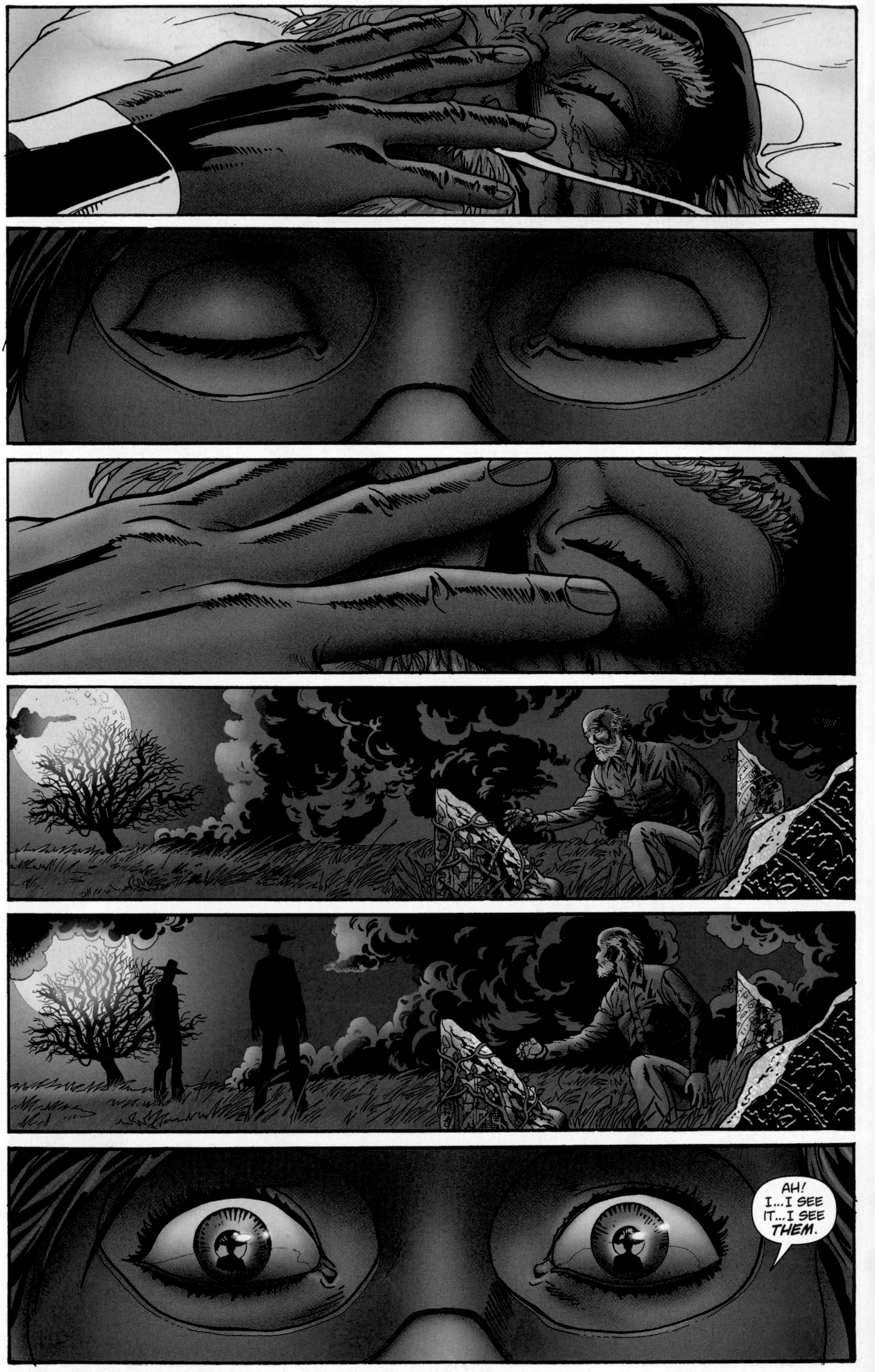
AH!
I...I SEE
IT...I SEE
THEM.

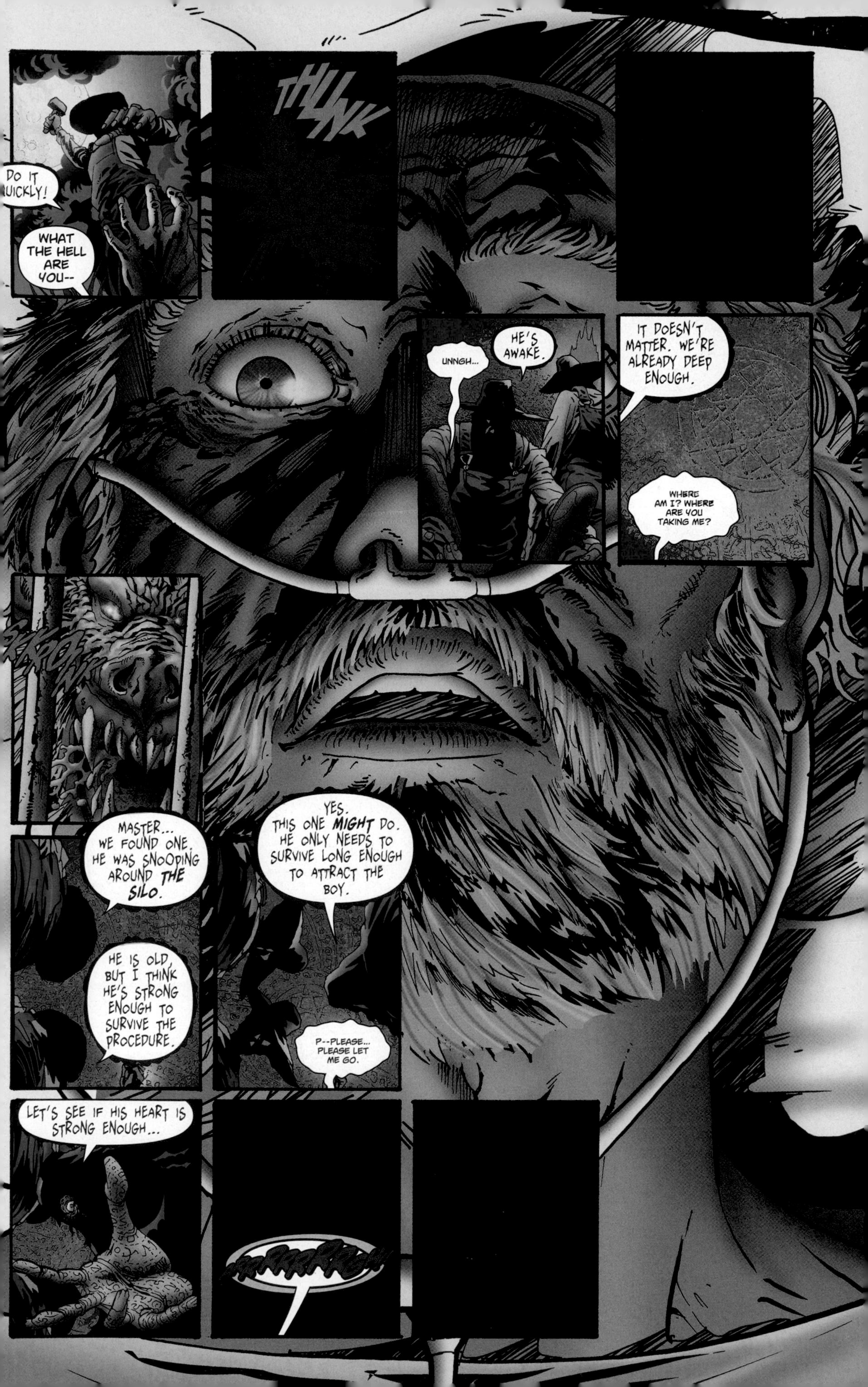

DO IT UICKLY!
WHAT THE HELL ARE YOU--
THUNK
UNNGH...
HE'S AWAKE.
IT DOESN'T MATTER. WE'RE ALREADY DEEP ENOUGH.
WHERE AM I? WHERE ARE YOU TAKING ME?
MASTER... WE FOUND ONE. HE WAS SNOOPING AROUND THE SILO.
HE IS OLD, BUT I THINK HE'S STRONG ENOUGH TO SURVIVE THE PROCEDURE.
YES. THIS ONE MIGHT DO. HE ONLY NEEDS TO SURVIVE LONG ENOUGH TO ATTRACT THE BOY.
P--PLEASE... PLEASE LET ME GO.
LET'S SEE IF HIS HEART IS STRONG ENOUGH...

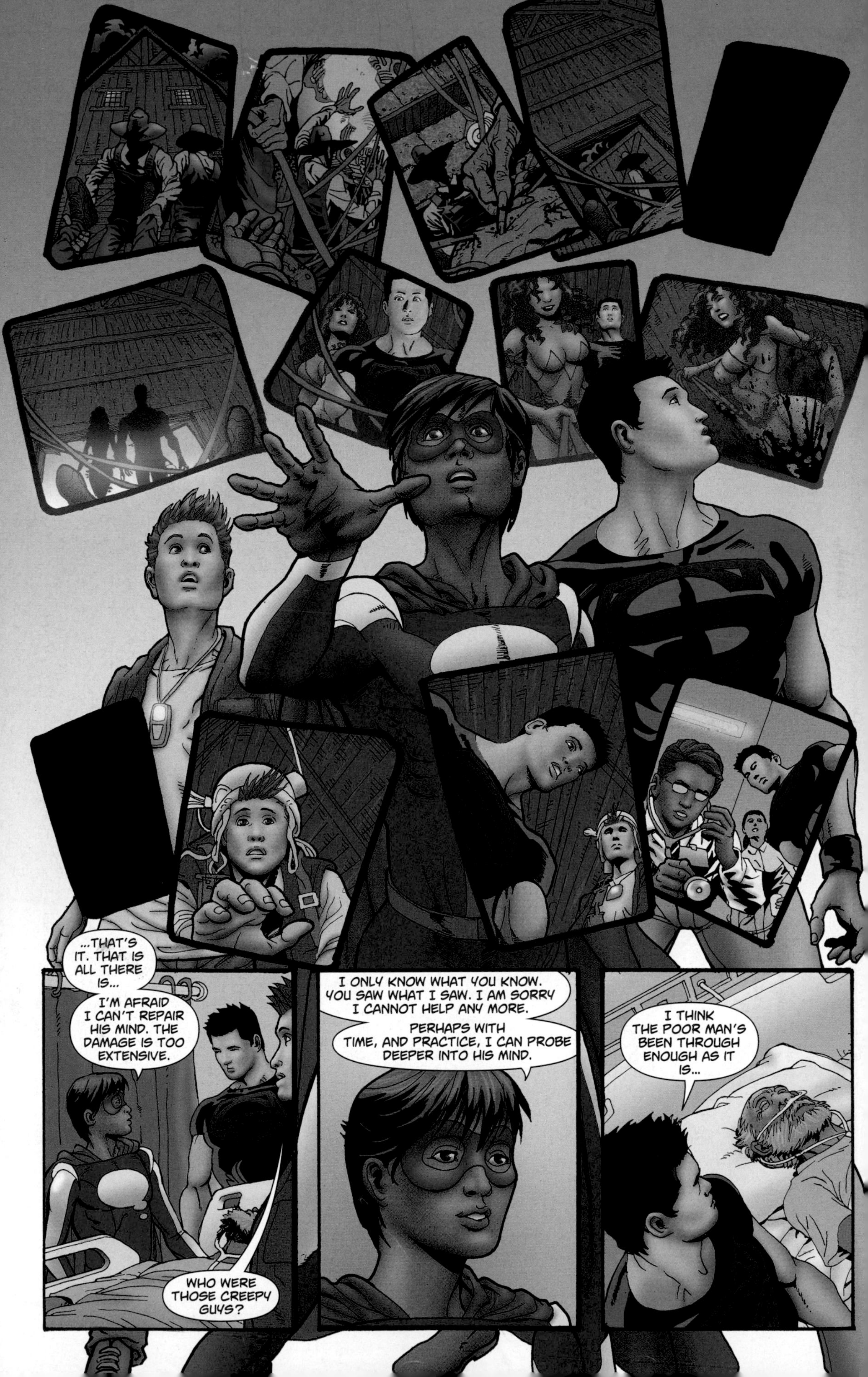
...THAT'S IT. THAT IS ALL THERE IS...
I'M AFRAID I CAN'T REPAIR HIS MIND. THE DAMAGE IS TOO EXTENSIVE.
WHO WERE THOSE CREEPY GUYS?
I ONLY KNOW WHAT YOU KNOW. YOU SAW WHAT I SAW. I AM SORRY I CANNOT HELP ANY MORE.
PERHAPS WITH TIME, AND PRACTICE, I CAN PROBE DEEPER INTO HIS MIND.
I THINK THE POOR MAN'S BEEN THROUGH ENOUGH AS IT IS...

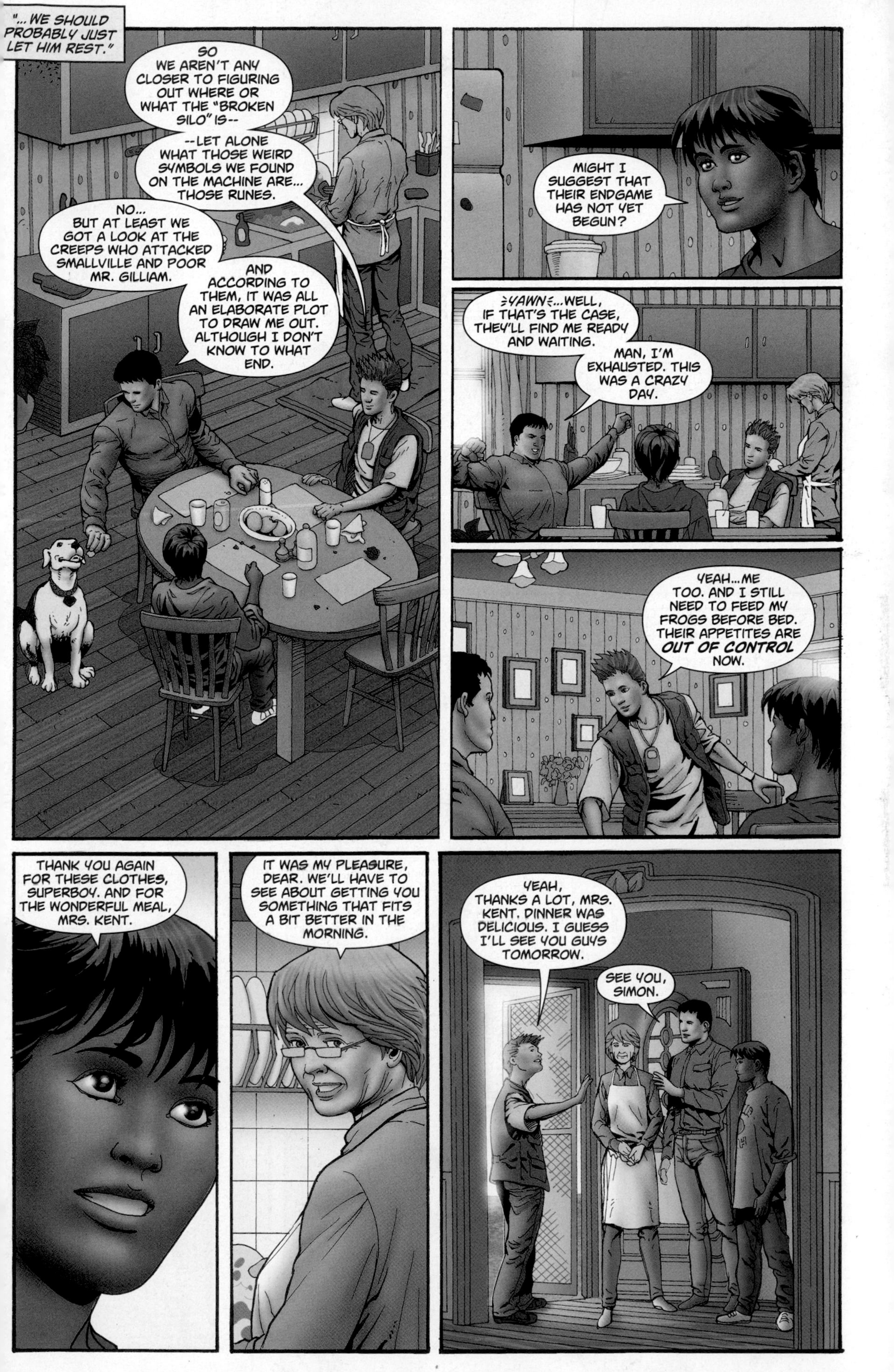
"...WE SHOULD PROBABLY JUST LET HIM REST."
SO WE AREN'T ANY CLOSER TO FIGURING OUT WHERE OR WHAT THE "BROKEN SILO" IS--
--LET ALONE WHAT THOSE WEIRD SYMBOLS WE FOUND ON THE MACHINE ARE... THOSE RUNES.
NO... BUT AT LEAST WE GOT A LOOK AT THE CREEPS WHO ATTACKED SMALLVILLE AND POOR MR. GILLIAM.
AND ACCORDING TO THEM, IT WAS ALL AN ELABORATE PLOT TO DRAW ME OUT. ALTHOUGH I DON'T KNOW TO WHAT END.
MIGHT I SUGGEST THAT THEIR ENDGAME HAS NOT YET BEGUN?
YAWN...WELL, IF THAT'S THE CASE, THEY'LL FIND ME READY AND WAITING.
MAN, I'M EXHAUSTED. THIS WAS A CRAZY DAY.
YEAH...ME TOO. AND I STILL NEED TO FEED MY FROGS BEFORE BED. THEIR APPETITES ARE OUT OF CONTROL NOW.
THANK YOU AGAIN FOR THESE CLOTHES, SUPERBOY. AND FOR THE WONDERFUL MEAL, MRS. KENT.
IT WAS MY PLEASURE, DEAR. WE'LL HAVE TO SEE ABOUT GETTING YOU SOMETHING THAT FITS A BIT BETTER IN THE MORNING.
YEAH, THANKS A LOT, MRS. KENT. DINNER WAS DELICIOUS. I GUESS I'LL SEE YOU GUYS TOMORROW.
SEE YOU, SIMON.

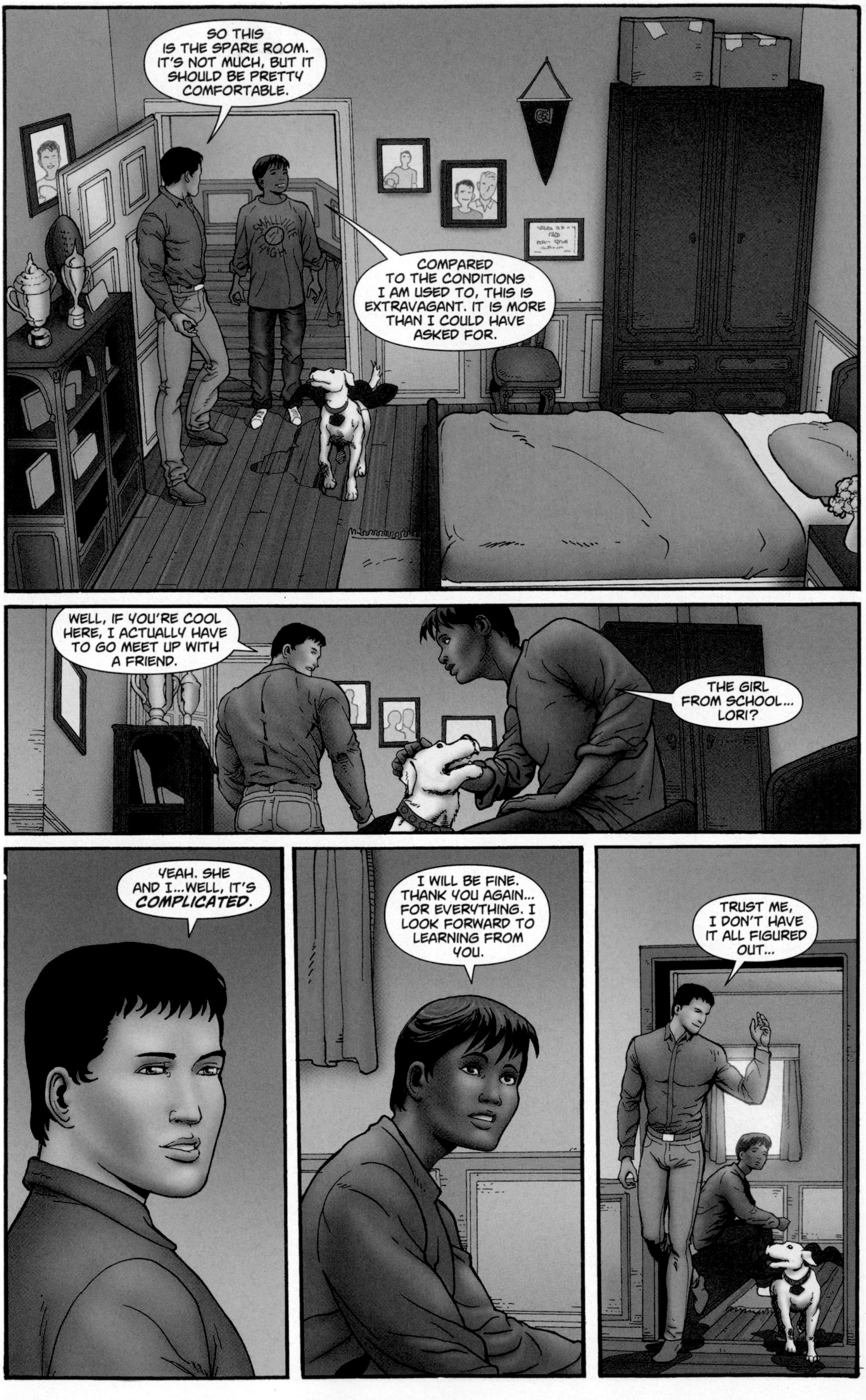
SO THIS IS THE SPARE ROOM. IT'S NOT MUCH, BUT IT SHOULD BE PRETTY COMFORTABLE.
COMPARED TO THE CONDITIONS I AM USED TO, THIS IS EXTRAVAGANT. IT IS MORE THAN I COULD HAVE ASKED FOR.
WELL, IF YOU'RE COOL HERE, I ACTUALLY HAVE TO GO MEET UP WITH A FRIEND.
THE GIRL FROM SCHOOL... LORI?
YEAH. SHE AND I...WELL, IT'S *COMPLICATED*.
I WILL BE FINE. THANK YOU AGAIN... FOR EVERYTHING. I LOOK FORWARD TO LEARNING FROM YOU.
TRUST ME, I DON'T HAVE IT ALL FIGURED OUT...

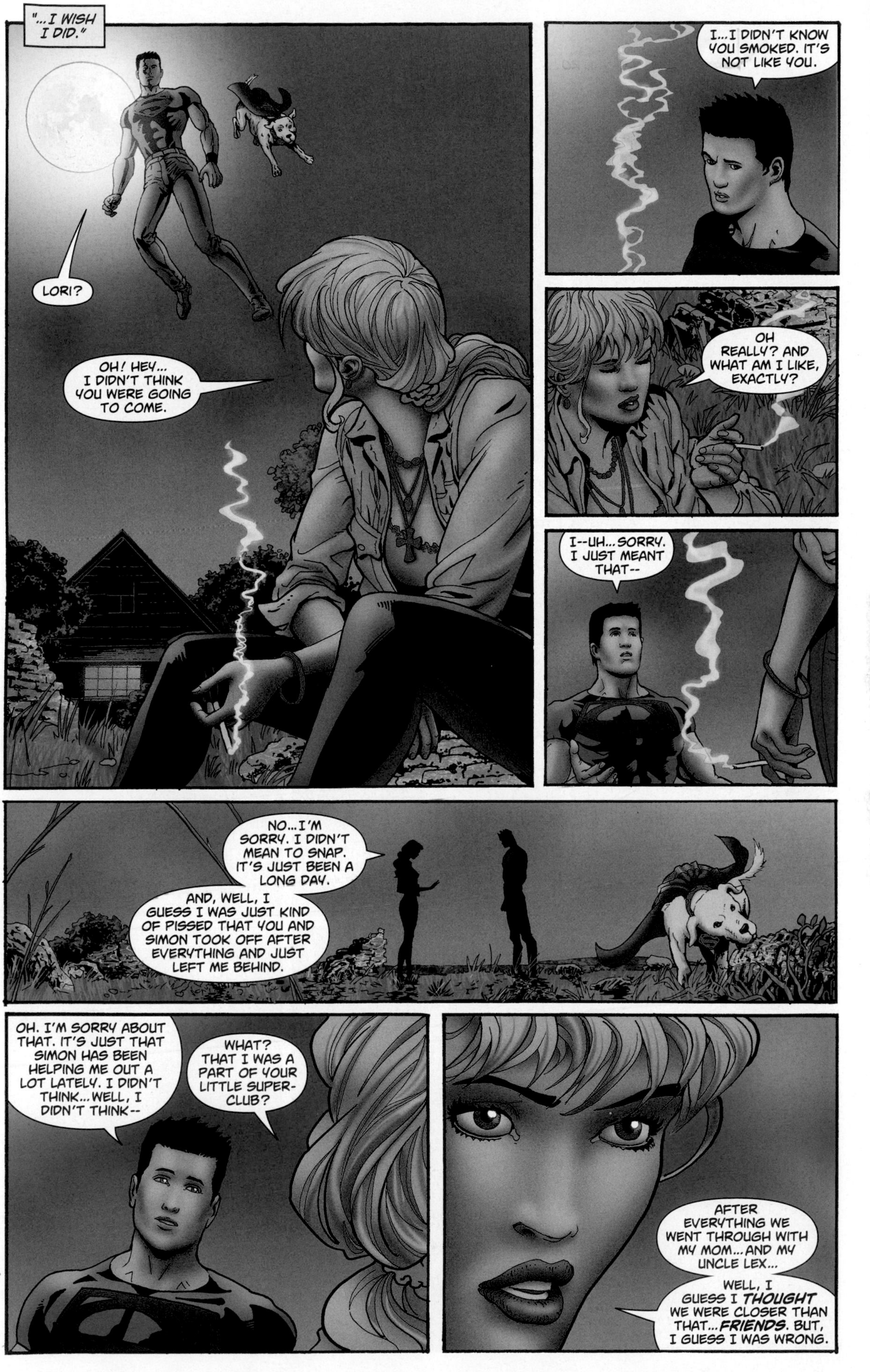
"...I WISH I DID."
LORI?
OH! HEY... I DIDN'T THINK YOU WERE GOING TO COME.
I...I DIDN'T KNOW YOU SMOKED. IT'S NOT LIKE YOU.
OH REALLY? AND WHAT AM I LIKE, EXACTLY?
I--UH... SORRY. I JUST MEANT THAT--
NO... I'M SORRY. I DIDN'T MEAN TO SNAP. IT'S JUST BEEN A LONG DAY.
AND, WELL, I GUESS I WAS JUST KIND OF PISSED THAT YOU AND SIMON TOOK OFF AFTER EVERYTHING AND JUST LEFT ME BEHIND.
OH. I'M SORRY ABOUT THAT. IT'S JUST THAT SIMON HAS BEEN HELPING ME OUT A LOT LATELY. I DIDN'T THINK... WELL, I DIDN'T THINK--
WHAT? THAT I WAS A PART OF YOUR LITTLE SUPER-CLUB?
AFTER EVERYTHING WE WENT THROUGH WITH MY MOM... AND MY UNCLE LEX...
WELL, I GUESS I *THOUGHT* WE WERE CLOSER THAN THAT... *FRIENDS*. BUT, I GUESS I WAS WRONG.

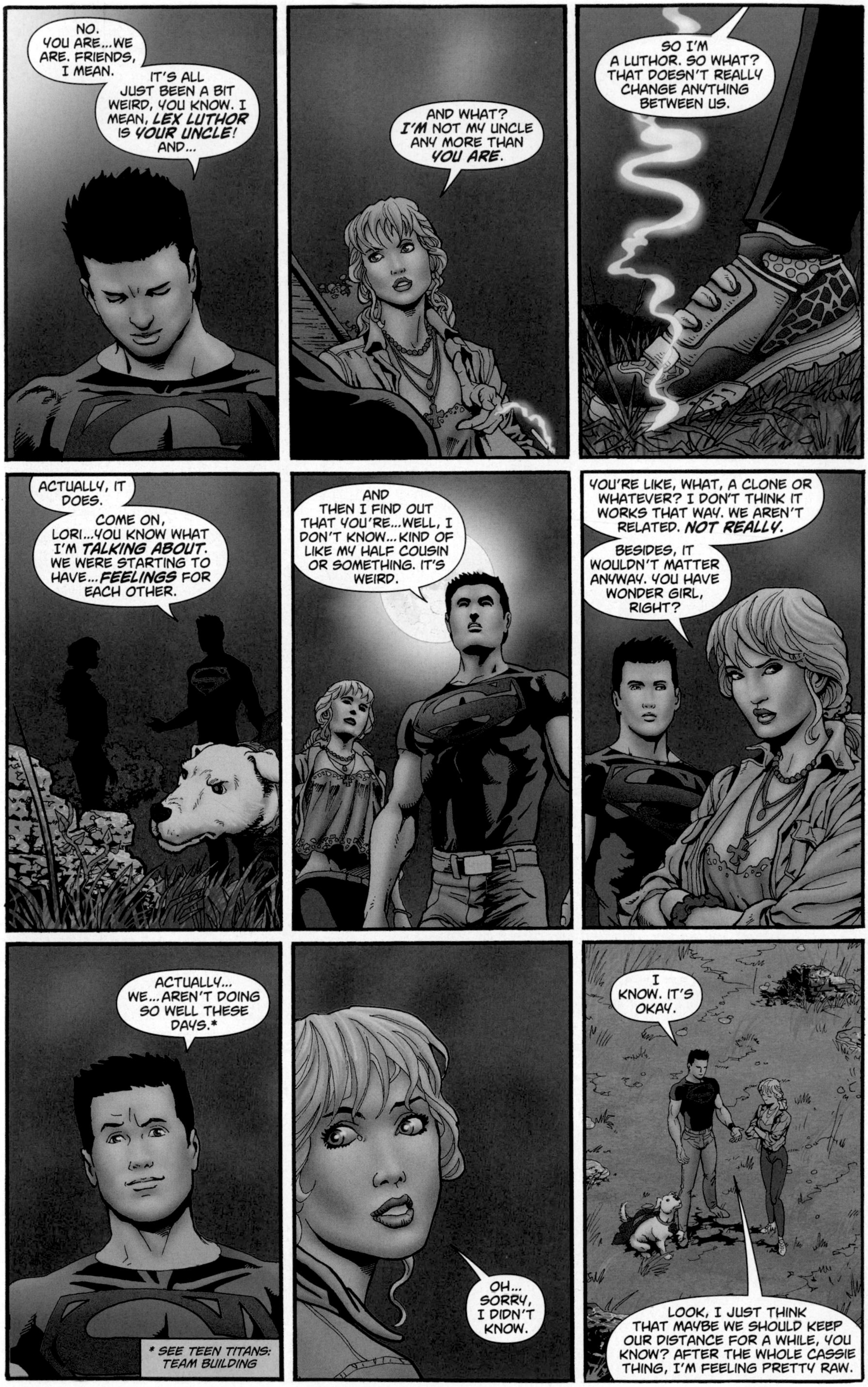
NO. YOU ARE...WE ARE. FRIENDS, I MEAN.
IT'S ALL JUST BEEN A BIT WEIRD, YOU KNOW. I MEAN, LEX LUTHOR IS YOUR UNCLE! AND...
AND WHAT? I'M NOT MY UNCLE ANY MORE THAN YOU ARE.
SO I'M A LUTHOR. SO WHAT? THAT DOESN'T REALLY CHANGE ANYTHING BETWEEN US.
ACTUALLY, IT DOES.
COME ON, LORI...YOU KNOW WHAT I'M TALKING ABOUT. WE WERE STARTING TO HAVE...FEELINGS FOR EACH OTHER.
AND THEN I FIND OUT THAT YOU'RE...WELL, I DON'T KNOW...KIND OF LIKE MY HALF COUSIN OR SOMETHING. IT'S WEIRD.
YOU'RE LIKE, WHAT, A CLONE OR WHATEVER? I DON'T THINK IT WORKS THAT WAY. WE AREN'T RELATED. NOT REALLY.
BESIDES, IT WOULDN'T MATTER ANYWAY. YOU HAVE WONDER GIRL, RIGHT?
ACTUALLY... WE...AREN'T DOING SO WELL THESE DAYS.*
* SEE TEEN TITANS: TEAM BUILDING
OH... SORRY, I DIDN'T KNOW.
I KNOW. IT'S OKAY.
LOOK, I JUST THINK THAT MAYBE WE SHOULD KEEP OUR DISTANCE FOR A WHILE, YOU KNOW? AFTER THE WHOLE CASSIE THING, I'M FEELING PRETTY RAW.

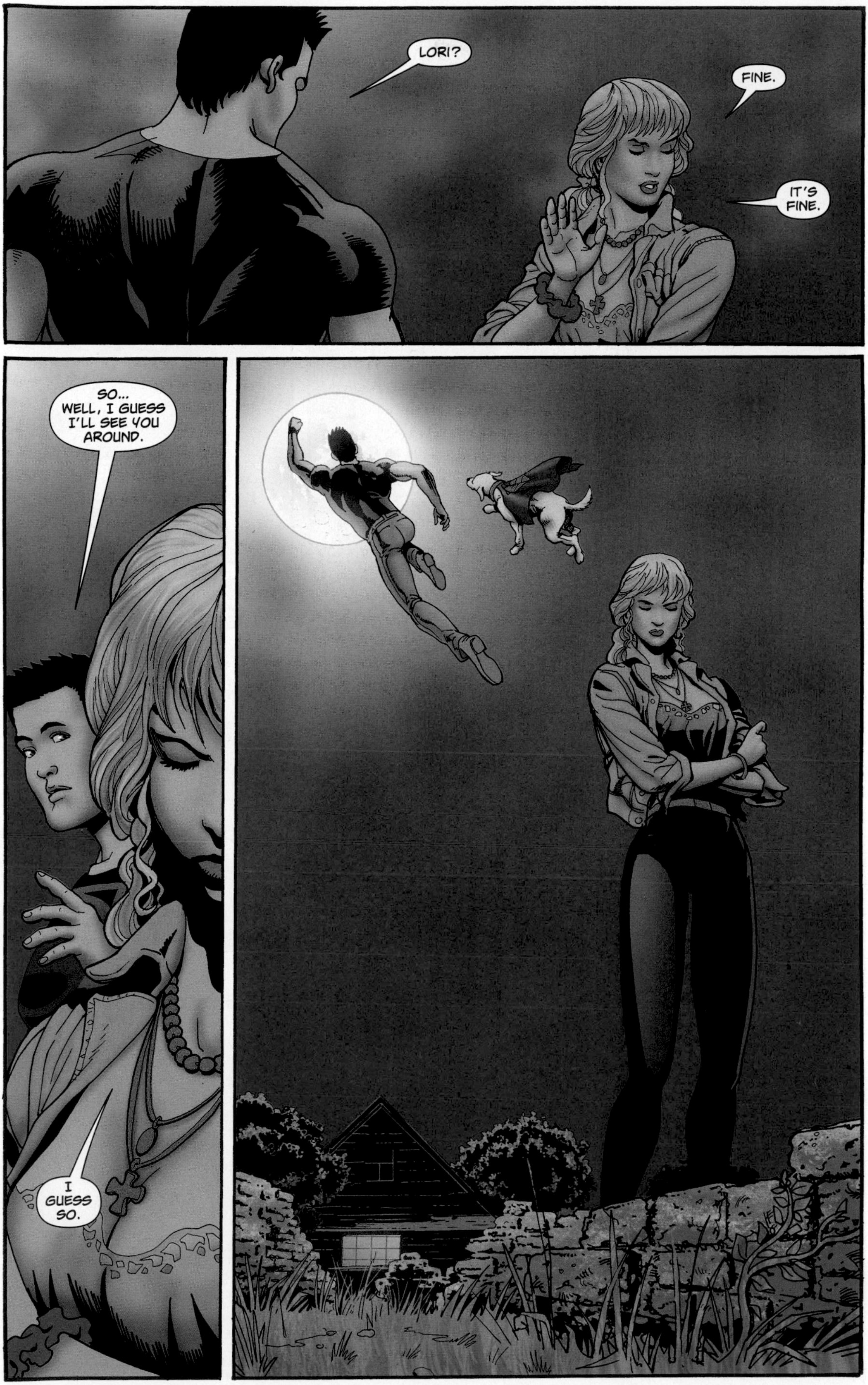
LORI?
FINE.
IT'S FINE.
SO... WELL, I GUESS I'LL SEE YOU AROUND.
I GUESS SO.

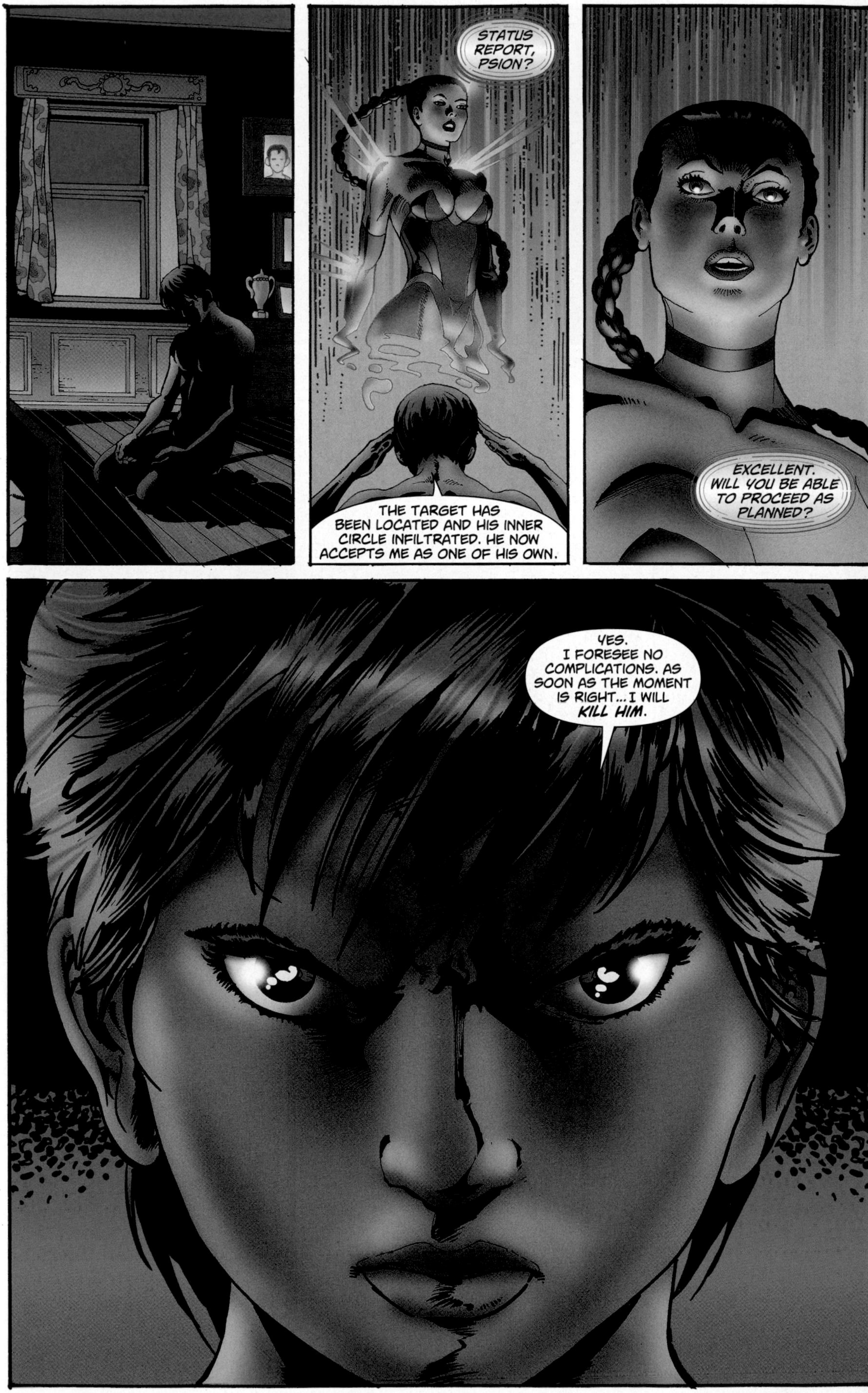
STATUS REPORT, PSION?
THE TARGET HAS BEEN LOCATED AND HIS INNER CIRCLE INFILTRATED. HE NOW ACCEPTS ME AS ONE OF HIS OWN.
EXCELLENT. WILL YOU BE ABLE TO PROCEED AS PLANNED?
YES. I FORESEE NO COMPLICATIONS. AS SOON AS THE MOMENT IS RIGHT... I WILL KILL HIM.

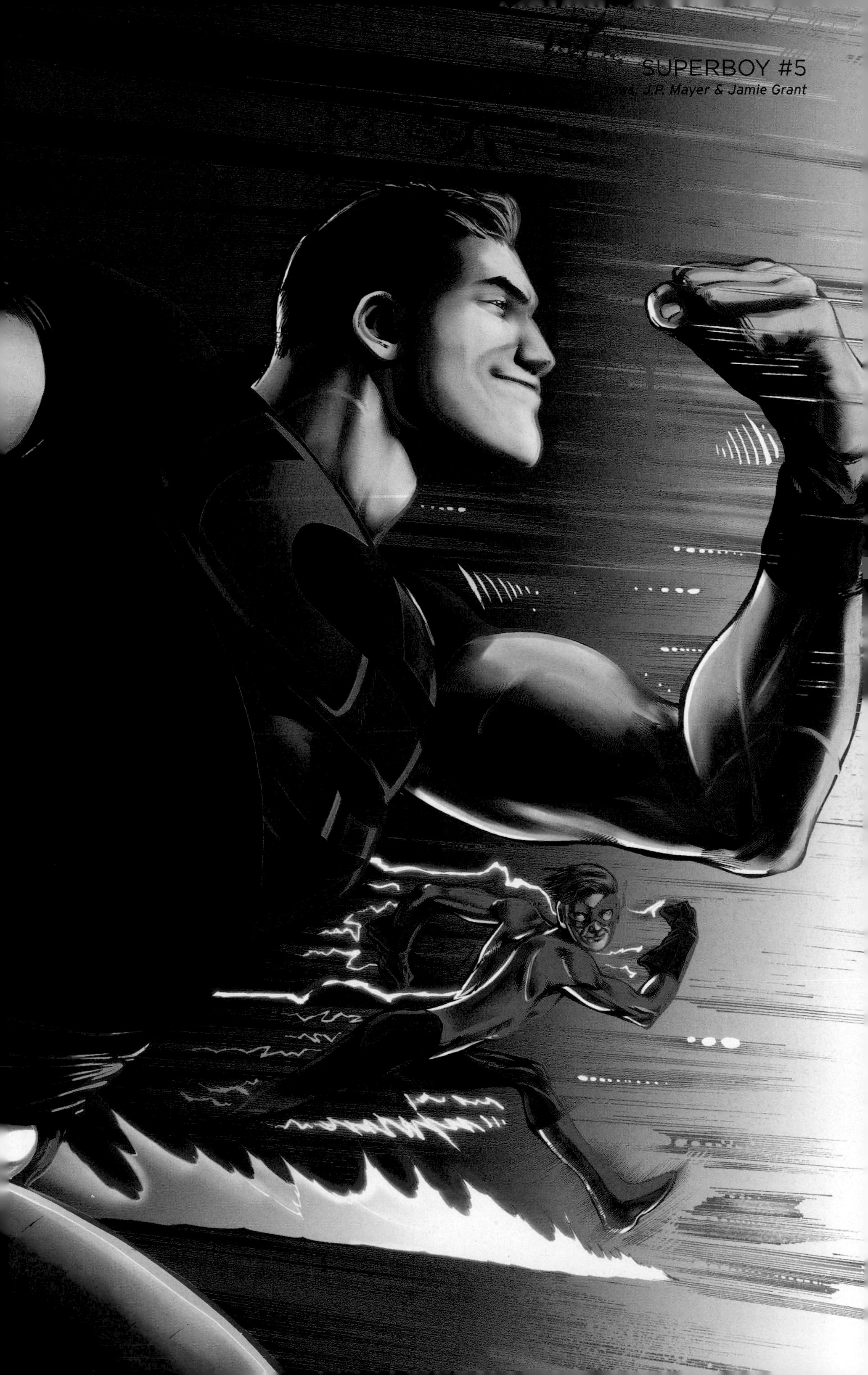

SUPERBOY #5

...ows, J.P. Mayer & Jamie Grant

SUPERBOY #5 | VARIANT

Cover by Francis Manapul

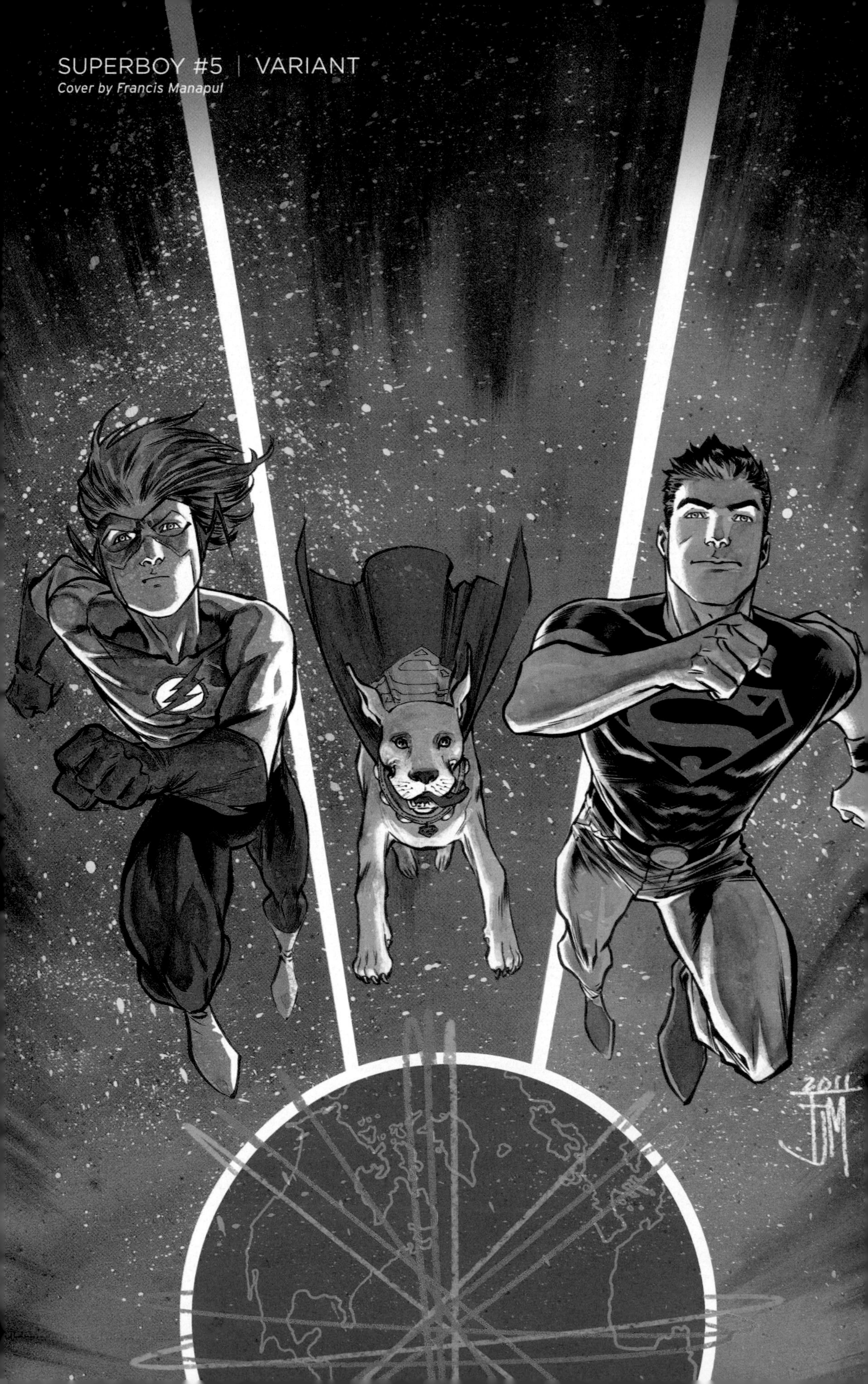

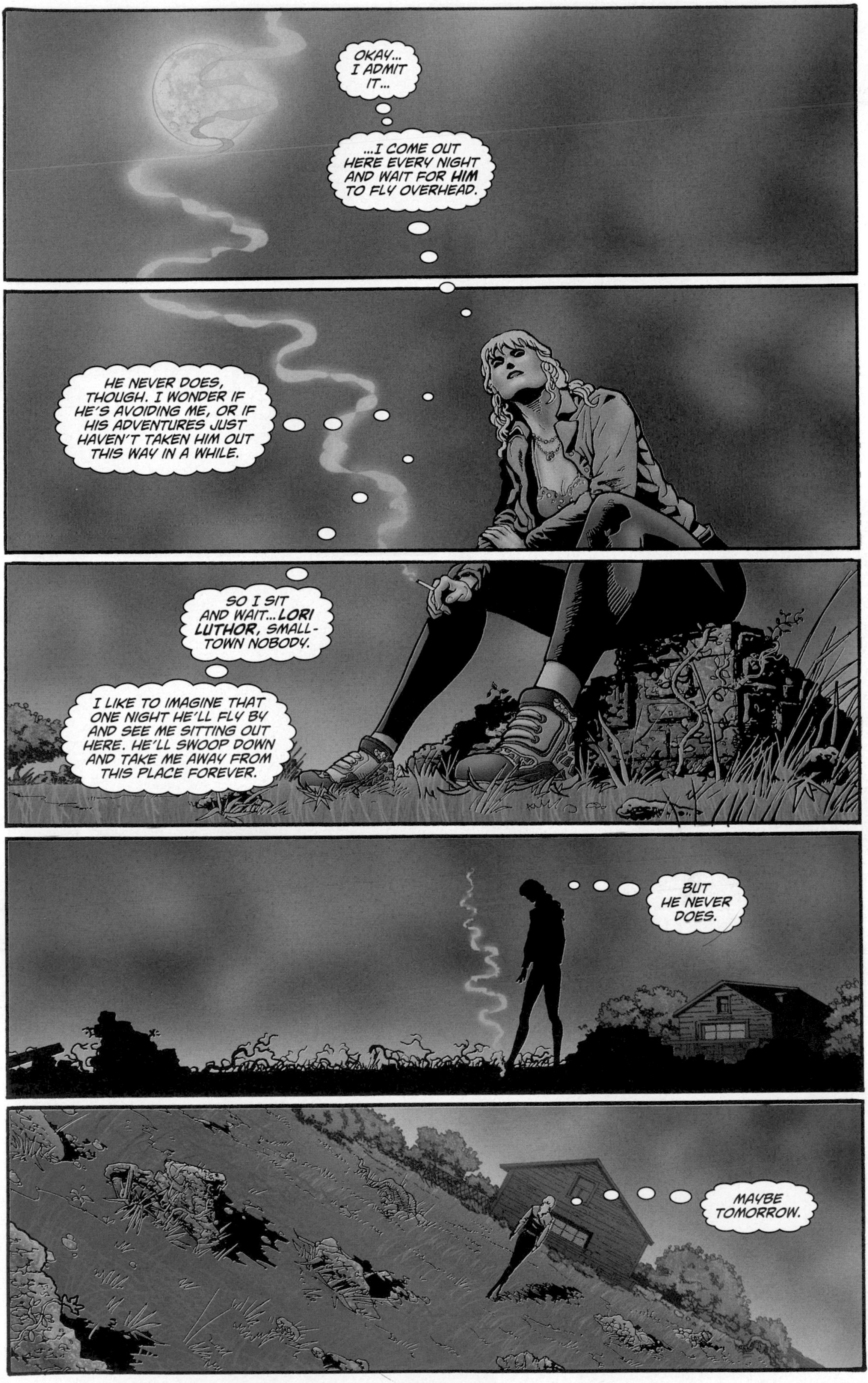
OKAY... I ADMIT IT...
...I COME OUT HERE EVERY NIGHT AND WAIT FOR HIM TO FLY OVERHEAD.
HE NEVER DOES, THOUGH. I WONDER IF HE'S AVOIDING ME, OR IF HIS ADVENTURES JUST HAVEN'T TAKEN HIM OUT THIS WAY IN A WHILE.
SO I SIT AND WAIT...LORI LUTHOR, SMALL-TOWN NOBODY.
I LIKE TO IMAGINE THAT ONE NIGHT HE'LL FLY BY AND SEE ME SITTING OUT HERE. HE'LL SWOOP DOWN AND TAKE ME AWAY FROM THIS PLACE FOREVER.
BUT HE NEVER DOES.
MAYBE TOMORROW.

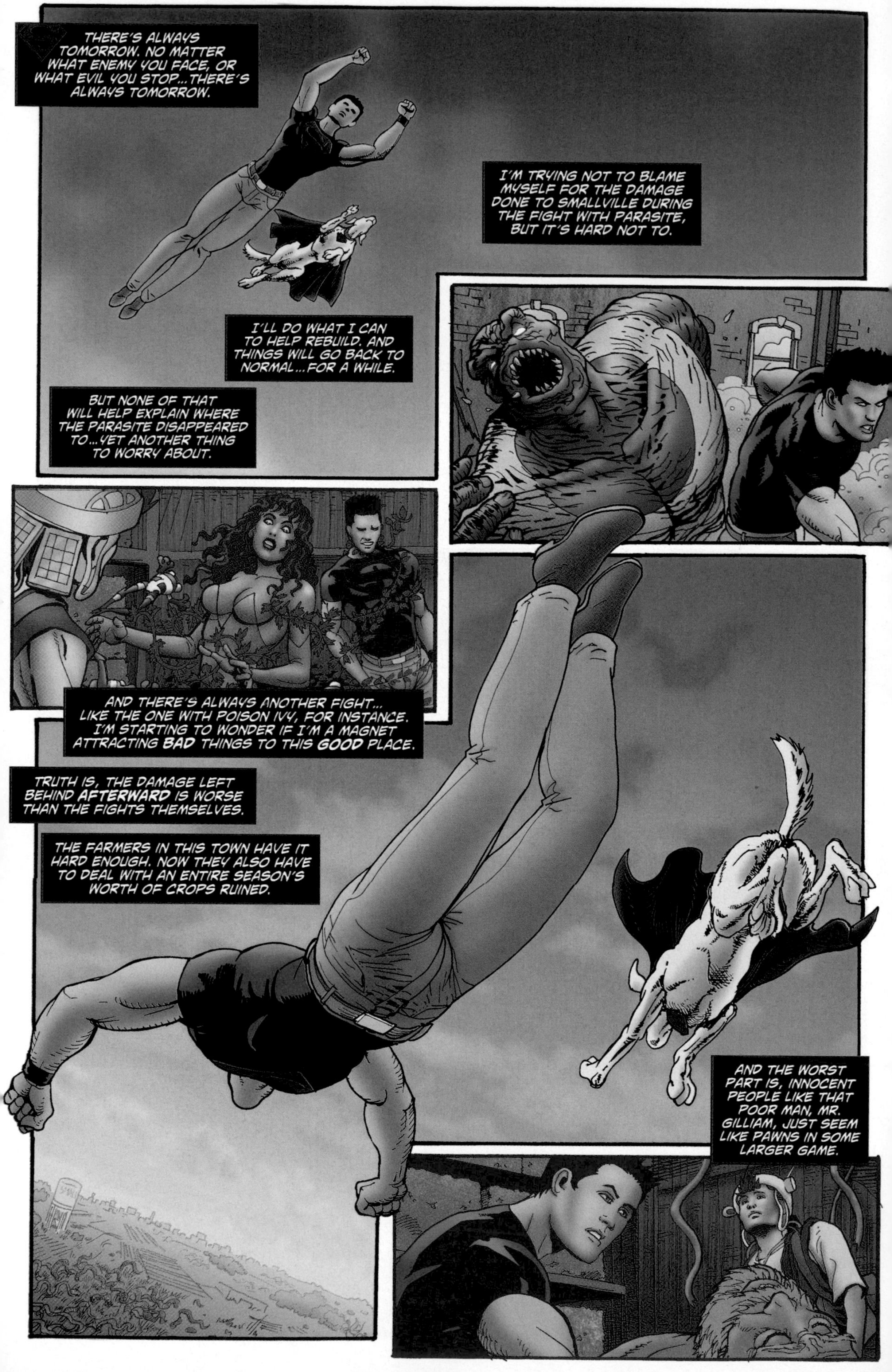
THERE'S ALWAYS TOMORROW. NO MATTER WHAT ENEMY YOU FACE, OR WHAT EVIL YOU STOP...THERE'S ALWAYS TOMORROW.
I'M TRYING NOT TO BLAME MYSELF FOR THE DAMAGE DONE TO SMALLVILLE DURING THE FIGHT WITH PARASITE, BUT IT'S HARD NOT TO.
I'LL DO WHAT I CAN TO HELP REBUILD. AND THINGS WILL GO BACK TO NORMAL...FOR A WHILE.
BUT NONE OF THAT WILL HELP EXPLAIN WHERE THE PARASITE DISAPPEARED TO...YET ANOTHER THING TO WORRY ABOUT.
AND THERE'S ALWAYS ANOTHER FIGHT... LIKE THE ONE WITH POISON IVY, FOR INSTANCE. I'M STARTING TO WONDER IF I'M A MAGNET ATTRACTING **BAD** THINGS TO THIS **GOOD** PLACE.
TRUTH IS, THE DAMAGE LEFT BEHIND **AFTERWARD** IS WORSE THAN THE FIGHTS THEMSELVES.
THE FARMERS IN THIS TOWN HAVE IT HARD ENOUGH. NOW THEY ALSO HAVE TO DEAL WITH AN ENTIRE SEASON'S WORTH OF CROPS RUINED.
AND THE WORST PART IS, INNOCENT PEOPLE LIKE THAT POOR MAN, MR. GILLIAM, JUST SEEM LIKE PAWNS IN SOME LARGER GAME.

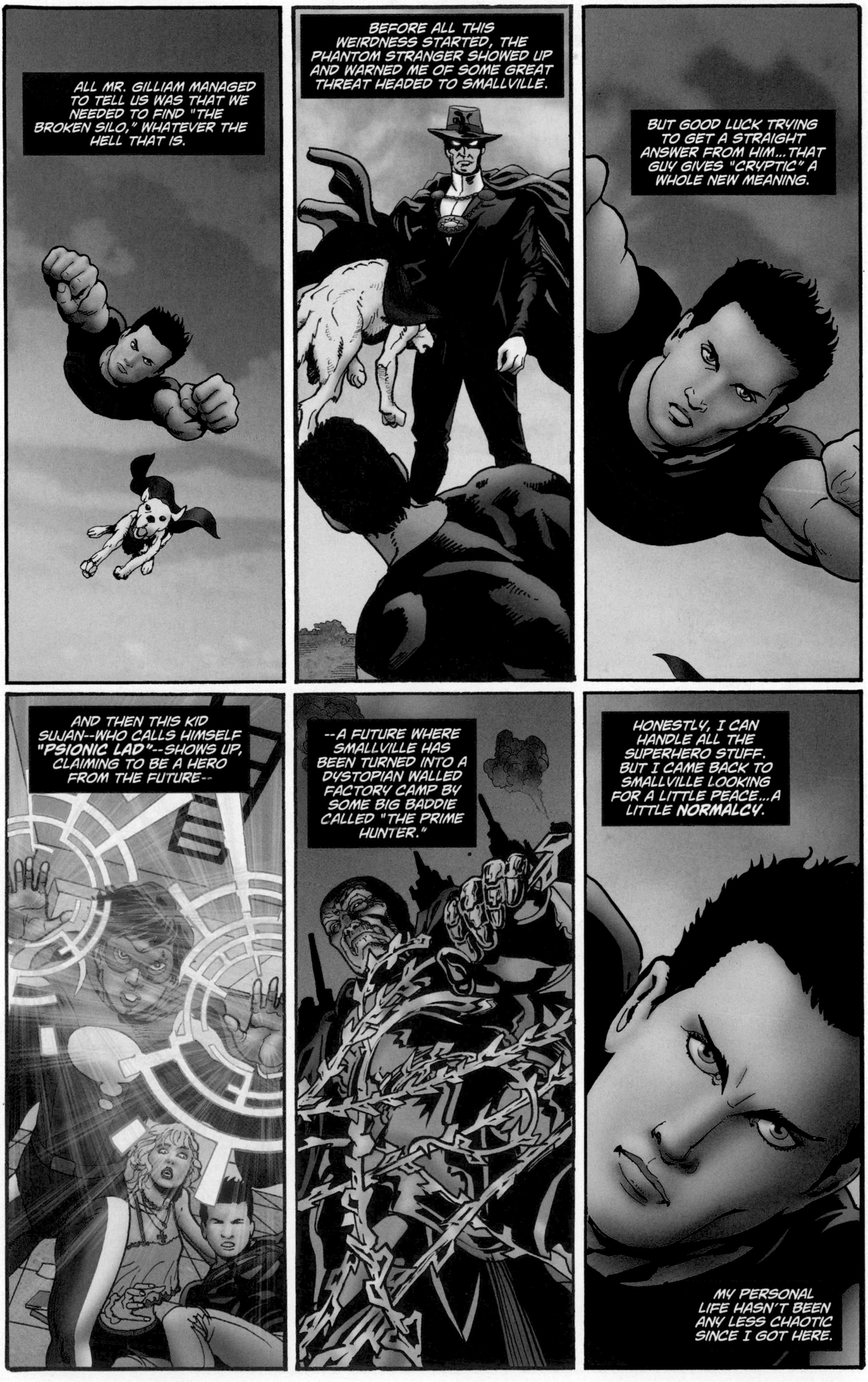
ALL MR. GILLIAM MANAGED TO TELL US WAS THAT WE NEEDED TO FIND "THE BROKEN SILO," WHATEVER THE HELL THAT IS.
BEFORE ALL THIS WEIRDNESS STARTED, THE PHANTOM STRANGER SHOWED UP AND WARNED ME OF SOME GREAT THREAT HEADED TO SMALLVILLE.
BUT GOOD LUCK TRYING TO GET A STRAIGHT ANSWER FROM HIM...THAT GUY GIVES "CRYPTIC" A WHOLE NEW MEANING.
AND THEN THIS KID SUJAN--WHO CALLS HIMSELF "PSIONIC LAD"--SHOWS UP, CLAIMING TO BE A HERO FROM THE FUTURE--
--A FUTURE WHERE SMALLVILLE HAS BEEN TURNED INTO A DYSTOPIAN WALLED FACTORY CAMP BY SOME BIG BADDIE CALLED "THE PRIME HUNTER."
HONESTLY, I CAN HANDLE ALL THE SUPERHERO STUFF. BUT I CAME BACK TO SMALLVILLE LOOKING FOR A LITTLE PEACE...A LITTLE NORMALCY.
MY PERSONAL LIFE HASN'T BEEN ANY LESS CHAOTIC SINCE I GOT HERE.

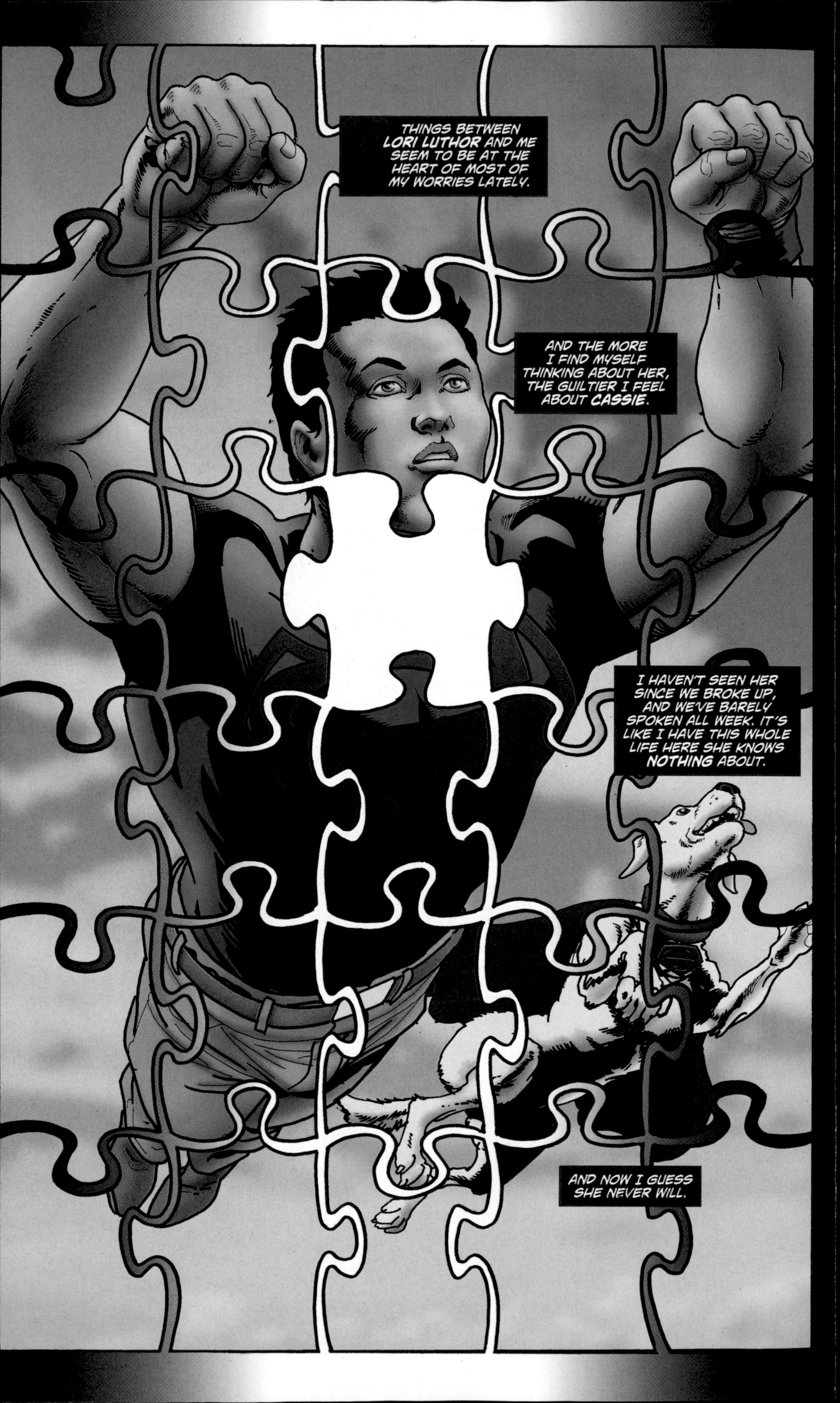
THINGS BETWEEN LORI LUTHOR AND ME SEEM TO BE AT THE HEART OF MOST OF MY WORRIES LATELY.
AND THE MORE I FIND MYSELF THINKING ABOUT HER, THE GUILTIER I FEEL ABOUT CASSIE.
I HAVEN'T SEEN HER SINCE WE BROKE UP, AND WE'VE BARELY SPOKEN ALL WEEK. IT'S LIKE I HAVE THIS WHOLE LIFE HERE SHE KNOWS NOTHING ABOUT.
AND NOW I GUESS SHE NEVER WILL.

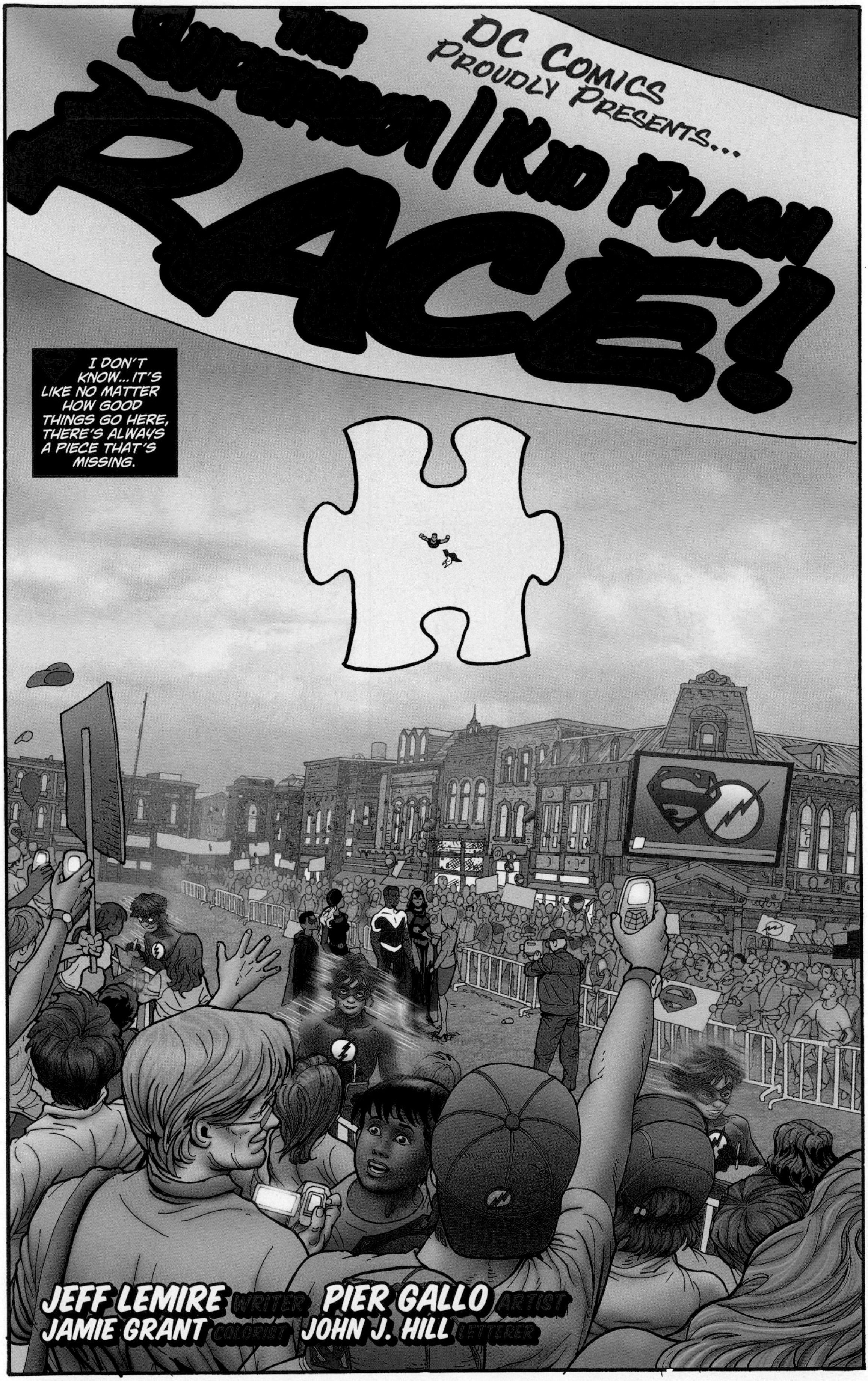
DC COMICS PROUDLY PRESENTS...
THE SUPERBOY/KID FLASH RACE!
I DON'T KNOW... IT'S LIKE NO MATTER HOW GOOD THINGS GO HERE, THERE'S ALWAYS A PIECE THAT'S MISSING.
JEFF LEMIRE WRITER PIER GALLO ARTIST
JAMIE GRANT COLORIST JOHN J. HILL LETTERER

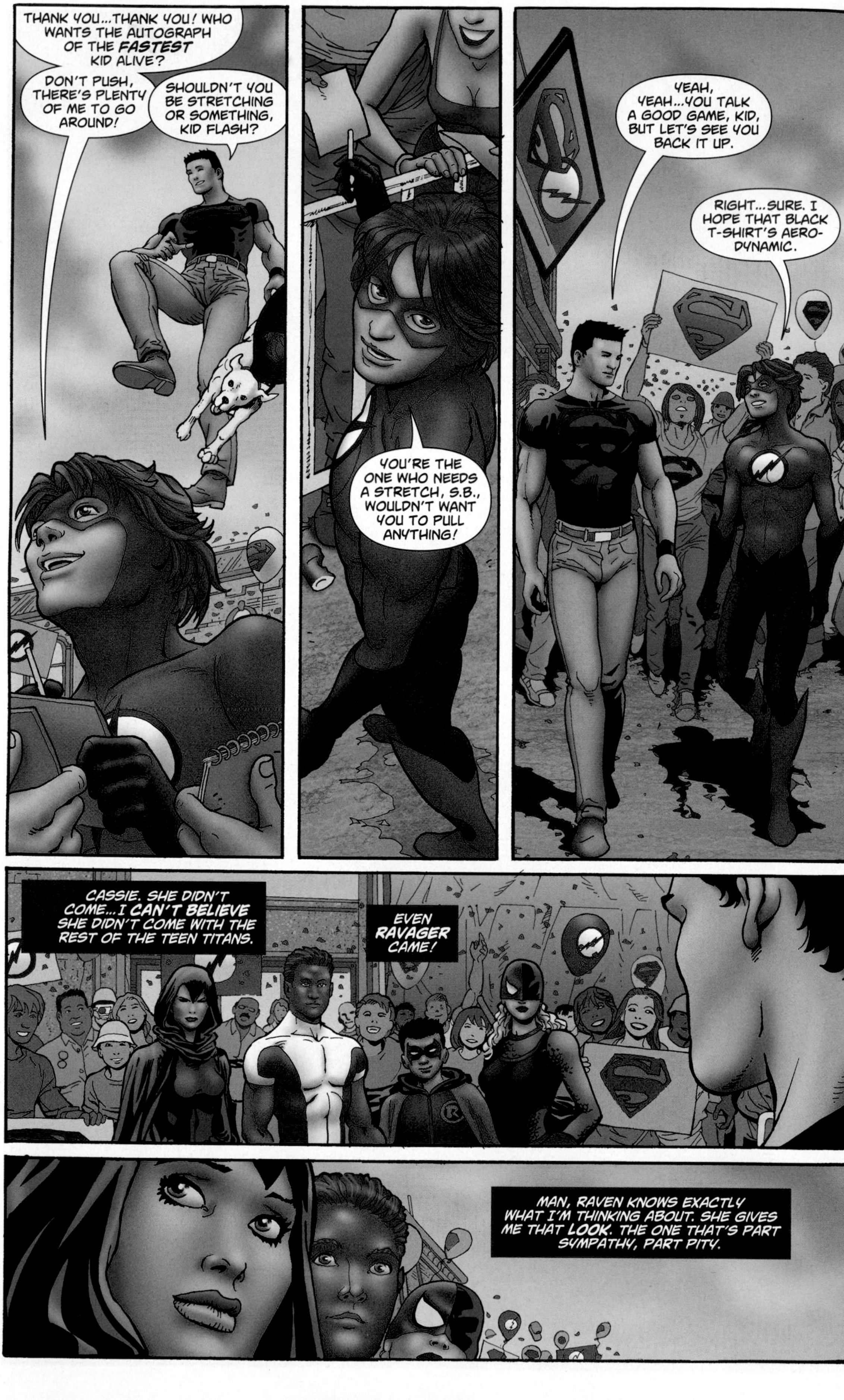
THANK YOU...THANK YOU! WHO WANTS THE AUTOGRAPH OF THE FASTEST KID ALIVE?
DON'T PUSH, THERE'S PLENTY OF ME TO GO AROUND!
SHOULDN'T YOU BE STRETCHING OR SOMETHING, KID FLASH?
YOU'RE THE ONE WHO NEEDS A STRETCH, S.B., WOULDN'T WANT YOU TO PULL ANYTHING!
YEAH, YEAH...YOU TALK A GOOD GAME, KID, BUT LET'S SEE YOU BACK IT UP.
RIGHT...SURE. I HOPE THAT BLACK T-SHIRT'S AERO-DYNAMIC.
CASSIE. SHE DIDN'T COME...I CAN'T BELIEVE SHE DIDN'T COME WITH THE REST OF THE TEEN TITANS.
EVEN RAVAGER CAME!
MAN, RAVEN KNOWS EXACTLY WHAT I'M THINKING ABOUT. SHE GIVES ME THAT LOOK. THE ONE THAT'S PART SYMPATHY, PART PITY.

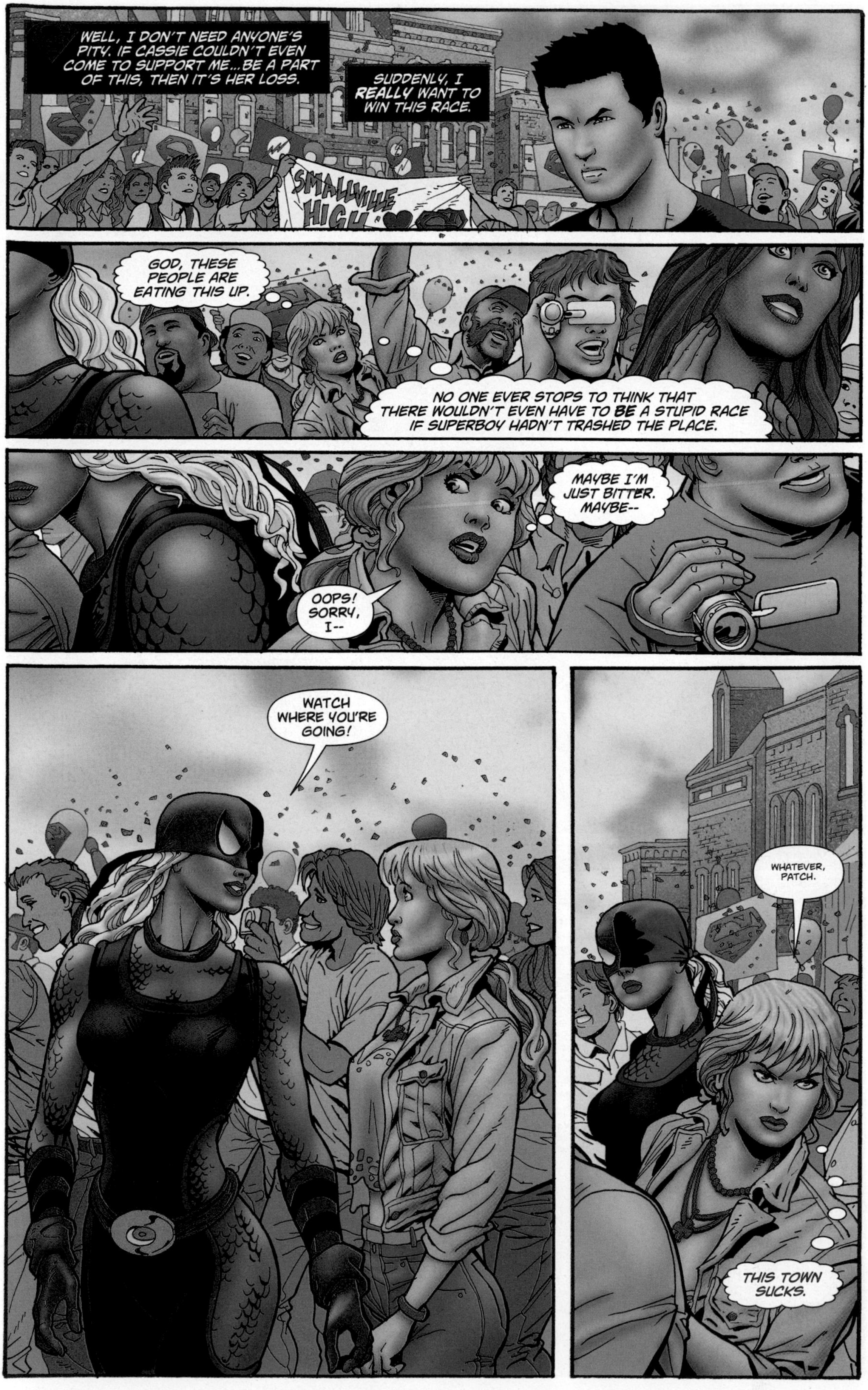
WELL, I DON'T NEED ANYONE'S PITY. IF CASSIE COULDN'T EVEN COME TO SUPPORT ME...BE A PART OF THIS, THEN IT'S HER LOSS.
SUDDENLY, I REALLY WANT TO WIN THIS RACE.
SMALLVILLE HIGH
GOD, THESE PEOPLE ARE EATING THIS UP.
NO ONE EVER STOPS TO THINK THAT THERE WOULDN'T EVEN HAVE TO BE A STUPID RACE IF SUPERBOY HADN'T TRASHED THE PLACE.
MAYBE I'M JUST BITTER. MAYBE--
OOPS! SORRY, I--
WATCH WHERE YOU'RE GOING!
WHATEVER, PATCH.
THIS TOWN SUCKS.

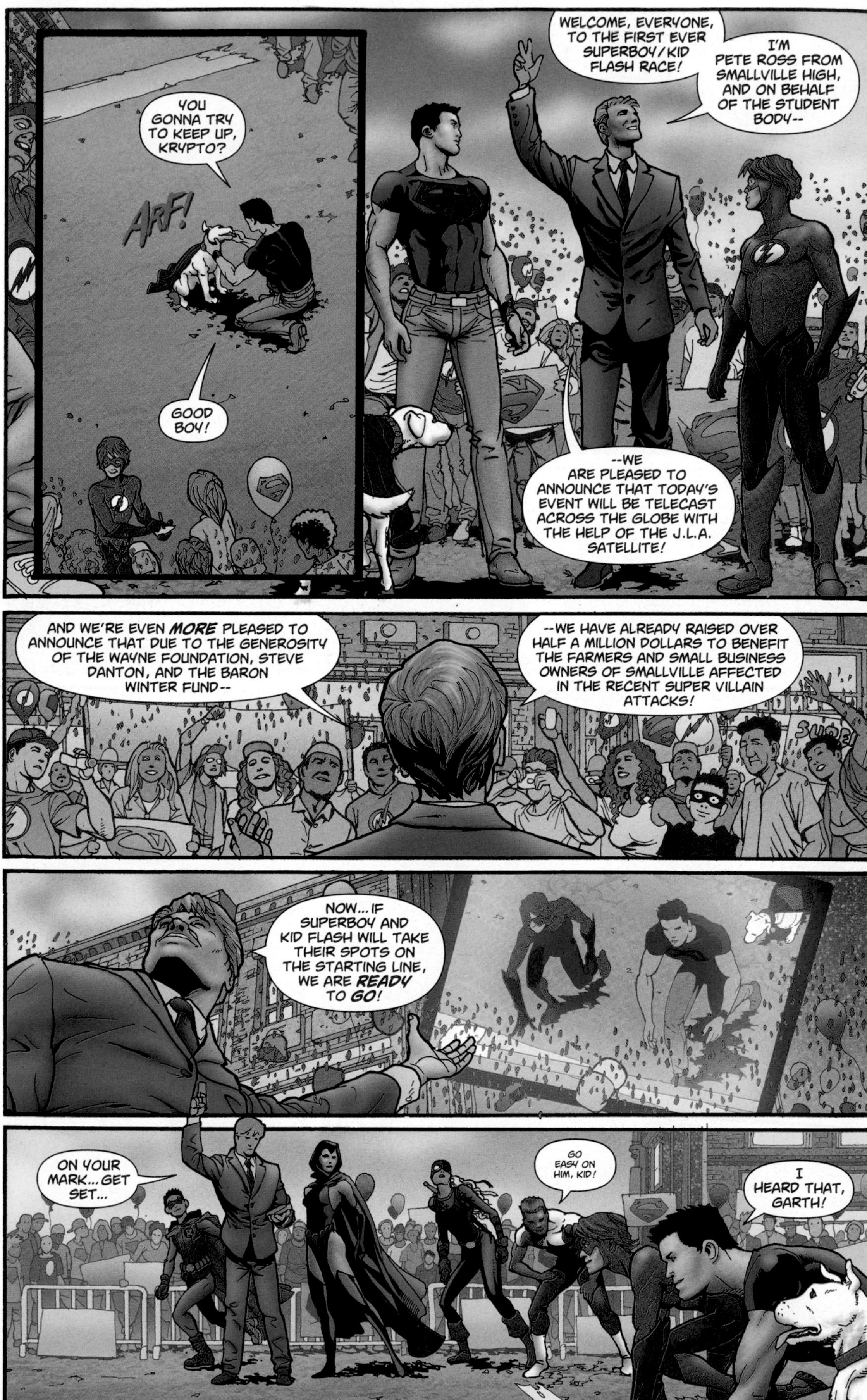
YOU GONNA TRY TO KEEP UP, KRYPTO?
ARF!
GOOD BOY!
WELCOME, EVERYONE, TO THE FIRST EVER SUPERBOY/KID FLASH RACE!
I'M PETE ROSS FROM SMALLVILLE HIGH, AND ON BEHALF OF THE STUDENT BODY--
--WE ARE PLEASED TO ANNOUNCE THAT TODAY'S EVENT WILL BE TELECAST ACROSS THE GLOBE WITH THE HELP OF THE J.L.A. SATELLITE!
AND WE'RE EVEN MORE PLEASED TO ANNOUNCE THAT DUE TO THE GENEROSITY OF THE WAYNE FOUNDATION, STEVE DANTON, AND THE BARON WINTER FUND--
--WE HAVE ALREADY RAISED OVER HALF A MILLION DOLLARS TO BENEFIT THE FARMERS AND SMALL BUSINESS OWNERS OF SMALLVILLE AFFECTED IN THE RECENT SUPER VILLAIN ATTACKS!
NOW... IF SUPERBOY AND KID FLASH WILL TAKE THEIR SPOTS ON THE STARTING LINE, WE ARE READY TO GO!
ON YOUR MARK... GET SET...
GO EASY ON HIM, KID!
I HEARD THAT, GARTH!

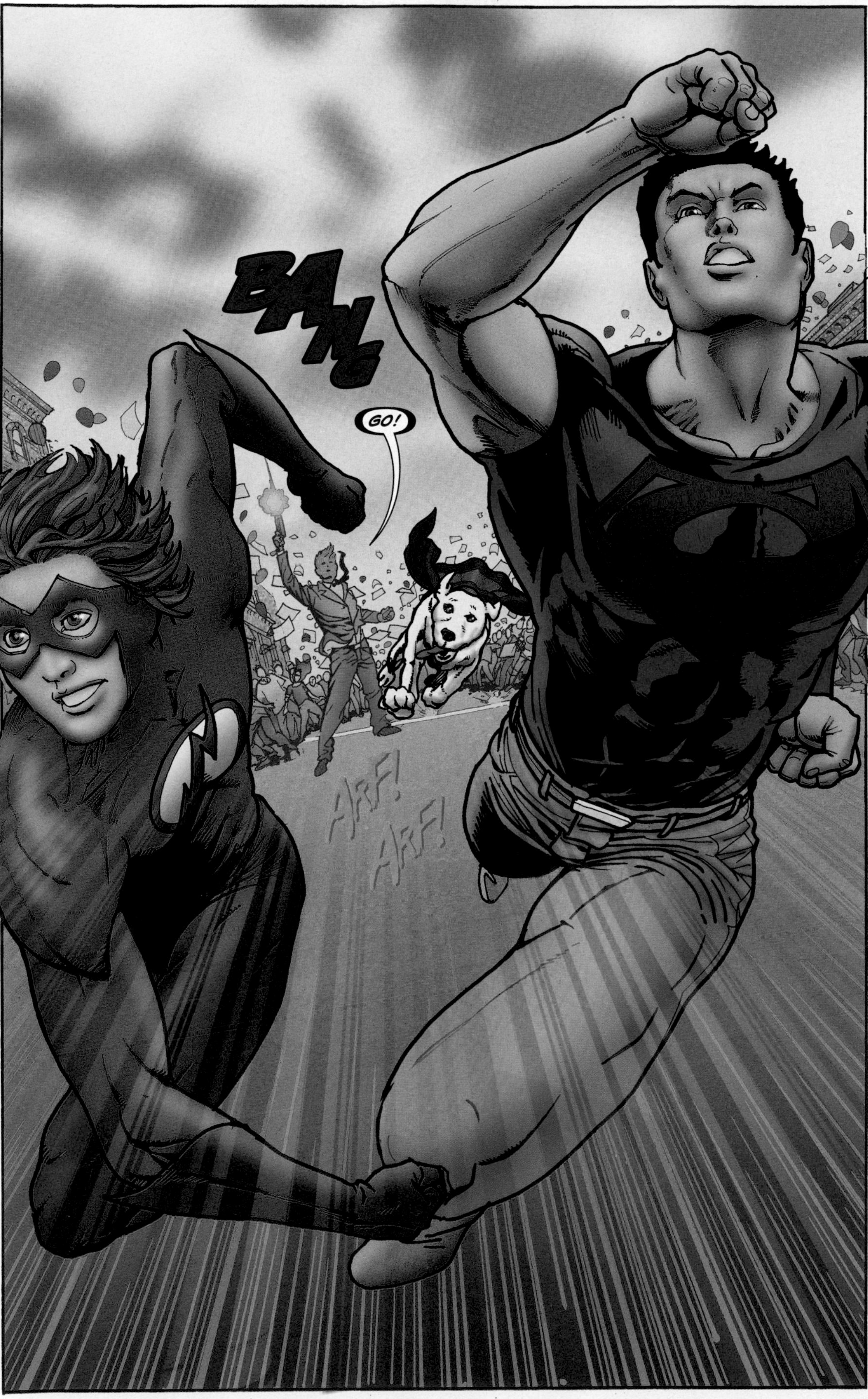
BANG
GO!
ARF! ARF!

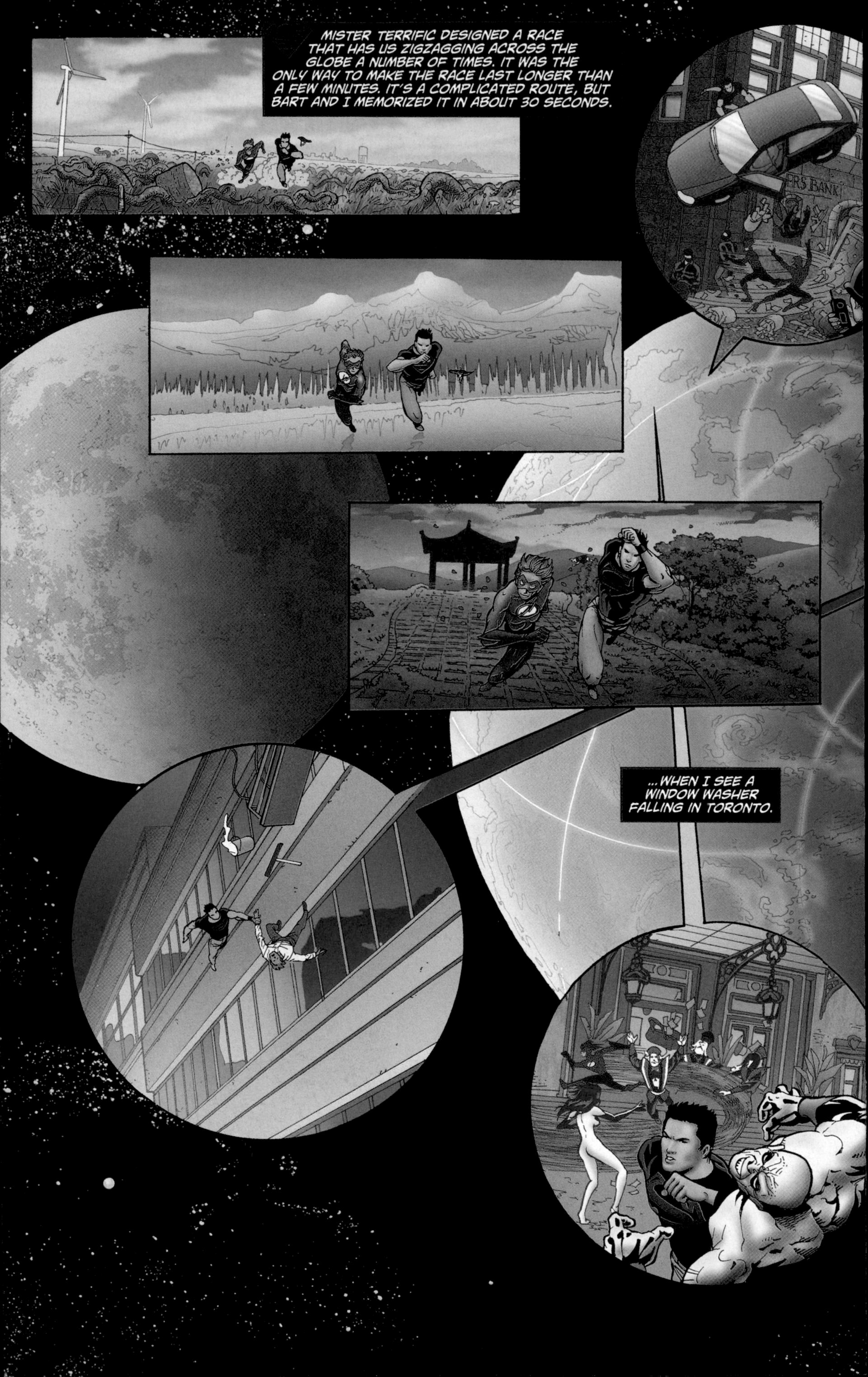

MISTER TERRIFIC DESIGNED A RACE THAT HAS US ZIGZAGGING ACROSS THE GLOBE A NUMBER OF TIMES. IT WAS THE ONLY WAY TO MAKE THE RACE LAST LONGER THAN A FEW MINUTES. IT'S A COMPLICATED ROUTE, BUT BART AND I MEMORIZED IT IN ABOUT 30 SECONDS.
...WHEN I SEE A WINDOW WASHER FALLING IN TORONTO.

EVEN SO, WE TAKE OUR TIME AND STOP FOR A FEW "DETOURS" ALONG THE WAY, JUST TO MAKE IT INTERESTING. WE PREVENT A BANK ROBBERY WHILE PASSING THROUGH LONDON.

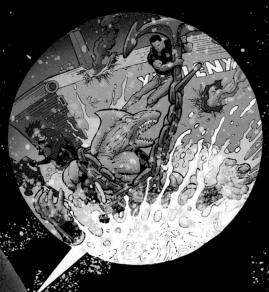

BART NOTICES ONE OF MY LAME OLD VILLAINS, KING SHARK, OFF THE COAST OF HAWAII, SO WE DEAL WITH HIM QUICKLY AND ARE ABOUT TO HEAD EAST...

WE EVEN STOP THE ROYAL FLUSH GANG'S ATTACK ON A CASINO IN THE SOUTH OF FRANCE.

THIS SHOULD BE FUN. JUST LIKE OLD TIMES... KID FLASH AND SUPERBOY IN ACTION. BUT I HAVE A HARD TIME ENJOYING MYSELF.

WHAT'S UP WITH YOU, CONNER?

WHAT? NOTHING. WHY?

DUDE, I KNOW YOU BETTER THAN THAT. YOUR HEART ISN'T IN THIS.

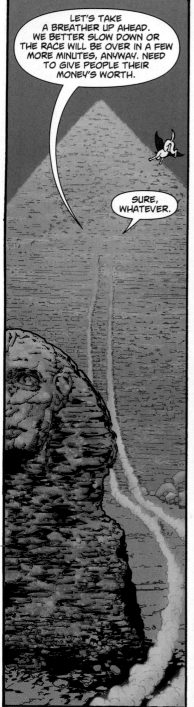

LET'S TAKE A BREATHER UP AHEAD. WE BETTER SLOW DOWN OR THE RACE WILL BE OVER IN A FEW MORE MINUTES, ANYWAY. NEED TO GIVE PEOPLE THEIR MONEY'S WORTH.

SURE, WHATEVER.

SHE WANTED TO COME, YOU KNOW.

WHAT?

CASSIE. SHE WANTED TO COME, SHE WAS JUST REALLY BUSY BACK AT TITANS TOWER.

BART... YOU DON'T HAVE TO DO THIS.

DO WHAT?

LIE FOR HER. I KNOW WHY SHE DIDN'T COME. SHE DIDN'T *WANT* TO.

IT'S OKAY. I MEAN, THINGS ARE WEIRD BETWEEN US SINCE WE BROKE UP.

I JUST STILL HAVEN'T REALLY GOTTEN USED TO IT, I GUESS.

SORRY, MAN.

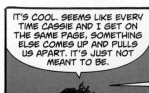

IT'S COOL. SEEMS LIKE EVERY TIME CASSIE AND I GET ON THE SAME PAGE, SOMETHING ELSE COMES UP AND PULLS US APART. IT'S JUST NOT MEANT TO BE.

COME ON, MAN, SUPERBOY AND WONDER GIRL--YOU'RE THE DREAM COUPLE. EVERYBODY WANTS WHAT YOU GUYS HAVE.

YOU'LL GET BACK TOGETHER. YOU ALWAYS DO.

NOT THIS TIME, BART.

RIGHT. SHE'S TOTALLY OUT OF YOUR LEAGUE, ANYWAY. I WAS JUST TRYING TO MAKE YOU FEEL BETTER.

...MAYBE I SHOULD GO FOR HER.

YOU SO MUCH AS TAKE A LIGHT SPEED GLANCE AT HER AND YOU'RE A DEAD MAN, ALLEN.

WELL... AT LEAST YOU HAVE KRYPTO, RIGHT?

RUF!

THANKS, BART.

FOR WHAT?

BEING YOU.

DON'T GO GETTING ALL SUPER-SENTIMENTAL ON ME, S.B.

I'M STILL GOING TO KICK YOUR BUTT IN THIS RACE!

ARF!

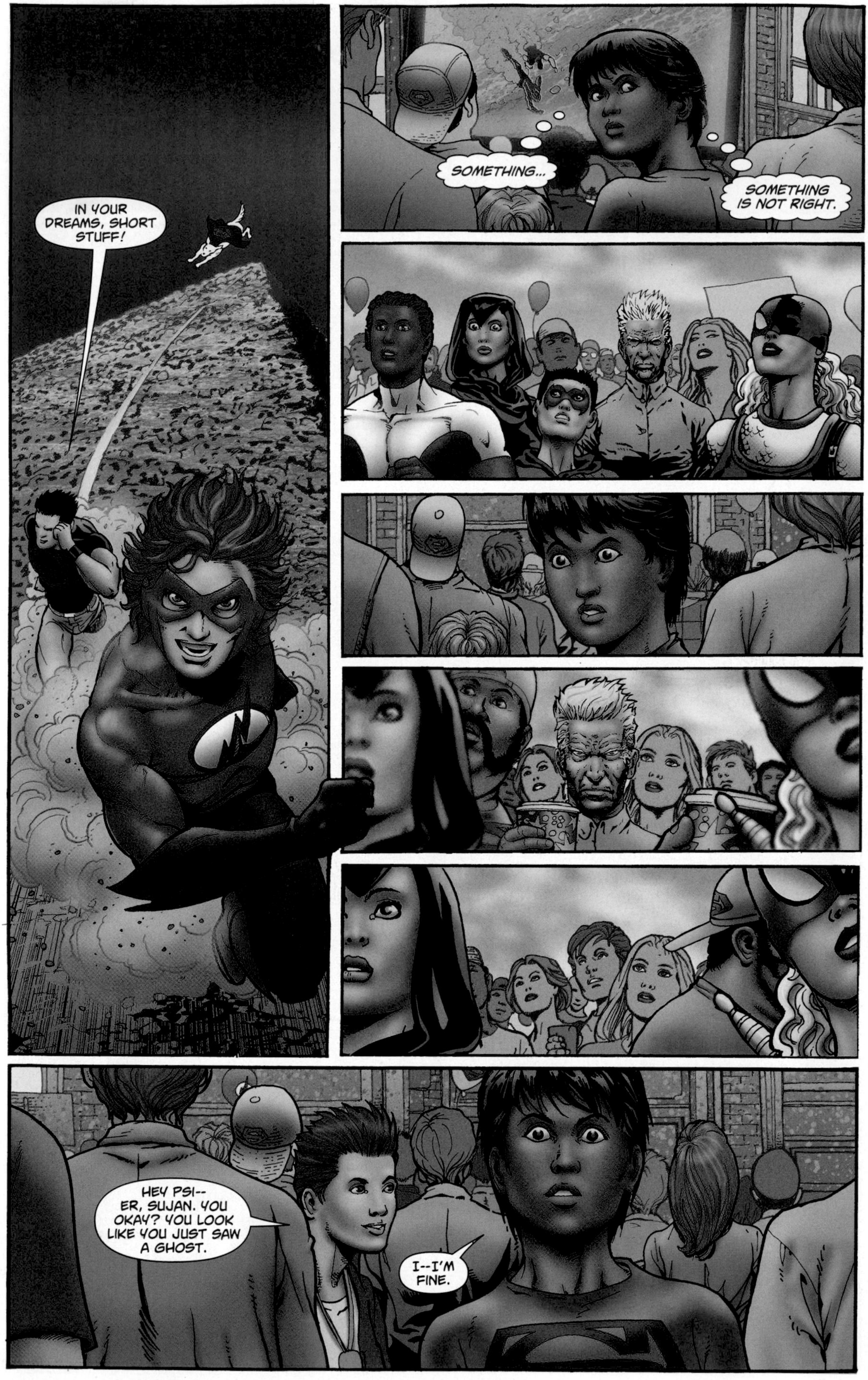
IN YOUR DREAMS, SHORT STUFF!
SOMETHING...
SOMETHING IS NOT RIGHT.
HEY PSI-- ER, SUJAN. YOU OKAY? YOU LOOK LIKE YOU JUST SAW A GHOST.
I--I'M FINE.

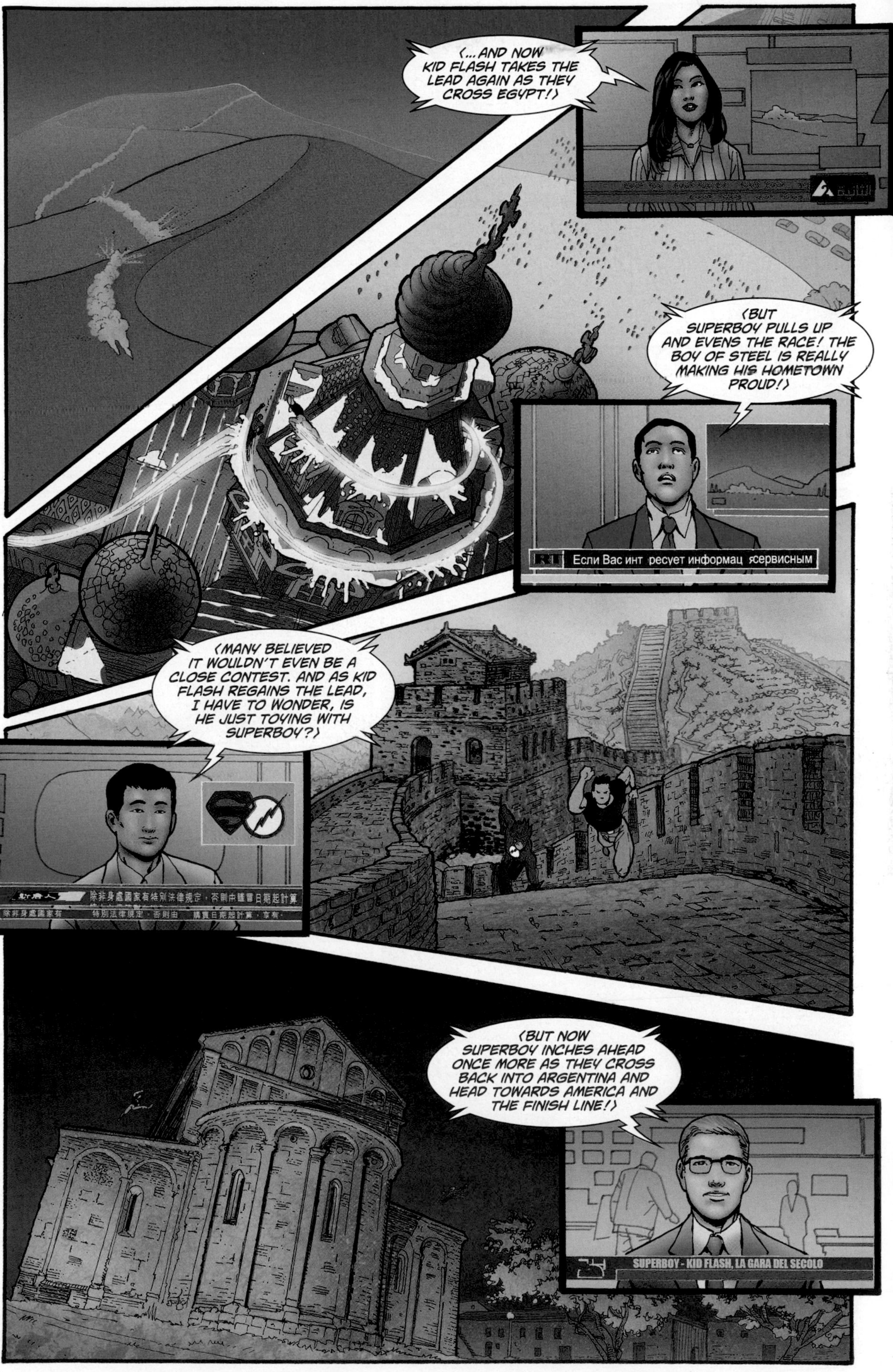
⟨...AND NOW KID FLASH TAKES THE LEAD AGAIN AS THEY CROSS EGYPT!⟩
⟨BUT SUPERBOY PULLS UP AND EVENS THE RACE! THE BOY OF STEEL IS REALLY MAKING HIS HOMETOWN PROUD!⟩
R1 Если Вас инт ресует информац ясервисным
⟨MANY BELIEVED IT WOULDN'T EVEN BE A CLOSE CONTEST. AND AS KID FLASH REGAINS THE LEAD, I HAVE TO WONDER, IS HE JUST TOYING WITH SUPERBOY?⟩
除非身處國家有特別法律規定，否則由購買日期起計算
除非身處國家有 特別法律規定，否則由 購買日期起計算，享有
⟨BUT NOW SUPERBOY INCHES AHEAD ONCE MORE AS THEY CROSS BACK INTO ARGENTINA AND HEAD TOWARDS AMERICA AND THE FINISH LINE!⟩
SUPERBOY - KID FLASH, LA GARA DEL SECOLO

ALMOST THERE, KENT... SHOULD I START TRYING YET?

KEEP RUNNING YOUR MOUTH, BART, IT'S ABOUT THE ONLY THING YOU GOT THAT'S FASTER THAN ME!

WHA--

PHANTOM STRANGER?!

HEY, WHAT ARE YOU DOING? WE'RE ALMOST DONE, MAN!

I...I THOUGHT I SAW SOMETHING... SOMEONE. OVER THERE, BY LORI'S HOUSE.

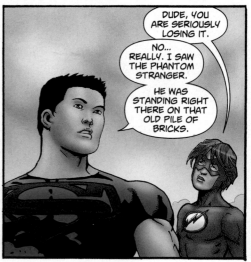

DUDE, YOU ARE SERIOUSLY LOSING IT.

NO... REALLY. I SAW THE PHANTOM STRANGER.

HE WAS STANDING RIGHT THERE ON THAT OLD PILE OF BRICKS.

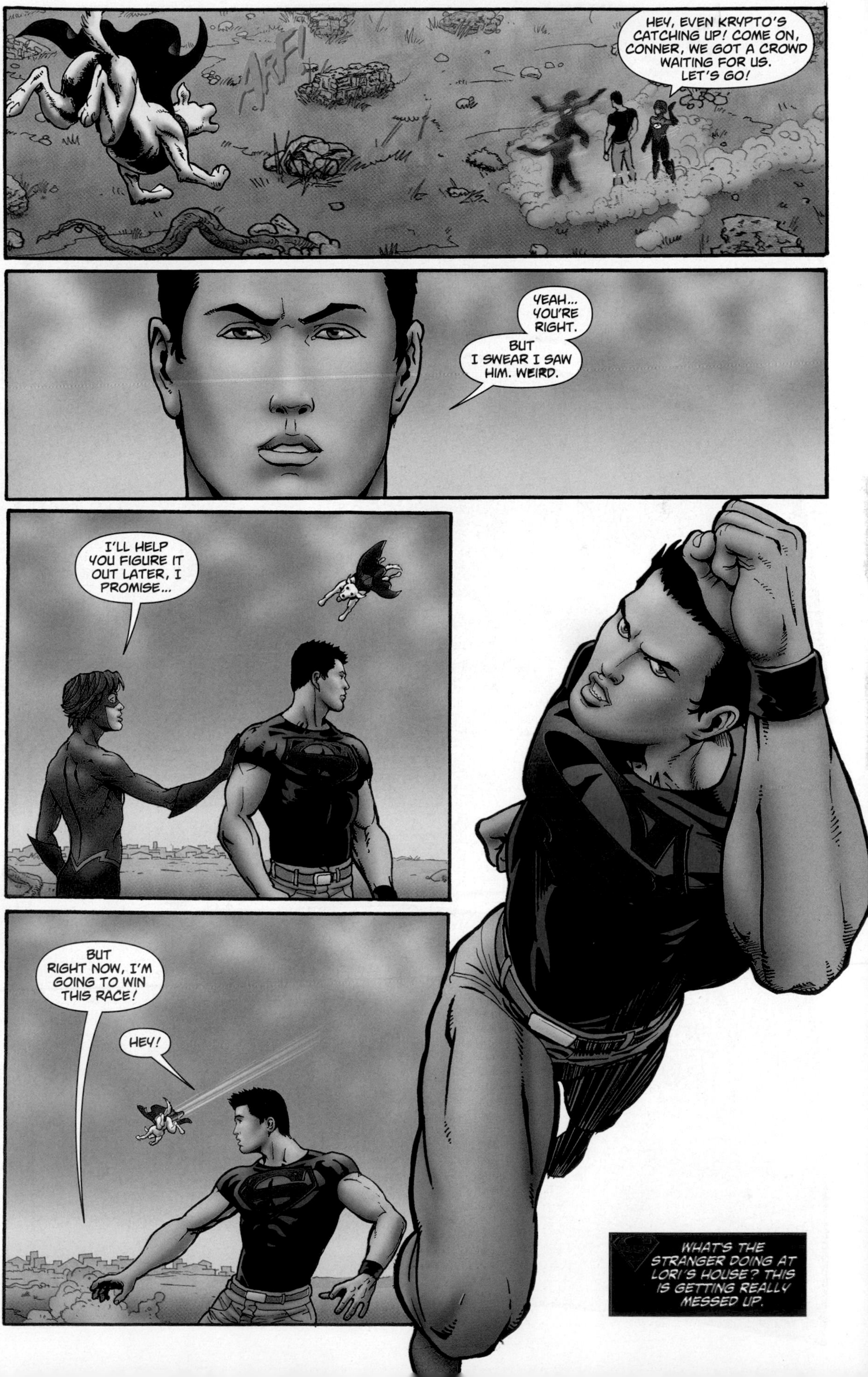
ARF!
HEY, EVEN KRYPTO'S CATCHING UP! COME ON, CONNER, WE GOT A CROWD WAITING FOR US. LET'S GO!
YEAH... YOU'RE RIGHT.
BUT I SWEAR I SAW HIM. WEIRD.
I'LL HELP YOU FIGURE IT OUT LATER, I PROMISE...
BUT RIGHT NOW, I'M GOING TO WIN THIS RACE!
HEY!
WHAT'S THE STRANGER DOING AT LORI'S HOUSE? THIS IS GETTING REALLY MESSED UP.

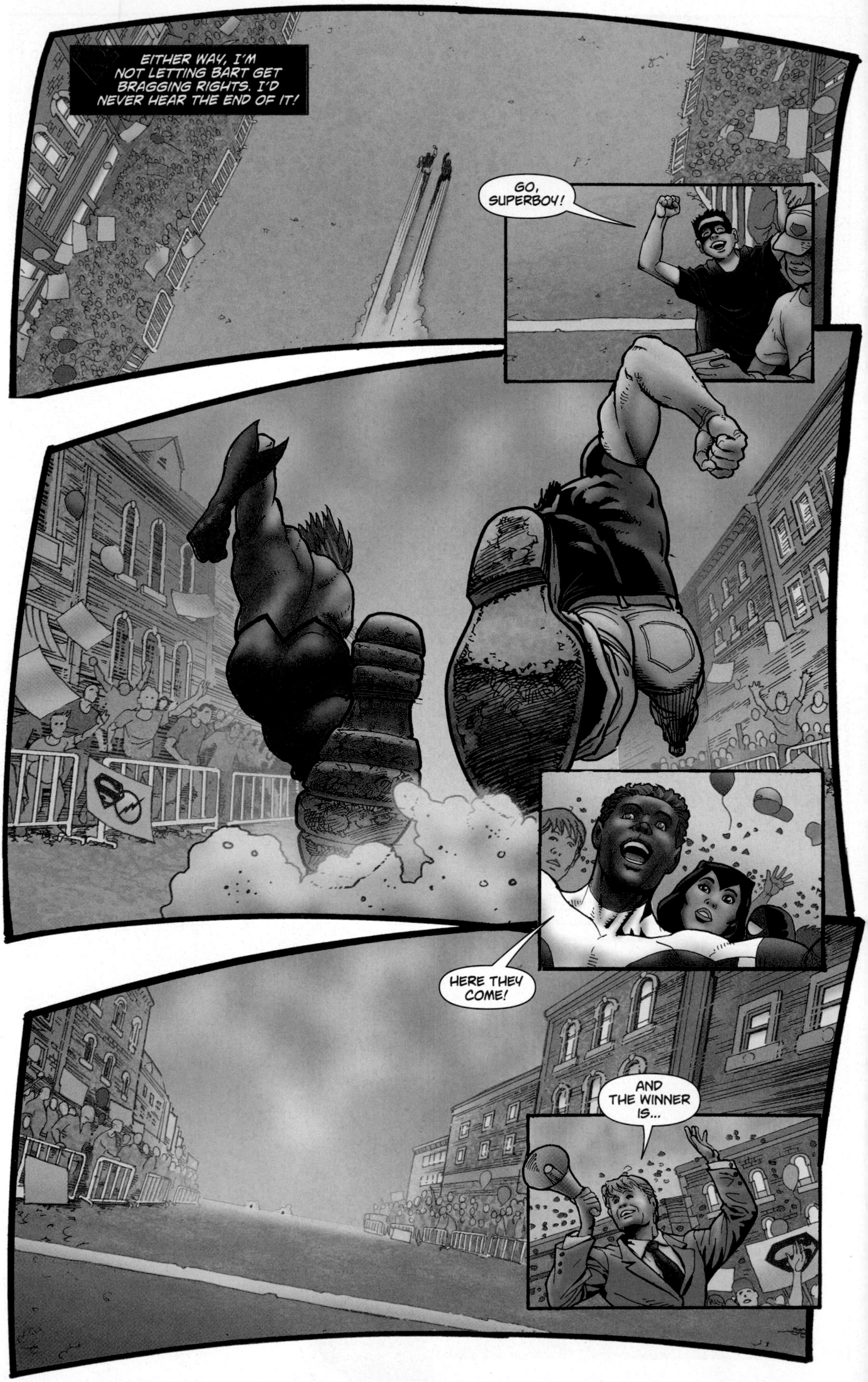
EITHER WAY, I'M NOT LETTING BART GET BRAGGING RIGHTS. I'D NEVER HEAR THE END OF IT!
GO, SUPERBOY!
HERE THEY COME!
AND THE WINNER IS...

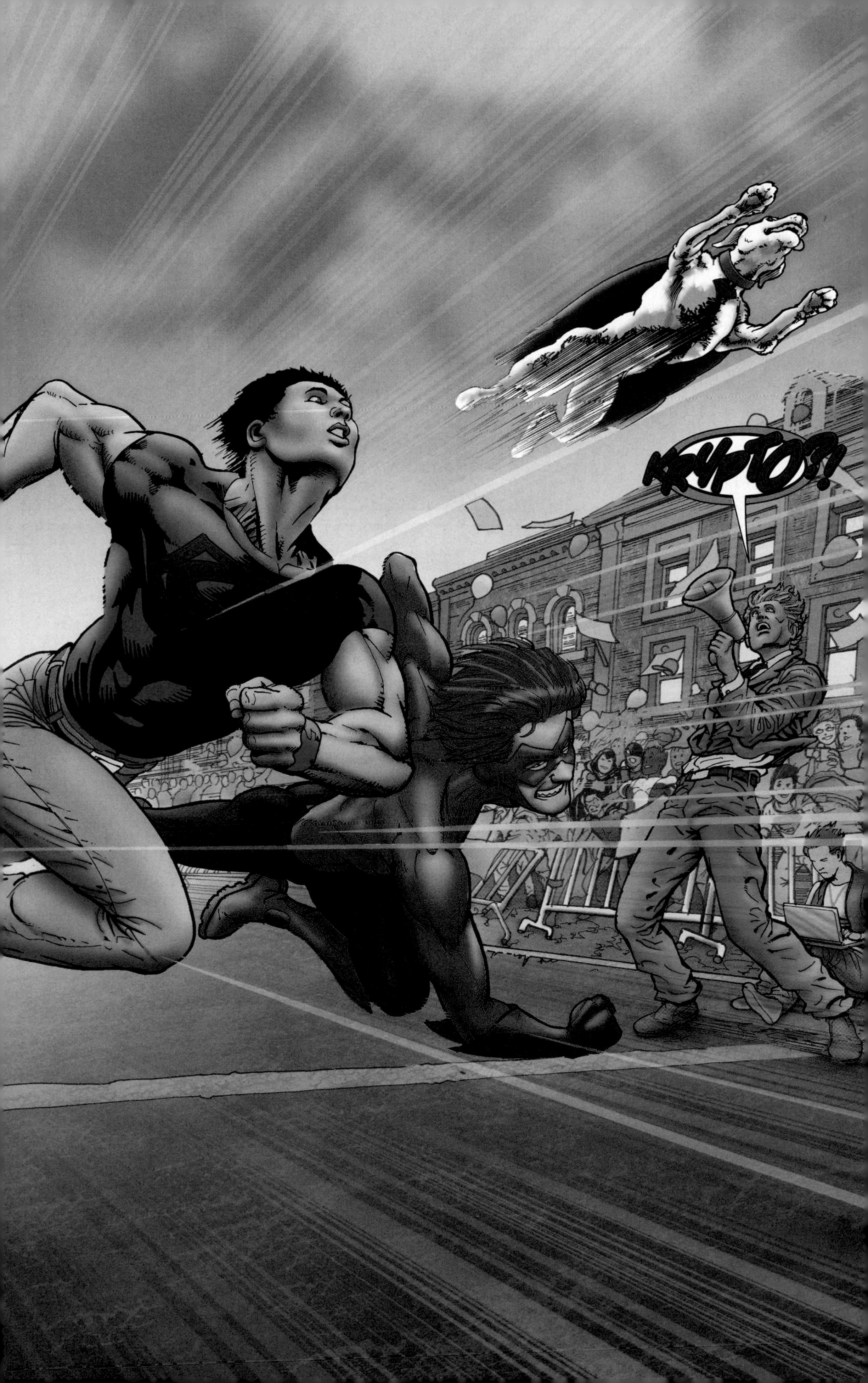
KRYPTO?!

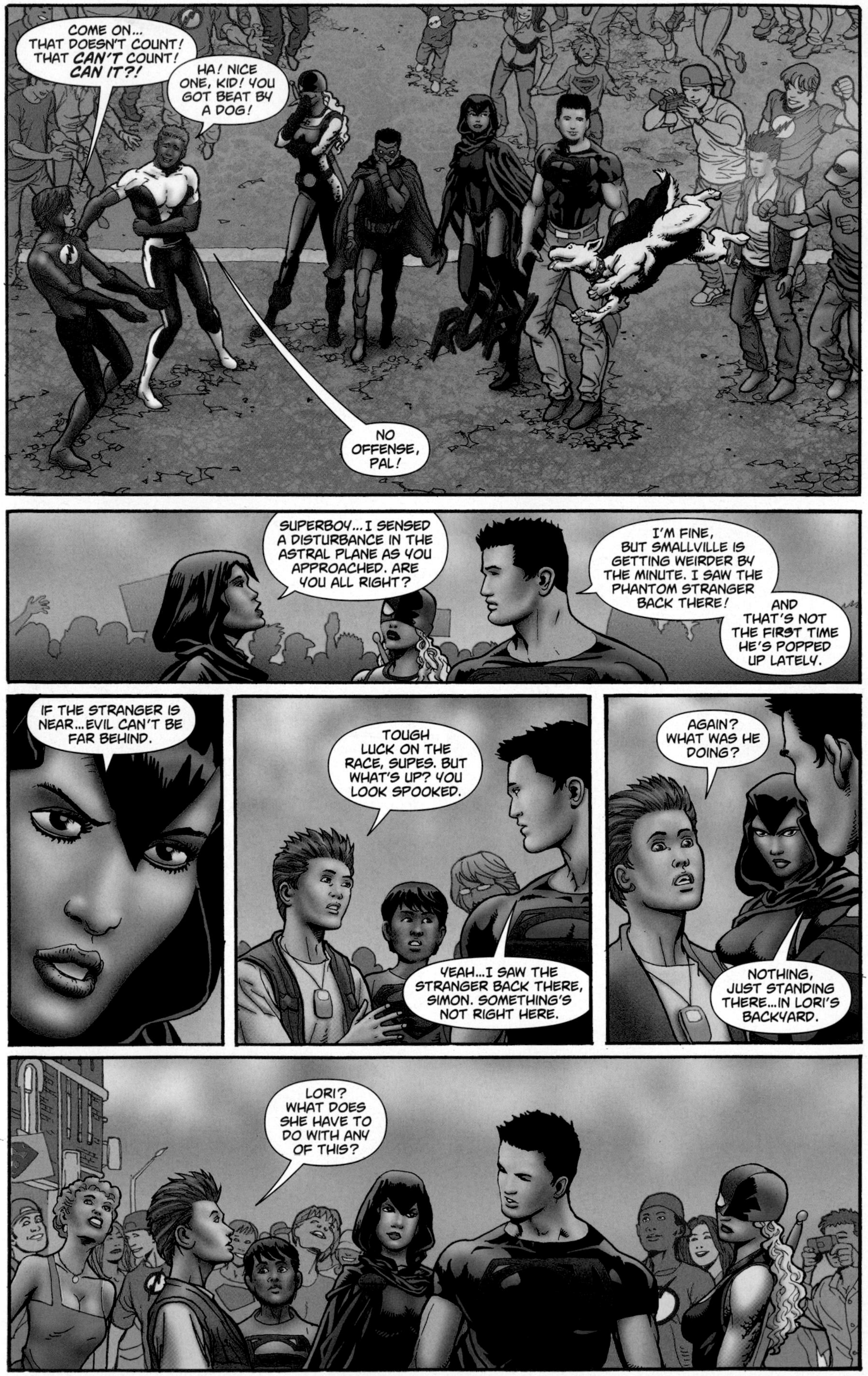
COME ON... THAT DOESN'T COUNT! THAT CAN'T COUNT! CAN IT?!
HA! NICE ONE, KID! YOU GOT BEAT BY A DOG!
NO OFFENSE, PAL!
SUPERBOY... I SENSED A DISTURBANCE IN THE ASTRAL PLANE AS YOU APPROACHED. ARE YOU ALL RIGHT?
I'M FINE, BUT SMALLVILLE IS GETTING WEIRDER BY THE MINUTE. I SAW THE PHANTOM STRANGER BACK THERE!
AND THAT'S NOT THE FIRST TIME HE'S POPPED UP LATELY.
IF THE STRANGER IS NEAR...EVIL CAN'T BE FAR BEHIND.
TOUGH LUCK ON THE RACE, SUPES. BUT WHAT'S UP? YOU LOOK SPOOKED.
YEAH...I SAW THE STRANGER BACK THERE, SIMON. SOMETHING'S NOT RIGHT HERE.
AGAIN? WHAT WAS HE DOING?
NOTHING, JUST STANDING THERE...IN LORI'S BACKYARD.
LORI? WHAT DOES SHE HAVE TO DO WITH ANY OF THIS?

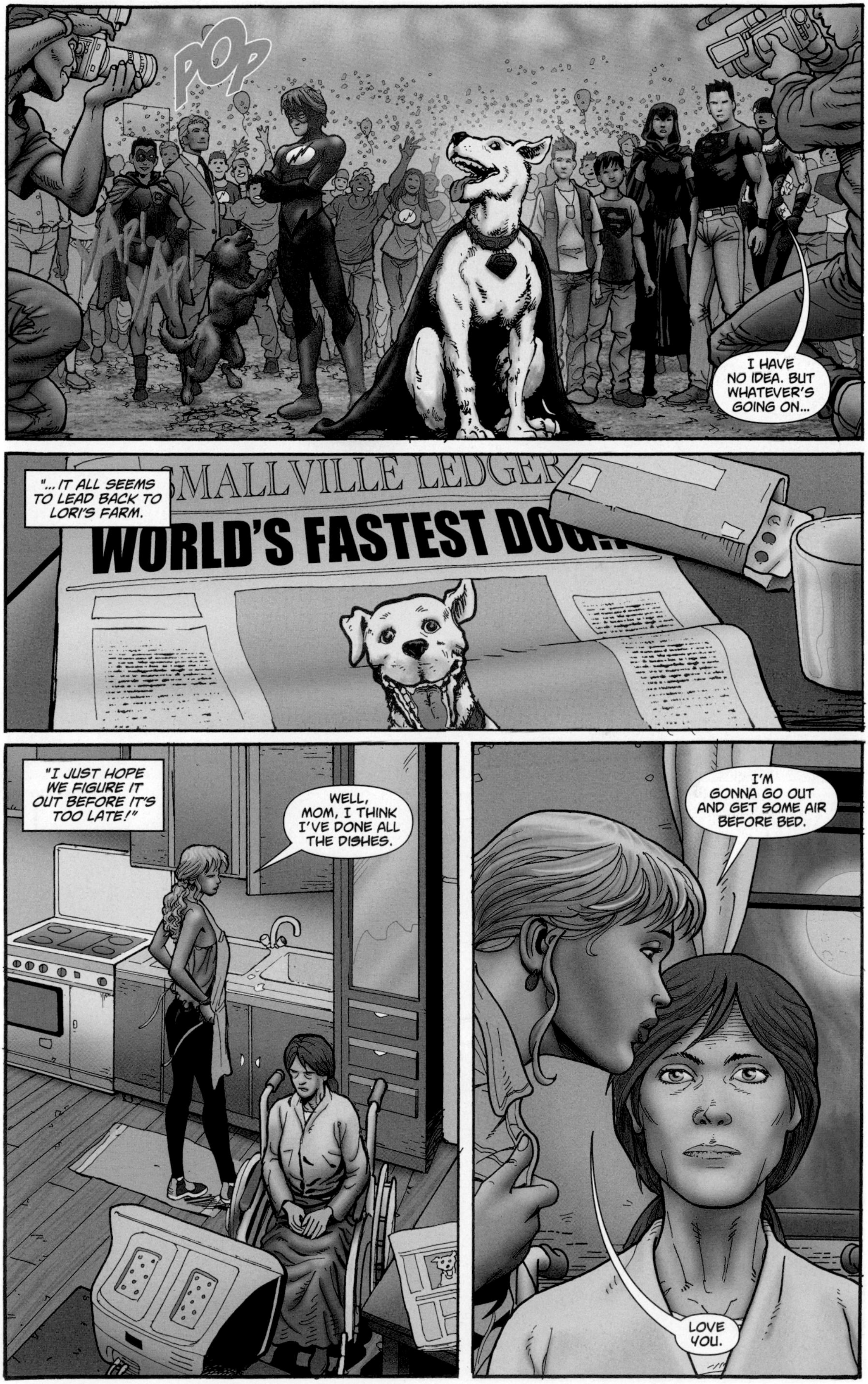
POP
YAP! YAP!
I HAVE NO IDEA. BUT WHATEVER'S GOING ON...
"...IT ALL SEEMS TO LEAD BACK TO LORI'S FARM.
SMALLVILLE LEDGER
WORLD'S FASTEST DOG!
"I JUST HOPE WE FIGURE IT OUT BEFORE IT'S TOO LATE!"
WELL, MOM, I THINK I'VE DONE ALL THE DISHES.
I'M GONNA GO OUT AND GET SOME AIR BEFORE BED.
LOVE YOU.

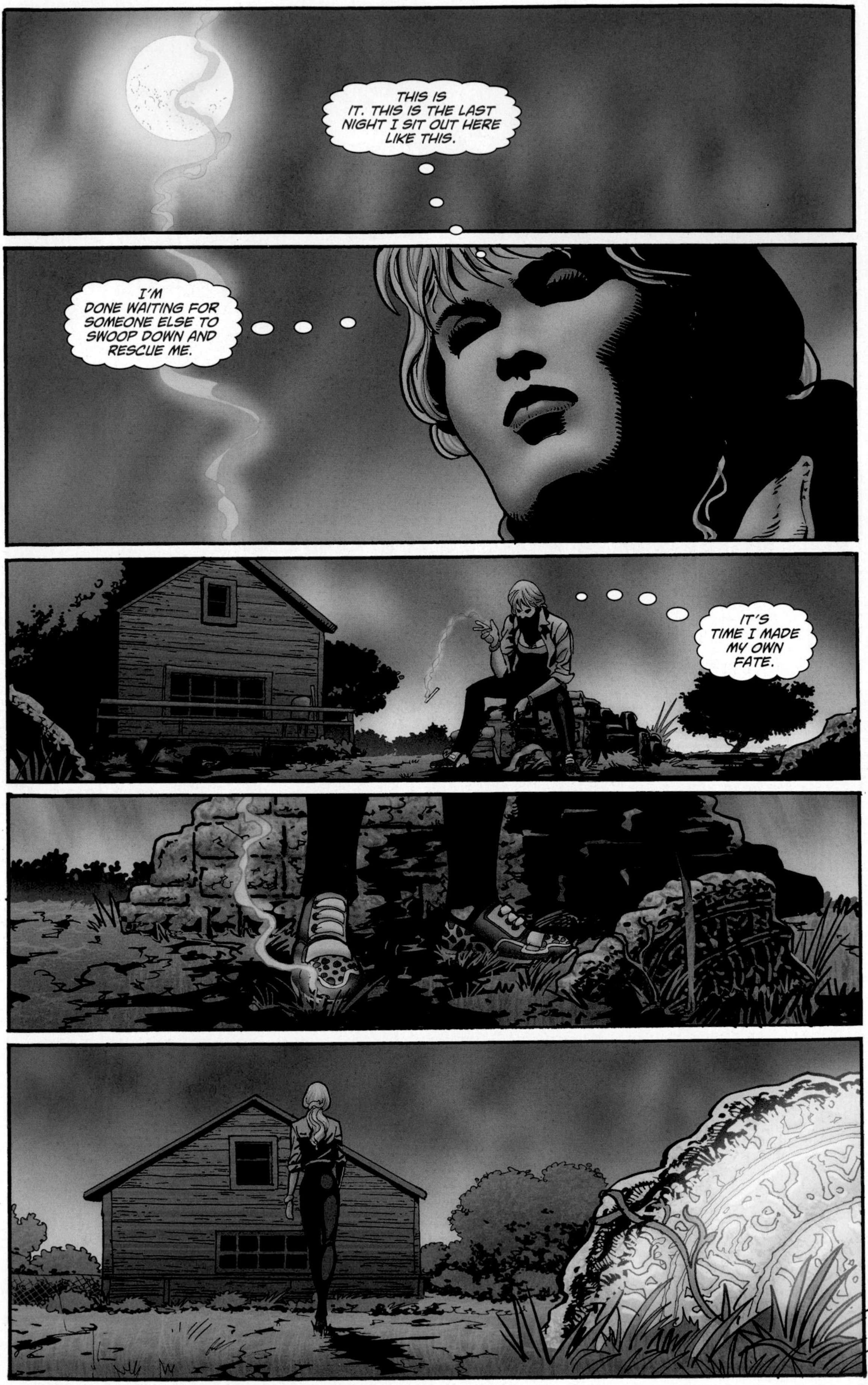
THIS IS IT. THIS IS THE LAST NIGHT I SIT OUT HERE LIKE THIS.
I'M DONE WAITING FOR SOMEONE ELSE TO SWOOP DOWN AND RESCUE ME.
IT'S TIME I MADE MY OWN FATE.

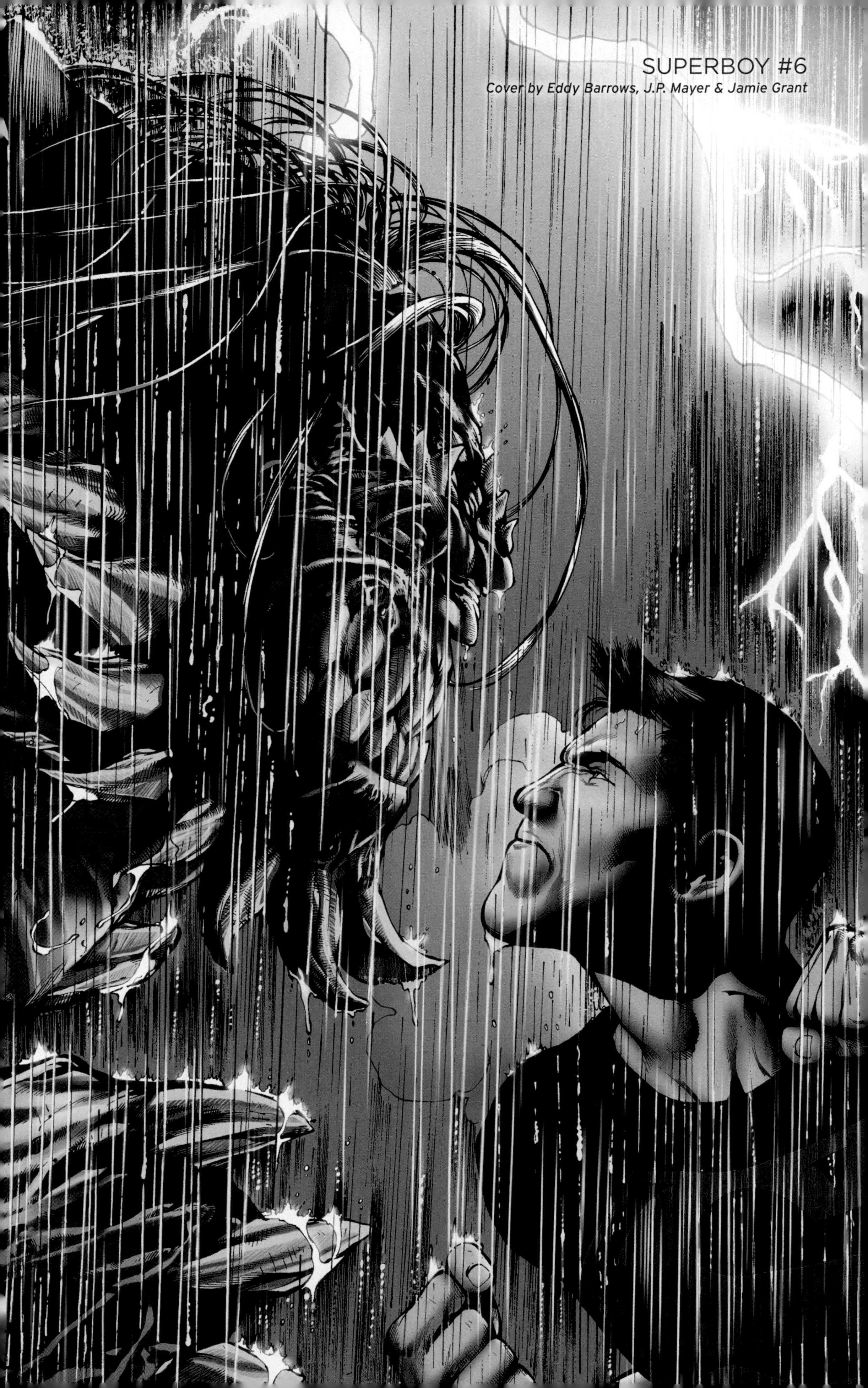
SUPERBOY #6
Cover by Eddy Barrows, J.P. Mayer & Jamie Grant

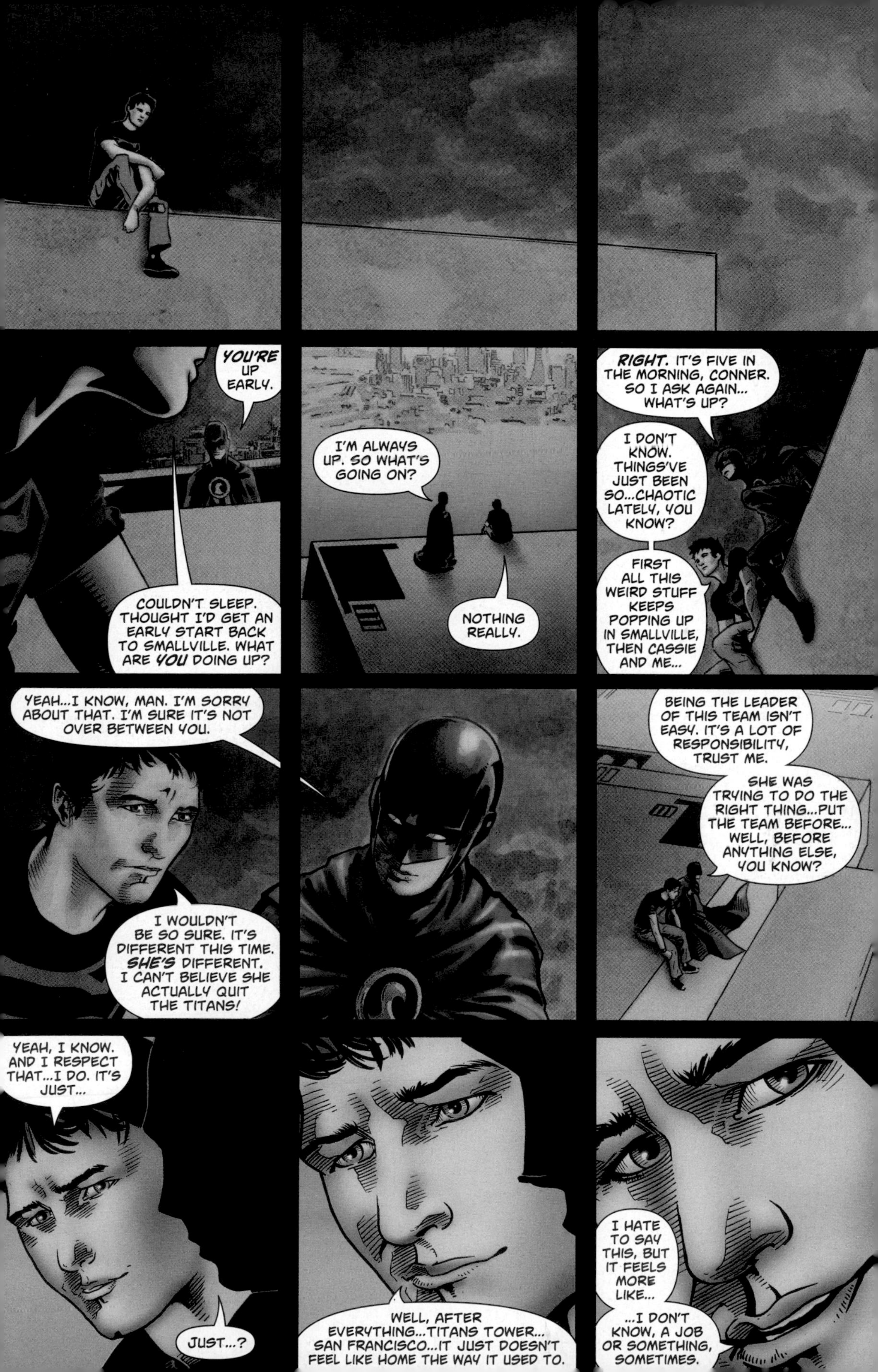
YOU'RE UP EARLY.
COULDN'T SLEEP. THOUGHT I'D GET AN EARLY START BACK TO SMALLVILLE. WHAT ARE YOU DOING UP?
I'M ALWAYS UP. SO WHAT'S GOING ON?
NOTHING REALLY.
RIGHT. IT'S FIVE IN THE MORNING, CONNER. SO I ASK AGAIN... WHAT'S UP?
I DON'T KNOW. THINGS'VE JUST BEEN SO...CHAOTIC LATELY, YOU KNOW?
FIRST ALL THIS WEIRD STUFF KEEPS POPPING UP IN SMALLVILLE, THEN CASSIE AND ME...
YEAH...I KNOW, MAN. I'M SORRY ABOUT THAT. I'M SURE IT'S NOT OVER BETWEEN YOU.
I WOULDN'T BE SO SURE. IT'S DIFFERENT THIS TIME. SHE'S DIFFERENT. I CAN'T BELIEVE SHE ACTUALLY QUIT THE TITANS!
BEING THE LEADER OF THIS TEAM ISN'T EASY. IT'S A LOT OF RESPONSIBILITY, TRUST ME.
SHE WAS TRYING TO DO THE RIGHT THING...PUT THE TEAM BEFORE... WELL, BEFORE ANYTHING ELSE, YOU KNOW?
YEAH, I KNOW. AND I RESPECT THAT...I DO. IT'S JUST...
JUST...?
WELL, AFTER EVERYTHING...TITANS TOWER... SAN FRANCISCO...IT JUST DOESN'T FEEL LIKE HOME THE WAY IT USED TO.
I HATE TO SAY THIS, BUT IT FEELS MORE LIKE...
...I DON'T KNOW, A JOB OR SOMETHING, SOMETIMES.

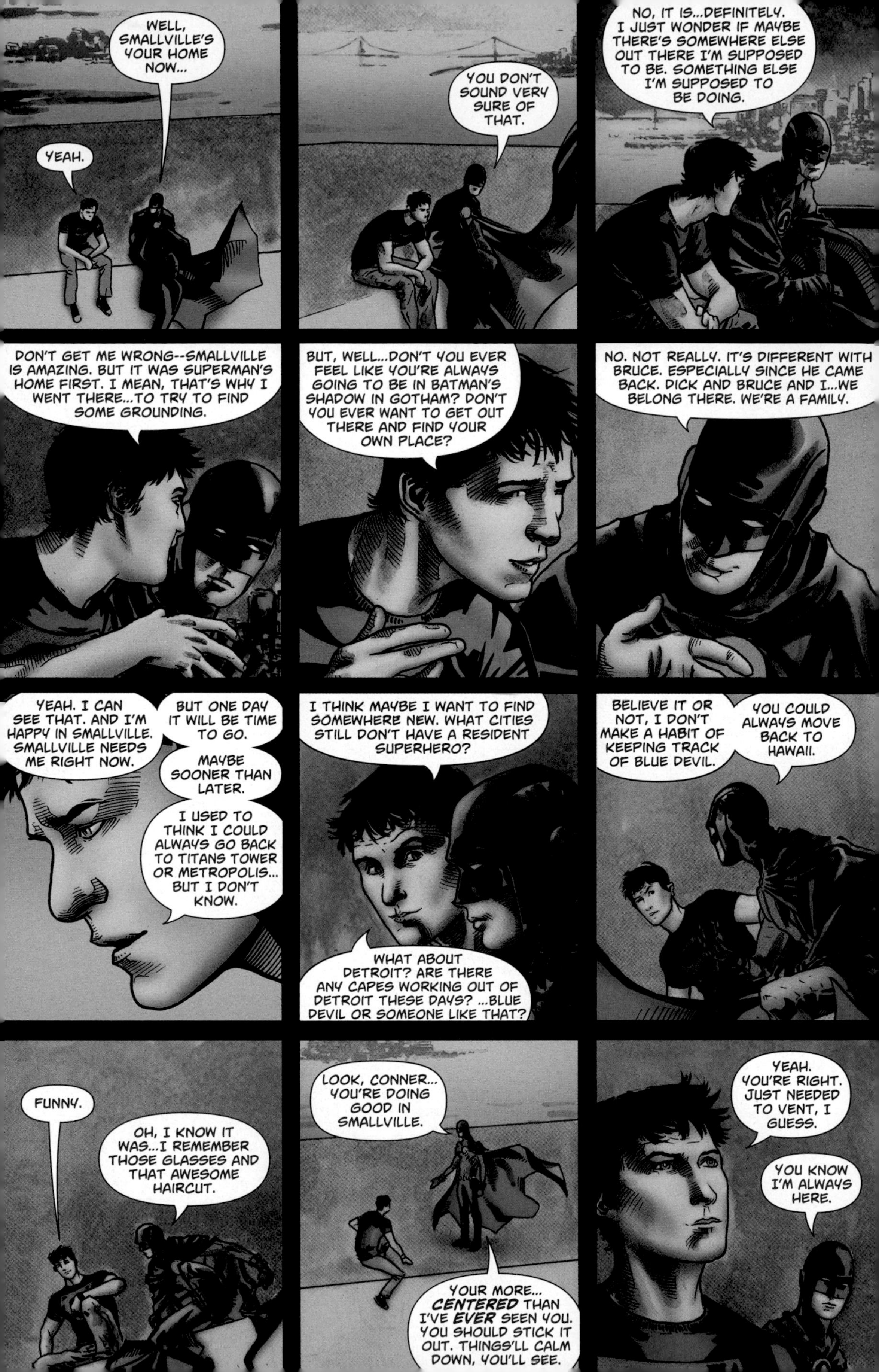
WELL, SMALLVILLE'S YOUR HOME NOW...
YEAH.
YOU DON'T SOUND VERY SURE OF THAT.
NO, IT IS...DEFINITELY. I JUST WONDER IF MAYBE THERE'S SOMEWHERE ELSE OUT THERE I'M SUPPOSED TO BE. SOMETHING ELSE I'M SUPPOSED TO BE DOING.
DON'T GET ME WRONG--SMALLVILLE IS AMAZING. BUT IT WAS SUPERMAN'S HOME FIRST. I MEAN, THAT'S WHY I WENT THERE...TO TRY TO FIND SOME GROUNDING.
BUT, WELL...DON'T YOU EVER FEEL LIKE YOU'RE ALWAYS GOING TO BE IN BATMAN'S SHADOW IN GOTHAM? DON'T YOU EVER WANT TO GET OUT THERE AND FIND YOUR OWN PLACE?
NO. NOT REALLY. IT'S DIFFERENT WITH BRUCE. ESPECIALLY SINCE HE CAME BACK. DICK AND BRUCE AND I...WE BELONG THERE. WE'RE A FAMILY.
YEAH. I CAN SEE THAT. AND I'M HAPPY IN SMALLVILLE. SMALLVILLE NEEDS ME RIGHT NOW.
BUT ONE DAY IT WILL BE TIME TO GO.
MAYBE SOONER THAN LATER.
I USED TO THINK I COULD ALWAYS GO BACK TO TITANS TOWER OR METROPOLIS... BUT I DON'T KNOW.
I THINK MAYBE I WANT TO FIND SOMEWHERE NEW. WHAT CITIES STILL DON'T HAVE A RESIDENT SUPERHERO?
WHAT ABOUT DETROIT? ARE THERE ANY CAPES WORKING OUT OF DETROIT THESE DAYS? ...BLUE DEVIL OR SOMEONE LIKE THAT?
BELIEVE IT OR NOT, I DON'T MAKE A HABIT OF KEEPING TRACK OF BLUE DEVIL.
YOU COULD ALWAYS MOVE BACK TO HAWAII.
FUNNY.
OH, I KNOW IT WAS...I REMEMBER THOSE GLASSES AND THAT AWESOME HAIRCUT.
LOOK, CONNER... YOU'RE DOING GOOD IN SMALLVILLE.
YOUR MORE... CENTERED THAN I'VE EVER SEEN YOU. YOU SHOULD STICK IT OUT. THINGS'LL CALM DOWN, YOU'LL SEE.
YEAH. YOU'RE RIGHT. JUST NEEDED TO VENT, I GUESS.
YOU KNOW I'M ALWAYS HERE.

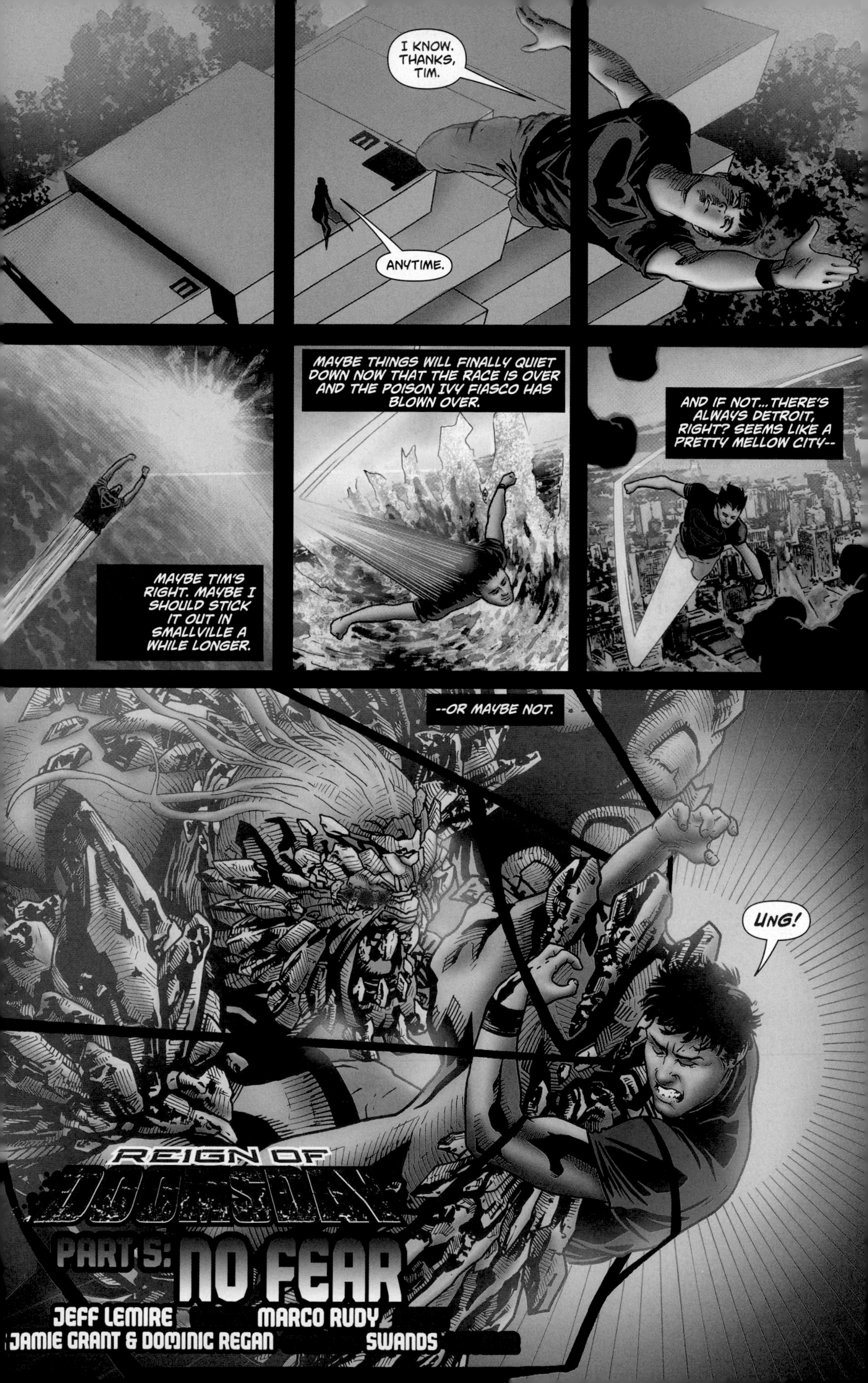
I KNOW. THANKS, TIM.
ANYTIME.
MAYBE TIM'S RIGHT. MAYBE I SHOULD STICK IT OUT IN SMALLVILLE A WHILE LONGER.
MAYBE THINGS WILL FINALLY QUIET DOWN NOW THAT THE RACE IS OVER AND THE POISON IVY FIASCO HAS BLOWN OVER.
AND IF NOT...THERE'S ALWAYS DETROIT, RIGHT? SEEMS LIKE A PRETTY MELLOW CITY--
--OR MAYBE NOT.
UNG!
REIGN OF DOOMSDAY
PART 5: NO FEAR
JEFF LEMIRE [redacted] MARCO RUDY [redacted]
JAMIE GRANT & DOMINIC REGAN [redacted] SWANDS [redacted]

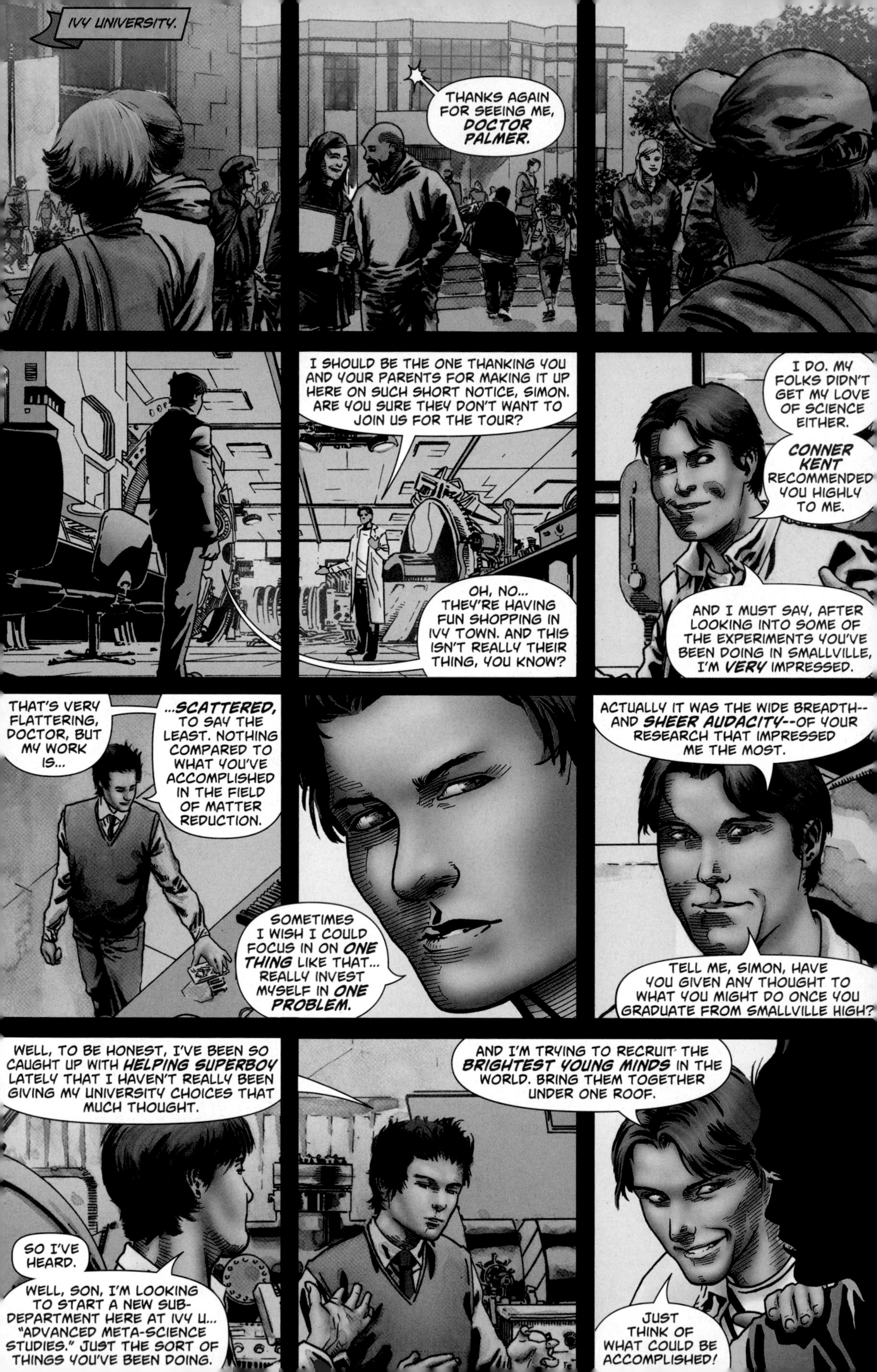
IVY UNIVERSITY.
THANKS AGAIN FOR SEEING ME, DOCTOR PALMER.
I SHOULD BE THE ONE THANKING YOU AND YOUR PARENTS FOR MAKING IT UP HERE ON SUCH SHORT NOTICE, SIMON. ARE YOU SURE THEY DON'T WANT TO JOIN US FOR THE TOUR?
OH, NO... THEY'RE HAVING FUN SHOPPING IN IVY TOWN. AND THIS ISN'T REALLY THEIR THING, YOU KNOW?
I DO. MY FOLKS DIDN'T GET MY LOVE OF SCIENCE EITHER.
CONNER KENT RECOMMENDED YOU HIGHLY TO ME.
AND I MUST SAY, AFTER LOOKING INTO SOME OF THE EXPERIMENTS YOU'VE BEEN DOING IN SMALLVILLE, I'M VERY IMPRESSED.
THAT'S VERY FLATTERING, DOCTOR, BUT MY WORK IS...
...SCATTERED, TO SAY THE LEAST. NOTHING COMPARED TO WHAT YOU'VE ACCOMPLISHED IN THE FIELD OF MATTER REDUCTION.
SOMETIMES I WISH I COULD FOCUS IN ON ONE THING LIKE THAT... REALLY INVEST MYSELF IN ONE PROBLEM.
ACTUALLY IT WAS THE WIDE BREADTH--AND SHEER AUDACITY--OF YOUR RESEARCH THAT IMPRESSED ME THE MOST.
TELL ME, SIMON, HAVE YOU GIVEN ANY THOUGHT TO WHAT YOU MIGHT DO ONCE YOU GRADUATE FROM SMALLVILLE HIGH?
WELL, TO BE HONEST, I'VE BEEN SO CAUGHT UP WITH HELPING SUPERBOY LATELY THAT I HAVEN'T REALLY BEEN GIVING MY UNIVERSITY CHOICES THAT MUCH THOUGHT.
SO I'VE HEARD.
WELL, SON, I'M LOOKING TO START A NEW SUB-DEPARTMENT HERE AT IVY U... "ADVANCED META-SCIENCE STUDIES." JUST THE SORT OF THINGS YOU'VE BEEN DOING.
AND I'M TRYING TO RECRUIT THE BRIGHTEST YOUNG MINDS IN THE WORLD. BRING THEM TOGETHER UNDER ONE ROOF.
JUST THINK OF WHAT COULD BE ACCOMPLISHED!

WELL, TO BE FRANK, DOCTOR PALMER...

I'VE ALWAYS PREFERRED TO *WORK ALONE.*

MOST PEOPLE LIKE US DO, SIMON. BUT EVEN THE MOST BRILLIANT MINDS NEED GUIDANCE...STRUCTURE. YOU MIGHT EVEN FIND IT WILL HELP GIVE YOU THE FOCUS YOU TALKED ABOUT.

I WON'T LIE TO YOU--ONE REASON I'M GATHERING YOUNG PEOPLE LIKE YOU IS TO TRY TO HELP KEEP THEM ON THE *RIGHT PATH.*

WE LIVE IN A *DANGEROUS WORLD*...WITH *DANGEROUS PEOPLE* LOOKING TO EXPLOIT GIFTED MINDS LIKE YOURS.

I CAN APPRECIATE THAT, DOCTOR PALMER. I JUST CAN'T HELP BUT FEEL THAT...

...WELL, THIS MIGHT SOUND STRANGE TO YOU, BUT I'VE ALWAYS KIND OF FELT LIKE I HAVE *SOMETHING* PULLING ME ALONG. A *GREATER DESTINY,* OR SOMETHING.

I KNOW THAT'S NOT A VERY *SCIENTIFIC* THING TO SAY. YOU MUST THINK I SOUND, I DON'T KNOW...FOOLISH.

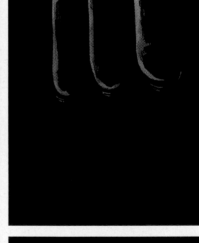

NOT AT ALL. JUST PROMISE ME YOU'LL CONSIDER MY OFFER. THERE WILL ALWAYS BE A PLACE FOR YOU HERE.

THIS IS MY DIRECT LINE. YOU CAN CALL ME ANY-TIME. *ANYTIME.*

I WILL, THANK YOU.

NOW...LET'S GO TOUR THE REST OF THE LAB. I THINK YOU'LL GET A KICK OUT OF MY NEW *NANO-VAPOR* PROTOTYPES.

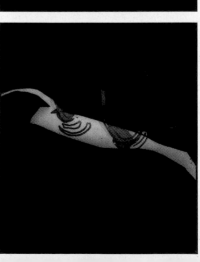

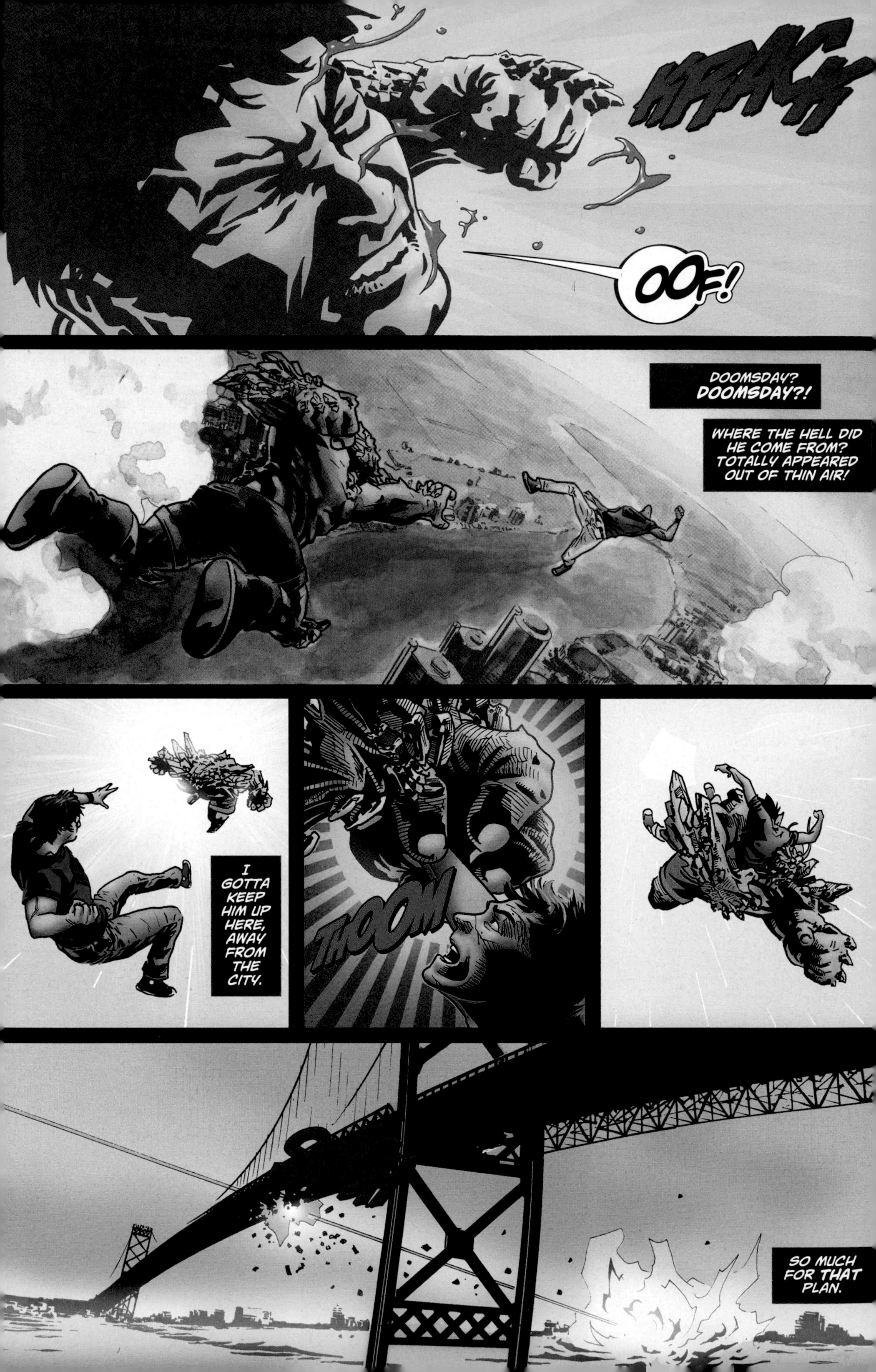
KRAKK
OOF!
DOOMSDAY? DOOMSDAY?!
WHERE THE HELL DID HE COME FROM? TOTALLY APPEARED OUT OF THIN AIR!
I GOTTA KEEP HIM UP HERE, AWAY FROM THE CITY.
THOOM
SO MUCH FOR THAT PLAN.

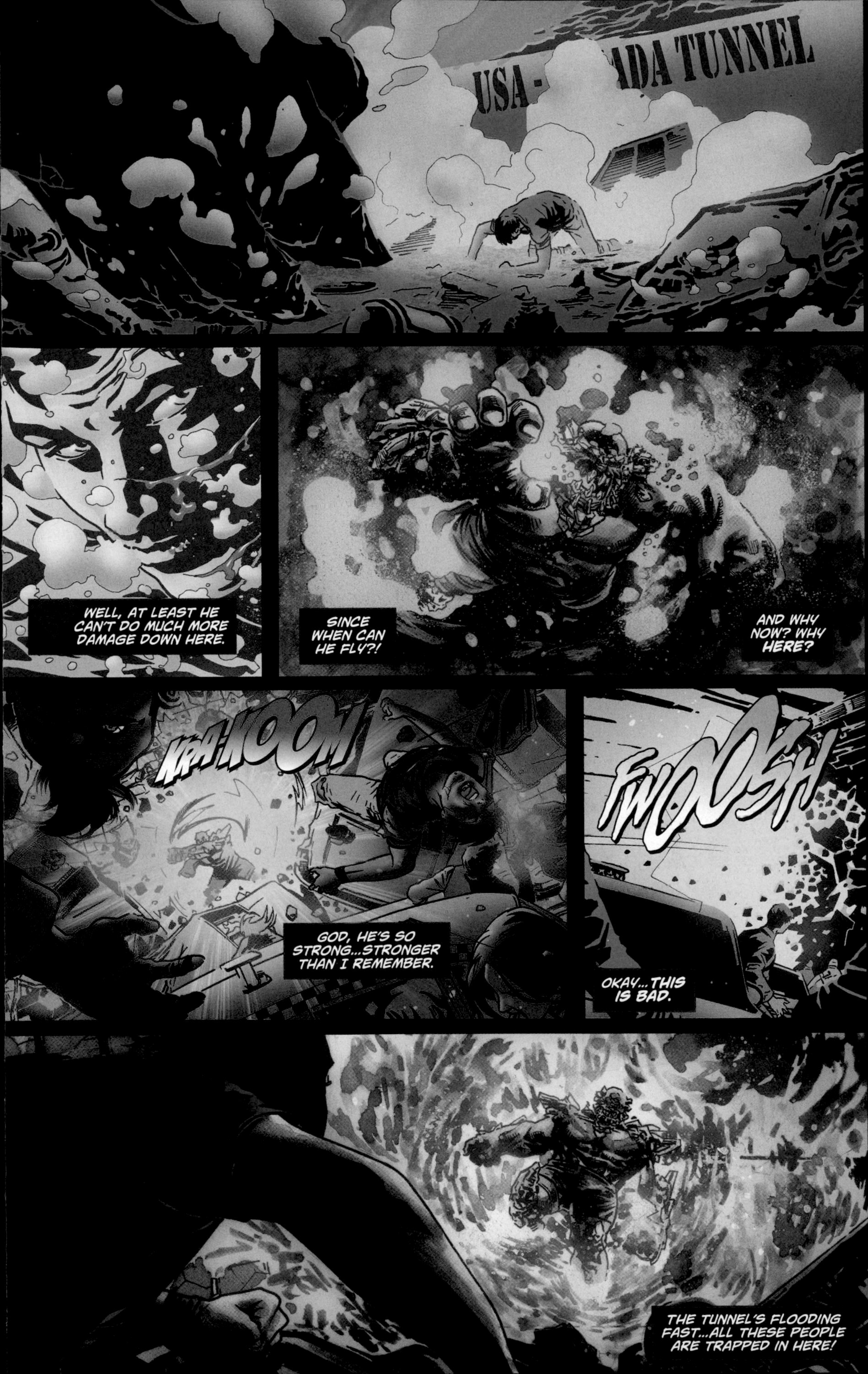
USA - ADA TUNNEL
WELL, AT LEAST HE CAN'T DO MUCH MORE DAMAGE DOWN HERE.
SINCE WHEN CAN HE FLY?!
AND WHY NOW? WHY HERE?
KRA-KOOM
GOD, HE'S SO STRONG...STRONGER THAN I REMEMBER.
FWOOSH
OKAY...THIS IS BAD.
THE TUNNEL'S FLOODING FAST...ALL THESE PEOPLE ARE TRAPPED IN HERE!

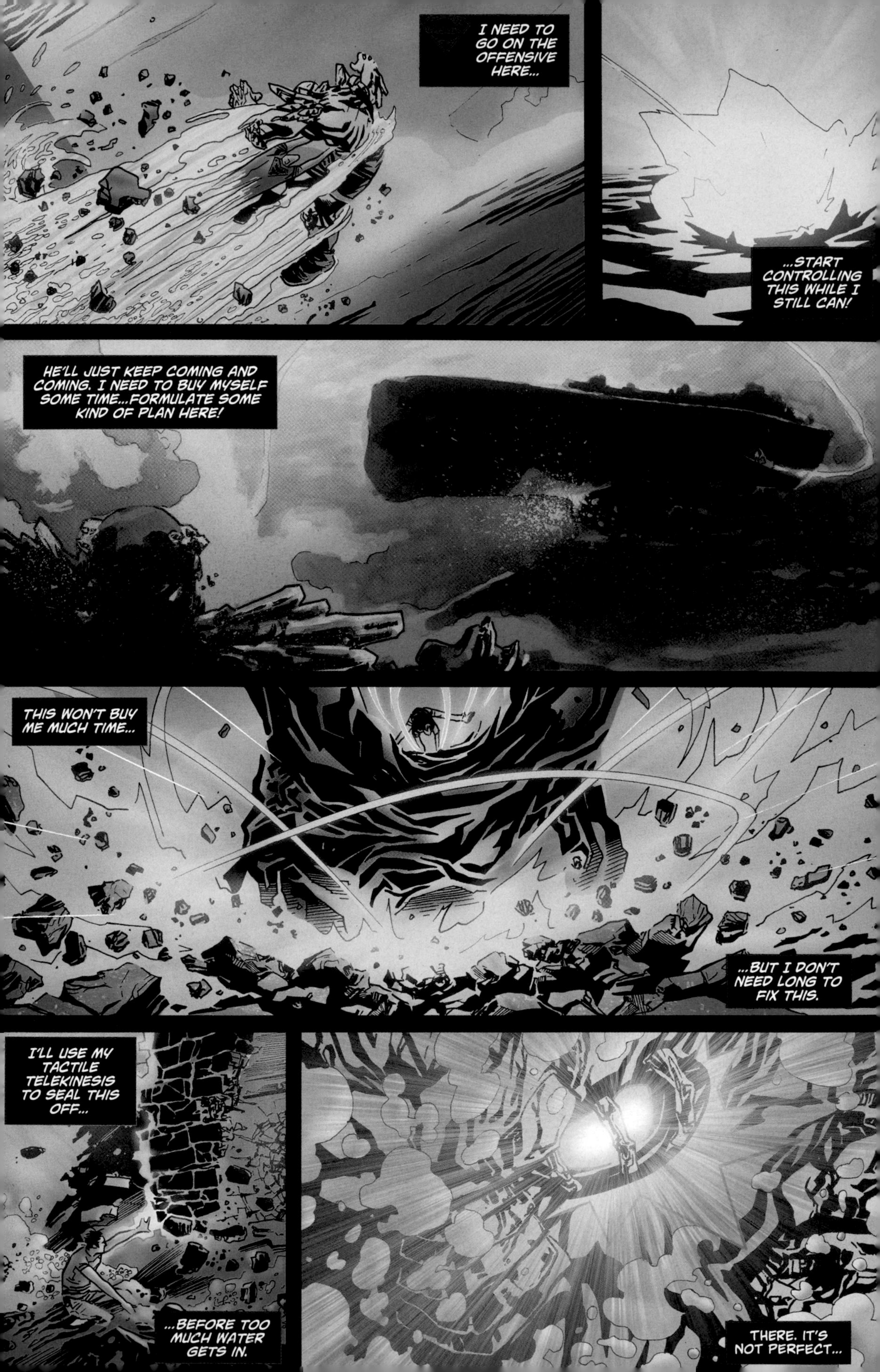
I NEED TO GO ON THE OFFENSIVE HERE...
...START CONTROLLING THIS WHILE I STILL CAN!
HE'LL JUST KEEP COMING AND COMING. I NEED TO BUY MYSELF SOME TIME...FORMULATE SOME KIND OF PLAN HERE!
THIS WON'T BUY ME MUCH TIME...
...BUT I DON'T NEED LONG TO FIX THIS.
I'LL USE MY TACTILE TELEKINESIS TO SEAL THIS OFF...
...BEFORE TOO MUCH WATER GETS IN.
THERE. IT'S NOT PERFECT...

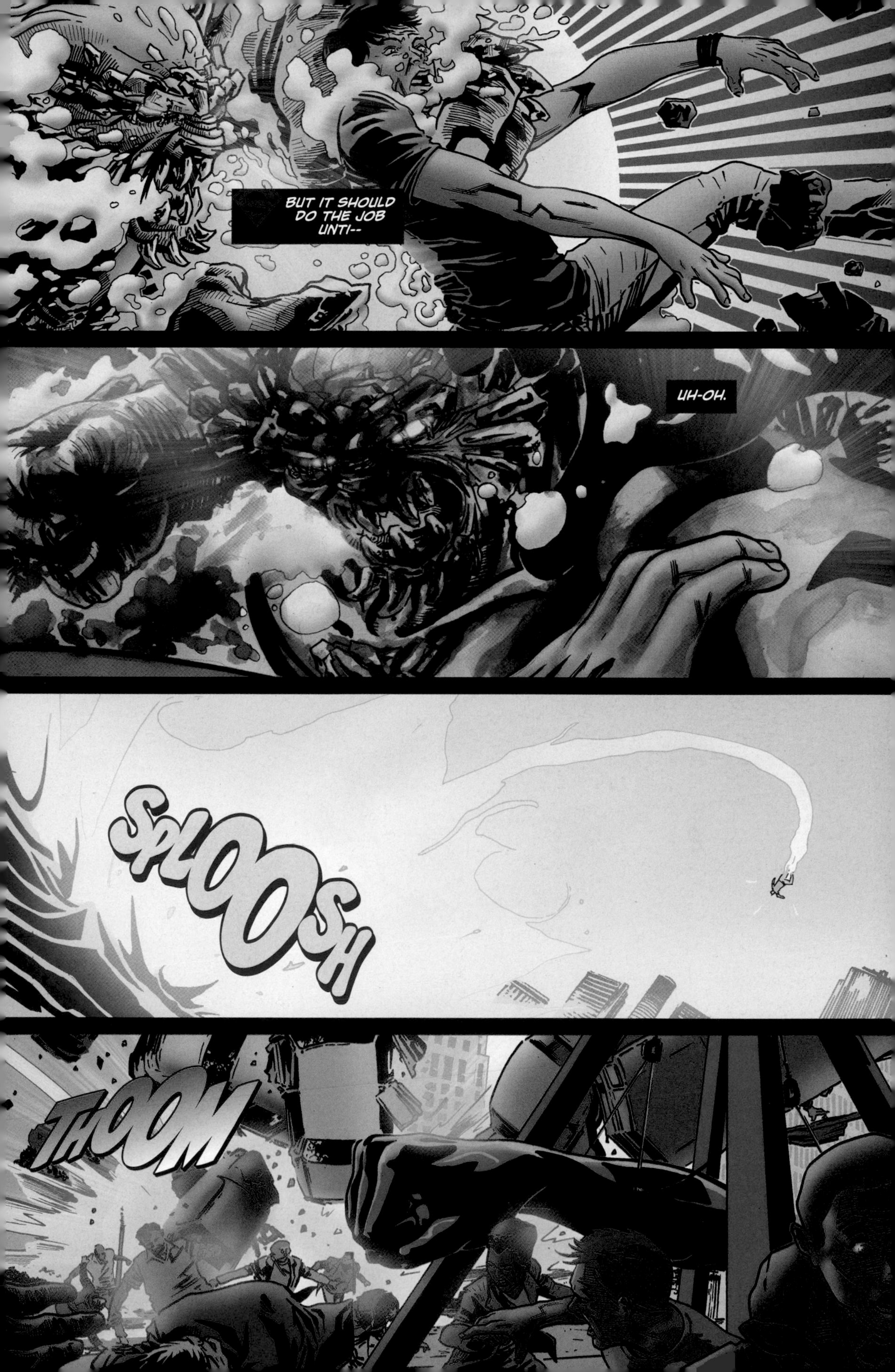
BUT IT SHOULD DO THE JOB UNTI--
UH-OH.
SPLOOSH
THOOM

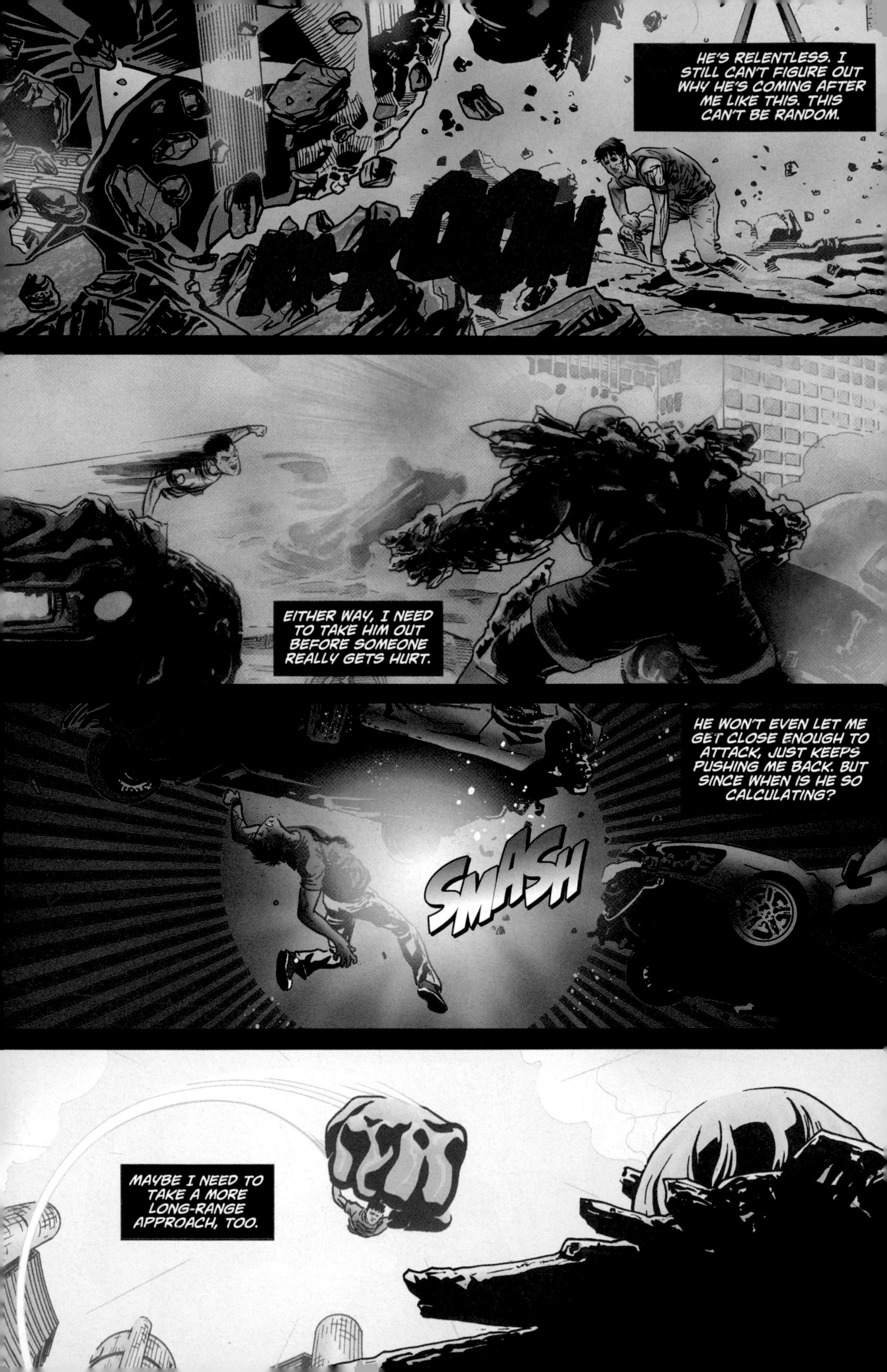
HE'S RELENTLESS. I STILL CAN'T FIGURE OUT WHY HE'S COMING AFTER ME LIKE THIS. THIS CAN'T BE RANDOM.
EITHER WAY, I NEED TO TAKE HIM OUT BEFORE SOMEONE REALLY GETS HURT.
HE WON'T EVEN LET ME GET CLOSE ENOUGH TO ATTACK, JUST KEEPS PUSHING ME BACK. BUT SINCE WHEN IS HE SO CALCULATING?
SMASH
MAYBE I NEED TO TAKE A MORE LONG-RANGE APPROACH, TOO.

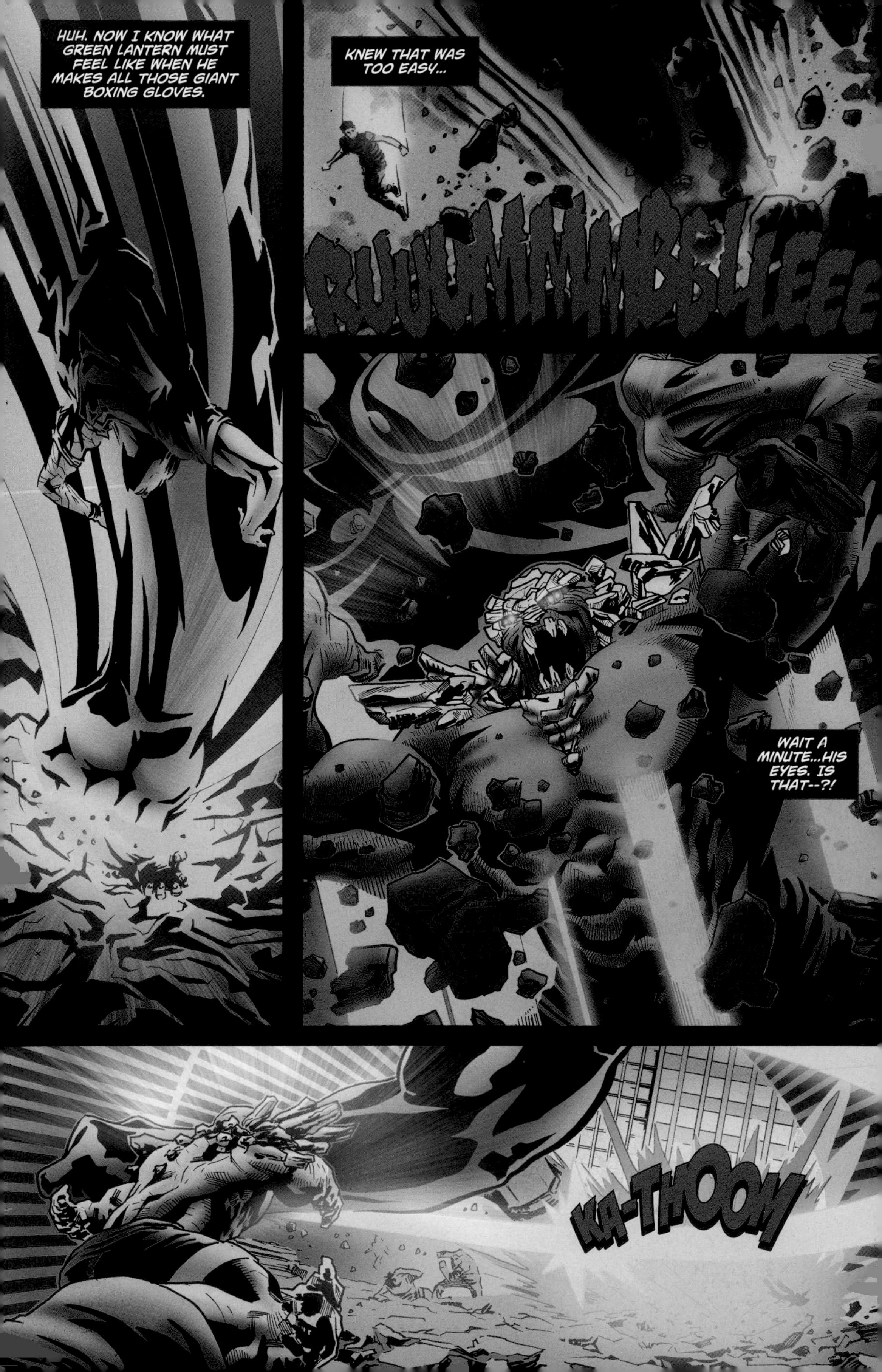

HUH. NOW I KNOW WHAT GREEN LANTERN MUST FEEL LIKE WHEN HE MAKES ALL THOSE GIANT BOXING GLOVES.
KNEW THAT WAS TOO EASY...
RUUUMMMMBBLLEEE
WAIT A MINUTE...HIS EYES. IS THAT--?!
KA-THOOM

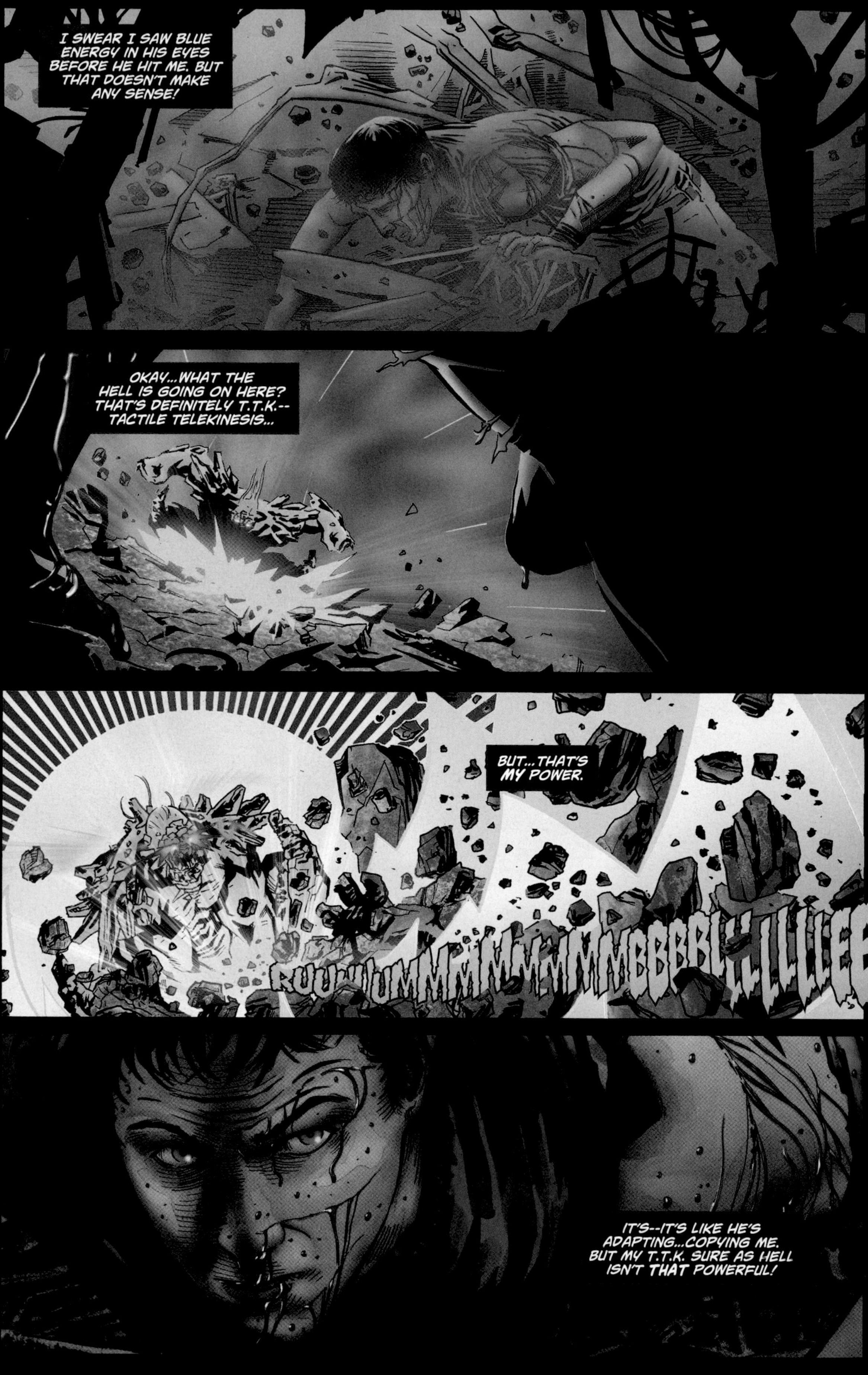
I SWEAR I SAW BLUE ENERGY IN HIS EYES BEFORE HE HIT ME. BUT THAT DOESN'T MAKE ANY SENSE!
OKAY...WHAT THE HELL IS GOING ON HERE? THAT'S DEFINITELY T.T.K.-- TACTILE TELEKINESIS...
BUT...THAT'S MY POWER.
IT'S--IT'S LIKE HE'S ADAPTING...COPYING ME. BUT MY T.T.K. SURE AS HELL ISN'T THAT POWERFUL!

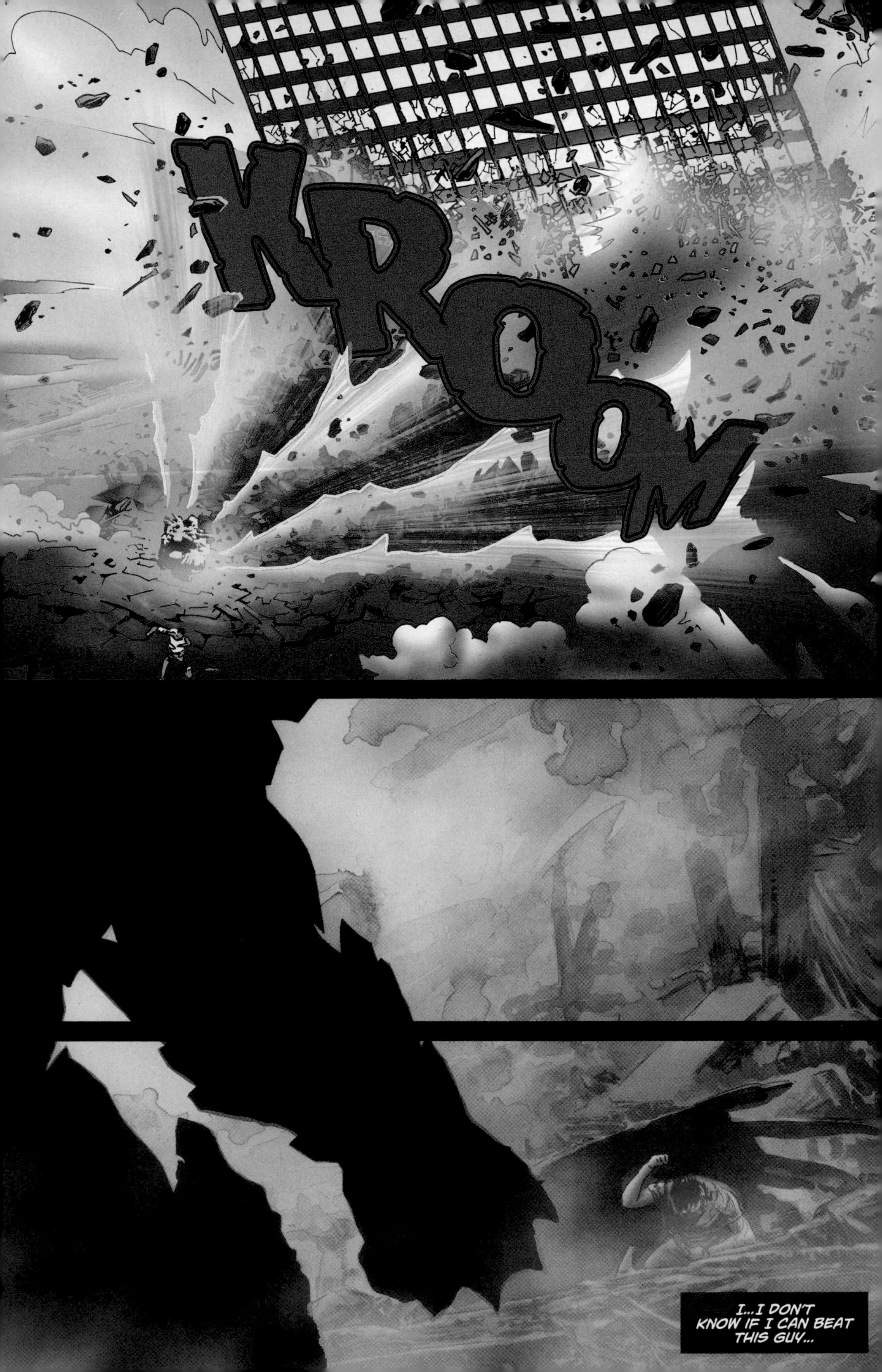
KROOOM
I...I DON'T KNOW IF I CAN BEAT THIS GUY...

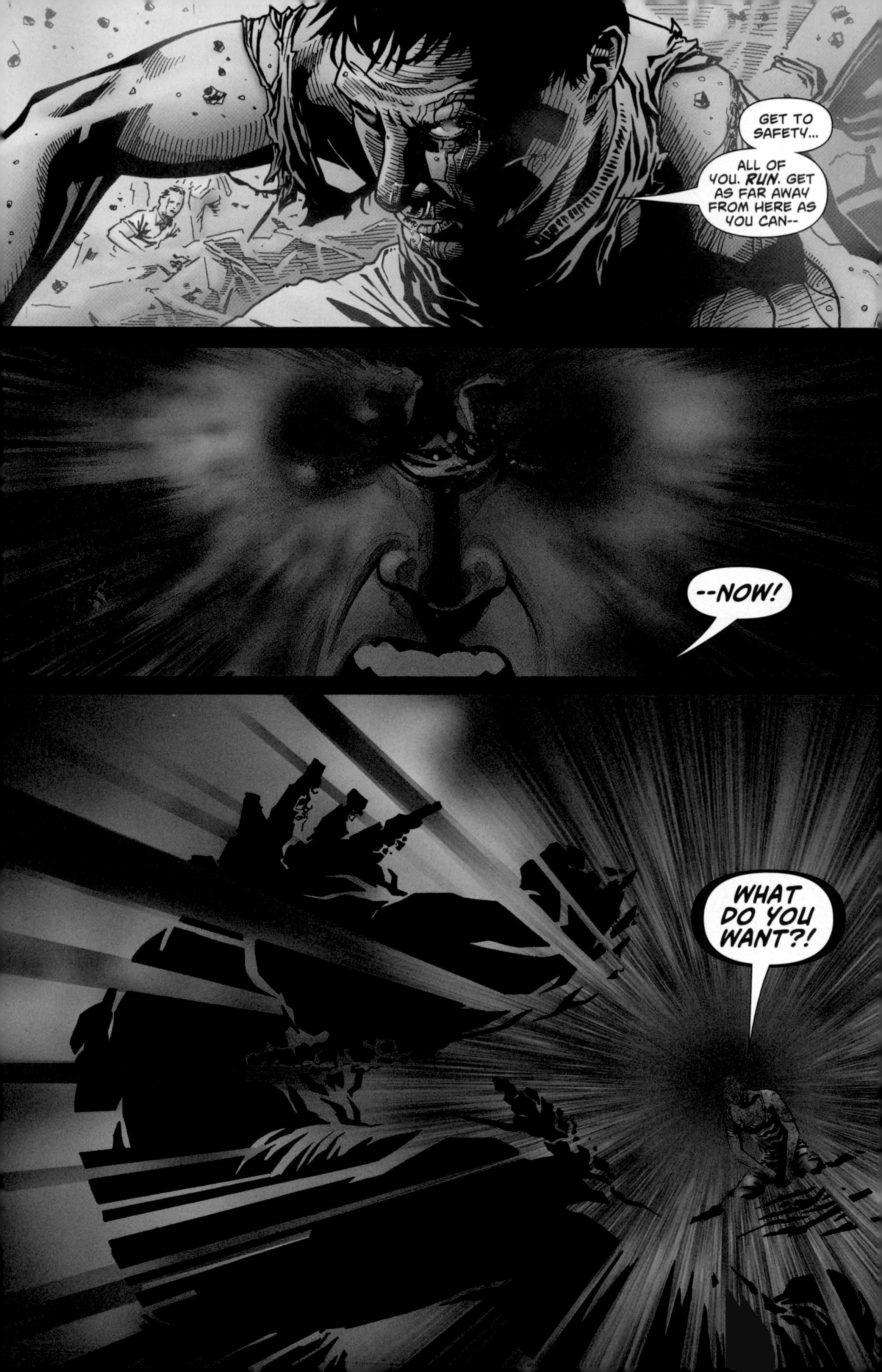
GET TO SAFETY...
ALL OF YOU. RUN. GET AS FAR AWAY FROM HERE AS YOU CAN--
--NOW!
WHAT DO YOU WANT?!

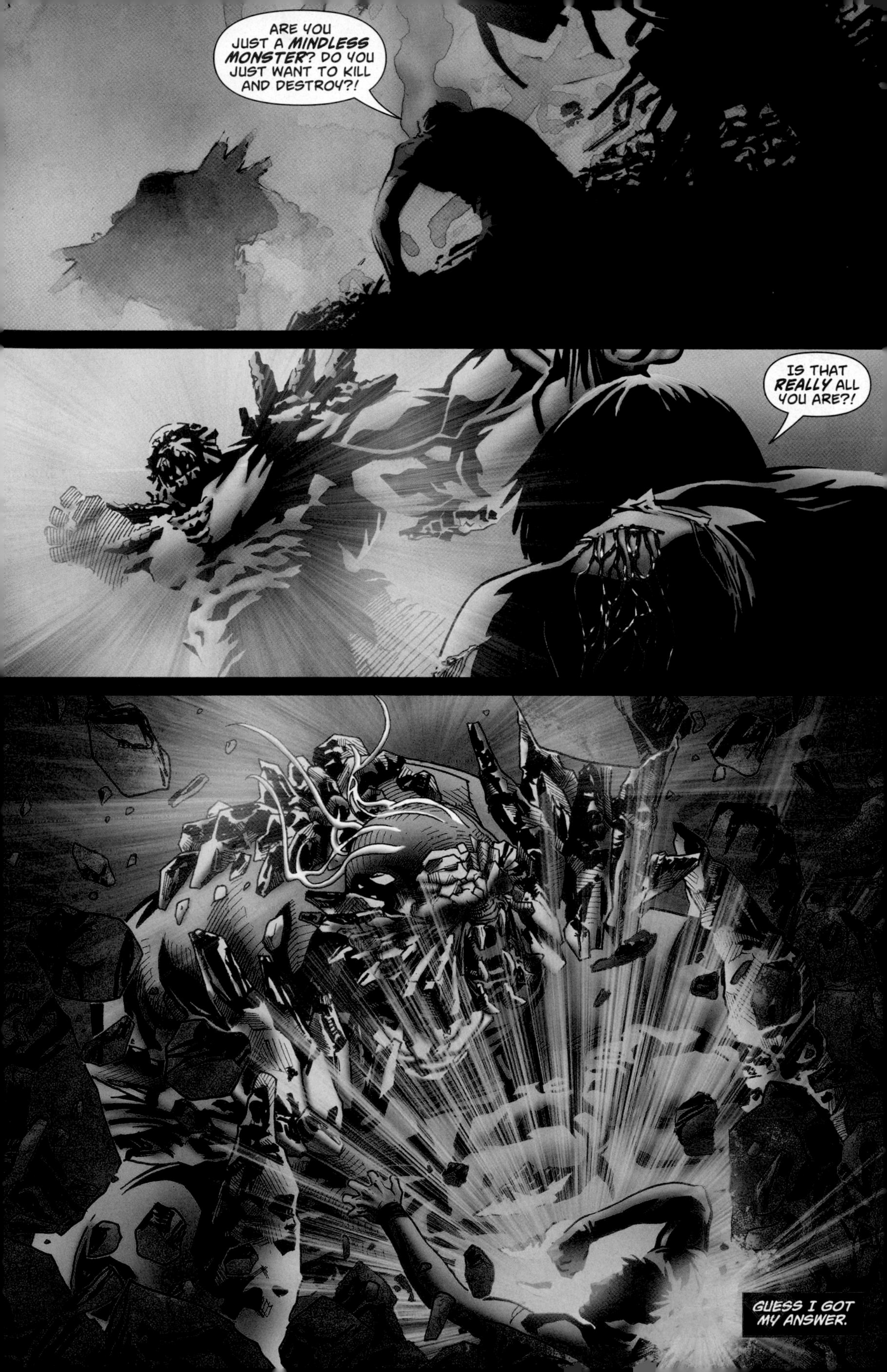
ARE YOU JUST A MINDLESS MONSTER? DO YOU JUST WANT TO KILL AND DESTROY?!
IS THAT REALLY ALL YOU ARE?!
GUESS I GOT MY ANSWER.

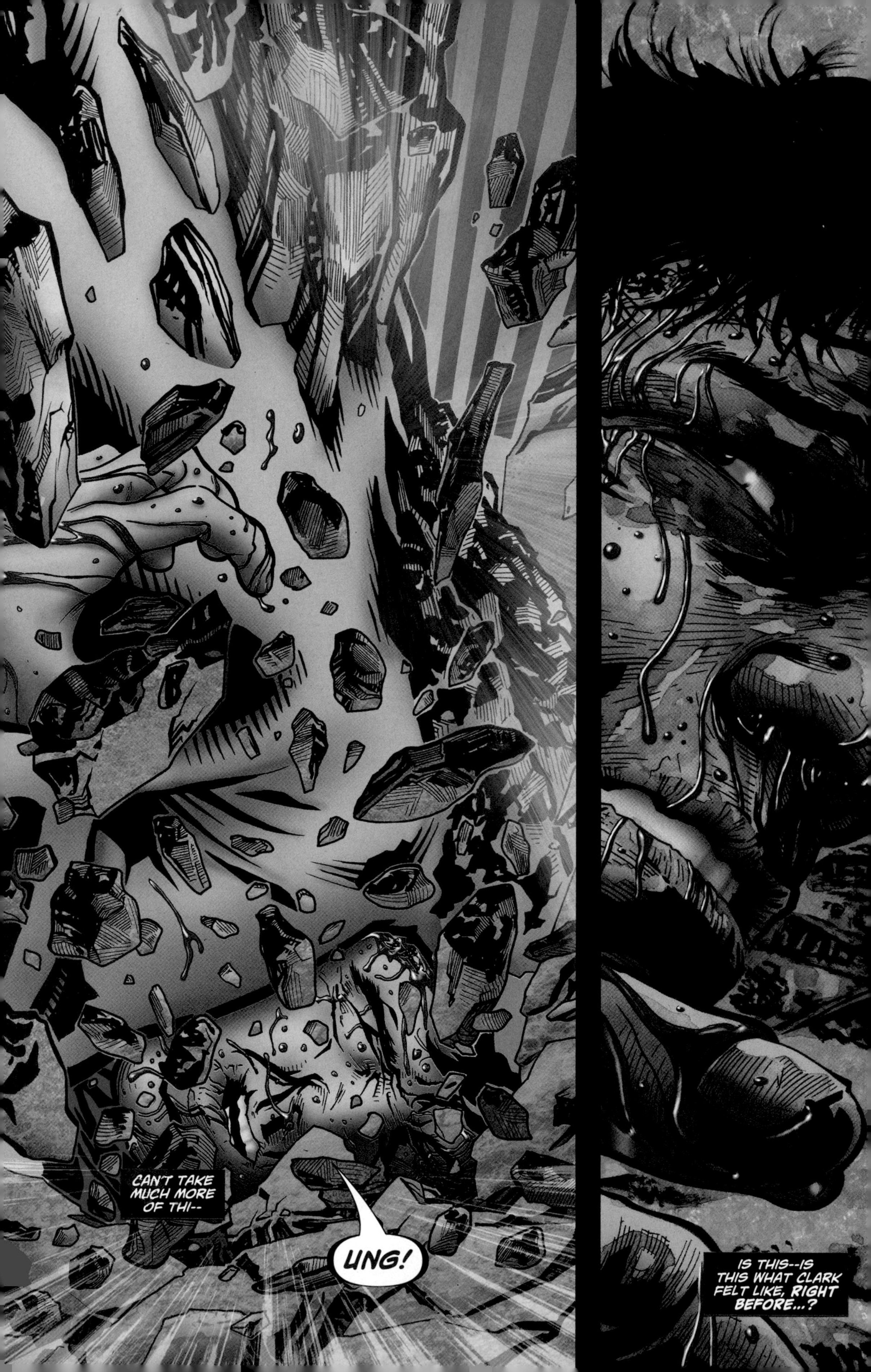
CAN'T TAKE MUCH MORE OF THI--
UNG!
IS THIS--IS THIS WHAT CLARK FELT LIKE, RIGHT BEFORE...?

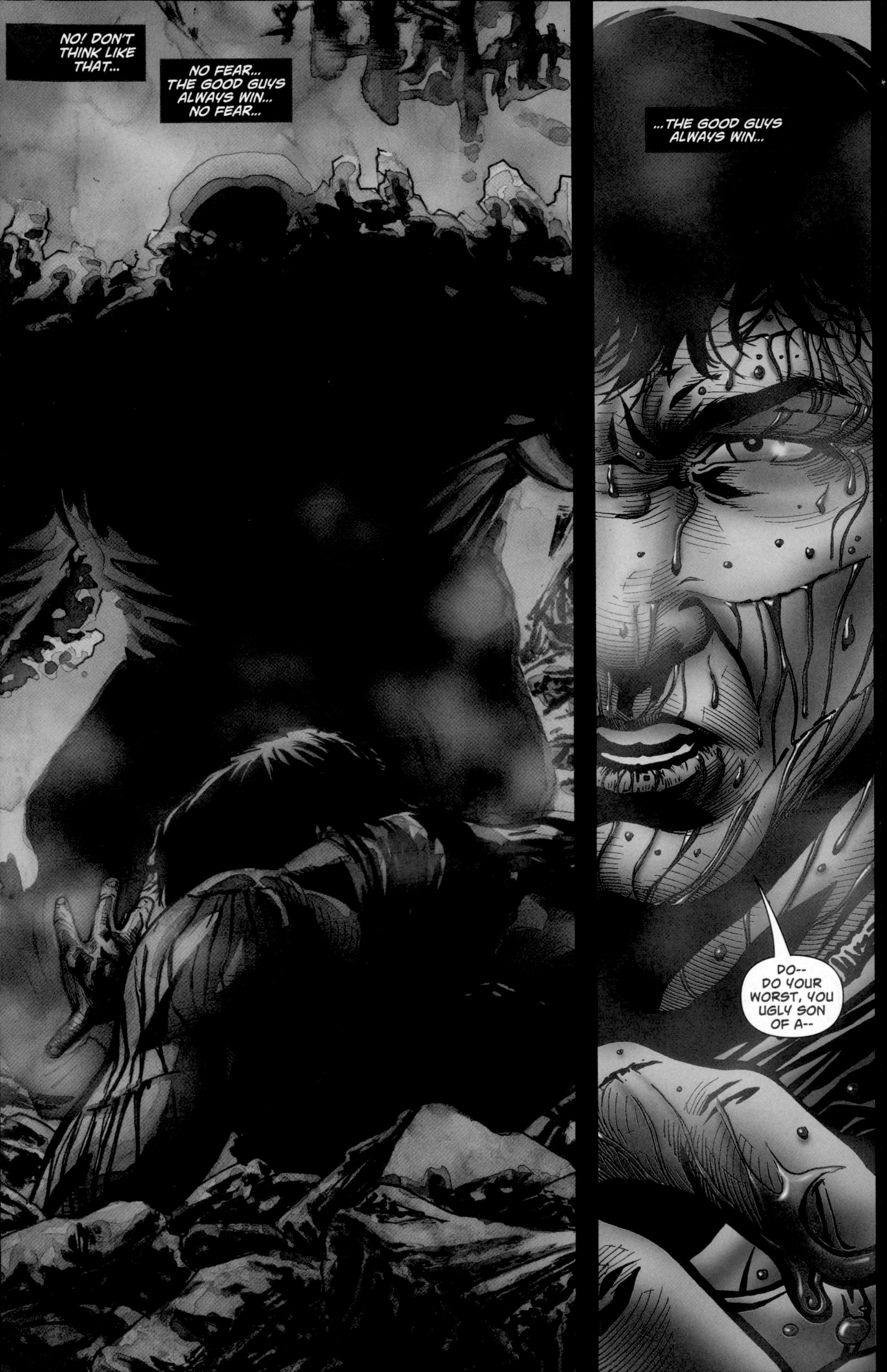
NO! DON'T THINK LIKE THAT...
NO FEAR... THE GOOD GUYS ALWAYS WIN... NO FEAR...
...THE GOOD GUYS ALWAYS WIN...
DO-- DO YOUR WORST, YOU UGLY SON OF A--

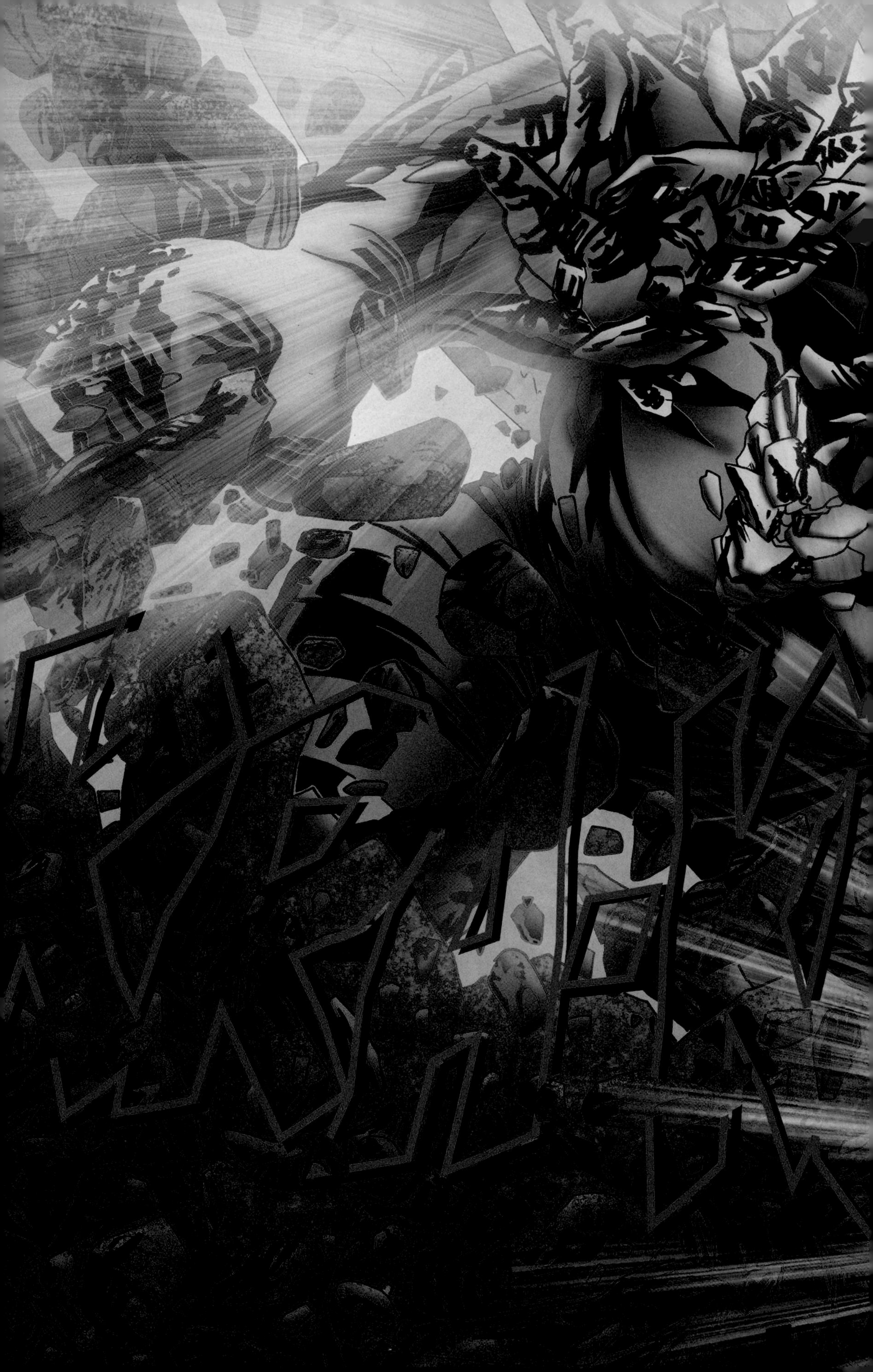

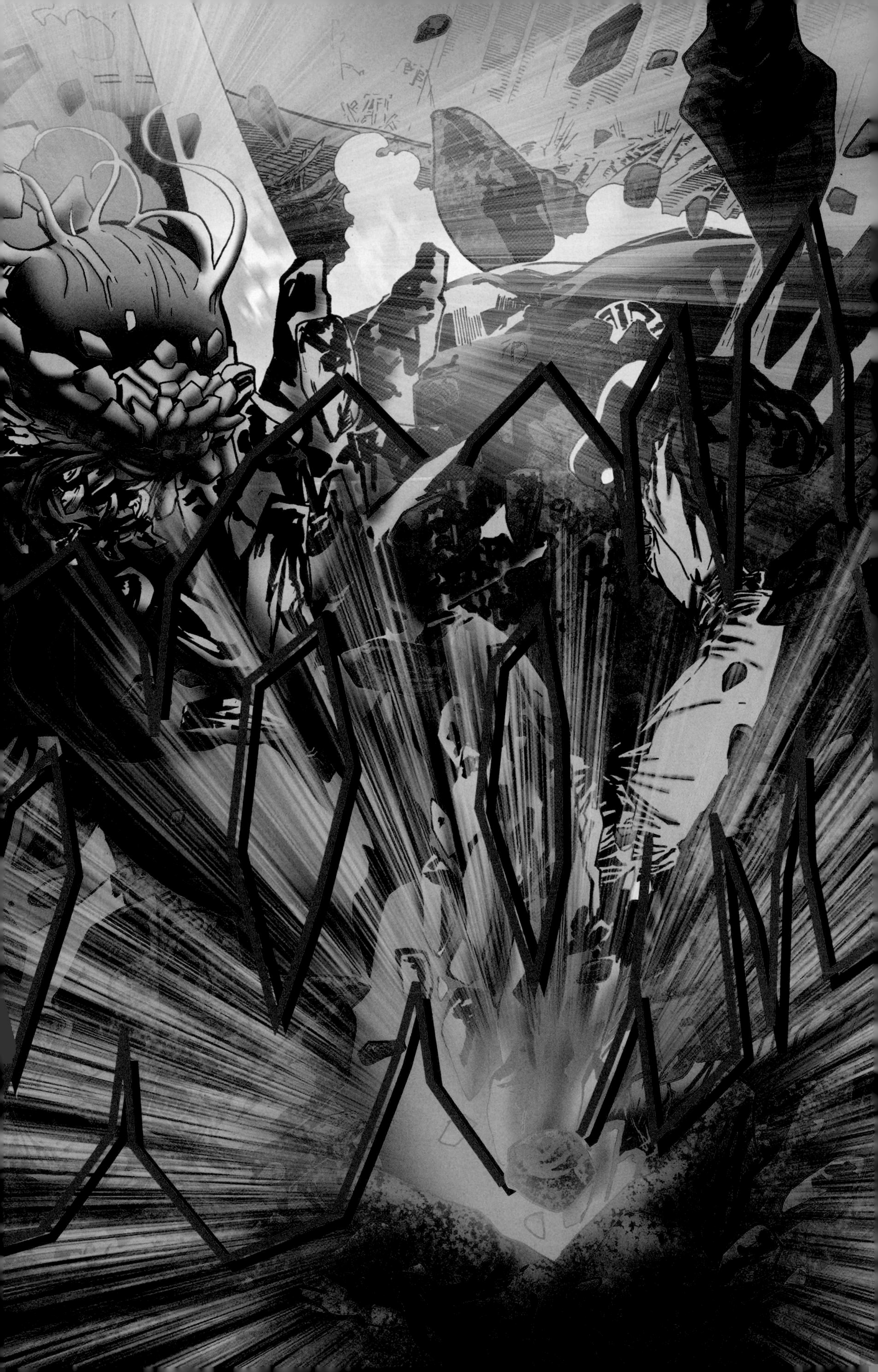

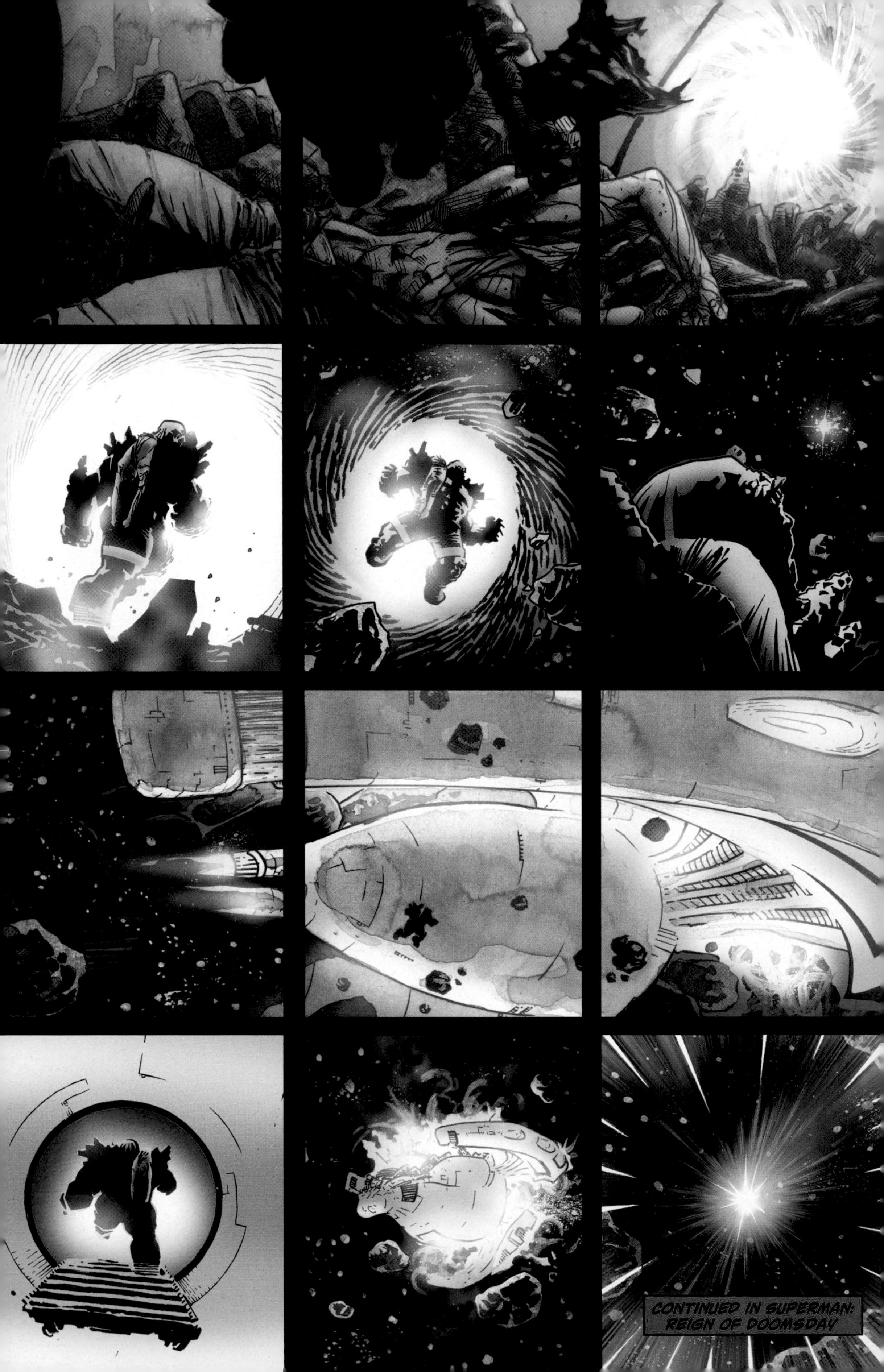
CONTINUED IN SUPERMAN: REIGN OF DOOMSDAY

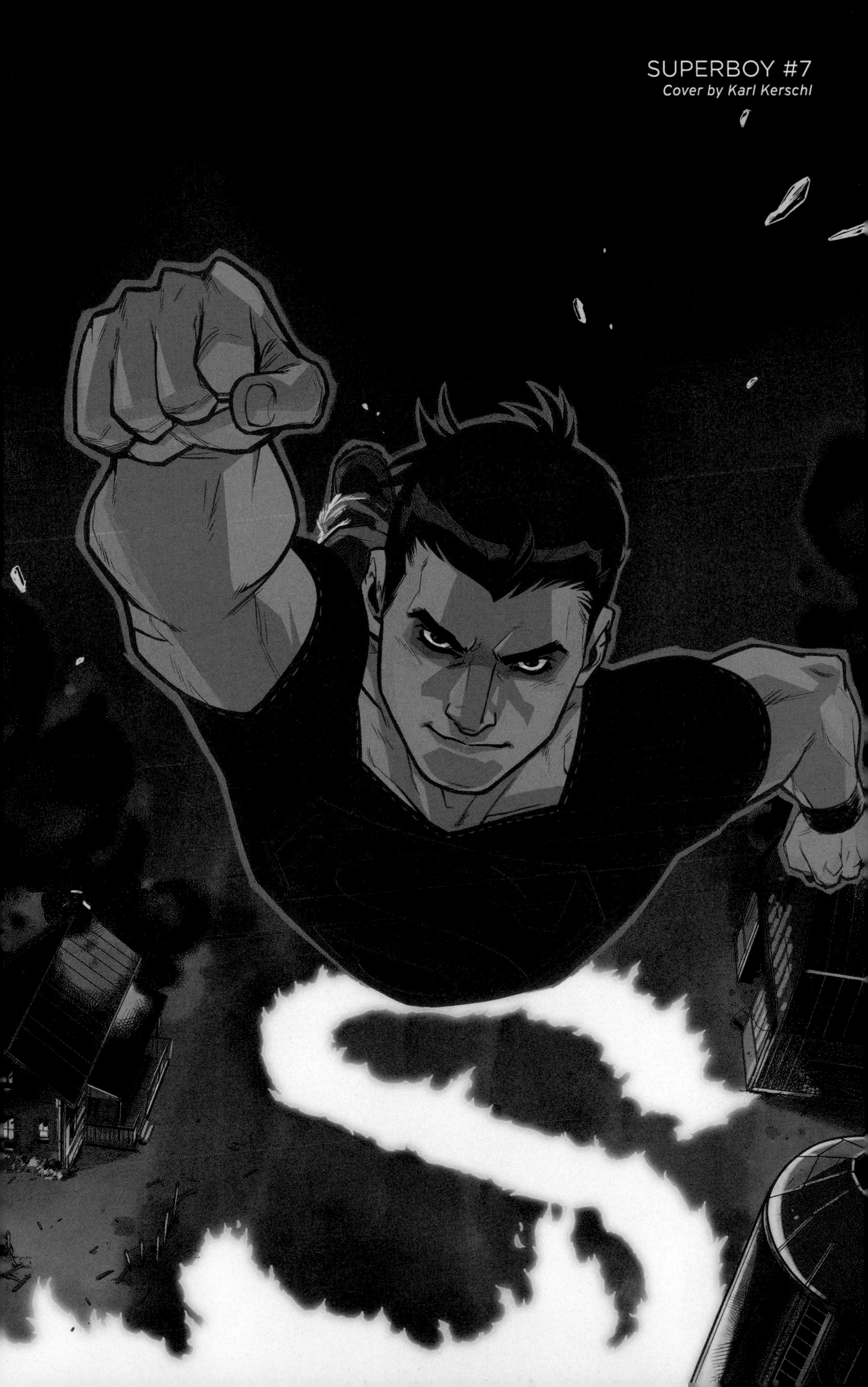

SUPERBOY #7

Cover by Karl Kerschl

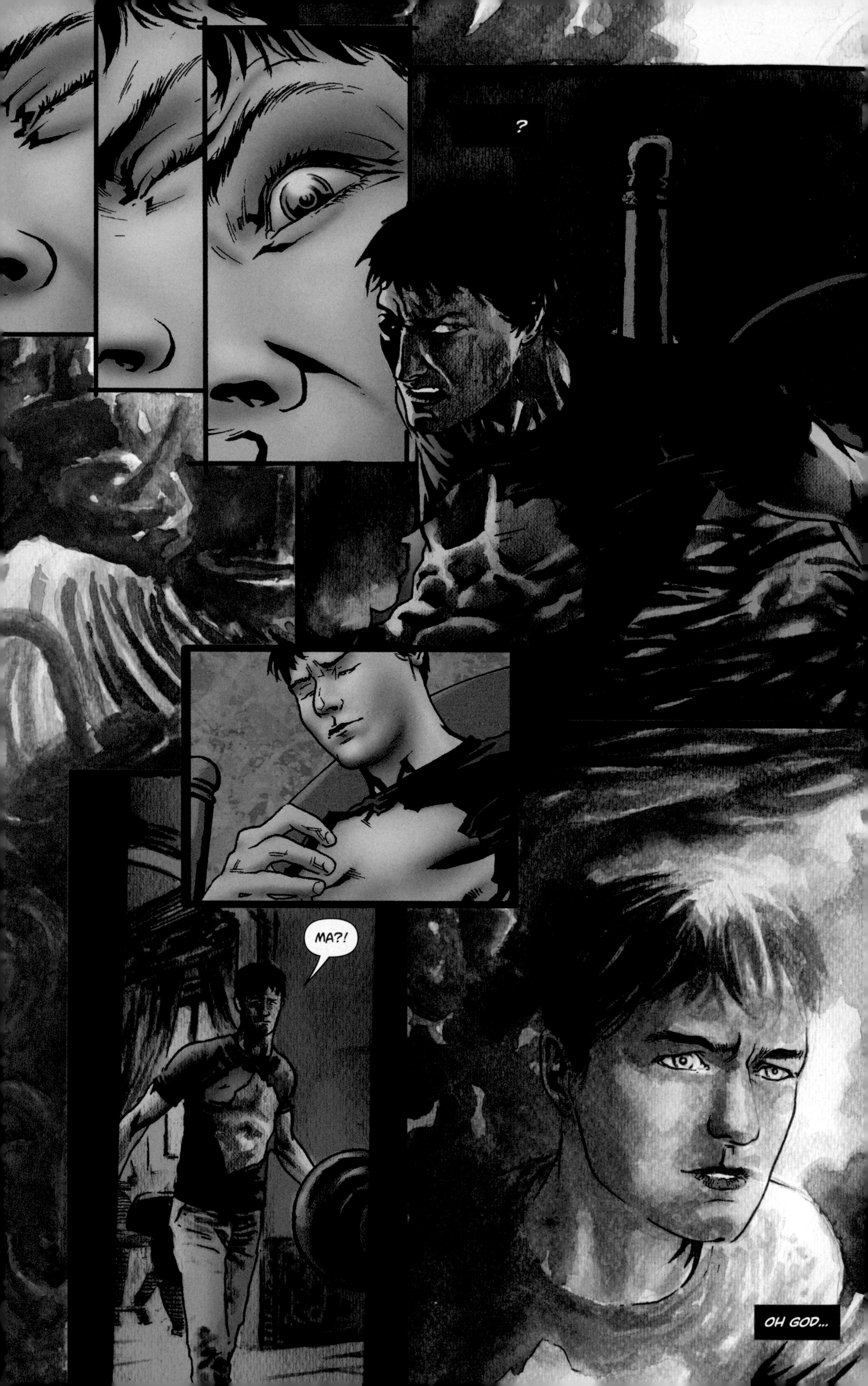
?
MA?!
OH GOD...

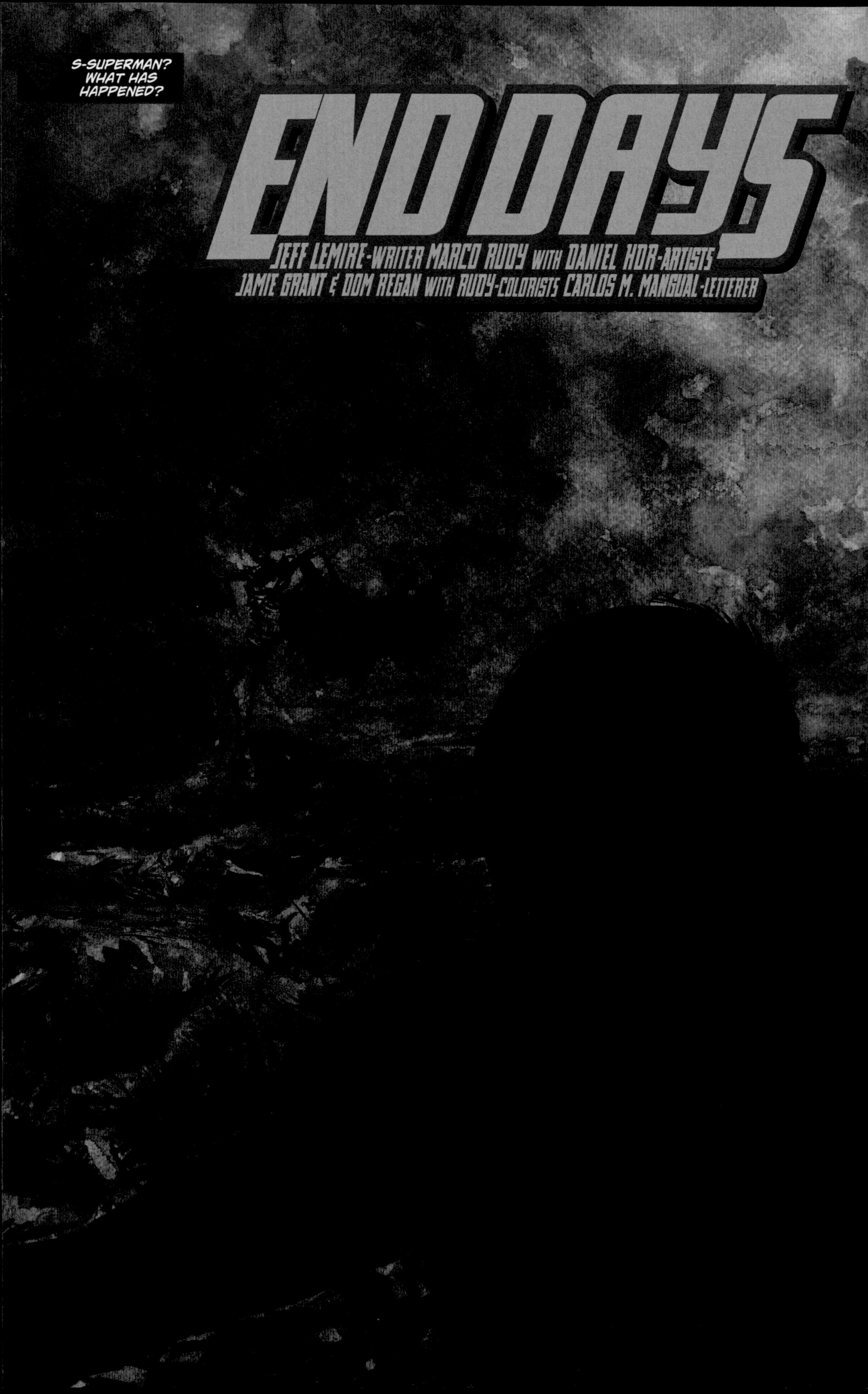
S-SUPERMAN? WHAT HAS HAPPENED?
END DAYS
JEFF LEMIRE-WRITER MARCO RUDY WITH DANIEL HDR-ARTISTS
JAMIE GRANT & DOM REGAN WITH RUDY-COLORISTS CARLOS M. MANGUAL-LETTERER

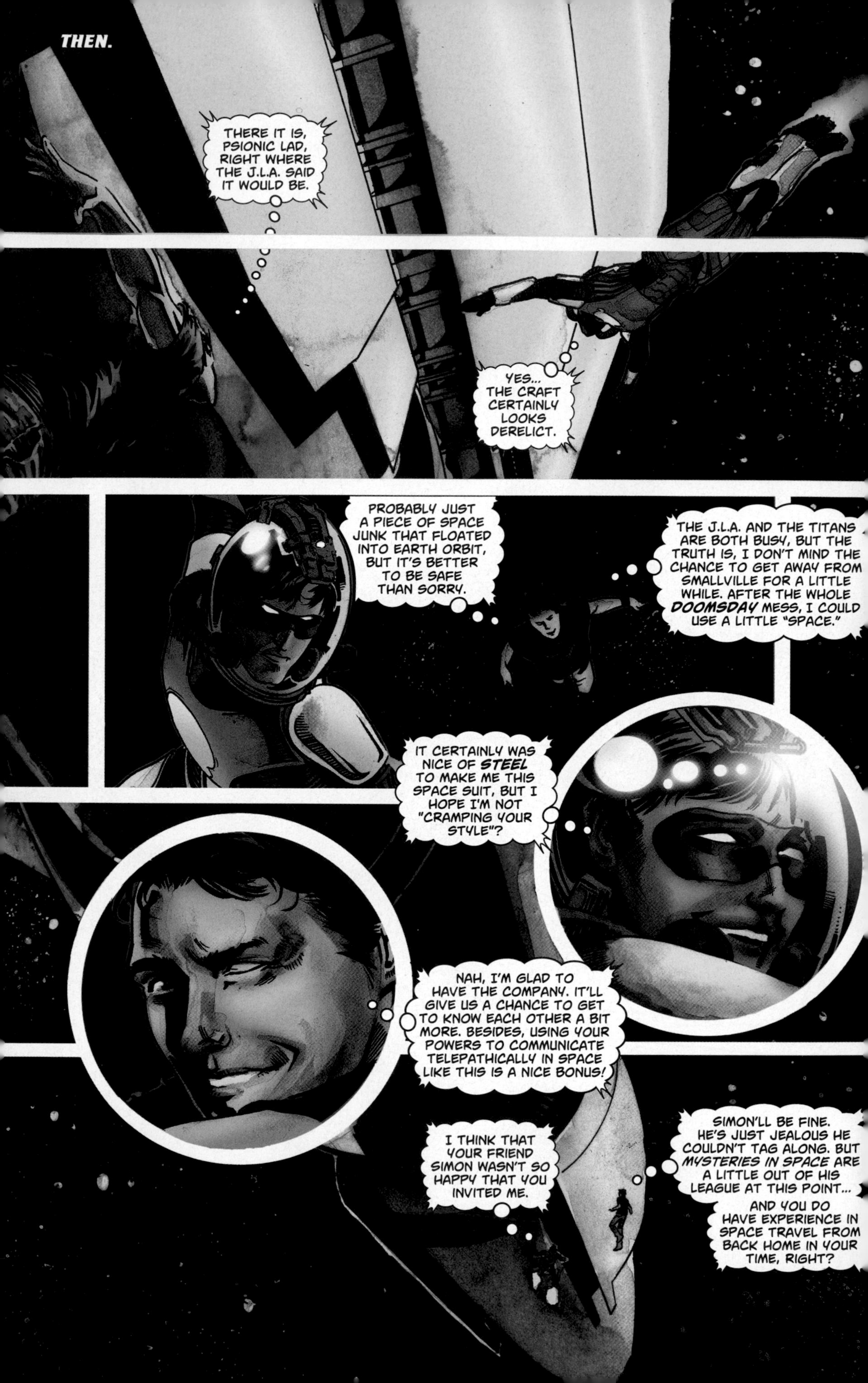
THEN.
THERE IT IS, PSIONIC LAD, RIGHT WHERE THE J.L.A. SAID IT WOULD BE.
YES... THE CRAFT CERTAINLY LOOKS DERELICT.
PROBABLY JUST A PIECE OF SPACE JUNK THAT FLOATED INTO EARTH ORBIT, BUT IT'S BETTER TO BE SAFE THAN SORRY.
THE J.L.A. AND THE TITANS ARE BOTH BUSY, BUT THE TRUTH IS, I DON'T MIND THE CHANCE TO GET AWAY FROM SMALLVILLE FOR A LITTLE WHILE. AFTER THE WHOLE DOOMSDAY MESS, I COULD USE A LITTLE "SPACE."
IT CERTAINLY WAS NICE OF STEEL TO MAKE ME THIS SPACE SUIT, BUT I HOPE I'M NOT "CRAMPING YOUR STYLE"?
NAH, I'M GLAD TO HAVE THE COMPANY. IT'LL GIVE US A CHANCE TO GET TO KNOW EACH OTHER A BIT MORE. BESIDES, USING YOUR POWERS TO COMMUNICATE TELEPATHICALLY IN SPACE LIKE THIS IS A NICE BONUS!
I THINK THAT YOUR FRIEND SIMON WASN'T SO HAPPY THAT YOU INVITED ME.
SIMON'LL BE FINE. HE'S JUST JEALOUS HE COULDN'T TAG ALONG. BUT MYSTERIES IN SPACE ARE A LITTLE OUT OF HIS LEAGUE AT THIS POINT...
AND YOU DO HAVE EXPERIENCE IN SPACE TRAVEL FROM BACK HOME IN YOUR TIME, RIGHT?

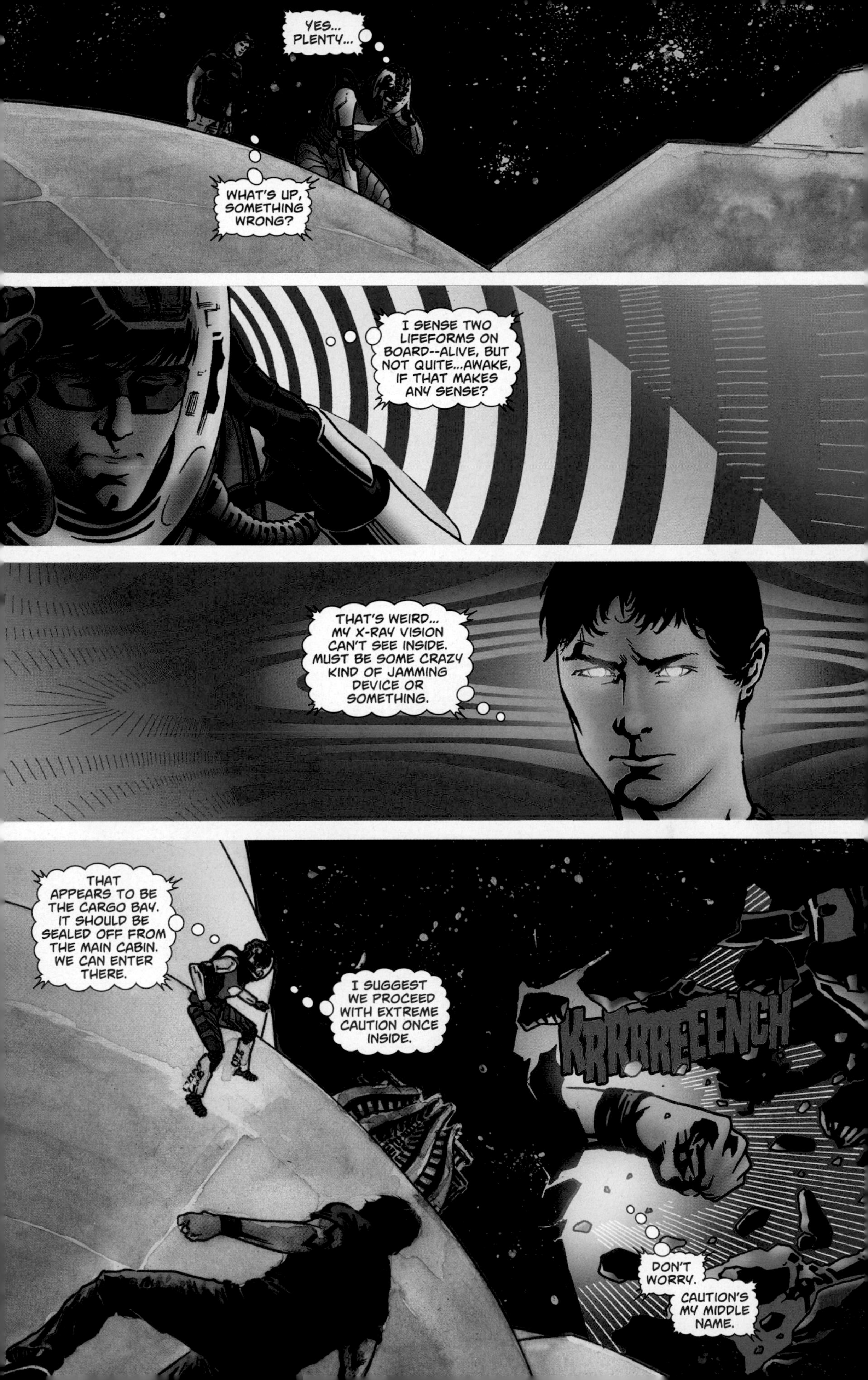
YES... PLENTY...
WHAT'S UP, SOMETHING WRONG?
I SENSE TWO LIFEFORMS ON BOARD--ALIVE, BUT NOT QUITE...AWAKE, IF THAT MAKES ANY SENSE?
THAT'S WEIRD... MY X-RAY VISION CAN'T SEE INSIDE. MUST BE SOME CRAZY KIND OF JAMMING DEVICE OR SOMETHING.
THAT APPEARS TO BE THE CARGO BAY. IT SHOULD BE SEALED OFF FROM THE MAIN CABIN. WE CAN ENTER THERE.
I SUGGEST WE PROCEED WITH EXTREME CAUTION ONCE INSIDE.
KRRRRREEENCH
DON'T WORRY.
CAUTION'S MY MIDDLE NAME.

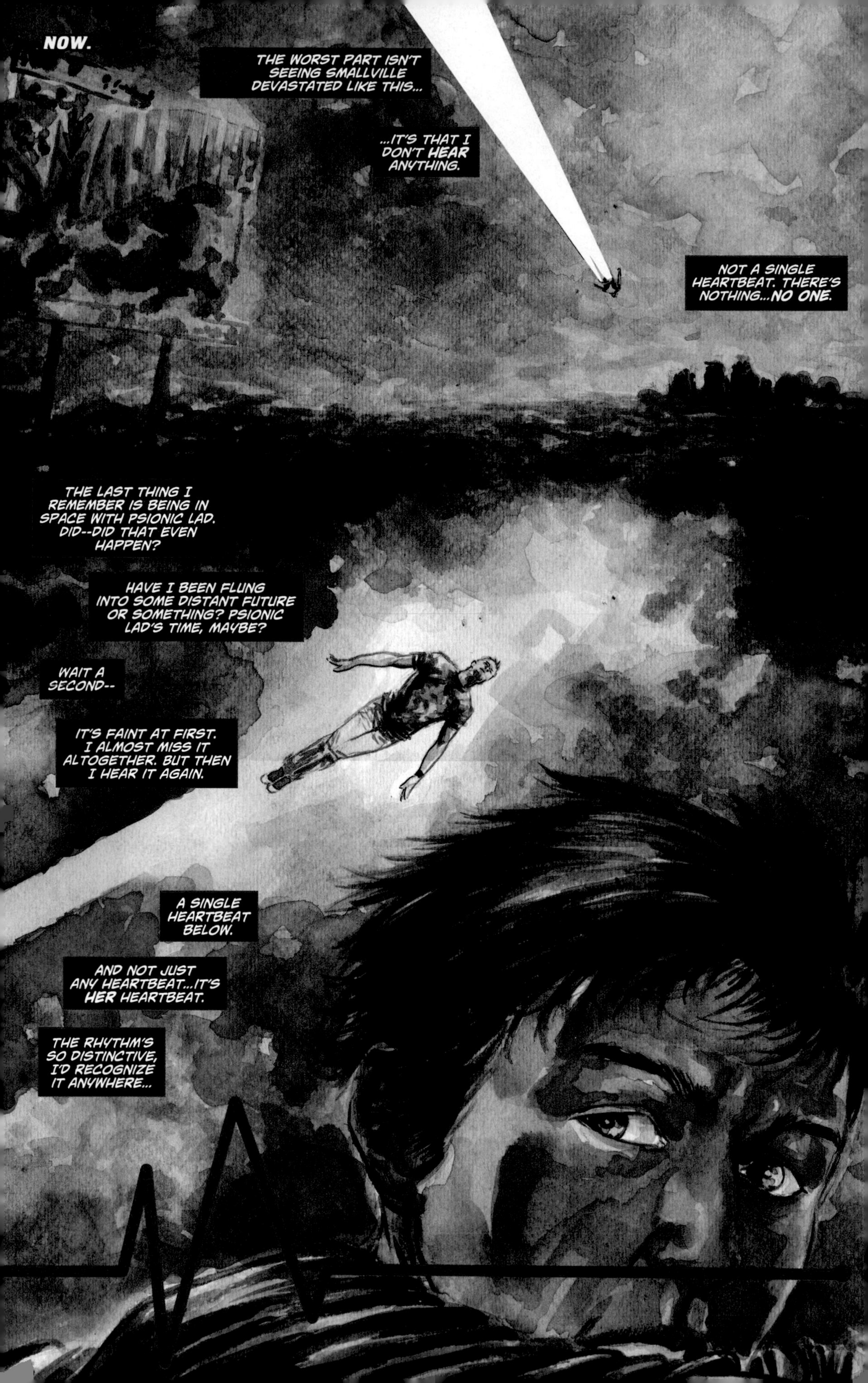
NOW.
THE WORST PART ISN'T SEEING SMALLVILLE DEVASTATED LIKE THIS...
...IT'S THAT I DON'T HEAR ANYTHING.
NOT A SINGLE HEARTBEAT. THERE'S NOTHING...NO ONE.
THE LAST THING I REMEMBER IS BEING IN SPACE WITH PSIONIC LAD. DID--DID THAT EVEN HAPPEN?
HAVE I BEEN FLUNG INTO SOME DISTANT FUTURE OR SOMETHING? PSIONIC LAD'S TIME, MAYBE?
WAIT A SECOND--
IT'S FAINT AT FIRST. I ALMOST MISS IT ALTOGETHER. BUT THEN I HEAR IT AGAIN.
A SINGLE HEARTBEAT BELOW.
AND NOT JUST ANY HEARTBEAT...IT'S HER HEARTBEAT.
THE RHYTHM'S SO DISTINCTIVE, I'D RECOGNIZE IT ANYWHERE...

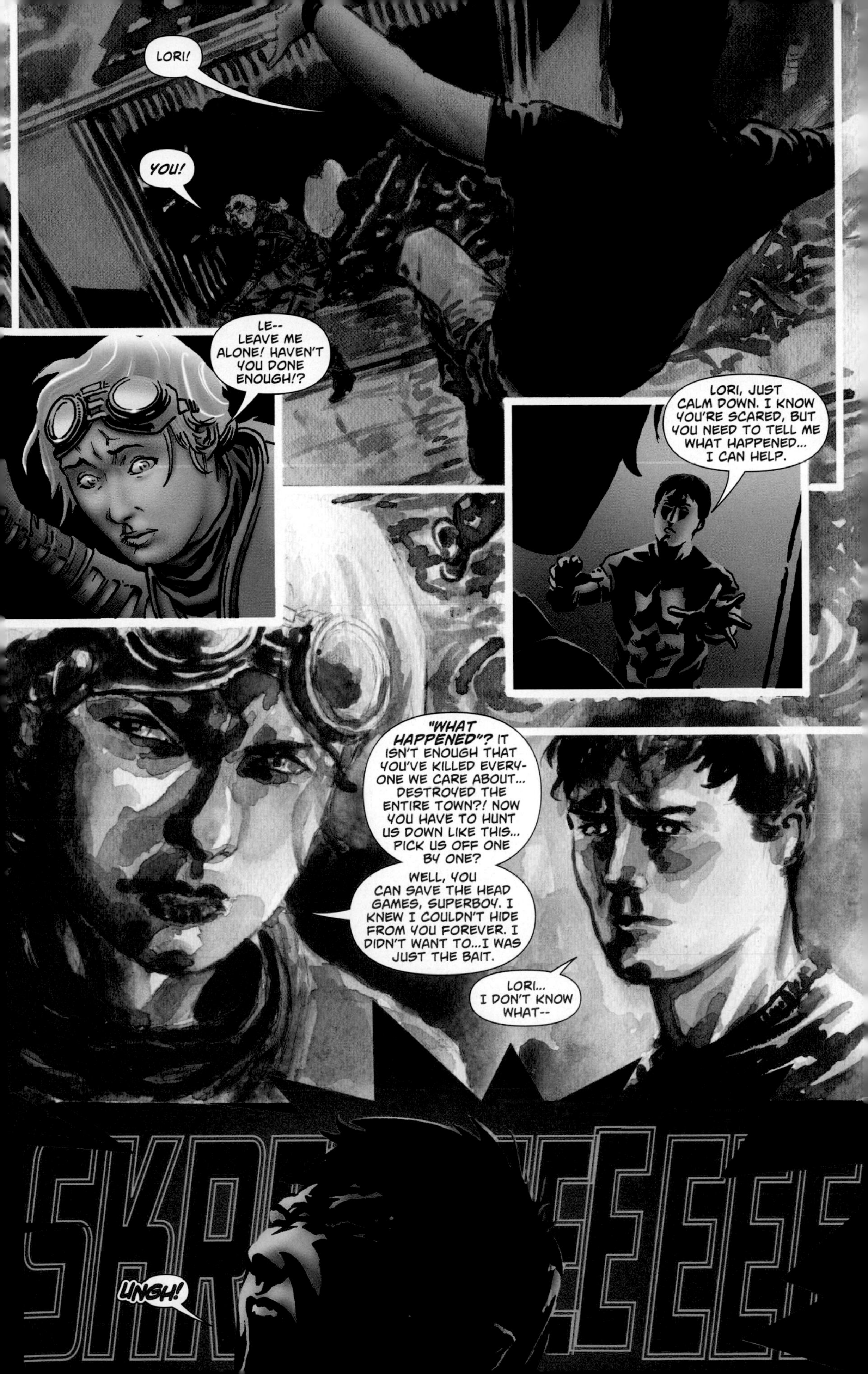
LORI!
YOU!
LE-- LEAVE ME ALONE! HAVEN'T YOU DONE ENOUGH!?
LORI, JUST CALM DOWN. I KNOW YOU'RE SCARED, BUT YOU NEED TO TELL ME WHAT HAPPENED... I CAN HELP.
"WHAT HAPPENED"? IT ISN'T ENOUGH THAT YOU'VE KILLED EVERY-ONE WE CARE ABOUT... DESTROYED THE ENTIRE TOWN?! NOW YOU HAVE TO HUNT US DOWN LIKE THIS... PICK US OFF ONE BY ONE?
WELL, YOU CAN SAVE THE HEAD GAMES, SUPERBOY. I KNEW I COULDN'T HIDE FROM YOU FOREVER. I DIDN'T WANT TO...I WAS JUST THE BAIT.
LORI... I DON'T KNOW WHAT--
UNGH!

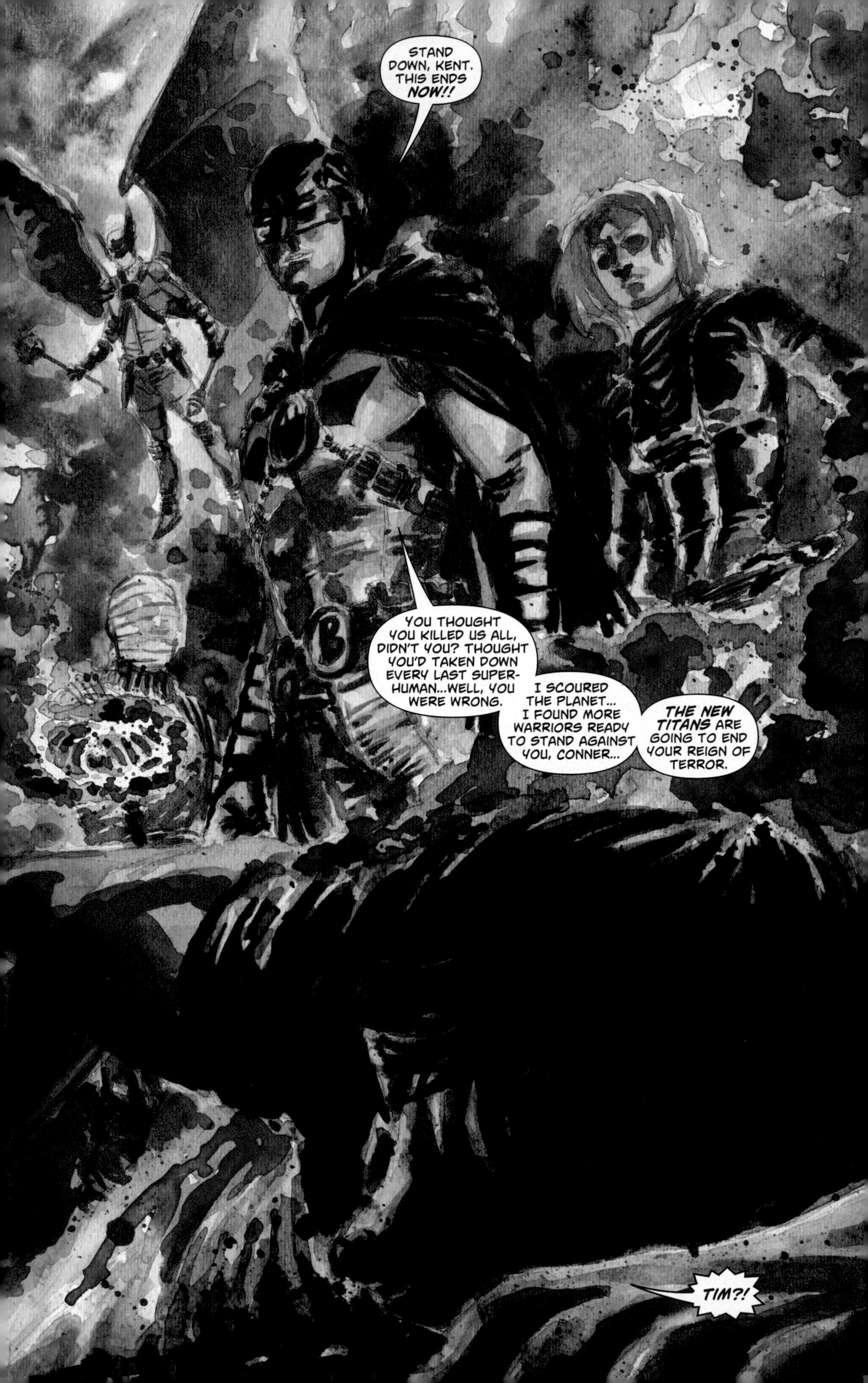
STAND DOWN, KENT. THIS ENDS NOW!!
YOU THOUGHT YOU KILLED US ALL, DIDN'T YOU? THOUGHT YOU'D TAKEN DOWN EVERY LAST SUPER-HUMAN...WELL, YOU WERE WRONG.
I SCOURED THE PLANET... I FOUND MORE WARRIORS READY TO STAND AGAINST YOU, CONNER...
THE NEW TITANS ARE GOING TO END YOUR REIGN OF TERROR.
TIM?!

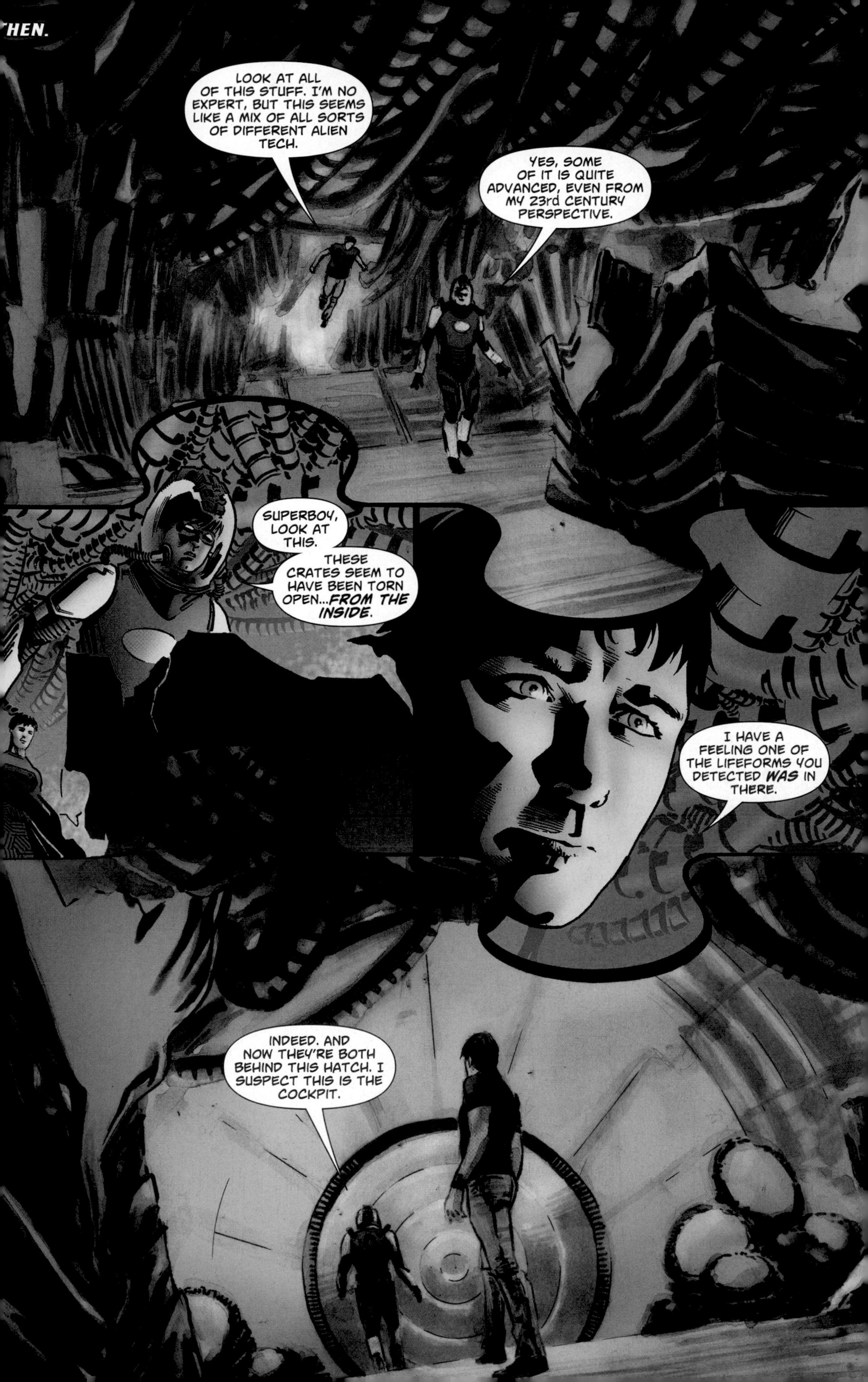
THEN.
LOOK AT ALL OF THIS STUFF. I'M NO EXPERT, BUT THIS SEEMS LIKE A MIX OF ALL SORTS OF DIFFERENT ALIEN TECH.
YES, SOME OF IT IS QUITE ADVANCED, EVEN FROM MY 23rd CENTURY PERSPECTIVE.
SUPERBOY, LOOK AT THIS.
THESE CRATES SEEM TO HAVE BEEN TORN OPEN...FROM THE INSIDE.
I HAVE A FEELING ONE OF THE LIFEFORMS YOU DETECTED WAS IN THERE.
INDEED. AND NOW THEY'RE BOTH BEHIND THIS HATCH. I SUSPECT THIS IS THE COCKPIT.

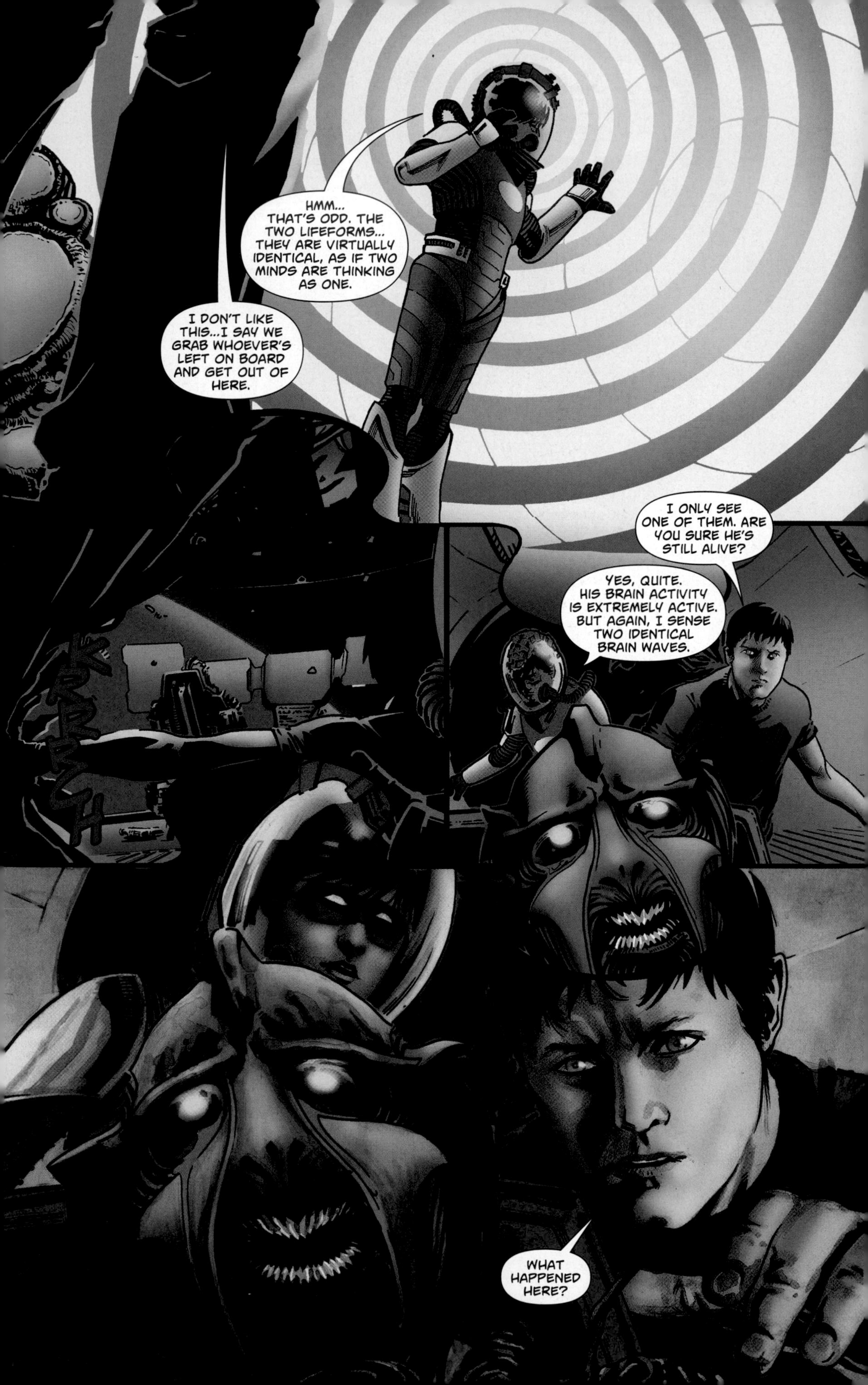
HMM... THAT'S ODD. THE TWO LIFEFORMS... THEY ARE VIRTUALLY IDENTICAL, AS IF TWO MINDS ARE THINKING AS ONE.
I DON'T LIKE THIS...I SAY WE GRAB WHOEVER'S LEFT ON BOARD AND GET OUT OF HERE.
I ONLY SEE ONE OF THEM. ARE YOU SURE HE'S STILL ALIVE?
YES, QUITE. HIS BRAIN ACTIVITY IS EXTREMELY ACTIVE. BUT AGAIN, I SENSE TWO IDENTICAL BRAIN WAVES.
WHAT HAPPENED HERE?

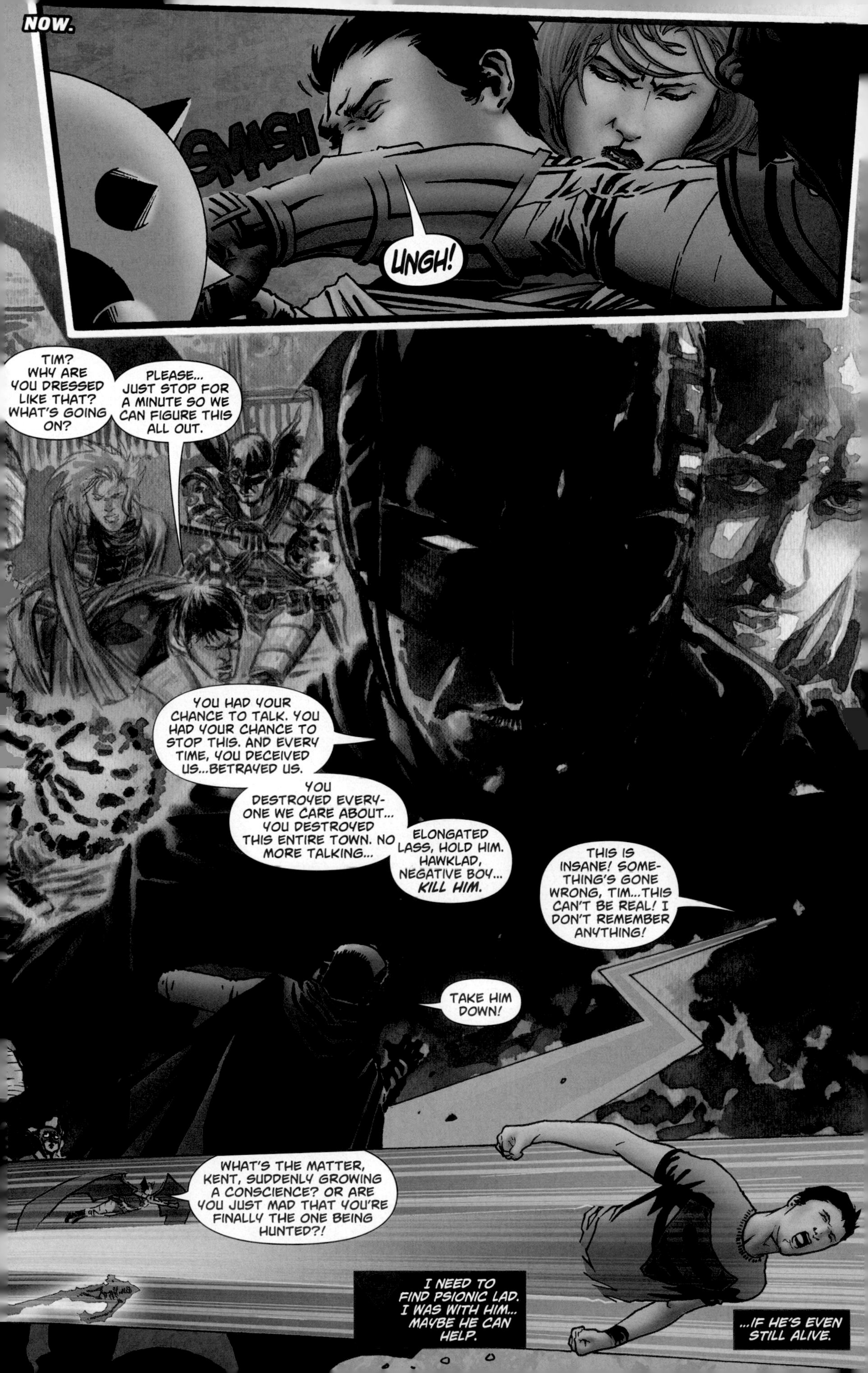
NOW.
SMASH
UNGH!
TIM? WHY ARE YOU DRESSED LIKE THAT? WHAT'S GOING ON?
PLEASE... JUST STOP FOR A MINUTE SO WE CAN FIGURE THIS ALL OUT.
YOU HAD YOUR CHANCE TO TALK. YOU HAD YOUR CHANCE TO STOP THIS. AND EVERY TIME, YOU DECEIVED US...BETRAYED US.
YOU DESTROYED EVERY-ONE WE CARE ABOUT... YOU DESTROYED THIS ENTIRE TOWN. NO MORE TALKING...
ELONGATED LASS, HOLD HIM. HAWKLAD, NEGATIVE BOY... KILL HIM.
THIS IS INSANE! SOME-THING'S GONE WRONG, TIM...THIS CAN'T BE REAL! I DON'T REMEMBER ANYTHING!
TAKE HIM DOWN!
WHAT'S THE MATTER, KENT, SUDDENLY GROWING A CONSCIENCE? OR ARE YOU JUST MAD THAT YOU'RE FINALLY THE ONE BEING HUNTED?!
I NEED TO FIND PSIONIC LAD. I WAS WITH HIM... MAYBE HE CAN HELP.
...IF HE'S EVEN STILL ALIVE.

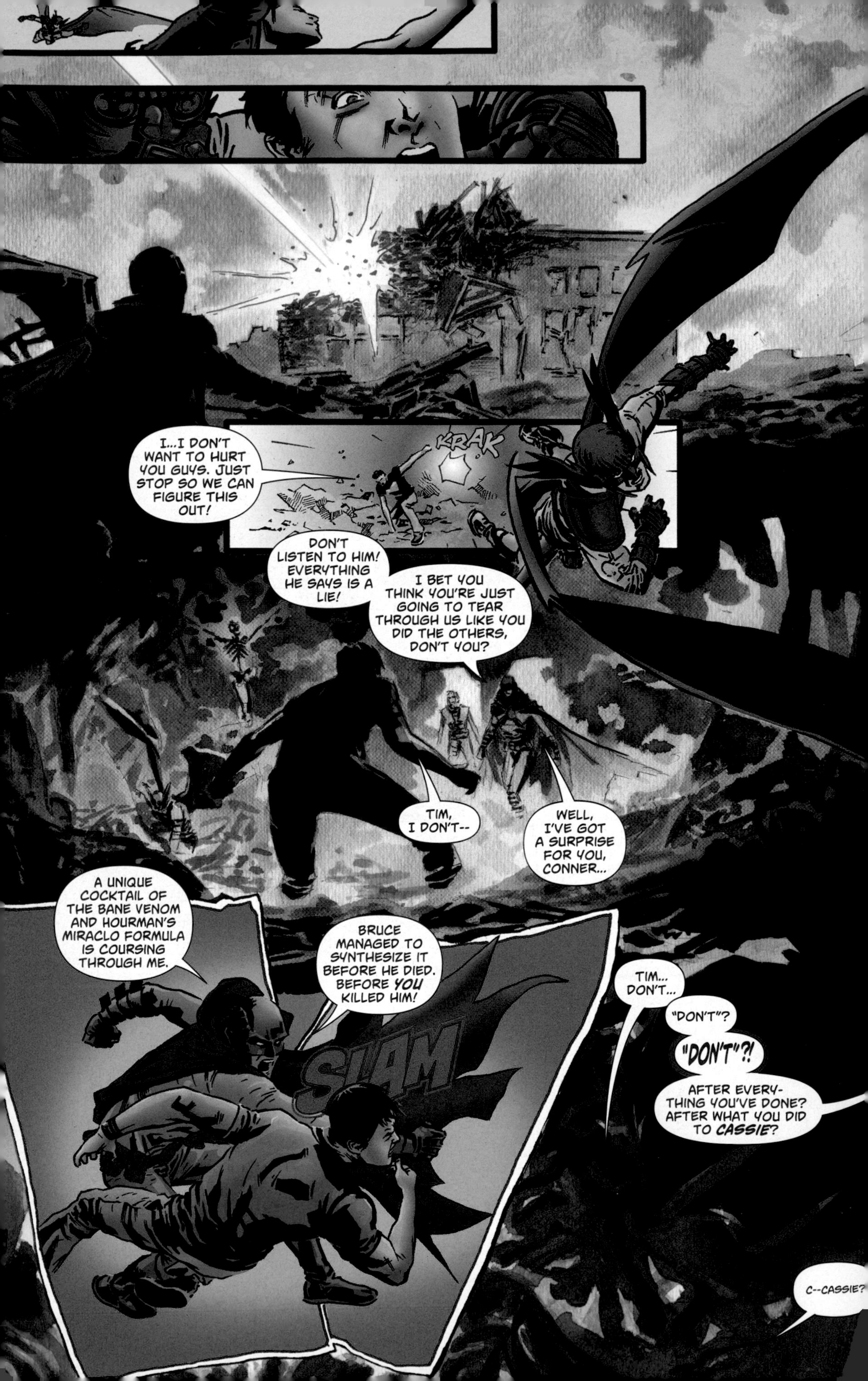
I...I DON'T WANT TO HURT YOU GUYS. JUST STOP SO WE CAN FIGURE THIS OUT!
KRAK
DON'T LISTEN TO HIM! EVERYTHING HE SAYS IS A LIE!
I BET YOU THINK YOU'RE JUST GOING TO TEAR THROUGH US LIKE YOU DID THE OTHERS, DON'T YOU?
TIM, I DON'T--
WELL, I'VE GOT A SURPRISE FOR YOU, CONNER...
A UNIQUE COCKTAIL OF THE BANE VENOM AND HOURMAN'S MIRACLO FORMULA IS COURSING THROUGH ME.
BRUCE MANAGED TO SYNTHESIZE IT BEFORE HE DIED. BEFORE *YOU* KILLED HIM!
SLAM
TIM... DON'T...
"DON'T"?
"DON'T"?!
AFTER EVERY-THING YOU'VE DONE? AFTER WHAT YOU DID TO *CASSIE*?
C--CASSIE?

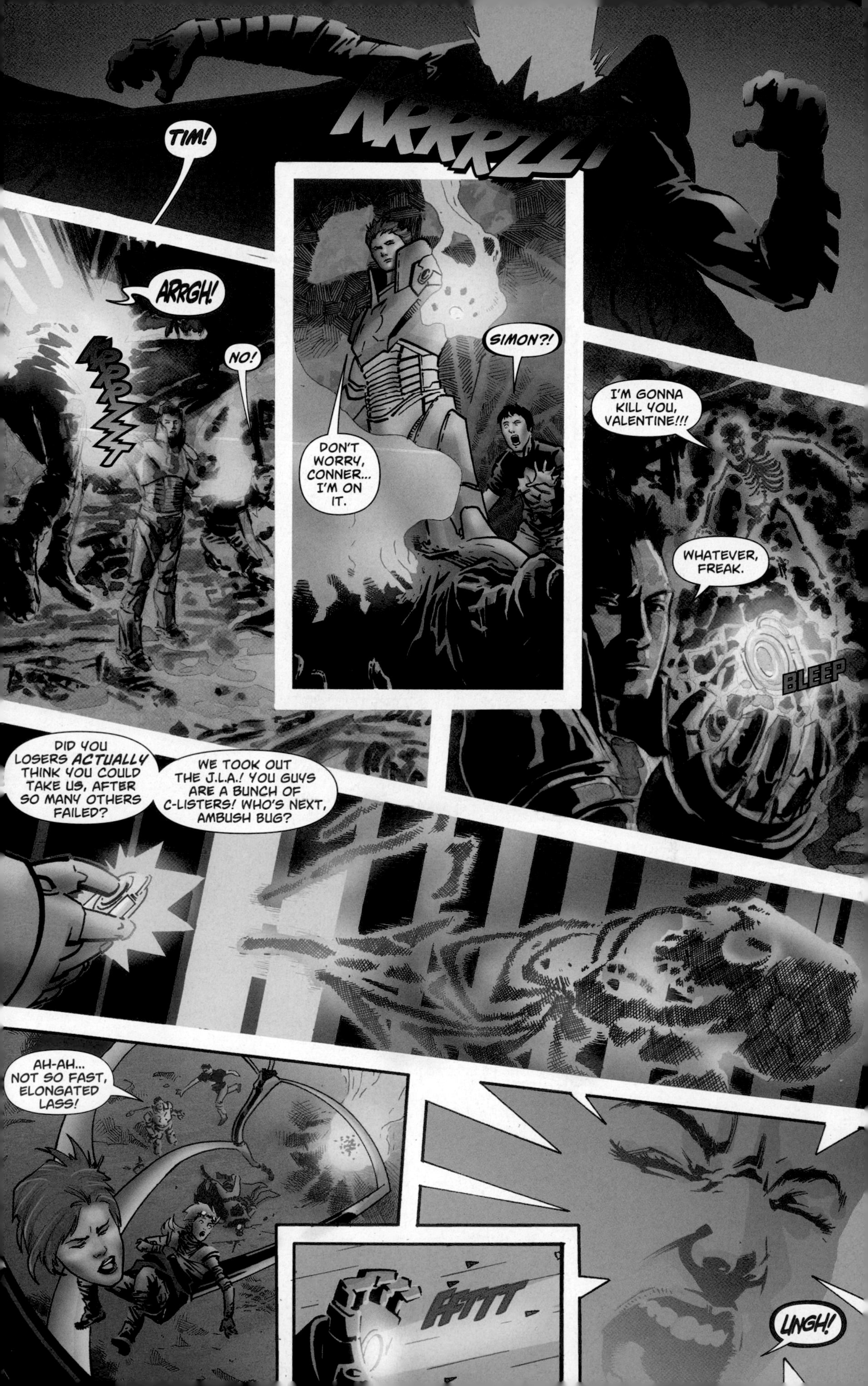

NRRRZZT
TIM!
ARRGH!
KRRRZZZT
NO!
SIMON?!
DON'T WORRY, CONNER... I'M ON IT.
I'M GONNA KILL YOU, VALENTINE!!!
WHATEVER, FREAK.
BLEEP
DID YOU LOSERS ACTUALLY THINK YOU COULD TAKE US, AFTER SO MANY OTHERS FAILED?
WE TOOK OUT THE J.L.A.! YOU GUYS ARE A BUNCH OF C-LISTERS! WHO'S NEXT, AMBUSH BUG?
AH-AH... NOT SO FAST, ELONGATED LASS!
UNGH!

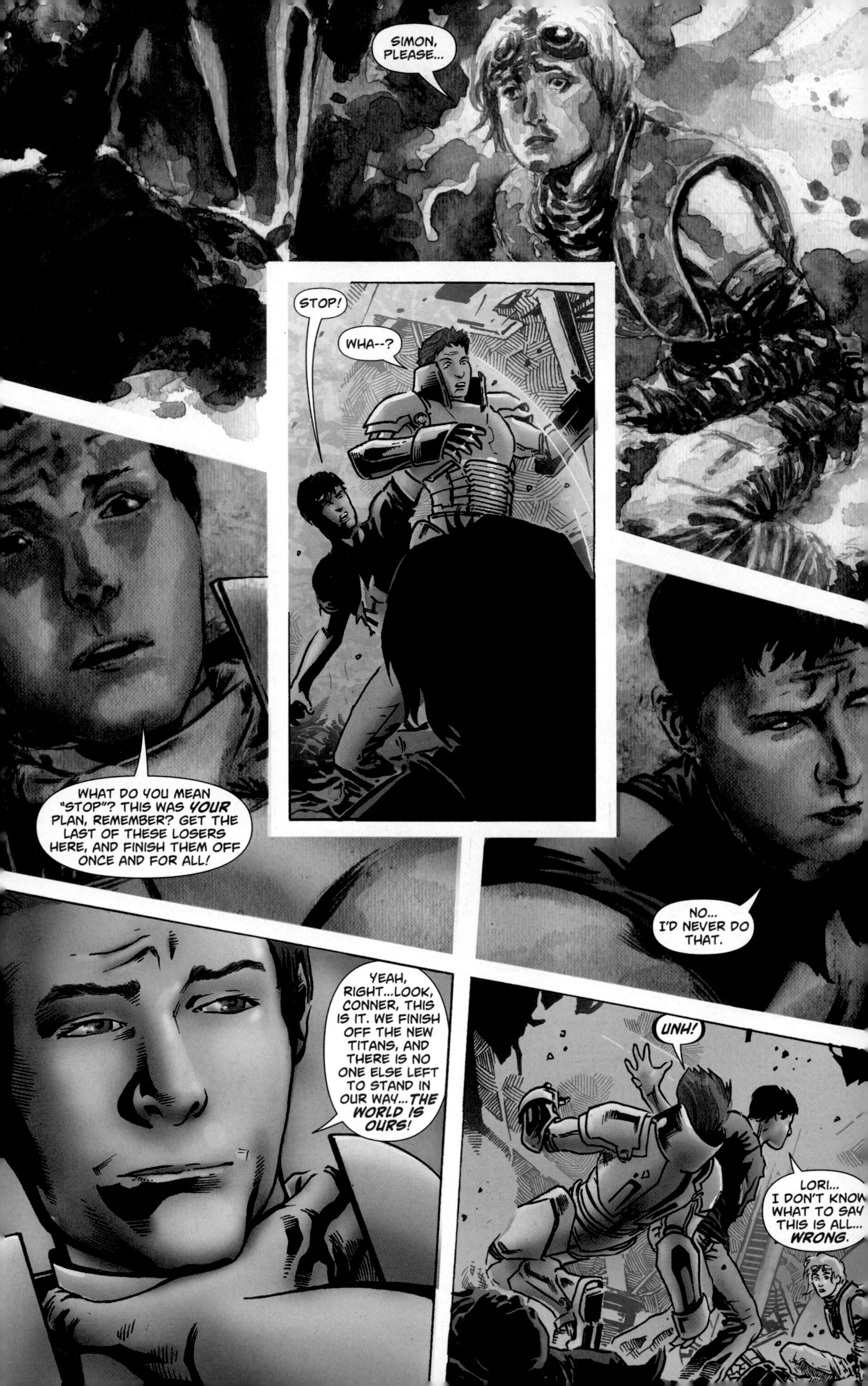
SIMON, PLEASE...
STOP!
WHA--?
WHAT DO YOU MEAN "STOP"? THIS WAS YOUR PLAN, REMEMBER? GET THE LAST OF THESE LOSERS HERE, AND FINISH THEM OFF ONCE AND FOR ALL!
NO... I'D NEVER DO THAT.
YEAH, RIGHT...LOOK, CONNER, THIS IS IT. WE FINISH OFF THE NEW TITANS, AND THERE IS NO ONE ELSE LEFT TO STAND IN OUR WAY...THE WORLD IS OURS!
UNH!
LORI... I DON'T KNOW WHAT TO SAY THIS IS ALL... WRONG.

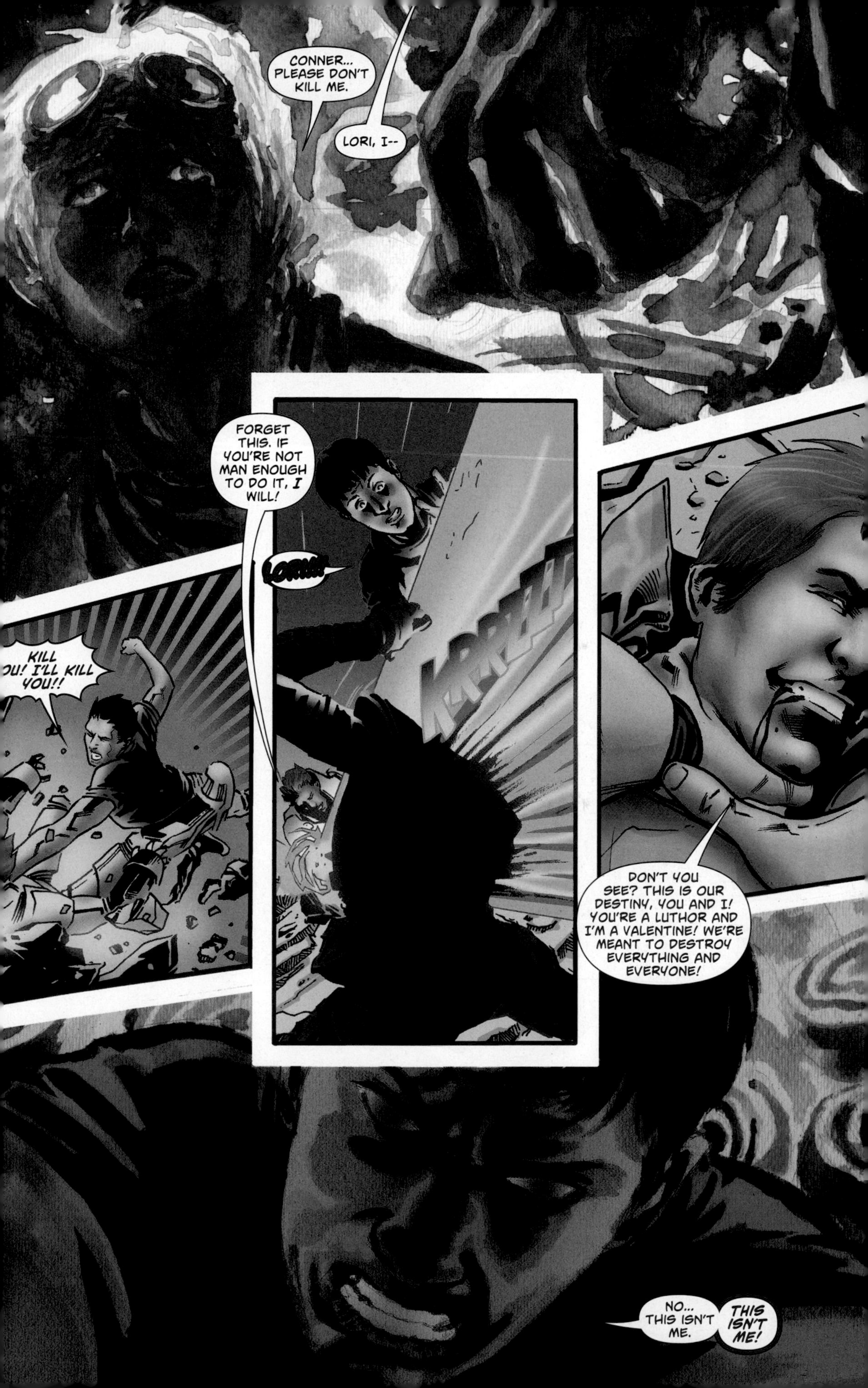
CONNER... PLEASE DON'T KILL ME.
LORI, I--
FORGET THIS. IF YOU'RE NOT MAN ENOUGH TO DO IT, *I* WILL!
KILL YOU! I'LL KILL YOU!!
DON'T YOU SEE? THIS IS OUR DESTINY, YOU AND I! YOU'RE A LUTHOR AND I'M A VALENTINE! WE'RE MEANT TO DESTROY EVERYTHING AND EVERYONE!
NO... THIS ISN'T ME.
THIS ISN'T ME!

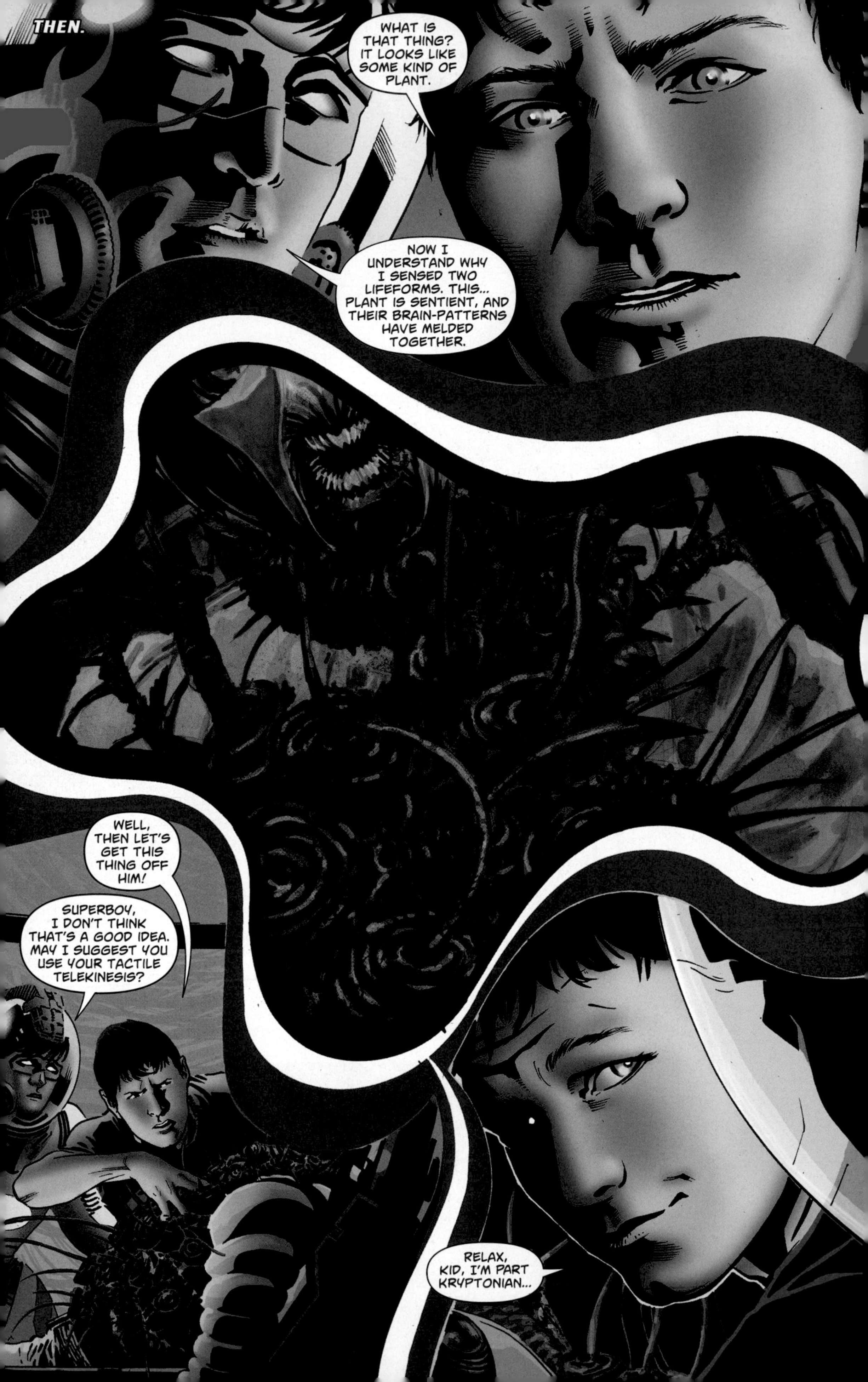
THEN.
WHAT IS THAT THING? IT LOOKS LIKE SOME KIND OF PLANT.
NOW I UNDERSTAND WHY I SENSED TWO LIFEFORMS. THIS... PLANT IS SENTIENT, AND THEIR BRAIN-PATTERNS HAVE MELDED TOGETHER.
WELL, THEN LET'S GET THIS THING OFF HIM!
SUPERBOY, I DON'T THINK THAT'S A GOOD IDEA. MAY I SUGGEST YOU USE YOUR TACTILE TELEKINESIS?
RELAX, KID, I'M PART KRYPTONIAN...

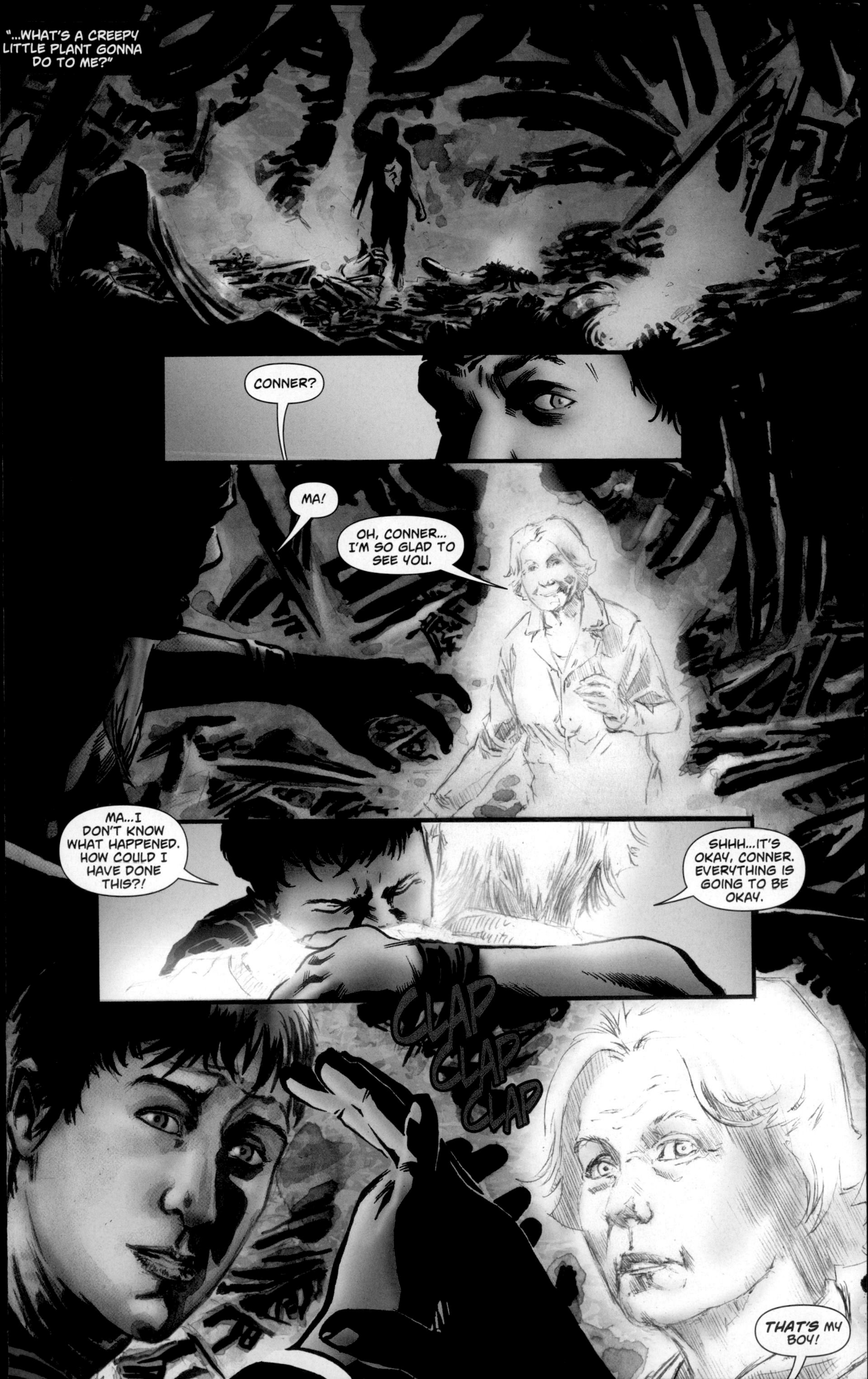
"...WHAT'S A CREEPY LITTLE PLANT GONNA DO TO ME?"
CONNER?
MA!
OH, CONNER... I'M SO GLAD TO SEE YOU.
MA...I DON'T KNOW WHAT HAPPENED. HOW COULD I HAVE DONE THIS?!
SHHH...IT'S OKAY, CONNER. EVERYTHING IS GOING TO BE OKAY.
CLAP CLAP CLAP
THAT'S MY BOY!

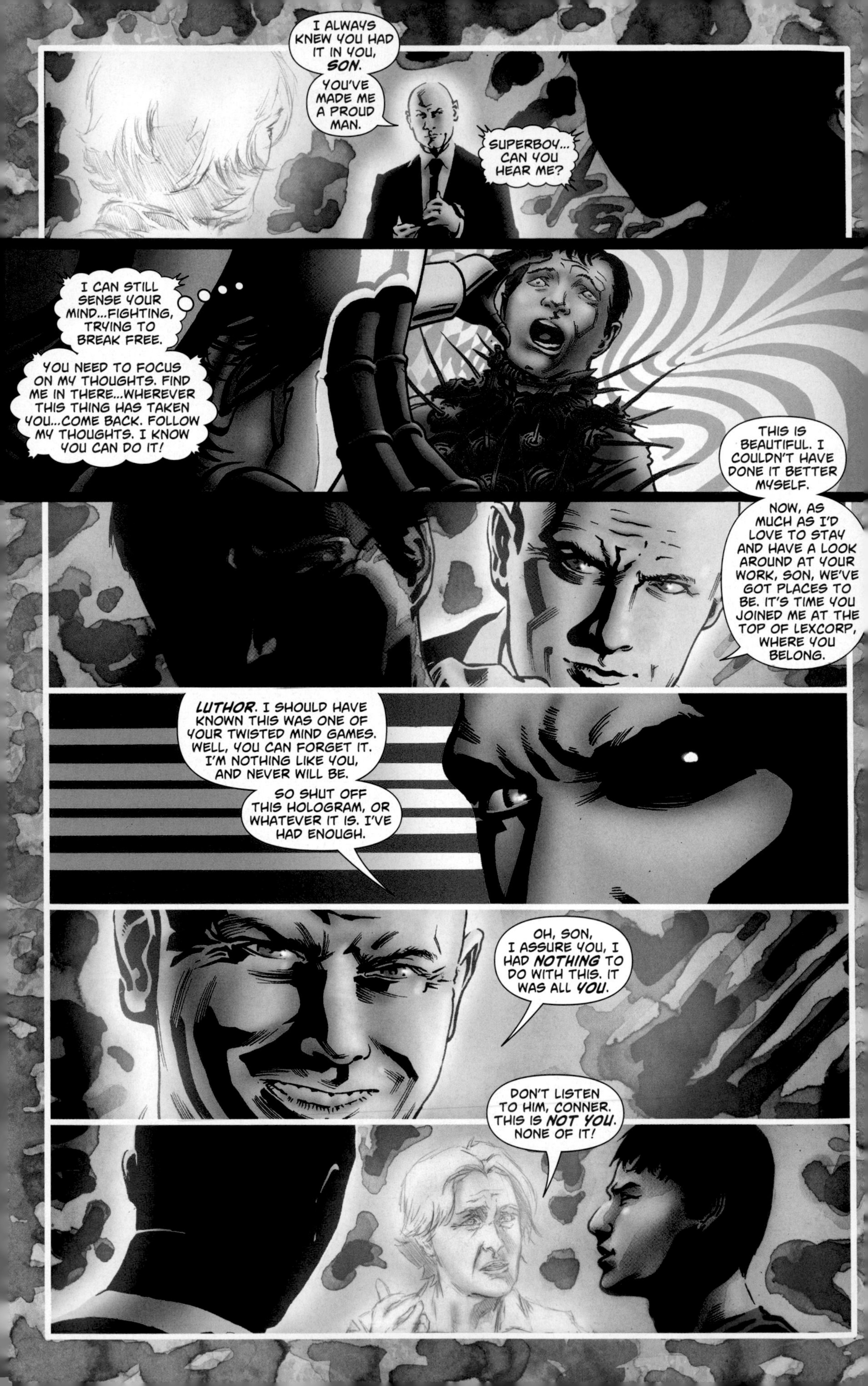
I ALWAYS KNEW YOU HAD IT IN YOU, **SON**. YOU'VE MADE ME A PROUD MAN.
SUPERBOY... CAN YOU HEAR ME?
I CAN STILL SENSE YOUR MIND...FIGHTING, TRYING TO BREAK FREE.
YOU NEED TO FOCUS ON MY THOUGHTS. FIND ME IN THERE...WHEREVER THIS THING HAS TAKEN YOU...COME BACK. FOLLOW MY THOUGHTS. I KNOW YOU CAN DO IT!
THIS IS BEAUTIFUL. I COULDN'T HAVE DONE IT BETTER MYSELF.
NOW, AS MUCH AS I'D LOVE TO STAY AND HAVE A LOOK AROUND AT YOUR WORK, SON, WE'VE GOT PLACES TO BE. IT'S TIME YOU JOINED ME AT THE TOP OF LEXCORP, WHERE YOU BELONG.
LUTHOR. I SHOULD HAVE KNOWN THIS WAS ONE OF YOUR TWISTED MIND GAMES. WELL, YOU CAN FORGET IT. I'M NOTHING LIKE YOU, AND NEVER WILL BE.
SO SHUT OFF THIS HOLOGRAM, OR WHATEVER IT IS. I'VE HAD ENOUGH.
OH, SON, I ASSURE YOU, I HAD ***NOTHING*** TO DO WITH THIS. IT WAS ALL ***YOU***.
DON'T LISTEN TO HIM, CONNER. THIS IS ***NOT YOU***. NONE OF IT!

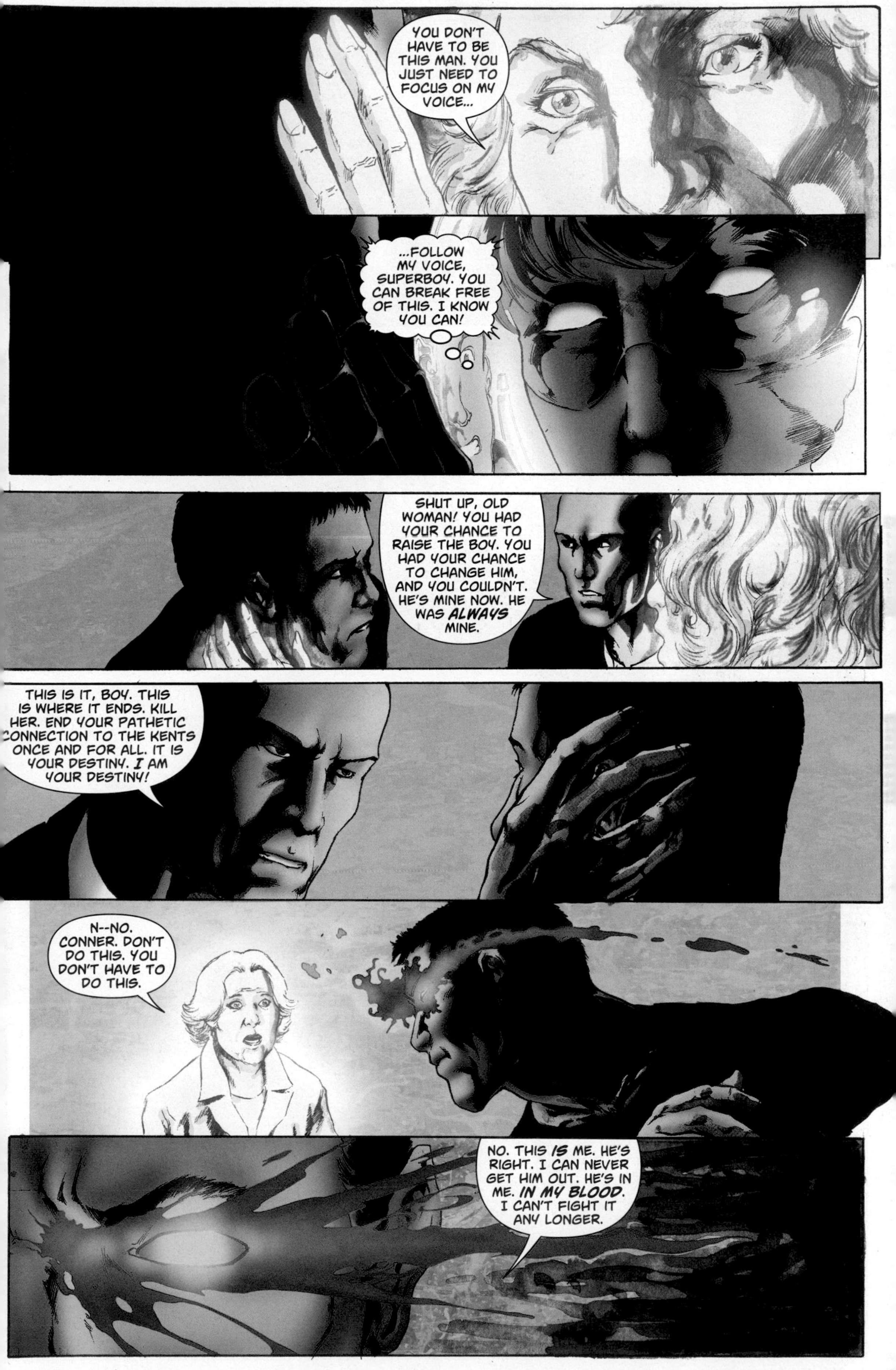
YOU DON'T HAVE TO BE THIS MAN. YOU JUST NEED TO FOCUS ON MY VOICE...
...FOLLOW MY VOICE, SUPERBOY. YOU CAN BREAK FREE OF THIS. I KNOW YOU CAN!
SHUT UP, OLD WOMAN! YOU HAD YOUR CHANCE TO RAISE THE BOY. YOU HAD YOUR CHANCE TO CHANGE HIM, AND YOU COULDN'T. HE'S MINE NOW. HE WAS *ALWAYS* MINE.
THIS IS IT, BOY. THIS IS WHERE IT ENDS. KILL HER. END YOUR PATHETIC CONNECTION TO THE KENTS ONCE AND FOR ALL. IT IS YOUR DESTINY. *I* AM YOUR DESTINY!
N--NO. CONNER. DON'T DO THIS. YOU DON'T HAVE TO DO THIS.
NO. THIS *IS* ME. HE'S RIGHT. I CAN NEVER GET HIM OUT. HE'S IN ME. *IN MY BLOOD*. I CAN'T FIGHT IT ANY LONGER.

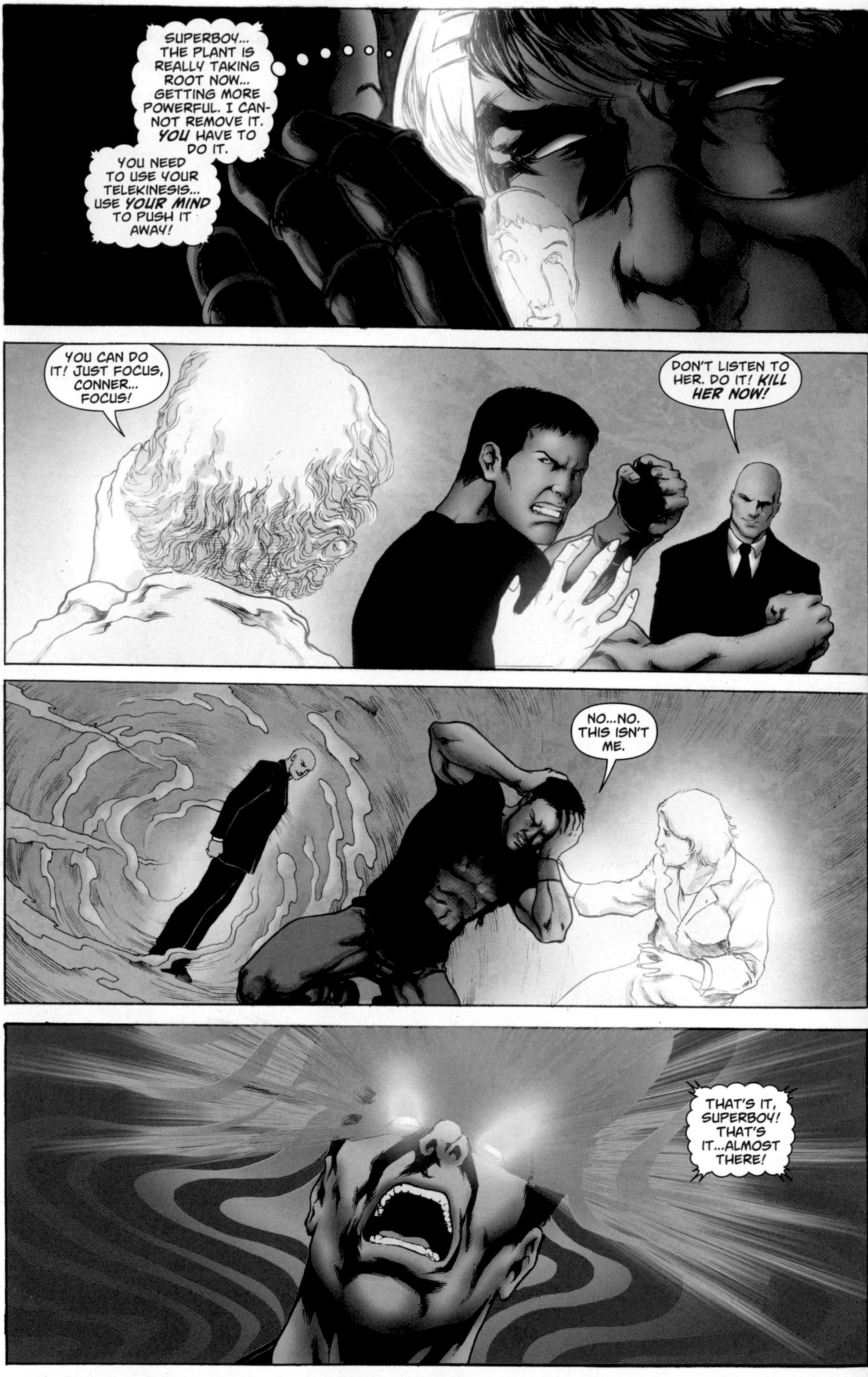
SUPERBOY... THE PLANT IS REALLY TAKING ROOT NOW... GETTING MORE POWERFUL. I CAN-NOT REMOVE IT. YOU HAVE TO DO IT.
YOU NEED TO USE YOUR TELEKINESIS... USE YOUR MIND TO PUSH IT AWAY!
YOU CAN DO IT! JUST FOCUS, CONNER... FOCUS!
DON'T LISTEN TO HER. DO IT! KILL HER NOW!
NO...NO. THIS ISN'T ME.
THAT'S IT, SUPERBOY! THAT'S IT...ALMOST THERE!

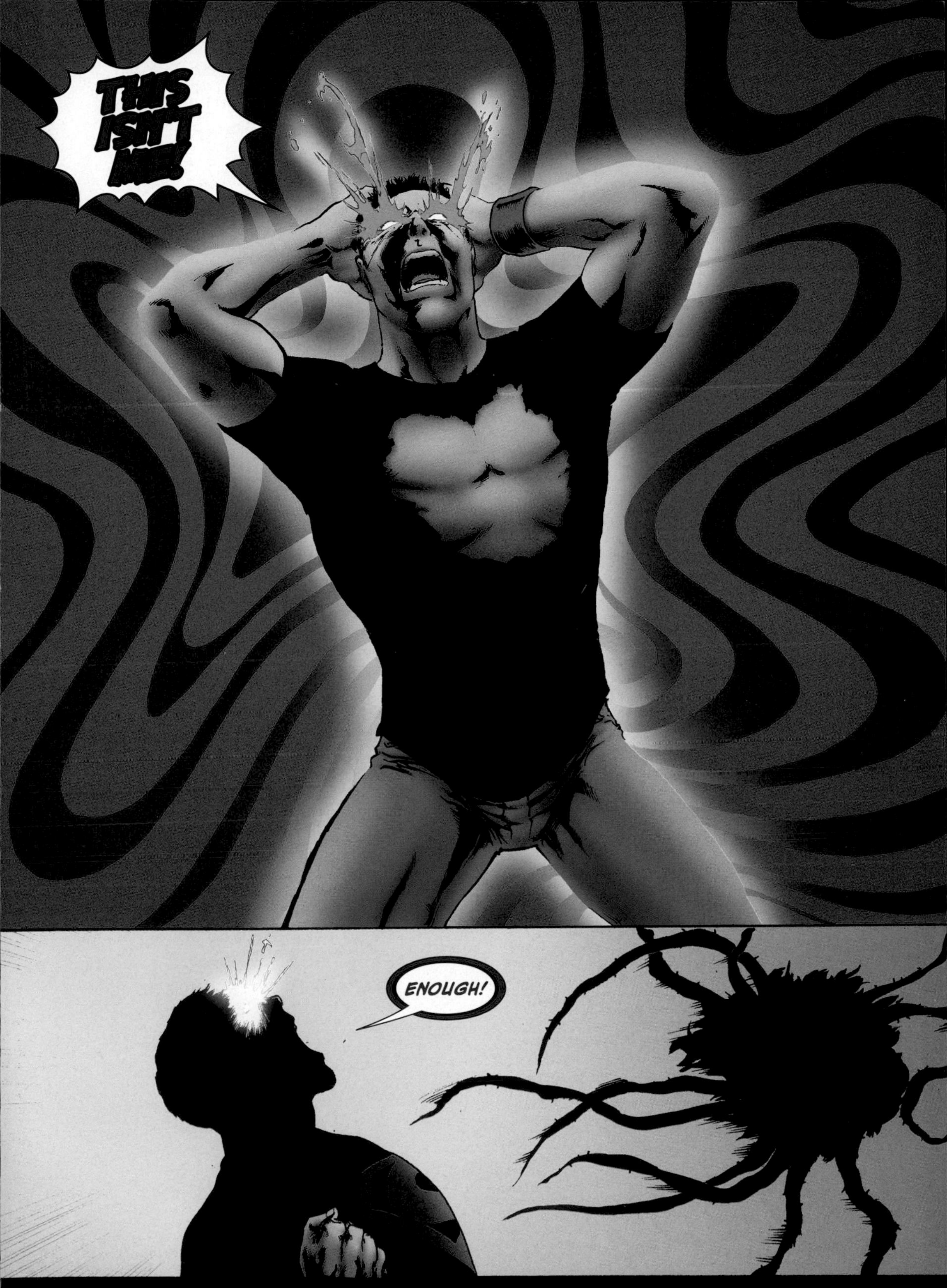
THIS ISN'T ME!
ENOUGH!

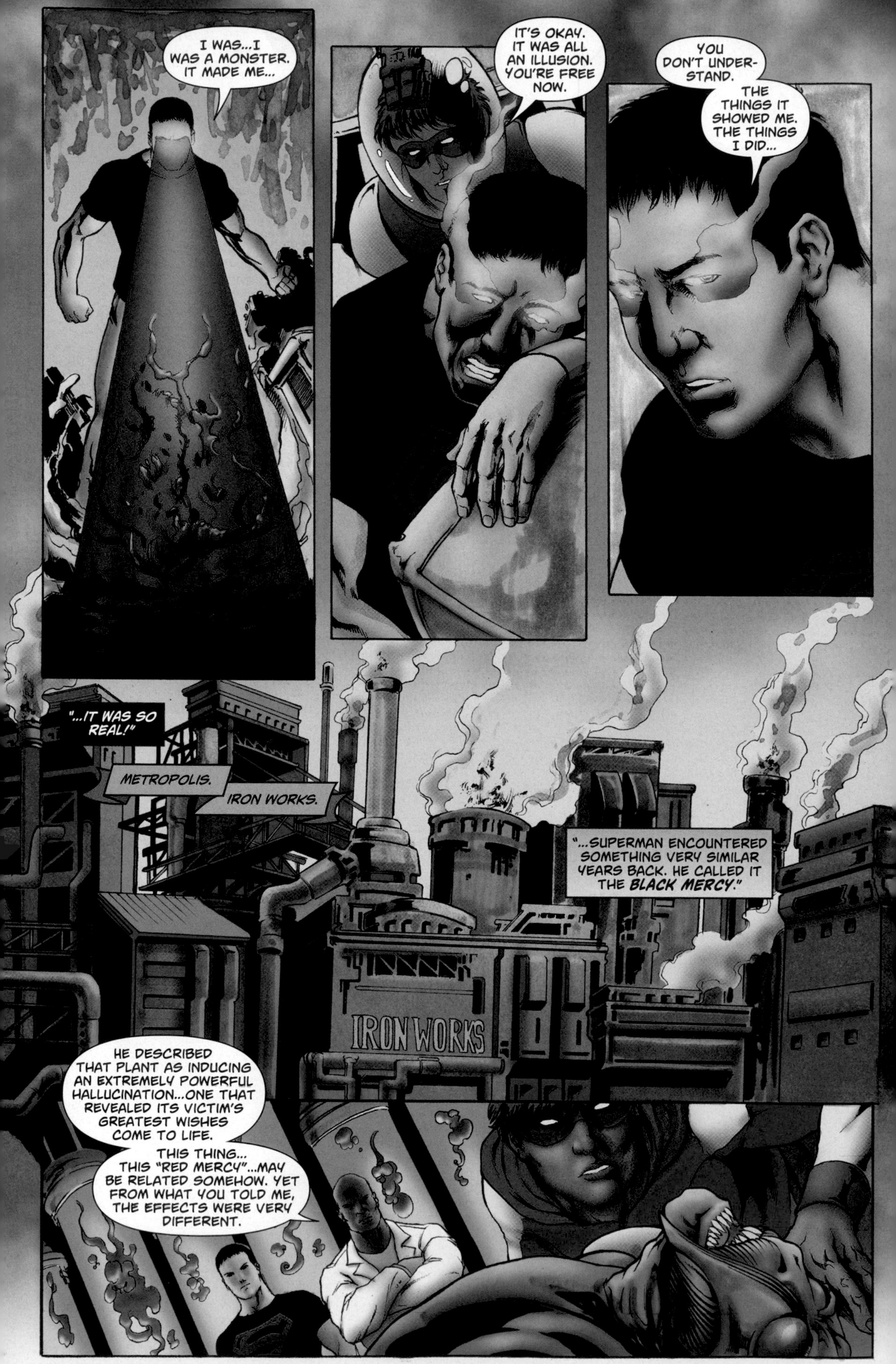

I WAS...I WAS A MONSTER. IT MADE ME...
IT'S OKAY. IT WAS ALL AN ILLUSION. YOU'RE FREE NOW.
YOU DON'T UNDER-STAND.
THE THINGS IT SHOWED ME. THE THINGS I DID...
"...IT WAS SO REAL!"
METROPOLIS.
IRON WORKS.
"...SUPERMAN ENCOUNTERED SOMETHING VERY SIMILAR YEARS BACK. HE CALLED IT THE BLACK MERCY."
IRON WORKS
HE DESCRIBED THAT PLANT AS INDUCING AN EXTREMELY POWERFUL HALLUCINATION...ONE THAT REVEALED ITS VICTIM'S GREATEST WISHES COME TO LIFE.
THIS THING... THIS "RED MERCY"...MAY BE RELATED SOMEHOW. YET FROM WHAT YOU TOLD ME, THE EFFECTS WERE VERY DIFFERENT.

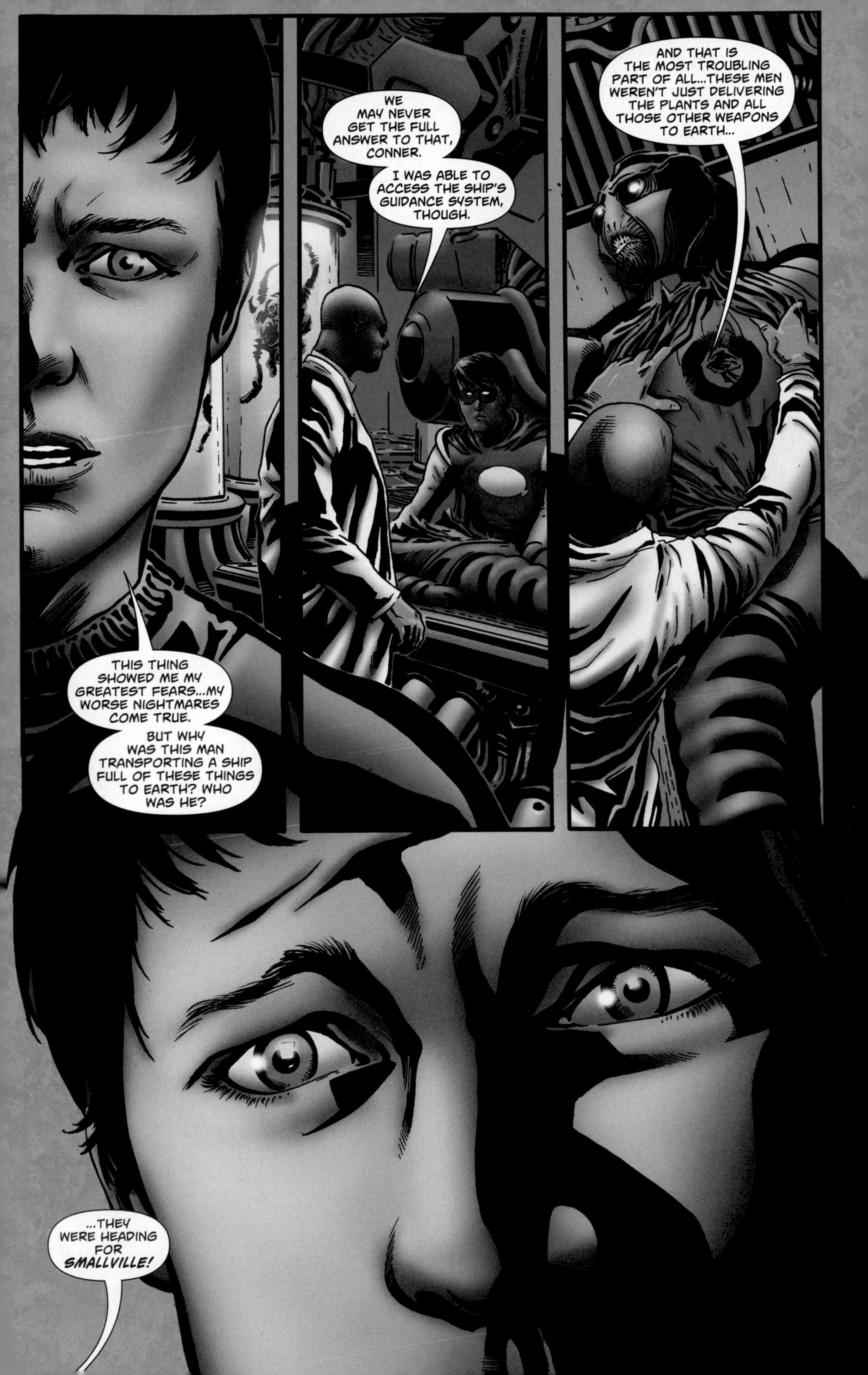
THIS THING SHOWED ME MY GREATEST FEARS...MY WORSE NIGHTMARES COME TRUE.
BUT WHY WAS THIS MAN TRANSPORTING A SHIP FULL OF THESE THINGS TO EARTH? WHO WAS HE?
WE MAY NEVER GET THE FULL ANSWER TO THAT, CONNER.
I WAS ABLE TO ACCESS THE SHIP'S GUIDANCE SYSTEM, THOUGH.
AND THAT IS THE MOST TROUBLING PART OF ALL...THESE MEN WEREN'T JUST DELIVERING THE PLANTS AND ALL THOSE OTHER WEAPONS TO EARTH...
...THEY WERE HEADING FOR SMALLVILLE!

SUPERBOY #8

Cover by Karl Kerschl

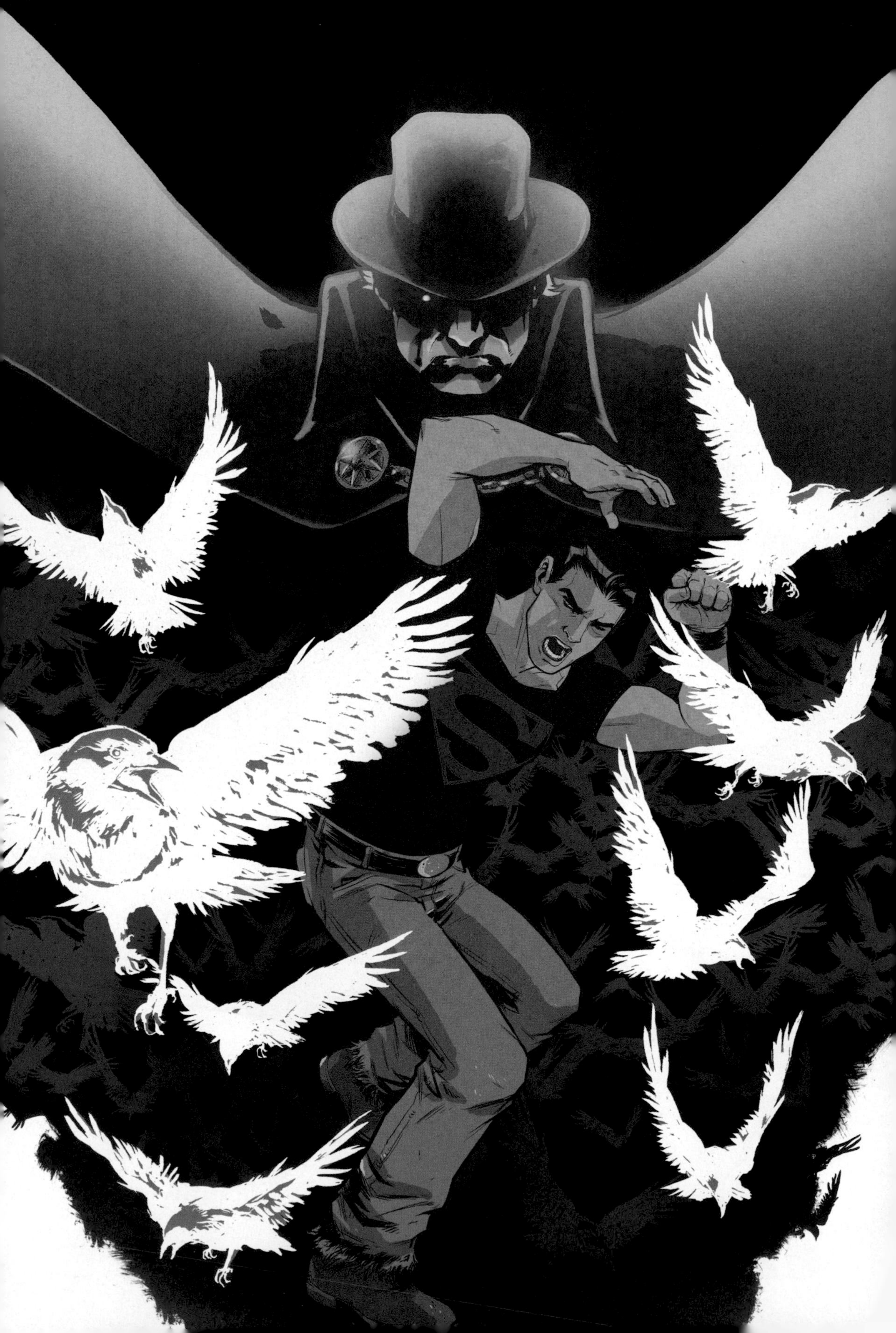

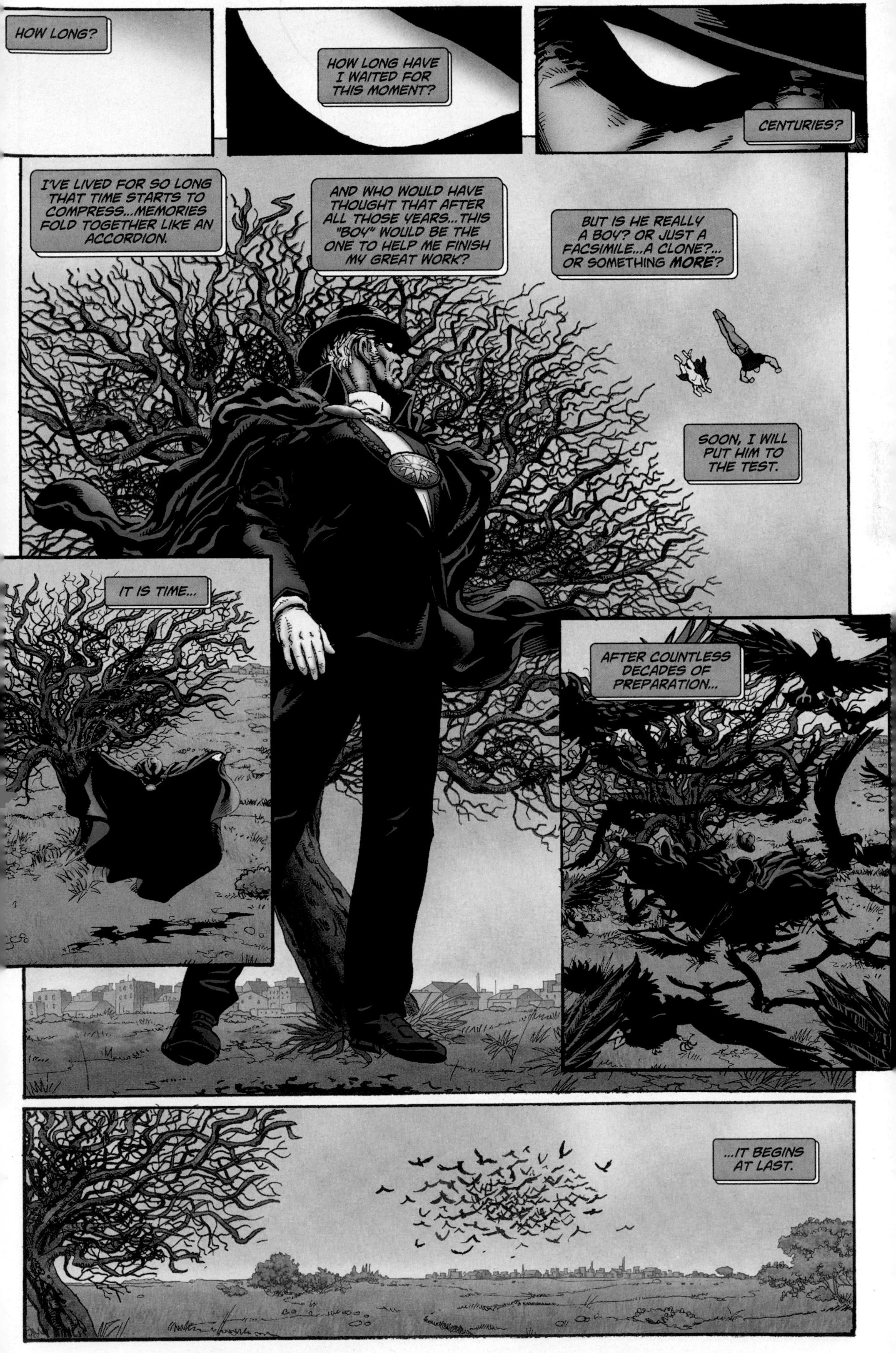
HOW LONG?
HOW LONG HAVE I WAITED FOR THIS MOMENT?
CENTURIES?
I'VE LIVED FOR SO LONG THAT TIME STARTS TO COMPRESS...MEMORIES FOLD TOGETHER LIKE AN ACCORDION.
AND WHO WOULD HAVE THOUGHT THAT AFTER ALL THOSE YEARS...THIS "BOY" WOULD BE THE ONE TO HELP ME FINISH MY GREAT WORK?
BUT IS HE REALLY A BOY? OR JUST A FACSIMILE...A CLONE?... OR SOMETHING MORE?
SOON, I WILL PUT HIM TO THE TEST.
IT IS TIME...
AFTER COUNTLESS DECADES OF PREPARATION...
...IT BEGINS AT LAST.

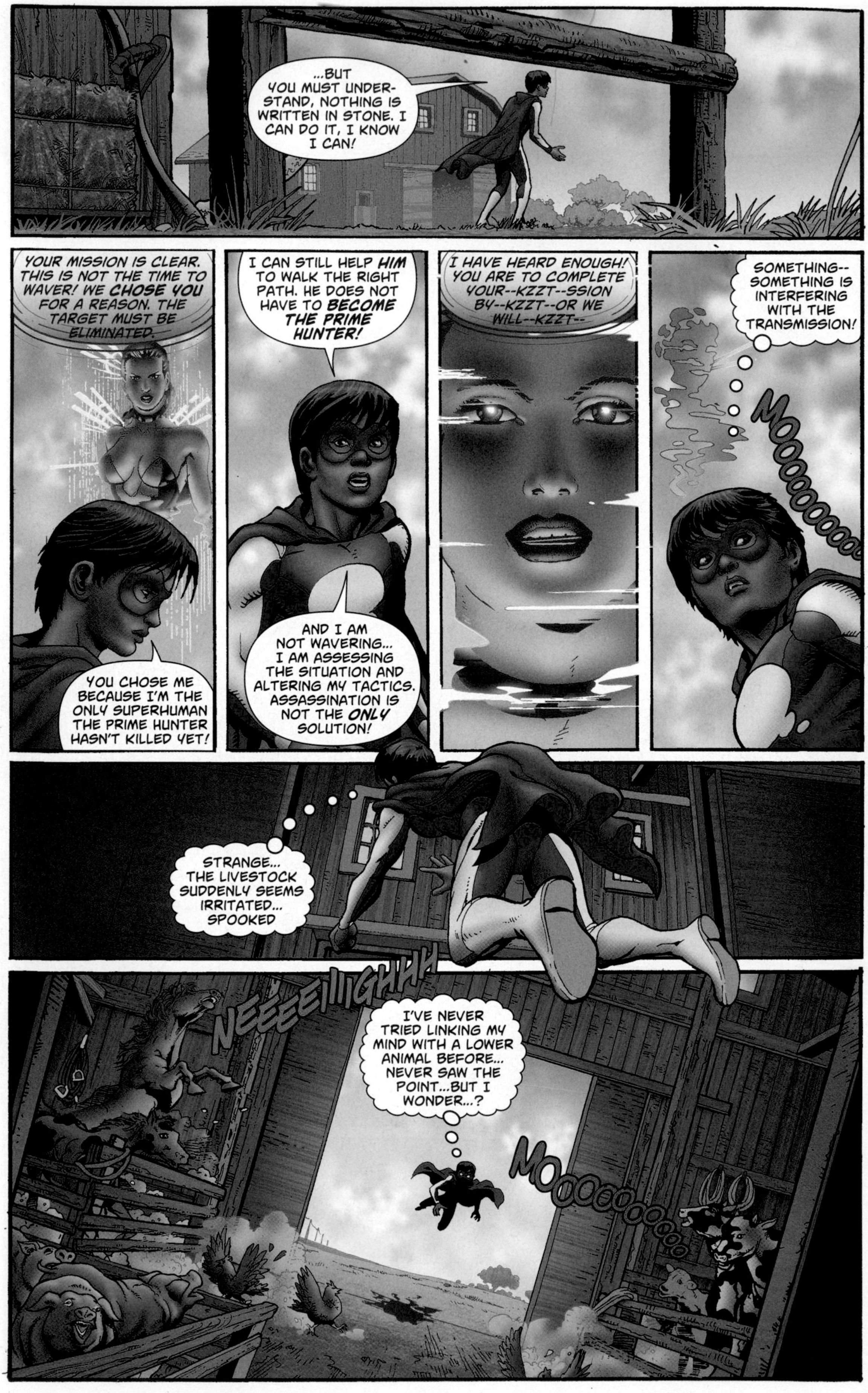
...BUT YOU MUST UNDERSTAND, NOTHING IS WRITTEN IN STONE. I CAN DO IT, I KNOW I CAN!
YOUR MISSION IS CLEAR. THIS IS NOT THE TIME TO WAVER! WE CHOSE YOU FOR A REASON. THE TARGET MUST BE ELIMINATED.
YOU CHOSE ME BECAUSE I'M THE ONLY SUPERHUMAN THE PRIME HUNTER HASN'T KILLED YET!
I CAN STILL HELP HIM TO WALK THE RIGHT PATH. HE DOES NOT HAVE TO BECOME THE PRIME HUNTER!
AND I AM NOT WAVERING... I AM ASSESSING THE SITUATION AND ALTERING MY TACTICS. ASSASSINATION IS NOT THE ONLY SOLUTION!
I HAVE HEARD ENOUGH! YOU ARE TO COMPLETE YOUR--KZZT--SSION BY--KZZT--OR WE WILL--KZZT--
SOMETHING-- SOMETHING IS INTERFERING WITH THE TRANSMISSION!
MOOOOOOOOOO
STRANGE... THE LIVESTOCK SUDDENLY SEEMS IRRITATED... SPOOKED
NEEEEIIIGHHH
I'VE NEVER TRIED LINKING MY MIND WITH A LOWER ANIMAL BEFORE... NEVER SAW THE POINT...BUT I WONDER...?
MOOOOOOOOOO

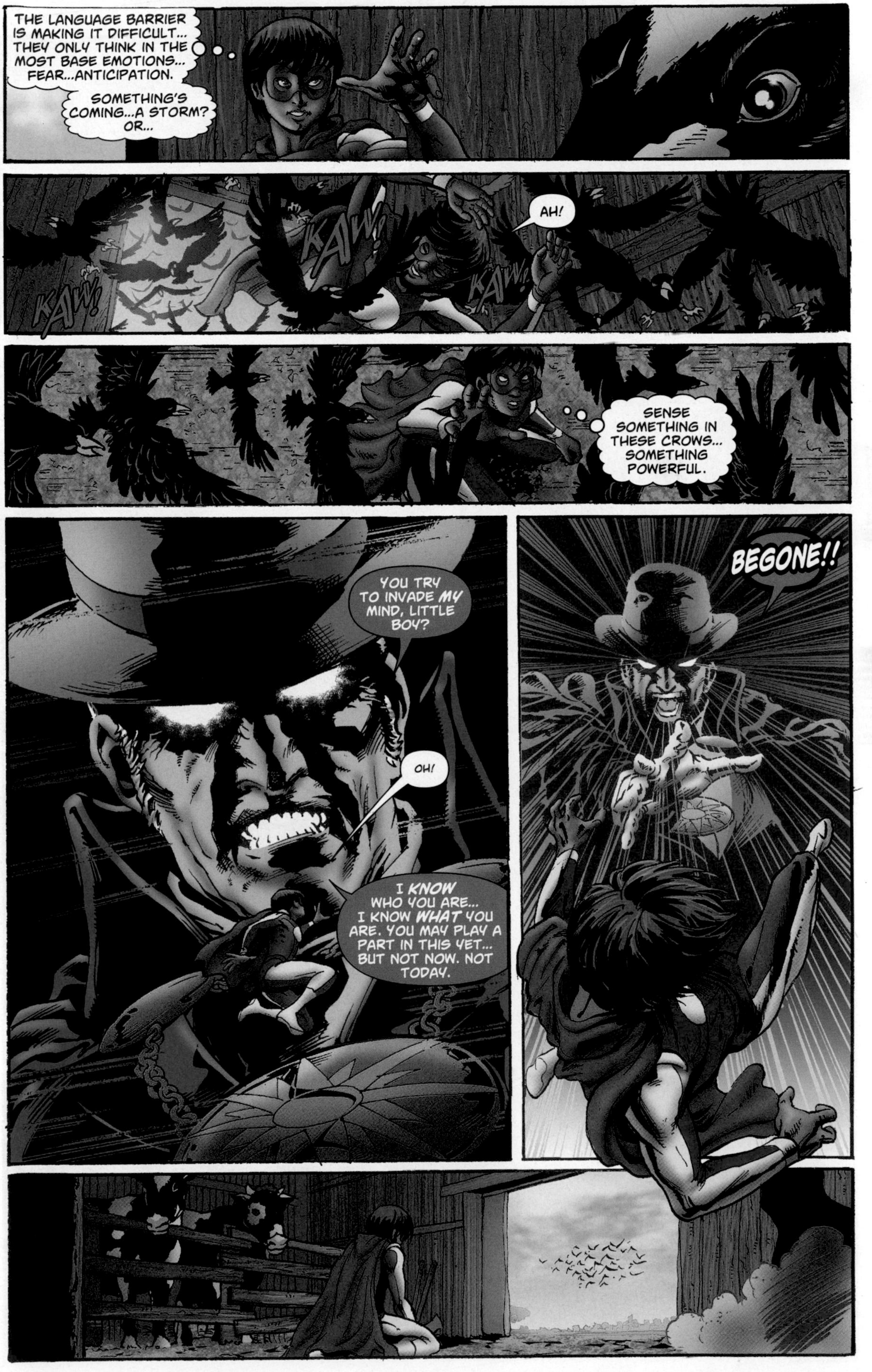
THE LANGUAGE BARRIER IS MAKING IT DIFFICULT... THEY ONLY THINK IN THE MOST BASE EMOTIONS... FEAR...ANTICIPATION.
SOMETHING'S COMING...A STORM? OR...
KAW!
KAW!
KAW!
AH!
SENSE SOMETHING IN THESE CROWS... SOMETHING POWERFUL.
YOU TRY TO INVADE MY MIND, LITTLE BOY?
OH!
I KNOW WHO YOU ARE... I KNOW WHAT YOU ARE. YOU MAY PLAY A PART IN THIS YET... BUT NOT NOW. NOT TODAY.
BEGONE!!

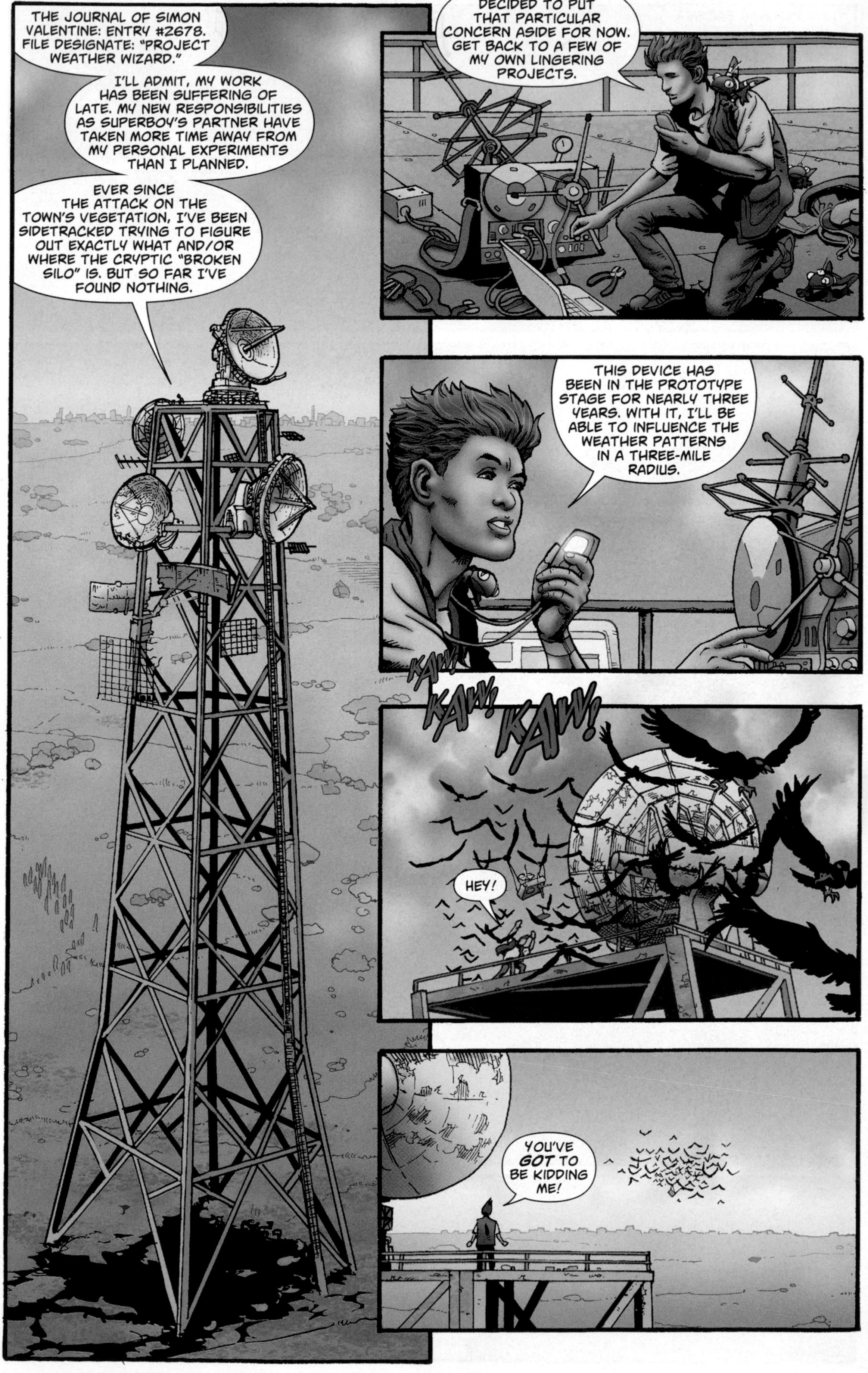
THE JOURNAL OF SIMON VALENTINE: ENTRY #2678. FILE DESIGNATE: "PROJECT WEATHER WIZARD."
I'LL ADMIT, MY WORK HAS BEEN SUFFERING OF LATE. MY NEW RESPONSIBILITIES AS SUPERBOY'S PARTNER HAVE TAKEN MORE TIME AWAY FROM MY PERSONAL EXPERIMENTS THAN I PLANNED.
EVER SINCE THE ATTACK ON THE TOWN'S VEGETATION, I'VE BEEN SIDETRACKED TRYING TO FIGURE OUT EXACTLY WHAT AND/OR WHERE THE CRYPTIC "BROKEN SILO" IS. BUT SO FAR I'VE FOUND NOTHING.
SO I'VE DECIDED TO PUT THAT PARTICULAR CONCERN ASIDE FOR NOW. GET BACK TO A FEW OF MY OWN LINGERING PROJECTS.
THIS DEVICE HAS BEEN IN THE PROTOTYPE STAGE FOR NEARLY THREE YEARS. WITH IT, I'LL BE ABLE TO INFLUENCE THE WEATHER PATTERNS IN A THREE-MILE RADIUS.
KAW! KAW! KAW!
HEY!
YOU'VE GOT TO BE KIDDING ME!

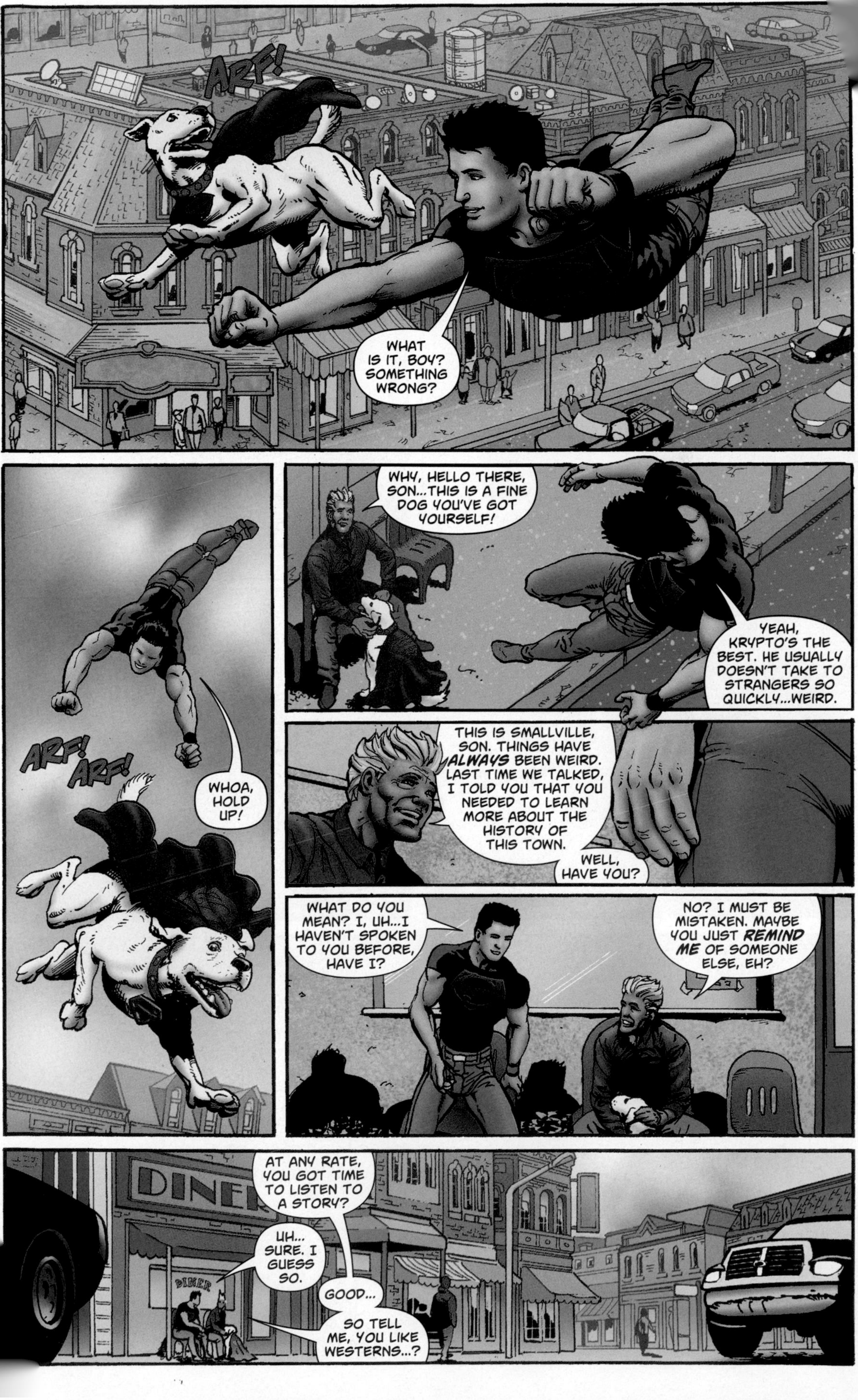
ARF!
WHAT IS IT, BOY? SOMETHING WRONG?
WHOA, HOLD UP!
ARF! ARF!
WHY, HELLO THERE, SON...THIS IS A FINE DOG YOU'VE GOT YOURSELF!
YEAH, KRYPTO'S THE BEST. HE USUALLY DOESN'T TAKE TO STRANGERS SO QUICKLY...WEIRD.
THIS IS SMALLVILLE, SON. THINGS HAVE ALWAYS BEEN WEIRD. LAST TIME WE TALKED, I TOLD YOU THAT YOU NEEDED TO LEARN MORE ABOUT THE HISTORY OF THIS TOWN.
WELL, HAVE YOU?
WHAT DO YOU MEAN? I, UH...I HAVEN'T SPOKEN TO YOU BEFORE, HAVE I?
NO? I MUST BE MISTAKEN. MAYBE YOU JUST REMIND ME OF SOMEONE ELSE, EH?
DINER
AT ANY RATE, YOU GOT TIME TO LISTEN TO A STORY?
UH... SURE. I GUESS SO.
GOOD...
SO TELL ME, YOU LIKE WESTERNS...?

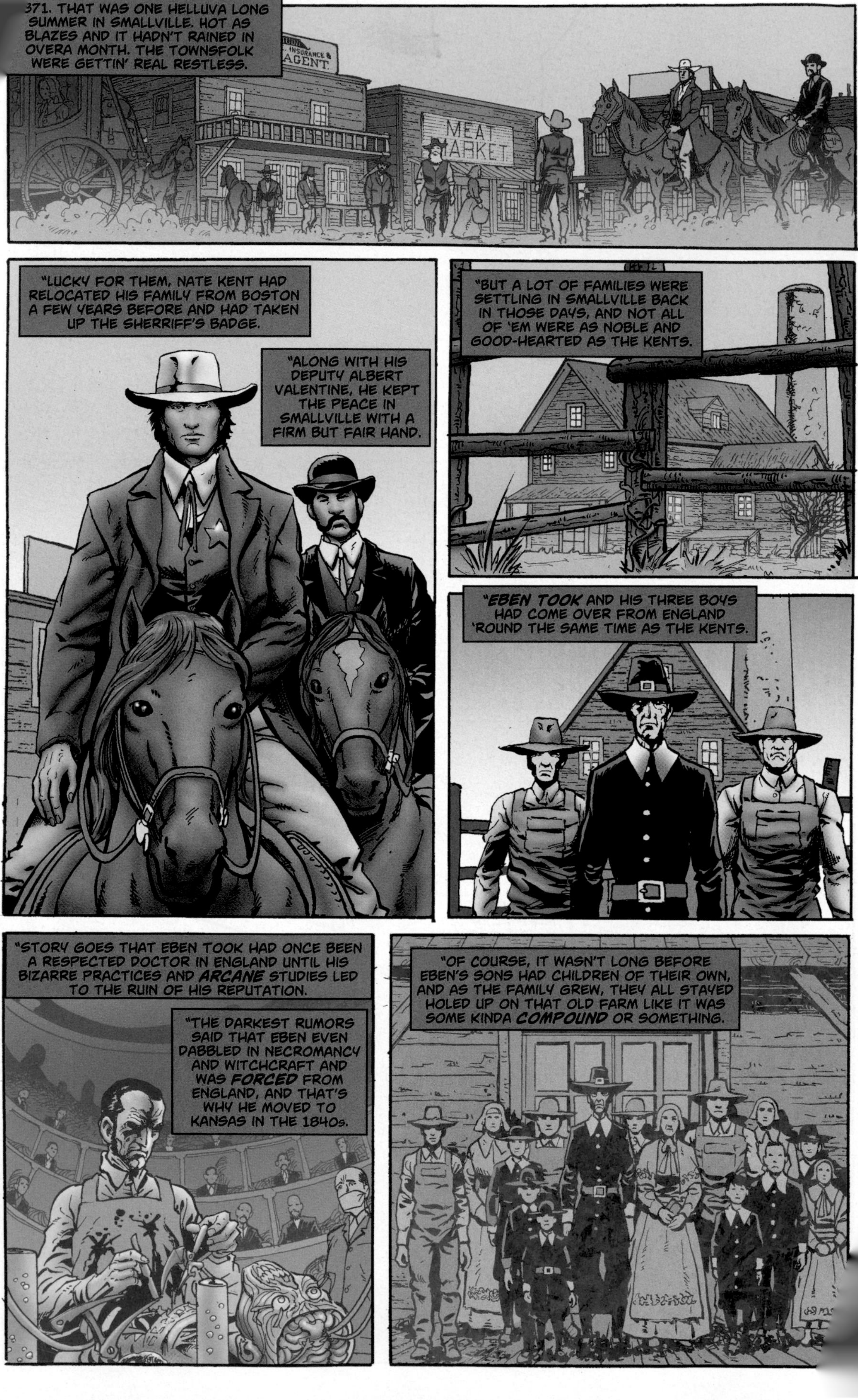
371. THAT WAS ONE HELLUVA LONG SUMMER IN SMALLVILLE. HOT AS BLAZES AND IT HADN'T RAINED IN OVERA MONTH. THE TOWNSFOLK WERE GETTIN' REAL RESTLESS.
INSURANCE & AGENT
MEAT MARKET
"LUCKY FOR THEM, NATE KENT HAD RELOCATED HIS FAMILY FROM BOSTON A FEW YEARS BEFORE AND HAD TAKEN UP THE SHERRIFF'S BADGE.
"ALONG WITH HIS DEPUTY ALBERT VALENTINE, HE KEPT THE PEACE IN SMALLVILLE WITH A FIRM BUT FAIR HAND.
"BUT A LOT OF FAMILIES WERE SETTLING IN SMALLVILLE BACK IN THOSE DAYS, AND NOT ALL OF 'EM WERE AS NOBLE AND GOOD-HEARTED AS THE KENTS.
"EBEN TOOK AND HIS THREE BOYS HAD COME OVER FROM ENGLAND 'ROUND THE SAME TIME AS THE KENTS.
"STORY GOES THAT EBEN TOOK HAD ONCE BEEN A RESPECTED DOCTOR IN ENGLAND UNTIL HIS BIZARRE PRACTICES AND ARCANE STUDIES LED TO THE RUIN OF HIS REPUTATION.
"THE DARKEST RUMORS SAID THAT EBEN EVEN DABBLED IN NECROMANCY AND WITCHCRAFT AND WAS FORCED FROM ENGLAND, AND THAT'S WHY HE MOVED TO KANSAS IN THE 1840s.
"OF COURSE, IT WASN'T LONG BEFORE EBEN'S SONS HAD CHILDREN OF THEIR OWN, AND AS THE FAMILY GREW, THEY ALL STAYED HOLED UP ON THAT OLD FARM LIKE IT WAS SOME KINDA COMPOUND OR SOMETHING.

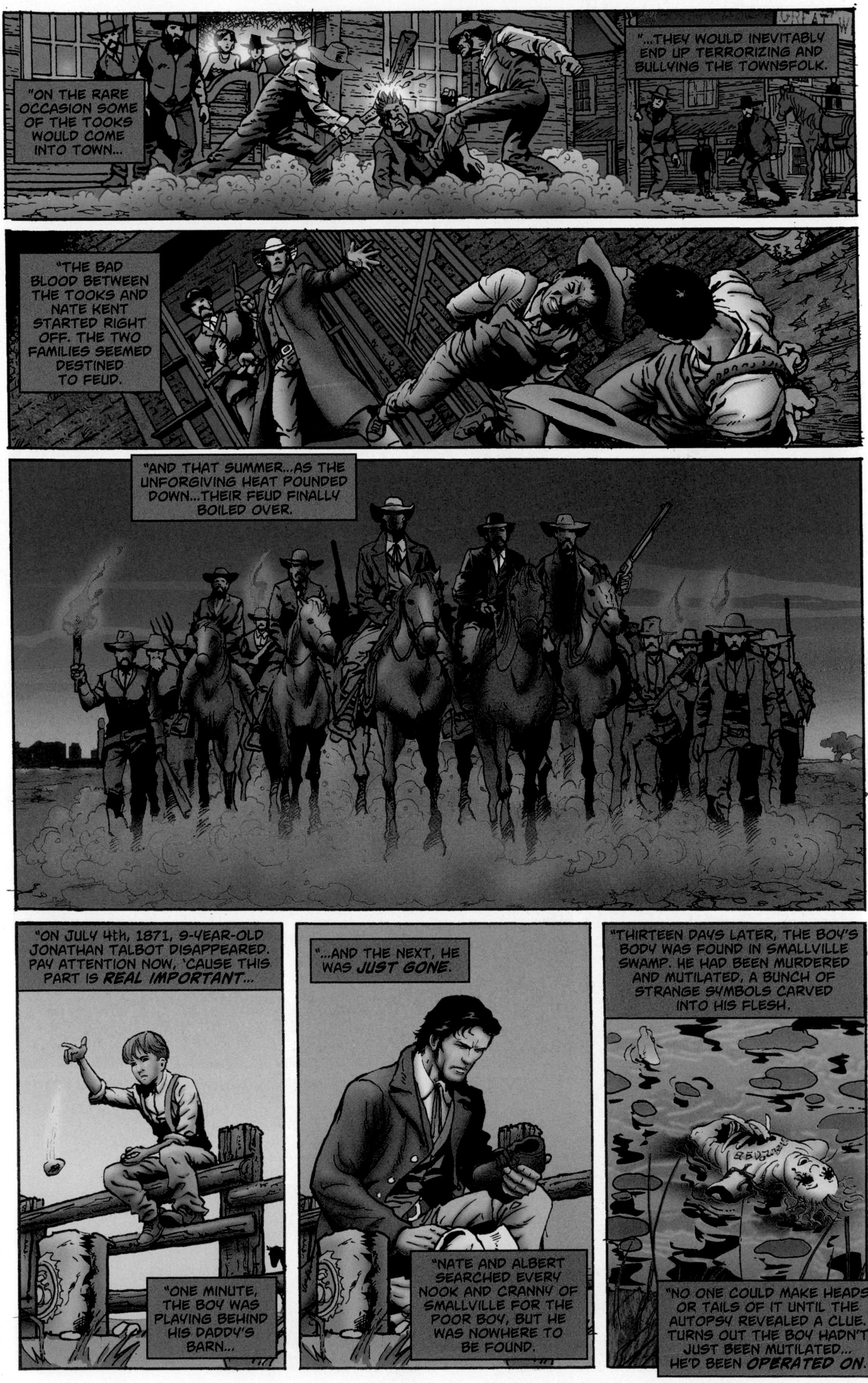
"ON THE RARE OCCASION SOME OF THE TOOKS WOULD COME INTO TOWN...
"...THEY WOULD INEVITABLY END UP TERRORIZING AND BULLYING THE TOWNSFOLK.
"THE BAD BLOOD BETWEEN THE TOOKS AND NATE KENT STARTED RIGHT OFF. THE TWO FAMILIES SEEMED DESTINED TO FEUD.
"AND THAT SUMMER...AS THE UNFORGIVING HEAT POUNDED DOWN...THEIR FEUD FINALLY BOILED OVER.
"ON JULY 4th, 1871, 9-YEAR-OLD JONATHAN TALBOT DISAPPEARED. PAY ATTENTION NOW, 'CAUSE THIS PART IS REAL IMPORTANT...
"ONE MINUTE, THE BOY WAS PLAYING BEHIND HIS DADDY'S BARN...
"...AND THE NEXT, HE WAS JUST GONE.
"NATE AND ALBERT SEARCHED EVERY NOOK AND CRANNY OF SMALLVILLE FOR THE POOR BOY, BUT HE WAS NOWHERE TO BE FOUND.
"THIRTEEN DAYS LATER, THE BOY'S BODY WAS FOUND IN SMALLVILLE SWAMP. HE HAD BEEN MURDERED AND MUTILATED, A BUNCH OF STRANGE SYMBOLS CARVED INTO HIS FLESH.
"NO ONE COULD MAKE HEADS OR TAILS OF IT UNTIL THE AUTOPSY REVEALED A CLUE. TURNS OUT THE BOY HADN'T JUST BEEN MUTILATED... HE'D BEEN OPERATED ON.

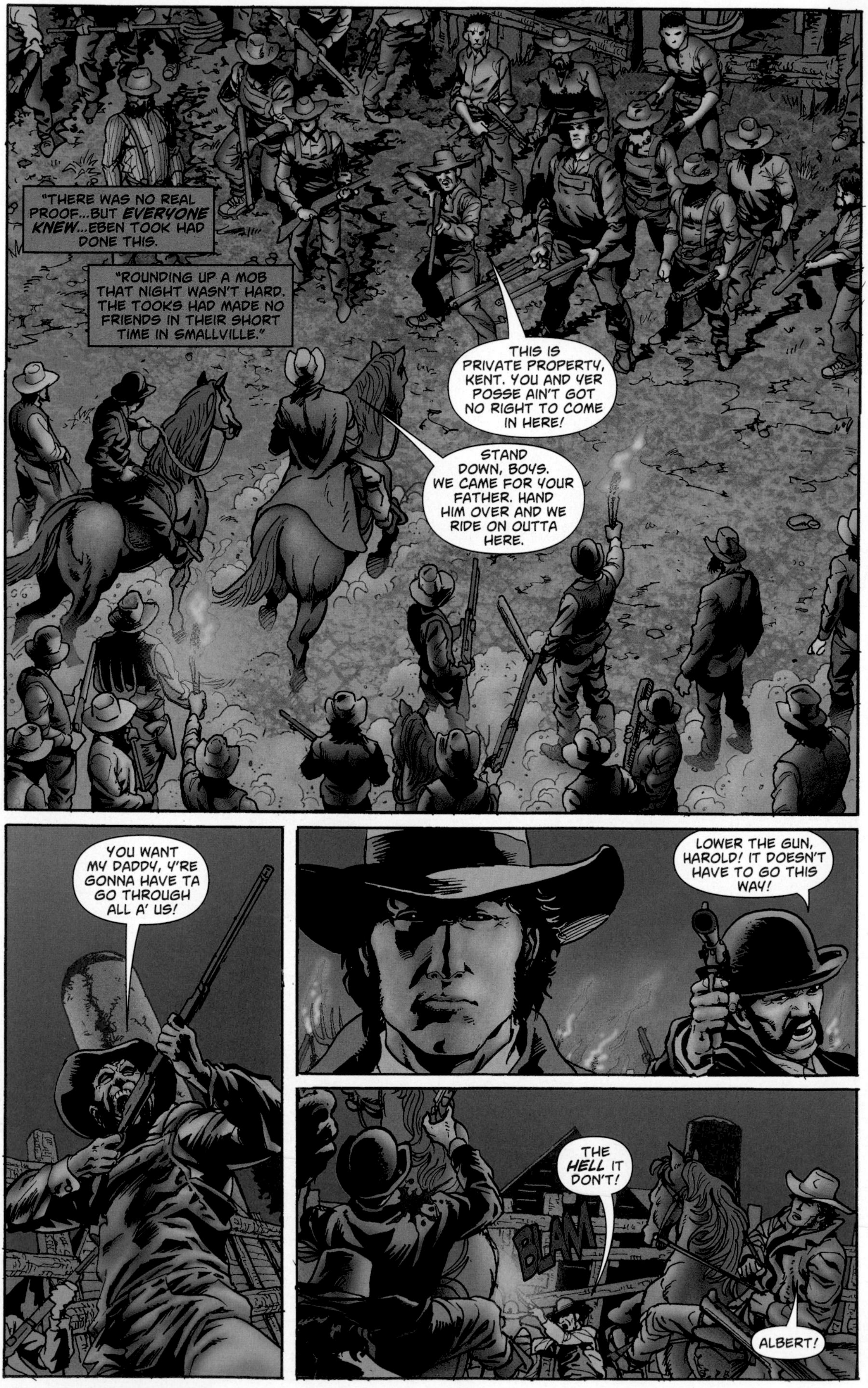
"THERE WAS NO REAL PROOF...BUT EVERYONE KNEW...EBEN TOOK HAD DONE THIS.
"ROUNDING UP A MOB THAT NIGHT WASN'T HARD. THE TOOKS HAD MADE NO FRIENDS IN THEIR SHORT TIME IN SMALLVILLE."
THIS IS PRIVATE PROPERTY, KENT. YOU AND YER POSSE AIN'T GOT NO RIGHT TO COME IN HERE!
STAND DOWN, BOYS. WE CAME FOR YOUR FATHER. HAND HIM OVER AND WE RIDE ON OUTTA HERE.
YOU WANT MY DADDY, Y'RE GONNA HAVE TA GO THROUGH ALL A' US!
LOWER THE GUN, HAROLD! IT DOESN'T HAVE TO GO THIS WAY!
THE HELL IT DON'T!
BLAM
ALBERT!

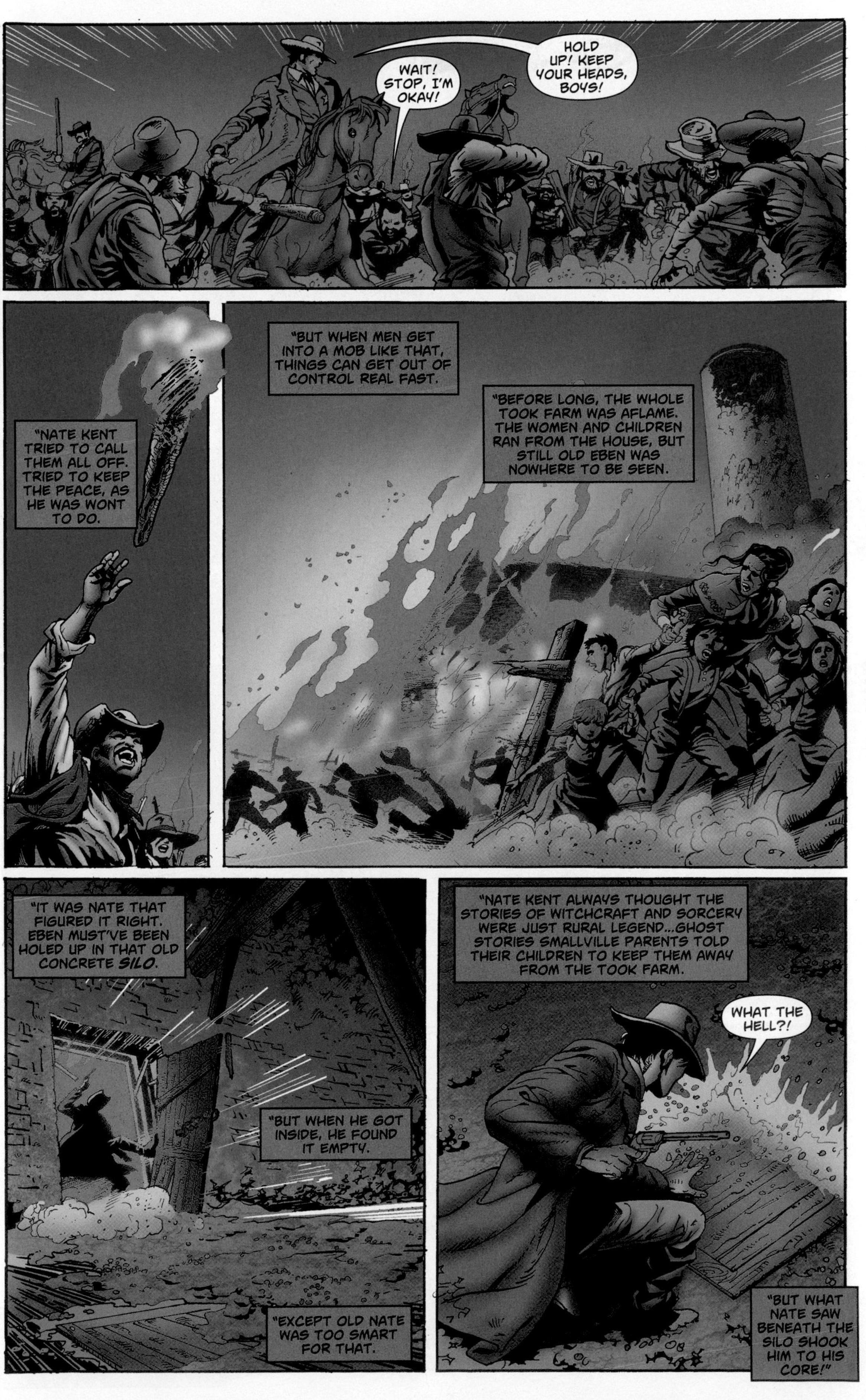
HOLD UP! KEEP YOUR HEADS, BOYS!
WAIT! STOP, I'M OKAY!
"NATE KENT TRIED TO CALL THEM ALL OFF. TRIED TO KEEP THE PEACE, AS HE WAS WONT TO DO.
"BUT WHEN MEN GET INTO A MOB LIKE THAT, THINGS CAN GET OUT OF CONTROL REAL FAST.
"BEFORE LONG, THE WHOLE TOOK FARM WAS AFLAME. THE WOMEN AND CHILDREN RAN FROM THE HOUSE, BUT STILL OLD EBEN WAS NOWHERE TO BE SEEN.
"IT WAS NATE THAT FIGURED IT RIGHT. EBEN MUST'VE BEEN HOLED UP IN THAT OLD CONCRETE SILO.
"BUT WHEN HE GOT INSIDE, HE FOUND IT EMPTY.
"EXCEPT OLD NATE WAS TOO SMART FOR THAT.
"NATE KENT ALWAYS THOUGHT THE STORIES OF WITCHCRAFT AND SORCERY WERE JUST RURAL LEGEND...GHOST STORIES SMALLVILLE PARENTS TOLD THEIR CHILDREN TO KEEP THEM AWAY FROM THE TOOK FARM.
WHAT THE HELL?!
"BUT WHAT NATE SAW BENEATH THE SILO SHOOK HIM TO HIS CORE!"

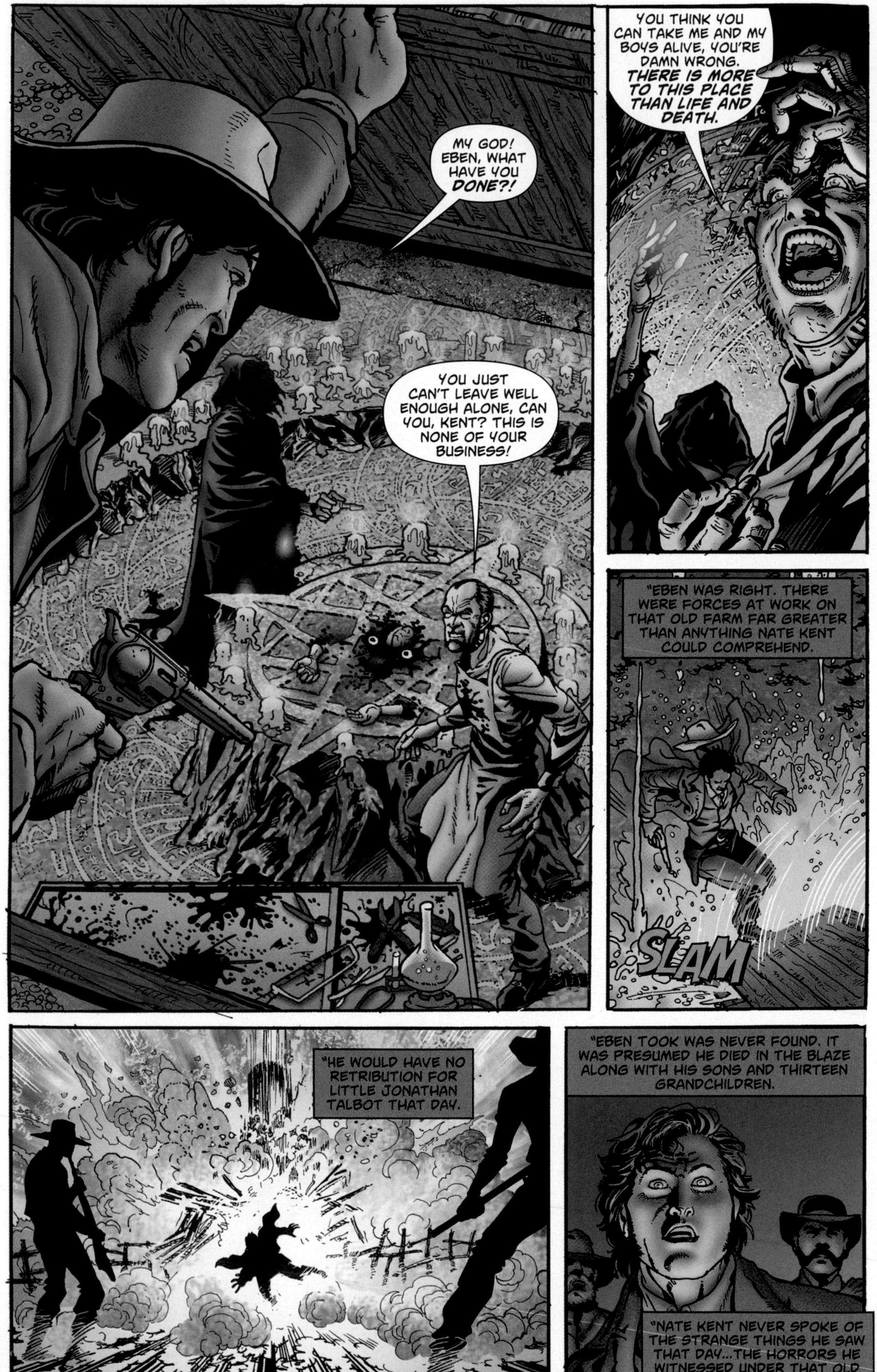
MY GOD! EBEN, WHAT HAVE YOU DONE?!
YOU JUST CAN'T LEAVE WELL ENOUGH ALONE, CAN YOU, KENT? THIS IS NONE OF YOUR BUSINESS!
YOU THINK YOU CAN TAKE ME AND MY BOYS ALIVE, YOU'RE DAMN WRONG. THERE IS MORE TO THIS PLACE THAN LIFE AND DEATH.
"EBEN WAS RIGHT. THERE WERE FORCES AT WORK ON THAT OLD FARM FAR GREATER THAN ANYTHING NATE KENT COULD COMPREHEND.
SLAM
"HE WOULD HAVE NO RETRIBUTION FOR LITTLE JONATHAN TALBOT THAT DAY.
"EBEN TOOK WAS NEVER FOUND. IT WAS PRESUMED HE DIED IN THE BLAZE ALONG WITH HIS SONS AND THIRTEEN GRANDCHILDREN.
"NATE KENT NEVER SPOKE OF THE STRANGE THINGS HE SAW THAT DAY...THE HORRORS HE WITNESSED UNDER THAT OLD BROKEN SILO..."

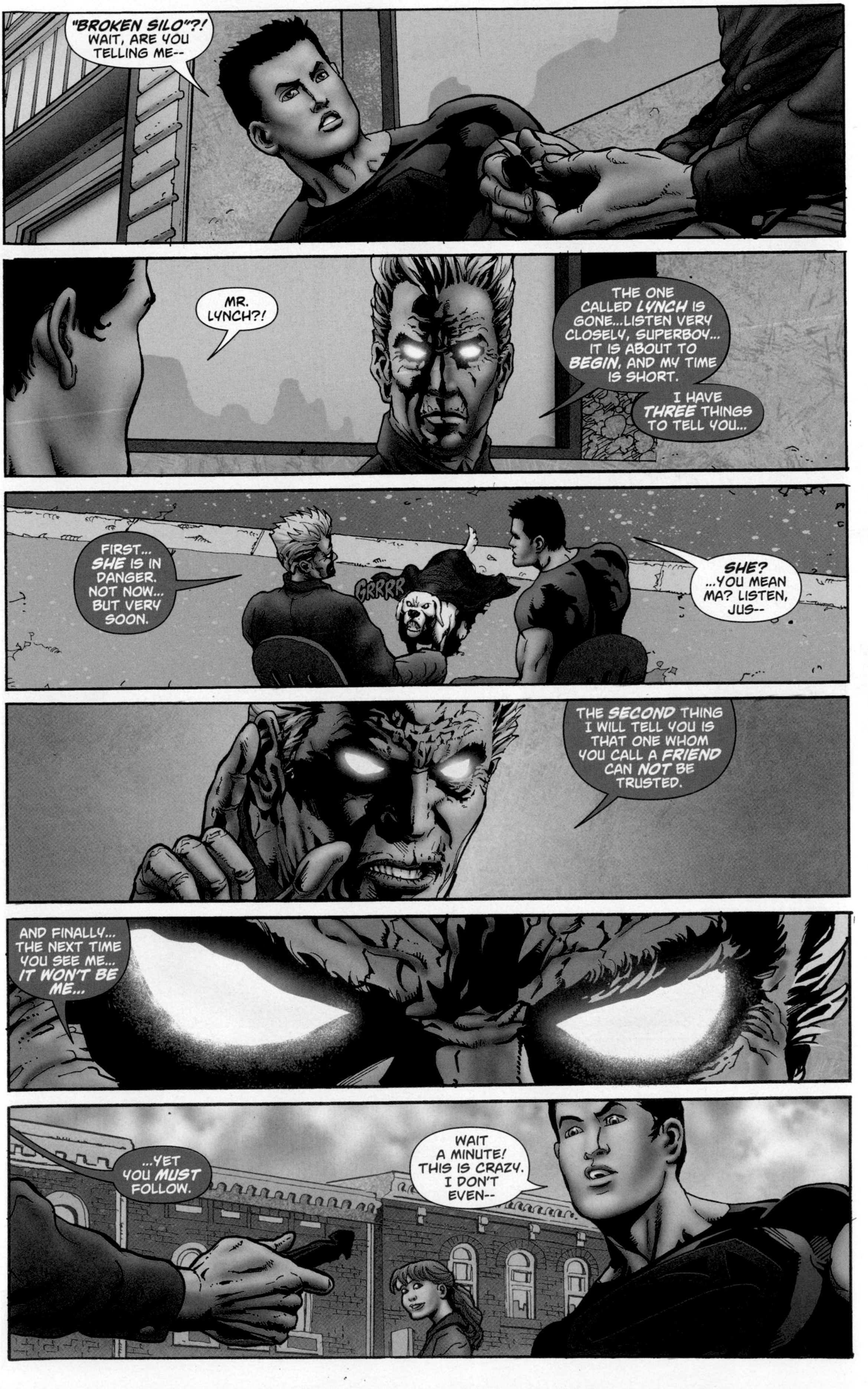
"BROKEN SILO"?! WAIT, ARE YOU TELLING ME--
MR. LYNCH?!
THE ONE CALLED LYNCH IS GONE...LISTEN VERY CLOSELY, SUPERBOY... IT IS ABOUT TO BEGIN, AND MY TIME IS SHORT.
I HAVE THREE THINGS TO TELL YOU...
FIRST... SHE IS IN DANGER. NOT NOW... BUT VERY SOON.
GRRRR
SHE? ...YOU MEAN MA? LISTEN, JUS--
THE SECOND THING I WILL TELL YOU IS THAT ONE WHOM YOU CALL A FRIEND CAN NOT BE TRUSTED.
AND FINALLY... THE NEXT TIME YOU SEE ME... IT WON'T BE ME...
...YET YOU MUST FOLLOW.
WAIT A MINUTE! THIS IS CRAZY. I DON'T EVEN--

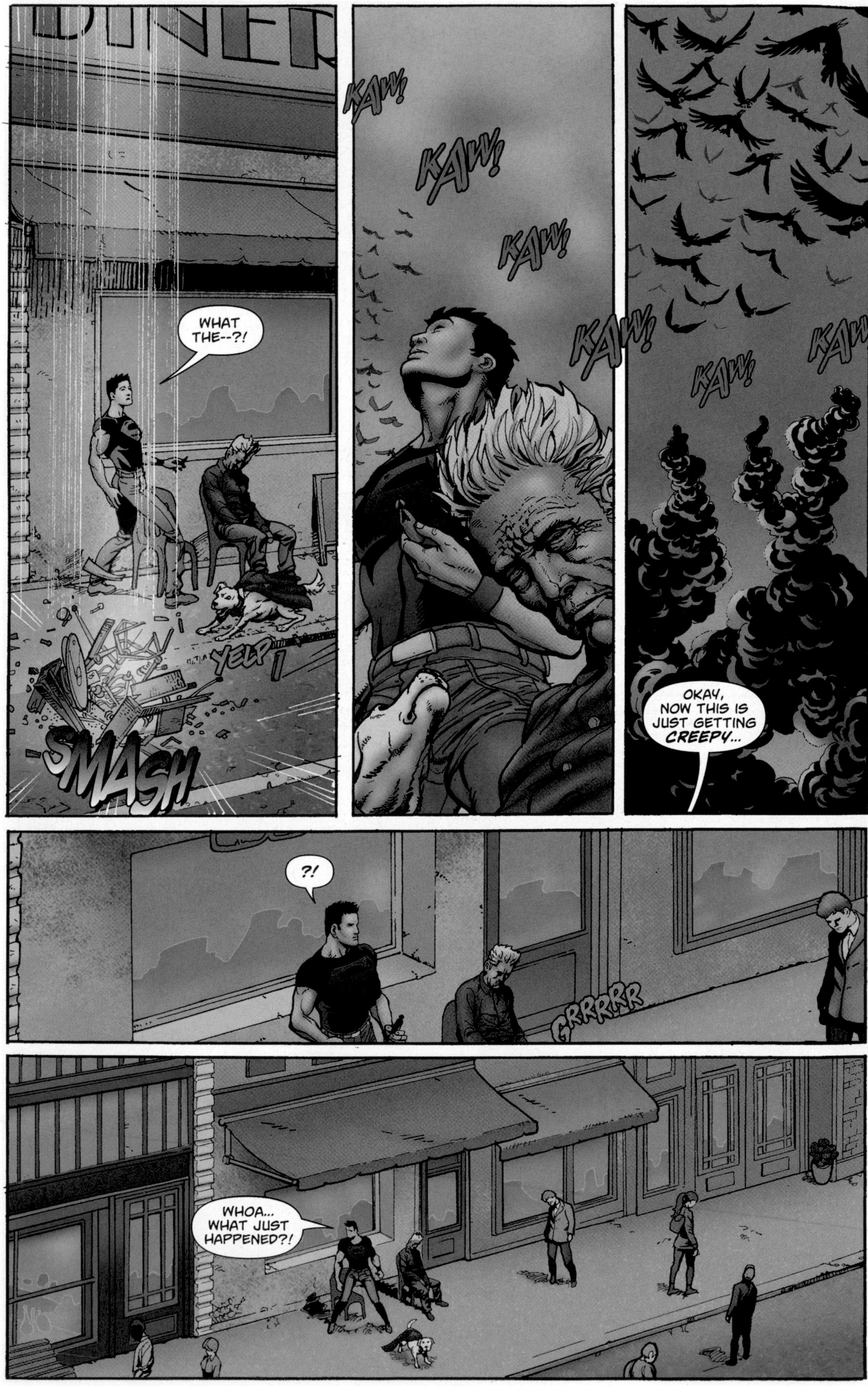
DINER
WHAT THE--?!
YELP
SMASH
KAW!
KAW!
KAW!
KAW!
KAW!
KAW!
OKAY, NOW THIS IS JUST GETTING CREEPY...
?!
GRRRRR
WHOA... WHAT JUST HAPPENED?!

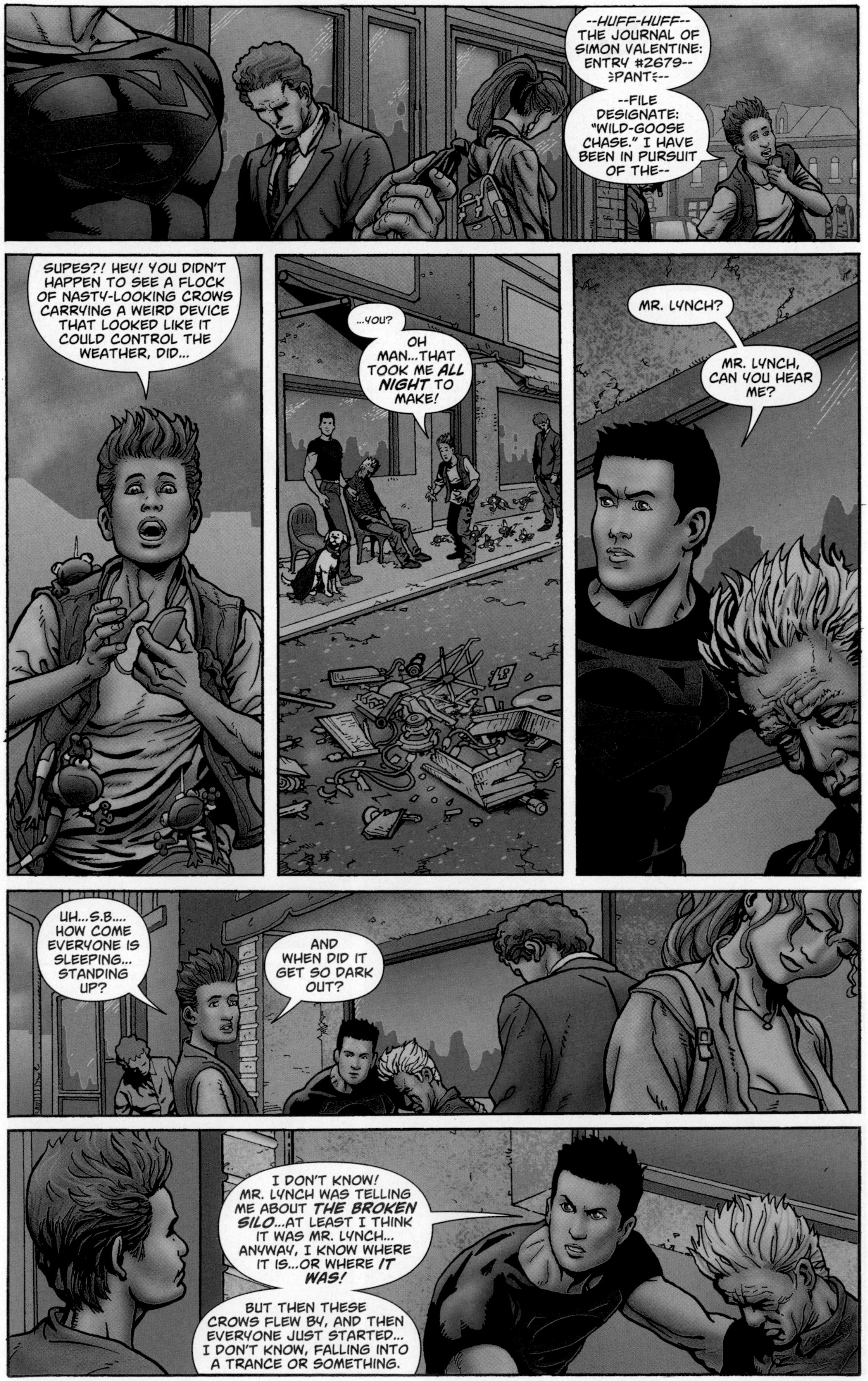
--HUFF-HUFF-- THE JOURNAL OF SIMON VALENTINE: ENTRY #2679-- PANT--
--FILE DESIGNATE: "WILD-GOOSE CHASE." I HAVE BEEN IN PURSUIT OF THE--
SUPES?! HEY! YOU DIDN'T HAPPEN TO SEE A FLOCK OF NASTY-LOOKING CROWS CARRYING A WEIRD DEVICE THAT LOOKED LIKE IT COULD CONTROL THE WEATHER, DID...
...YOU?
OH MAN...THAT TOOK ME ALL NIGHT TO MAKE!
MR. LYNCH?
MR. LYNCH, CAN YOU HEAR ME?
UH...S.B.... HOW COME EVERYONE IS SLEEPING... STANDING UP?
AND WHEN DID IT GET SO DARK OUT?
I DON'T KNOW! MR. LYNCH WAS TELLING ME ABOUT THE BROKEN SILO...AT LEAST I THINK IT WAS MR. LYNCH... ANYWAY, I KNOW WHERE IT IS...OR WHERE IT WAS!
BUT THEN THESE CROWS FLEW BY, AND THEN EVERYONE JUST STARTED... I DON'T KNOW, FALLING INTO A TRANCE OR SOMETHING.

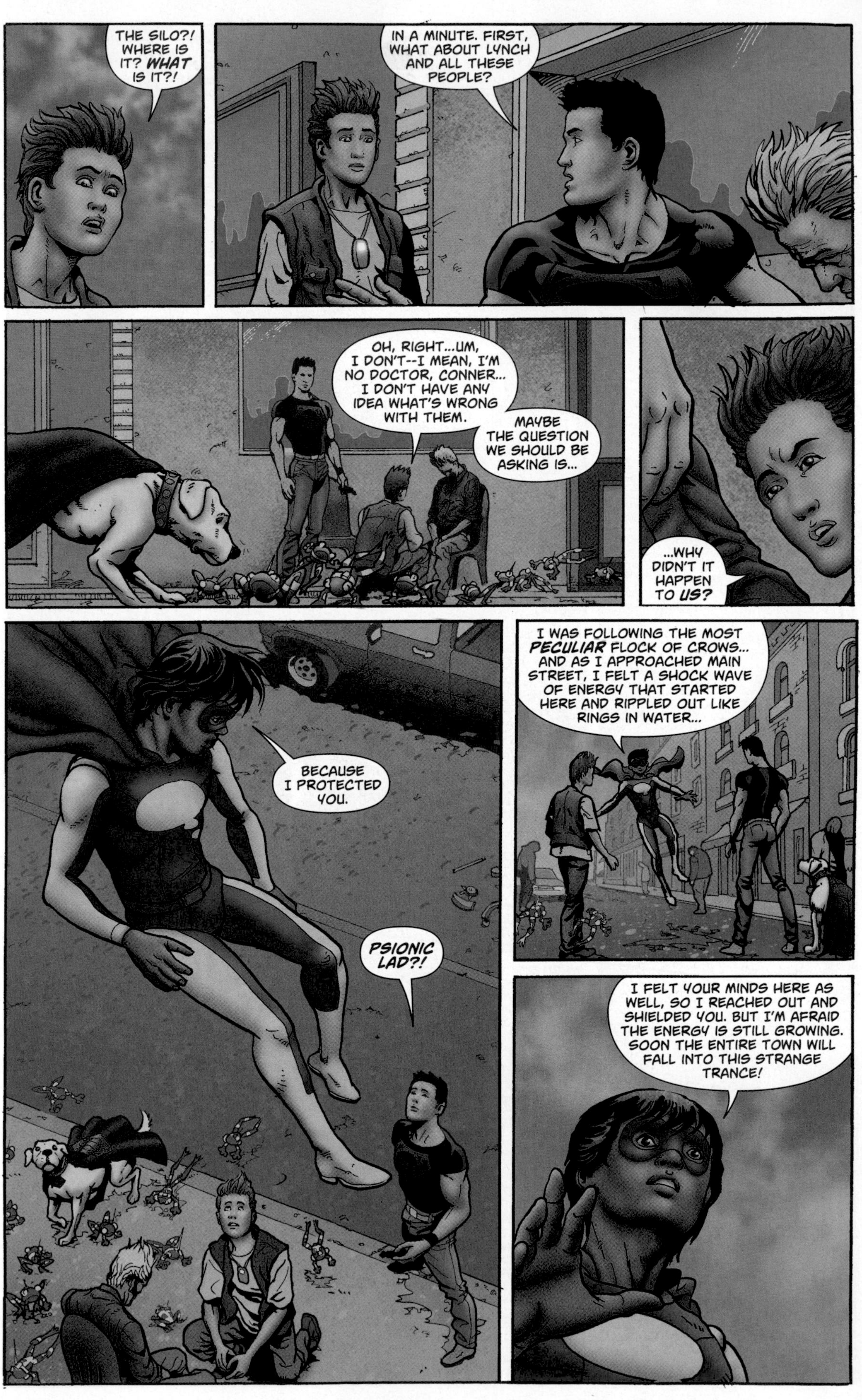
THE SILO?! WHERE IS IT? WHAT IS IT?!
IN A MINUTE. FIRST, WHAT ABOUT LYNCH AND ALL THESE PEOPLE?
OH, RIGHT...UM, I DON'T--I MEAN, I'M NO DOCTOR, CONNER... I DON'T HAVE ANY IDEA WHAT'S WRONG WITH THEM.
MAYBE THE QUESTION WE SHOULD BE ASKING IS...
...WHY DIDN'T IT HAPPEN TO US?
BECAUSE I PROTECTED YOU.
PSIONIC LAD?!
I WAS FOLLOWING THE MOST PECULIAR FLOCK OF CROWS... AND AS I APPROACHED MAIN STREET, I FELT A SHOCK WAVE OF ENERGY THAT STARTED HERE AND RIPPLED OUT LIKE RINGS IN WATER...
I FELT YOUR MINDS HERE AS WELL, SO I REACHED OUT AND SHIELDED YOU. BUT I'M AFRAID THE ENERGY IS STILL GROWING. SOON THE ENTIRE TOWN WILL FALL INTO THIS STRANGE TRANCE!

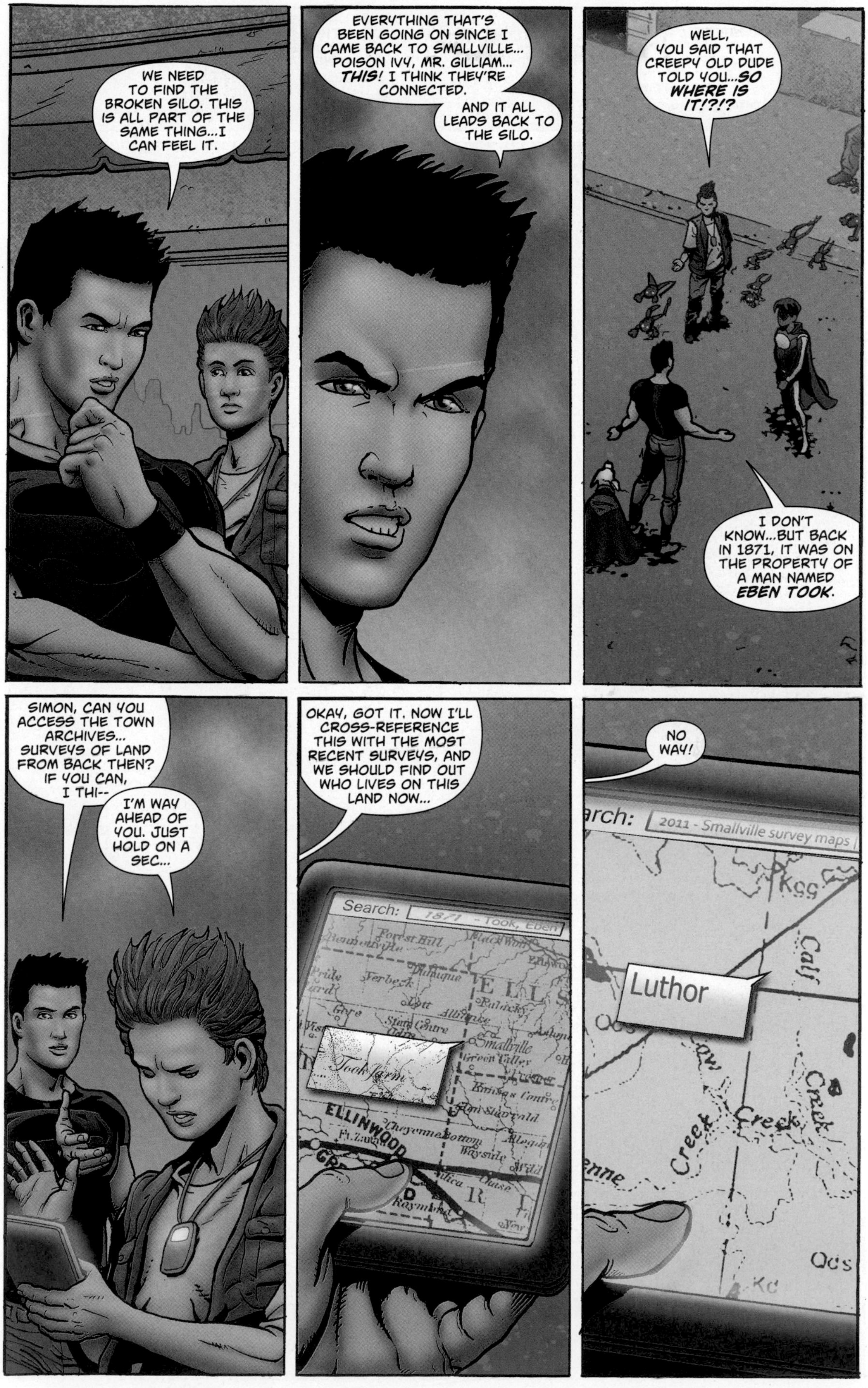
WE NEED TO FIND THE BROKEN SILO. THIS IS ALL PART OF THE SAME THING...I CAN FEEL IT.
EVERYTHING THAT'S BEEN GOING ON SINCE I CAME BACK TO SMALLVILLE... POISON IVY, MR. GILLIAM... THIS! I THINK THEY'RE CONNECTED.
AND IT ALL LEADS BACK TO THE SILO.
WELL, YOU SAID THAT CREEPY OLD DUDE TOLD YOU...SO WHERE IS IT!?!?
I DON'T KNOW...BUT BACK IN 1871, IT WAS ON THE PROPERTY OF A MAN NAMED EBEN TOOK.
SIMON, CAN YOU ACCESS THE TOWN ARCHIVES... SURVEYS OF LAND FROM BACK THEN? IF YOU CAN, I THI--
I'M WAY AHEAD OF YOU. JUST HOLD ON A SEC...
OKAY, GOT IT. NOW I'LL CROSS-REFERENCE THIS WITH THE MOST RECENT SURVEYS, AND WE SHOULD FIND OUT WHO LIVES ON THIS LAND NOW...
Search: 1871 - Took, Eben
Took farm
Smallville
ELLINWOOD
NO WAY!
Search: 2011 - Smallville survey maps
Luthor
Creek
Creek

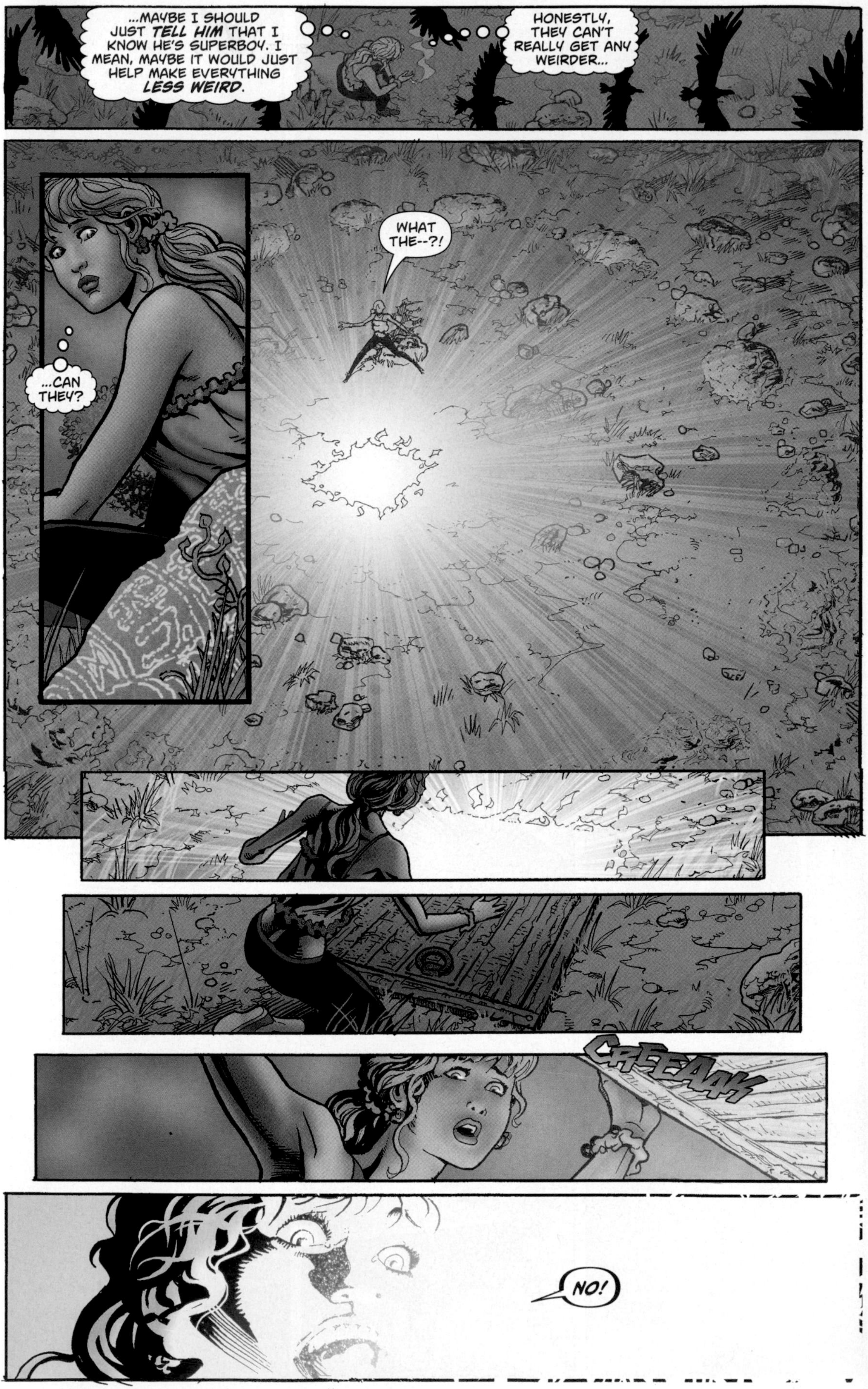
...MAYBE I SHOULD JUST TELL HIM THAT I KNOW HE'S SUPERBOY. I MEAN, MAYBE IT WOULD JUST HELP MAKE EVERYTHING LESS WEIRD.
HONESTLY, THEY CAN'T REALLY GET ANY WEIRDER...
...CAN THEY?
WHAT THE--?!
CREEAAK
NO!

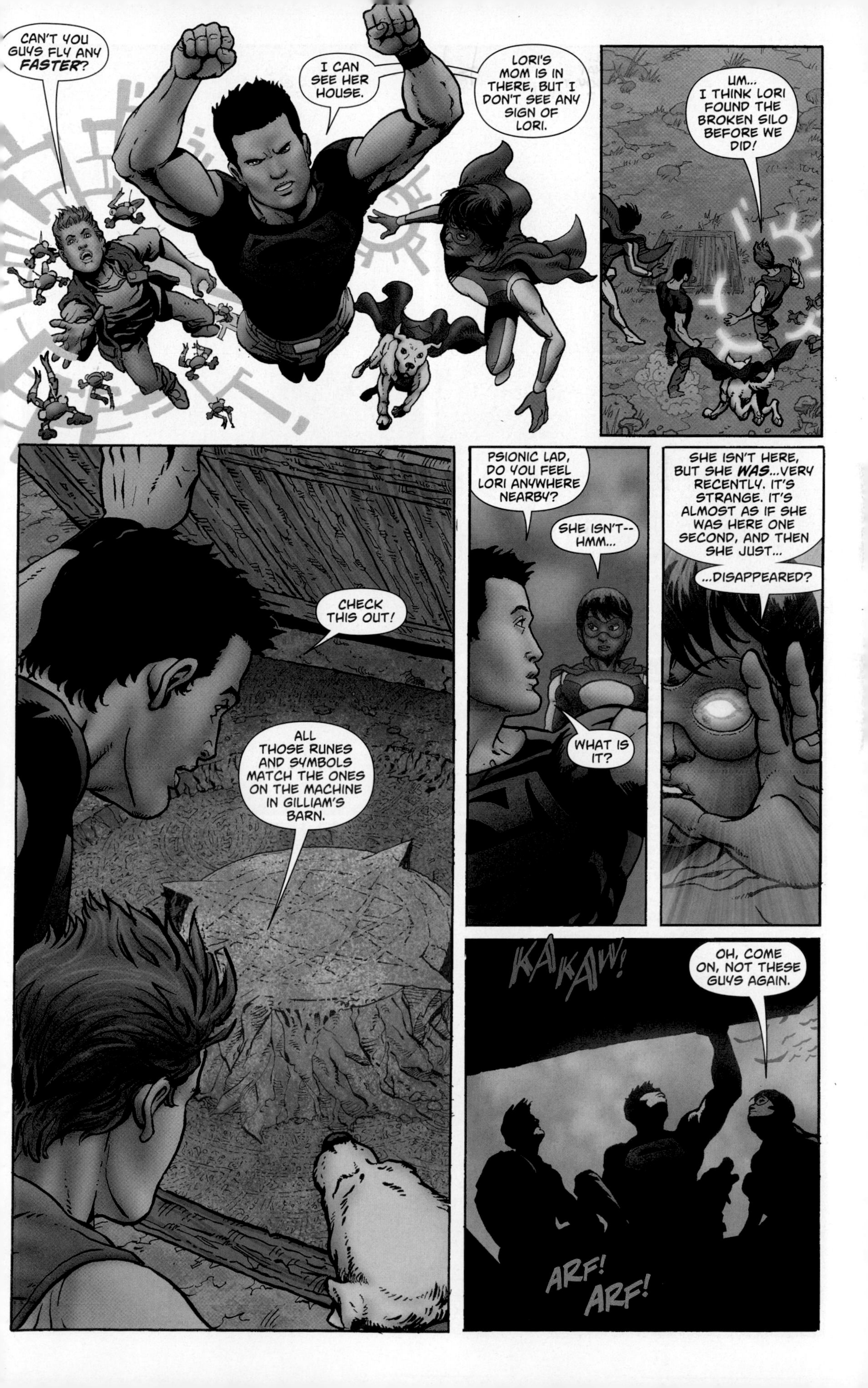
CAN'T YOU GUYS FLY ANY FASTER?
I CAN SEE HER HOUSE.
LORI'S MOM IS IN THERE, BUT I DON'T SEE ANY SIGN OF LORI.
UM... I THINK LORI FOUND THE BROKEN SILO BEFORE WE DID!
CHECK THIS OUT!
ALL THOSE RUNES AND SYMBOLS MATCH THE ONES ON THE MACHINE IN GILLIAM'S BARN.
PSIONIC LAD, DO YOU FEEL LORI ANYWHERE NEARBY?
SHE ISN'T-- HMM...
WHAT IS IT?
SHE ISN'T HERE, BUT SHE WAS...VERY RECENTLY. IT'S STRANGE. IT'S ALMOST AS IF SHE WAS HERE ONE SECOND, AND THEN SHE JUST...
...DISAPPEARED?
KAKAW!
OH, COME ON, NOT THESE GUYS AGAIN.
ARF! ARF!

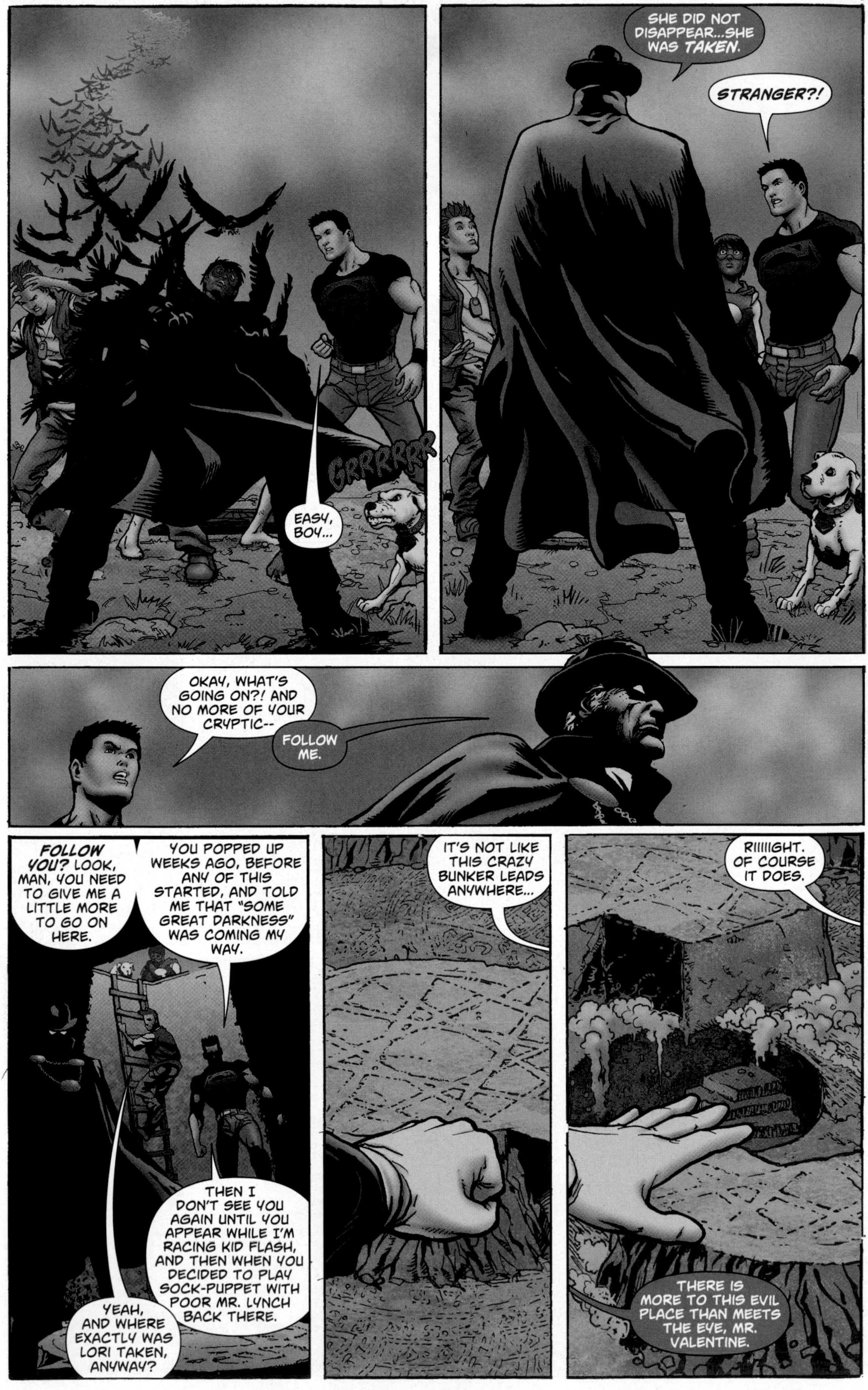
GRRRRRR
EASY, BOY...
SHE DID NOT DISAPPEAR...SHE WAS TAKEN.
STRANGER?!
OKAY, WHAT'S GOING ON?! AND NO MORE OF YOUR CRYPTIC--
FOLLOW ME.
FOLLOW YOU? LOOK, MAN, YOU NEED TO GIVE ME A LITTLE MORE TO GO ON HERE.
YOU POPPED UP WEEKS AGO, BEFORE ANY OF THIS STARTED, AND TOLD ME THAT "SOME GREAT DARKNESS" WAS COMING MY WAY.
THEN I DON'T SEE YOU AGAIN UNTIL YOU APPEAR WHILE I'M RACING KID FLASH, AND THEN WHEN YOU DECIDED TO PLAY SOCK-PUPPET WITH POOR MR. LYNCH BACK THERE.
YEAH, AND WHERE EXACTLY WAS LORI TAKEN, ANYWAY?
IT'S NOT LIKE THIS CRAZY BUNKER LEADS ANYWHERE...
RIIIIIGHT. OF COURSE IT DOES.
THERE IS MORE TO THIS EVIL PLACE THAN MEETS THE EYE, MR. VALENTINE.

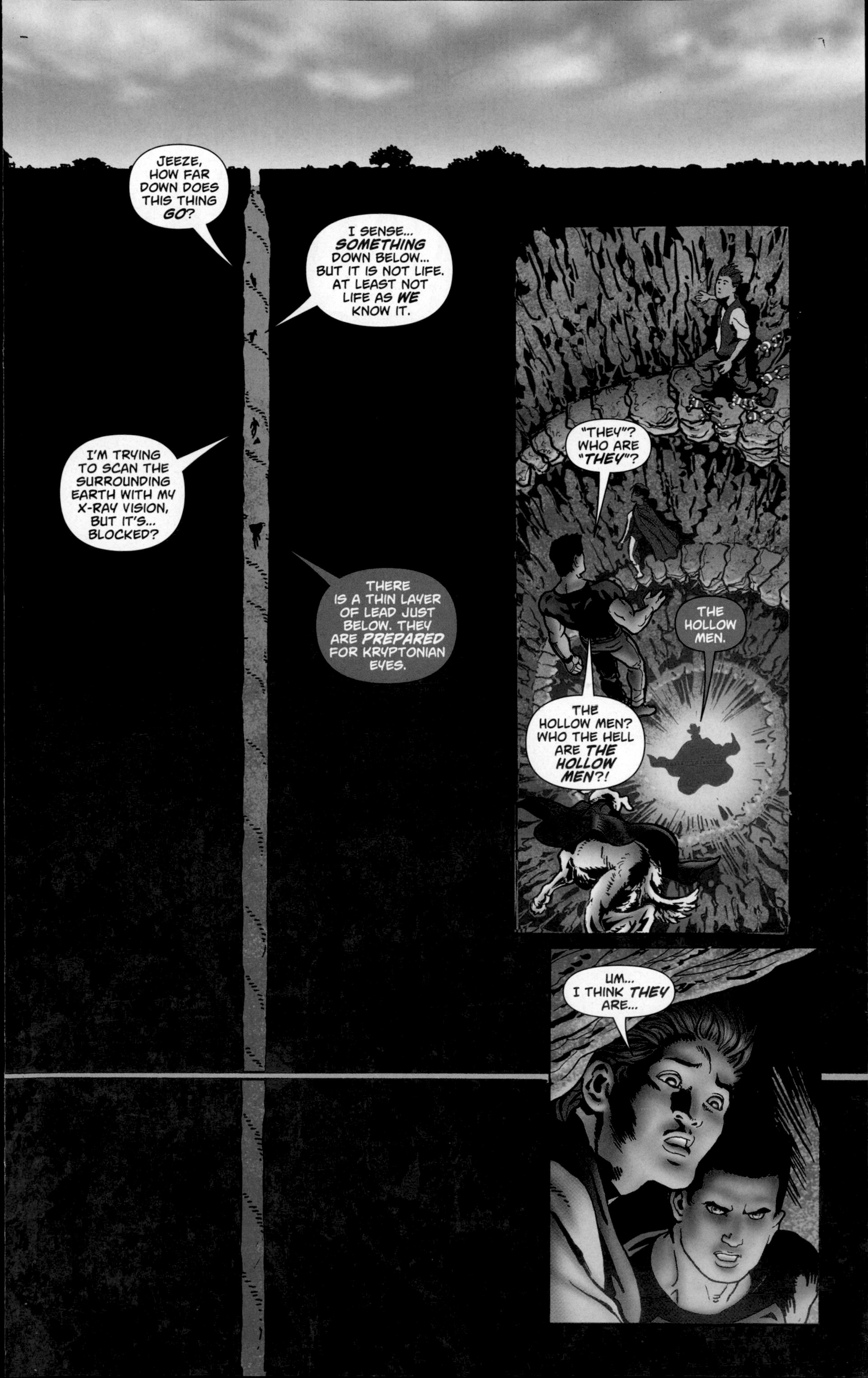
JEEZE, HOW FAR DOWN DOES THIS THING GO?
I SENSE... SOMETHING DOWN BELOW... BUT IT IS NOT LIFE. AT LEAST NOT LIFE AS WE KNOW IT.
I'M TRYING TO SCAN THE SURROUNDING EARTH WITH MY X-RAY VISION, BUT IT'S... BLOCKED?
THERE IS A THIN LAYER OF LEAD JUST BELOW. THEY ARE PREPARED FOR KRYPTONIAN EYES.
"THEY"? WHO ARE "THEY"?
THE HOLLOW MEN.
THE HOLLOW MEN? WHO THE HELL ARE THE HOLLOW MEN?!
UM... I THINK THEY ARE...

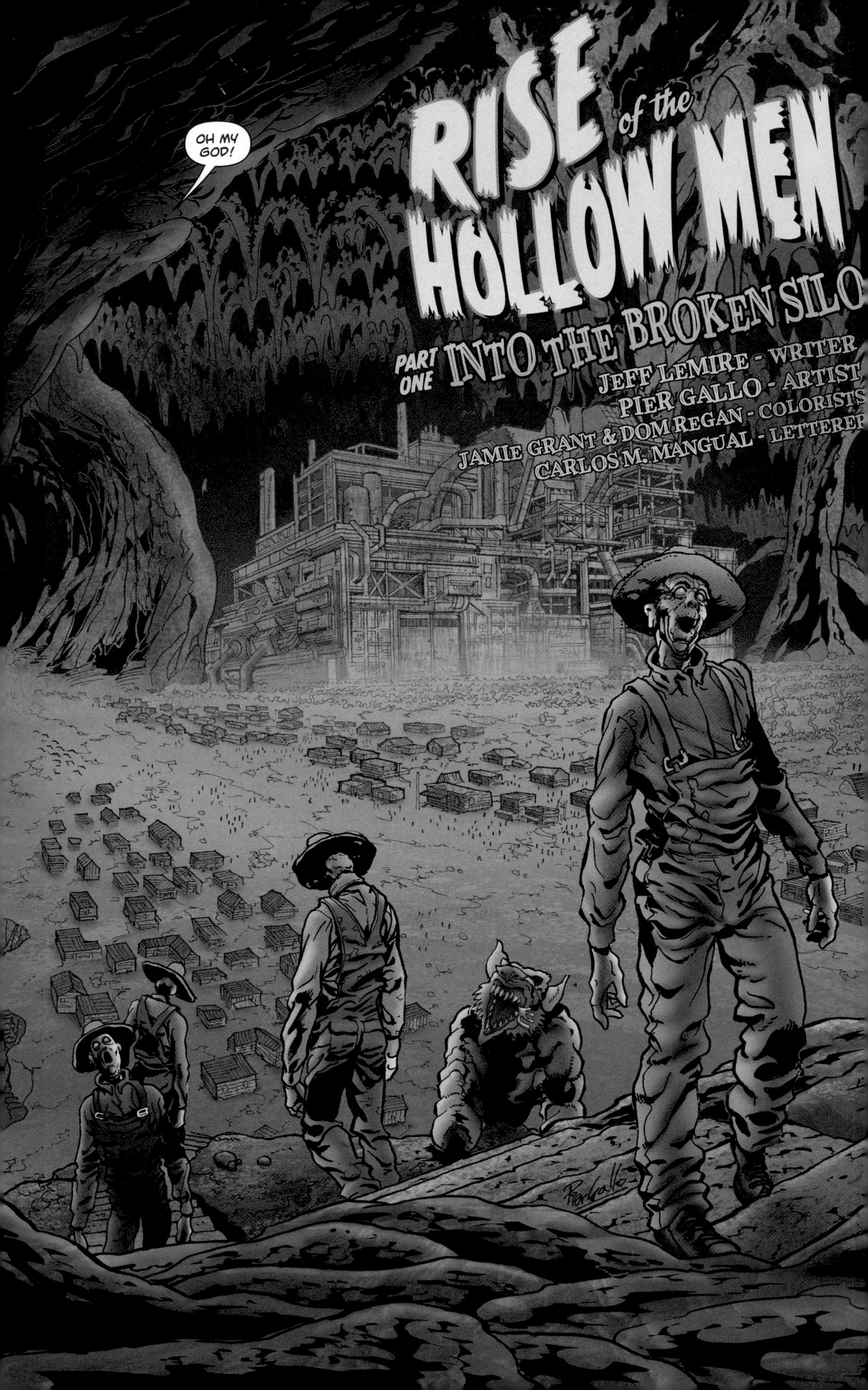
OH MY GOD!
RISE of the HOLLOW MEN
PART ONE INTO THE BROKEN SILO
JEFF LEMIRE - WRITER
PIER GALLO - ARTIST
JAMIE GRANT & DOM REGAN - COLORISTS
CARLOS M. MANGUAL - LETTERER

SUPERBOY #9

Cover by Karl Kerschl

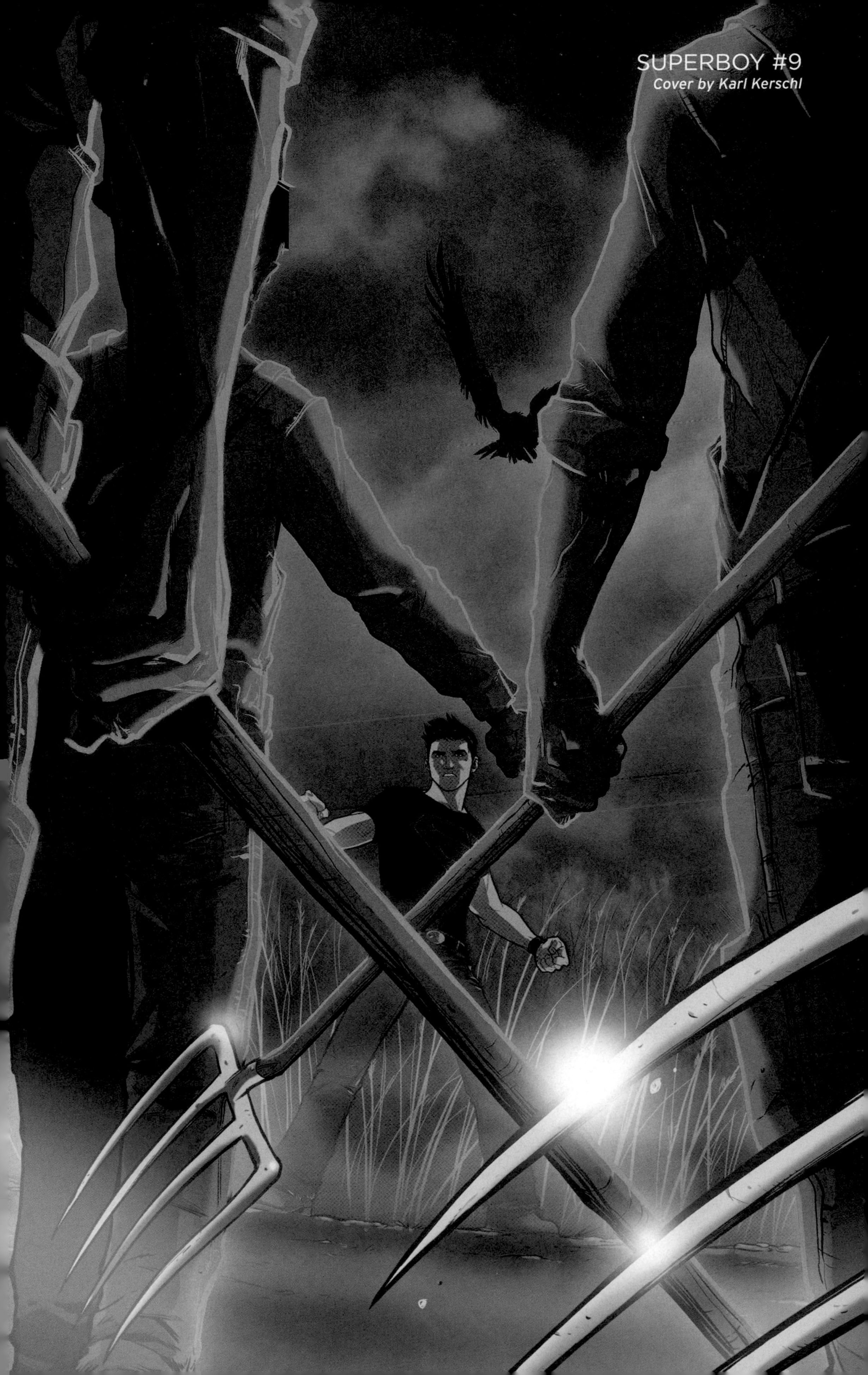

SUPERBOY #10
Cover by Karl Kerschl

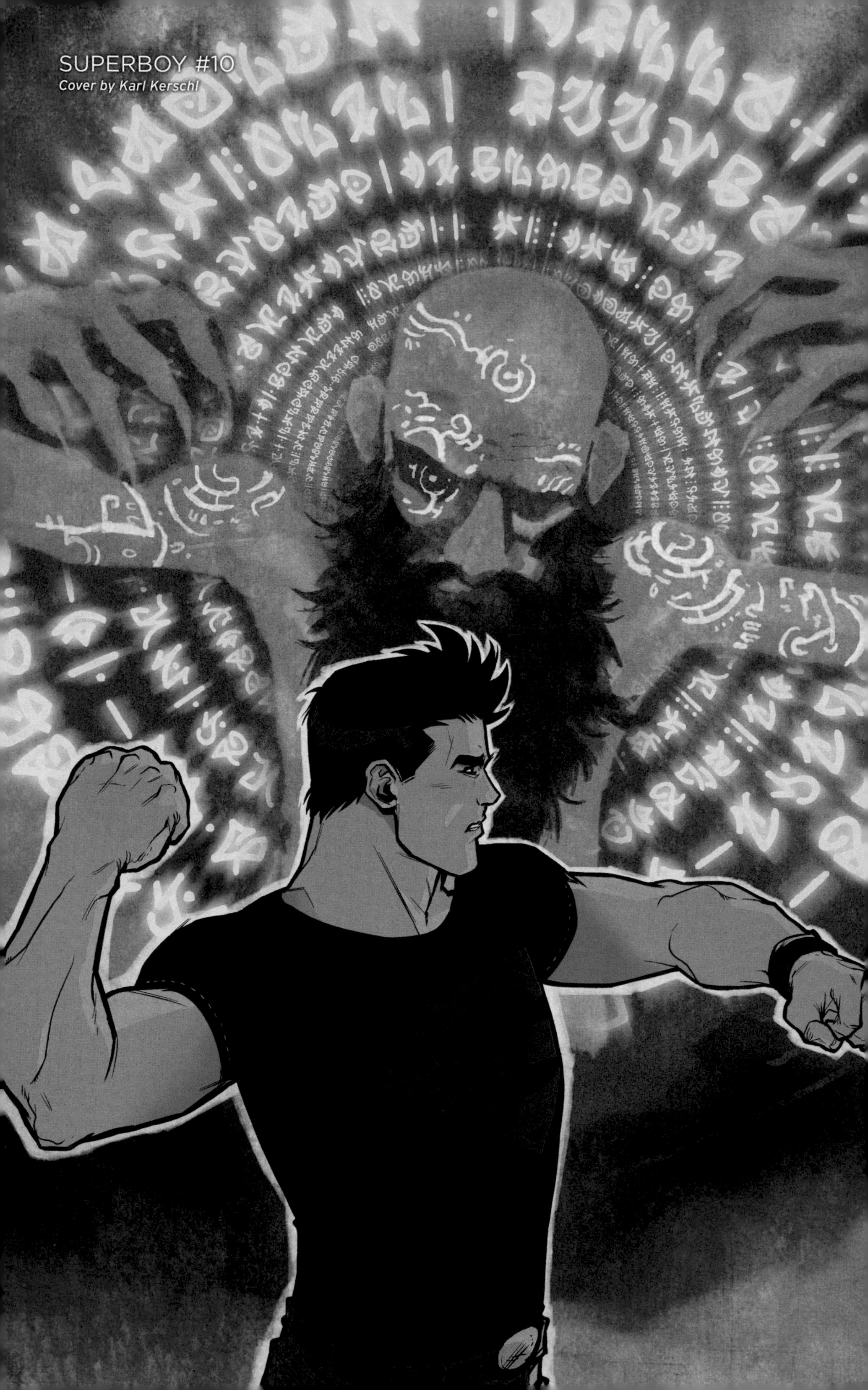

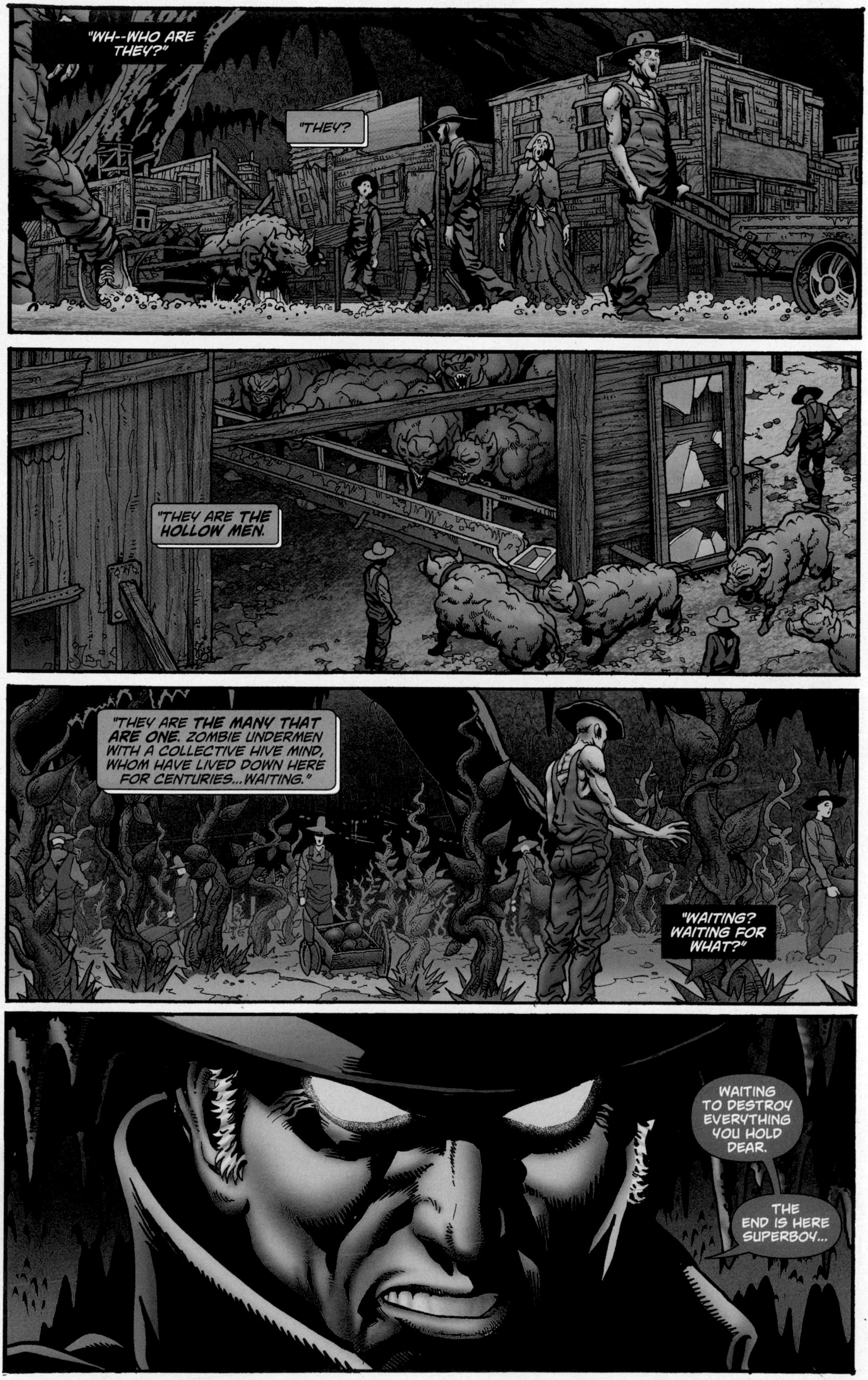
"WH--WHO ARE THEY?"
"THEY?
"THEY ARE THE HOLLOW MEN.
"THEY ARE THE MANY THAT ARE ONE. ZOMBIE UNDERMEN WITH A COLLECTIVE HIVE MIND, WHOM HAVE LIVED DOWN HERE FOR CENTURIES...WAITING."
"WAITING? WAITING FOR WHAT?"
WAITING TO DESTROY EVERYTHING YOU HOLD DEAR.
THE END IS HERE SUPERBOY...

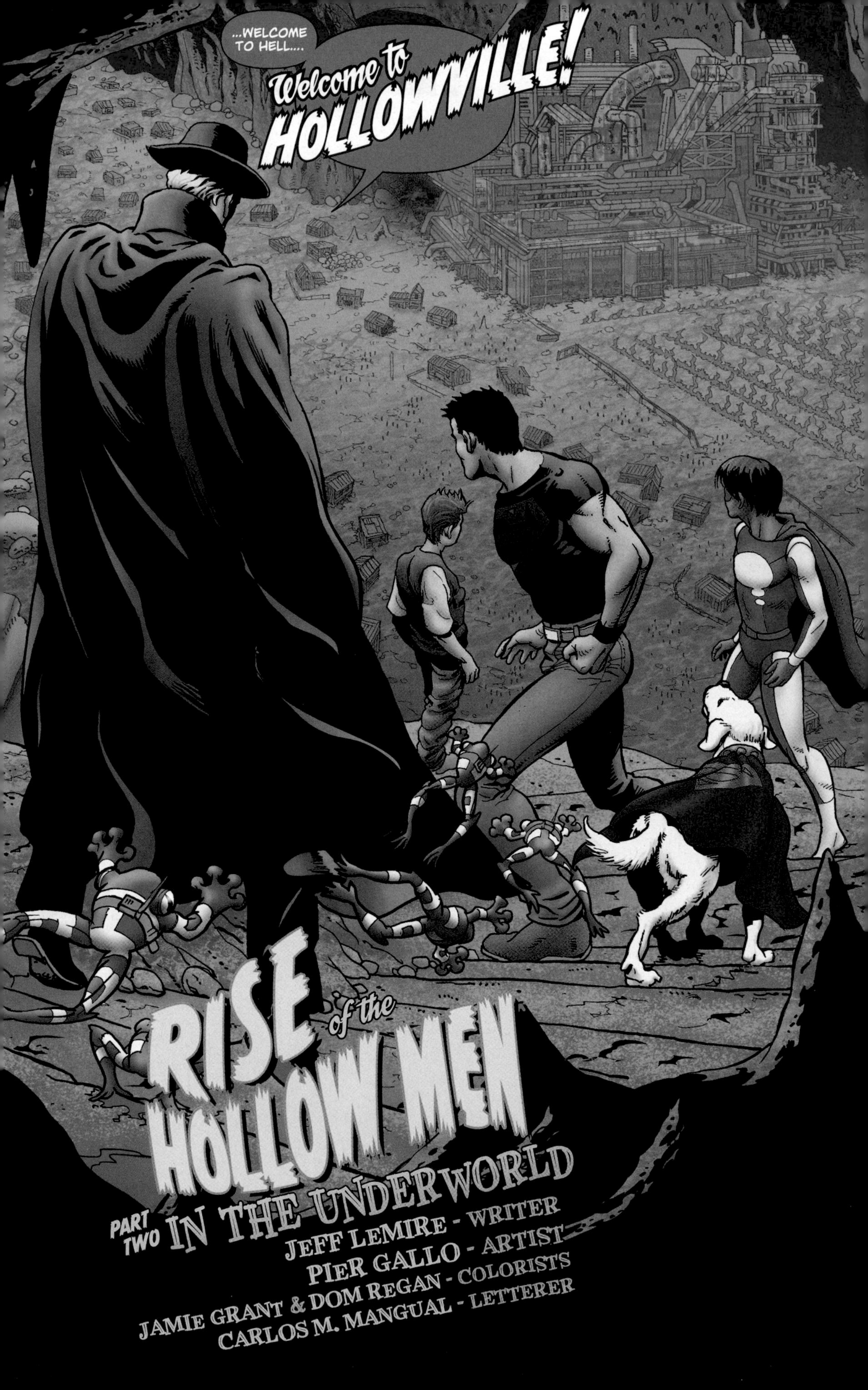
...WELCOME TO HELL....
Welcome to HOLLOWVILLE!
RISE of the HOLLOW MEN
PART TWO IN THE UNDERWORLD
JEFF LEMIRE - WRITER
PIER GALLO - ARTIST
JAMIE GRANT & DOM REGAN - COLORISTS
CARLOS M. MANGUAL - LETTERER

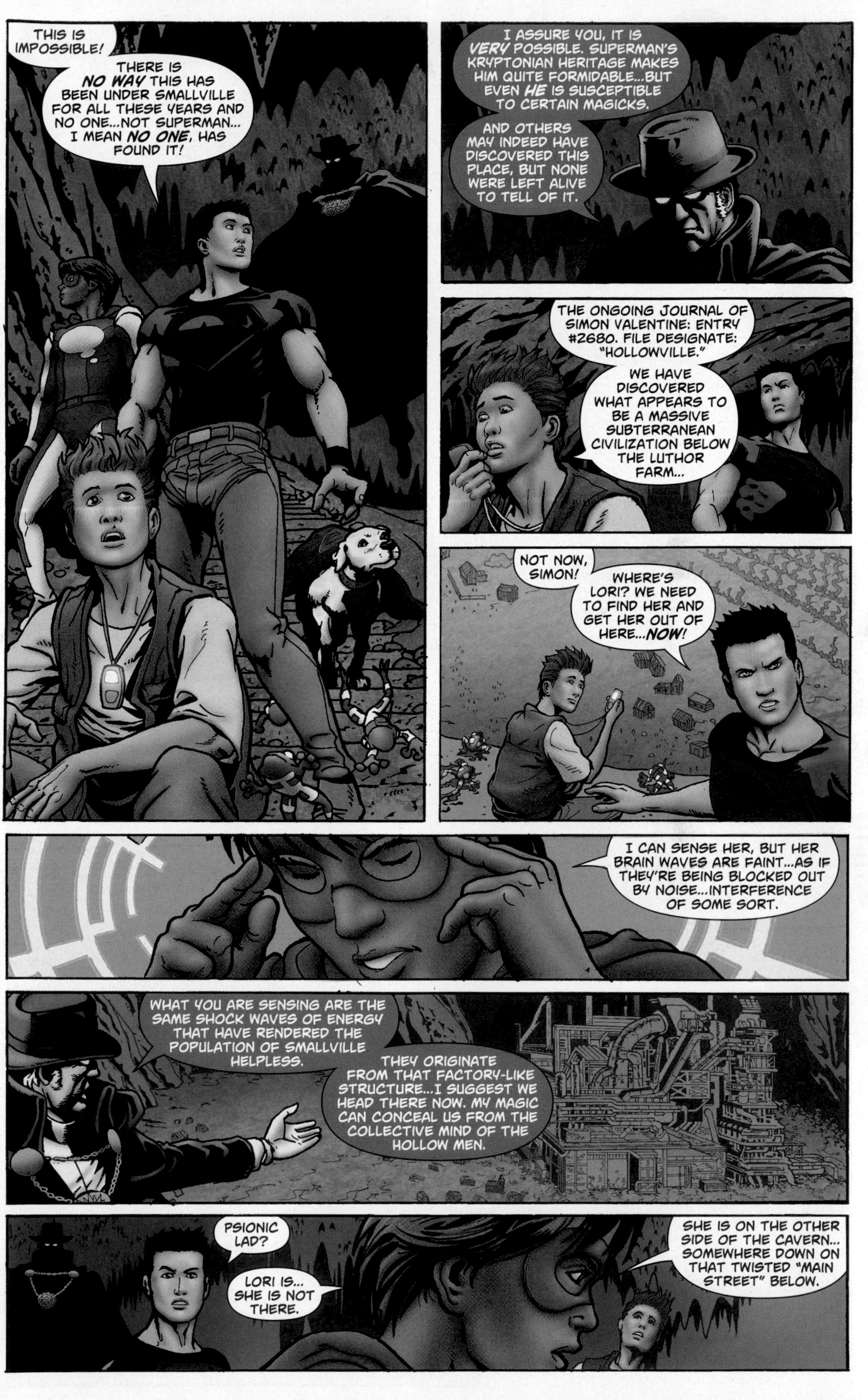

THIS IS IMPOSSIBLE!
THERE IS NO WAY THIS HAS BEEN UNDER SMALLVILLE FOR ALL THESE YEARS AND NO ONE...NOT SUPERMAN... I MEAN NO ONE, HAS FOUND IT!
I ASSURE YOU, IT IS VERY POSSIBLE. SUPERMAN'S KRYPTONIAN HERITAGE MAKES HIM QUITE FORMIDABLE...BUT EVEN HE IS SUSCEPTIBLE TO CERTAIN MAGICKS.
AND OTHERS MAY INDEED HAVE DISCOVERED THIS PLACE, BUT NONE WERE LEFT ALIVE TO TELL OF IT.
THE ONGOING JOURNAL OF SIMON VALENTINE: ENTRY #2680. FILE DESIGNATE: "HOLLOWVILLE."
WE HAVE DISCOVERED WHAT APPEARS TO BE A MASSIVE SUBTERRANEAN CIVILIZATION BELOW THE LUTHOR FARM...
NOT NOW, SIMON!
WHERE'S LORI? WE NEED TO FIND HER AND GET HER OUT OF HERE...NOW!
I CAN SENSE HER, BUT HER BRAIN WAVES ARE FAINT...AS IF THEY'RE BEING BLOCKED OUT BY NOISE...INTERFERENCE OF SOME SORT.
WHAT YOU ARE SENSING ARE THE SAME SHOCK WAVES OF ENERGY THAT HAVE RENDERED THE POPULATION OF SMALLVILLE HELPLESS.
THEY ORIGINATE FROM THAT FACTORY-LIKE STRUCTURE...I SUGGEST WE HEAD THERE NOW. MY MAGIC CAN CONCEAL US FROM THE COLLECTIVE MIND OF THE HOLLOW MEN.
PSIONIC LAD?
LORI IS... SHE IS NOT THERE.
SHE IS ON THE OTHER SIDE OF THE CAVERN... SOMEWHERE DOWN ON THAT TWISTED "MAIN STREET" BELOW.

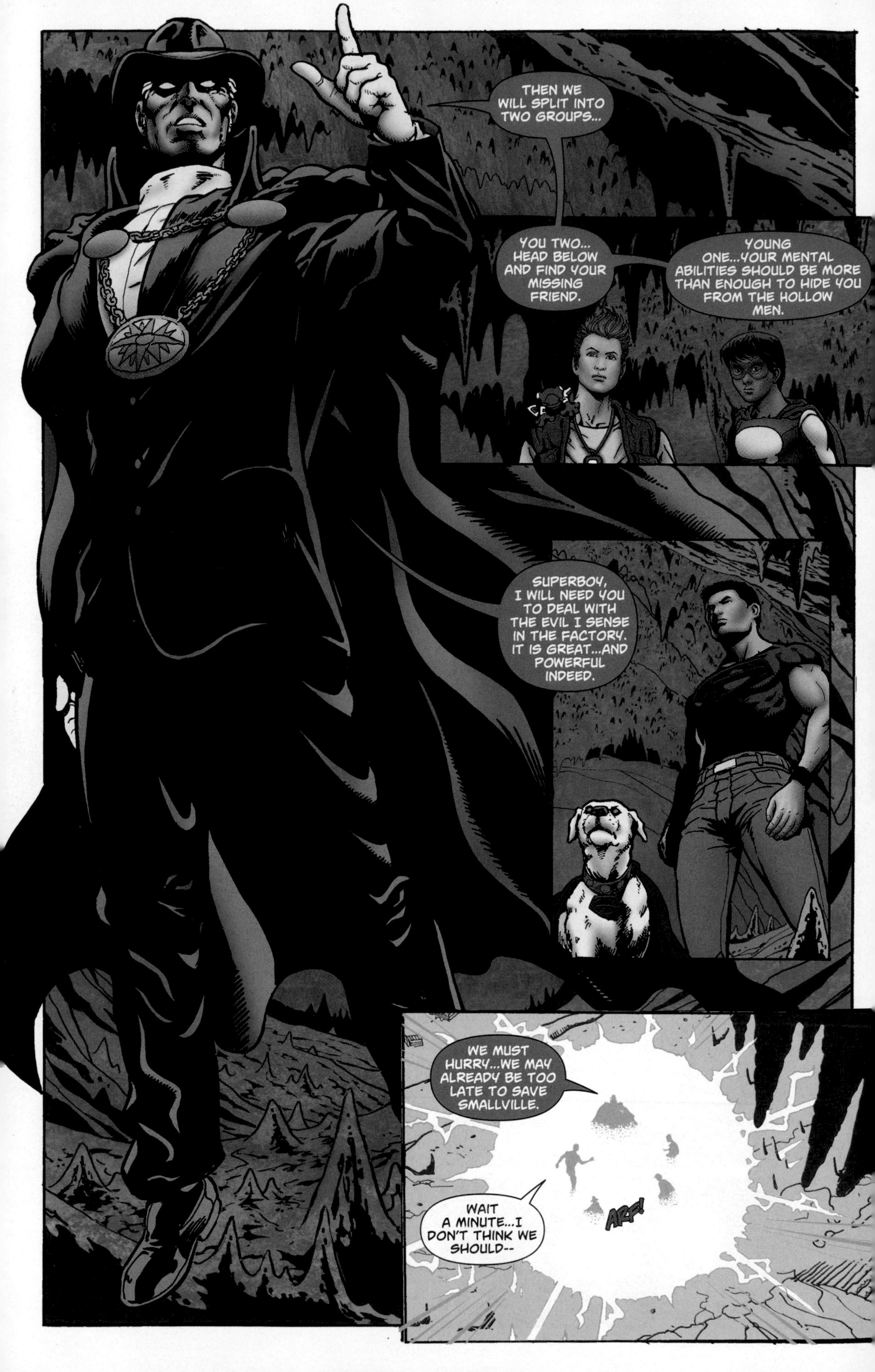
THEN WE WILL SPLIT INTO TWO GROUPS...
YOU TWO... HEAD BELOW AND FIND YOUR MISSING FRIEND.
YOUNG ONE...YOUR MENTAL ABILITIES SHOULD BE MORE THAN ENOUGH TO HIDE YOU FROM THE HOLLOW MEN.
SUPERBOY, I WILL NEED YOU TO DEAL WITH THE EVIL I SENSE IN THE FACTORY. IT IS GREAT...AND POWERFUL INDEED.
WE MUST HURRY...WE MAY ALREADY BE TOO LATE TO SAVE SMALLVILLE.
WAIT A MINUTE...I DON'T THINK WE SHOULD--
ARF!

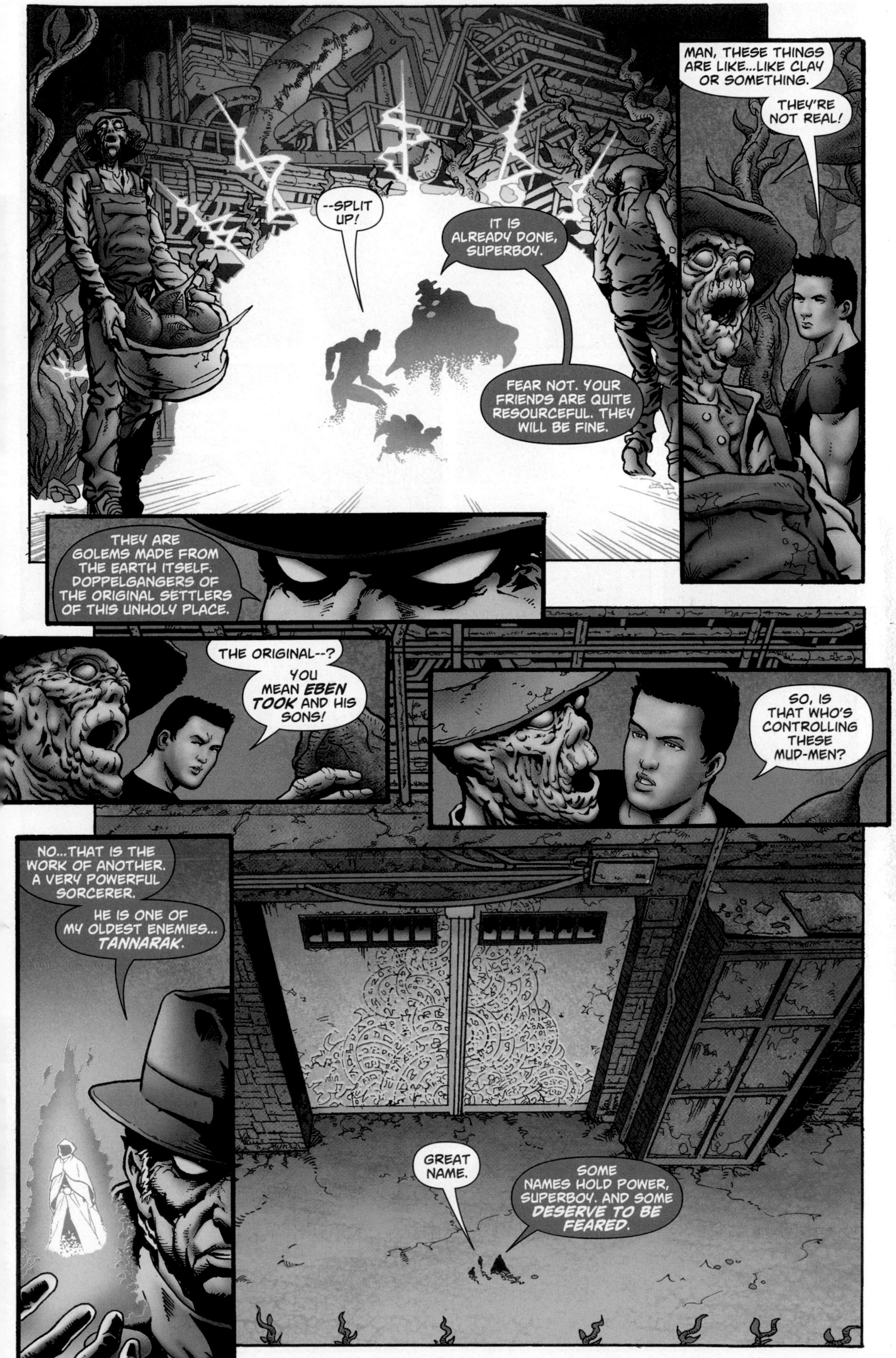
--SPLIT UP!
IT IS ALREADY DONE, SUPERBOY.
FEAR NOT. YOUR FRIENDS ARE QUITE RESOURCEFUL. THEY WILL BE FINE.
MAN, THESE THINGS ARE LIKE...LIKE CLAY OR SOMETHING.
THEY'RE NOT REAL!
THEY ARE GOLEMS MADE FROM THE EARTH ITSELF. DOPPELGANGERS OF THE ORIGINAL SETTLERS OF THIS UNHOLY PLACE.
THE ORIGINAL--?
YOU MEAN EBEN TOOK AND HIS SONS!
SO, IS THAT WHO'S CONTROLLING THESE MUD-MEN?
NO...THAT IS THE WORK OF ANOTHER. A VERY POWERFUL SORCERER.
HE IS ONE OF MY OLDEST ENEMIES... TANNARAK.
GREAT NAME.
SOME NAMES HOLD POWER, SUPERBOY. AND SOME DESERVE TO BE FEARED.

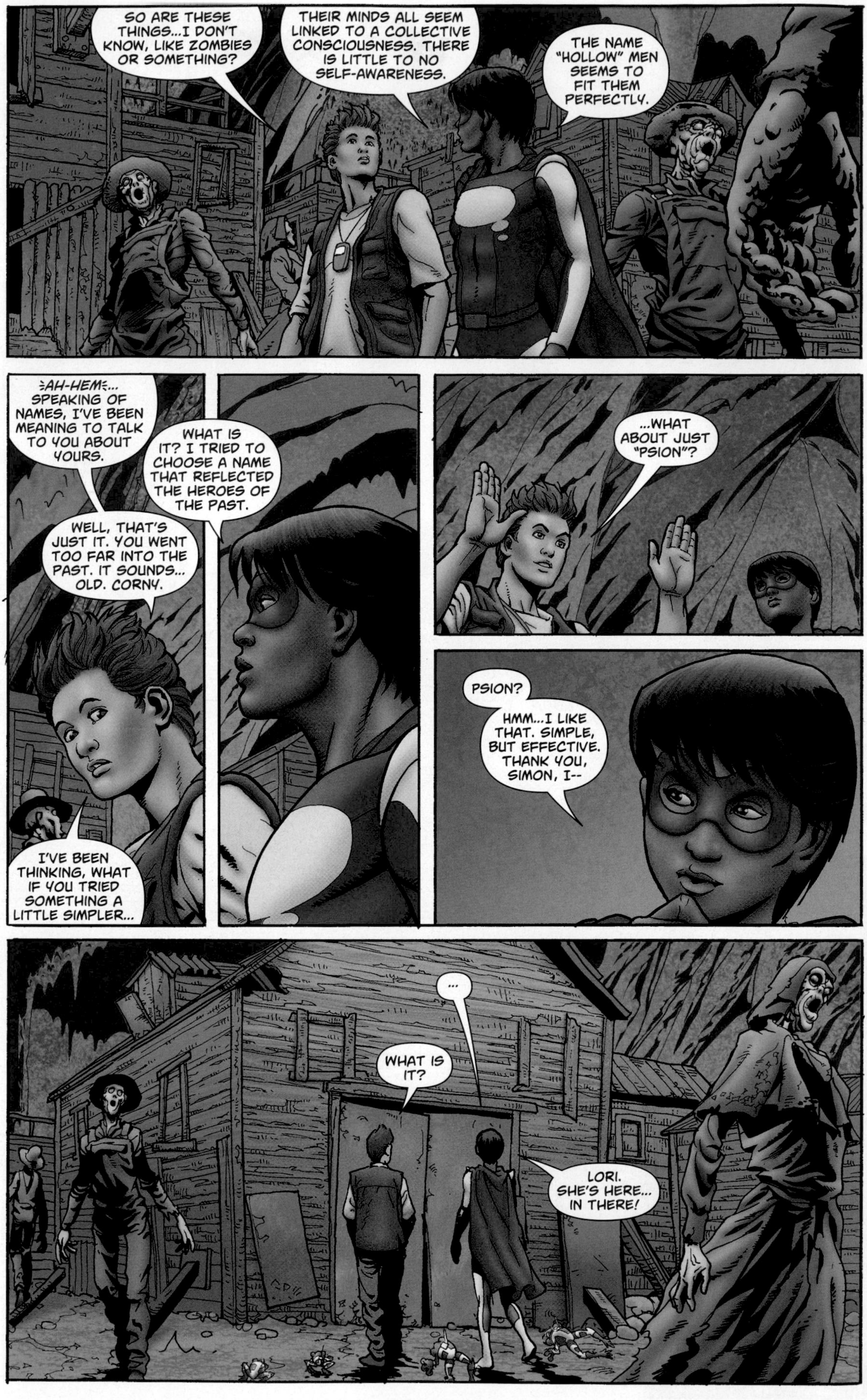
SO ARE THESE THINGS...I DON'T KNOW, LIKE ZOMBIES OR SOMETHING?
THEIR MINDS ALL SEEM LINKED TO A COLLECTIVE CONSCIOUSNESS. THERE IS LITTLE TO NO SELF-AWARENESS.
THE NAME "HOLLOW" MEN SEEMS TO FIT THEM PERFECTLY.
AH-HEM... SPEAKING OF NAMES, I'VE BEEN MEANING TO TALK TO YOU ABOUT YOURS.
WHAT IS IT? I TRIED TO CHOOSE A NAME THAT REFLECTED THE HEROES OF THE PAST.
WELL, THAT'S JUST IT. YOU WENT TOO FAR INTO THE PAST. IT SOUNDS... OLD. CORNY.
I'VE BEEN THINKING, WHAT IF YOU TRIED SOMETHING A LITTLE SIMPLER...
...WHAT ABOUT JUST "PSION"?
PSION?
HMM...I LIKE THAT. SIMPLE, BUT EFFECTIVE. THANK YOU, SIMON, I--
...
WHAT IS IT?
LORI. SHE'S HERE... IN THERE!

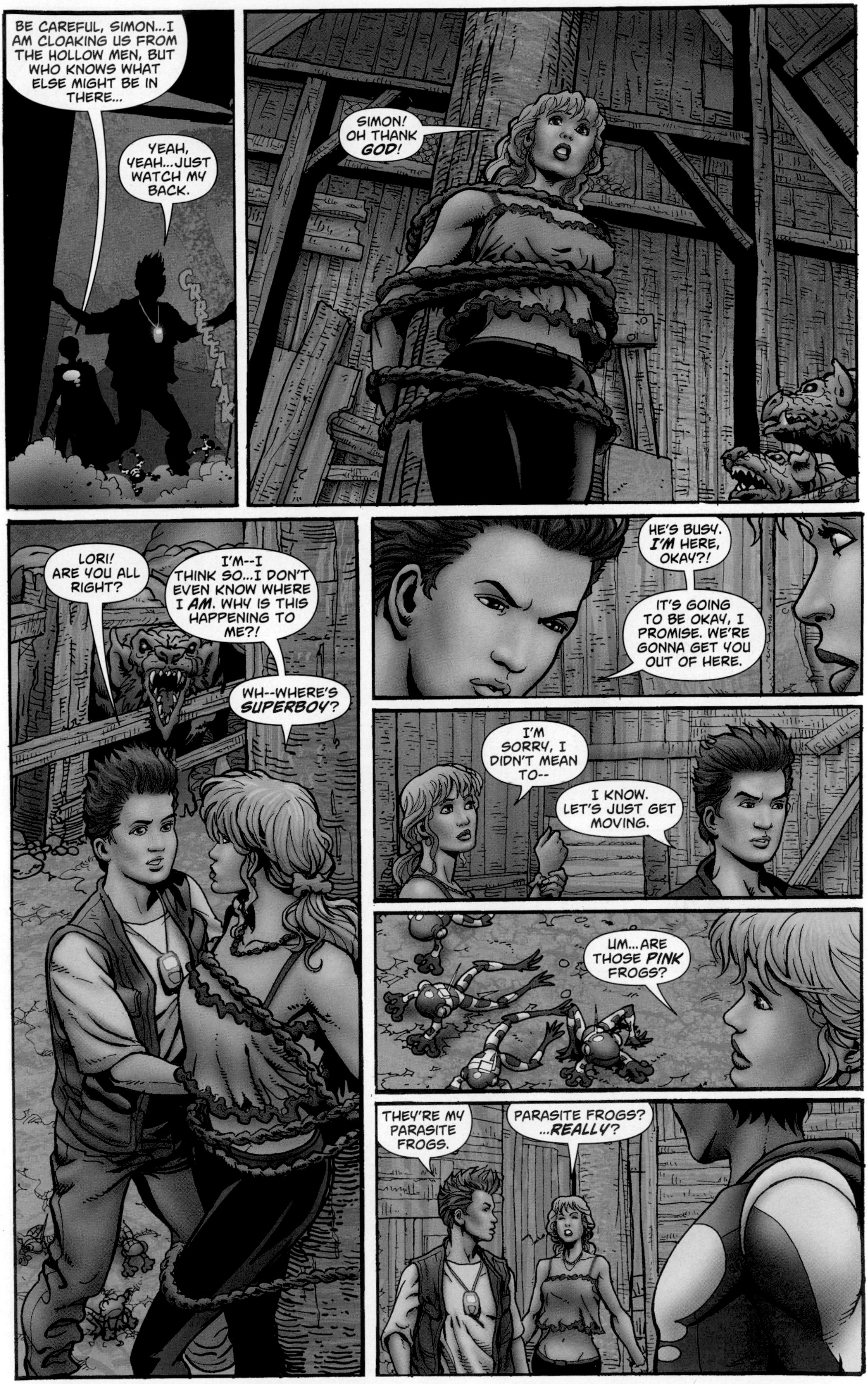
BE CAREFUL, SIMON...I AM CLOAKING US FROM THE HOLLOW MEN, BUT WHO KNOWS WHAT ELSE MIGHT BE IN THERE...
YEAH, YEAH...JUST WATCH MY BACK.
CRREEEAAK
SIMON! OH THANK GOD!
LORI! ARE YOU ALL RIGHT?
I'M--I THINK SO...I DON'T EVEN KNOW WHERE I AM. WHY IS THIS HAPPENING TO ME?!
WH--WHERE'S SUPERBOY?
HE'S BUSY. I'M HERE, OKAY?!
IT'S GOING TO BE OKAY, I PROMISE. WE'RE GONNA GET YOU OUT OF HERE.
I'M SORRY, I DIDN'T MEAN TO--
I KNOW. LET'S JUST GET MOVING.
UM...ARE THOSE PINK FROGS?
THEY'RE MY PARASITE FROGS.
PARASITE FROGS? ...REALLY?

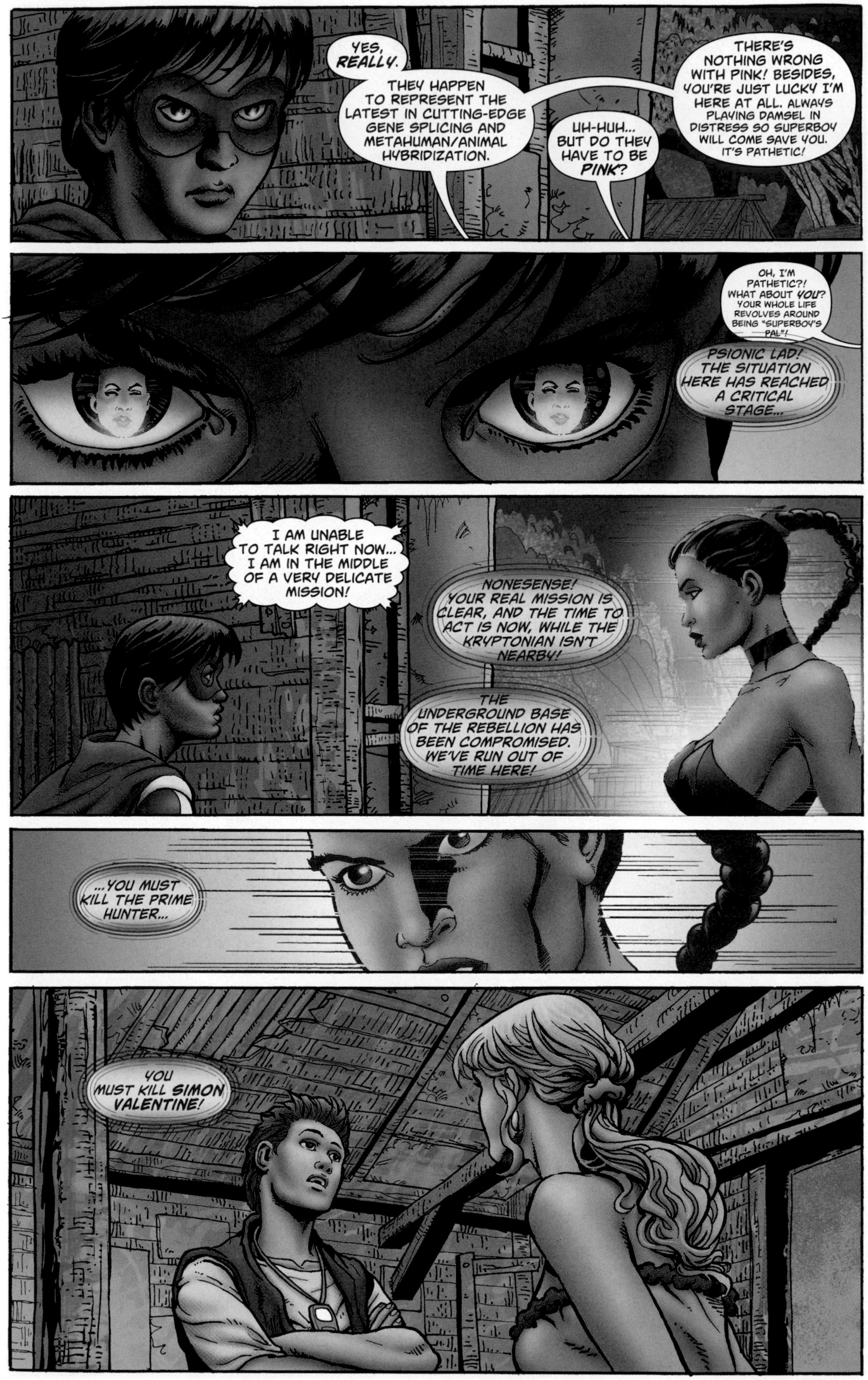
YES, REALLY.
THEY HAPPEN TO REPRESENT THE LATEST IN CUTTING-EDGE GENE SPLICING AND METAHUMAN/ANIMAL HYBRIDIZATION.
UH-HUH... BUT DO THEY HAVE TO BE PINK?
THERE'S NOTHING WRONG WITH PINK! BESIDES, YOU'RE JUST LUCKY I'M HERE AT ALL. ALWAYS PLAYING DAMSEL IN DISTRESS SO SUPERBOY WILL COME SAVE YOU. IT'S PATHETIC!
OH, I'M PATHETIC?! WHAT ABOUT YOU? YOUR WHOLE LIFE REVOLVES AROUND BEING "SUPERBOY'S PAL"!
PSIONIC LAD! THE SITUATION HERE HAS REACHED A CRITICAL STAGE...
I AM UNABLE TO TALK RIGHT NOW... I AM IN THE MIDDLE OF A VERY DELICATE MISSION!
NONESENSE! YOUR REAL MISSION IS CLEAR, AND THE TIME TO ACT IS NOW, WHILE THE KRYPTONIAN ISN'T NEARBY!
THE UNDERGROUND BASE OF THE REBELLION HAS BEEN COMPROMISED. WE'VE RUN OUT OF TIME HERE!
...YOU MUST KILL THE PRIME HUNTER...
YOU MUST KILL SIMON VALENTINE!

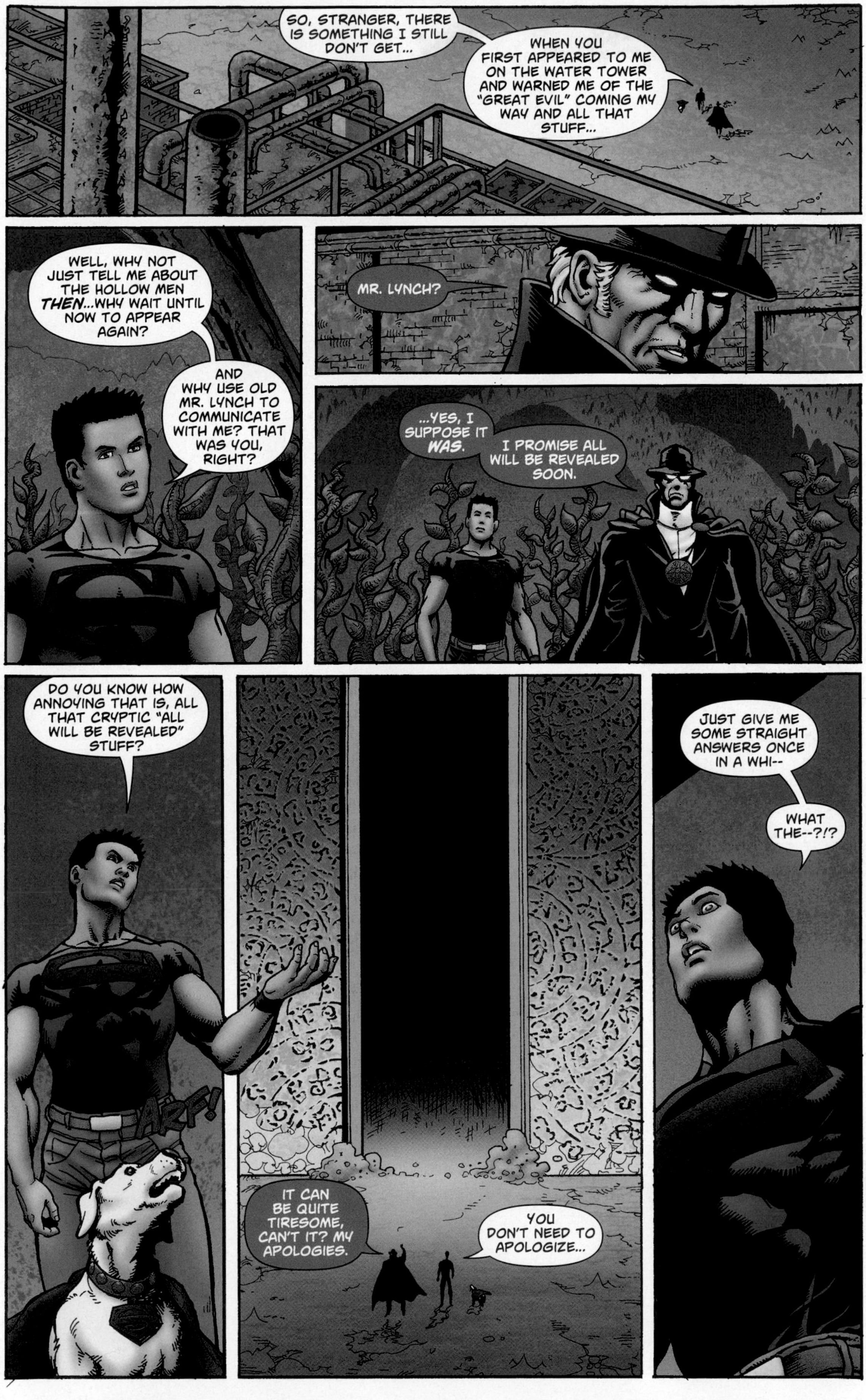
SO, STRANGER, THERE IS SOMETHING I STILL DON'T GET...
WHEN YOU FIRST APPEARED TO ME ON THE WATER TOWER AND WARNED ME OF THE "GREAT EVIL" COMING MY WAY AND ALL THAT STUFF...
WELL, WHY NOT JUST TELL ME ABOUT THE HOLLOW MEN THEN...WHY WAIT UNTIL NOW TO APPEAR AGAIN?
AND WHY USE OLD MR. LYNCH TO COMMUNICATE WITH ME? THAT WAS YOU, RIGHT?
MR. LYNCH?
...YES, I SUPPOSE IT WAS.
I PROMISE ALL WILL BE REVEALED SOON.
DO YOU KNOW HOW ANNOYING THAT IS, ALL THAT CRYPTIC "ALL WILL BE REVEALED" STUFF?
ARF!
IT CAN BE QUITE TIRESOME, CAN'T IT? MY APOLOGIES.
YOU DON'T NEED TO APOLOGIZE...
JUST GIVE ME SOME STRAIGHT ANSWERS ONCE IN A WHI--
WHAT THE--?!?

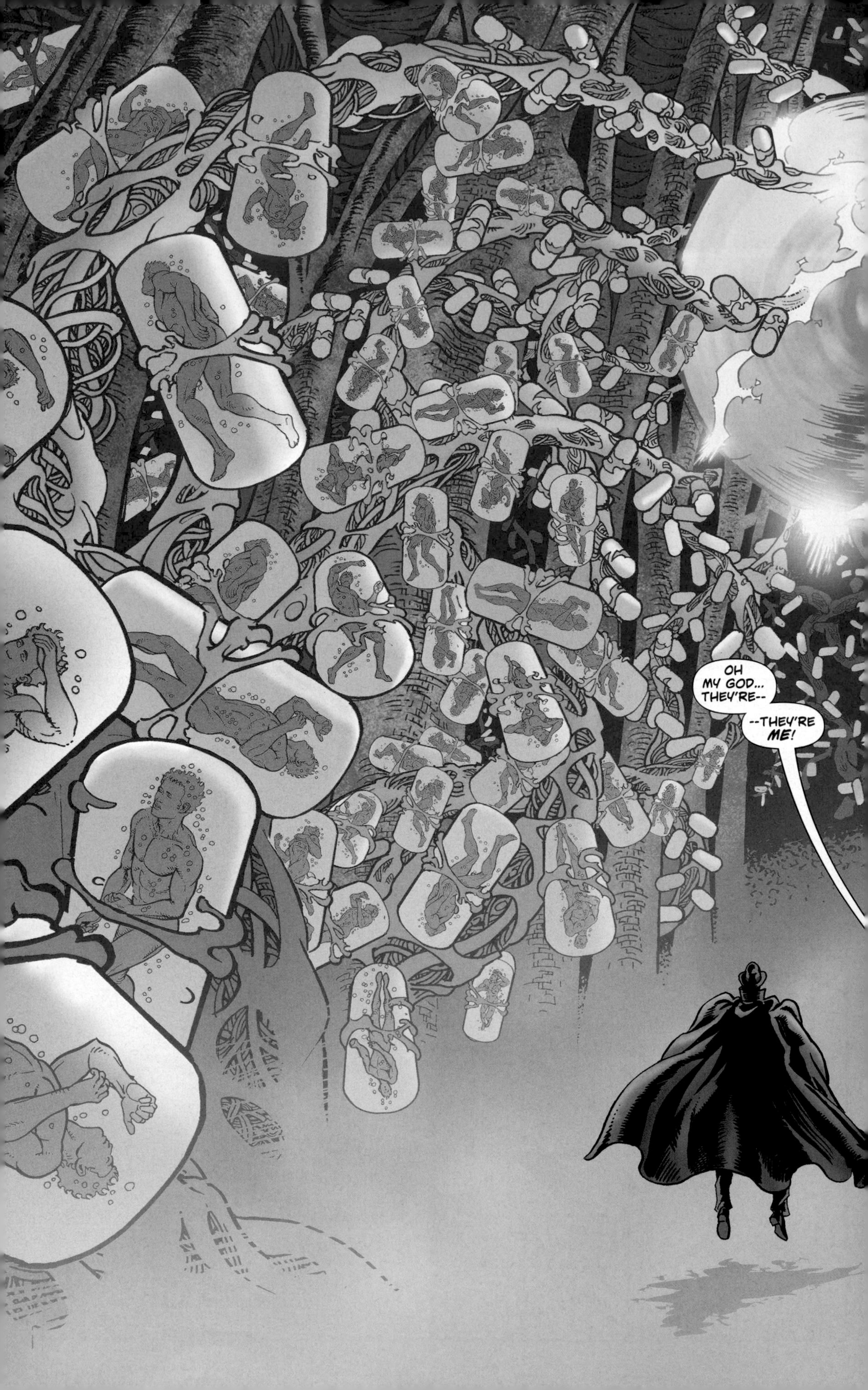
OH MY GOD... THEY'RE--
--THEY'RE ME!

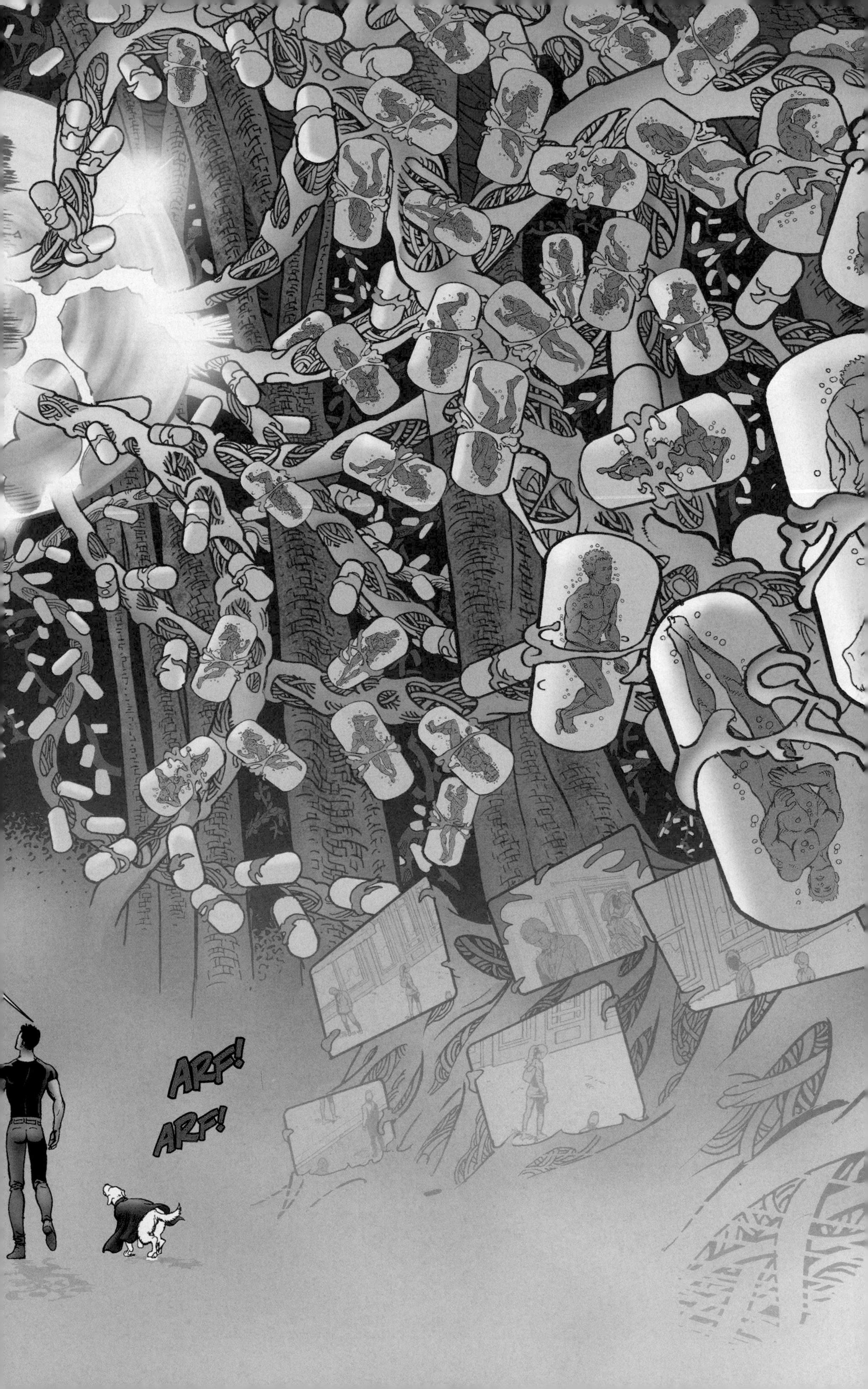
ARF!
ARF!

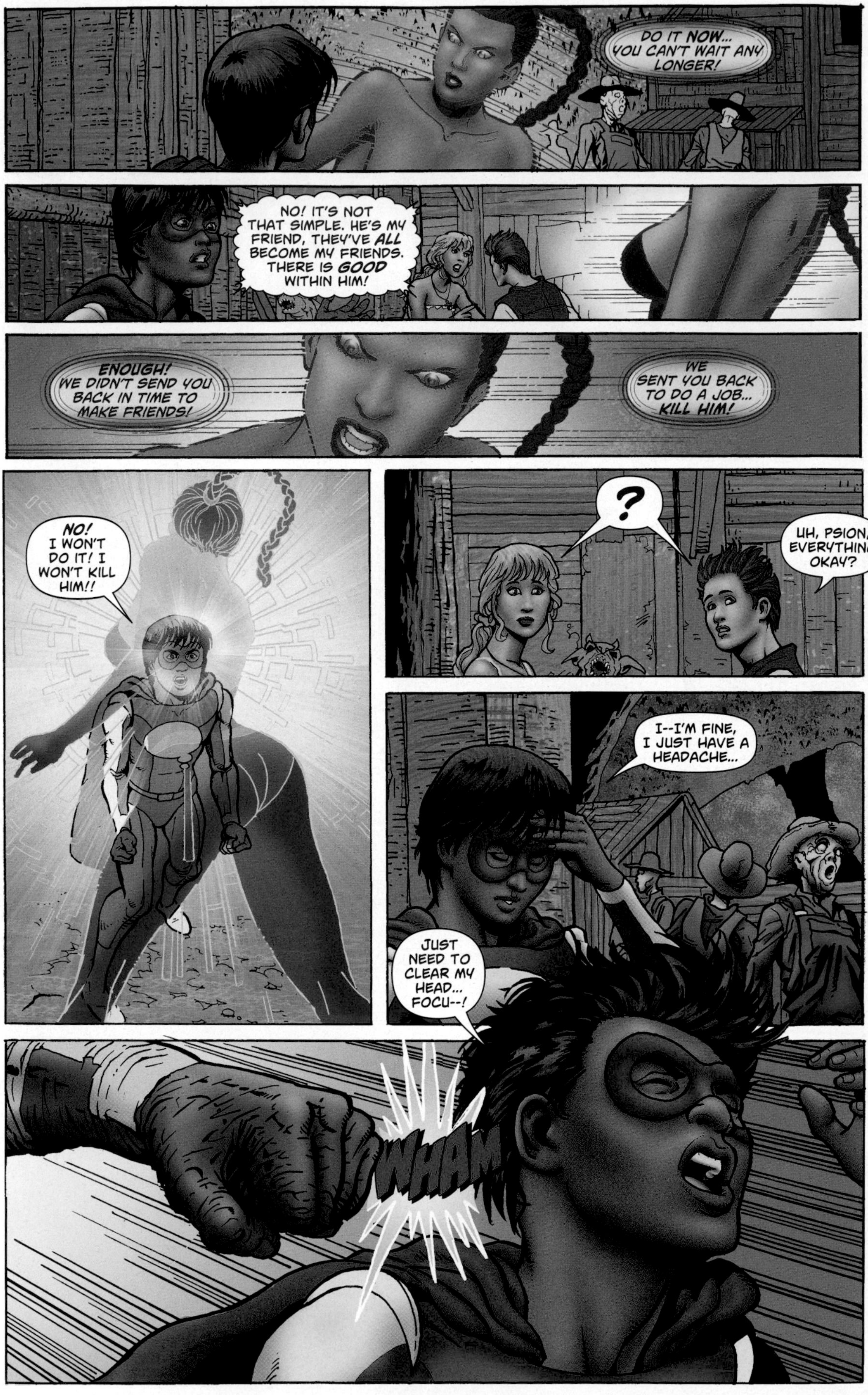
DO IT NOW... YOU CAN'T WAIT ANY LONGER!
NO! IT'S NOT THAT SIMPLE. HE'S MY FRIEND, THEY'VE ALL BECOME MY FRIENDS. THERE IS GOOD WITHIN HIM!
ENOUGH! WE DIDN'T SEND YOU BACK IN TIME TO MAKE FRIENDS!
WE SENT YOU BACK TO DO A JOB... KILL HIM!
NO! I WON'T DO IT! I WON'T KILL HIM!!
?
UH, PSION, EVERYTHING OKAY?
I--I'M FINE, I JUST HAVE A HEADACHE...
JUST NEED TO CLEAR MY HEAD... FOCU--!
WHAM

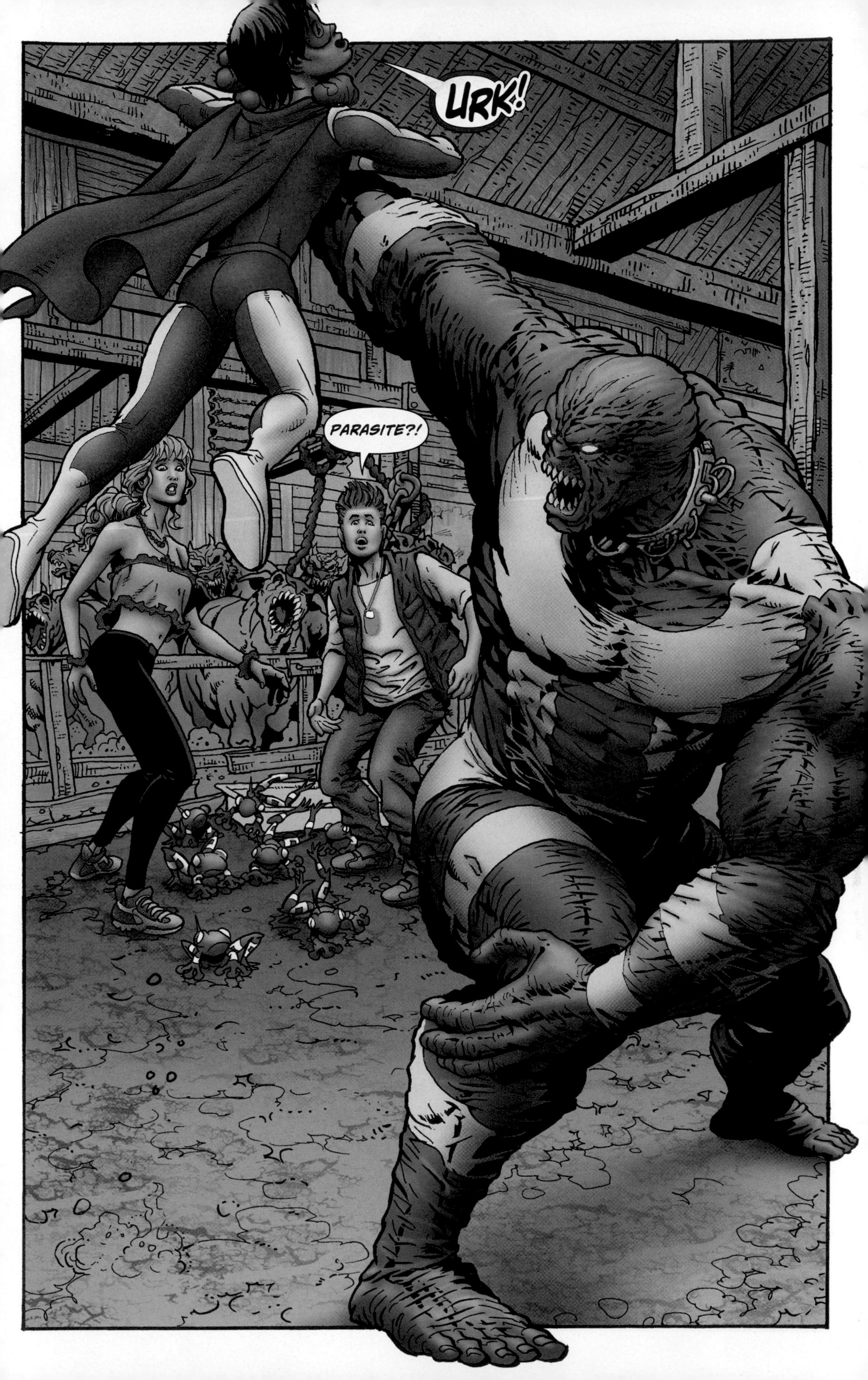
URK!
PARASITE?!

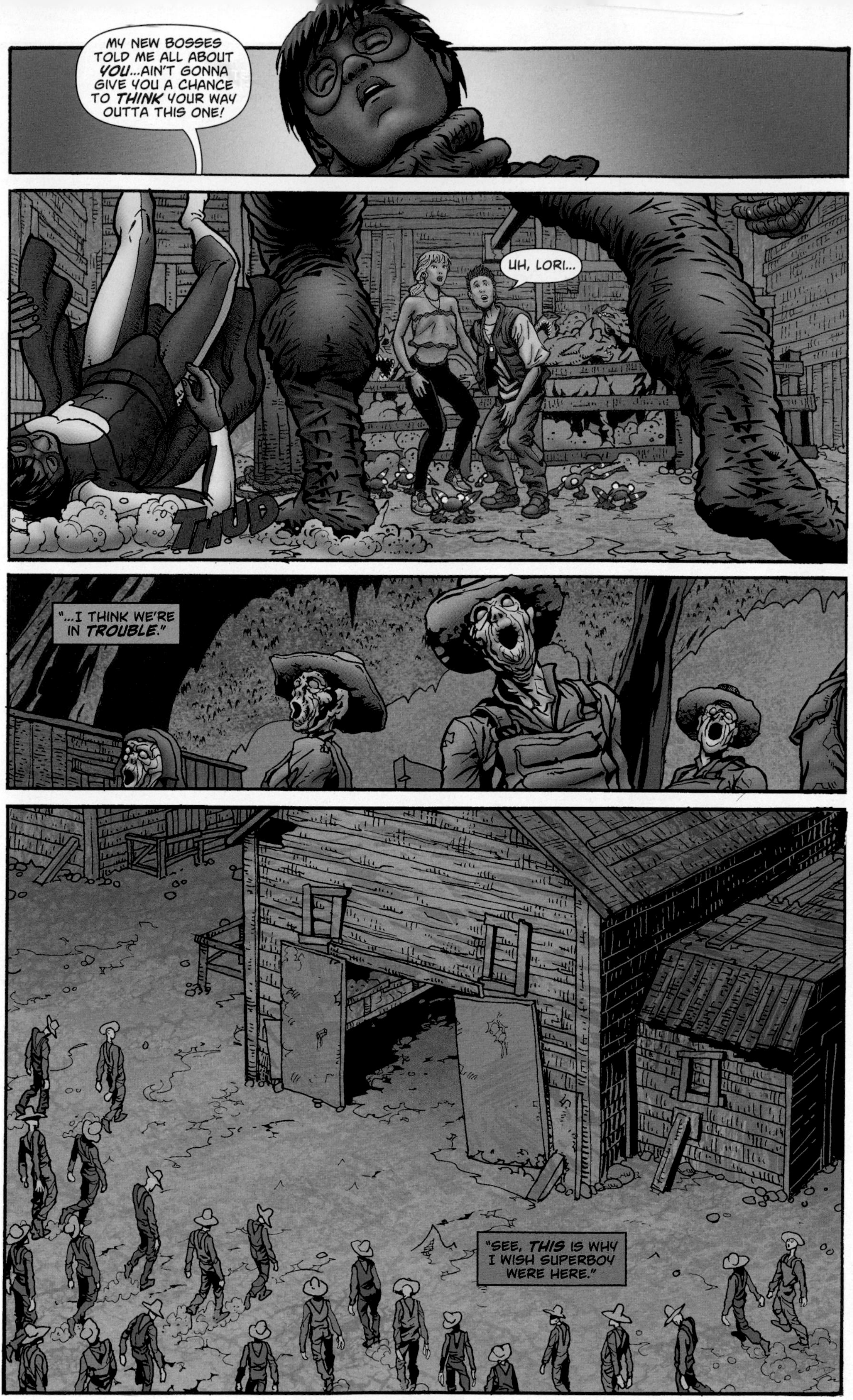
MY NEW BOSSES TOLD ME ALL ABOUT YOU...AIN'T GONNA GIVE YOU A CHANCE TO THINK YOUR WAY OUTTA THIS ONE!
THUD
UH, LORI...
"...I THINK WE'RE IN TROUBLE."
"SEE, THIS IS WHY I WISH SUPERBOY WERE HERE."

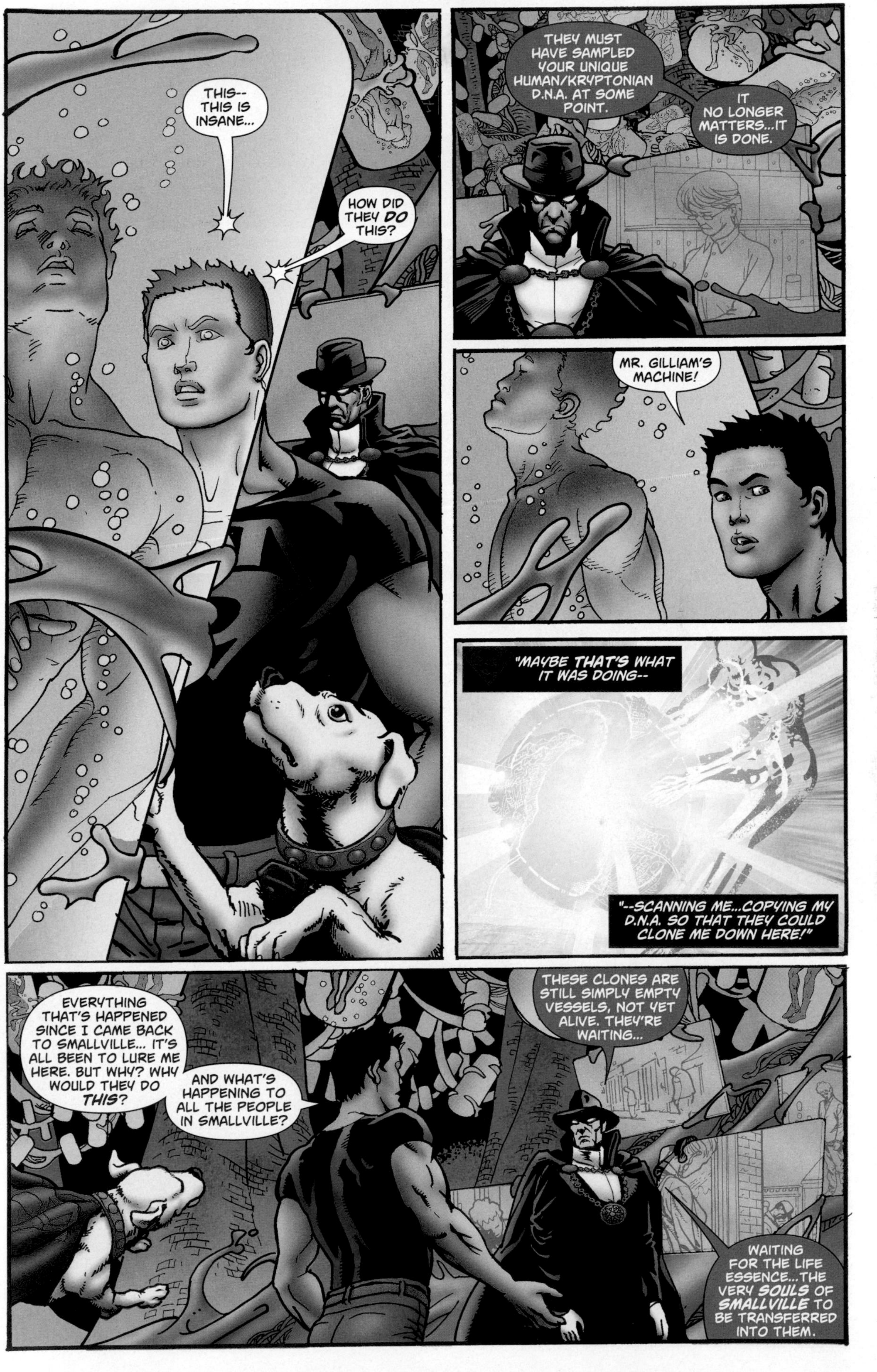

THIS-- THIS IS INSANE...
HOW DID THEY DO THIS?
THEY MUST HAVE SAMPLED YOUR UNIQUE HUMAN/KRYPTONIAN D.N.A. AT SOME POINT.
IT NO LONGER MATTERS...IT IS DONE.
MR. GILLIAM'S MACHINE!
"MAYBE THAT'S WHAT IT WAS DOING--
"--SCANNING ME...COPYING MY D.N.A. SO THAT THEY COULD CLONE ME DOWN HERE!"
EVERYTHING THAT'S HAPPENED SINCE I CAME BACK TO SMALLVILLE... IT'S ALL BEEN TO LURE ME HERE. BUT WHY? WHY WOULD THEY DO THIS?
AND WHAT'S HAPPENING TO ALL THE PEOPLE IN SMALLVILLE?
THESE CLONES ARE STILL SIMPLY EMPTY VESSELS, NOT YET ALIVE. THEY'RE WAITING...
WAITING FOR THE LIFE ESSENCE...THE VERY SOULS OF SMALLVILLE TO BE TRANSFERRED INTO THEM.

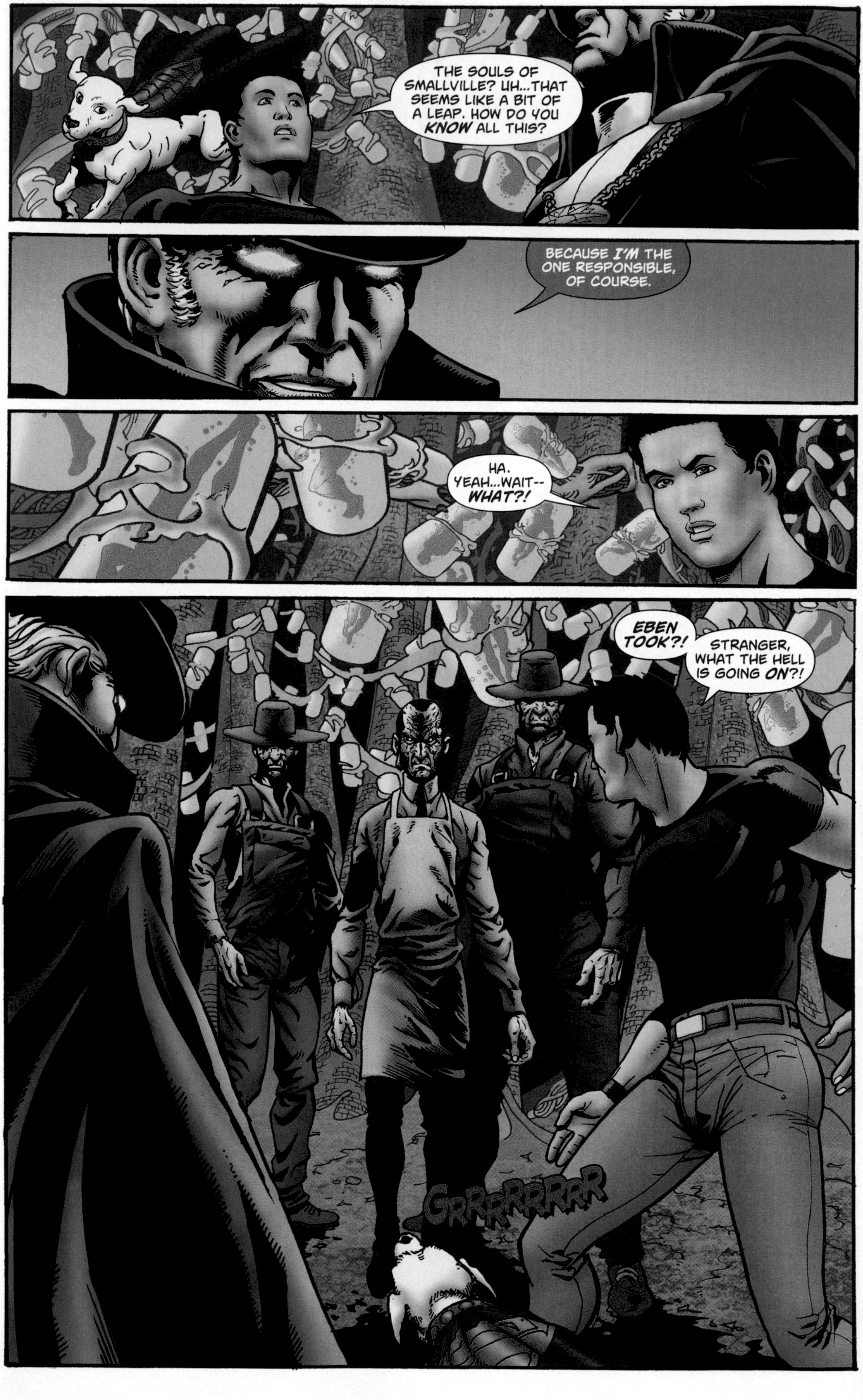
THE SOULS OF SMALLVILLE? UH...THAT SEEMS LIKE A BIT OF A LEAP. HOW DO YOU KNOW ALL THIS?
BECAUSE I'M THE ONE RESPONSIBLE, OF COURSE.
HA. YEAH...WAIT-- WHAT?!
EBEN TOOK?!
STRANGER, WHAT THE HELL IS GOING ON?!
GRRRRRRRR

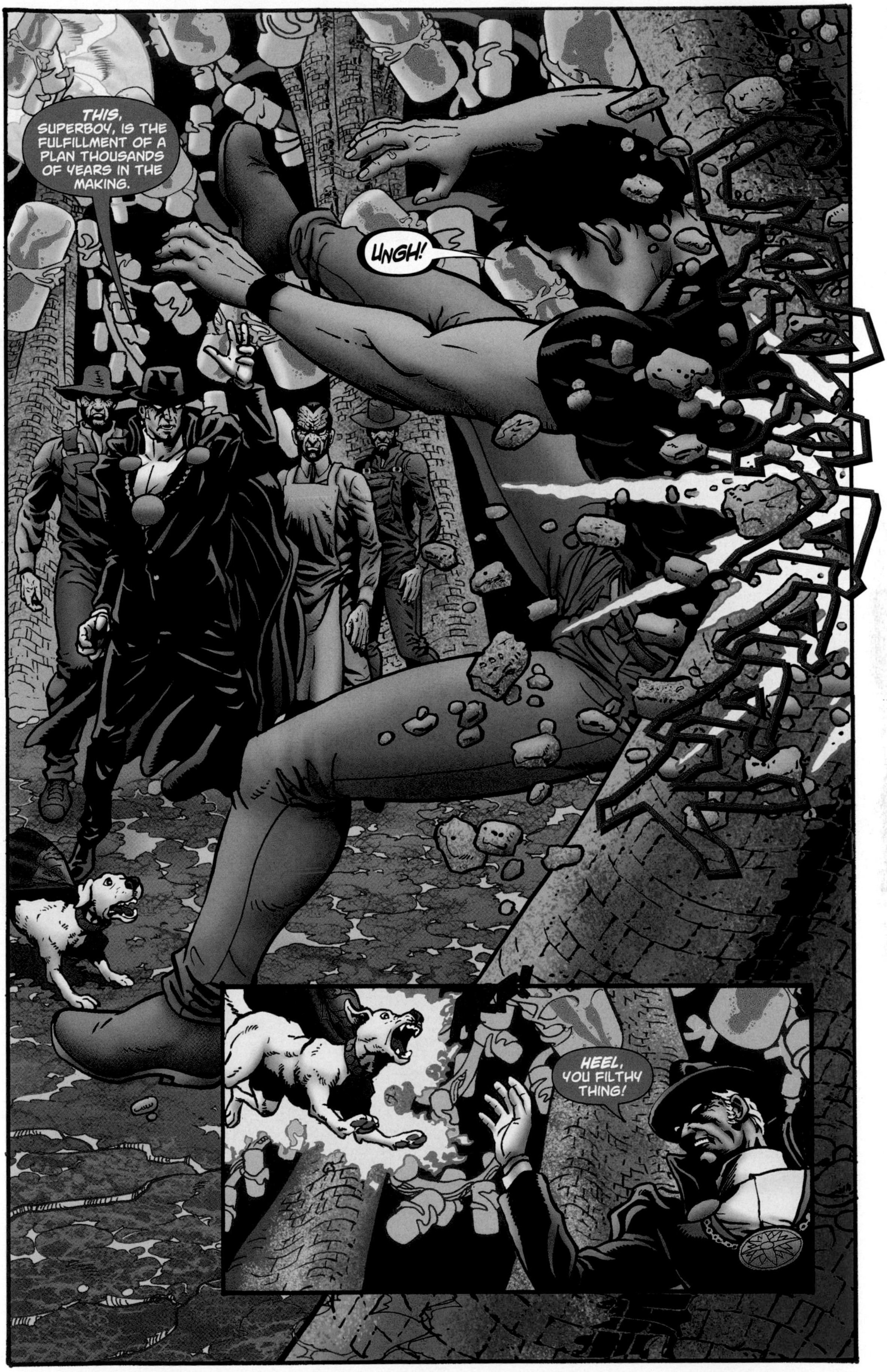

THIS, SUPERBOY, IS THE FULFILLMENT OF A PLAN THOUSANDS OF YEARS IN THE MAKING.
UNGH!
HEEL, YOU FILTHY THING!

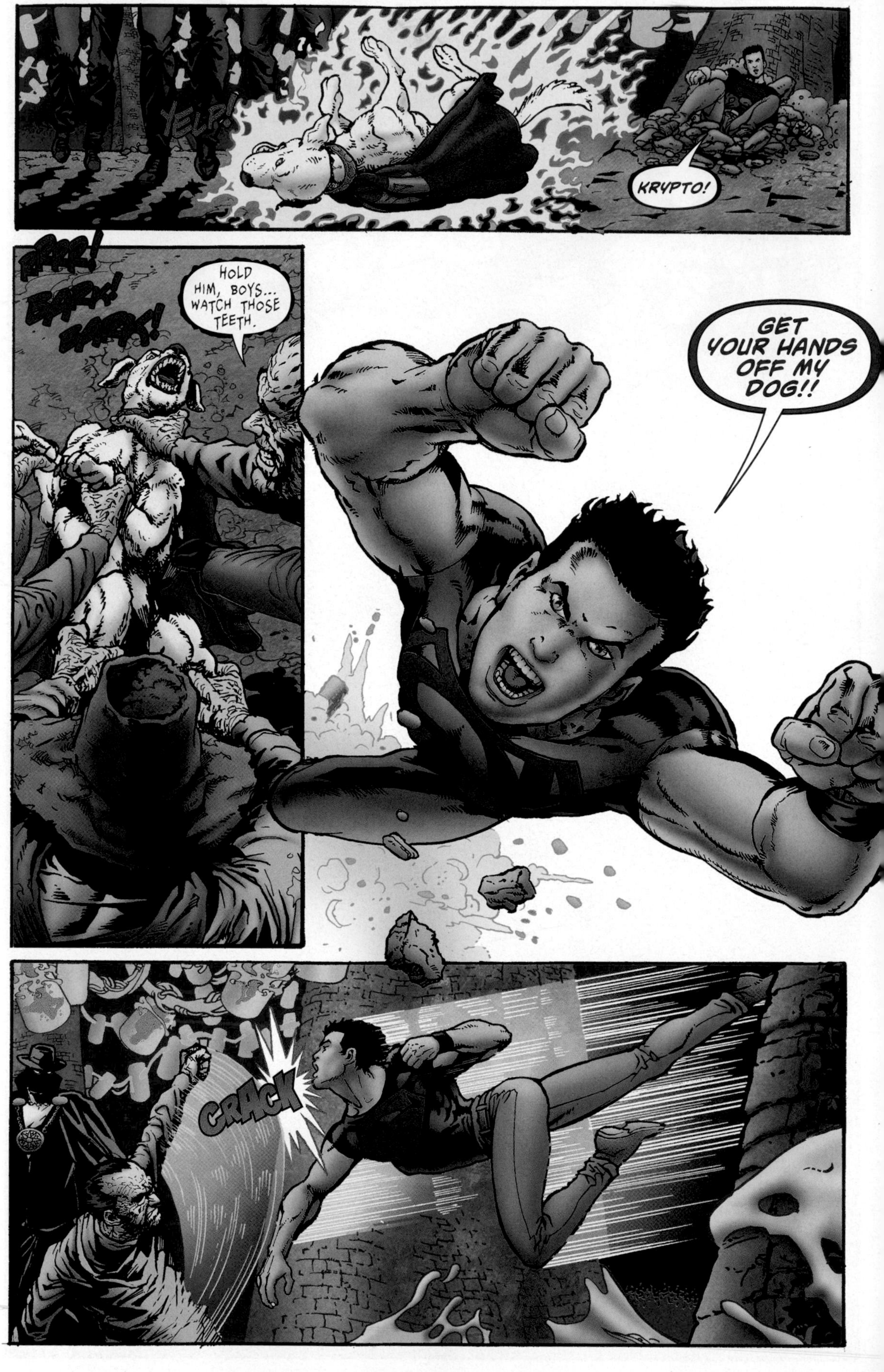
YELP!
KRYPTO!
RRRR!
BARK!
BARK!
HOLD HIM, BOYS... WATCH THOSE TEETH.
GET YOUR HANDS OFF MY DOG!!
CRACK

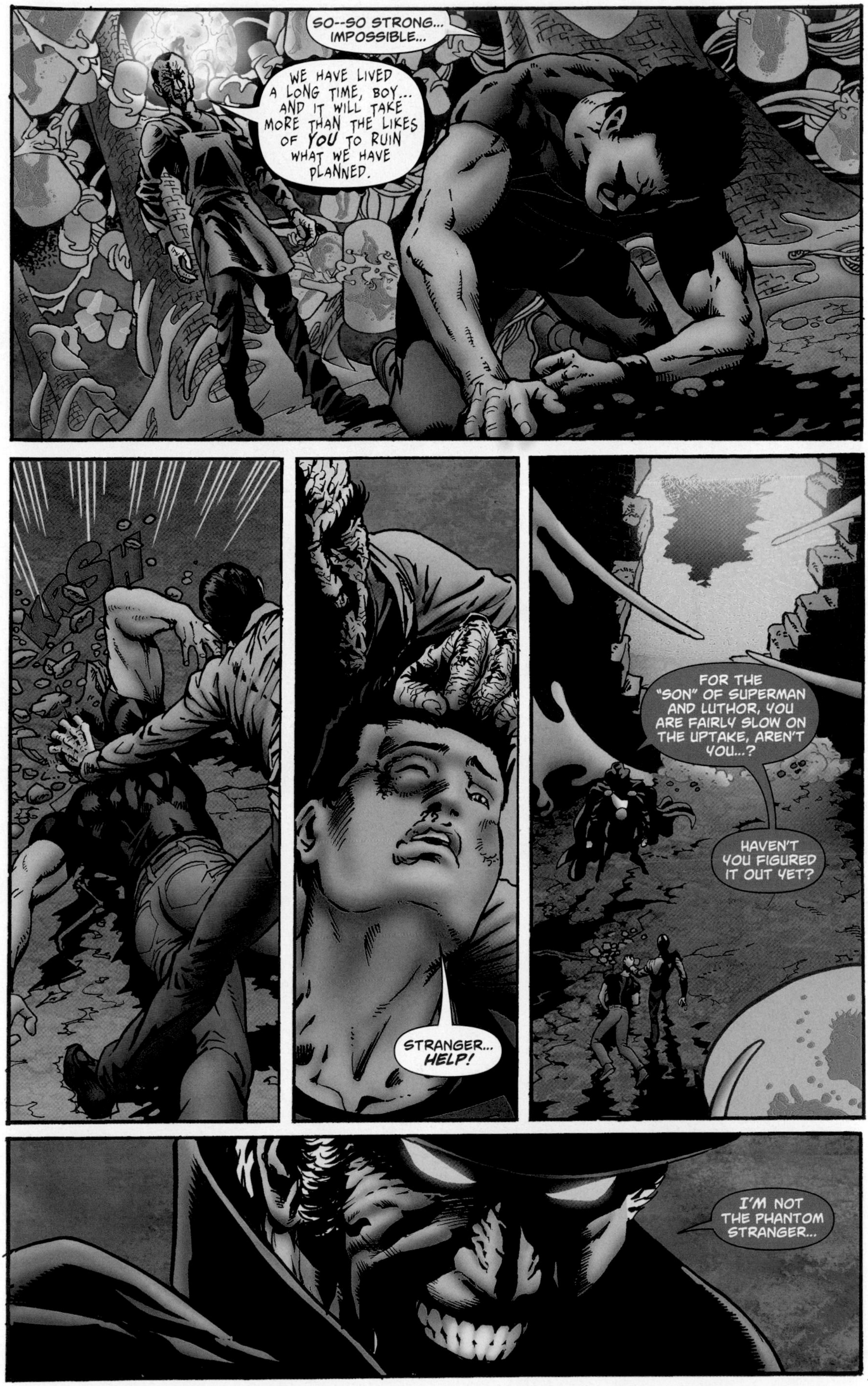
SO--SO STRONG... IMPOSSIBLE...
WE HAVE LIVED A LONG TIME, BOY... AND IT WILL TAKE MORE THAN THE LIKES OF YOU TO RUIN WHAT WE HAVE PLANNED.
KRSH
STRANGER... HELP!
FOR THE "SON" OF SUPERMAN AND LUTHOR, YOU ARE FAIRLY SLOW ON THE UPTAKE, AREN'T YOU...?
HAVEN'T YOU FIGURED IT OUT YET?
I'M NOT THE PHANTOM STRANGER...

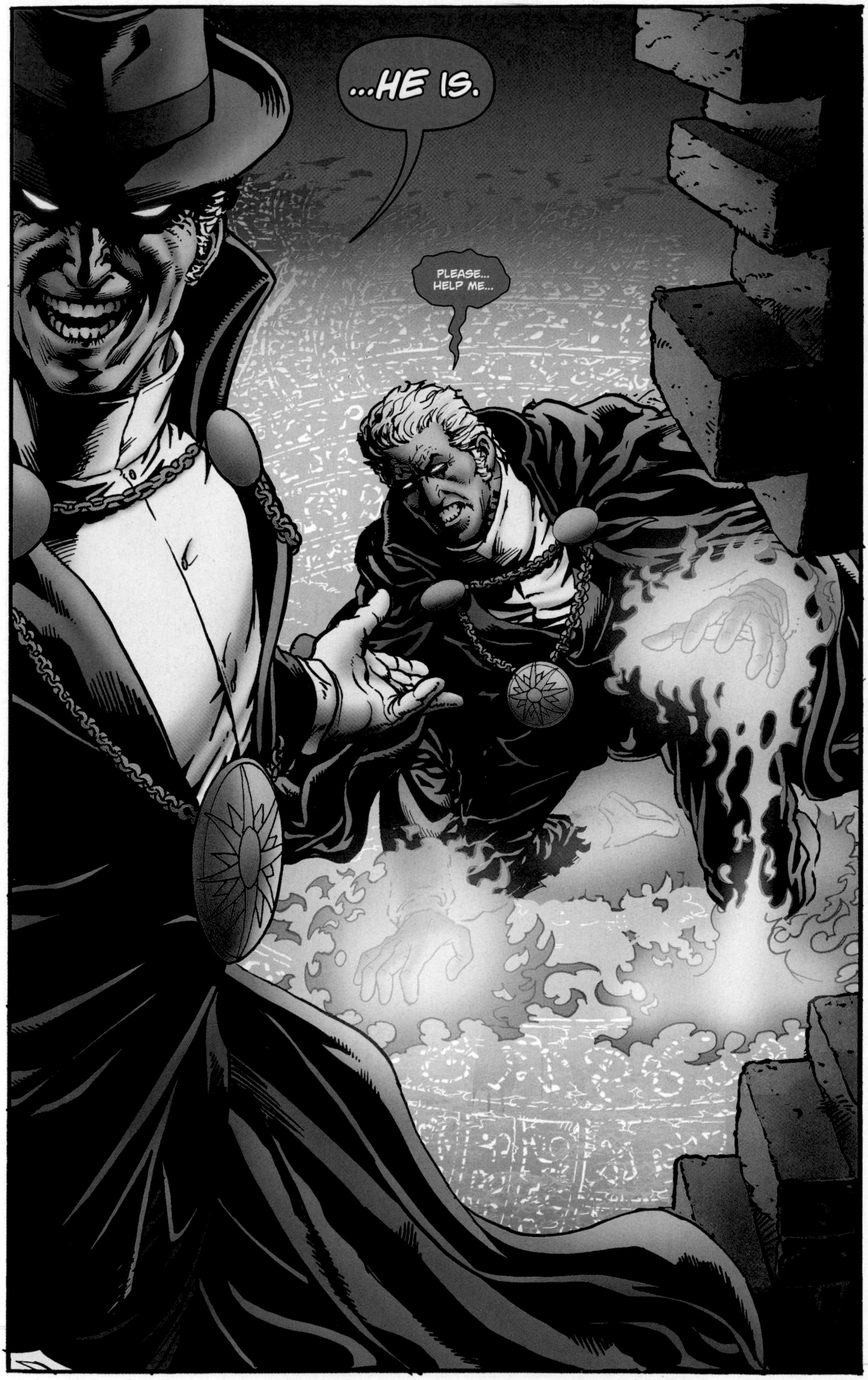
...HE IS.
PLEASE... HELP ME...

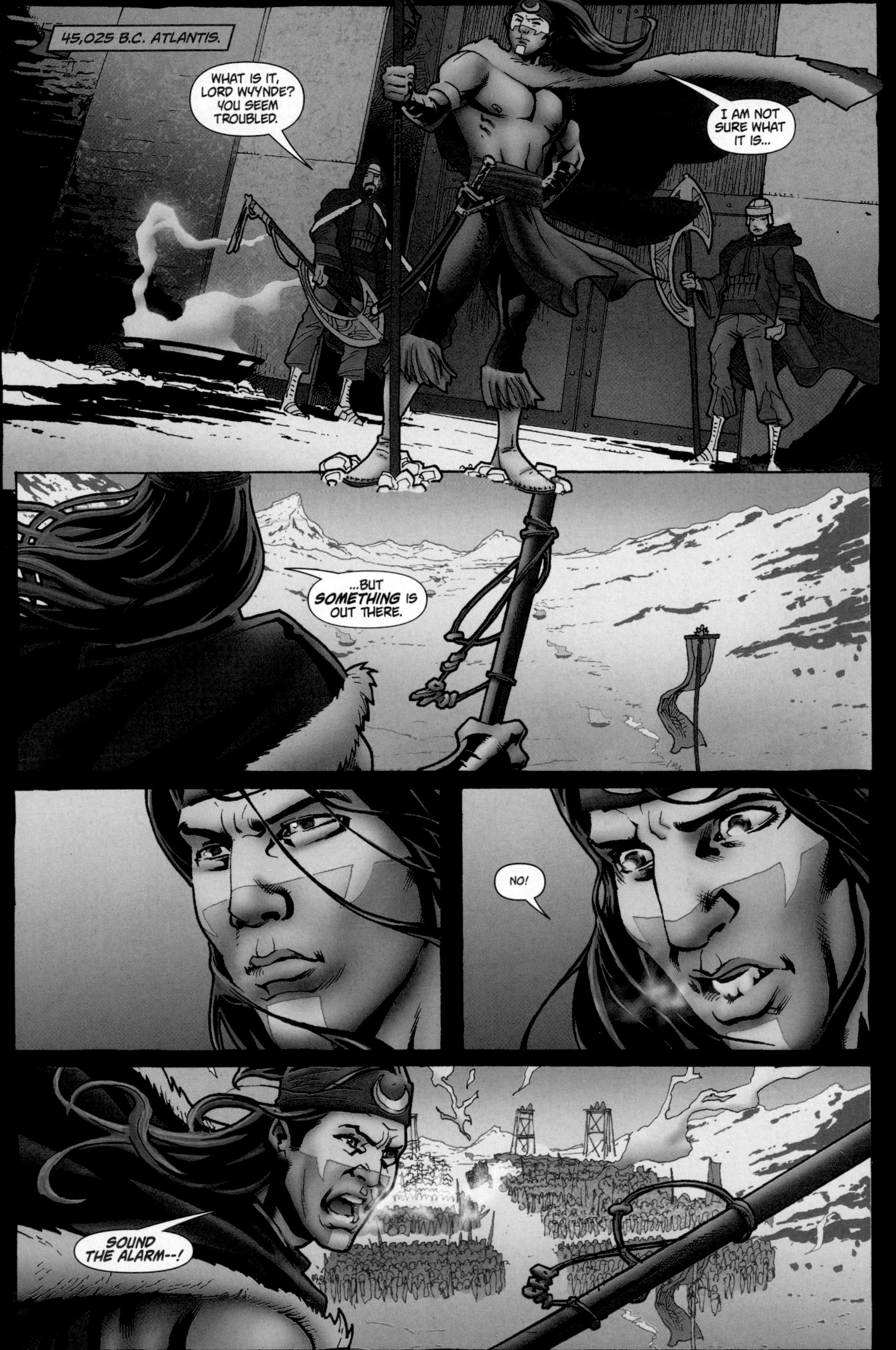
45,025 B.C. ATLANTIS.
WHAT IS IT, LORD WYYNDE? YOU SEEM TROUBLED.
I AM NOT SURE WHAT IT IS...
...BUT SOMETHING IS OUT THERE.
NO!
SOUND THE ALARM--!

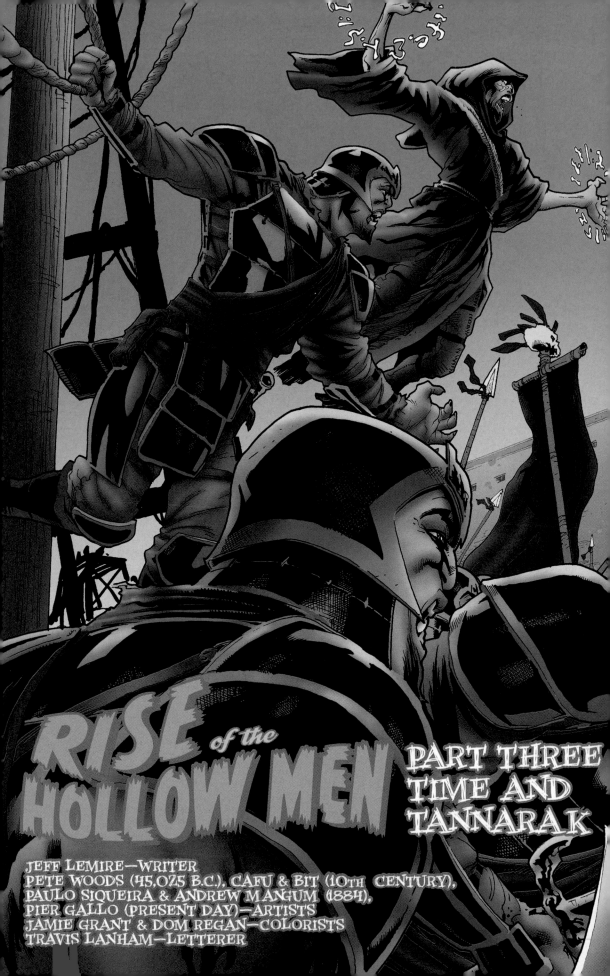

RISE of the HOLLOW MEN

PART THREE TIME AND TANNARAK

JEFF LEMIRE—WRITER
PETE WOODS (45,025 B.C.), CAFU & BIT (10TH CENTURY),
PAULO SIQUEIRA & ANDREW MANGUM (1884),
PIER GALLO (PRESENT DAY)—ARTISTS
JAMIE GRANT & DOM REGAN—COLORISTS
TRAVIS LANHAM—LETTERER

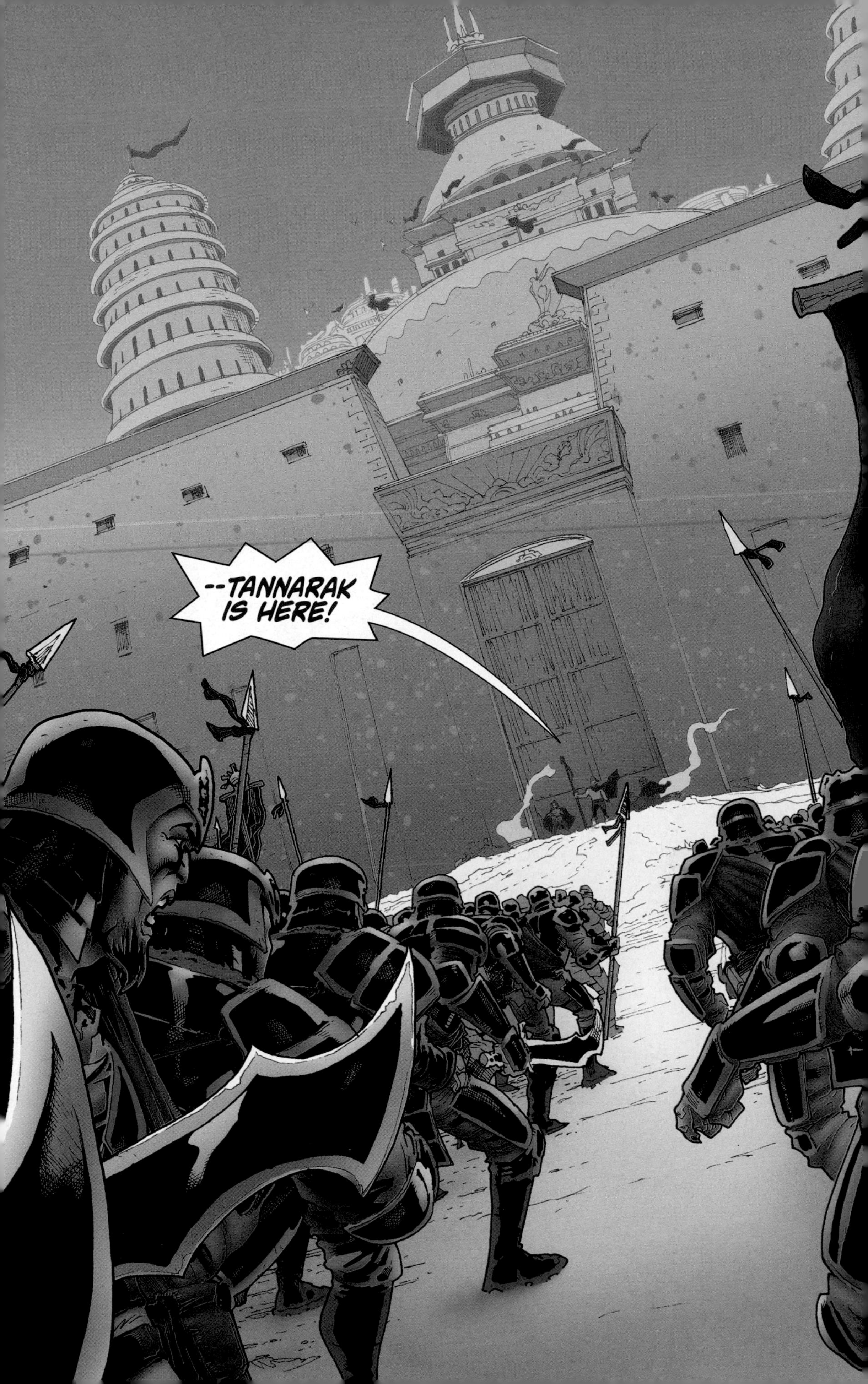
--TANNARAK IS HERE!

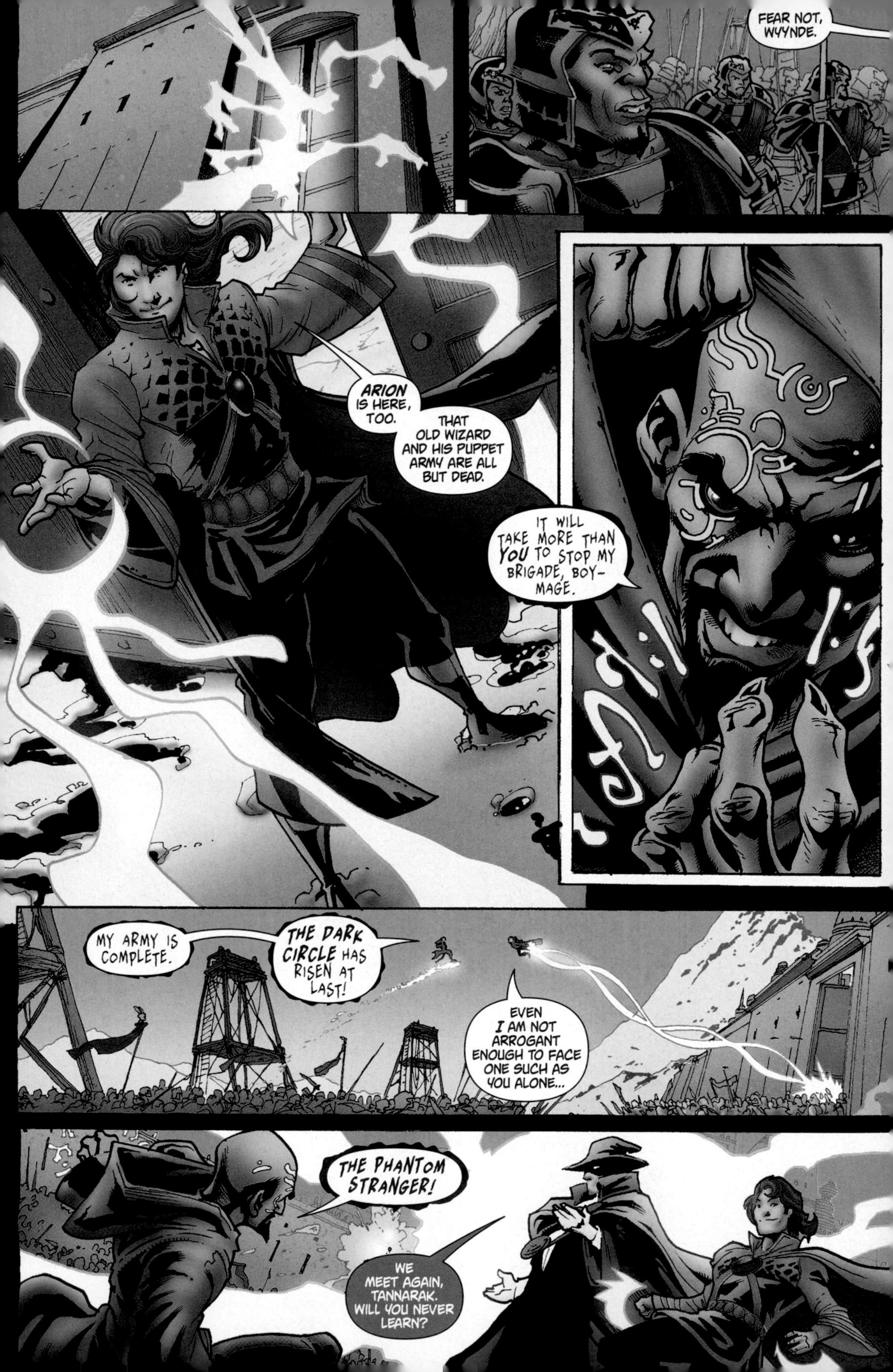
FEAR NOT, WYYNDE.
ARION IS HERE, TOO.
THAT OLD WIZARD AND HIS PUPPET ARMY ARE ALL BUT DEAD.
IT WILL TAKE MORE THAN YOU TO STOP MY BRIGADE, BOY-MAGE.
MY ARMY IS COMPLETE.
THE DARK CIRCLE HAS RISEN AT LAST!
EVEN I AM NOT ARROGANT ENOUGH TO FACE ONE SUCH AS YOU ALONE...
THE PHANTOM STRANGER!
WE MEET AGAIN, TANNARAK. WILL YOU NEVER LEARN?

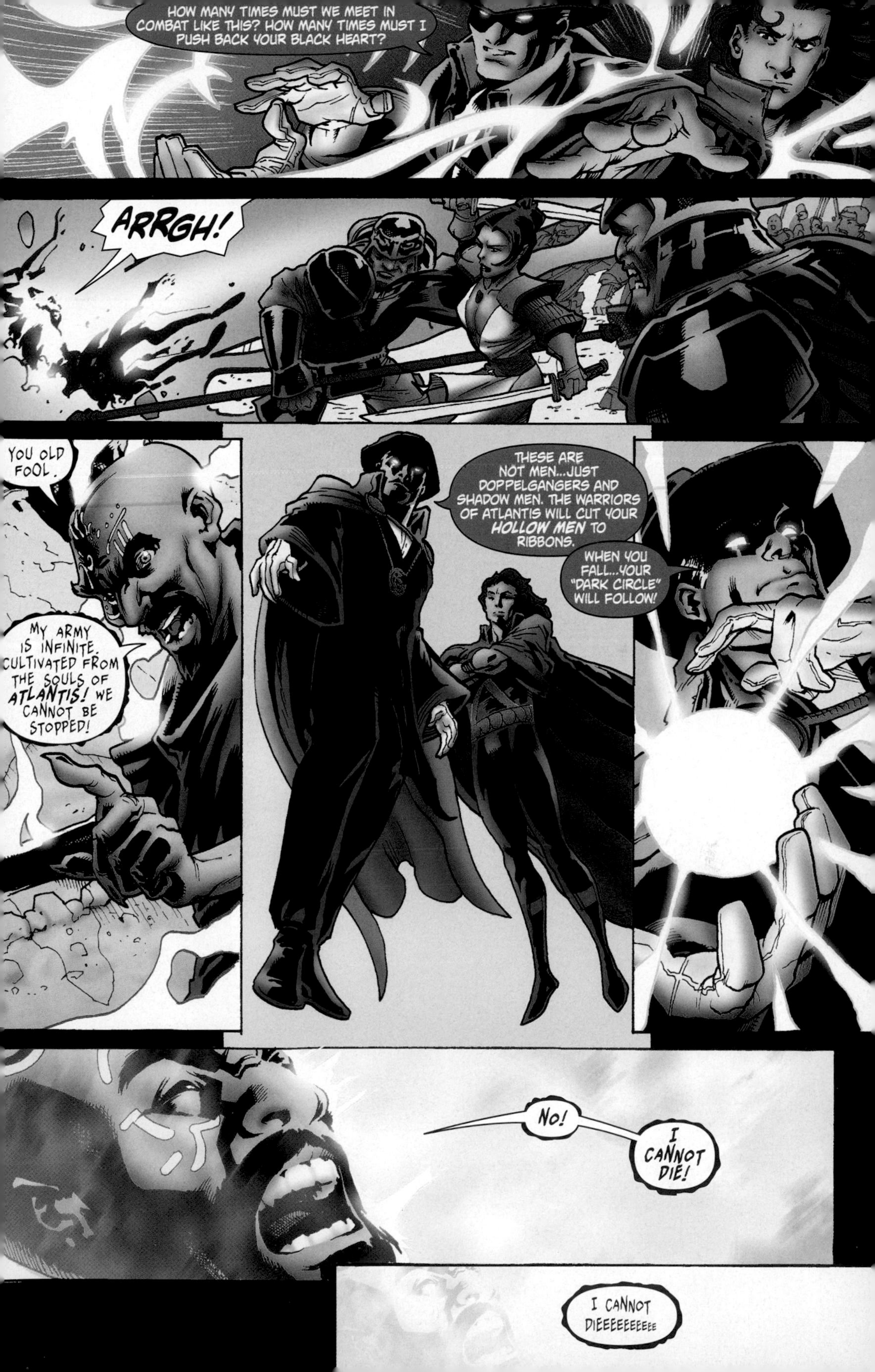
HOW MANY TIMES MUST WE MEET IN COMBAT LIKE THIS? HOW MANY TIMES MUST I PUSH BACK YOUR BLACK HEART?
ARRGH!
YOU OLD FOOL.
MY ARMY IS INFINITE. CULTIVATED FROM THE SOULS OF ATLANTIS! WE CANNOT BE STOPPED!
THESE ARE NOT MEN...JUST DOPPELGANGERS AND SHADOW MEN. THE WARRIORS OF ATLANTIS WILL CUT YOUR HOLLOW MEN TO RIBBONS.
WHEN YOU FALL...YOUR "DARK CIRCLE" WILL FOLLOW!
NO!
I CANNOT DIE!
I CANNOT DIEEEEEEEEEEE

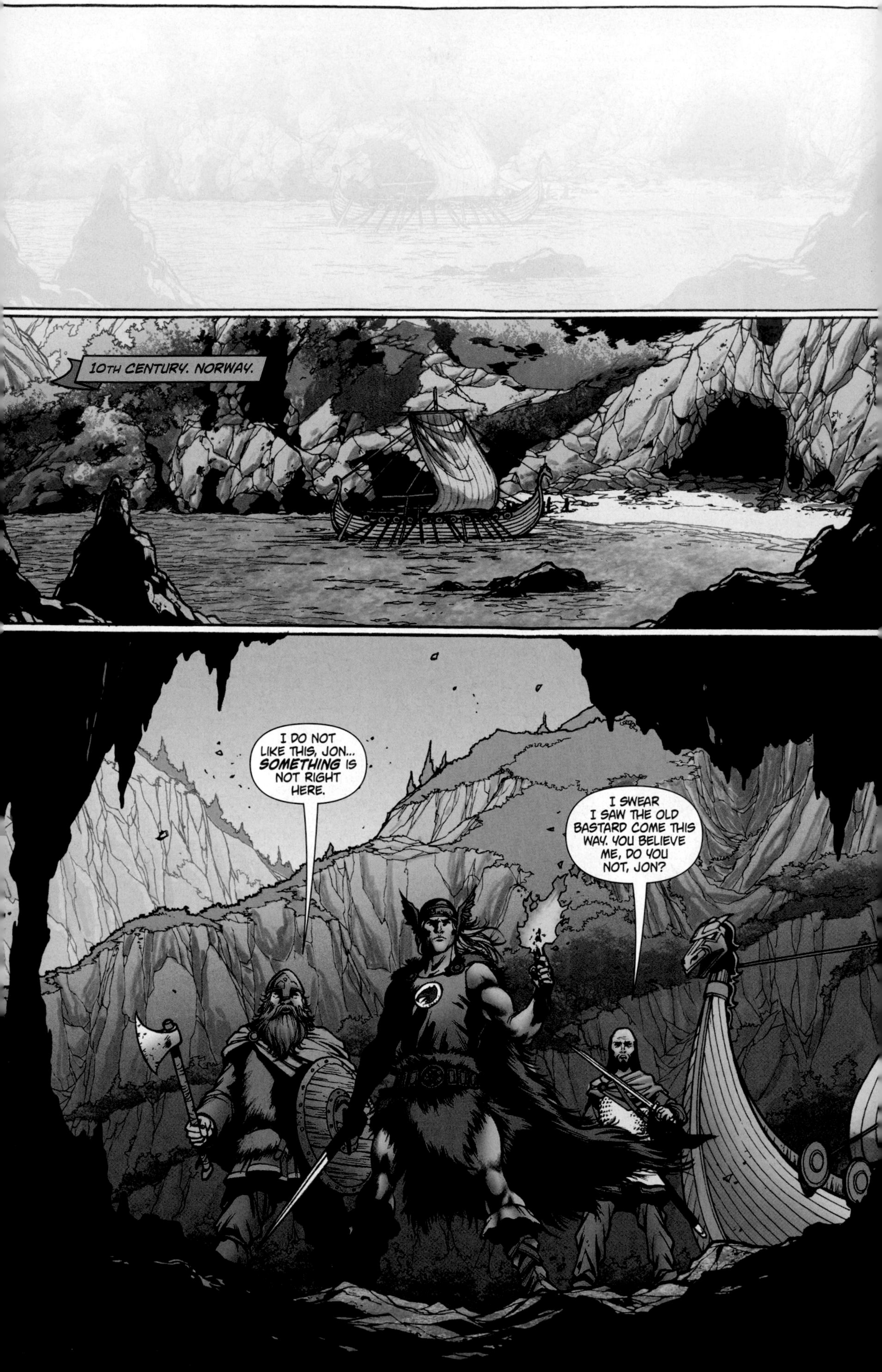
10TH CENTURY. NORWAY.
I DO NOT LIKE THIS, JON... SOMETHING IS NOT RIGHT HERE.
I SWEAR I SAW THE OLD BASTARD COME THIS WAY. YOU BELIEVE ME, DO YOU NOT, JON?

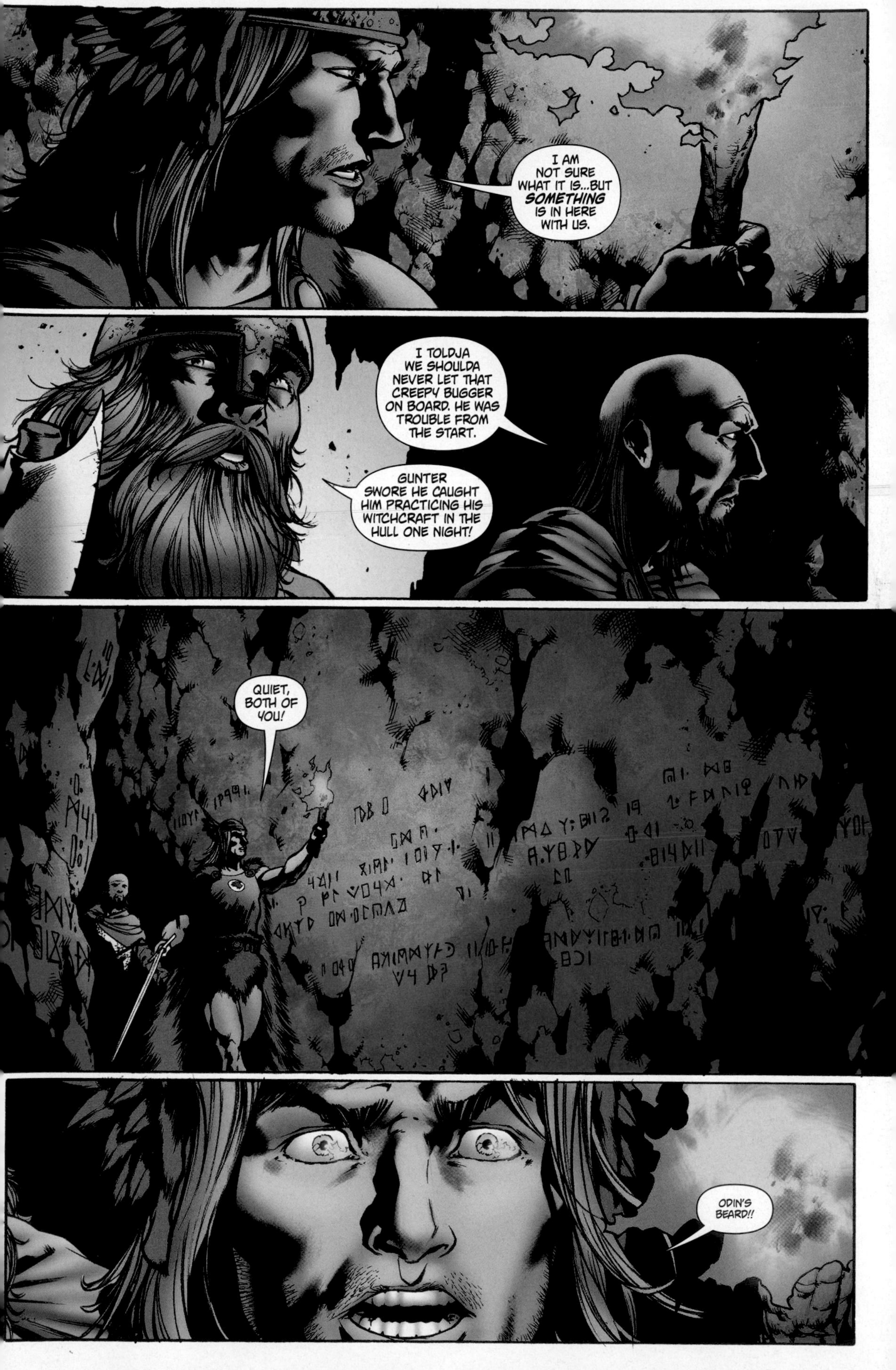
I AM NOT SURE WHAT IT IS...BUT SOMETHING IS IN HERE WITH US.
I TOLDJA WE SHOULDA NEVER LET THAT CREEPY BUGGER ON BOARD. HE WAS TROUBLE FROM THE START.
GUNTER SWORE HE CAUGHT HIM PRACTICING HIS WITCHCRAFT IN THE HULL ONE NIGHT!
QUIET, BOTH OF YOU!
ODIN'S BEARD!!

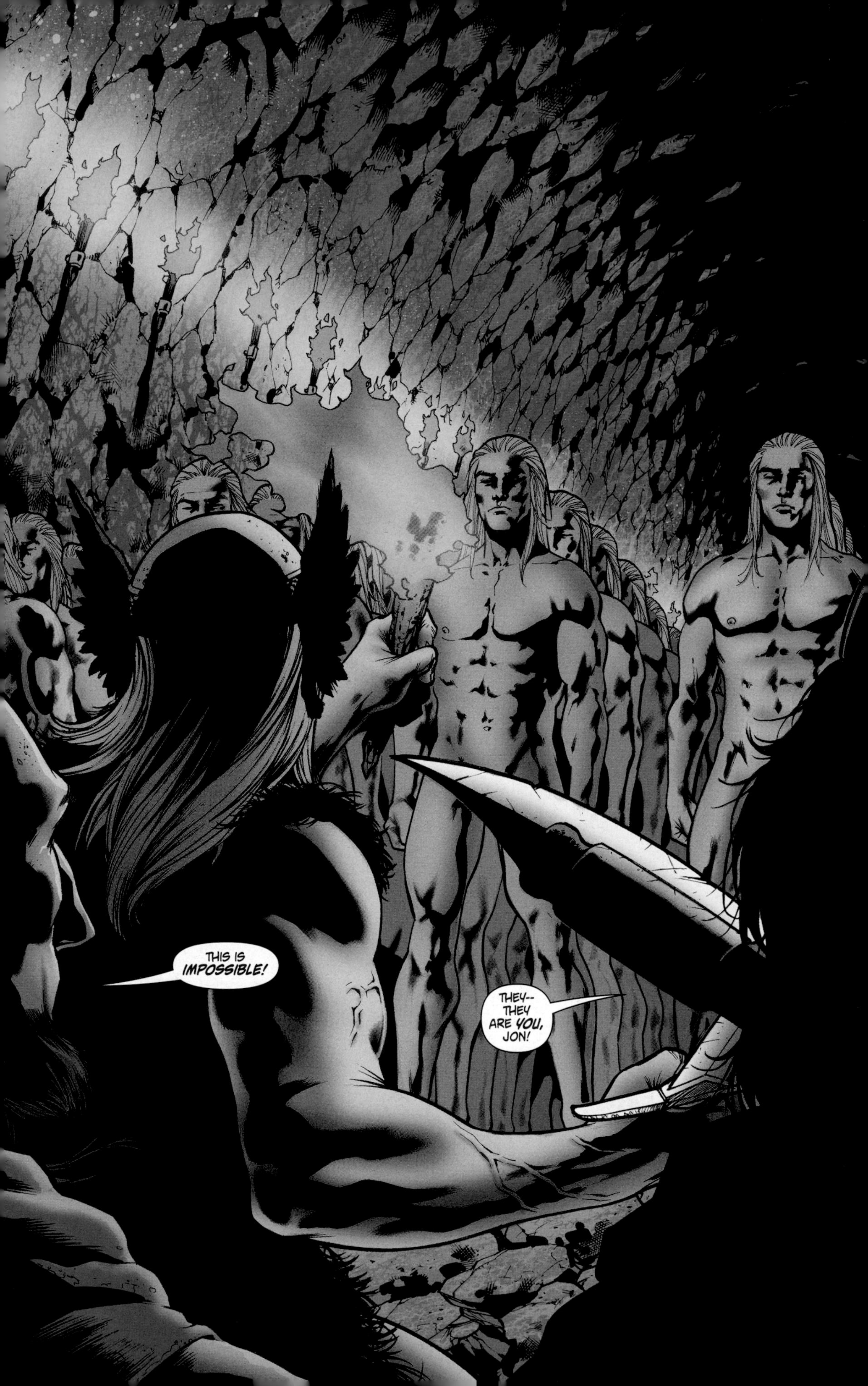
THIS IS IMPOSSIBLE!
THEY-- THEY ARE YOU, JON!

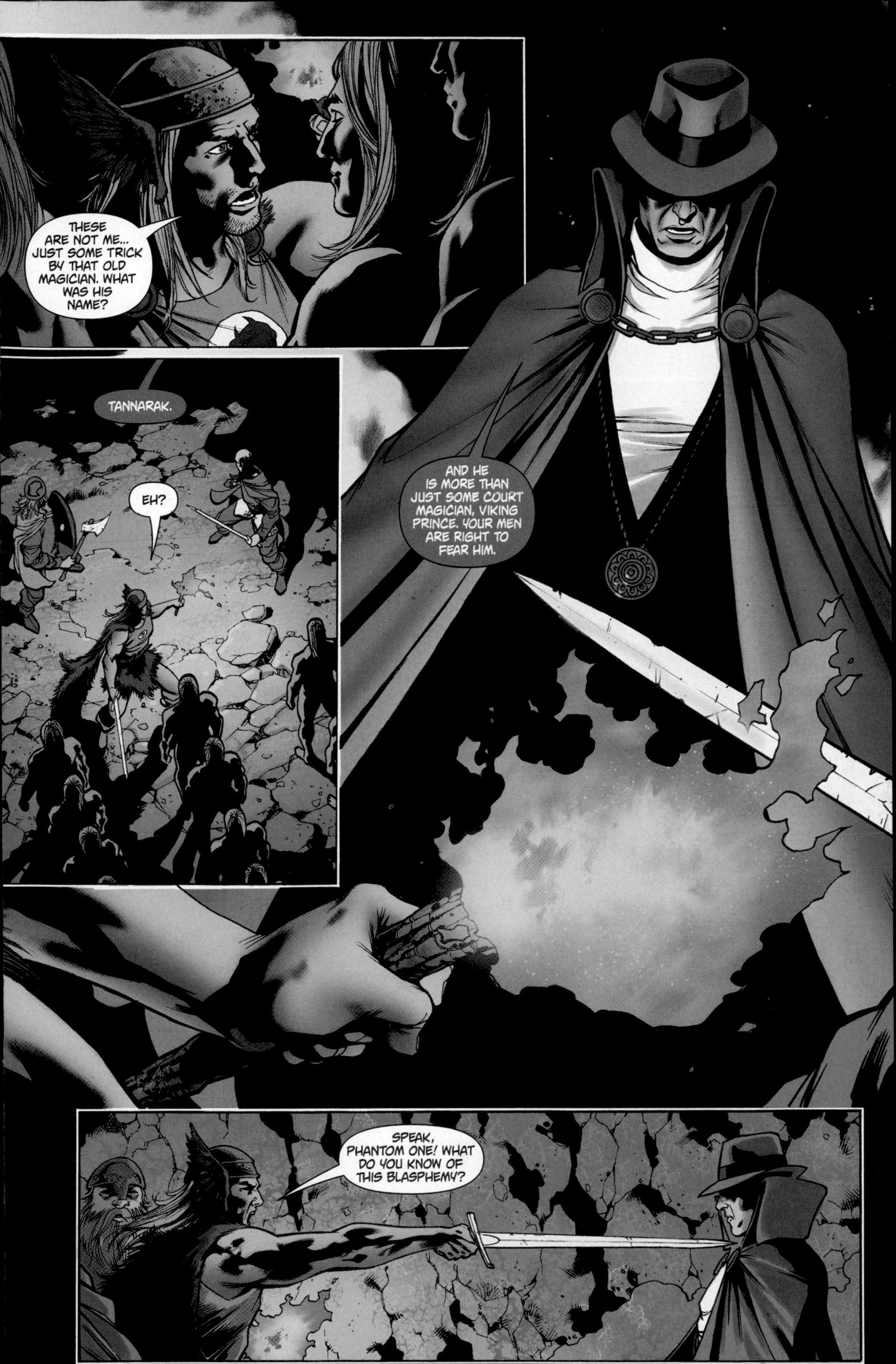

THESE ARE NOT ME... JUST SOME TRICK BY THAT OLD MAGICIAN. WHAT WAS HIS NAME?
TANNARAK.
EH?
AND HE IS MORE THAN JUST SOME COURT MAGICIAN, VIKING PRINCE. YOUR MEN ARE RIGHT TO FEAR HIM.
SPEAK, PHANTOM ONE! WHAT DO YOU KNOW OF THIS BLASPHEMY?

UNFORTUNATELY, I KNOW MUCH. I HAVE FACED THE WIZARD WHO INFILTRATED YOUR RANKS ON MANY OCCASIONS.

HE HAS ATTEMPTED TO COPY YOU...REBUILD HIS LOST ARMY IN YOUR LIKENESS.

HE HAS DONE THIS BEFORE, BUT THIS TIME HE FAILED TO WAIT LONG ENOUGH BETWEEN DEFEATS...HE IS STILL WEAK, AND SO ARE HIS EMPTY MEN.

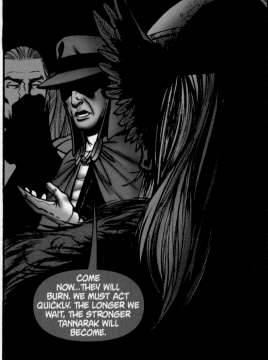

COME NOW...THEY WILL BURN. WE MUST ACT QUICKLY. THE LONGER WE WAIT, THE STRONGER TANNARAK WILL BECOME.

I SHALL GLADLY BE DONE WITH THESE ABERRATIONS.

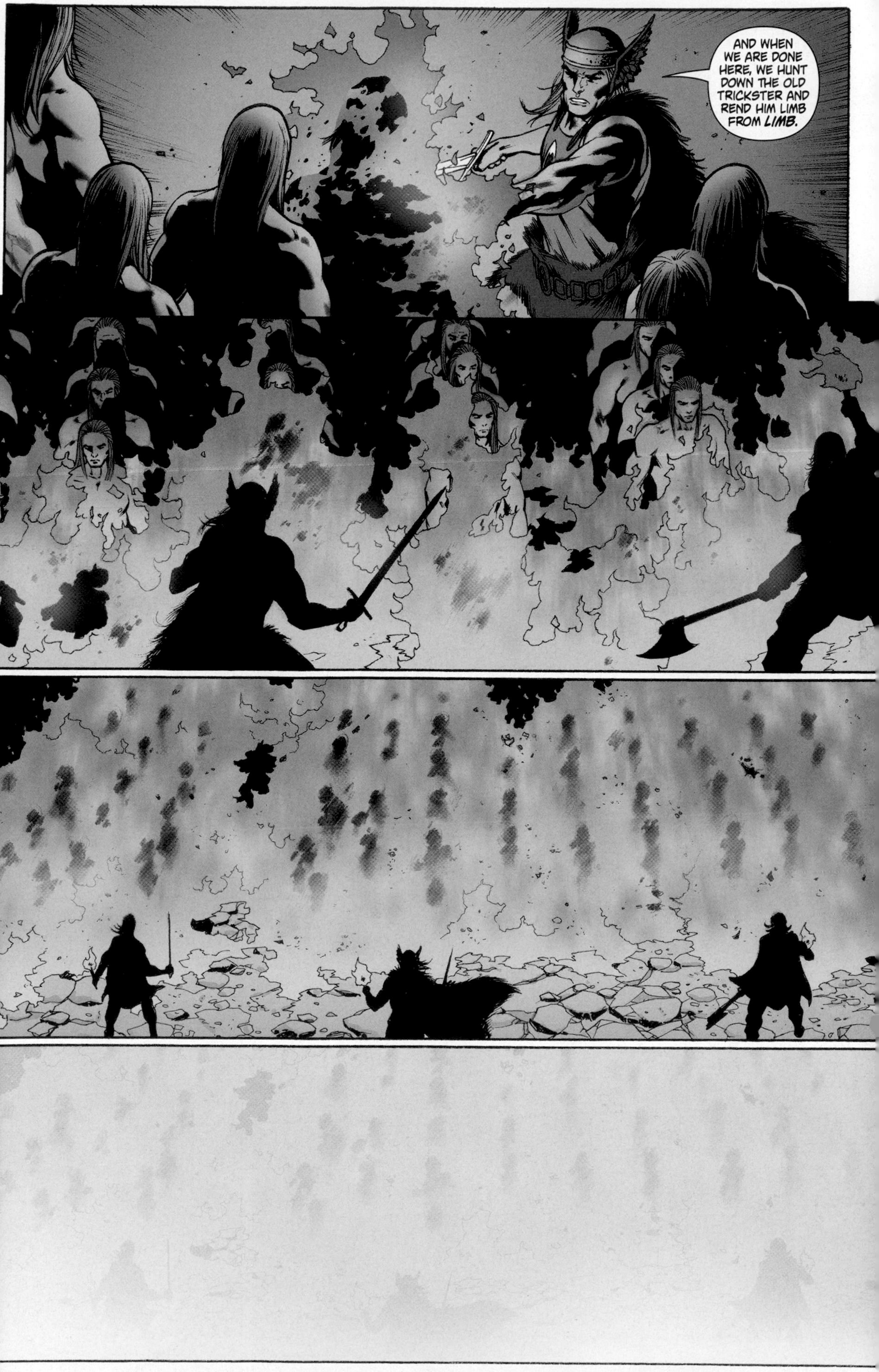
AND WHEN WE ARE DONE HERE, WE HUNT DOWN THE OLD TRICKSTER AND REND HIM LIMB FROM LIMB.

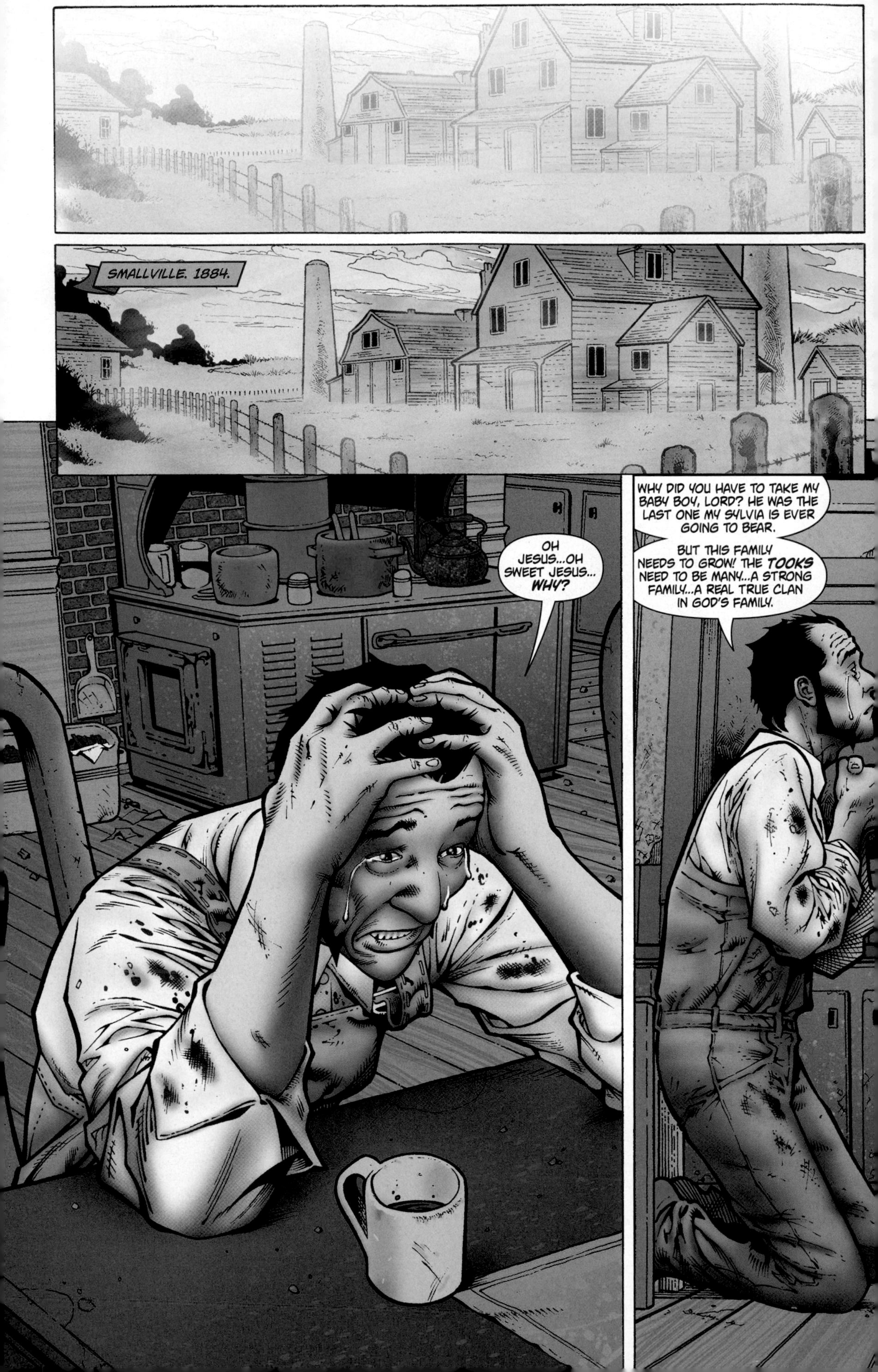
SMALLVILLE. 1884.
OH JESUS...OH SWEET JESUS... WHY?
WHY DID YOU HAVE TO TAKE MY BABY BOY, LORD? HE WAS THE LAST ONE MY SYLVIA IS EVER GOING TO BEAR.
BUT THIS FAMILY NEEDS TO GROW! THE TOOKS NEED TO BE MANY...A STRONG FAMILY...A REAL TRUE CLAN IN GOD'S FAMILY.

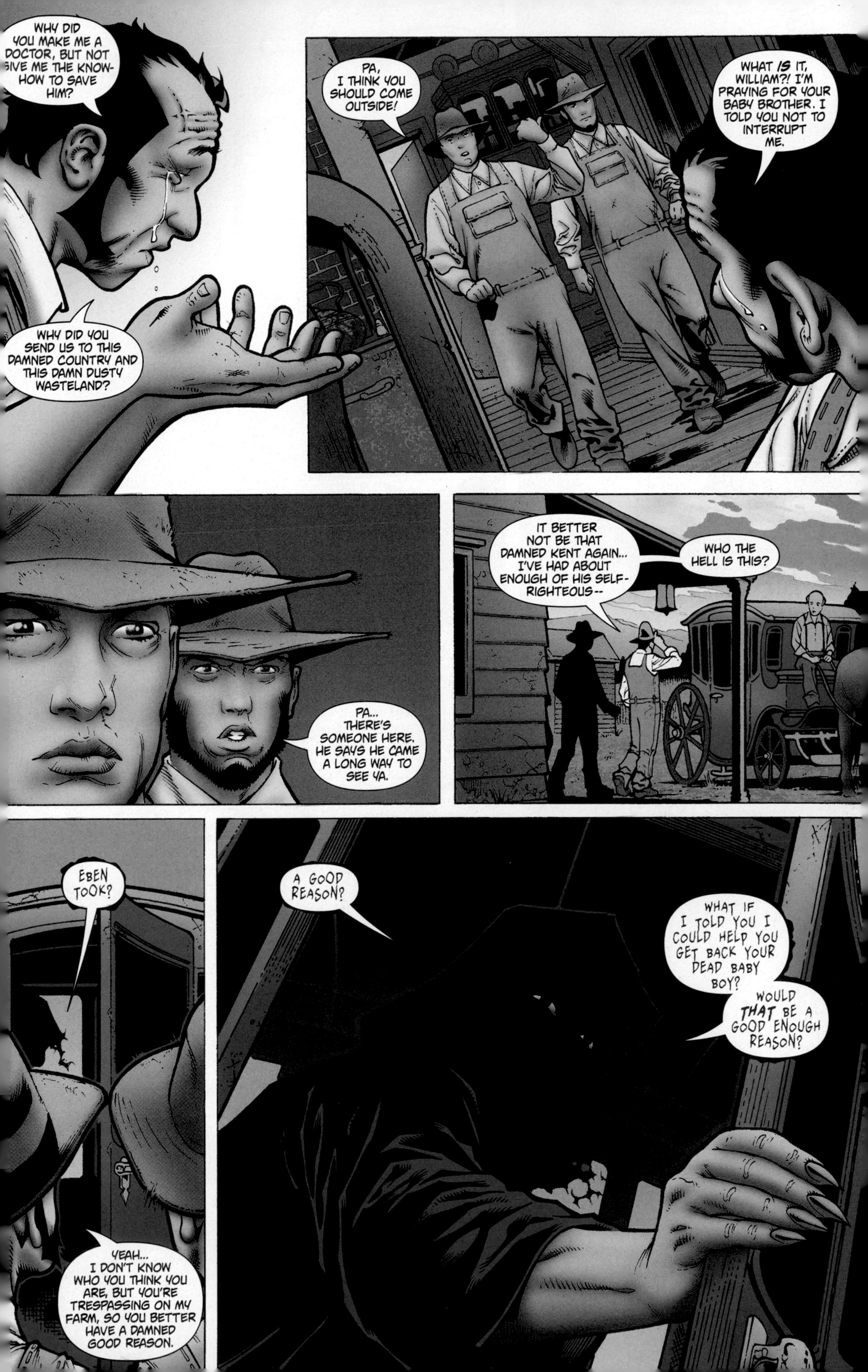
WHY DID YOU MAKE ME A DOCTOR, BUT NOT GIVE ME THE KNOW-HOW TO SAVE HIM?
WHY DID YOU SEND US TO THIS DAMNED COUNTRY AND THIS DAMN DUSTY WASTELAND?
PA, I THINK YOU SHOULD COME OUTSIDE!
WHAT IS IT, WILLIAM?! I'M PRAYING FOR YOUR BABY BROTHER. I TOLD YOU NOT TO INTERRUPT ME.
PA... THERE'S SOMEONE HERE. HE SAYS HE CAME A LONG WAY TO SEE YA.
IT BETTER NOT BE THAT DAMNED KENT AGAIN... I'VE HAD ABOUT ENOUGH OF HIS SELF-RIGHTEOUS--
WHO THE HELL IS THIS?
EBEN TOOK?
YEAH... I DON'T KNOW WHO YOU THINK YOU ARE, BUT YOU'RE TRESPASSING ON MY FARM, SO YOU BETTER HAVE A DAMNED GOOD REASON.
A GOOD REASON?
WHAT IF I TOLD YOU I COULD HELP YOU GET BACK YOUR DEAD BABY BOY?
WOULD THAT BE A GOOD ENOUGH REASON?

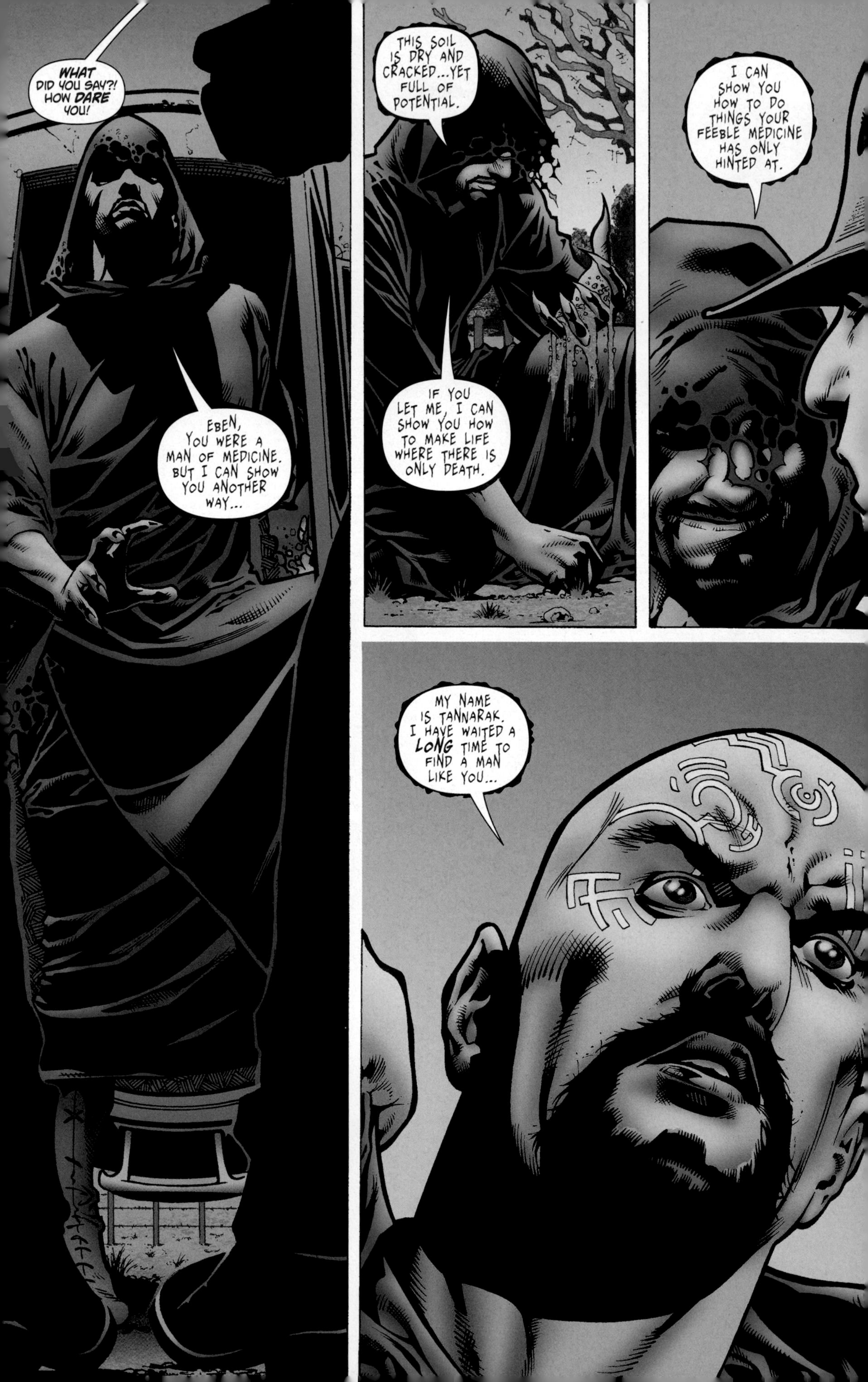
WHAT DID YOU SAY?! HOW DARE YOU!
EBEN, YOU WERE A MAN OF MEDICINE. BUT I CAN SHOW YOU ANOTHER WAY...
THIS SOIL IS DRY AND CRACKED...YET FULL OF POTENTIAL.
IF YOU LET ME, I CAN SHOW YOU HOW TO MAKE LIFE WHERE THERE IS ONLY DEATH.
I CAN SHOW YOU HOW TO DO THINGS YOUR FEEBLE MEDICINE HAS ONLY HINTED AT.
MY NAME IS TANNARAK. I HAVE WAITED A LONG TIME TO FIND A MAN LIKE YOU...

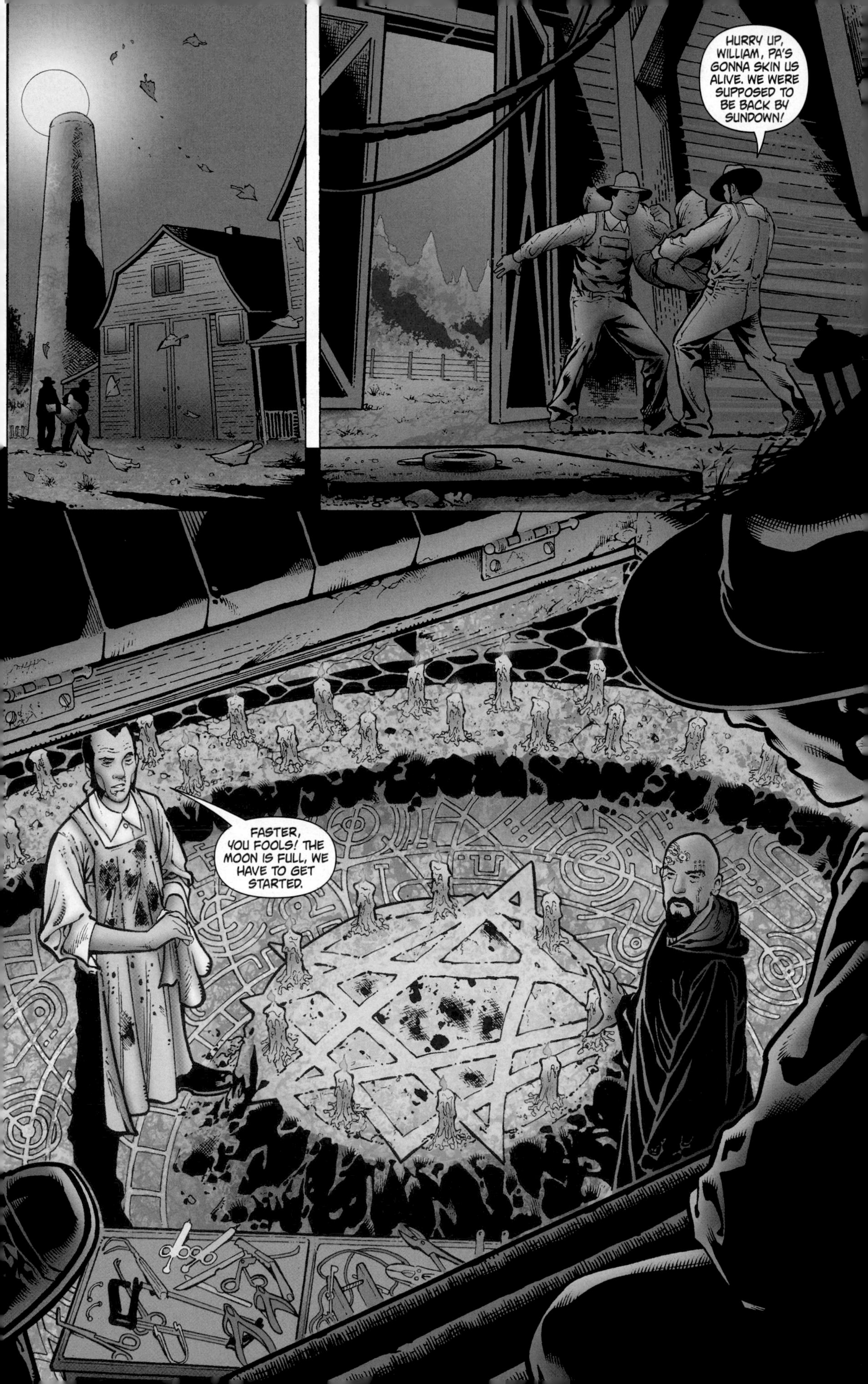
HURRY UP, WILLIAM, PA'S GONNA SKIN US ALIVE. WE WERE SUPPOSED TO BE BACK BY SUNDOWN!
FASTER, YOU FOOLS! THE MOON IS FULL, WE HAVE TO GET STARTED.

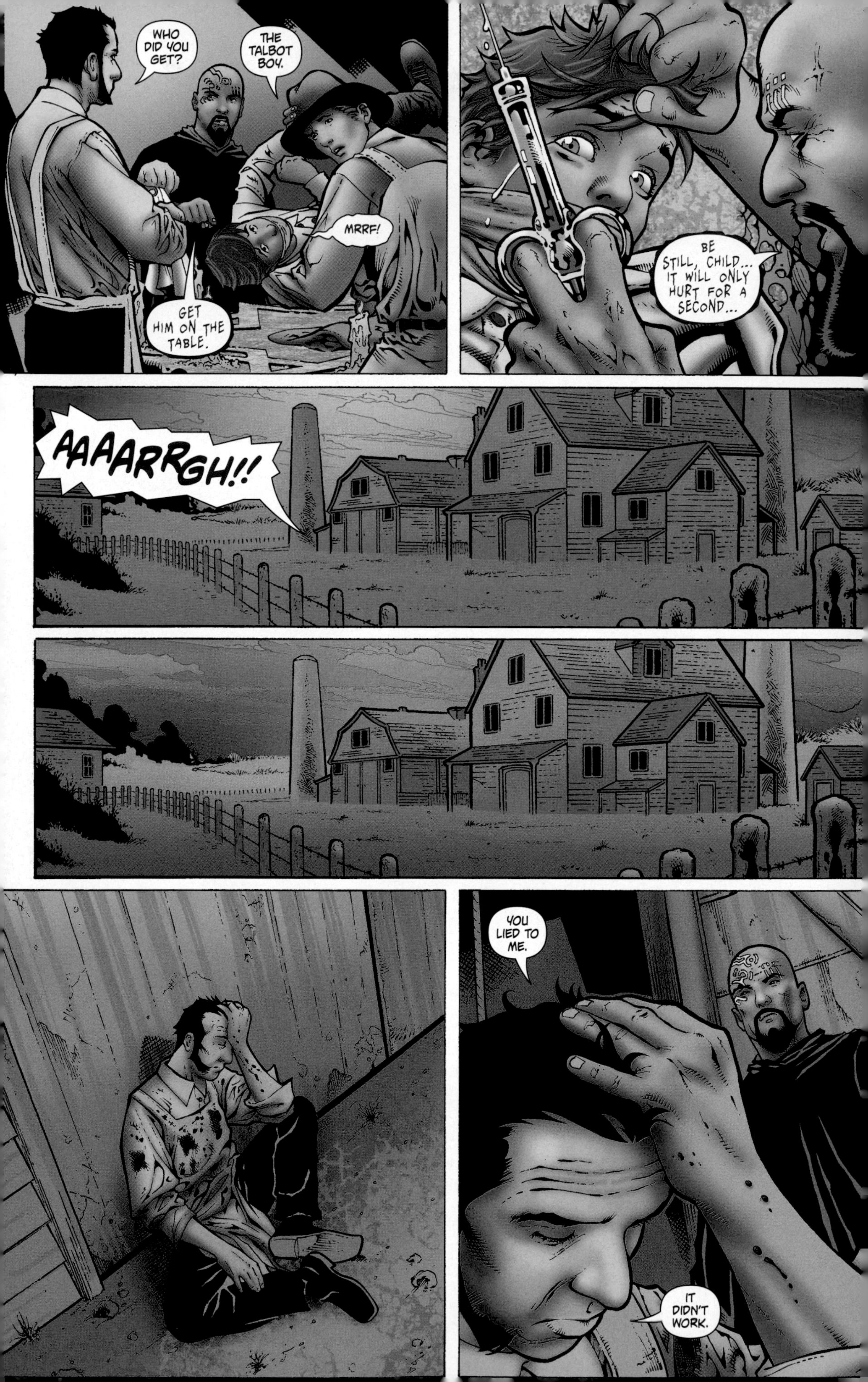
WHO DID YOU GET?
THE TALBOT BOY.
MRRF!
GET HIM ON THE TABLE.
BE STILL, CHILD... IT WILL ONLY HURT FOR A SECOND...
AAAARRGH!!
YOU LIED TO ME.
IT DIDN'T WORK.

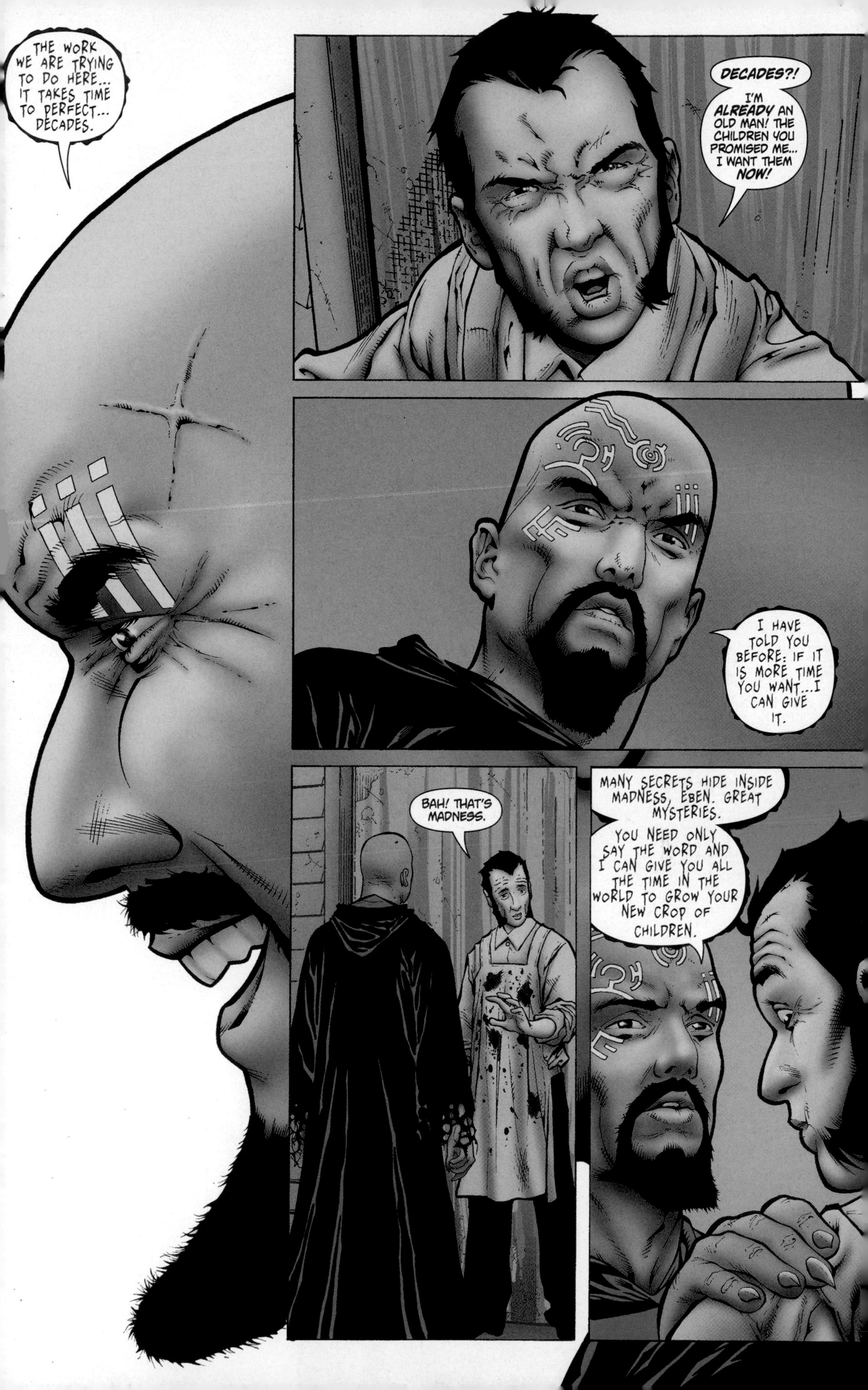
THE WORK WE ARE TRYING TO DO HERE... IT TAKES TIME TO PERFECT... DECADES.
DECADES?!
I'M ALREADY AN OLD MAN! THE CHILDREN YOU PROMISED ME... I WANT THEM NOW!
I HAVE TOLD YOU BEFORE: IF IT IS MORE TIME YOU WANT...I CAN GIVE IT.
BAH! THAT'S MADNESS.
MANY SECRETS HIDE INSIDE MADNESS, EBEN. GREAT MYSTERIES.
YOU NEED ONLY SAY THE WORD AND I CAN GIVE YOU ALL THE TIME IN THE WORLD TO GROW YOUR NEW CROP OF CHILDREN.

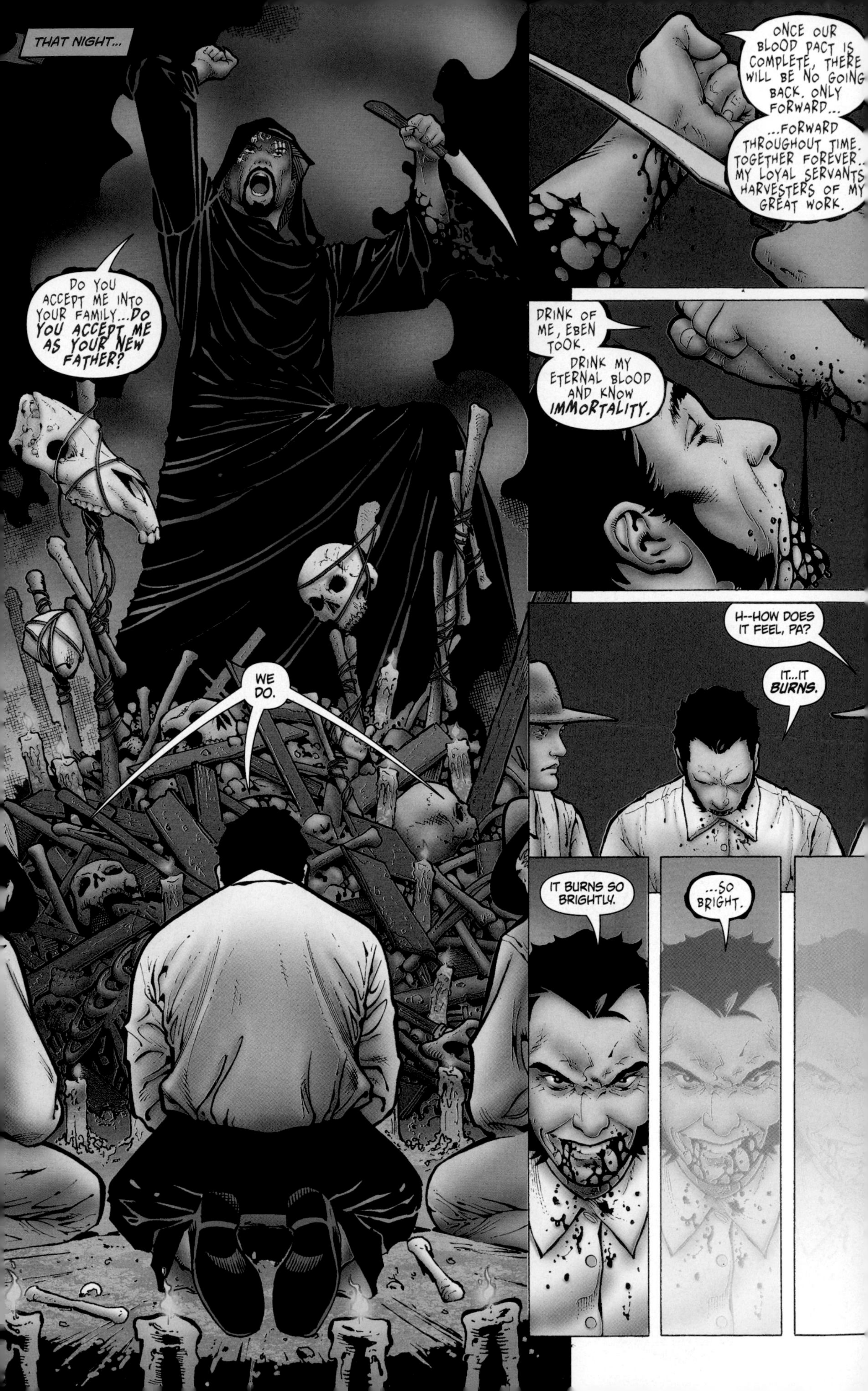
THAT NIGHT...
DO YOU ACCEPT ME INTO YOUR FAMILY...DO YOU ACCEPT ME AS YOUR NEW FATHER?
WE DO.
ONCE OUR BLOOD PACT IS COMPLETE, THERE WILL BE NO GOING BACK. ONLY FORWARD...
...FORWARD THROUGHOUT TIME. TOGETHER FOREVER. MY LOYAL SERVANTS. HARVESTERS OF MY GREAT WORK.
DRINK OF ME, EBEN TOOK.
DRINK MY ETERNAL BLOOD AND KNOW IMMORTALITY.
H--HOW DOES IT FEEL, PA?
IT...IT BURNS.
IT BURNS SO BRIGHTLY.
...SO BRIGHT.

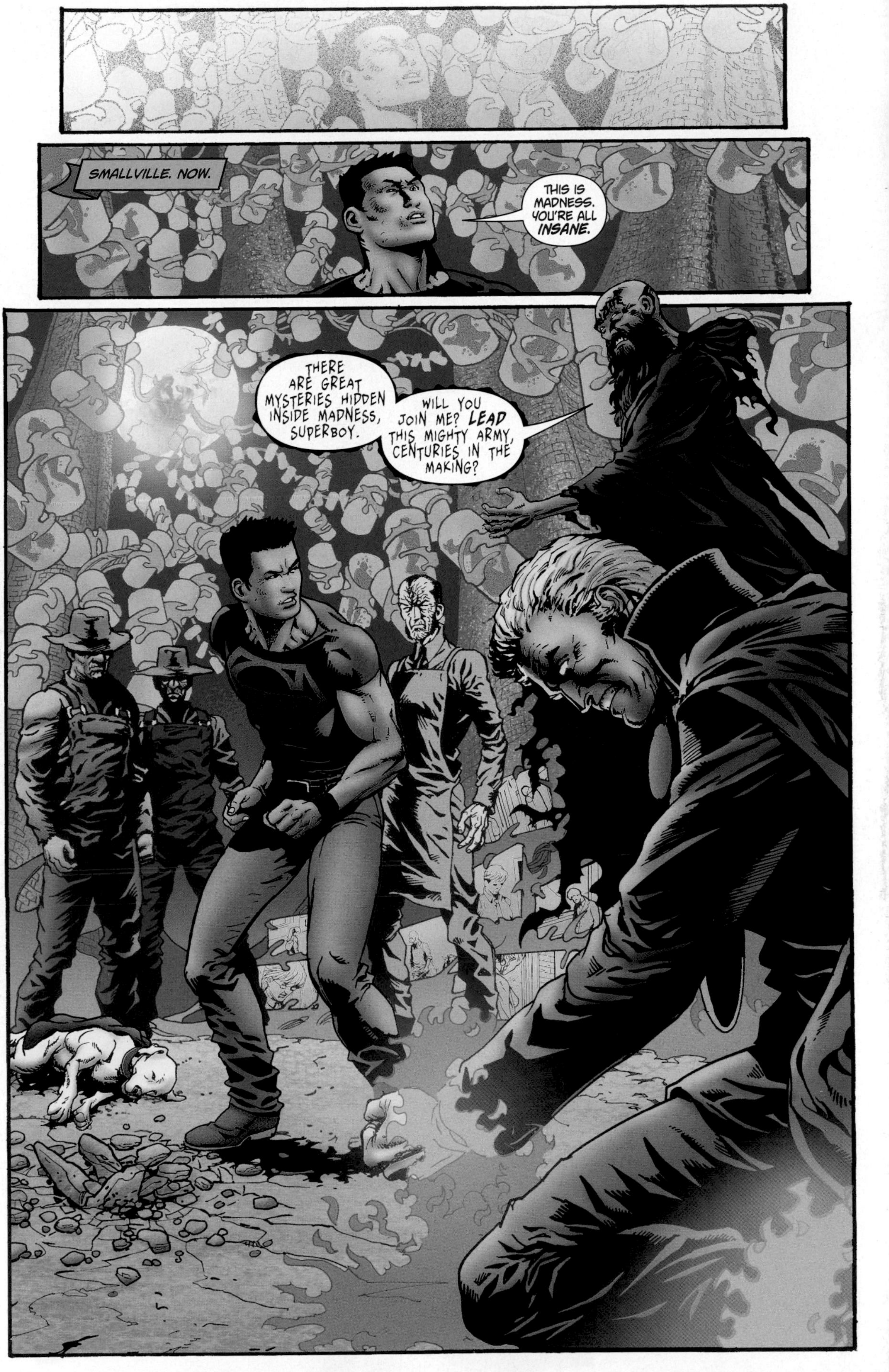
SMALLVILLE. NOW.
THIS IS MADNESS. YOU'RE ALL INSANE.
THERE ARE GREAT MYSTERIES HIDDEN INSIDE MADNESS, SUPERBOY.
WILL YOU JOIN ME? LEAD THIS MIGHTY ARMY, CENTURIES IN THE MAKING?

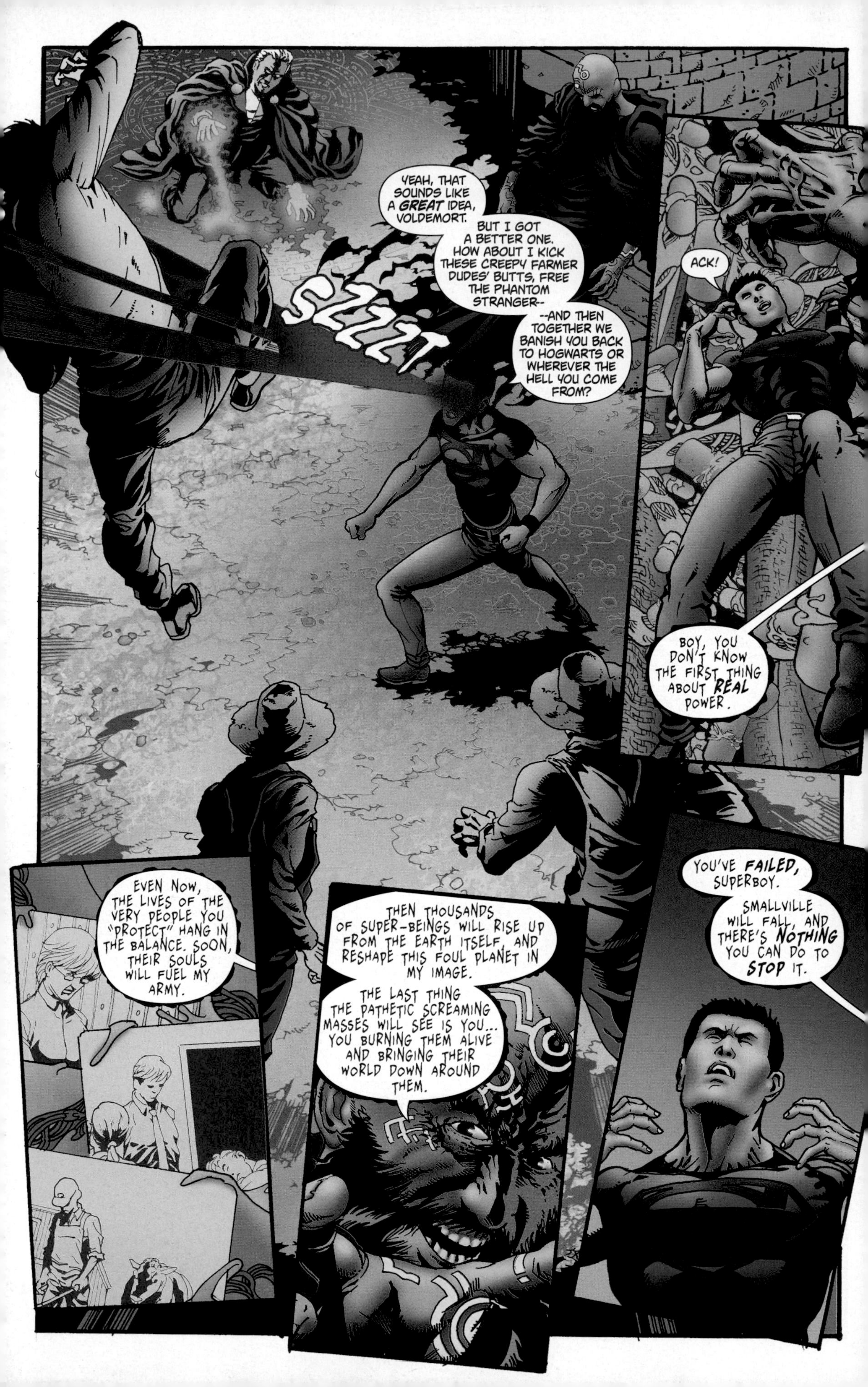
YEAH, THAT SOUNDS LIKE A GREAT IDEA, VOLDEMORT.
BUT I GOT A BETTER ONE. HOW ABOUT I KICK THESE CREEPY FARMER DUDES' BUTTS, FREE THE PHANTOM STRANGER--
--AND THEN TOGETHER WE BANISH YOU BACK TO HOGWARTS OR WHEREVER THE HELL YOU COME FROM?
SZZZT
ACK!
BOY, YOU DON'T KNOW THE FIRST THING ABOUT REAL POWER.
EVEN NOW, THE LIVES OF THE VERY PEOPLE YOU "PROTECT" HANG IN THE BALANCE. SOON, THEIR SOULS WILL FUEL MY ARMY.
THEN THOUSANDS OF SUPER-BEINGS WILL RISE UP FROM THE EARTH ITSELF, AND RESHAPE THIS FOUL PLANET IN MY IMAGE.
THE LAST THING THE PATHETIC SCREAMING MASSES WILL SEE IS YOU... YOU BURNING THEM ALIVE AND BRINGING THEIR WORLD DOWN AROUND THEM.
YOU'VE FAILED, SUPERBOY.
SMALLVILLE WILL FALL, AND THERE'S NOTHING YOU CAN DO TO STOP IT.

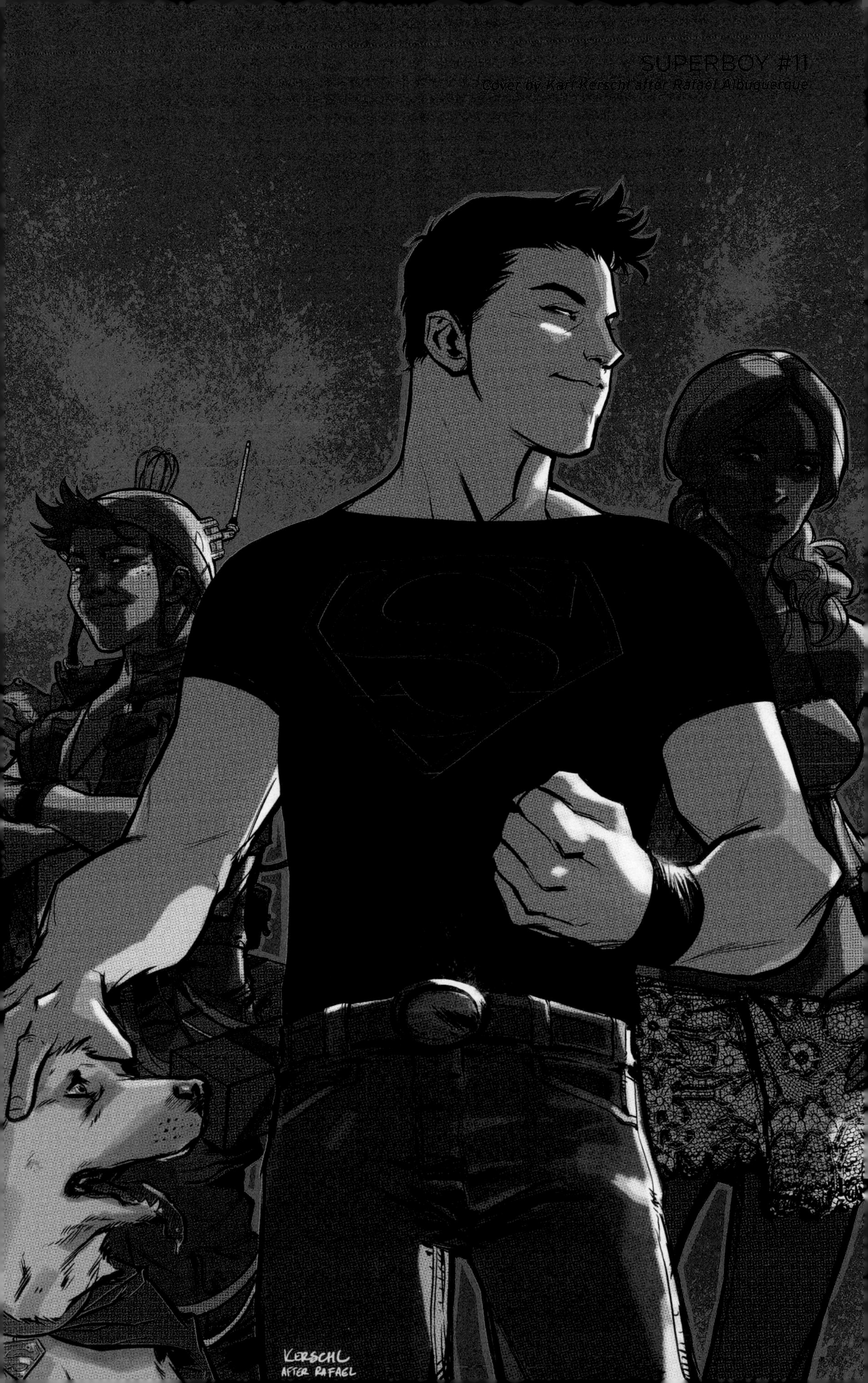
KERSCHL
AFTER RAFAEL

SUPERBOY #11
Cover by Karl Kerschl after Rafael Albuquerque

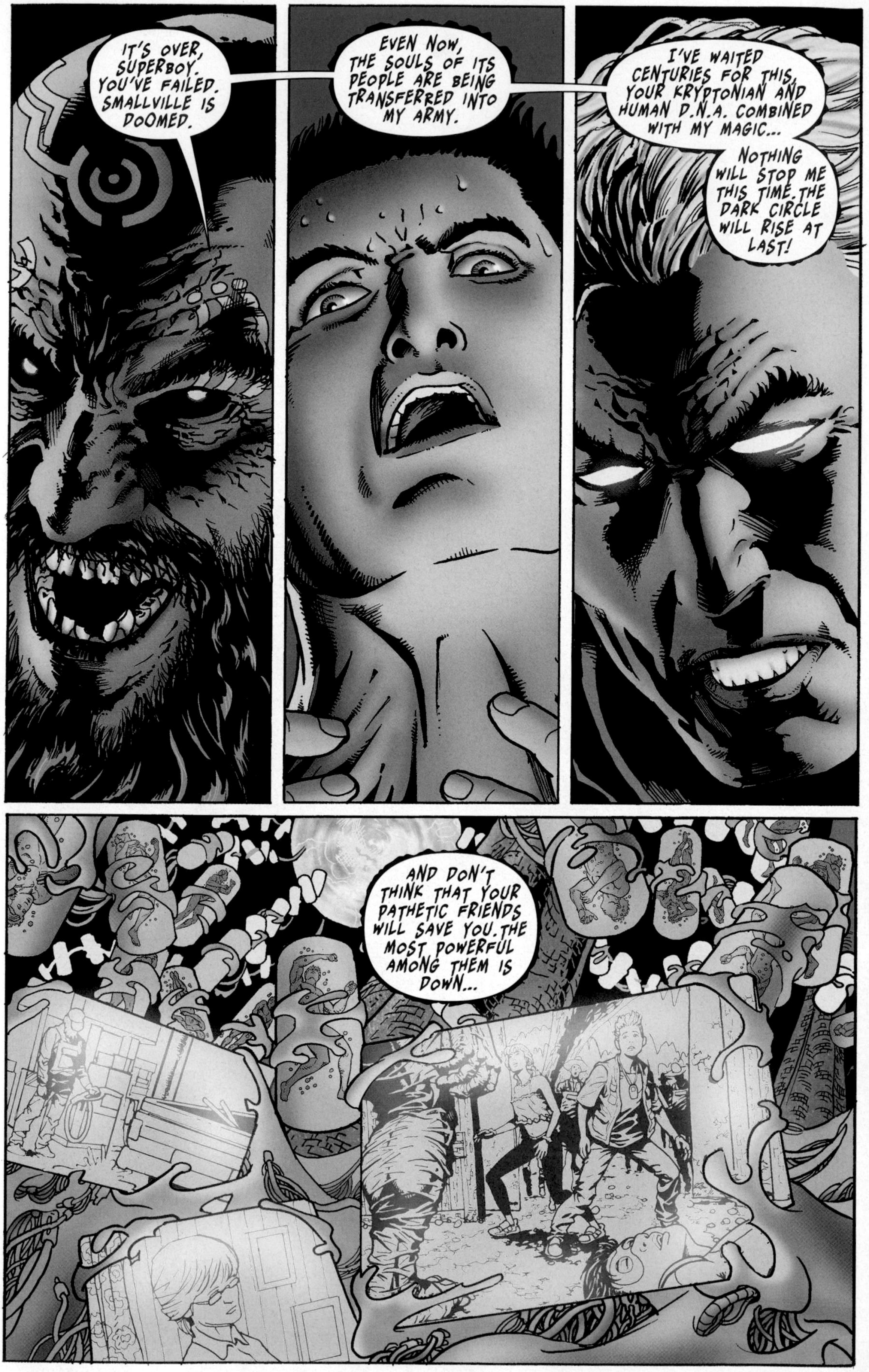
IT'S OVER, SUPERBOY. YOU'VE FAILED. SMALLVILLE IS DOOMED.
EVEN NOW, THE SOULS OF ITS PEOPLE ARE BEING TRANSFERRED INTO MY ARMY.
I'VE WAITED CENTURIES FOR THIS, YOUR KRYPTONIAN AND HUMAN D.N.A. COMBINED WITH MY MAGIC...
NOTHING WILL STOP ME THIS TIME. THE DARK CIRCLE WILL RISE AT LAST!
AND DON'T THINK THAT YOUR PATHETIC FRIENDS WILL SAVE YOU. THE MOST POWERFUL AMONG THEM IS DOWN...

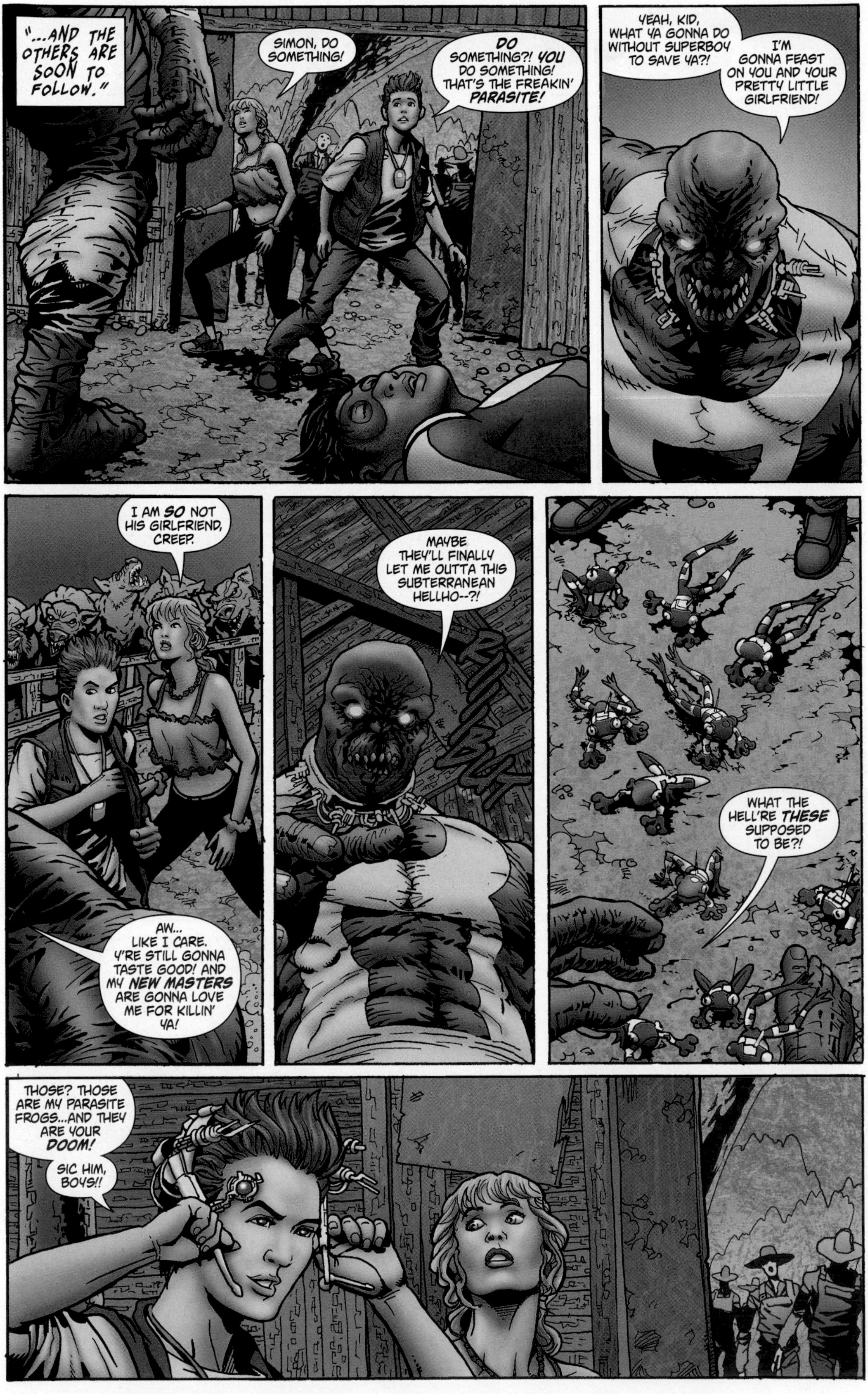
"...AND THE OTHERS ARE SOON TO FOLLOW."
SIMON, DO SOMETHING!
DO SOMETHING?! YOU DO SOMETHING! THAT'S THE FREAKIN' PARASITE!
YEAH, KID, WHAT YA GONNA DO WITHOUT SUPERBOY TO SAVE YA?!
I'M GONNA FEAST ON YOU AND YOUR PRETTY LITTLE GIRLFRIEND!
I AM SO NOT HIS GIRLFRIEND, CREEP.
AW... LIKE I CARE. Y'RE STILL GONNA TASTE GOOD! AND MY NEW MASTERS ARE GONNA LOVE ME FOR KILLIN' YA!
MAYBE THEY'LL FINALLY LET ME OUTTA THIS SUBTERRANEAN HELLHO--?!
RIBBIT
WHAT THE HELL'RE THESE SUPPOSED TO BE?!
THOSE? THOSE ARE MY PARASITE FROGS...AND THEY ARE YOUR DOOM!
SIC HIM, BOYS!!

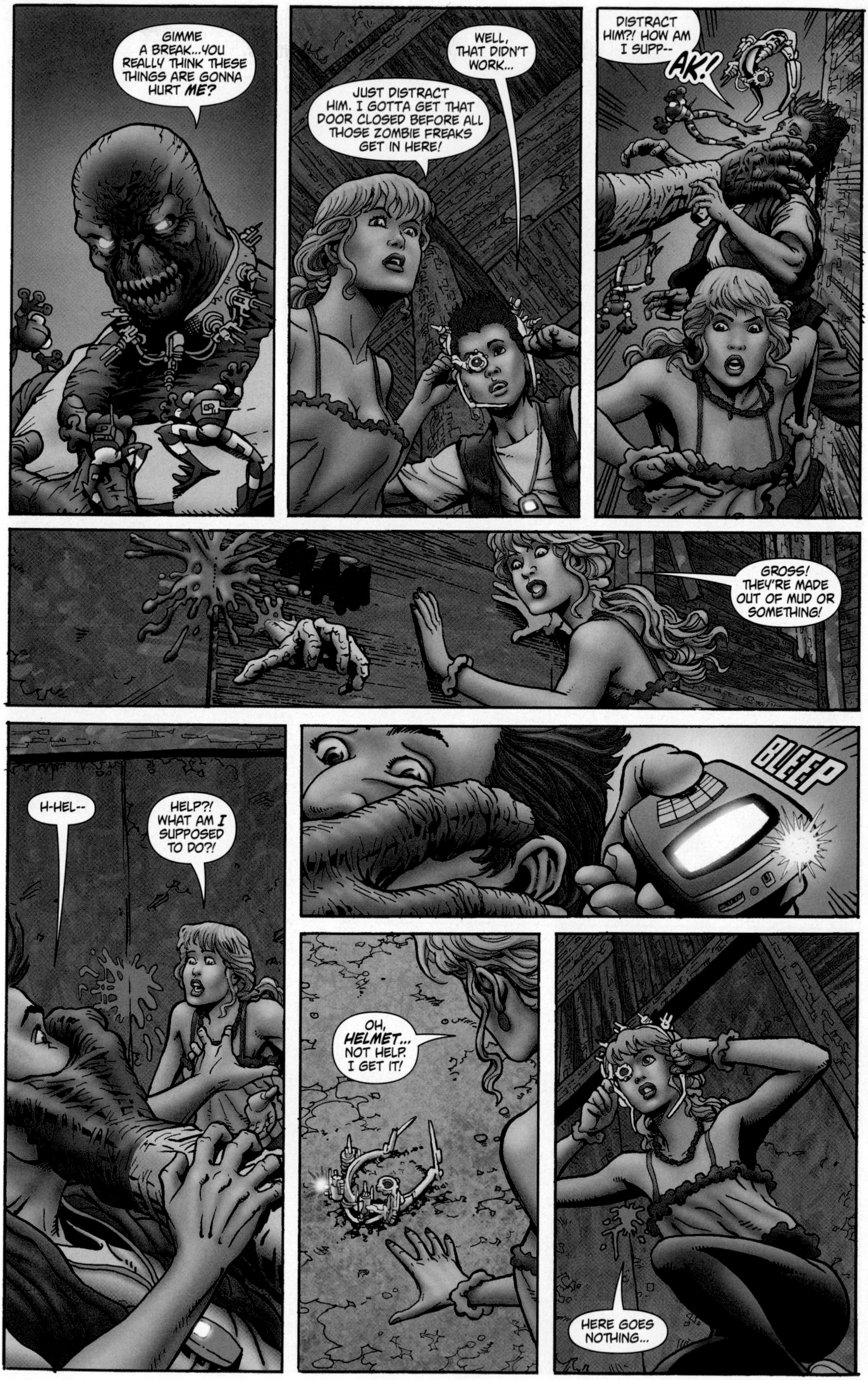

GIMME A BREAK...YOU REALLY THINK THESE THINGS ARE GONNA HURT ME?
WELL, THAT DIDN'T WORK...
JUST DISTRACT HIM. I GOTTA GET THAT DOOR CLOSED BEFORE ALL THOSE ZOMBIE FREAKS GET IN HERE!
DISTRACT HIM?! HOW AM I SUPP--
AK!
GROSS! THEY'RE MADE OUT OF MUD OR SOMETHING!
H-HEL--
HELP?! WHAT AM I SUPPOSED TO DO?!
BLEEP
OH, HELMET... NOT HELP. I GET IT!
HERE GOES NOTHING...

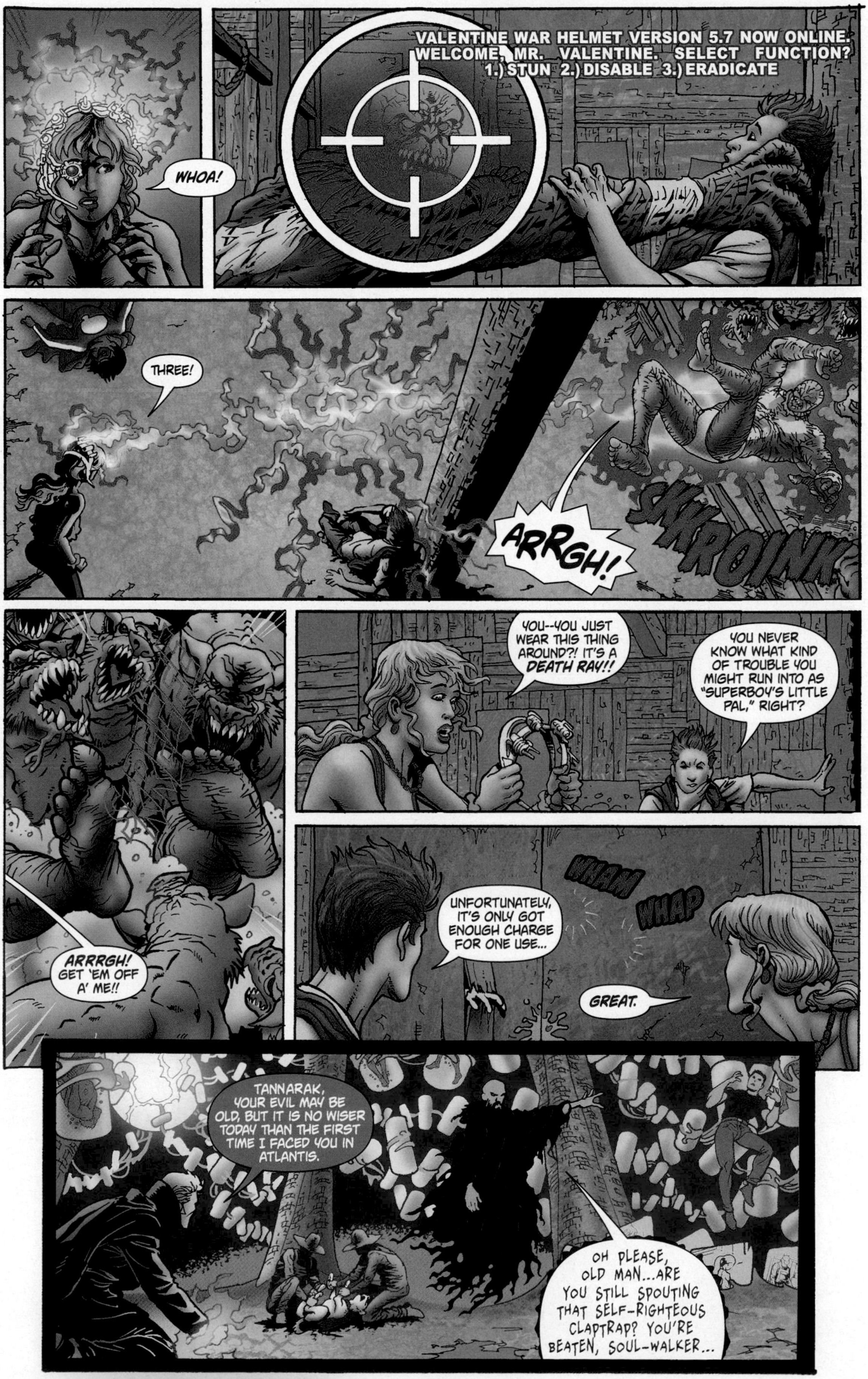
VALENTINE WAR HELMET VERSION 5.7 NOW ONLINE. WELCOME, MR. VALENTINE. SELECT FUNCTION? 1.) STUN 2.) DISABLE 3.) ERADICATE
WHOA!
THREE!
ARRGH!
SKKROINK
YOU--YOU JUST WEAR THIS THING AROUND?! IT'S A DEATH RAY!!
YOU NEVER KNOW WHAT KIND OF TROUBLE YOU MIGHT RUN INTO AS "SUPERBOY'S LITTLE PAL," RIGHT?
ARRRGH! GET 'EM OFF A' ME!!
WHAM
WHAP
UNFORTUNATELY, IT'S ONLY GOT ENOUGH CHARGE FOR ONE USE...
GREAT.
TANNARAK, YOUR EVIL MAY BE OLD, BUT IT IS NO WISER TODAY THAN THE FIRST TIME I FACED YOU IN ATLANTIS.
OH PLEASE, OLD MAN...ARE YOU STILL SPOUTING THAT SELF-RIGHTEOUS CLAPTRAP? YOU'RE BEATEN, SOUL-WALKER...

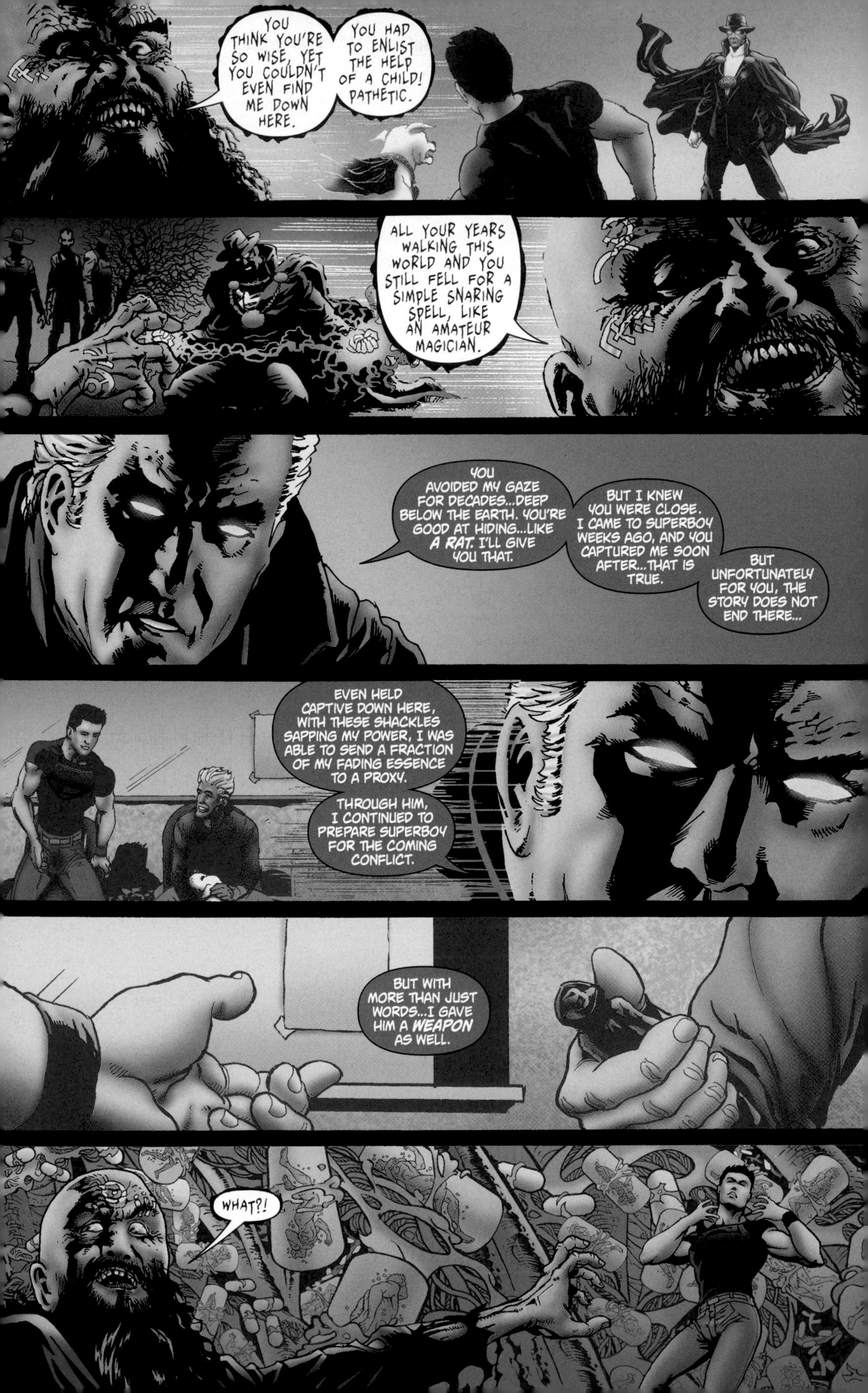
YOU THINK YOU'RE SO WISE, YET YOU COULDN'T EVEN FIND ME DOWN HERE.
YOU HAD TO ENLIST THE HELP OF A CHILD! PATHETIC.
ALL YOUR YEARS WALKING THIS WORLD AND YOU STILL FELL FOR A SIMPLE SNARING SPELL, LIKE AN AMATEUR MAGICIAN.
YOU AVOIDED MY GAZE FOR DECADES...DEEP BELOW THE EARTH. YOU'RE GOOD AT HIDING...LIKE *A RAT.* I'LL GIVE YOU THAT.
BUT I KNEW YOU WERE CLOSE. I CAME TO SUPERBOY WEEKS AGO, AND YOU CAPTURED ME SOON AFTER...THAT IS TRUE.
BUT UNFORTUNATELY FOR YOU, THE STORY DOES NOT END THERE...
EVEN HELD CAPTIVE DOWN HERE, WITH THESE SHACKLES SAPPING MY POWER, I WAS ABLE TO SEND A FRACTION OF MY FADING ESSENCE TO A PROXY.
THROUGH HIM, I CONTINUED TO PREPARE SUPERBOY FOR THE COMING CONFLICT.
BUT WITH MORE THAN JUST WORDS...I GAVE HIM A *WEAPON* AS WELL.
WHAT?!

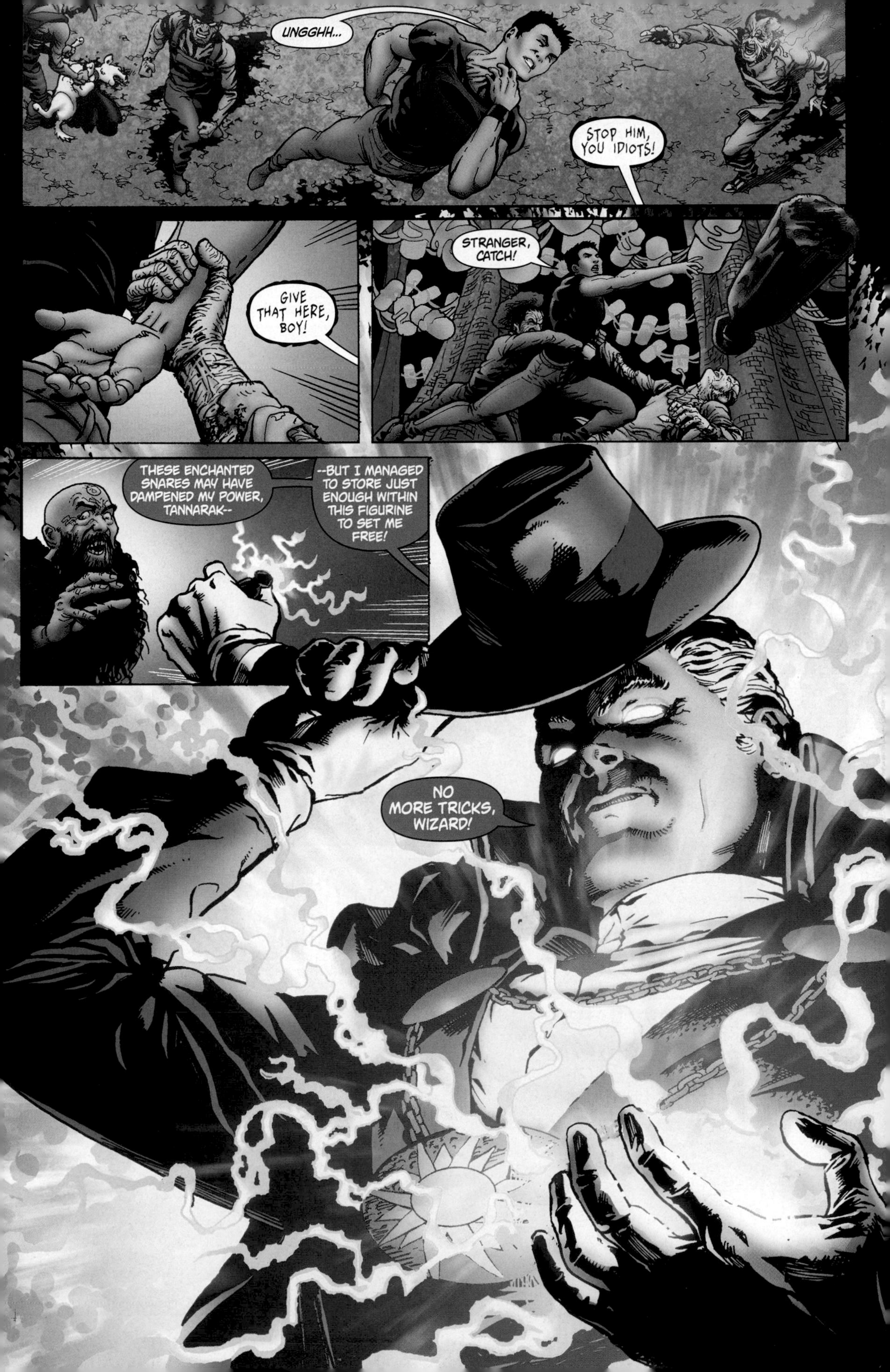
UNGGHH...
STOP HIM, YOU IDIOTS!
GIVE THAT HERE, BOY!
STRANGER, CATCH!
THESE ENCHANTED SNARES MAY HAVE DAMPENED MY POWER, TANNARAK--
--BUT I MANAGED TO STORE JUST ENOUGH WITHIN THIS FIGURINE TO SET ME FREE!
NO MORE TRICKS, WIZARD!

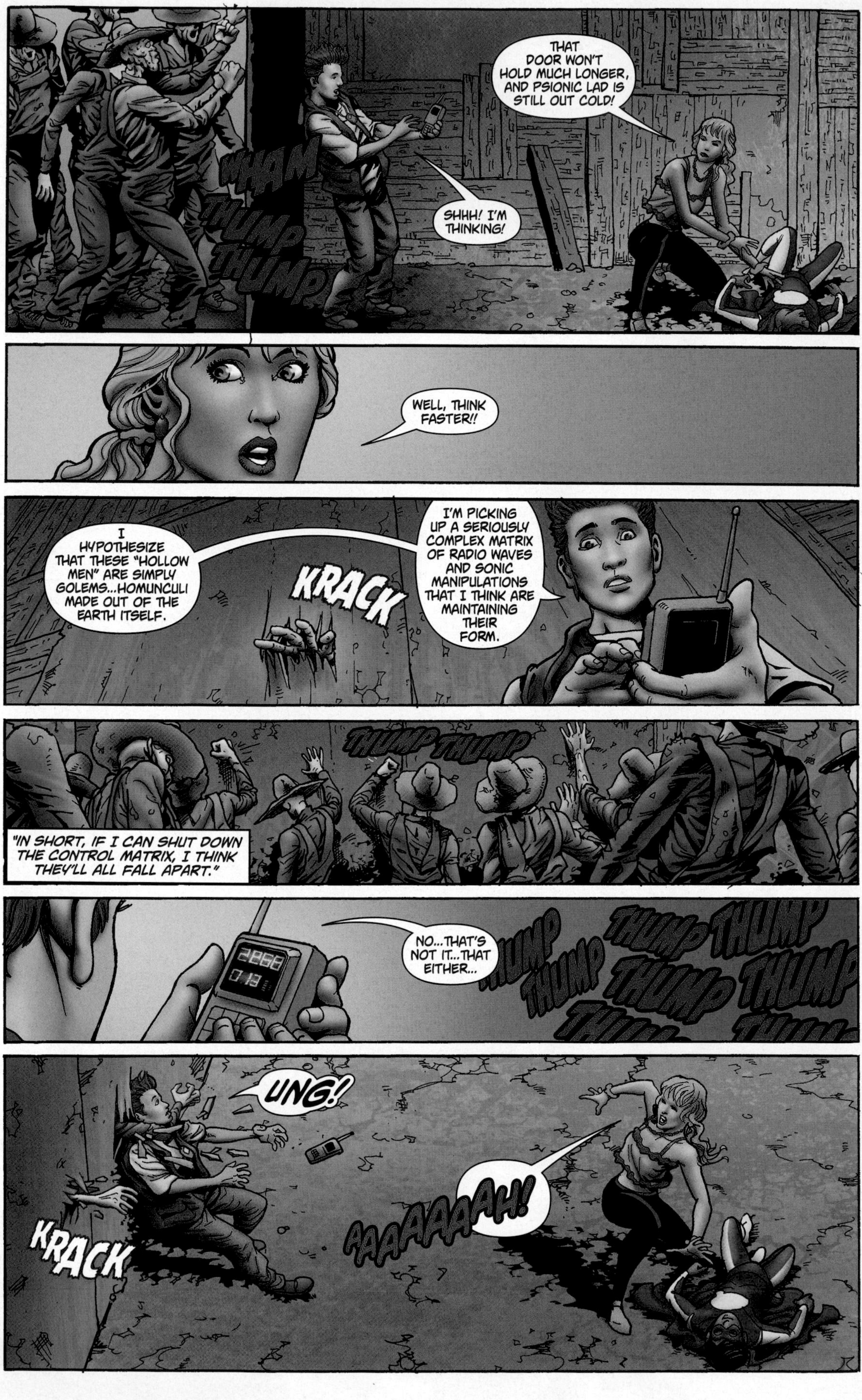
THAT DOOR WON'T HOLD MUCH LONGER, AND PSIONIC LAD IS STILL OUT COLD!
WHAM
THUMP
THUMP
SHHH! I'M THINKING!
WELL, THINK FASTER!!
I HYPOTHESIZE THAT THESE "HOLLOW MEN" ARE SIMPLY GOLEMS...HOMUNCULI MADE OUT OF THE EARTH ITSELF.
I'M PICKING UP A SERIOUSLY COMPLEX MATRIX OF RADIO WAVES AND SONIC MANIPULATIONS THAT I THINK ARE MAINTAINING THEIR FORM.
KRACK
THUMP THUMP
"IN SHORT, IF I CAN SHUT DOWN THE CONTROL MATRIX, I THINK THEY'LL ALL FALL APART."
NO...THAT'S NOT IT...THAT EITHER...
THUMP THUMP THUMP
THUMP THUMP THUMP
UNG!
AAAAAAAAH!
KRACK

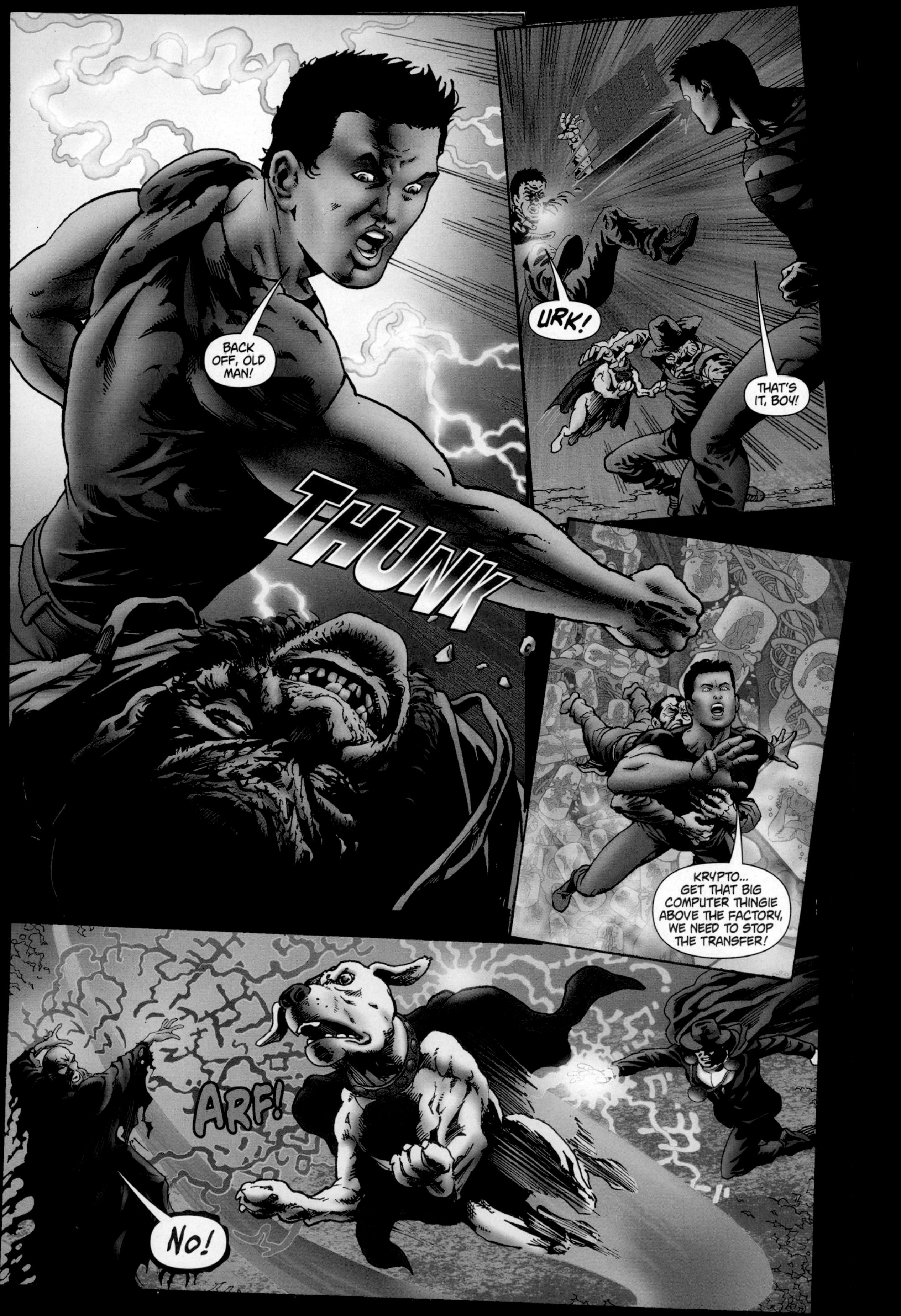
BACK OFF, OLD MAN!
THUNK
URK!
THAT'S IT, BOY!
KRYPTO... GET THAT BIG COMPUTER THINGIE ABOVE THE FACTORY, WE NEED TO STOP THE TRANSFER!
ARF!
NO!

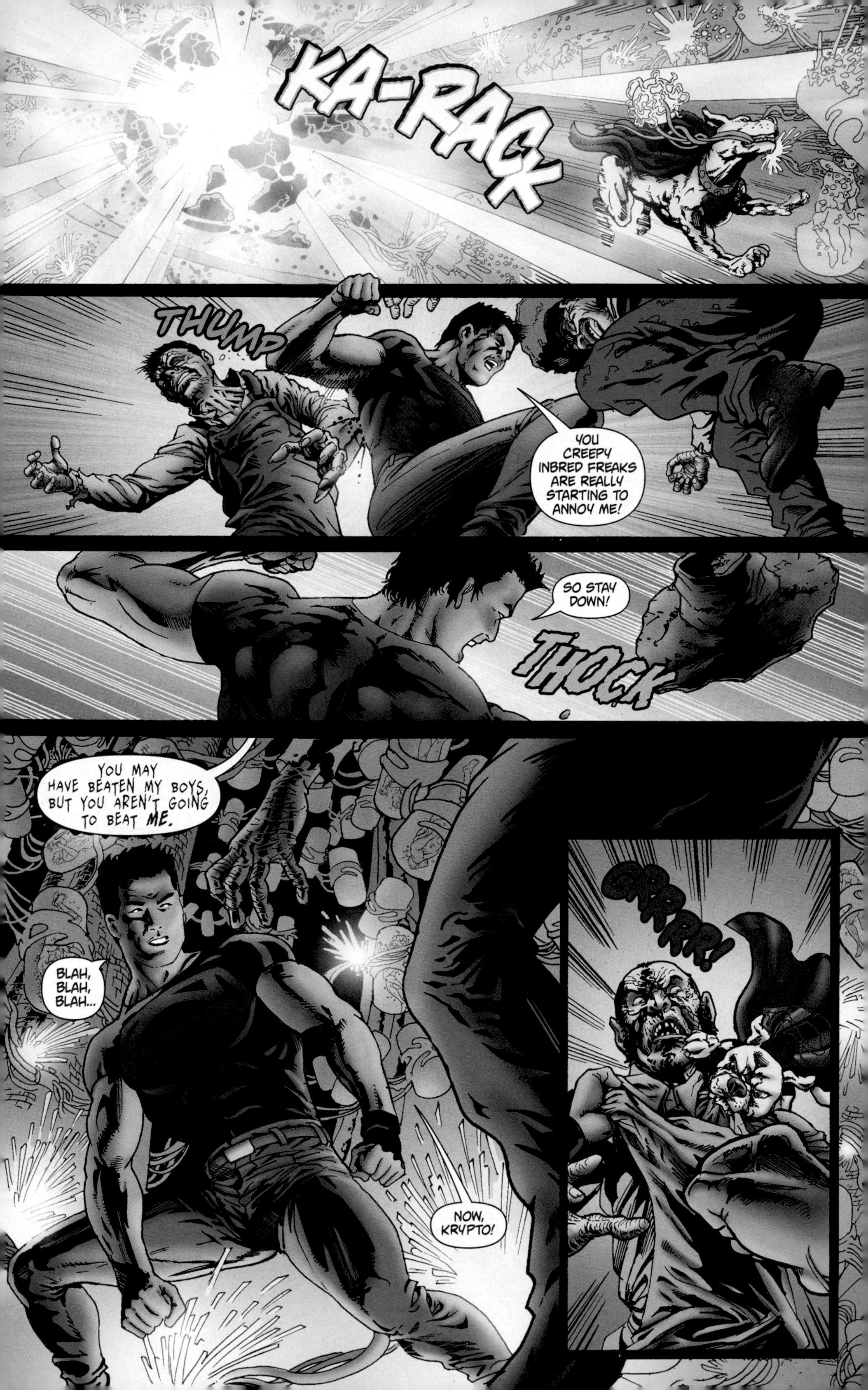
KA-RACK
THUMP
YOU CREEPY INBRED FREAKS ARE REALLY STARTING TO ANNOY ME!
SO STAY DOWN!
THOCK
YOU MAY HAVE BEATEN MY BOYS, BUT YOU AREN'T GOING TO BEAT ME.
BLAH, BLAH, BLAH...
NOW, KRYPTO!
GRRRR!

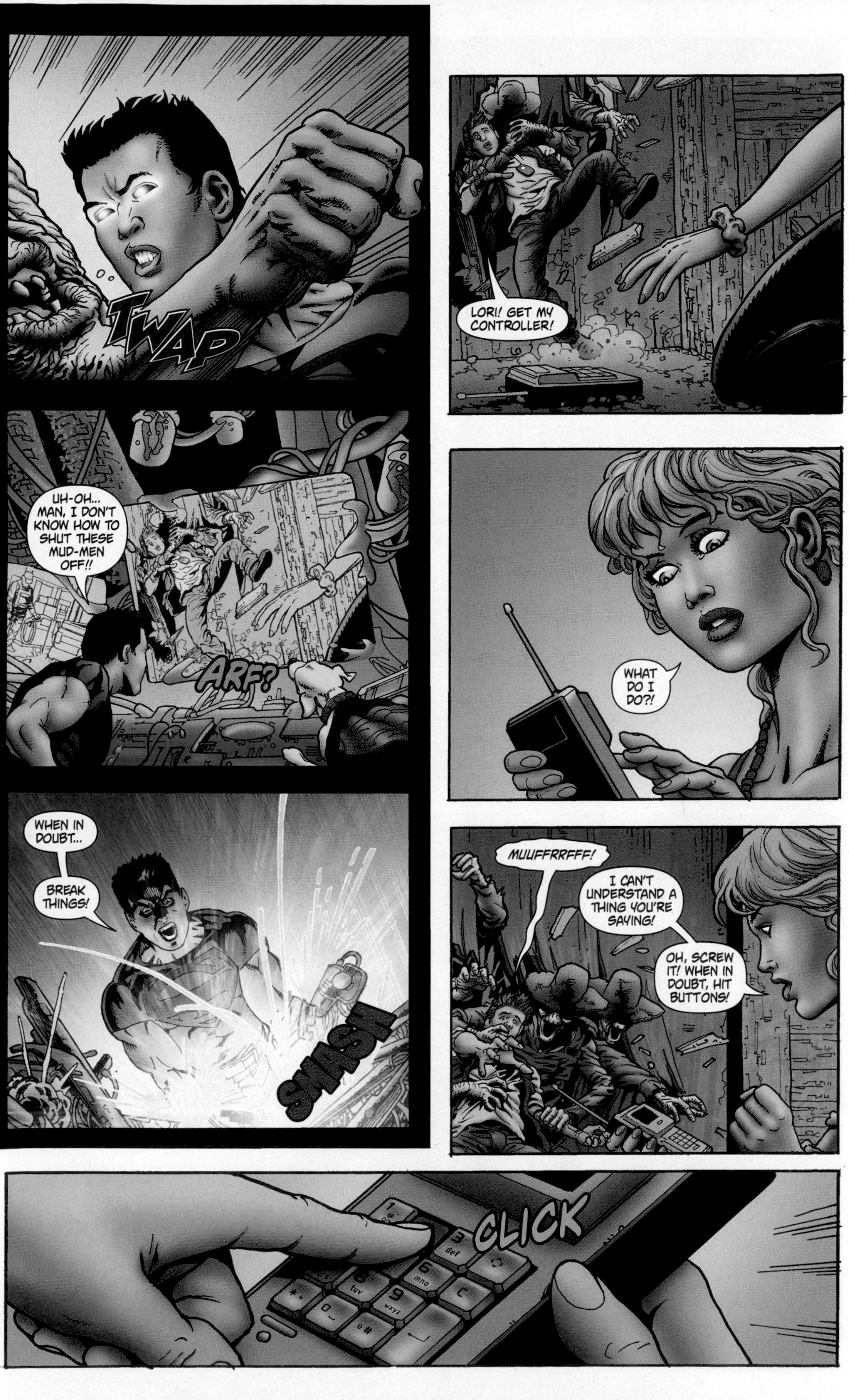
TWAP
LORI! GET MY CONTROLLER!
UH-OH... MAN, I DON'T KNOW HOW TO SHUT THESE MUD-MEN OFF!!
ARF?
WHAT DO I DO?!
WHEN IN DOUBT...
BREAK THINGS!
SMASH
MUUFFRRFFF!
I CAN'T UNDERSTAND A THING YOU'RE SAYING!
OH, SCREW IT! WHEN IN DOUBT, HIT BUTTONS!
CLICK

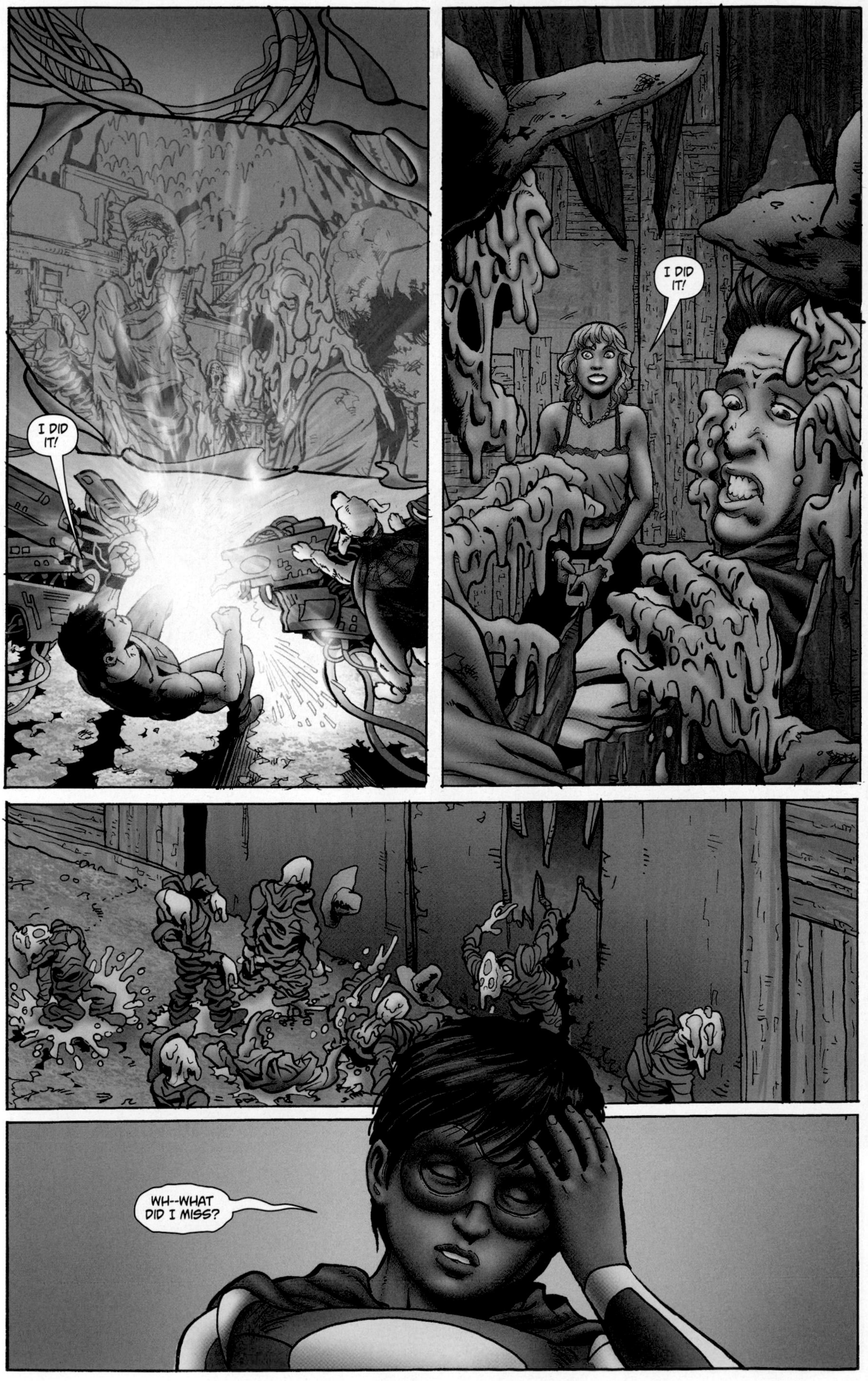
I DID IT!
I DID IT!
WH--WHAT DID I MISS?

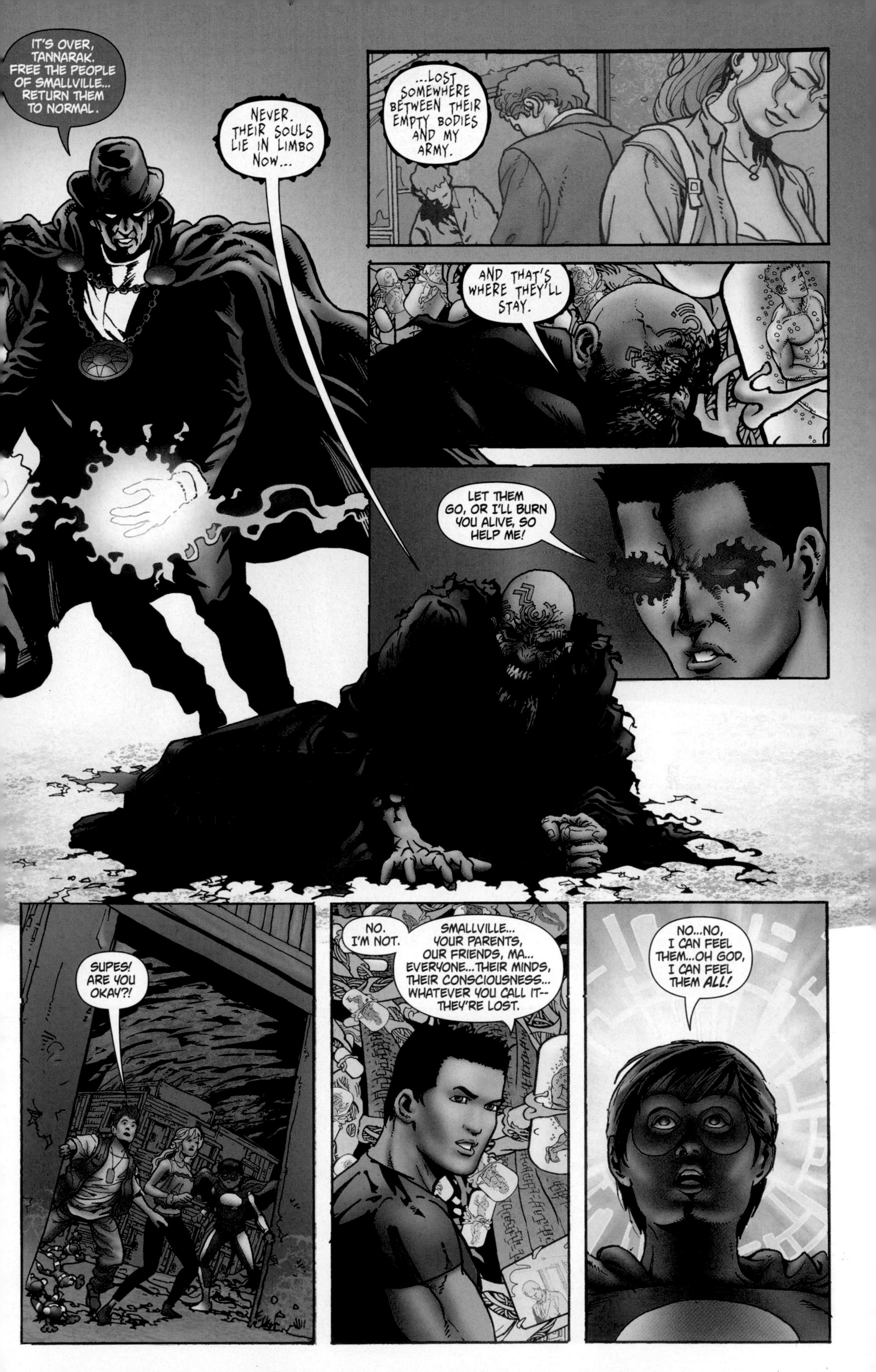
IT'S OVER, TANNARAK. FREE THE PEOPLE OF SMALLVILLE... RETURN THEM TO NORMAL.
NEVER. THEIR SOULS LIE IN LIMBO NOW...
...LOST SOMEWHERE BETWEEN THEIR EMPTY BODIES AND MY ARMY.
AND THAT'S WHERE THEY'LL STAY.
LET THEM GO, OR I'LL BURN YOU ALIVE, SO HELP ME!
SUPES! ARE YOU OKAY?!
NO. I'M NOT.
SMALLVILLE... YOUR PARENTS, OUR FRIENDS, MA... EVERYONE...THEIR MINDS, THEIR CONSCIOUSNESS... WHATEVER YOU CALL IT-- THEY'RE LOST.
NO...NO, I CAN FEEL THEM...OH GOD, I CAN FEEL THEM ALL!

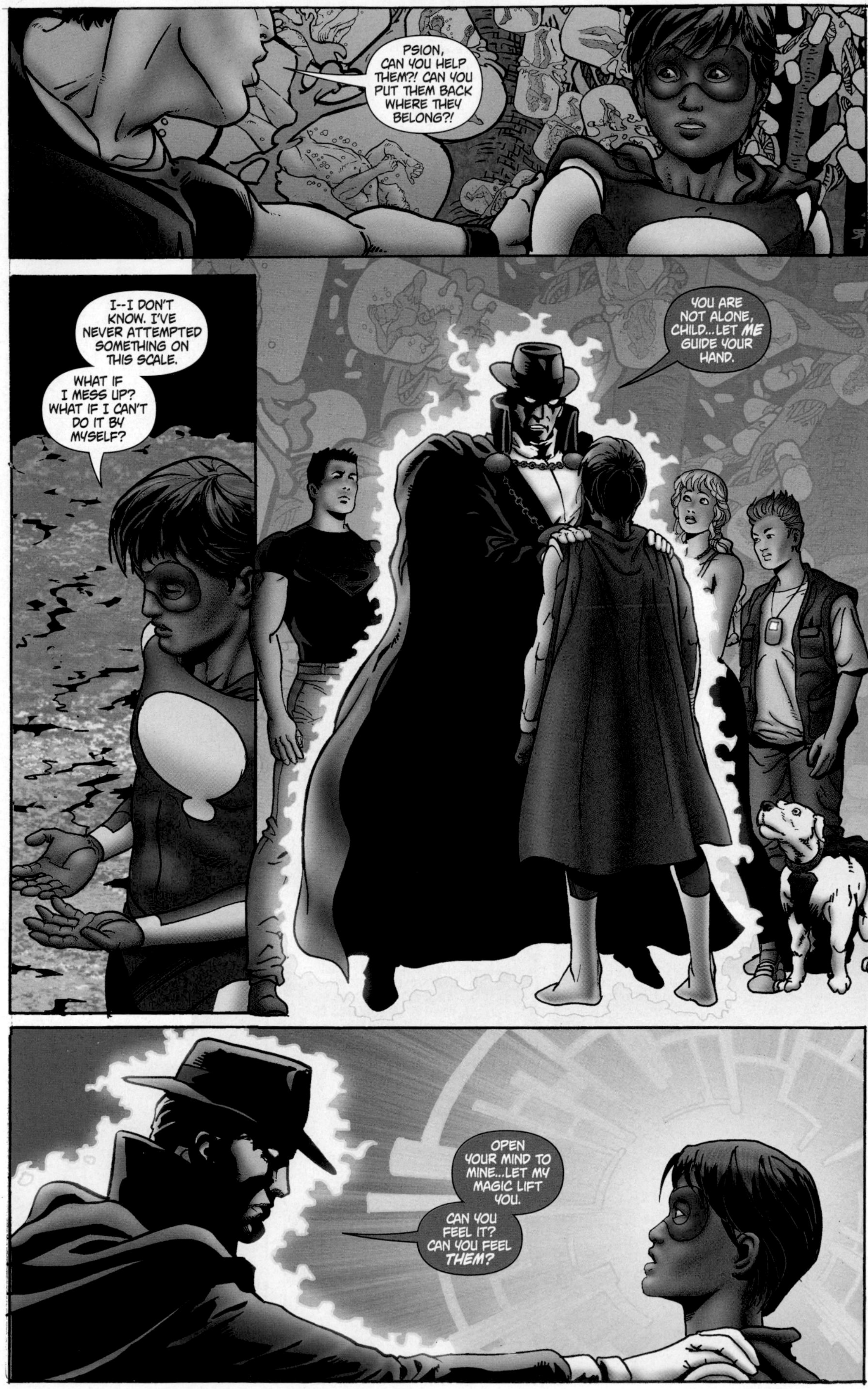
PSION, CAN YOU HELP THEM?! CAN YOU PUT THEM BACK WHERE THEY BELONG?!
I--I DON'T KNOW. I'VE NEVER ATTEMPTED SOMETHING ON THIS SCALE.
WHAT IF I MESS UP? WHAT IF I CAN'T DO IT BY MYSELF?
YOU ARE NOT ALONE, CHILD...LET ME GUIDE YOUR HAND.
OPEN YOUR MIND TO MINE...LET MY MAGIC LIFT YOU.
CAN YOU FEEL IT? CAN YOU FEEL THEM?

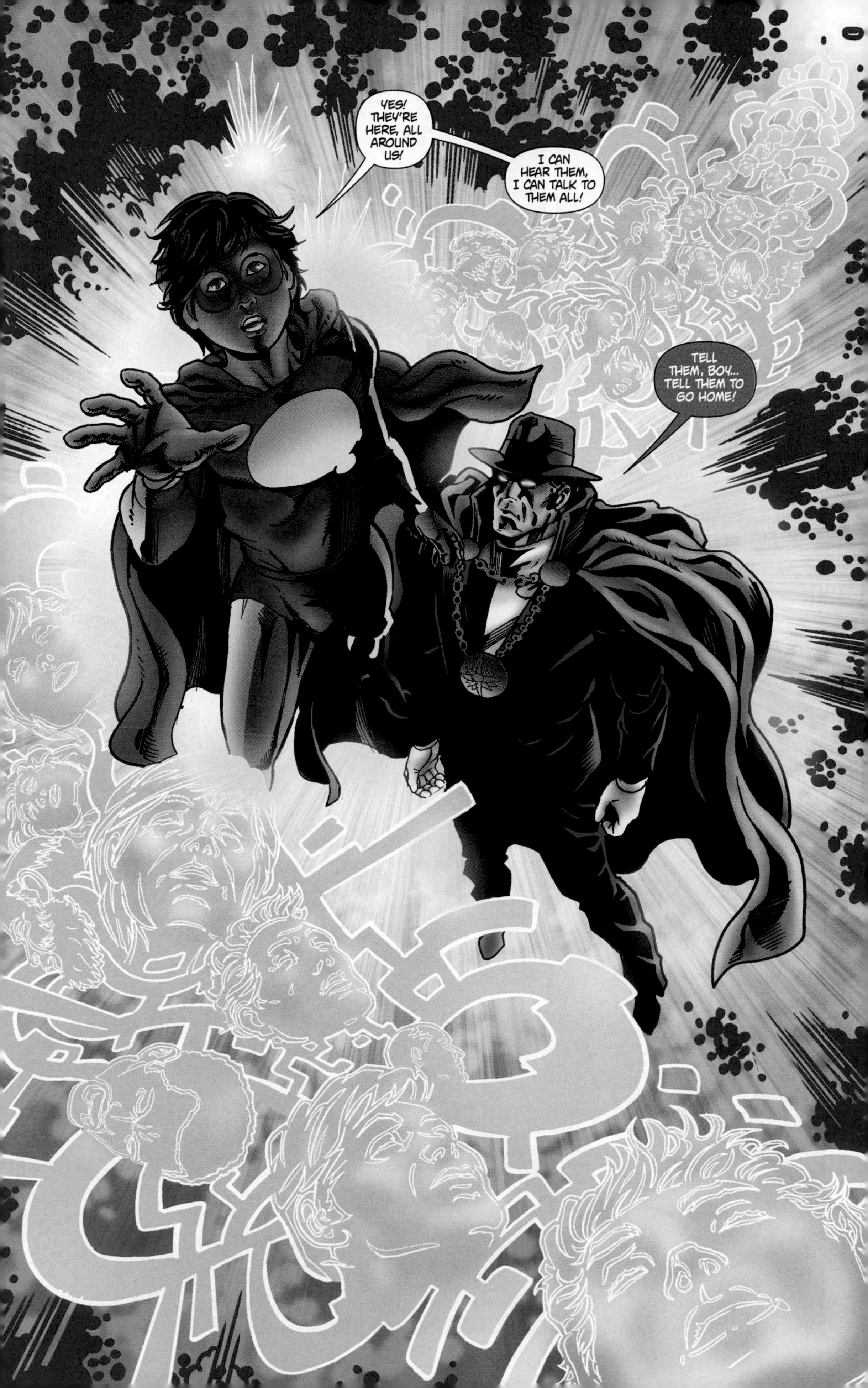
YES! THEY'RE HERE, ALL AROUND US!
I CAN HEAR THEM, I CAN TALK TO THEM ALL!
TELL THEM, BOY... TELL THEM TO GO HOME!

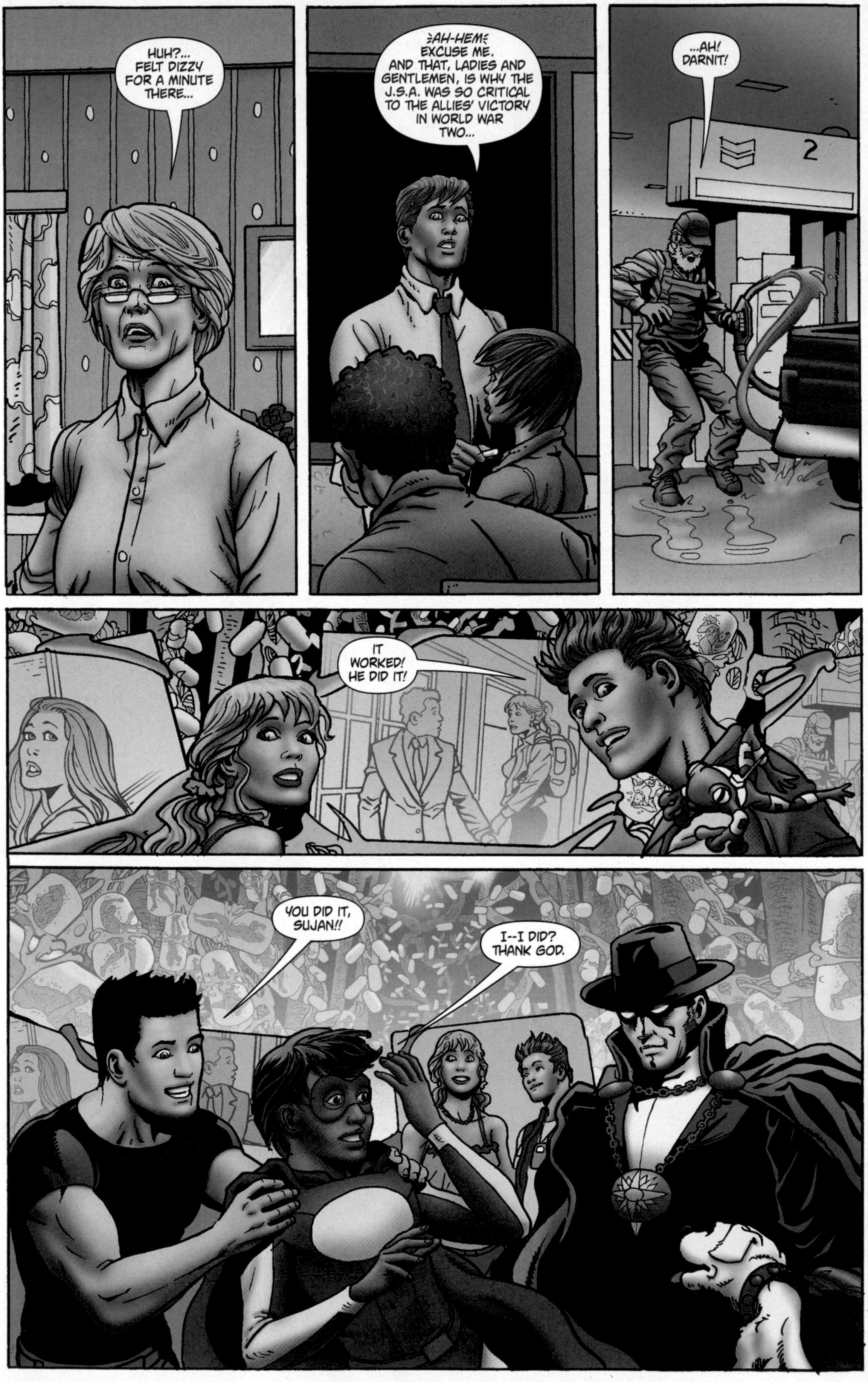
HUH?... FELT DIZZY FOR A MINUTE THERE...
AH-HEM EXCUSE ME. AND THAT, LADIES AND GENTLEMEN, IS WHY THE J.S.A. WAS SO CRITICAL TO THE ALLIES' VICTORY IN WORLD WAR TWO...
...AH! DARNIT!
2
IT WORKED! HE DID IT!
YOU DID IT, SUJAN!!
I--I DID? THANK GOD.

DON'T YOU KNOW...I'LL NEVER STOP, I'LL KEEP COMING BACK... KEEP BUILDING MY ARMY.

AND ONE DAY, LONG AFTER YOU'RE ALL DEAD, I'LL LEAD THE DARK CIRCLE ACROSS THE ROTTING HUSK OF THIS WORLD.

AND YOU, STRANGER... YOU'RE NOT THE ONLY ONE WITH AN ACE UP HIS SLEEVE...

EBEN TOOK, YOU AND YOUR BOYS HAVE BEEN LOYAL SERVANTS... AND I ONLY NEED ONE FINAL THING FROM YOU...

NOOOOOOOO!!!

FWOOOSH!

HE'S GONE!

AND THAT'S NOT ALL. THIS PLACE IS COMING DOWN!

HURRY, GATHER AROUND. I'LL TRANSPORT US ALL TOPSIDE BEFORE IT'S TOO LATE!

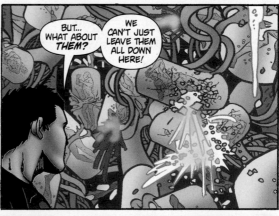

BUT... WHAT ABOUT THEM?

WE CAN'T JUST LEAVE THEM ALL DOWN HERE!

THESE ARE NOT ALIVE, SUPERBOY. THEY ARE ONLY HUSKS. FLESH AND BLOOD, PERHAPS...BUT NO MINDS OR SOULS.

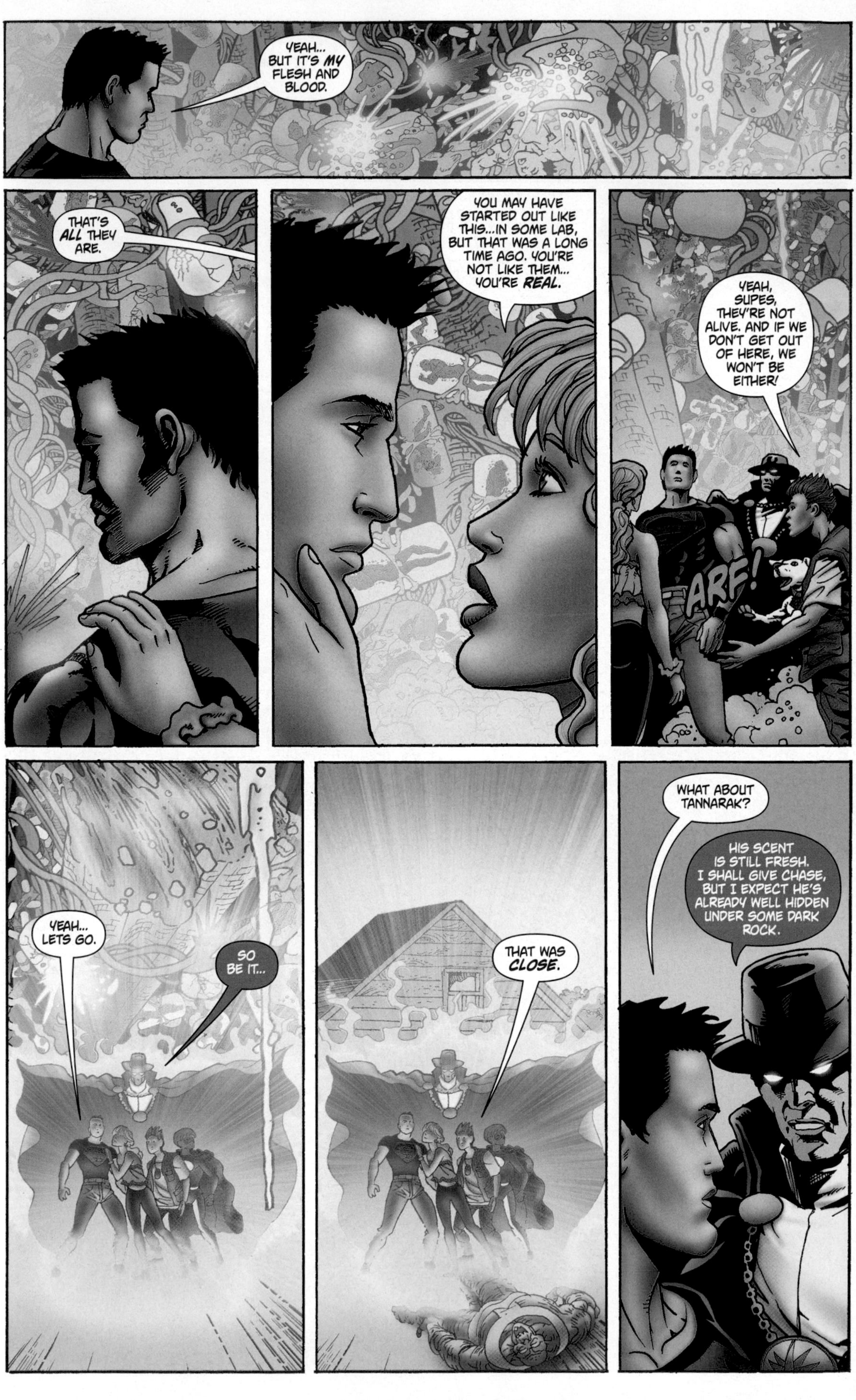
YEAH... BUT IT'S MY FLESH AND BLOOD.
THAT'S ALL THEY ARE.
YOU MAY HAVE STARTED OUT LIKE THIS...IN SOME LAB, BUT THAT WAS A LONG TIME AGO. YOU'RE NOT LIKE THEM... YOU'RE REAL.
YEAH, SUPES, THEY'RE NOT ALIVE. AND IF WE DON'T GET OUT OF HERE, WE WON'T BE EITHER!
ARF!
YEAH... LETS GO.
SO BE IT...
THAT WAS CLOSE.
WHAT ABOUT TANNARAK?
HIS SCENT IS STILL FRESH. I SHALL GIVE CHASE, BUT I EXPECT HE'S ALREADY WELL HIDDEN UNDER SOME DARK ROCK.

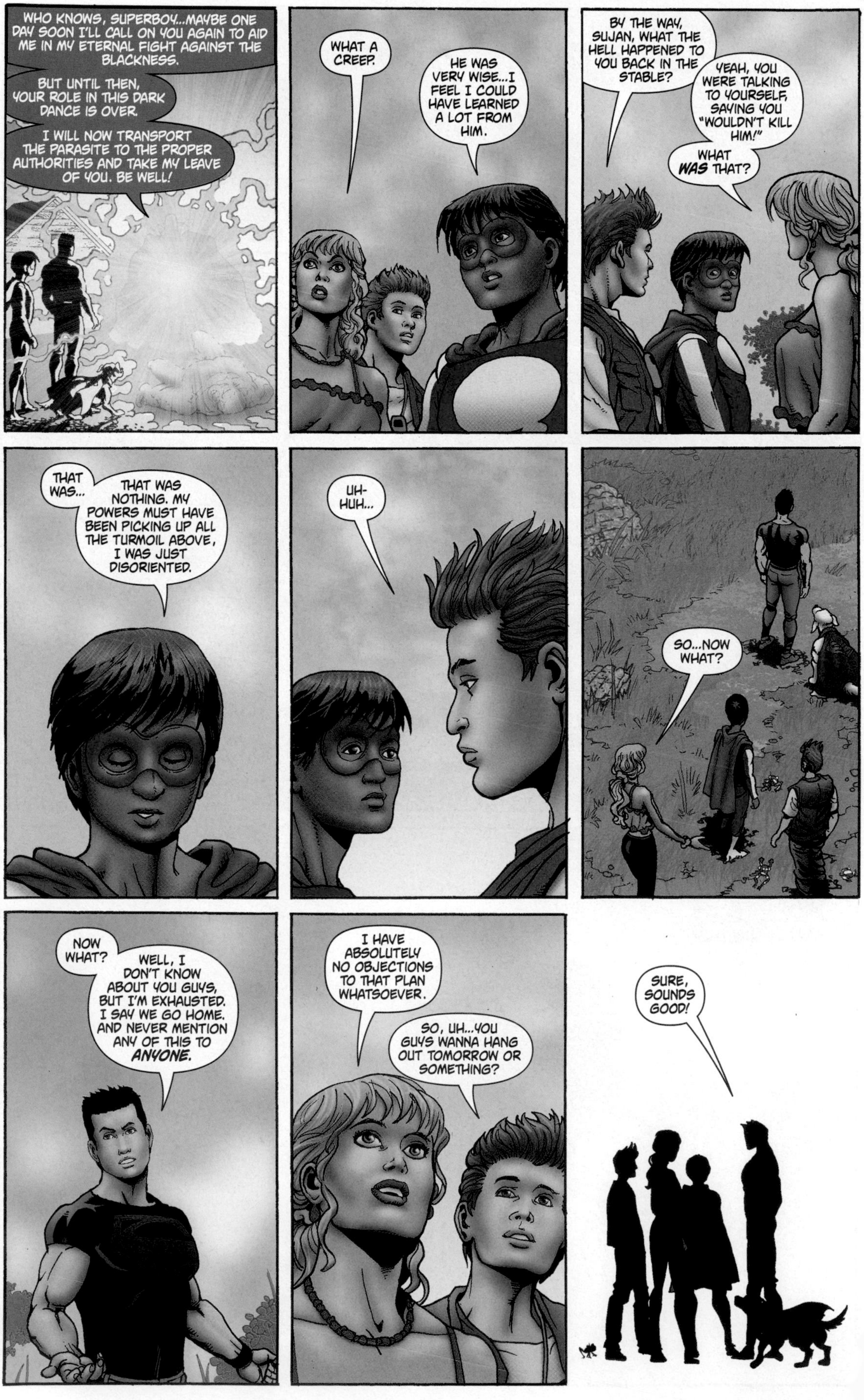
WHO KNOWS, SUPERBOY...MAYBE ONE DAY SOON I'LL CALL ON YOU AGAIN TO AID ME IN MY ETERNAL FIGHT AGAINST THE BLACKNESS.
BUT UNTIL THEN, YOUR ROLE IN THIS DARK DANCE IS OVER.
I WILL NOW TRANSPORT THE PARASITE TO THE PROPER AUTHORITIES AND TAKE MY LEAVE OF YOU. BE WELL!
WHAT A CREEP.
HE WAS VERY WISE...I FEEL I COULD HAVE LEARNED A LOT FROM HIM.
BY THE WAY, SUJAN, WHAT THE HELL HAPPENED TO YOU BACK IN THE STABLE?
YEAH, YOU WERE TALKING TO YOURSELF, SAYING YOU "WOULDN'T KILL HIM!"
WHAT *WAS* THAT?
THAT WAS...
THAT WAS NOTHING. MY POWERS MUST HAVE BEEN PICKING UP ALL THE TURMOIL ABOVE, I WAS JUST DISORIENTED.
UH-HUH...
SO...NOW WHAT?
NOW WHAT?
WELL, I DON'T KNOW ABOUT YOU GUYS, BUT I'M EXHAUSTED. I SAY WE GO HOME. AND NEVER MENTION ANY OF THIS TO *ANYONE*.
I HAVE ABSOLUTELY NO OBJECTIONS TO THAT PLAN WHATSOEVER.
SO, UH...YOU GUYS WANNA HANG OUT TOMORROW OR SOMETHING?
SURE, SOUNDS GOOD!

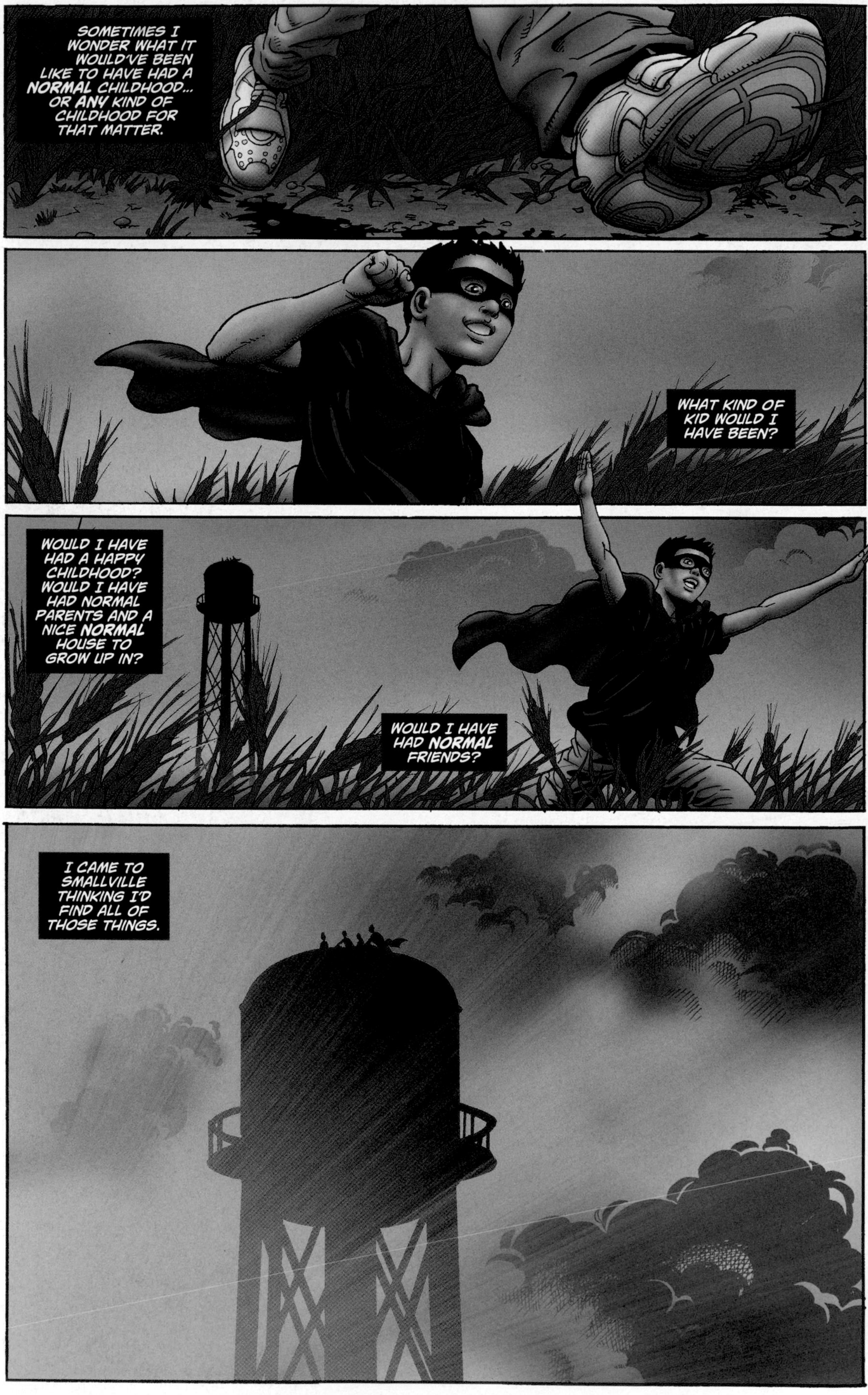
SOMETIMES I WONDER WHAT IT WOULD'VE BEEN LIKE TO HAVE HAD A NORMAL CHILDHOOD... OR ANY KIND OF CHILDHOOD FOR THAT MATTER.
WHAT KIND OF KID WOULD I HAVE BEEN?
WOULD I HAVE HAD A HAPPY CHILDHOOD? WOULD I HAVE HAD NORMAL PARENTS AND A NICE NORMAL HOUSE TO GROW UP IN?
WOULD I HAVE HAD NORMAL FRIENDS?
I CAME TO SMALLVILLE THINKING I'D FIND ALL OF THOSE THINGS.

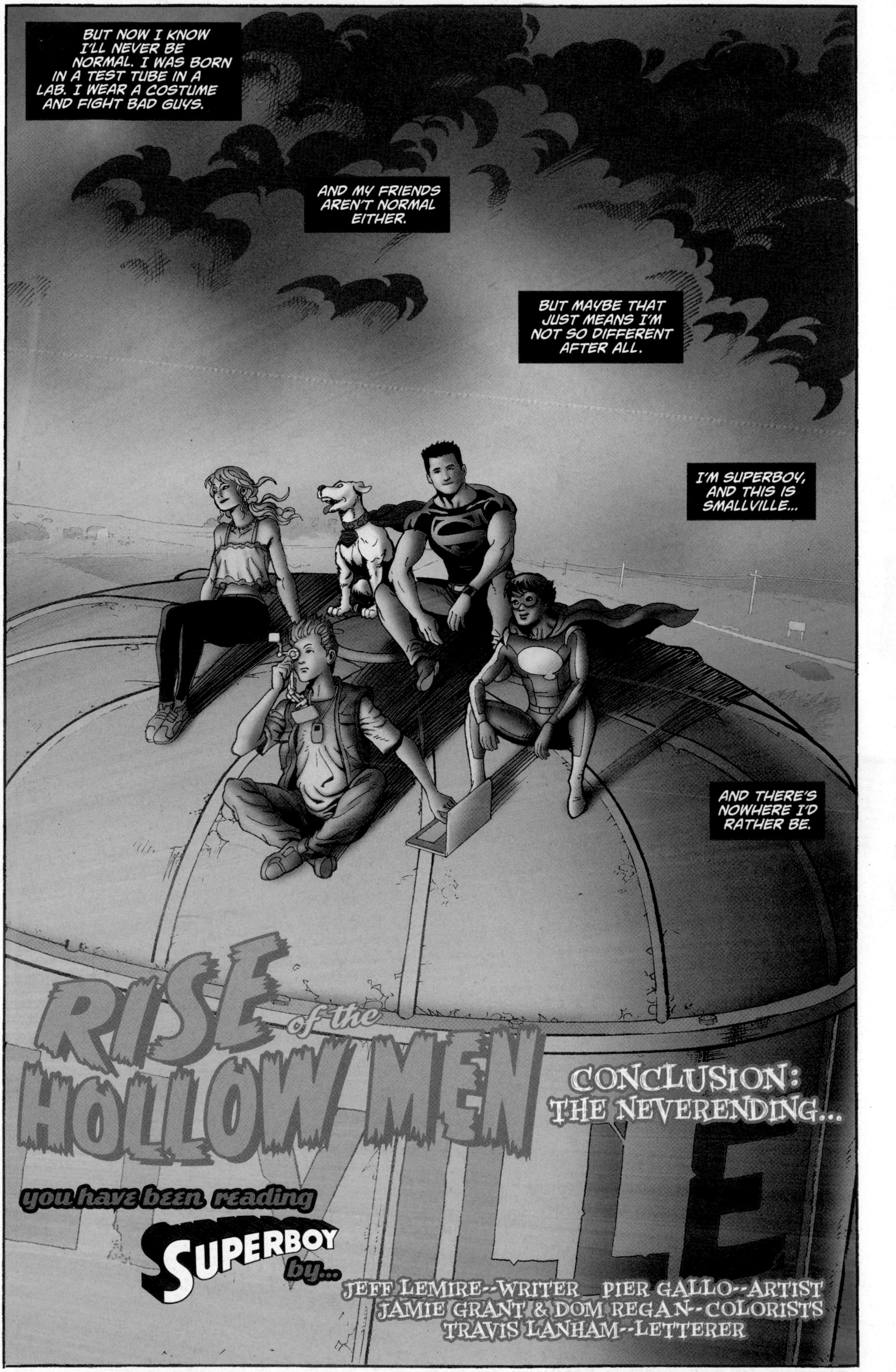
BUT NOW I KNOW I'LL NEVER BE NORMAL. I WAS BORN IN A TEST TUBE IN A LAB. I WEAR A COSTUME AND FIGHT BAD GUYS.
AND MY FRIENDS AREN'T NORMAL EITHER.
BUT MAYBE THAT JUST MEANS I'M NOT SO DIFFERENT AFTER ALL.
I'M SUPERBOY, AND THIS IS SMALLVILLE...
AND THERE'S NOWHERE I'D RATHER BE.
RISE of the HOLLOW MEN
CONCLUSION: THE NEVERENDING...
you have been reading
SUPERBOY
by...
JEFF LEMIRE--WRITER PIER GALLO--ARTIST
JAMIE GRANT & DOM REGAN--COLORISTS
TRAVIS LANHAM--LETTERER

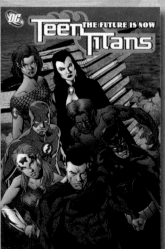